Geography Alive!

Regions and People

Student Edition

Teachers' Curriculum Institute

Director of Development: Liz Russell
Editorial Project Manager: Laura Alavosus
Content Editors: John Bergez, John Burner
Production Editors: Mali Apple, Beverly Cory
Editorial Assistant: Anna Embree
Art Director: John F. Kelly
Production Manager: Lynn Sanchez
Senior Graphic Designer: Christy Uyeno
Graphic Designers: Katy Haun, Paul Rebello, Don Taka
Photo Edit Manager: Margee Robinson
Art Editor: Eric Houts
Audio Director: Katy Haun

 Teachers' Curriculum Institute
P.O. Box 50996
Palo Alto, CA 94303

ISBN13: 978-1-58371-427-0   ISBN10: 1-58371-427-8
3 4 5 6 7 8 9 10 WC 12 11 10 09 08 07

Teacher and Content Consultants (cont.)

Miles Lawrence
NOAA TPC/National Hurricane
Center
Miami, Florida

Patrick McCrystle
Bellarmine College Preparatory
San Jose, California

Deanna Morrow
Martinez Middle School
Hillsborough County School
District
Lutz, Florida

Michael Radcliffe
Greenville High School
Greenville Public Schools
Greenville, Michigan

Betsy Sheffield
National Snow and Ice Data
Center
Boulder, Colorado

Stacy Stewart
NOAA TPC/National Hurricane
Center
Miami, Florida

Fred Walk (NCGE)
Normal Community High School
McLean County Unit District No. 5
Normal, Illinois

Department of Geography
Illinois State University
Normal, Illinois

Scholars

Dr. Siaw Akwawua
College of Humanities and
Social Sciences
University of Northern Colorado

Dr. Robert Bednarz (NCGE)
College of Geosciences
Texas A&M University

Dr. James Dunn (NCGE)
College of Humanities and
Social Sciences
University of Northern Colorado

Dr. Bill Fraser
Polar Oceans Research Group
Palmer Station, Antarctica
Sheridan, Montana

Dr. Patricia Gober (NCGE)
Department of Geography
Arizona State University

Dr. Susan Hardwick (NCGE)
Department of Geography
University of Oregon

Professor Gail Hobbs (NCGE)
Department of Anthropological
and Geographical Sciences
Los Angeles Pierce College

Dr. Phil Klein (NCGE)
College of Humanities and
Social Sciences
University of Northern Colorado

Dr. Gwenda Rice (NCGE)
College of Education
Western Oregon University

Dr. Kit Salter (retired; NCGE)
Department of Geography
University of Missouri

Dr. Earl Scott (retired)
Department of Geography
University of Minnesota

Music Consultant

Melanie Pinkert
Music Faculty
Montgomery College, Maryland

Geography Specialist

Mapping Specialists
Madison, Wisconsin

Internet Consultant

Clinton Couse
Educational Technology
Consultant
Seattle, Washington

Researcher

Jessica Efron
Library Faculty
Appalachian State University

Contents

Unit

1

The Geographer's World

Unit

2

Canada and the United States

Unit 3

Latin America

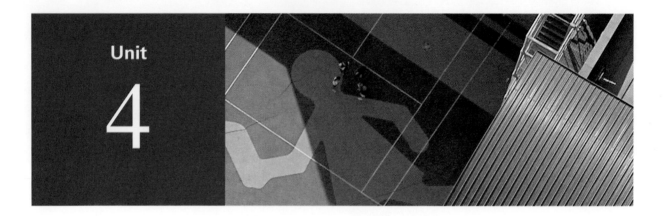

Unit 4

Europe and Russia

Unit 5

Africa

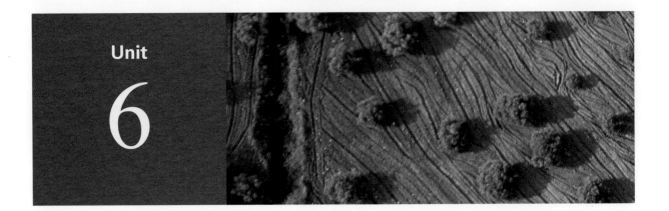

Unit

6

Southwest and Central Asia

Unit

7

Monsoon Asia

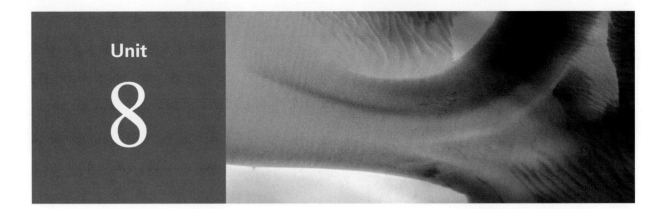

Unit

8

Oceania and Antarctica

Maps

Diagrams, Graphs, and Tables

Aerial Photographs and Satellite Imagery

Aerial Photography

Aerial photography is the taking of photographs from above the surface of Earth. A photographer in an airplane or helicopter may hold the camera used to take an aerial photograph. Or the camera may be mounted on an aircraft, a balloon, a rocket, or even a kite. Aerial photographs help geographers see the world in new ways. They show land use patterns and features that may not be visible to a person standing on the ground.

At the beginning of each unit in this book, you will see aerial photographs that may puzzle you. They were taken by a French photographer named Yann Arthus-Bertrand. For more information about these photographs, see pages 514 and 515.

Some of the aerial photographs that appear in this book are listed below.

Satellite Imagery

Satellite imagery is the taking of photographs of Earth or other planets from satellites. A satellite is any object that revolves around a planet. The moon is Earth's largest natural satellite. It revolves around Earth every $27\frac{1}{3}$ days. Today thousands of much smaller artificial satellites circle Earth each day. These satellites are made on Earth and then launched into space on rockets.

The first satellite photographs of Earth were taken in 1960 by a weather satellite. In 1972, the United States started the Landsat program. This program has sent several satellites into space to take photographs of Earth. These pictures are used for many purposes including mapping geographic features, locating mineral deposits, studying environmental problems, finding crop problems, and locating fish at sea.

The satellite images that appear in this book are listed below.

Geography Alive!

Regions and People

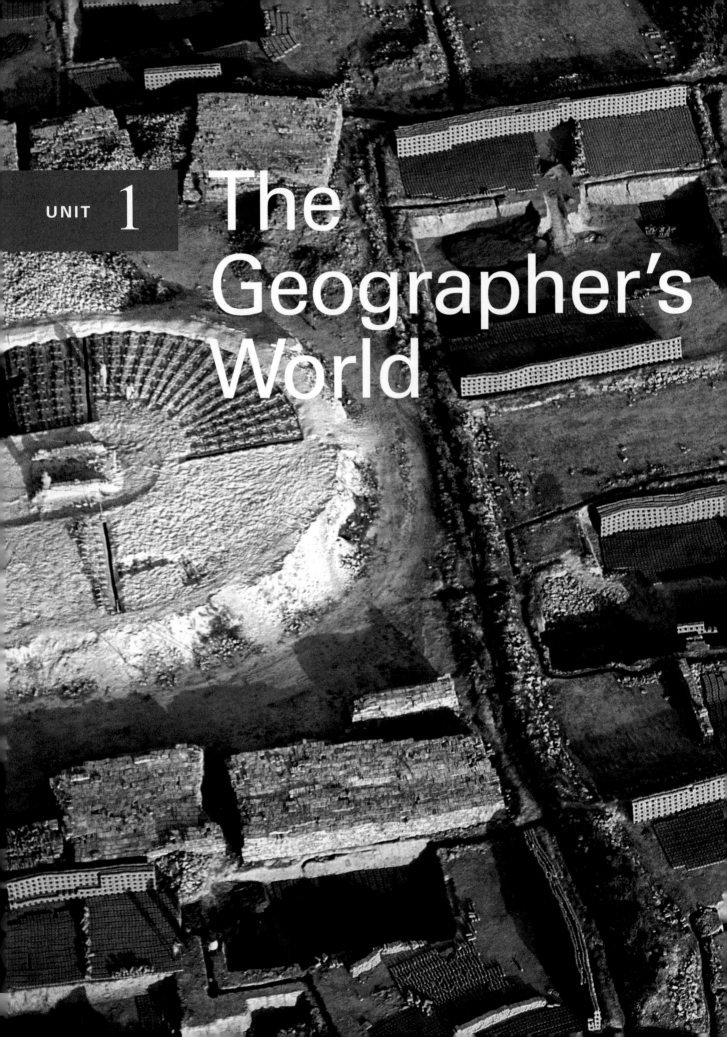

UNIT 1

The Geographer's World

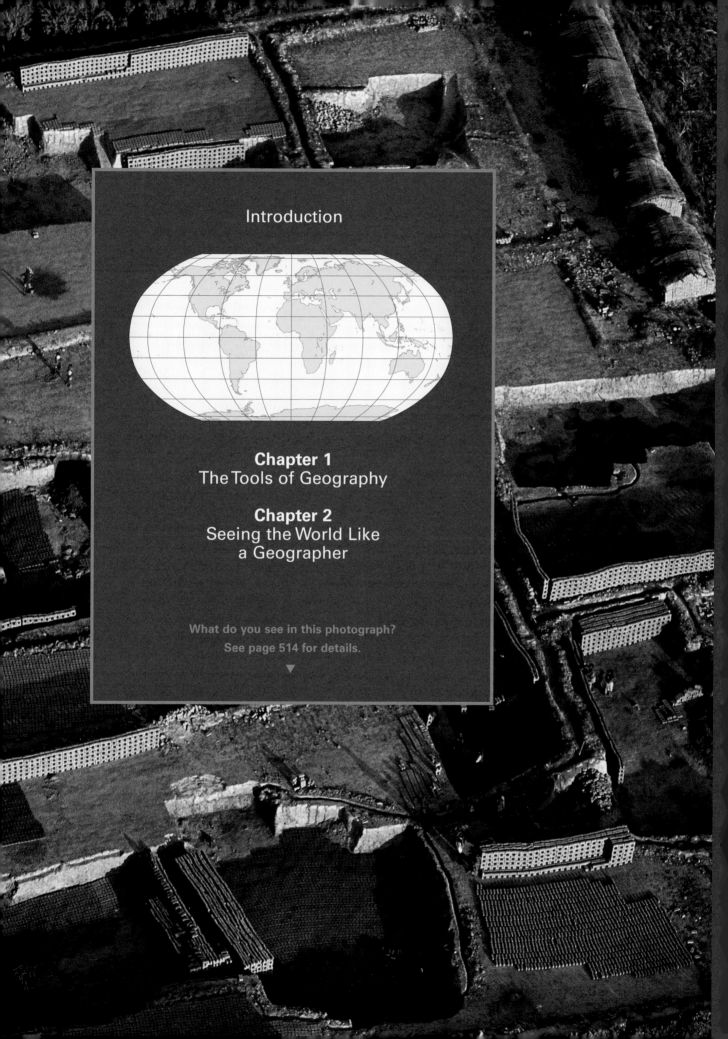

Introduction

Chapter 1
The Tools of Geography

Chapter 2
Seeing the World Like
a Geographer

What do you see in this photograph?
See page 514 for details.

▼

Welcome to *Geography Alive! Regions and People.* You have just begun an active, hands-on journey into the world around you. That journey started with the dramatic photograph you saw on the previous page.

Before going back to look at that photo again, picture yourself in a tiny airplane. You are sitting next to a famous landscape photographer named Yann Arthus-Bertrand. You can't talk to him because he is hanging out of his window snapping pictures with his camera. To see what he sees, turn back to the previous page.

What a strange landscape, you think to yourself. As you look more, your mind is flooded with questions. Where are we? Who lives down there? What are they doing? Why does the land look this way? With such questions tickling your brain, you have just entered the geographer's world.

The Field of Geography

Geography is a field of study that tries to make sense of the world around us. It helps us understand how people, places, and environments came to be and how they affect each other.

When geographers look at something on Earth, they ask questions. Where is it? Why is it there? How did it get there? How does it affect the people living there? How does it affect the natural environment in this area? That "something" could be as ordinary as a nearby factory. Or it could be as extraordinary as a distant, fire-belching volcano.

To answer such questions, geographers look at the world in **spatial** terms. This means they look at how things are arranged in space. Look at the photograph of the camels below. The first question to pop into a geographer's mind about this photo would be a spatial one. Of all the places on Earth, where were these camels on the day this picture was taken?

Physical Geography

Geographers divide their field into two broad branches: physical and human. The word *physical* means relating to things that can be seen, tasted, or felt. **Physical geography** is the study of natural features on the surface of Earth. These are things that can be seen (and sometimes tasted), such as mountains, plants, and animals. They also include things that can be felt more than seen, such as temperature, wind, and weather.

Physical geographers looking at the camel photograph below would be interested in its desert landscape. They would wonder how this place got to be so very dry and what might live in this sea of sand.

Human Geography

Human geography is the study of people as they have spread across Earth. Human geographers seek to understand who lives where, how, and why. They are also interested in human-made features such as towns, farms, dams, and roads.

Viewing the same camel picture, a human geographer would wonder who is driving those camels. Where did the people come from? Where are they going? And why are they traveling through such a harsh, dry land?

The Geographic Inquiry Process

Geography is a very old field of study. Around 450 B.C.E., a Greek scholar named Herodotus created the first map of the known world. You can see a modern version of it at the bottom of this page. Looking at his map, you may notice two things. First, how much of the world it shows. Second, how much of the world is missing. What you cannot see is how Herodotus created his map. He followed a series of steps known as the *geographic inquiry process.*

Asking Geographic Questions

Herodotus began by asking geographic questions. What is the world like? What lands and seas cover Earth? What peoples does the world contain? Where do they live?

Acquiring Geographic Information

To answer his questions, Herodotus needed geographic information. He traveled widely to see the world. He interviewed other travelers and traders. They told him many tales, some true and some tall, about distant lands. In this way, Herodotus learned about peoples and places he would never see.

Geographers today still travel in search of geographic information. Those travels may take them to nearby places or to distant lands. Like Herodotus, they also look for information gathered by others. This information can often found in books and on the Internet.

Organizing Geographic Information

Once Herodotus had collected his information, he needed to organize it in some way.

There are many ways to organize geographic information. The most common, however, is the one he chose to organize information about all of the places he had learned about: a map.

A map is a way of showing how things are arranged in space. On his map, Herodotus showed what he had learned about the locations of land, seas, and peoples.

Analyzing Geographic Information

To analyze means to examine something in detail in order to discover more about it. Analyzing geographic information involves seeing patterns and making connections.

As Herodotus analyzed his information, he compared different ways of life. He noticed that Egyptians, for example, did many things "backward" from a Greek point of view. They wrote from right to left, instead of from left to right. They ate outdoors but washed indoors, while the Greeks did just the opposite.

Answering Geographic Questions

At the end of his inquiry, Herodotus tried to answer the questions he had started with. He wrote down all that he had learned. He also recorded conclusions about peoples based on his analysis. People still read his books today.

Throughout this course, you will be engaged in the geographic inquiry process. You will ask questions and gather information. You will organize and analyze that information. Finally, you will try to answer your questions. You may find, however, that each answer leads to new questions. When that happens, you are thinking like a geographer.

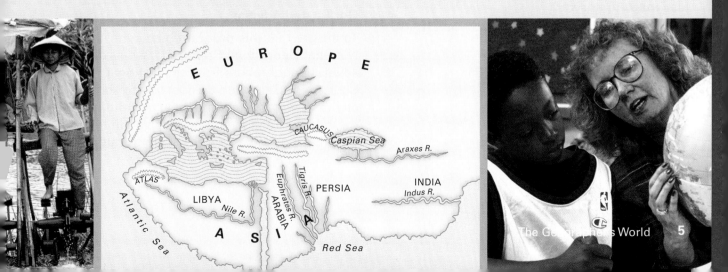

Program Overview

The goal of *Geography Alive! Regions and People* is to help you see the world through a geographer's eyes. With those eyes, you will be able to make better sense of the world around you. Each element of this program has been designed to help you not only to reach this goal, but to have fun doing it.

Mastering the Basics

In this first unit, you will master the basic concepts, skills, and tools that you will be using all year. Chapter 1 introduces the most important tools of geography: maps and globes. In Chapter 2, you will explore different kinds of maps. You will also learn map-reading skills that you will use throughout this program.

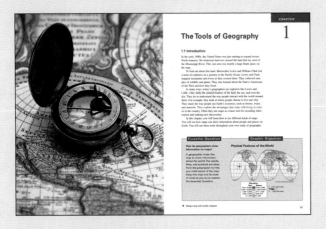

Regions and Mapping Labs

After Unit 1, the program is divided into seven world regions. The study of each region begins with a Mapping Lab. In these labs, you will be challenged to use maps to answer questions about a region. Sometimes you will have to organize and analyze information from several maps to find your answer.

While completing your Mapping Lab, take time to read the unit introduction. It will give you a broad overview of the region that you will be studying for the next few weeks.

Chapter Case Studies

You will explore each region through a series of case studies. Each case study takes you to a new place while focusing on a key topic in geography. In one, you will learn how oil has affected countries in Southwest Asia. In another, you will experience what it is like to climb the world's tallest mountain. In still another, you will "step into" an image of a hurricane to learn how such storms form.

A Standards-Based Program

Geography Alive! Regions and People is closely based on the National Geography Standards. These standards set out what every young person should know and be able to do in geography. You can read more about those standards on the next three pages.

Our Trusted Advisors

To ensure that this program meets the National Geography Standards, we asked several geographers from the National Council for Geographic Education to serve as our advisors. We are deeply grateful to them for helping everyone involved in this program's creation see the world through the eyes of a geographer.

The World in Spatial Terms

Geographers look at the world in spatial terms. (Remember that *spatial* means relating to or happening in space.) They are interested in where things are located on Earth and why. They use a number of tools to help show these spatial relationships. Standards 1–3 say that a person educated in geography should know and understand these things:

Standard 1 How to use maps and other geographic representations, tools, and technologies to acquire, process, and report information from a spatial perspective

Standard 2 How to use mental maps to organize information about people, places, and environments in a spatial context

Standard 3 How to analyze the spatial organization of people, places, and environments on Earth's surface

Sample Case Study: Chapter 6
National Parks: Saving the Natural Heritage of the U.S. and Canada

In this case study, you will use topographic maps to plan adventure tours of three national parks. Geographers use this type of map to show the surface features of an area. Topographic maps of national parks show many of the special features that make these places worth preserving.

Places and Regions

You live in particular place. That place may be in a city, small town, or rural area. It has a name and an address. You also live in a region. A region is not a specific place. Rather, it is a way of thinking about a group of places that have something in common. The Sunbelt, for example, is a region of the United States made up of warm-weather states. Standards 4–6 say that a person educated in geography should know and understand these things:

Standard 4 The physical and human characteristics of places

Standard 5 That people create regions to interpret Earth's complexity

Standard 6 How culture and experience influence people's perceptions of places and regions

Sample Case Study: Chapter 22
Nigeria: A Country of Many Cultures

This case study will introduce you to the more than 250 different ethnic groups that live in the country of Nigeria. You will see how dividing Nigeria into cultural regions helps geographers make sense of this complex country. You will also design an educational Web page about the regions of Nigeria.

National Geography Standards

Physical Systems

Physical geography focuses on processes that shape and change Earth's surface. The wearing away of coastlines by ocean waves is a physical process. Most physical processes work very slowly over time. But they create the **ecosystems,** or natural environments, in which we live. Standards 7 and 8 say that a person educated in geography should know and understand these things:

Standard 7 The physical processes that shape the patterns of Earth's surface

Standard 8 The characteristics and spatial distribution of ecosystems on Earth's surface

Sample Case Study: Chapter 17
**Russia's Varied Landscape:
Physical Processes at Work**

In this case study, you will learn about four physical processes: volcanic activity, glaciation, erosion, and tectonic movement. You will act out each of these processes to show how they shape Earth's surface. You will also do research on physical processes close to home.

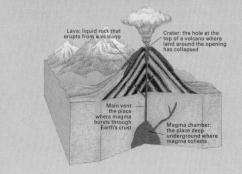

Lava: liquid rock that erupts from a volcano

Crater: the hole at the top of a volcano where land around the opening has collapsed

Main vent: the place where magma bursts through Earth's crust

Magma chamber: the place deep underground where magma collects

Human Systems

People are central in the study of geography. Human activities—such as trade, migration, settlement, and warfare—affect where and how people live. Standards 9–13 say that a person educated in geography should know and understand these things:

Standard 9 The characteristics, distribution, and migration of human populations on Earth's surface

Standard 10 The characteristics, distribution, and complexity of Earth's cultural mosaics

Standard 11 The patterns and networks of economic interdependence on Earth's surface

Standard 12 The processes, patterns, and functions of human settlement

Standard 13 How the forces of cooperation and conflict among people influence the division and control of Earth's surface

Sample Case Study: Chapter 32
**The Global Sneaker:
From Asia to Everywhere**

In this case study, you will learn how economic interdependence brings you sneakers. You will see how making sneakers has become a global business. You will also find and map other "global" products in your home.

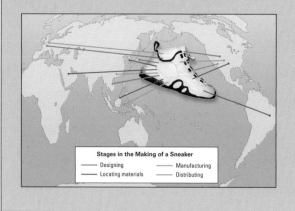

Stages in the Making of a Sneaker

—— Designing   —— Manufacturing
—— Locating materials   —— Distributing

Environment and Society

People constantly interact with their physical, or natural, environment. Human geographers look at how physical environments shape the way people live. They also study how human activities change physical environments. Standards 14–16 say that a person educated in geography should know and understand these things:

Standard 14 How human actions modify the physical environment

Standard 15 How physical systems affect human systems

Standard 16 The changes that occur in the meaning, use, distribution, and importance of resources

Sample Case Study: Chapter 26

The Aral Sea: Central Asia's Shrinking Water Source

This case study takes you to what was once a large freshwater lake in Central Asia. You will learn how human activities have turned this lake into a shrinking, saltwater sea. You will also create documentaries that explore how the shrinking of the Aral Sea has affected people living in this region.

The Uses of Geography

Geography opens up a window on the world we live in today. It helps us to understand the past and to plan for the future. Standards 17 and 18 say that a person educated in geography should know and understand these things:

Standard 17 How to apply geography to interpret the past

Standard 18 How to apply geography to interpret the present and plan for the future

Sample Case Study: Chapter 35

Antarctica: Researching Global Warming at the Coldest Place on Earth

You will travel to Antarctica in this case study to do research on global warming. You will visit research stations to gather data on air temperatures, ice shelves, and penguins. After analyzing your data, you will write a dialogue that explores different views about global warming and how it may affect our future.

The Tools of Geography

1.1 Introduction

In the early 1800s, the United States was just beginning to expand west across North America. No American had ever crossed the territory that lay west of the Mississippi River. This vast area was mostly a mysterious blank space on the map.

To find out about this unknown territory, President Thomas Jefferson sent Meriwether Lewis and William Clark to explore the western frontier. Lewis and Clark led a team of explorers on a two-year expedition to the Pacific Ocean. The team mapped mountains and rivers as they crossed them. They collected samples of wildlife and plants that they had never seen before. The explorers also met the Native Americans of the West and learned how they lived.

In many ways, today's geographers are explorers like Lewis and Clark. They study the natural features of the land, the sea, and even the sky above. They try to understand the way people interact with the world around them. For example, they look at where people choose to live and why. They study the way people use Earth's resources, such as forests, water, and minerals. They explore the advantages that come with living in cities or in the country. Often geographers use maps as a basic tool for recording information and making new discoveries.

In this chapter, you will learn how to use different kinds of maps. You will see how maps can illustrate information about people and places on Earth. You will then put these tools to use in your own study of geography.

Essential Question

How do geographers show information on maps?

A geographer made this map to show information about the world. The words, lines, and symbols are clues from the geographer to help you make sense of the map. Keep this map and its clues in mind as you try to answer the Essential Question.

Graphic Organizer

Physical Features of the World

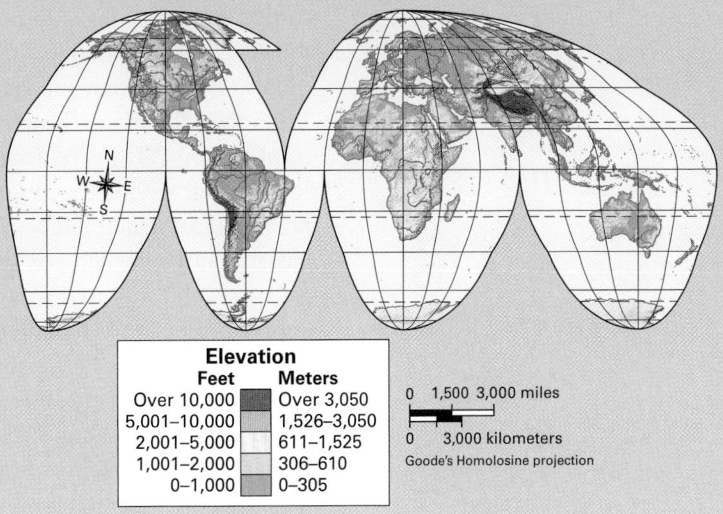

Elevation		
Feet		**Meters**
Over 10,000		Over 3,050
5,001–10,000		1,526–3,050
2,001–5,000		611–1,525
1,001–2,000		306–610
0–1,000		0–305

0   1,500 3,000 miles

0   3,000 kilometers

Goode's Homolosine projection

◀ Antique map and sundial compass

1.2 The Geographic Setting

In September 1805, the Lewis and Clark expedition crossed the Rocky Mountains on the way to the Pacific Ocean. Lewis and Clark wanted to explore the Columbia River, which could take them to the ocean, but they didn't know how to find it. A Native American chief named Twisted Hair came to the rescue. He drew a map on a white elk skin that showed the explorers how to reach the Columbia and indicated that the river was "five sleeps" away.

Today we still use maps to find the locations of places and determine how far apart they are. Like Twisted Hair's drawing, the most basic map is a diagram that shows what is where.

Locating Things on Earth: The Main Purpose of Maps For geographers, maps are tools that show where things are on Earth. With these tools, we can find the **absolute location** of any place in the world. Every feature is located at a precise, or absolute, point on Earth, and there are many ways to describe this precise point. Your street address, for example, indicates the absolute location of your home. Later in this chapter, you'll learn how a grid, or system of lines, can be used to show the absolute location of places on a map.

Maps also show the **relative location** of places on Earth. This is the location of one place compared to another. For instance, one place might be located east or west of another one. You probably use relative location when you give someone directions. Suppose you want to tell a friend how to locate the street where you live. You might tell her to proceed along a main street and then turn right one block past the park. With these directions, you would be telling her your street's location relative to a place she knows well.

Distortion: The Big Problem with Maps Maps are great tools, but they're not perfect pictures of Earth's surface. Maps are two-dimensional, or flat. In contrast, Earth is three-dimensional and shaped like a sphere, which is much like a basketball. The only way to show a spherical Earth on a flat map is by stretching some parts of it—a process that changes the shape, size, and position of Earth's features. These changes are called **distortion**. The photographs at the right show just how severe this distortion can be.

One way geographers deal with the problem of distortion is to use globes. Because they are spheres, globes are better models of the whole Earth than flat maps. They show the size, shape, distance, and direction of places on Earth very accurately. Unfortunately, globes cannot show a lot of detail without becoming huge. Maps, in contrast, can show smaller areas of Earth and include much more detail. In addition, maps are much easier than globes to carry around.

A second way to deal with distortion is to use **map projections**. A map projection is a particular way of showing Earth on a flat surface. All map projections have some kind of distortion. For example, one projection that accurately shows the sizes of places will distort their shapes, while another that shows accurate shapes will distort sizes and distances. Geographers choose the projection that best suits the kind of information they want the map to show.

▶ Geoterms

absolute location the precise point where a place is located on Earth

distortion a change in the shape, size, or position of a place when it is shown on a map

map projection a way of representing the spherical Earth on a flat surface

relative location where a place is located in relation to another place

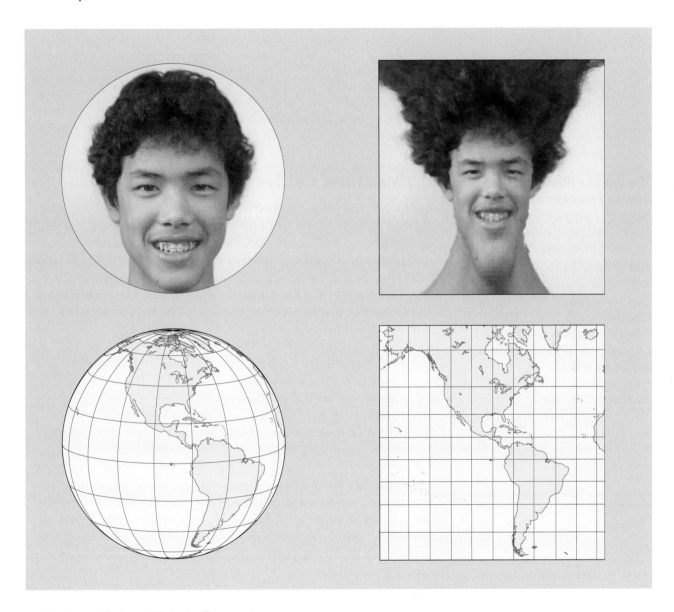

Flattening a Sphere Distorts Features
A person's head is shaped almost like a sphere. If you try to flatten a head, its features stretch and change shape. As a result, the person becomes almost unrecognizable. In a similar way, flat maps can distort information about Earth's features.

Political Boundaries of the World

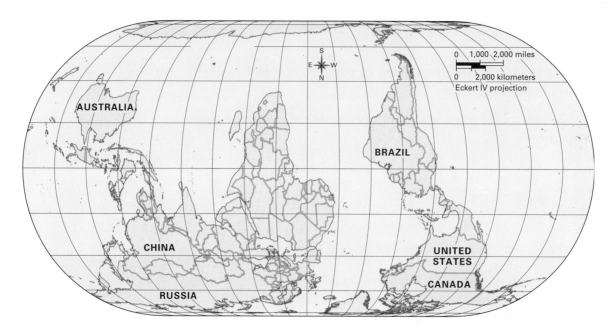

The Top of a Map Doesn't Always Point North

On most maps, the top of the map points north, but not all maps work this way. This map turns our usual view of Earth upside down. The map isn't right or wrong. After all, Earth does not have a "right" side up as seen from space. When you look at any map, be sure to check the compass rose so you know which direction is which.

1.3 Map Titles and Symbols

Like Lewis and Clark, early explorers often had no maps to guide them on their journeys. Lewis Carroll, the well-known English author of *Alice in Wonderland* and *Through the Looking Glass,* made fun of their situation in a poem called *The Hunting of the Snark.* The poem tells of sailors searching for an imaginary creature called a *snark*. To assist them, the ship's captain unrolls a large map of the sea without a trace of land or even a mark indicating where anything was. The snark-hunting sailors, Carroll wrote,

> *were much pleased when they found it to be*
> *A map they could all understand....*
> *"A perfect and absolute blank!"*

Luckily for us, instead of being blank, the maps we use today are filled with information.

The Title Tells What a Map Shows A map's title gives us our first clue about its content. The title usually describes the area shown on the map and identifies the map's main topic. The topic might be gold or silver mining, politics, agriculture, or even the night sky. Often the title also includes a date. The date tells us that the map shows the locations of places at a certain time.

A Compass Rose Shows Directions on a Map Have you ever used a magnetic compass to find your way when you were lost and in a strange place? If so, you know that the needle of a compass always points in a northward direction—toward the North Pole. Knowing where north is can help you determine which way to go.

Mapmakers use a small diagram called a **compass rose** to indicate directions on a map. Because these diagrams often resembled a flower on early maps, sailors called this direction-finding tool a compass rose. It gave them courage to sail out of sight of land.

A simple compass rose has two short lines that cross at right angles. The points at the ends of the lines are labeled with the **cardinal directions**—north, south, east, and west. You can see such a compass rose on the map to the right. A more elaborate compass rose has lines between the cardinal points showing the **intermediate directions**—northeast, southeast, southwest, and northwest.

A Legend Identifies Symbols on a Map

A compass rose is one of many symbols used to show information on a map. Some symbols incorporate color to show features. Blue lines, for example, are symbols that indicate the locations of rivers; lakes and oceans are often colored blue as well. Other symbols use shapes to show information. A bold star is a common symbol for the capital of a state or country, while miniature airplanes are often used to show the locations of airports.

The symbols used on a map are usually identified in a box known as the **map legend,** or sometimes the **map key**. The map legend lists each symbol and explains what it shows on the map. The legend for the map on this page appears in the upper right corner.

Marshall Gold Discovery State Historic Park

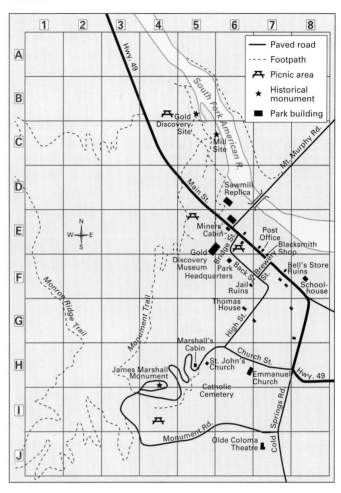

A Grid Organizes Space on a Map Mapmakers often use a system of imaginary lines called a **map grid** to divide up space on their maps. You can see an example of a grid on the map above. To form this grid, the mapmaker drew a network of evenly spaced horizontal lines and vertical lines that meet at 90-degree angles. (Remember that horizontal lines go straight across, while vertical lines go up and down.)

Geographers make map grids useful by giving each line a label. For instance, on some maps the horizontal lines are labeled with letters and the vertical lines are labeled with numbers. Each number and letter identifies a particular section of the map. Once the grid has been labeled, a letter and number such as A9 or C3 can be used to specify the location of any place or feature on the map. The letter and number indicate the intersection of a horizontal and a vertical line on the map. Find the intersection of these two lines, and you will have found the place or feature you are looking for close by.

One very useful type of grid is the system of latitude and longitude. This **global grid** allows people to locate any point on Earth's surface with the use of a simple numeric code. You will learn more about the global grid in the next section.

Using a Map's Title, Compass Rose, Legend, and Grid

You can use this map to tour a historic site. The map title tells which site you will be exploring. The compass rose shows which way north is on the map. The map legend tells you what the symbols on the map mean. Once you know what you want to visit, the map grid will help you locate it on the map.

1.4 The Global Grid: Longitude and Latitude

In early November of 2003, a hiker set up camp high in the Adirondack Mountains of New York. Sudden, heavy snows trapped him there with no way to hike out. Luckily, the hiker had brought his Personal Locator Beacon, and he pressed a button to call for help. A helicopter crew soon rescued the hiker and flew him to safety.

How did the rescuers find the stranded hiker? His locator beacon showed his exact location on the same global grid that geographers use to show the absolute location of every place on Earth.

Lines of Latitude Parallel the Equator The global grid system is made up of two sets of imaginary lines. The first set of lines, **parallels of latitude,** run east and west around the globe.

The equator is the most important parallel of latitude. It circles Earth exactly midway between the North and South poles. All other lines of latitude are parallel to the equator. Parallels of latitude are measured in degrees (°), with the equator marking 0° latitude. Other parallels are measured with reference to the equator.

32° North, 4° West

Any place on Earth, no matter how lonely, has an exact address on the global grid. This lonely spot lies 32° north of the equator and 4° west of the prime meridian.

Latitude Lines Run East to West

Latitude Is Measured from the Equator

Lines of Longitude Run from Pole to Pole The other set of lines in the global grid are half-circles, called **meridians of longitude,** that run from the North Pole to the South Pole. These lines are not parallel to each other, so the distance between them varies.

The most important of these north-south lines is the **prime meridian,** which runs through Greenwich, England. Like parallels of latitude, meridians are measured in degrees, with the prime meridian marking 0° longitude. The prime meridian is a reference for measuring other meridians.

The next most important meridian is the **International Date Line**. This line runs though the Pacific Ocean exactly halfway around the world from the prime meridian. When travelers cross the International Date Line, they cross over to a different day. Travelers moving west across the line go forward a day, while those traveling east across the line go back a day.

Longitude Lines Run North to South

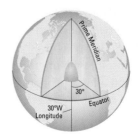

Longitude Is Measured from the Prime Meridian

Cities Around the World

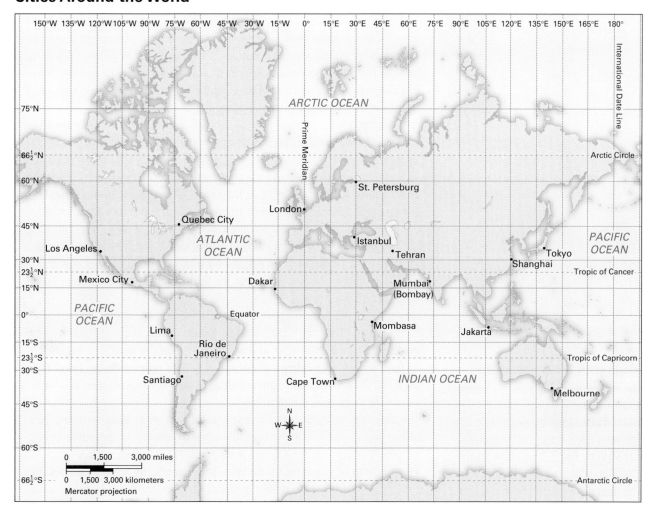

Latitude and Longitude Mark Absolute Location The numbering system of the global grid helps make it easy for you to locate any place on Earth.

Moving north from the equator, the parallels of latitude increase in number from 0° up to 90°N (north) at the North Pole. A similar thing happens moving south of the equator, where the numbers of the parallels increase from 0° to 90°S (south) at the South Pole. One degree of latitude covers about 69 miles, or 111 kilometers.

Meridians of longitude start from 0° at the prime meridian. Traveling east from there, the numbers on lines of longitude increase until they reach 180° at the International Date Line. These numbers are labeled E (east). The same thing occurs going west from the prime meridian. The numbers increase until they reach 180° at the date line and are labeled W (west).

The absolute location of any place on Earth can be described as the meeting point of a parallel of latitude and a meridian of longitude. The numbers of these lines are the geographic **coordinates** of a place. These coordinates are like a street address for your house. They tell exactly where that place is located.

The Absolute Location of Cities

Latitude and longitude mark the absolute location of cities. The coordinates of Rio de Janeiro are 23°S, 43°W. To find this location, look for the parallel of latitude that is 23 degrees south of the equator. Move your finger along it until you come to the prime meridian. Now move west along the same line until you reach 43 degrees. You should be pointing to Rio de Janeiro.

1.5 Dealing with Distances: Map Scale

In Ithaca, New York, a winding path called the Sagan Planet Walk takes people on a journey past models of the sun and the planets. In less than a mile, walkers pass through a model of the entire solar system. The model shrinks the vast distances of space to make them easier to understand. For instance, people can see that the planet Mars is about one and a half times Earth's distance from the sun.

A map does a similar thing for the area it shows. The scale on a map tells you how the distances on the map compare to the actual distances on Earth.

How Scale Affects Details A map can be large scale or small scale. A large-scale map gives a close-up view of a small area with a lot of detail such as street names and interesting places to visit. You could use a large-scale map to find a store in a mall or on a neighborhood street. A small-scale map, in contrast, shows a larger area but with fewer details. Small-scale maps are best for finding your way between cities, states, and larger areas.

Estimating Distance with a Map Scale Many maps include a **map scale,** which tells you how to read distances on the map. For instance, an inch on a map might equal 10 miles or 100 miles or even 1,000 miles on Earth. The map scale appears either inside the map legend box or in a relatively open area on the map.

The map scale is usually made up of two short lines with notches along them, one line measuring distance in miles and the other in kilometers. The easiest way to use a map scale is to make a scale strip. Place a strip of paper under the map scale, mark the scale's notches on the paper, and label the marks with the numbers of miles or kilometers. Then place your strip with the "0" mark at one point on the map, and line up the strip with a second point. Now read the closest number on your strip to this second point. You've just figured out the distance between those two points.

Maps with Different Scales

The map on the left is a small-scale map. It shows where Washington, D.C., is located in relation to nearby cities. The map does not show details like city streets. But it does show larger features, such as major highways.

The map on the right is a large-scale map. It focuses on Washington, D.C. You could use it to find your way through the city's streets to the White House or other monuments.

Washington, D.C., and Surrounding Areas

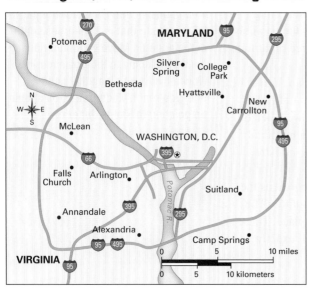

Downtown Washington, D.C.

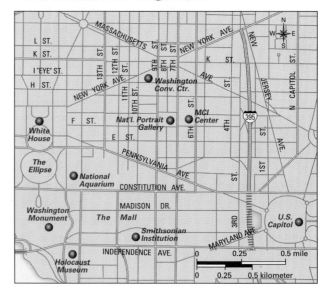

1.6 Hemispheres, Continents, and Oceans

"One of my favorite things to do when I have time off is to just watch the world go by," said astronaut Ed Lu about his experience in space. In 2003, Lu watched Earth go by while he was living aboard the International Space Station. "It isn't exactly seeing Earth like a big blue marble," he explained. "It's more like having your face up against a big blue beach ball." On the "big blue beach ball," he saw Earth's wide continents and blue oceans.

Few of us will ever see Earth from an astronaut's point of view, but we can use maps and globes to get a bird's-eye view of our planet's natural wonders. Geographers make these features easier to understand by dividing Earth into different areas.

A Hemisphere Is a World Geographers divide Earth into halves called **hemispheres**. The equator divides Earth into two hemispheres. The northern half is called the Northern Hemisphere, and the southern half is called the Southern Hemisphere.

Geographers also divide Earth in half by longitude. The Western Hemisphere lies west of the prime meridian, and the Eastern Hemisphere lies to the east of it. The two hemispheres divide again at the International Date Line.

Continents and Oceans Cover Earth Geographers also divide Earth's lands and seas into areas. Ocean water covers more than 70 percent of Earth's surface. In fact, this ocean is really just one big body of water. But geographers usually divide it into four oceans—the Atlantic, Pacific, Indian, and Arctic oceans. Sometimes the Atlantic and Pacific oceans are divided at the equator into the North and South Atlantic and the North and South Pacific.

These oceans lap the shores of continents, the largest areas of land on our planet. The seven continents identified by geographers are, from largest to smallest, Asia, Africa, North America, South America, Antarctica, Europe, and Australia. Europe and Asia are actually parts of one huge **landmass,** but geographers usually think of them as two continents because they have different cultures and histories.

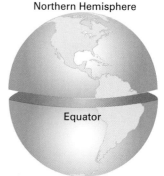

Northern Hemisphere

Equator

Southern Hemisphere

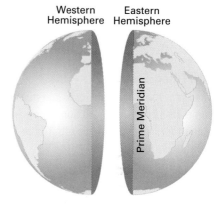

Western Hemisphere   Eastern Hemisphere

Prime Meridian

Hemispheres

The equator splits the globe into Northern and Southern hemispheres. The prime meridian and International Date Line split the globe into Eastern and Western hemispheres.

The World

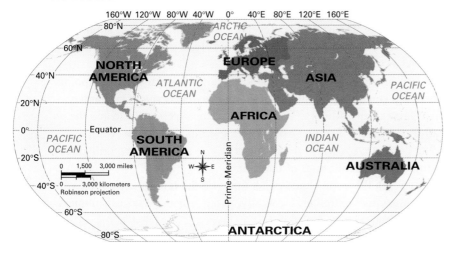

Earth's Continents and Oceans

You can see from this map that oceans cover most of Earth. The four major oceans are actually a single body of water that surrounds the seven continents.

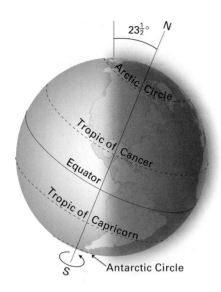

The Tilted Earth

The tilt of Earth on its axis means that some areas receive more sunshine than others each day. This difference creates Earth's seasons.

1.7 Earth and the Sun

For centuries, most people believed that Earth stood still in space. Today we know that our planet is in constant motion, moving at an average speed of about 67,000 miles per hour. That motion creates our years, months, and days and also helps to create our seasons.

The Moving Earth Earth moves around the sun in a nearly circular path called an *orbit*. One round trip, called a **revolution,** takes about $365\frac{1}{4}$ days, which makes an Earth year.

As Earth revolves around the sun, it spins like a giant top upon its **axis**. The axis is an imaginary line that runs from the North Pole to the South Pole through the center of Earth. The spinning motion of Earth is called **rotation**.

Earth makes one full rotation about every 24 hours. As Earth spins, it is daytime on the side facing the sun. Meanwhile, on the side facing away from the sun, it is night.

Earth's Tilt Creates the Seasons Earth's axis is tilted at an angle relative to the sun. Because of this tilt, the Northern and Southern hemispheres receive different amounts of sunlight as Earth moves around the sun. These differences create Earth's seasons.

Look at the diagram on the opposite page to see the changing seasons in the Northern Hemisphere. During the north's summer, this half of Earth is tilted toward the sun. At this time the Northern Hemisphere receives more sunlight and enjoys long, hot days. Winter, the colder part of the year, comes when this hemisphere tilts away from the sun and the days grow short and cool.

Of course, during these same months of winter, the Southern Hemisphere tilts toward the sun, so in the south it is summer. Similarly, when it is summer in the Northern Hemisphere, it is winter in Earth's southern half.

Tropics, Circles, and Zones Because of Earth's tilt, the sun never beats straight down on places in the far north and south. Two lines of latitude mark the northernmost and southernmost points where the sun's rays ever beat straight down. The northern line is called the **Tropic of Cancer,** and the southern line is called the **Tropic of Capricorn**. The Tropic of Cancer and the Tropic of Capricorn are equidistant from the equator.

The areas between these two lines and the equator are known as **tropical zones**. Tropical zones receive a lot of sunshine and are hot all year round. Considerable rain falls, especially in the hot rainy season, but there is no winter season.

Two other lines of latitude mark the farthest north and south points where the sun doesn't shine at all on one day each year. On that day, night lasts a full 24 hours. These lines are the **Arctic Circle** and the **Antarctic Circle**. The areas between these circles and the North and South poles are known as **polar zones**. These zones receive little direct sunlight and are cold most of the year.

Between the tropical and polar zones lie the **temperate zones,** which lack temperature extremes. Generally, in the temperate zones summers are warm and winters are cool.

The Revolution of Earth Around the Sun

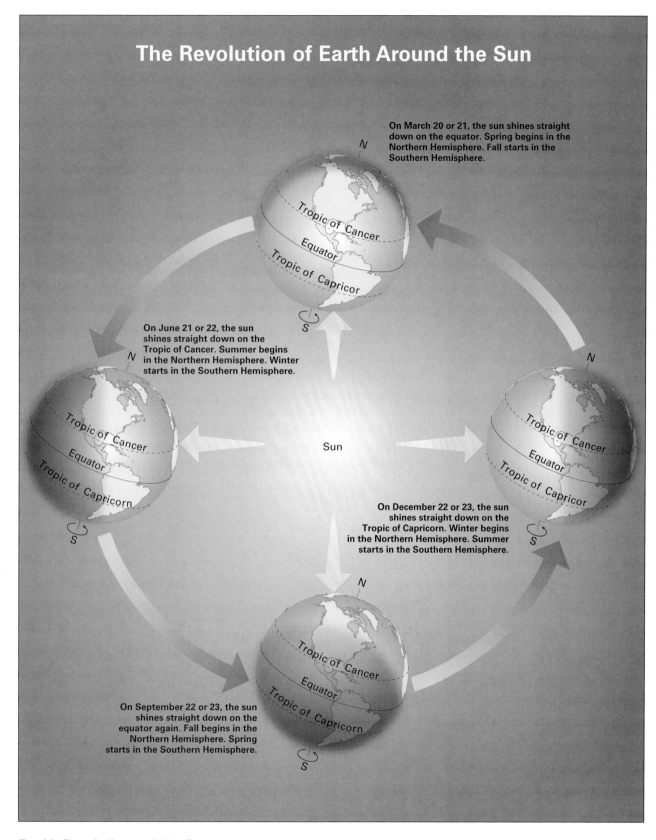

On March 20 or 21, the sun shines straight down on the equator. Spring begins in the Northern Hemisphere. Fall starts in the Southern Hemisphere.

On June 21 or 22, the sun shines straight down on the Tropic of Cancer. Summer begins in the Northern Hemisphere. Winter starts in the Southern Hemisphere.

On December 22 or 23, the sun shines straight down on the Tropic of Capricorn. Winter begins in the Northern Hemisphere. Summer starts in the Southern Hemisphere.

On September 22 or 23, the sun shines straight down on the equator again. Fall begins in the Northern Hemisphere. Spring starts in the Southern Hemisphere.

Sun

Earth's Revolution and the Seasons

This diagram shows how Earth's tilt creates the seasons during our planet's year-long trip around the sun. Notice that the seasons are reversed in the Northern and Southern hemispheres.

The World

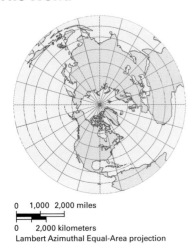

0   1,000 2,000 miles

0   2,000 kilometers
Lambert Azimuthal Equal-Area projection

Lambert Projections Show Polar Areas that Other Maps Distort

A Lambert projection is a circular map. It shows size accurately at its center, but not distance or shape. It is good for showing the areas around the North or South pole. Most other map projections distort the shape and size of the Arctic and Antarctica.

1.8 Showing a Round World on a Flat Map

In this chapter, you learned how geographers show information on maps. Exploring a map's title, compass rose, legend, and symbols can help you understand what a map shows.

You learned how geographers describe where a place is in terms of its absolute location. The global grid allows mapmakers to indicate the exact location of any place on Earth using lines of latitude and longitude labeled with letters and numbers. Map scales are useful for describing the relative location of two places. Using a scale, you can estimate about how far two places are from each other.

All Flat Maps Have Distortion Geographers use maps to show important features of Earth, such as its oceans and continents. But every flat map of Earth involves some distortion. As a result, the size or shape of landmasses or large bodies of water may be distorted, and the distances between places may not be accurately shown.

To deal with distortions, mapmakers use different map projections. Many projections are named after the mapmakers who designed them. For example, Arthur Robinson designed the Robinson projection. The world map on page 19 is a Robinson projection. It is a popular projection because it balances the distortions of size and shape, resulting in a fairly accurate picture of the world.

You can see several map projections on this and the following page. Notice how each projection does some things better than others. As you compare the shapes and sizes of the oceans and continents displayed on the various maps, think about what type of information each projection might show best.

The World

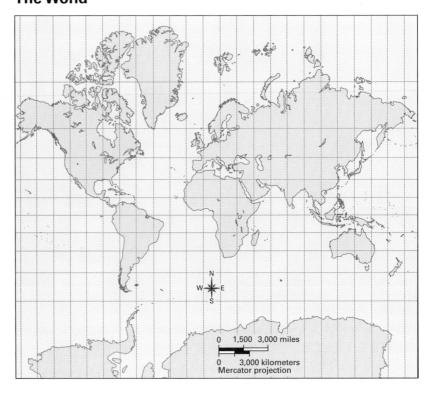

0   1,500 3,000 miles

0   3,000 kilometers
Mercator projection

Mercator Projections Show Direction but Distort Size

Gerardus Mercator designed his map projection in 1569. It shows directions between places accurately near the equator. But it distorts the size of continents, especially near the North and South poles. This is called *area distortion*.

The World

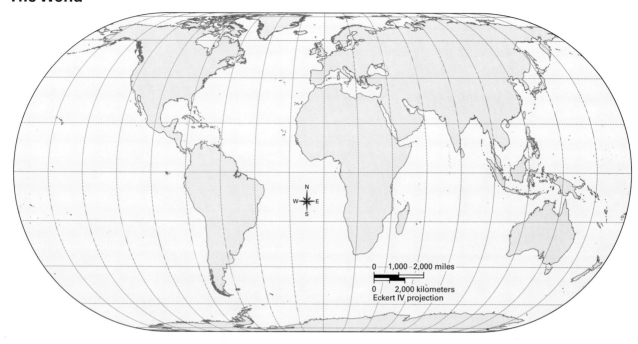

Eckert IV Projections Show Size but Distort Shape

The Eckert IV projection is an equal-area map. Equal-area maps show the sizes of places accurately. However, they distort shape near the poles. This is called *shape distortion*. Geographers often use Eckert IV projections to show the number of people in different areas.

The World

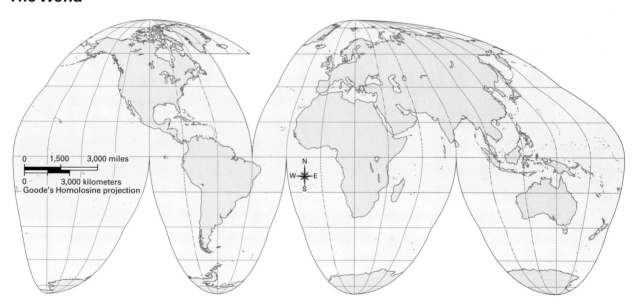

Goode's Homolosine Projections Show Continents but Distort Oceans

Goode's Homolosine projection uses a trick to help us see how the continents compare in size. It snips bits out of the oceans. This trick allows the continents to stretch without distorting their shapes. But it distorts the shape and size of the oceans.

AMAZON
BASIN

SOUTH
AMERICA

W N E
S

Amazon R.

Equator

BRAZILIAN
HIGHLANDS

São Francisco R.

Manaus

Sucre

Brasília

Salv

Equator

Equator

Equator

0   500   1,000 miles
0   500   1,000 kilometers
Lambert Azimuthal Equal-Area projection

Seeing the World Like a Geographer

2.1 Introduction

In the late summer of 1854, a highly contagious disease called *cholera* struck a neighborhood in London, England. People suddenly began suffering cramps, vomiting, and terrible thirst. So severe was the disease that many people died within hours of their first symptoms. In just 10 days, the disease killed about 500 people. Wagons groaned under the weight of corpses being taken away for mass burial.

No one knew how cholera spread or had any idea how to contain the outbreak—except a doctor named John Snow. Snow convinced officials to remove the handle from a water pump on Broad Street so that no one could draw water from the well located there. As the cholera outbreak slowed, Snow knew he had correctly identified the source of infection: polluted drinking water.

By thinking like a geographer, John Snow solved the mystery of how cholera was spreading through the city so quickly. He had surveyed the infected area to find out where people were dying. Later he showed his findings on a map by marking each house where people had succumbed to cholera. The map clearly showed that most of the deaths were clustered around the Broad Street pump.

John Snow's map is an example of a **thematic map**. A thematic map presents information related to only one theme, or topic. In this chapter, you will learn how to identify and read different types of thematic maps. In addition, you will see how geographers use these tools to make sense of Earth's physical and human features.

Essential Question

Why do geographers use a variety of maps to represent the world?

Geographers use maps for many purposes. A map legend tells you what kind of information the map shows. Colors, for example, can show different climates. Symbols can show physical features like rivers. Or they can identify human features such as roads and cities. Keep this map and its legend in mind as you try to answer the Essential Question.

Graphic Organizer

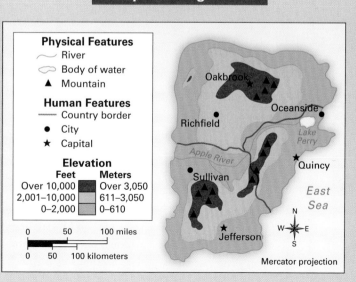

◀ Thematic maps of South America

2.2 The Geographic Setting

Thematic maps are all around us. Tune in to a news program and you're likely to see a weather map with the high and low temperatures for towns in your area. To find your way on the local bus system, you might use a map showing bus routes. By focusing on a specific topic, or theme, maps like these show information about some aspect of physical or human geography.

The Steep Rock Walls of Canyon de Chelly

Canyons are a landform found in Arizona. Canyon de Chelly was once home to Anasazi Indians. They built their villages in the steep canyon walls. You can find Canyon de Chelly on a physical features map of Arizona.

Thematic Maps Can Show Physical Geography Some thematic maps focus on physical geography. For instance, they may display Earth's **physical features**—the natural parts of Earth's surface. Such features include **landforms** like mountains, valleys, plains, and **plateaus**. Physical features also include bodies of water such as oceans, seas, rivers, and lakes.

Thematic maps can also illustrate other aspects of the physical environment. For example, some maps focus on **climate,** or long-term weather patterns. Climate maps show how much rainfall different areas receive. They also show how hot or cold various places tend to be in winter and summer.

Climate has a tremendous effect on the types of **vegetation,** or trees and other plants, that will grow in an area. You can see this by comparing a climate map of Earth with a vegetation map. A vegetation map shows the kinds of trees and other plants that grow in various places. In many ways it looks like a climate map, although other factors also affect what will grow where.

Thematic Maps Can Show Human Geography Thematic maps can also focus on human geography. John Snow's map of the cholera deaths near the Broad Street pump is a good example. Another example is a political map. The political map on the next page shows the borders of the 50 U.S. states. Political maps of larger areas show the borders between countries. In addition to borders, political maps also show important cities, such as the capitals of states and countries.

Another type of thematic map shows **population density**. This is the average number of people living in a unit of area, such as a square mile. The higher the number, the more crowded an area is. A population density map reveals where large numbers of people cluster.

Besides showing where people live, a thematic map can show what they do. A map of **economic activity** focuses on the ways people produce, buy, and sell goods and services. This kind of map might show the main types of business and industry in an area. It might also show the **natural resources** that fuel the area's economy. Natural resources are useful items found in nature, such as wood, coal, and oil.

A Map's Title and Legend State Its Theme To read a thematic map, first look at a map's title. The title usually states the topic of the map. Then look at the **map legend** to determine how to read the map's symbols. On the U.S. political map, the legend shows the symbols for the national and state capitals. A map legend may also explain how the map uses colors. For instance, a thematic map might use colors to show differences in elevation or population density.

▶ Geoterms

climate the pattern of weather over a long period of time

economic activity any action that relates to the making, buying, and selling of goods and services

landform any natural feature of Earth's surface that has a distinct shape. Landforms include major features such as continents, plains, plateaus, and mountain ranges. They also include minor features such as hills, valleys, canyons, and dunes.

physical feature any natural characteristic of Earth's surface, such as landforms and bodies of water

population density the average number of people who live in a unit of area, such as a square mile. Population density measures how crowded an area is.

region an area defined by one or more natural or cultural characteristics that set it apart from other areas

thematic map a map that shows a particular theme, or topic

vegetation all the plants and trees in an area

Political Maps

Political maps are one type of thematic map. These maps help us see where countries, states, and important cities are located. On this map of the United States, you can see the borders of your state. A star marks the state's capital. A star with a circle around it shows the nation's capital.

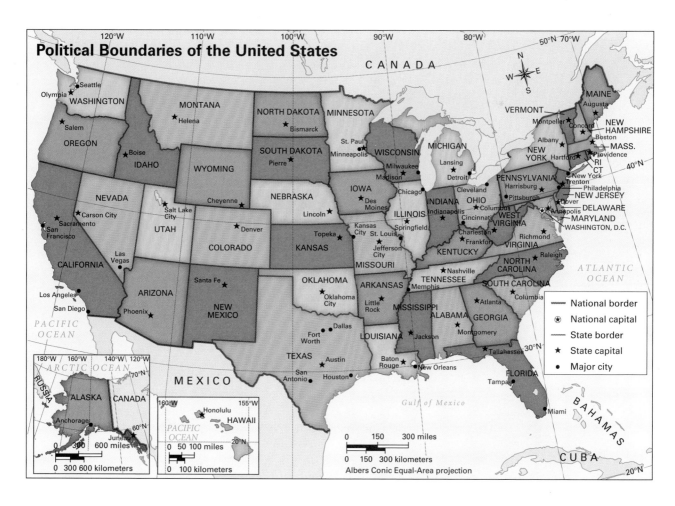

Political Boundaries of the United States

2.3 Mapping Earth's Physical Features

In the winter, snowboarders look for a snowy mountain to practice their sport on. In the summer, vacationers seek to cool off by a lake or river. These are just three of the landforms and bodies of water that you might see on a physical features map.

Common Landforms Geographers have given names to the many landforms found on Earth. Some landforms have distinctive shapes when viewed from above. A long, narrow **peninsula,** for example, juts out from a continent into the ocean and is surrounded by water on three sides. Other landforms have distinct shapes when viewed from ground level. Mountain ranges tower over low, flat plains. A **plateau** is a raised, flat area of land. A canyon is a deep, narrow valley with steep sides.

Physical features maps show the shapes of features as seen from above. They also show the elevation, or height above sea level, of various features. These maps typically use colors and shading to show changes in elevation.

Bodies of Water Geographers also label bodies of water on physical features maps. Many kinds of water bodies appear on continents. For instance, rivers flow down from mountains and make their way to the sea. Lakes are entirely surrounded by land. Other water bodies are created where oceans and seas meet continents. A bay is part of an ocean that is enclosed by an inward-curving stretch of coastline. A **gulf** is a body of water that cuts deeply into the shoreline and is enclosed by land on three sides.

Landforms and Water Bodies

You will see both landforms and bodies of water labeled on maps. This diagram shows many of these physical features.

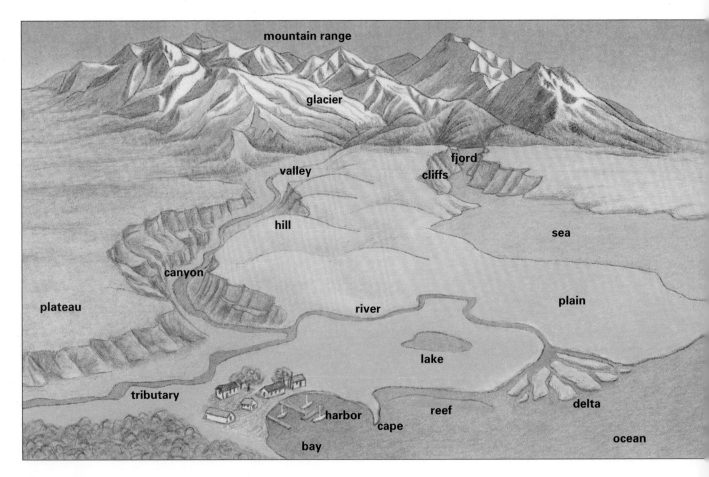

Physical Features of India

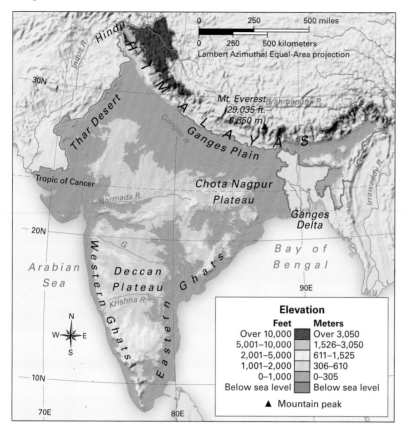

Physical Features Maps

This map shows major physical features in India. The Himalayas are India's highest physical feature. Two long rivers, the Ganges and the Brahmaputra, flow out of the Himalayas. They form one of the world's largest river deltas where they meet the Bay of Bengal.

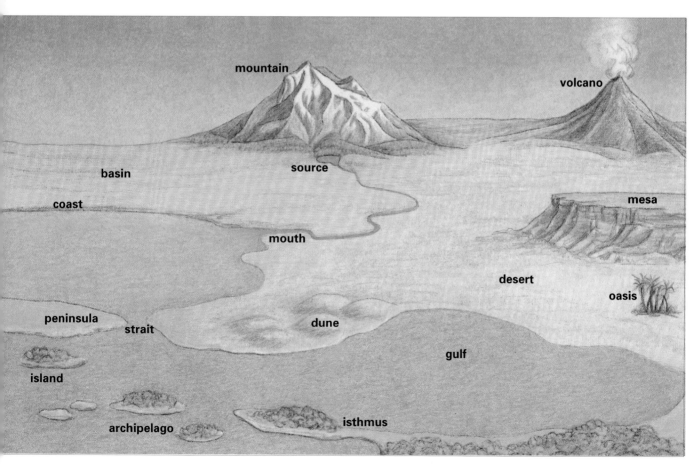

2.4 Hot, Cold, Wet, Dry: Earth's Climates

Do you check a weather report each morning to see what the day will be like? Are most days sunny? Or does it rain a lot where you live? Such long-term patterns in weather are called *climate*.

Climate Zones To study climates, geographers divide Earth into **climate zones**. Each zone has a particular pattern of temperature and **precipitation:** rain, snow, or other forms of moisture. This pattern is often shown on a **climagraph,** like those you see below.

A climagraph shows the average temperature and precipitation in a place over a year. The letters at the bottom of the graph stand for the months of the year. The curved line indicates the average monthly temperatures, while the bars show the average monthly precipitation.

Location Affects Climate Many factors affect a location's climate, but none is more important than latitude. Places in tropical latitudes, close to the equator, get the most direct rays from the sun all year—and have hot weather year-round. Places at high latitudes, close to the North and South poles, receive much less sunlight and remain quite cold all year.

Elevation, or altitude, also affects climate. Places at high elevations have colder climates than those lower down. Large bodies of water can also affect an area's climate. In coastal areas, ocean winds and warm-water currents keep temperatures even year-round. Places farther inland have more extreme climates, with hotter summers and colder winters. You'll learn more about the factors that affect climate throughout this book.

World Climate Zones

Climagraphs for the 12 climate zones found around the world are shown below.

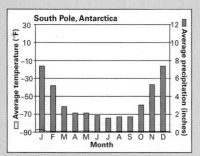

ice cap very cold all year with permanent ice and snow

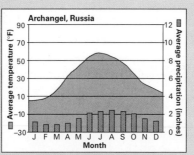

subarctic cold, snowy winters and cool, rainy summers

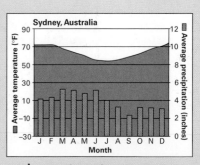

marine west coast warm summers, cool winters, and rainfall all year

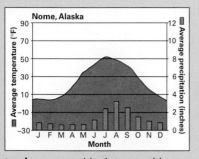

tundra very cold winters, cold summers, and little rain or snow

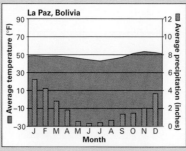

highlands temperature and precipitation vary with latitude and elevation

humid continental warm, rainy summers and cool, snowy winters

Climate Zones of Australia

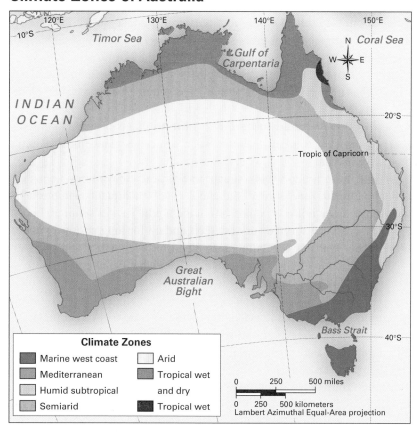

Climate Zones

- Marine west coast
- Mediterranean
- Humid subtropical
- Semiarid
- Arid
- Tropical wet and dry
- Tropical wet

0   250   500 miles
0   250   500 kilometers
Lambert Azimuthal Equal-Area projection

Climate Maps

Australia has seven climate zones. This climate map shows each zone in a different color.

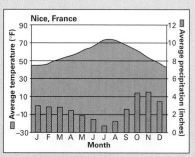

Mediterranean warm all year with dry summers and short, rainy winters

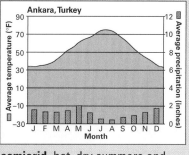

semiarid hot, dry summers and cool, dry winters

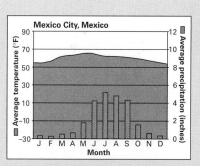

tropical wet and dry hot all year with rainy and dry seasons

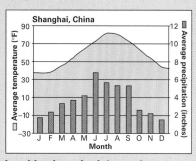

humid subtropical hot, rainy summers and mild winters with some rain

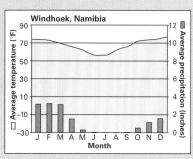

arid hot and dry all year with very little rain

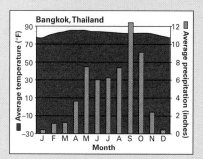

tropical wet hot and rainy all year

2.5 Trees and Other Plants: Earth's Vegetation

Think about the climate where you live. Now think about the kinds of trees and other plants that grow nearby. In an **arid** climate like a **desert**, you might see hardy cacti and scrubby brush. In a **humid continental** climate, you might see lofty fir and pine trees that stay green all year. Climate has a major effect on the kind of vegetation that grows in a place.

Vegetation Is Adapted to Its Environment Plants of some kind grow nearly everywhere on Earth. But in order to survive, plants must adapt to their environment.

Plants have found ways to adapt to even extreme environments. A tundra climate zone is very cold and dry, yet small plants and bushes grow there and wildflowers blossom in the tundra's short summer. In arid climates, cacti can survive very hot days and go for long periods without water. Other kinds of vegetation need plentiful precipitation to thrive.

In addition to climate, other factors affect what plants grow where. Among them are elevation, amount of sunlight, and richness of the soil.

Global Vegetation Zones Geographers study where different plants grow by dividing the world into **vegetation zones**. In each zone, a certain mix of plants has adapted to similar conditions.

Like climate zones, vegetation zones are affected by latitude and elevation. They range from the barren ice cap zones at the poles to the dense broadleaf evergreen forest zones near the equator. Highlands vegetation zones are usually on mountain slopes.

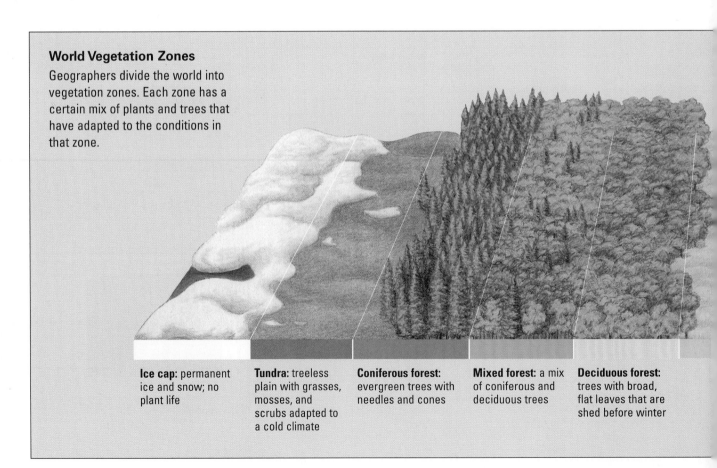

World Vegetation Zones

Geographers divide the world into vegetation zones. Each zone has a certain mix of plants and trees that have adapted to the conditions in that zone.

Ice cap: permanent ice and snow; no plant life

Tundra: treeless plain with grasses, mosses, and scrubs adapted to a cold climate

Coniferous forest: evergreen trees with needles and cones

Mixed forest: a mix of coniferous and deciduous trees

Deciduous forest: trees with broad, flat leaves that are shed before winter

Vegetation Zones of North Africa

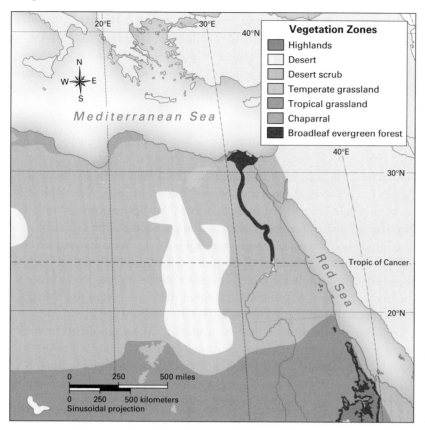

Vegetation Zones
- Highlands
- Desert
- Desert scrub
- Temperate grassland
- Tropical grassland
- Chaparral
- Broadleaf evergreen forest

Vegetation Maps

This map shows the vegetation zones found in North Africa. Chaparral thrives beside the Mediterranean Sea. Desert and desert scrub are found in the dry Sahara. A narrow band of broadleaf evergreen forest appears in the northeast corner of North Africa. What do you think allows tropical trees to survive in such an arid region?

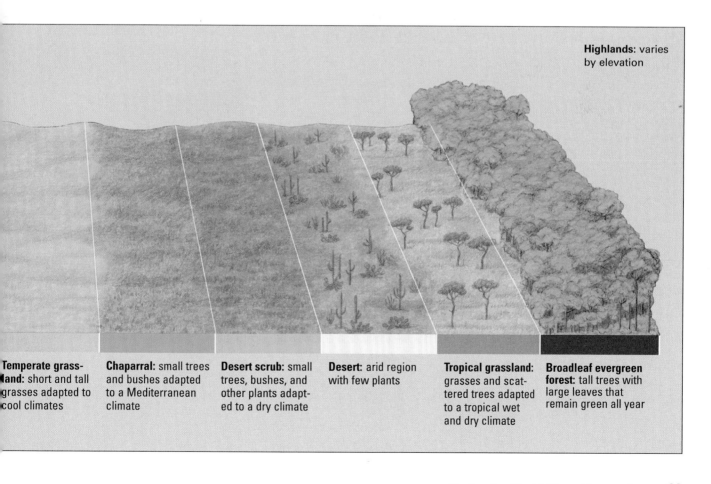

Highlands: varies by elevation

Temperate grassland: short and tall grasses adapted to cool climates

Chaparral: small trees and bushes adapted to a Mediterranean climate

Desert scrub: small trees, bushes, and other plants adapted to a dry climate

Desert: arid region with few plants

Tropical grassland: grasses and scattered trees adapted to a tropical wet and dry climate

Broadleaf evergreen forest: tall trees with large leaves that remain green all year

2.6 Where People Live: Population Density

In 2000, about 8 million people resided in New York City. They were jammed into an area of about 300 square miles. Compare this with the town of Skwentna, Alaska, where 111 people were spread out over about 450 square miles. When it comes to crowding, these two places are about as different as they can be. Geographers show these kinds of differences using population density maps.

Population Density Measures Crowding Population density tells us how crowded a place is. To calculate the density of a place, divide the total number of people living there by the location's total land area. The higher the result, the more crowded the place is. In 2000, New York City had a population density of more than 26,000 people per square mile. In contrast, Skwentna had less than 1 person per square mile.

Population density affects how people live. In Skwentna, houses are so spread out that people rarely see their neighbors. There are no roads so residents use airplanes, boats, or snowmobiles to get to the local store and the post office. Skwentna's version of rush hour comes in February, when dogsled racers speed through town.

Things are far different in New York City. Many people live in high-rise apartments, where they may have hundreds of neighbors just in their own building. Every day at rush hour, New Yorkers pour into railroads, ferries, and underwater tunnels to get to their destinations. Millions of "straphangers" hold on tight as they jostle one another in the city's crowded subways.

Population Density from High to Low

Population density is a measure of crowding. Some countries are very densely populated. Others are not. These photographs show places with different population densities.

More Than 250 People per Square Mile

Dhaka, Bangladesh, is one of the most crowded places on Earth. On average, many more than 250 people live in a square mile of this busy city.

125 to 250 People per Square Mile

Austria is a fairly crowded country. On average, between 125 and 250 people live in every square mile of this mountainous land.

Population Density of China

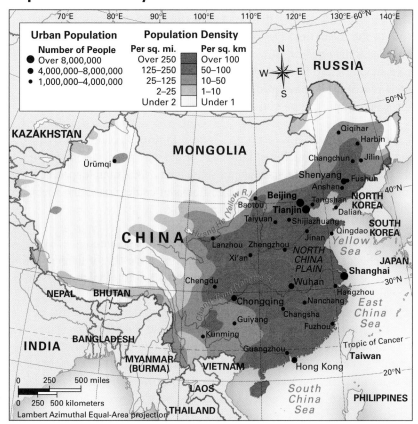

Population Density Maps

Population density maps show patterns of where people live. On this map, much of the North China Plain is colored purple. So are many coastal areas. These are the most crowded parts of China.

25 to 125 People per Square Mile

This uncrowded New England village has a lot of space for living. On average, between 25 and 125 people live in every square mile of the town.

2 to 25 People per Square Mile

This photograph of Ireland's countryside shows a thinly populated country. Ireland has some big cities. But in most of Ireland, there is an average of 2 to 25 people per square mile.

Fewer Than 2 People per Square Mile

These herders in Mongolia live in an almost empty country. Fewer than 2 people live in every square mile of areas like this one.

2.7 Economic Activity: Land and Resources

Do you like chocolate? This sweet treat comes from cocoa beans, the fruit of the cacao tree. The cacao tree grows only in hot, humid tropical areas near the equator. However, the factories that convert cocoa beans into chocolate are found mostly in Europe and the United States. The locations of cacao **plantations** and chocolate factories are examples of the kind of information you might see on an economic activity map.

Land Use Shows How People Make a Living Economic activity maps often show patterns of **land use,** or the way people use the land they live on to meet their needs. In some areas, for example, people use land for farming or for grazing large flocks of cattle, goats, and sheep. In other areas, they may use land for mining.

Natural Resources Affect Economic Activities Economic activity also depends on a country's natural resources. **Forestry,** or the harvesting of trees to produce wood products, is important in forested areas. Near oceans, fishing is an important industry.

Some resources lie concealed beneath the ground. This is true of mineral resources such as iron, copper, and gold. **Fossil fuels** such as oil, coal, and natural gas are extracted from Earth and burned to meet people's energy needs. Uranium, another underground energy resource, provides fuel for nuclear power plants. In contrast, moving water is an easy-to-find energy resource. Dams can be built on rivers to harness the moving water's energy and convert it to **hydroelectric power**.

Land Use and Resources

How people use land depends on the natural resources in their area. Some still get their food by hunting and gathering. Some grow crops and raise animals to sell. Others make and sell goods created from natural resources.

Hunting and Gathering in Greenland

Many people still hunt animals and gather plants for food. Most live in small groups that move from place to place. This hunter in Greenland tracks polar bears and seals across ice and snow.

Subsistence Farming in Africa

Some farmers grow only enough crops to feed their own families. This is called *subsistence farming*. More than half of the land in Africa is used for subsistence farming. Most of the subsistence farmers in Africa are women.

Commercial Farming in Colombia

Commercial farmers raise crops or livestock to sell. Commercial farms are often very large. Many grow a variety of crops. Others, like this coffee farm in Colombia, specialize in just one crop.

Nomadic Herding in China

Millions of people around the world are nomadic herders. They move around often to find food and water for their animals. This herder in China uses the animals' milk, hides, and other products.

Economic Activity of Europe

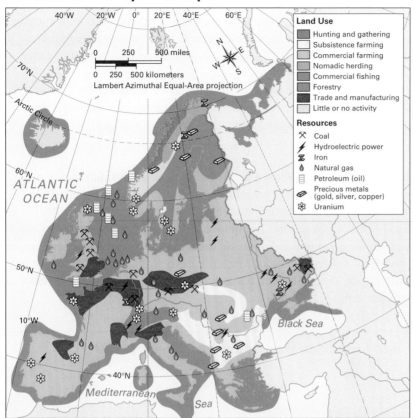

Economic Activity Maps

The colors on this map show land use patterns in Europe. The most widespread land use is commercial farming. The symbols show the locations of important resources in Europe. Where is petroleum, or oil, found in Europe?

Livestock Raising in Australia

Cattle, sheep, and goats are raised on huge ranches. More than half of the farmland in Australia is used for raising sheep and cows. Australian livestock raisers lead the world in production of wool for clothing and carpets.

Commercial Fishing in Asia

Many people make their living by fishing the world's oceans, lakes, and rivers. The Pacific Ocean yields more than half the world supply of fish. In 2000, 35 million people worked in the fishing industry. More than 80 percent were in Asia.

Forestry in the United States

Forestry uses trees as a resource for making homes, furniture, and paper. In 2003, the United States was the leading supplier of wood in the world. The United States also used up more forest resources than any other country.

Trade and Manufacturing in Ireland

Manufacturing turns resources into goods to sell. In this Irish factory, workers assemble computers for shipment around the world.

2.8 Organizing Earth's Surface: Regions

As you have learned, geographers use many kinds of maps to help make sense of the world. Some of these maps focus on physical geography; others focus on human geography. All of them reveal interesting patterns to explore.

Geographers use these patterns to organize Earth's surface into **regions**. A region is an area with one or more features that set it apart from other areas. As you will see, the concept of region allows geographers to divide the world in useful ways.

Unique Features Define a Region Think about the community in which you live. Does it have a business district? A shopping mall? An industrial park? A civic or community center? A residential neighborhood? Each of these areas has unique features that set it apart from other parts of the community. You might think of one area as a business region, another as a shopping region, and still another as a residential region. Each region looks different, has a different purpose, and has different requirements.

Transportation Region Maps

A region is an area with one or more features that set it apart from other areas. A feature might be something physical like climate. Or it might be a human feature such as roads and train lines. The network of routes on this map defines a transportation region in the San Francisco Bay Area.

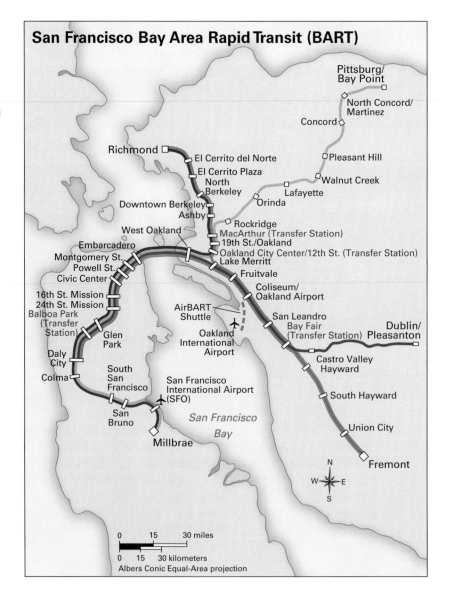

San Francisco Bay Area Rapid Transit (BART)

Geographers define regions in several ways. The Sunbelt is a region defined by physical, or natural, features. It is a region made up of states in the southern and southwestern United States, from Florida to California. What sets the Sunbelt apart from other regions is its warm, sunny climate. The Corn Belt, in contrast, is a region defined by human features. It is made up of states in the center of the country, such as Indiana, Illinois, and Iowa, where raising corn is an important economic activity.

Dividing the World into Seven Major Regions The world is a very large place to make sense of. For this reason, geographers usually divide it into regions to study. These world regions are still very large, but each has its own distinct features.

This book divides the world into seven major regions. Each region is shown in a different color on the world regions map below. These colors are your guide to finding each region in this book. Your study of a region will begin with an introduction to its most important physical and human features. In that introduction, you will begin to see what makes each of these regions unique.

World Regions Maps

This book divides the world into seven large regions. Each region has certain distinct physical features. Each also has unique human features.

Regions of the World

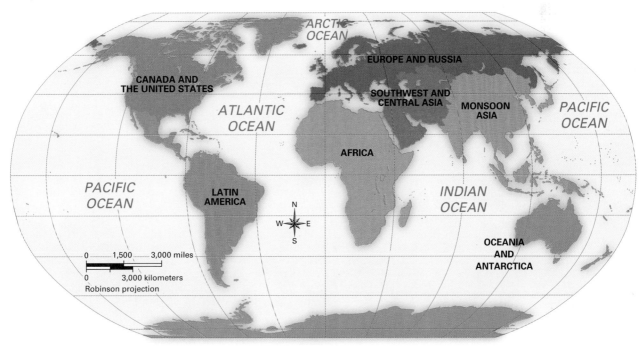

Canada and the United States

Introducing the Region:
Physical and Human Geography

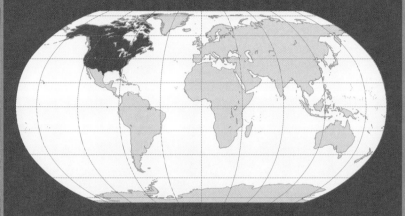

What do you see in this photograph?

See page 514 for details.

▼

Canada and the United States make up the region that covers most of North America. This region is bounded by the Atlantic Ocean on the east and the Pacific Ocean on the west. The Arctic Ocean lies to the north of this region. The Gulf of Mexico lies to the south. North America is the third largest continent in the world.

This large region contains two subregions. Canada and Alaska make up the northern part. The 48 continental United States make up the southern part. West of the Great Lakes, the two subregions are separated by the 49th parallel of latitude. East of the Great Lakes, the St. Lawrence River separates the two subregions.

Physical Features of Canada and the United States

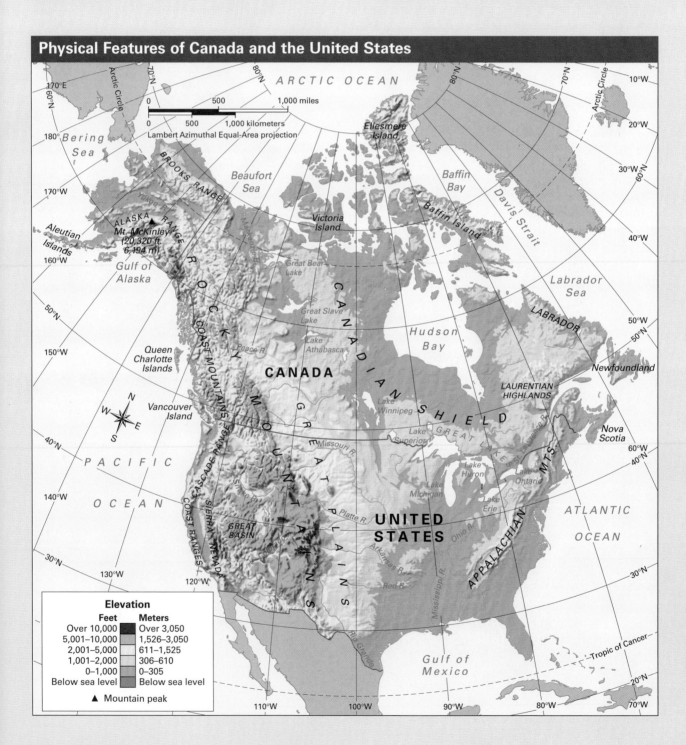

Physical Features

If you look at a physical map of this region, you see mountains running along both sides with a large, flat area in the center. This flat area runs from the Arctic Ocean to the Gulf of Mexico. It is made up of **shield** and plains.

The term *shield* refers to the large core of very old rock that lies at the base of each continent. In North America, this rock core was exposed thousands of years ago. During the ice ages, **glaciers** scraped across the land, taking the soil with them. They left just a thin layer of soil in eastern and central Canada.

Plains are flat or gently rolling areas of land. Much of the soil that glaciers scraped from the Canadian Shield ended up on the plains of Canada and the United States.

Canada and Alaska

The Canadian Shield covers almost half of Canada. The rest of this subregion contains islands, lakes, plains, and mountains.

The glaciers that scraped the shield also dug the huge holes that became the Great Lakes. These lakes lie between Canada and the United States. They are the world's largest group of **freshwater** lakes. The St. Lawrence River connects the Great Lakes to the ocean.

To the far north are many smaller lakes and Hudson Bay. The region extends past the Arctic Circle and ends with a scattering of islands. The largest is named Baffin Island.

In the Atlantic Ocean, off the southeast coast of Newfoundland, lie the Grand Banks. The ocean is very shallow here.

The Rocky Mountains stretch over 3,000 miles through North America.

Far to the west, in the Alaska Range, is the highest peak in North America. Mount McKinley rises 20,320 feet above sea level.

Continental United States

Two major mountain ranges run through the continental United States. In the east, the Appalachians are a gentle range of rounded peaks and deep valleys. In the west, the Rocky Mountains jut up into jagged, snow-capped peaks. The Rockies reach all the way from Alaska to New Mexico.

Between these two ranges, wide plains stretch across the middle of the continent. This vast, mostly flat region extends about 2,500 miles north and south. From the Rockies, the dry and treeless Great Plains slope down to the central lowlands.

A large system of rivers drains most of the plains between the Rocky Mountains and the Appalachians. These rivers all flow into the muddy Mississippi River. The Mississippi empties into the Gulf of Mexico.

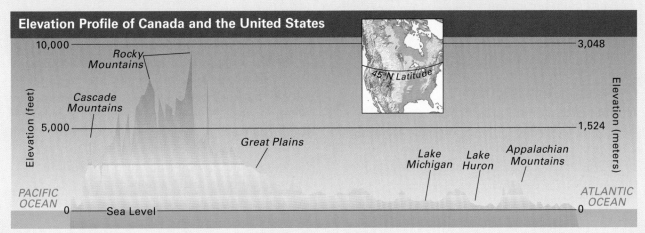

Elevation Profile of Canada and the United States

Elevation (feet)

10,000

Rocky Mountains

Cascade Mountains

5,000

Great Plains

PACIFIC OCEAN

0   Sea Level

45°N Latitude

Lake Michigan

Lake Huron

Appalachian Mountains

ATLANTIC OCEAN

0

Elevation (meters)

3,048

1,524

Climate

Climate varies widely across this large region, which reaches from the chilly Arctic to the warm waters of the Gulf of Mexico.

The northern parts of this landmass fall in **tundra** and **subarctic** climate zones. In subarctic climates, winters are very long, cold, and snowy. Summers are very short. They may be cool and rainy.

The tundra climate zone is even more severe. Here it is cold all year, even in summer. Winter temperatures are usually well below 0°F. In summer, the high temperatures may not be far above freezing (32°F). Areas with tundra climate get very little rain or snow. Beneath the surface, the ground is always frozen.

These colder climates occur in places that don't get a lot of direct sunlight. The sun's rays are most direct at the equator. In general, the farther a region is from the equator, the colder the climate will be. Since the northern part of this region is very far from the equator, it is very cold.

Canada and Alaska

Most of Canada and Alaska have either a tundra or a subarctic climate. But the climate warms up as you move farther south. The area closest to the continental United States enjoys a mostly **humid continental** climate. Winters are still freezing cold, but summers can be hot and steamy.

Nearly all of Canada and Alaska have heavy snows in the winter. But on the west coast of British Columbia, the **marine west coast** climate brings more rain than snow. There, and in the southern part of Canada, summers are warmer and drier.

Continental United States

No part of the continental United States has a tundra or subarctic climate. The climate here can vary greatly, depending on where you are. One state, California, has as many as five different climate zones.

The southern part of the United States is generally warm year-round. The Southeast

Mount Washington in New Hampshire has been called "Home of the World's Worst Weather." The fastest recorded wind speed ever, 231 mph, was recorded there in 1934. The research station is open year-round. In what month do you think this picture was probably taken?

has a **humid subtropical** climate, influenced by the Gulf of Mexico. Hot, rainy summers follow mild winters that see some rain. The climate of Florida's southern tip is **tropical wet and dry**. There, it is hot all year with both rainy and dry seasons.

Arid and **semiarid** climates are common in the Southwest. This area is hot and dry in the summer and pleasant in the winter, with very little rain. Many older people from colder climates choose to retire in the Southwest.

The rest of the western United States has a variety of climates. The Sierra Nevada and Rocky mountains have a **highlands** climate. Along the northern Pacific Coast, a marine west coast climate brings mild winters and lots of rain.

Most parts of the Midwest and Northeast have a humid continental climate. People here enjoy four distinct seasons. Summers are quite warm and winters are cold, often with snow and ice storms.

Vegetation

Just as the climate varies across Canada and the United States, so does the vegetation.

One widespread **vegetation zone** in this region is **temperate grassland**. Mainly short and tall grasses grow in temperate grasslands. Few trees grow in this zone because there is not enough rain. The Great Plains area of the United States and Canada is one of the world's largest temperate grasslands. This area combines a long growing season with fertile soil. As a result, the Great Plains provide very productive farmland.

Another special vegetation zone in this region is **tundra**. This vegetation zone shares a name with the tundra climate zone, where it is cold year-round. The tundra vegetation zone is like a very cold **desert**. Few large plants can grow here.

Like temperate grasslands, the tundra is treeless. Because the ground is frozen, trees cannot send their roots down into the soil. Only very low grasses, mosses, and scrub cover the ground during the short summer. They provide food for the grazing animals that live on the tundra.

Canada and Alaska

The tundra spreads across the far northern islands and coasts of Canada. Much of Alaska's land is tundra as well. In the **ice cap** on Alaska's highest peaks and glaciers, no plant life grows at all. Most of Canada and the rest of Alaska are covered in **coniferous forests**, filled with trees such as cedar, fir, pine, and spruce. The needle-like leaves of these trees stay green all year.

The warmer climate in southeastern Canada supports **mixed forest**. Here you find a mix of both coniferous and deciduous trees. Deciduous trees, such as oak, elm, and birch, have broad leaves that they shed each fall. The south-central part of Canada is temperate grassland.

Continental United States

The vegetation of the continental United States ranges from tropical palms to desert sagebrush. There are thick pine forests in the West, grasses on the central plains, and forested swamps in the South.

Spreading up and down the East Coast are forests of all types—coniferous, deciduous, and mixed. The extreme Southeast—along the Gulf Coast and in Florida's Everglades—is home to **tropical grasslands**. The tough sawgrass and scattered trees in the Everglades are adapted to the tropical wet and dry climate.

Across the central part of the United States is a wide band of temperate grassland. This area was once thick with prairie grasses. However, much of the land has been plowed for farming. It is now covered with fields of corn, wheat, and other crops.

In the West, coniferous forests blanket the mountains. **Desert scrub** grows throughout the deserts and canyons of the Southwest and Great Basin. Along the California coast, **chaparral** dots the Coast Ranges.

Mangrove trees grow in the swamps of Everglades National Park in Florida.

All of the other regions of the world are made up of many countries. However, this region is made up of just two large countries: Canada and the United States. In land area, Canada is the second largest country in the world. Yet its population is quite small for its size. The United States is almost as large as Canada in land area. But the U.S. population is nine times the size of Canada's.

The two countries share a common cultural background. Most of the people are English-speaking, although Canada officially uses French as well. Both countries have native populations. Both countries were colonized by settlers from Europe about 500 years ago. In later years, immigration from all parts of the world has enriched the two countries with a wide variety of cultures.

Political Boundaries of Canada and the United States

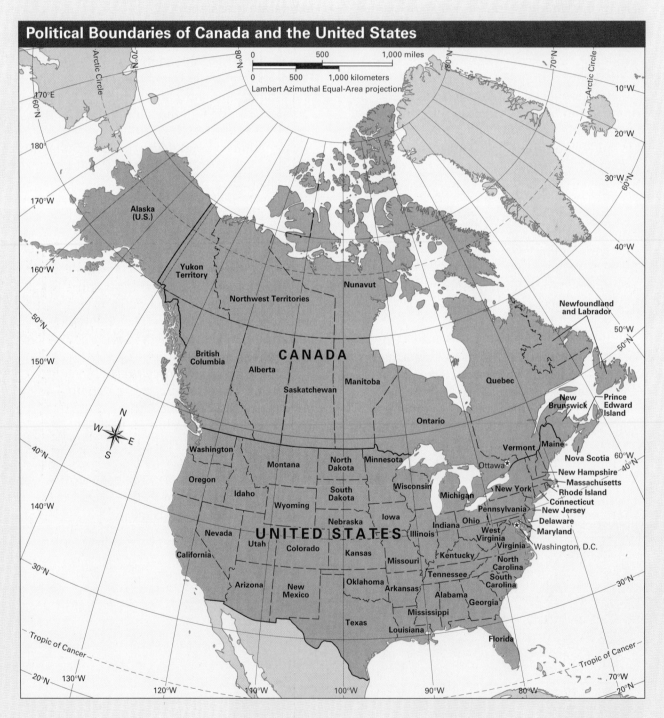

History

The histories of Canada and the United States reveal why these countries are so similar.

Early Times

Scholars believe that North American history began when bands of hunters migrated to Alaska from Asia. This happened more than 10,000 years ago. Over time, these first bands settled throughout the region. As they adapted to their environment, each group developed its own culture.

The Inuit, or Eskimo, people stayed in the far north. They hunted Arctic animals for food and clothing. Other groups settled along the west coast of the continent. Fish and trees were plentiful there and provided food, clothing, and shelter. Many groups settled in the central and eastern parts of the region. A group called the Anasazi built cliff houses in the southwestern United States.

The Colonial Period

Europeans began coming to North America in the 1500s. The French and British set up colonies along the eastern coast. The Spanish colonized Florida, Texas, and California.

The American colonies revolted against Britain in 1775. A successful war for independence followed. In 1783, the United States became an independent country.

Yet there was not freedom for everyone. Millions of slaves lived in the United States.

The country split over the question of slavery. It fought a **civil war** between 1861 and 1865. In 1865, slavery ended in the United States.

Canada was first colonized by the French. After a war, France turned Canada over to Great Britain in 1763. French culture still remains strong in Canada. Many Canadians speak French as their first language.

In 1867, Canadians won the right to govern themselves. Yet Canada still was part of the British Empire.

The Modern Era

In the twentieth century, Canada and the United States formed a strong bond. Canada gained its independence from Great Britain in 1931. People on both sides of the U.S.–Canadian border welcomed this event.

In 1939, war broke out in Europe. War was also raging in Asia. This global conflict is known as World War II. The United States and Canada worked closely together to end this war. Since then, they have continued to work together for world peace.

Today Canada and the United States are closely linked by trade. Canadians buy many products that are made or grown in the United States. Americans also buy many Canadian products. In 1994, the North American Free Trade Agreement (NAFTA) took effect. NAFTA made trade between the two countries easier. This trade pact allows most goods to move freely among Canada, the United States, and Mexico.

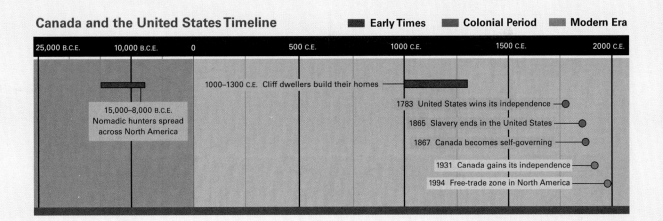

Canada and the United States Timeline   ■ Early Times   ■ Colonial Period   ■ Modern Era

25,000 B.C.E.   10,000 B.C.E.   0   500 C.E.   1000 C.E.   1500 C.E.   2000 C.E.

1000–1300 C.E. Cliff dwellers build their homes

15,000–8,000 B.C.E. Nomadic hunters spread across North America

1783 United States wins its independence

1865 Slavery ends in the United States

1867 Canada becomes self-governing

1931 Canada gains its independence

1994 Free-trade zone in North America

Population

More than 325 million people altogether live in Canada and the United States. This is about 6 percent of the world's population. The population of this region is growing very slowly compared with other parts of the world.

Some parts of this region are almost empty. The western deserts are too dry, and the far north is too cold for settlement. Very few people live in these places. Northern Canada is thinly settled, with a **population density** as low as one person per 43 square miles.

Most Canadians live close to the U.S. border. Toronto is the largest **urban** area in Canada. Throughout the region people tend to cluster in or near cities, where more jobs can be found.

Most people in Canada and the United States are Christian. Almost one fourth of these are Roman Catholics. Islam is the fastest growing religion here. Other faiths include Judaism, Buddhism, and Hinduism. One out of 10 people have no religion.

Canada and the United States: Major Religions

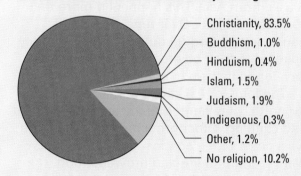

- Christianity, 83.5%
- Buddhism, 1.0%
- Hinduism, 0.4%
- Islam, 1.5%
- Judaism, 1.9%
- Indigenous, 0.3%
- Other, 1.2%
- No religion, 10.2%

Canada and the United States: Urban and Rural Population, 2000

Urban, 79.1%
Rural, 20.9%
10% of = the total population

Canada and the United States: Population Growth, 1950–2050

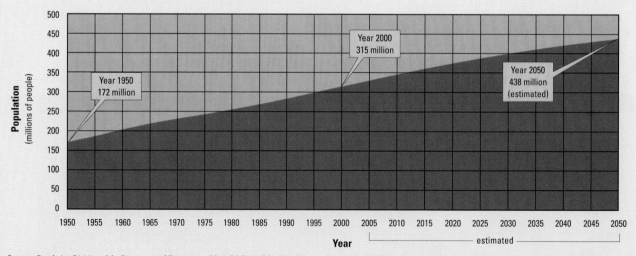

Year 1950
172 million

Year 2000
315 million

Year 2050
438 million
(estimated)

Sources: *Population Division of the Department of Economic and Social Affairs of the United Nations Secretariat,* "World Population Prospects: The 2004 Revision" and "World Urbanization Prospects: The 2003 Revision," esa.un.org/unpp. "Religion," *Encyclopædia Britannica,* 2005, Encyclopædia Britannica Premium Service, www.britannica.com.

Economic Activity

Canada and the United States are rich in many kinds of resources. One of these is good farmland. As a result, **commercial farming** is an important **economic activity** in this region.

Commercial farming is the growing of farm products for sale to others. Wheat, for example, is a commercial crop. It is grown widely in the U.S. Midwest and in the prairie provinces of Canada—Alberta, Manitoba, and Saskatchewan. The farmers of this region sell their crops around the world. They produce about half of the world's grain exports. From California and Florida, farmers ship fruits and vegetables. They help make this region the world's leading food exporter.

Forestry is also important to this region. Forestry is the planting, growing, and harvesting of trees. North America was once covered with thick forests. Over time, many of the trees were cut down for fuel and lumber. In southern Canada and in several corners of the United States, logging is still a big industry.

Resources

Canada and the United States also have a wealth of mineral resources. Oil and coal, used for energy, are the most important. Texas, Alaska, and Alberta have thriving oil industries. Coal is plentiful in the Appalachian

Cold winters have little impact on oil fields in Alberta, Canada. Oil is pumped all year, regardless of the season.

and Rocky mountains. It is also mined in the river valleys of the central United States.

Mines in Quebec, Ontario, and British Columbia produce gold, nickel, and copper. In the western United States, New Mexico has large reserves of uranium. Arizona is rich in copper deposits.

Land Use

Much of this region is used for livestock raising. Cattle graze widely across the western range. Sheep ranches are also common.

Trade and manufacturing are strong in the urban centers of this region. In the United States, manufacturing plays an especially big role in the Midwest and Northeast. Factories there produce cars, steel, plastics, glass, and textiles.

Orange groves need lots of sunshine and frost-free winters. Oranges are an important crop in Florida and California.

Settlement Patterns and Ways of Life in Canada

3

3.1 Introduction

James is a sixth grade student in Pond Inlet, a town in Nunavut. Located in the far northern part of Canada, Nunavut is the homeland for the Inuit people. When James goes to school in January, the sun never comes up. Looking out of his classroom window in the dark winter months, all he sees are streetlights and the lights of cars. Some of his classes at school are taught in English while others are in Inuktitut, the language of the Inuit. The majority of sixth graders, including James, also speak Inuktitut at home. In fact, in their language, the town's name is Mittimatalik.

Compare James with Marie, a sixth grader in Quebec City, which is in eastern Canada. Marie is French Canadian, and all of her classes are in taught in French. Because of Quebec City's location, it is always light outside when Marie is in school—she can watch many people passing by on the streets outdoors. James and Marie live in the same country, but their experiences are very different.

Canada is such a large, diverse country that it is often called a **plural society**. This term reflects the fact that the Canadian people have come from many countries and cultures. While most people share a Canadian identity, many also keep the traditions of their parents and grandparents.

Canadians often divide their country into five **regions**. In this chapter, you will explore these regions and determine how differently people live in each one. You will also discover how location influences people's lives.

Essential Question

How does where you live influence how you live?

This illustration shows the five regions of Canada. Each region has a different climate. Each region's history and economy are different too. These differences affect how people live in Canada. Keep this illustration in mind as you try to answer the Essential Question.

Graphic Organizer

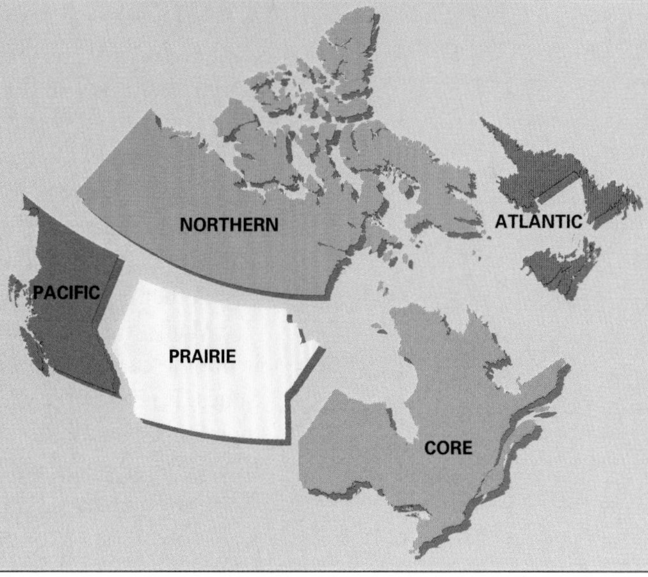

◀ Satellite image of Canada and the United States in winter

Canada's Population

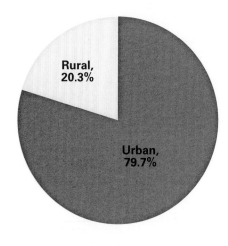

Most Canadians Live in Cities

Eight out of 10 Canadians live in urban areas. Only one fifth live in rural areas. Most Canadians live in the ecumene as well. This is found in the southern part of the country, mainly the southeast.

3.2 The Geographic Setting

In area, Canada is the world's second largest country, covering most of the northern part of the North American continent. The United States is Canada's neighbor to the south, and the two countries share a border that is about 5,000 miles long. This is the longest unguarded border in the world.

Canada's Three "Founding Peoples" The first people to settle in Canada probably came from Asia thousands of years ago. Pursuing mammoth, huge bison, and other game, the people crossed over a broad land bridge linking the continents of Asia and North America. In time, their descendants became the Inuit and other Native American groups. Groups moved southward, gradually spreading throughout the Americas. But the native peoples who still live in Canada are known as Canada's first "founding peoples."

Canada's second and third founding peoples came from Europe. In the early 1600s, the French established a settlement, calling the place by its Native American name, Quebec. Meanwhile, English colonists had settled on the Atlantic coast in what is now the state of Virginia. France and Great Britain struggled for power worldwide and in the mid-1700s fought a war for control of North America. When the war ended in 1763, Great Britain was victorious. As a result, France gave up Canada to Great Britain.

In the 1800s, large numbers of English settlers came to Canada, but the French Canadians held on to their language and way of life. Meanwhile, Canada attracted settlers from Ireland, Scotland, Sweden, Norway, and Germany. By the early 1900s, Italians, Ukrainians, and Jews were arriving from southern and eastern Europe. Some settled in the big eastern cities while others began farms on the flat land in central Canada. Chinese, Japanese, and Filipino people came from Asia as well, and many settled along Canada's Pacific coast.

All of these groups have helped to shape Canada's plural society. Its founding peoples have kept their languages and traditions. Newer settlers have also held on to traditional ways. Yet all are Canadians.

A Thinly Settled Country Canada is large in area but small in population. In 2001, just over 30 million people lived there. That is fewer people than lived in the state of California.

Nearly 8 out of every 10 Canadians live in an **urban** area. These are areas in or around cities. The rest of the population make their homes in **rural** areas. These are parts of the country that are not near cities.

Most of Canada's people live within 100 miles of the United States. This strip of land lies within Canada's **ecumene**. An ecumene is a region that is well suited for people to live permanently.

Many Americans think that Canadians' lives are just like theirs. This is not the case. It is true that many Canadians live close to the United States. It is also true that Canada and the United States are each other's most important trading partner. And it is true that they are good allies. But there are many political, economic, and cultural differences between the two countries.

► Geoterms

ecumene a geographic region that is well suited for permanent settlement by people. Areas not included in the ecumene are generally too dry, too cold, or too rugged for permanent human settlement.

plural society a society in which different cultural groups keep their own identity, beliefs, and traditions

rural found in or living in areas that are not close to cities

urban found in or living in a city

Canadians Cling to the Border

Canada has only about one tenth as many people as the United States. Much of the Canadian north lies outside the ecumene. It is so cold that few people choose to live there. Most of Canada's people live within 100 miles of the U.S. border.

Population Density of Canada

3.3 Canada's Five Regions

Canada is divided into provinces and territories. There are 10 provinces, each with its own government—much like states in the United States. A territory is an area that cannot become a province until its population is larger.

Geographers often divide Canada into five large regions, which are outlined in black on the map at the right. As you will see, each region has its own geography, history, and way of life.

Atlantic Region This region lines the Atlantic coast of Canada. The island of Newfoundland with Labrador on the mainland forms one province. The peninsula of Nova Scotia with an island to the northeast forms another. Two other provinces are Prince Edward Island and New Brunswick on the mainland.

Core Region This region in eastern Canada stretches north of the Great Lakes. It includes the two large provinces of Ontario and Quebec. It was in Quebec that the French, Canada's second founding people, made their first permanent settlement.

Prairie Region This region covers Canada's central plains—from grasslands to wooded country to plateaus. The region includes the provinces of Manitoba, Saskatchewan, and Alberta.

Pacific Region This region on Canada's Pacific coast is made up of the province of British Columbia. It has many islands and good harbors for ocean trade. It is also the most mountainous province.

Northern Region This region lies to the north of the provinces and reaches far into the Arctic Ocean. It includes Canada's three territories: the Yukon Territory, the Northwest Territories, and Nunavut. Nunavut, which means "our land," was carved from the Northwest Territories as a homeland for the Inuit people.

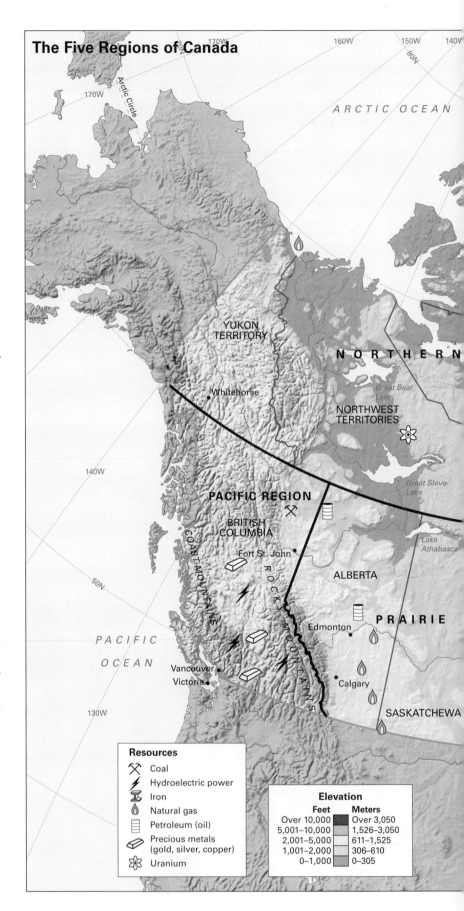

The Five Regions of Canada

Resources
- Coal
- Hydroelectric power
- Iron
- Natural gas
- Petroleum (oil)
- Precious metals (gold, silver, copper)
- Uranium

Elevation

Feet	Meters
Over 10,000	Over 3,050
5,001–10,000	1,526–3,050
2,001–5,000	611–1,525
1,001–2,000	306–610
0–1,000	0–305

3.4 Settlement Patterns: Who Lives Where?

Imagine that you could spread Canada's people out evenly. About eight people would live in every square mile of land. But Canada's people do not live like this. Outside of the large cities, an average of only two people live in every square mile.

The Atlantic Region This was the first area where Europeans settled in Canada. They came because fishing was so good in the North Atlantic. Until recent years, most people here made a living by fishing, but the ocean has been overfished. The government now limits fishing to make sure there will be fish in the future. As a result, many people have moved away.

The Core Region Most Canadians live in Canada's core region. This region has three of Canada's largest cities: Toronto, Montreal, and the **capital city** of Ottawa. In the past, people came to Ontario to work in its many factories. More recently they have come for jobs in banks, computer companies, and other businesses.

The Prairie Region About 5 million people live in the three prairie provinces. Farming was once the main activity here, but today the oil and gas business is booming in Alberta. As a result, Alberta is the fastest-growing province in Canada. Its largest cities, Edmonton and Calgary, are popular urban areas.

The Pacific Region British Columbia is home to more than 4 million people. Most live around the cities of Vancouver and Victoria. People also

A Population on the Move

Parts of Canada lost people between 1996 and 2001. Other parts gained people. The numbers show the percent of the loss (–) or gain (+) compared to the 1996 population. Although Nunavut shows a large population growth, its total population in 1991 was only 27,000 people.

Population Change in Canada, 1996–2001

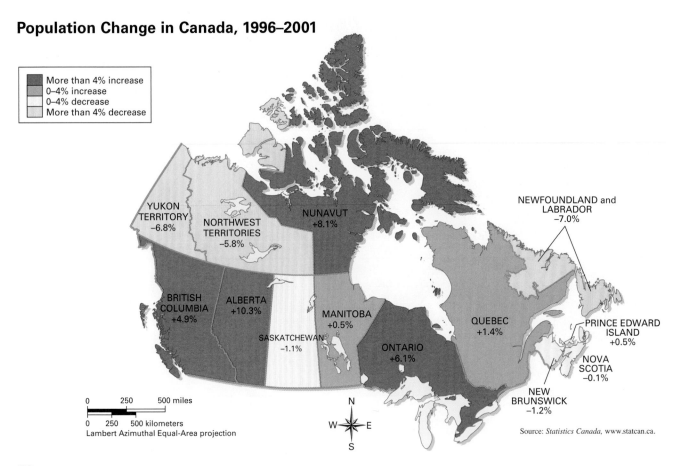

Legend:
- More than 4% increase
- 0–4% increase
- 0–4% decrease
- More than 4% decrease

YUKON TERRITORY −6.8%
NORTHWEST TERRITORIES −5.8%
NUNAVUT +8.1%
NEWFOUNDLAND and LABRADOR −7.0%
BRITISH COLUMBIA +4.9%
ALBERTA +10.3%
SASKATCHEWAN −1.1%
MANITOBA +0.5%
ONTARIO +6.1%
QUEBEC +1.4%
PRINCE EDWARD ISLAND +0.5%
NOVA SCOTIA −0.1%
NEW BRUNSWICK −1.2%

0   250   500 miles
0   250   500 kilometers
Lambert Azimuthal Equal-Area projection

Source: *Statistics Canada*, www.statcan.ca.

live on the western slopes of the Rocky Mountains. Many people from Asia have moved to this region because of its location on the Pacific Ocean.

The Northern Region This is the largest region in land area, but it has the smallest number of people. Only about 100,000 people live in all three territories. Living in the region is costly because it is so far from other places. In addition, there are so few roads that goods often have to be flown in by plane.

3.5 A Plural Society: Who Speaks What?

If you walked around Toronto, Ontario, you would hear people speaking a variety of languages. Of course, you would hear English and French, but many other cultural groups live there as well. Toronto has one of the most multicultural school districts in the world. More than half of the students in the city speak a language other than English at home.

The Atlantic Region Most people in this region speak English as their first language because their families came from Great Britain to farm or fish many years ago. Some French speakers settled here as well, and French remains their first language.

The Core Region In Ontario most people speak English; in Quebec most people speak French. Other languages spoken in this region include Chinese, Italian, and Portuguese. For many years, Canadians argued about which language their government should use. The government finally ended the argument by making both French and English the country's official languages.

Some people in Quebec think their province should be a separate country. In 1995, the people of Quebec voted whether to make the province its own state, independent of Canada. In a very close vote, the measure was rejected by just 1 percent.

The Prairie Region European settlers first came to this region to farm. Now oil in Alberta attracts newcomers. English is the first language for more than four out of five people who live in this region. But people who speak French, German, and Ukrainian have moved here too, seeking work and homes.

The Pacific Region Here English is the first language, but many people from Asia also live in this region. Chinese is the second most common language. In addition, people from India speak Punjabi, and people from the Philippines speak Tagalog.

The Northern Region Almost two thirds of the people in the north speak English as their first language. Many are English-speaking Canadians who moved here to work for the government. Most of the founding peoples, such as the Inuit, have retained their cultures. The Inuit, for instance, continue to speak Inuktitut.

Canada's Official Languages
Canada has two official languages. Signs all over the country are in both English and French. The 2001 census showed that about 22 percent of Canadians speak French most often at home. Almost 68 percent speak English most often at home. The third most spoken language is Chinese.

Surf's Up in the Winter
In the winter, storms slam into Vancouver Island, often creating 15-foot waves. Winter surfing is attempted by only the most dedicated surfers. To survive the cold, they wear rubber suits with hoods, gloves, and booties.

Winterlude: A Festival of Winter
Winterlude celebrations take place in Ottawa in February. Here, people play on an ice slide in a park. In the background is a snow sculpture of one of the Parliament Buildings. These buildings are the center of the national government.

3.6 Having Fun in the Cold

Winters are long and summers are short in this northern country, so Canadians have adjusted by finding ways to have fun in all seasons. In summer, for example, people use the Rideau Canal in Ottawa for boating. But in the winter the canal freezes, and for a few months it becomes the longest skating rink in the world.

The Atlantic Region This area has a **humid continental** climate, which is fairly mild. Winters can be very wet, though. Halifax, the capital of Nova Scotia, for instance, gets around five inches of **precipitation** in January alone.

Nova Scotia is said to be the birthplace of ice hockey. The story goes that Canadians were unhappy spending the long winter months indoors. They knew of a game that is like field hockey. Then someone thought to put on skates, and ice hockey was born. Today ice hockey is popular in the United States too.

The Core Region The southern part of this area also has a humid continental climate. The average temperature of Toronto, Ontario, in July is a pleasant 63°F.

Every February, Canadians celebrate Winterlude in Ottawa, in southeast Ontario. People ice skate and ride in horse-drawn sleighs along the Rideau Canal. There are ice-skating races and figure-skating contests. You can learn how to make ice carvings—or eat at a cafe carved from ice!

The Prairie Region The southern part of this region has a **semiarid** to humid continental climate. The northern part has a **subarctic** climate. In Churchill, located on Hudson Bay in northeast Manitoba, the average January temperature is a frosty –16°F.

Churchill is called the "Polar Bear Capital of the World." In the fall more than a thousand polar bears pass through the town to gather at Hudson Bay. There they wait for the bay to freeze so they can hunt for food. And every fall, people travel to Churchill to see this event.

The Pacific Region The coast of British Columbia has a **marine west coast** climate. In Vancouver, January temperatures average 37°F. This is much warmer than most parts of Canada.

Winter surfing is a popular sport off the Pacific coast, where large waves from winter storms challenge surfers. Farther inland lie the Coast Mountains and, even farther, the Rocky Mountains. The Rockies' highest peak in Canada is Mt. Robson, which soars 12,972 feet in British Columbia. The high altitudes here definitely mean long, cold winters, and you will find some of Canada's best ski resorts in this region.

The Northern Region Much of this area is treeless **tundra**. The most northern part has very few plants. The southern part has a subarctic climate. The temperature in the town of Whitehorse, Yukon Territory, in July averages 57°F.

The all-terrain vehicle has replaced the traditional dog sled in the north. People still love to compete in dog sled races, though. A long-distance race in winter, over mountains, frozen rivers, and other rough terrain, can cover 1,000 miles and take up to two weeks.

3.7 Different Traditions and Needs: What's Built Where?

Let's say you are visiting the Museum of Civilization, a short trip from Ottawa. You see houses of Canada's native peoples. Later you look at a lumber camp and then walk past an oil derrick and a fishing village. You soon see how people's needs and traditions, as well as their locations, have led them to build different kinds of structures.

The Atlantic Region Lighthouses dot the coast in this region because of the importance of fishing. Lighthouses help sailors determine their position on the ocean. They also guide ships, letting them know that land is near or warning them about dangerous rocks. Canada still has about 275 lighthouses in operation. The powerful light at the top of each lighthouse continues to flash. But there are new tools as well—radar beams, radio links, cellular phones, and even, perhaps, a helicopter and helipad atop a lighthouse.

The Core Region Many buildings here combine French and British influences. The Parliament Buildings in Ottawa were built in the Gothic revival style of architecture, which French and British settlers brought from western Europe. These large stone buildings have tall, pointed windows, pointed arches, and carved ornaments. Another example of the Gothic revival style is the Château Frontenac, a famous hotel in Quebec City.

The Prairie Region Farms cover the southern part of this region, with the typical farm sitting on hundreds of acres of land. Beside the barn is a silo, a tall, round structure used for storing grain. Farmers in this rural region usually grow spring wheat. This crop is planted in spring and harvested in late summer and grows well in climates with harsh winters. Farmers here also grow barley, another grain crop, and usually raise livestock as well.

The Pacific Region British influence is strong here. In the mid-1800s, Victoria—named for ruling Queen Victoria—became the first city in British Columbia and eventually its capital. Located off the mainland, on Vancouver Island, Victoria is known as the most British of Canadian cities. Some buildings there look almost like castles.

The Northern Region This region has long, cold winters. In the past, some Inuit made winter igloos from snow blocks. The word *igloo* translates to "house." Igloos can also be made of other materials, such as sod, stone, or wood. Today, most Inuit have houses made from kits. Such a house is put together from sections made in factories. Inuit live in widely scattered villages along the Arctic Ocean or Hudson Bay.

A Variety of Building Styles
Each region of Canada has its own styles of buildings. Sometimes these styles grow out of the needs of the people living there. Sometimes they reflect ideas that settlers brought with them from Europe about what buildings should look like.

3.8 How People Make a Living

Canada is rich in **natural resources**. Fish, furs, and lumber were early exports. Today oil and minerals are important as well. Even so, most Canadians today work in service industries—industries that produce a service for people rather than goods. Examples include restaurants, dry cleaners, and banks.

The Atlantic Region In the 1800s, this region had a strong economy. Good fishing in the Atlantic Ocean made it easy to make a living. In recent years, however, overfishing has led to limits on fishing. Many cod-fishing grounds, for instance, were closed by the government in the 1990s. That, in turn, has put many people out of work.

Farming is also important, but poor soil limits farming to small, scattered patches of good land. **Forestry,** in contrast, is a growing industry. Forestry companies are producing lumber as well as pulp for paper.

The Core Region Most of Canada's factories are located here. This region is also a strong farming center—more than a third of Canada's farm products are grown here. Recently, the region has become a large producer of **hydroelectric power,** which is electricity generated from flowing rivers. Some power plants are located on rivers in northern Quebec while others are situated near Niagara Falls or along the St. Lawrence River.

Canada's Plentiful Resources

This map shows the natural resources found in Canada. The location of natural resources tells much about a region's economy. It also shapes land use in a region.

Economic Activity in Canada

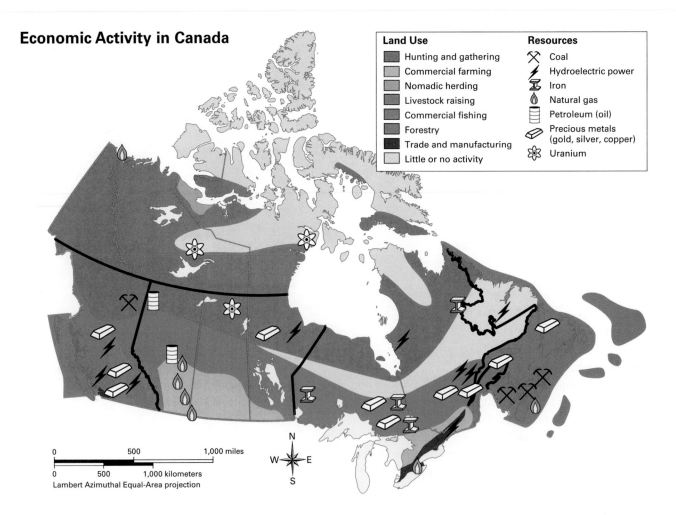

Land Use
- Hunting and gathering
- Commercial farming
- Nomadic herding
- Livestock raising
- Commercial fishing
- Forestry
- Trade and manufacturing
- Little or no activity

Resources
- Coal
- Hydroelectric power
- Iron
- Natural gas
- Petroleum (oil)
- Precious metals (gold, silver, copper)
- Uranium

0   500   1,000 miles
0   500   1,000 kilometers
Lambert Azimuthal Equal-Area projection

N
W   E
S

The Prairie Region This region produces half of the country's farm products. Its southern plains are good for raising grains, such as wheat and barley, as well as livestock. Mining is also important—more than half of Canada's minerals are mined here. They include coal, nickel, copper, zinc, and uranium.

Much oil is trapped in the oil sands of northern Alberta. In fact, this area is thought to contain more oil than the entire Middle East. It is expensive to separate oil from sand, but demand for oil is high and Alberta's oil business is booming. The same is true in Edmonton, where major oil reserves were discovered nearby. Now it is one of the fastest-growing cities in Canada.

The Pacific Region Forestry and fishing are important in British Columbia, but now newer industries have passed these by. Both metals and coal are mined in this region. The shipping industry is growing as well. Shippers on the coast carry Canadian products to all parts of the world. In addition, many rivers have been dammed to produce hydroelectric power. Much of the electricity generated in British Columbia is sold to the United States.

The Northern Region Some native peoples still follow the nomadic, or wandering, life of herders and hunters, but most are settled in small villages. Because there is little business in most villages, jobs are few. Canadians from the south sometimes travel here to work for short periods, finding jobs with the government, churches, or mining companies. Many people in the territories believe that there are undiscovered precious minerals still to be found here.

3.9 Beginning to Think Globally

In this chapter, you learned about settlement patterns and ways of life in Canada. You read about the various groups that make up Canada's plural society. You also learned about urban and rural areas in Canada.

For the most part, people have settled in Canada's ecumene. But not all Canadians live in the ecumene. Some people live in the subarctic region of Canada, and a few even make their homes in the far northern tundra climate zone.

This variety in settlement patterns is found in many places around the world. Consider Australia, for example. Many aborigines, the native people of Australia, choose to live in remote **deserts,** where they are able to retain their traditional way of life. But they face other problems there, such as lack of work and the challenge of keeping their culture alive. Think about these relationships between location and ways of life as you explore settlement patterns around the world in the next section.

Living Outside the Ecumene
People who live outside the ecumene have adapted to harsh conditions. This Inuit hunter is warmly dressed even on a summer day.

3.10 Global Connections

This map shows where people live around the world. The areas in purple represent the most densely populated regions—these are population hot spots in the global ecumene. The gray areas represent very thinly populated regions, which lie outside the global ecumene. Notice that different parts of the ecumene have different population densities. Why do you think this might be so?

What climate zones are likely to be found in the global ecumene?

The climates found in the ecumene are neither too hot nor too cold for people to live comfortably. Areas outside of the ecumene, however, often have extreme temperatures. Few crops, for instance, can be grown in such climate regions. That helps explain why the regions are not part of the ecumene.

Which physical features are likely to lie outside the global ecumene?

Some of Earth's physical features are not well suited for human settlement. Relatively few people live in major deserts because these areas are too dry to support life. Most mountainous regions are thinly settled because they are too rugged for most people. Many large swamps—wet, spongy lands that are submerged in water much of the time—also lie outside the ecumene.

What might life be like for people who live outside the ecumene?

Most of the world's people live within the global ecumene, but some people live in less populated areas. They survive by finding ways to stay warm, keep cool, find water, or keep dry—even in the harshest conditions. In later chapters, you will look at different ways people adapt to living in extreme environments outside the ecumene.

Ecumene Around the World

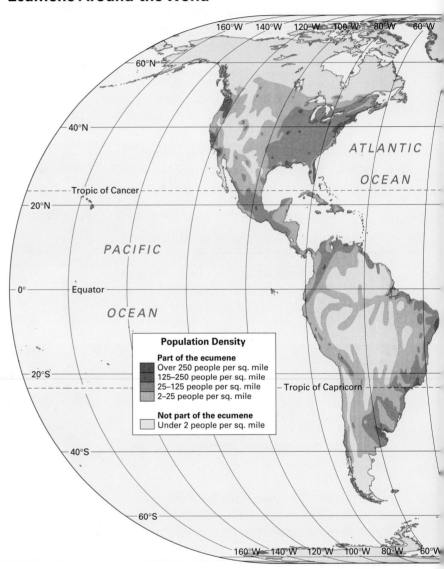

Population Density

Part of the ecumene
- Over 250 people per sq. mile
- 125–250 people per sq. mile
- 25–125 people per sq. mile
- 2–25 people per sq. mile

Not part of the ecumene
- Under 2 people per sq. mile

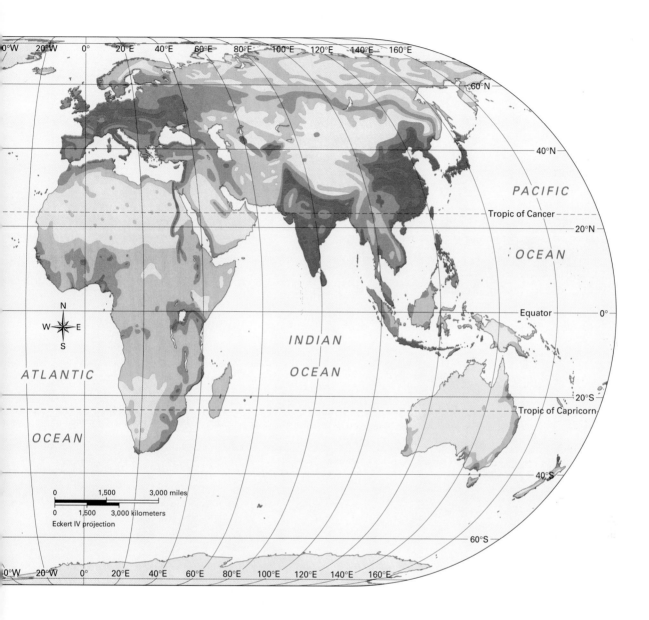

20°W 20°W 0° 20°E 40°E 60°E 80°E 100°E 120°E 140°E 160°E

60°N

40°N

PACIFIC

Tropic of Cancer

20°N

OCEAN

N
W   E
S

Equator 0°

ATLANTIC

INDIAN

OCEAN

OCEAN

20°S

Tropic of Capricorn

40°S

0   1,500   3,000 miles

0   1,500   3,000 kilometers
Eckert IV projection

60°S

0°W 20°W 0° 20°E 40°E 60°E 80°E 100°E 120°E 140°E 160°E

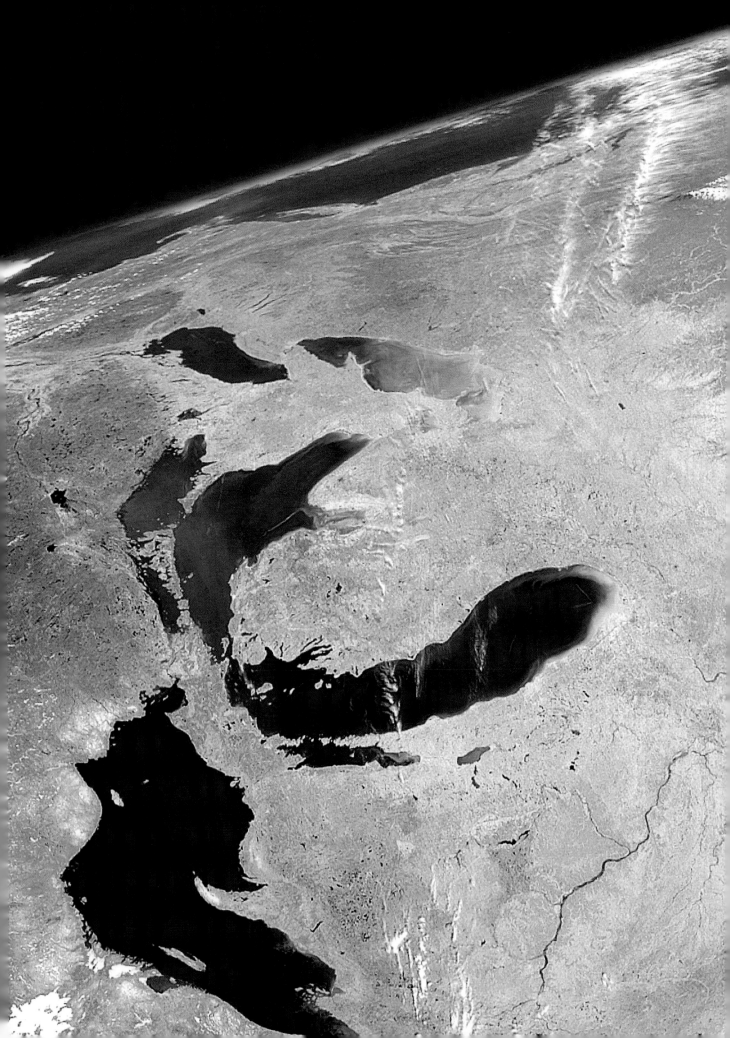

The Great Lakes: The U.S. and Canada's Freshwater Treasures

4.1 Introduction

A massive sheet of ice, the last of the Ice Age **glaciers,** crept across the North American continent. Covering thousands of miles, the ice sheet inched south across the vast region that is now Canada and what is today the northern United States. Finally, it slid to an icy stop near the present-day city of Chicago. All the while, the sheer weight of the huge glacier reshaped the landscape, grinding rocks into "rock flour," obstructing streambeds, and flattening mountains.

After thousands of years, Earth began to warm, and the vast blanket of ice began retreating. It left behind a transformed land, with high ridges and huge holes that the ice sheet had gouged into the land. As the ice melted, clear, fresh water filled the huge holes, and the Great Lakes were born.

Over time, a rich **ecosystem** developed on the land left bare when the glaciers retreated. An ecosystem is a community of all the living things in an area, including plants, animals, and the physical environment in which they live. Ecosystems can be as small as a lawn or as large as Earth. The Great Lakes make up the world's largest **freshwater** ecosystem.

It took thousands of years for the movement of glaciers to create the Great Lakes. In just decades, however, human activity has greatly changed this region. In this chapter, you will learn how people can upset an ecosystem. You will also find out what can be done to solve some of the problems that human activity has created in the Great Lakes ecosystem.

Essential Question

How can people best use and protect Earth's freshwater ecosystems?

The diagram shows some of the main ways that people use the Great Lakes. All of these uses affect the lakes' ecosystem in some way, large or small. Keep this diagram in mind as you try to answer the Essential Question.

Graphic Organizer

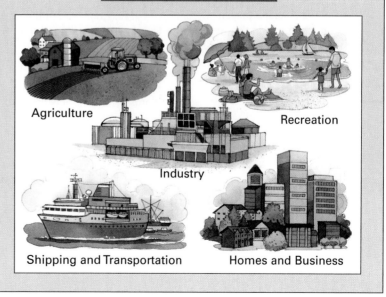

Agriculture

Recreation

Industry

Shipping and Transportation

Homes and Business

◀ Satellite photograph of the Great Lakes looking eastward toward the Atlantic Ocean

Herring gull eggs: 124 ppm

Lake trout: 4.83 ppm

Smelt: 1.04 ppm

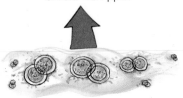

Phytoplankton: 0.025 ppm

Source: U.S. Environmental Protection Agency.

The Food Web and Toxic Waste

When poisons enter a waterway, they may also enter the food web. Some toxic chemicals are stored in living things. When a larger animal eats smaller animals, the poison becomes concentrated in the larger animal. In this diagram, notice how chemicals called PCBs build up within a food chain. PCBs are measured in parts per million, or ppm.

4.2 The Geographic Setting

Five lakes—Superior, Michigan, Huron, Erie, and Ontario—make up the Great Lakes. Only one of the lakes, Lake Michigan, is entirely within U.S. territory; the other four are shared by Canada and the United States. In fact, the U.S.-Canada boundary runs through the four lakes. Together, the Great Lakes form the largest group of freshwater lakes on Earth.

More than one tenth of the U.S. population and one fourth of the Canadian population live in the Great Lakes region, and they use the lakes in many ways. People in both countries depend on the lakes for drinking water. They also rely on lake water for use in factories, irrigation on farms, and generation of electric power. In addition, the lakes provide opportunities for shipping, fishing, and recreation, such as boating and swimming.

One of North America's Largest Watersheds Think of standing on a hill and pouring water from a large container onto the ground, and then watching the water flow downhill. While running downhill, some of the water would soak into the ground and, if there were a hole along the way, water would fill it to form a tiny lake. You would have created your own tiny **watershed**.

A watershed is a geographic area that includes all of the land and waterways that drain into a body of water. Watersheds come in many shapes and sizes, including hills and valleys and cities and towns. Smaller watersheds can drain into larger watersheds. The Great Lakes region is one of the largest watersheds in North America.

The Great Lakes are so large that they look and act like oceans. In fact, people have called them "the fourth seacoast" of the United States. Unlike the oceans, though, the lakes are filled with fresh water that has little or no salt. Thus they are also called "the sweetwater seas."

A Vast and Varied Ecosystem The Great Lakes region is a vast ecosystem. One way to understand how the living things in the Great Lakes ecosystem are related to one another is to look at who eats what. These relationships make up what scientists call a **food web**. Food webs include both plants and animals that feed on each other.

Every ecosystem has its own food web, which is made up of many **food chains**. A food chain is a series of plants and animals, each of which depends on the next for food. In the Great Lakes ecosystem, for example, one food chain might begin with plants that grow in lakes and rivers. The next link in the chain might be insects that feed on those plants. These insects are eaten by tiny fish, which are then eaten by larger fish. Eagles sitting at the top of the food chain, in turn, may eat the larger fish. Another food chain might begin with tiny organisms known as algae and end with a river otter.

The food web is an important part of any ecosystem. If one part of a food web is harmed, it affects all of the living things in the ecosystem. For instance, if a fish is poisoned by **pollution,** any animal that eats that fish will be poisoned as well. Or, if a type of plant or fish is lost from an ecosystem, all animals that feed on that plant or fish will lose part of their food supply. In this way, all living things in a food web depend on one another for their survival.

▶ Geoterms

ecosystem a community of all the living things in an area and the environment in which they live

food chain a series of plants and animals, each of which depends on the one below it for food. A food chain usually forms part of a much larger food web.

food web all of the feeding relationships within an ecosystem. Each living thing in a food web provides food energy to other living things within that ecosystem.

freshwater made up of water that is fresh, not salty. This term is also used to describe creatures that live in fresh water, such as freshwater fish.

watershed a geographic area that includes all of the land and waterways that drain into a body of water. Sometimes a watershed is also called a *drainage basin*.

An Enormous Ecosystem

The Great Lakes region includes eight U.S. states and one Canadian province. The lakes and waterways contain almost one fifth of the world's supply of fresh water.

The Great Lakes Region

4.3 The Great Lakes in 1969

For many years, people didn't worry about the Great Lakes ecosystem. The Great Lakes and its rivers were so large that most people didn't think human activity could affect them much. By the late 1960s, though, it was clear that there were problems. News articles similar to the one below made people aware that the Great Lakes were heavily polluted—and of how dangerous such pollution could be.

The Sad State of Our Once-Great Lakes
July 28, 1969

The Cuyahoga River in Cleveland, Ohio, looks like a melted chocolate mess. It is mud-brown, with a layer of oil on top. Gases bubble strangely on its surface. So it was not surprising when the filthy river, part of the Lake Erie watershed, burst into flames last month.

A Burning River and Dead Ducks

No one knows exactly what started the Cuyahoga River fire on June 22. It might have been a spark from a passing train. Whatever the source, the spark ignited picnic benches, piles of logs, and other garbage in the river. The burning debris set fire to oil floating on the river's surface. The flames blazed across the river and up in the air. They reached about five stories in height.

While the Cuyahoga River burned in Cleveland, another event was taking place on the Detroit River. A Detroit official was showing news reporters around the waterfront. As he assured them that the water was not as polluted as it looked, two ducks flew in for a landing. They paddled around the polluted river for a brief moment. Suddenly, they began choking, keeled over, and died.

These events show the terrible condition of the rivers that flow into the Great Lakes. But what of the Great Lakes themselves? Local residents have described the lakes as "cesspools" and "industrial wastebaskets." They claim that the lakes are used

A River in Flames
It's hard to believe that a river could catch on fire. But as this 1952 photograph shows, the Cuyahoga River did. And it burned again this year. Cleveland mayor Carl Stokes said that the river's polluted state is "a longstanding condition that must be brought to an end."

as dumping grounds for every kind of pollutant, from sewage to toxic chemicals.

Out-of-Control Algae

Television ads boast about the long-lasting suds of laundry detergents. Those suds may not cost a lot at the supermarket. But detergents are taking a toll on the Great Lakes.

Visitors to Lake Erie today see large mats of algae near the shore. This algae explosion is caused by phosphorus, a chemical in detergents. Algae need phosphorus to grow, but too much of it causes algae to grow out of control. Lake Erie is covered with algae mats that are up to two feet thick.

Algae mats create many problems. They choke fish. They clog filters in water treatment plants. They cover beaches in slime. And they make lake water taste like rotting vegetation.

DDT Kills More Than Mosquitoes

For years, the pesticide DDT has been used in the Great Lakes region to control insects. It is sprayed on crops and on waterways to kill mosquitoes and other pests. But when DDT enters rivers and streams, it also enters the Great Lakes food web.

Today, America's national bird, the bald eagle, has almost disappeared from the Great Lakes because of DDT poisoning. The eagles feed on fish that live in water polluted with the pesticide. Over time, a toxic amount of DDT builds up in their bodies.

The DDT doesn't kill the adult birds. Instead, it weakens the eagles' eggshells. The shells of eggs laid by female eagles are so thin that most break before the young are ready to hatch. The few eaglets that do hatch may already have DDT in their blood.

Invading Lampreys and Alewives

Bald eagles are not the only disappearing species. For the past century, people have fished the lakes for fun and profit. Fishing boats once harvested millions of pounds of fish every year. Now, due partly to overfishing, whole populations of fish have almost disappeared.

While some fish are disappearing, species that are not native to this area are overrunning the lakes. The invasion of nonnative species began in 1829 when the Welland Canal connected the Great Lakes to the Atlantic Ocean. The canal allowed species from the Atlantic Ocean to swim or be carried by boats to the Great Lakes.

One deadly invader is an eel-like animal known as the sea lamprey. Lampreys act like vampires. They suck the blood out of fish. Over time, sea lampreys have killed most of the whitefish, lake trout, and other fish native to the Great Lakes.

Another invader is the alewife, a type of herring. Alewives are small but have huge appetites. They have devoured entire species of fish. They also compete with other fish for food. The first alewife wasn't discovered in Lake Michigan until 1949. Yet by the mid-1960s, alewives made up 9 pounds of every 10 pounds of fish swimming in the lake.

Alewives die off in the spring. Every year, tons of dead alewives wash up on lake beaches. Clouds of flies lay eggs on the rotting fish. Soon, the smelly fish are riddled with maggots. As a result, most beaches are unbearable during the die-off season.

Can the Lakes Be Saved?

Scientists today have begun to talk about the death of the Great Lakes. They warn that unless the lakes are cleaned up soon, they may become lifeless ponds. The question is, will people do what is needed to save them?

A week ago, two American astronauts became the first humans to walk on the moon. If the United States can accomplish such an incredible feat, then surely Americans can meet the challenge of restoring the Great Lakes.

4.4 The Great Lakes Today: Pollution

During the 1960s and 1970s, the state of the Great Lakes worried many people, both Americans and Canadians. Dr. Seuss, the famous children's author, wrote about Lake Erie in his book *The Lorax*. In this 1971 book, fish living in a polluted lake decide to look for a new home. Dr. Seuss wrote,

> *They'll walk on their fins and get woefully weary,*
> *In search of some water that isn't so smeary.*
> *I hear things are just as bad up in Lake Erie.*

By 1991, however, Lake Erie had improved so much that this last line was removed from *The Lorax*. This amazing change was due to cleanup work done on both sides of the U.S.-Canada border.

Making Laws to Reduce Pollution In 1972, the United States and Canada created the first Great Lakes Water Quality Agreement, pledging to clean up and protect the Great Lakes ecosystem. The first cleanup efforts involved **point-source pollution**—pollution from a single source, such as a discharge pipe at a sewage treatment plant or a factory.

New laws put strict limits on the amount of phosphorus and other chemicals that factories and sewage treatment plants could release into the lakes. Detergent makers stopped putting phosphorus in their products. Industries stopped dumping oil and other pollutants into rivers draining into the lakes. Other laws banned the use of a number of **toxic chemicals,** like PCBs and DDT.

The new laws gradually worked. The Cuyahoga River was no longer flammable, or likely to catch fire. Algae growth was greatly reduced, and the lakes turned from green back to blue. PCBs and DDT in the food chain declined. And, as the amount of DDT in fish declined, the bald eagle made a comeback.

The Chicago Waterfront

The city of Chicago lies on the shores of Lake Michigan. For years, the city dumped untreated sewage and factory wastes into the lake. At the same time, it depended on the lake for its water supply. By 2003, the city was drawing 1 billion gallons of water a day from the lake. This water met the needs of Chicago and 124 neighboring towns. Today, Chicago treats its wastewater. The result is a cleaner lake and safer drinking water for millions of people.

Continuing Pollution Challenges One great challenge in the Great Lakes today is **non-point-source pollution,** or pollution that comes from many sources. One source, for example, is rainfall or snowmelt. **Runoff**—the water not absorbed by soil—travels over the ground, picking up **pollutants** from soil, and then into lakes and rivers. Runoff from storms also picks up waste from industrial and construction sites.

Old toxic waste dumps also pollute since many contain poisons that leak into waterways. There are as many as 250 dumps on the shores of the Niagara River alone.

Pollution from the air damages watersheds as well. Mercury, among other things, is released into the air when coal is burned. This highly toxic metal falls back to Earth mixed with rain or as dust and then enters waterways and the food web.

Canada and the United States are working to clean up non-point-source pollution, and new laws have been passed to limit harmful chemicals in the air, water, and soil. The two nations are also working to clean up toxic **sediment,** or polluted soil that has settled at the bottom of lakes and rivers. Removing such sediment is both difficult and costly. Water flows so slowly out of most of the Great Lakes that pollutants entering the lakes are likely to stay. Lake Superior, the largest and deepest Great Lake, retains water for 170 years or longer.

The best way to deal with pollution is to prevent it. Today education programs encourage prevention. As a result, people in industry and farming are using fewer harmful chemicals, and consumers are choosing products that are safer for the environment.

The Toronto Skyline

Toronto lies on the shores of Lake Ontario. The Great Lakes provide drinking water for three fourths of Ontario's people.

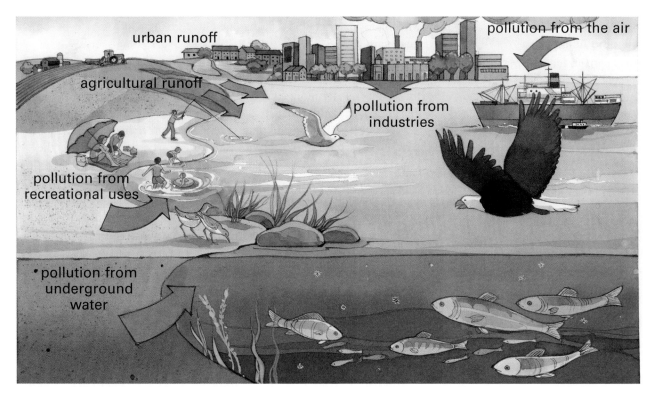

Sources of Pollution in the Great Lakes

This diagram shows several sources of pollution in the Great Lakes region. The United States and Canada have both passed laws to reduce pollution of the air, water, and soil.

Invasive Zebra Mussels

Zebra mussels are native to Eastern Europe. They are a threat to the food supplies of native fish in the Great Lakes. One problem they cause for humans is clogging water pipes.

Invading Asian Carp

Asian carp invaded the Mississippi, Missouri, and Ohio rivers in the 1980s. They pose a danger to boaters and water skiers. They jump into the air and slam into boats and people.

4.5 The Great Lakes Today: Invasive Species

Scientists estimate that there are more than 170 **invasive species** in the Great Lakes today. Invasive species are nonnative plants and animals that invade a new ecosystem. The sea lamprey described earlier in this chapter is one such invader.

Most Invaders Arrive by Sea Most invasive species travel to the Great Lakes by water. Some even come in the ballast water of ships. Ballast water is water that is pumped into the bottom of a ship to keep it stable. After arriving at a port, the ship releases the ballast water—and any creatures that were in it.

Other invaders, like the zebra mussel, hitch rides on the underside of ships. Once zebra mussels reach a suitable location, they multiply rapidly. In fact, up to 70,000 mussels can thrive in a single square meter of water.

Invasive Species Upset the Ecosystem Invaders like the zebra mussel, sea lamprey, and alewife have all damaged the Great Lakes ecosystem. Zebra mussels, for example, steal food from native species, clog water pipes, and attach to docks. They also make swimming dangerous because of their sharp shells.

The Asian carp is another major threat to the Great Lakes. Catfish farmers in the American South brought this large, ever-hungry fish from Asia to clean algae and other things from their ponds. However, during floods, many of these ponds overflowed, and carp escaped into rivers. Now carp in the Mississippi River are migrating northward toward Lake Michigan. Many people fear that the Great Lakes will someday become giant carp ponds.

The United States and Canada are working to prevent more nonnatives from entering the Great Lakes. Shippers are being asked to treat their ballast water more carefully. A barrier has been constructed to keep Asian carp and other nonnative fish in the Mississippi River from entering the Great Lakes. In addition, several states have banned the sale of live Asian carp for fear they will have disastrous consequences on the Great Lakes food chain.

Another approach has been to stock the Great Lakes with species that will eat the invaders. Pacific salmon, for example, have been introduced into the lakes to control alewives. Alewife numbers have dropped greatly as a result, and native fish have begun to recover.

4.6 The Great Lakes Today: Habitat Loss

A century ago, loggers in the Great Lakes region told folktales of a giant lumberjack named Paul Bunyan. Bunyan was so gigantic that he could cut down a forest in minutes. One tale tells of how he scooped out ponds to provide drinking water for his big blue ox, Babe. Today those ponds are the Great Lakes.

In Paul Bunyan's day, dense forests covered the Great Lakes region, so nobody worried about **habitat** loss. A habitat is the natural environment in which a plant or an animal lives. But habitat loss is a big worry in the region today.

Restoring Forest Habitat When settlers moved into the Great Lakes region in the 1800s, they cleared patches of forest for farms. Later, loggers cut down more, and still later more land was cleared for factories and cities. In time, almost half of the region's original forest was lost to development. When habitats are lost, the plants and animals that live there are often lost as well.

Today people are working to reverse forest loss in the Great Lakes watershed. Timber companies are cutting trees in ways that are less harmful to forests, and they replant trees in areas that have been logged. The result is that forests around the Great Lakes are now expanding instead of shrinking.

Protecting Precious Wetlands Like forests, **wetlands** were gradually lost as the Great Lakes region developed. A wetland is an area where the soil is usually wet all year, such as marshes, bogs, and swamps. Wetlands provide habitats for a wide variety of wildlife. At the same time, they help to control flooding during storms.

In the past, wetlands were viewed by many people as worthless bogs, and over time, more than half of the wetlands in the Great Lakes region disappeared. Only in recent years have people begun to see the value of wetlands habitat.

Today public and private groups are working to protect wetland habitats. One way is by creating nature preserves on existing wetlands. Another is by teaching landowners how to protect wetland areas. In some places, developers must create more than one acre of new wetland for every acre they destroy.

Population Pressures

The Great Lakes region has become densely populated. Each yellow dot below represents 2,500 people. The areas that are almost solid yellow have the most people. As the population has grown, forests and wetlands have disappeared. More habitats will be lost unless they are protected from development.

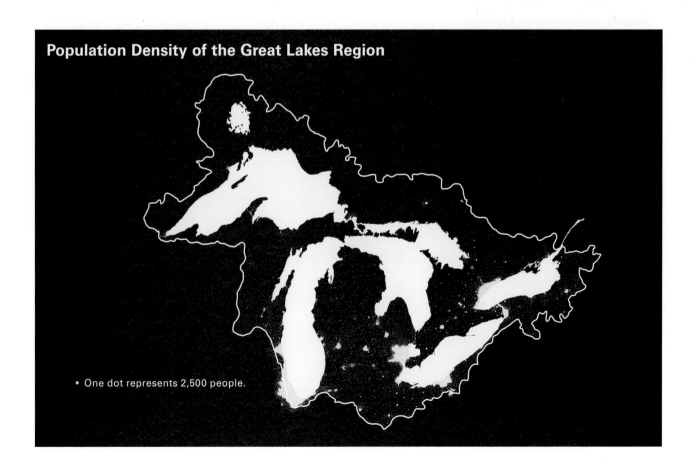

Population Density of the Great Lakes Region

• One dot represents 2,500 people.

Getting Water from a Well
This well in India draws large crowds every day. In many rural areas, the task of finding water falls to women. They often walk many miles each day to get water for their families.

4.7 Beginning to Think Globally

In this chapter, you read that the Great Lakes are the world's largest freshwater ecosystem. You saw how plants and animals in this ecosystem form a complex food web. You also learned how pollution and the invasion of nonnative species of fish are threatening the health of the Great Lakes. Finally, you found out how people are working to clean up and preserve this large watershed.

Water Is Essential to Life Managing freshwater ecosystems is of major importance around the world. All living things need water. Approximately 70 percent of Earth's surface is covered by water. However, nearly 98 percent of that water is too salty for human use. Of the remaining 2 percent that is fresh water, three fourths is frozen in ice caps, or permanent coverings of ice. That leaves less than 1 percent of Earth's water to meet human needs.

People obtain fresh water from many sources. Some draw water from rivers, lakes, and streams while others depend on wells that tap into underground water supplies. In other places, people collect and store rainwater to meet their needs. And in still other places, people desalinate seawater, or remove the salt from it.

Not all fresh water is safe for human use. Of the world's more than 6 billion people, at least 1 billion lack a steady supply of clean, safe drinking water. Unsafe water creates huge health problems. For instance, every day 6,000 children die from diseases that could have been prevented by having clean water to drink. And every year more than 2.2 million people die from diseases, such as cholera, related to unsafe drinking water.

Water Shortages Are Increasing The number of people on Earth grows larger by the year, but the supply of fresh water is not increasing. As a result, 31 countries now face water shortages.

China is one of those countries. To meet the water needs of its large population, China is pumping large amounts of water out of underground supplies. However, these supplies are slowly shrinking because more water is being pumped out than is replaced by rainfall each year. Also, some rivers in China are so polluted that their water can't be used to irrigate crops.

Competition for limited water supplies can result in conflict since some rivers flow through many countries. When one country dams a river for irrigation water, it may reduce the amount of water flowing to countries downstream.

Egypt, for example, has a population of more than 77 million people, but it receives almost no rainfall. Instead, Egyptians depend on the Nile River to meet their water needs. Before reaching Egypt, though, the Nile travels through several countries. If any of those countries reduced the flow of the Nile, Egypt could be starved for water—and the result could be a water war.

Climate Change May Shrink Water Supplies In the last 25 years, Earth's climate has warmed slightly, and many scientists hypothesize that this warming trend will continue. (See Chapter 35 for more information on the theory of **global warming**.) Such a shift in climate could have an effect on water supplies. Some areas, for instance, might get less rainfall than they do today while others might experience much more rain and frequent flooding.

If these changes occur, managing water supplies will become more important than ever. Countries with shortages will need to improve their water collection and storage methods. On the other hand, those with too much water will need to improve their flood defenses. Think about these potential problems as you examine maps showing changes in the world's freshwater supplies in the next section.

A Thirsty World

Asia uses more water than any other continent, in part because it has such a large population. However, North Americans and Europeans use more water *per person* than people in other continents.

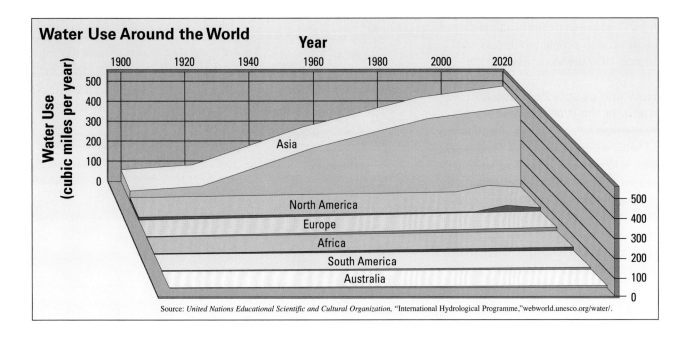

Water Use Around the World

Source: *United Nations Educational Scientific and Cultural Organization,* "International Hydrological Programme,"webworld.unesco.org/water/.

4.8 Global Connections

The maps at the right show the world's freshwater supplies for three different years. Each map indicates the amount of water available per person in each country. The maps do not show the total amounts of fresh water available in each year. The map for the year 2025 is based on population estimates for that year.

What factors might cause the changes in freshwater availability you see in the maps? Population is growing rapidly in places like India and Africa, but the amount of fresh water is not increasing. As a result, far more people must share the same amount of water. Climate changes in the future may also reduce the amount of clean, fresh water available. In addition, some sources of fresh water, such as wells, may have been polluted, and now these sources are no longer safe.

What concerns for the future can be drawn from the maps? The maps show that freshwater shortages are likely to increase over time. This situation could lead to rising water costs. It could also lead to less food production, since many crops require regular irrigation. In addition, public health problems could arise as people turn to less safe sources of water to survive.

How can people best use and manage the world's freshwater resources? People can do many things to better manage sources of fresh water. One is to prevent all kinds of water pollution. Another is to find better ways to store and distribute existing water supplies. Using less water in homes, industries, and on farms can stretch limited supplies. So can recycling water so that it can be used again and again.

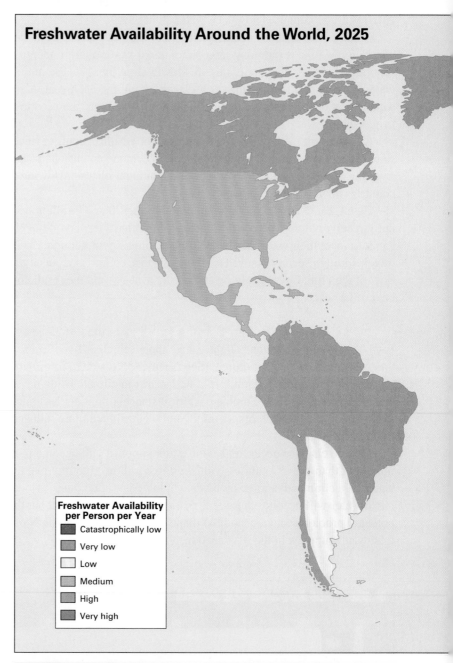

Freshwater Availability Around the World, 2025

Freshwater Availability per Person per Year

- Catastrophically low
- Very low
- Low
- Medium
- High
- Very high

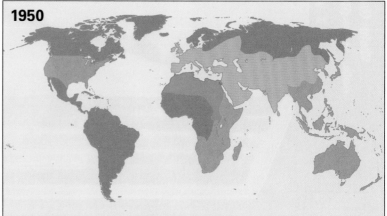

1950

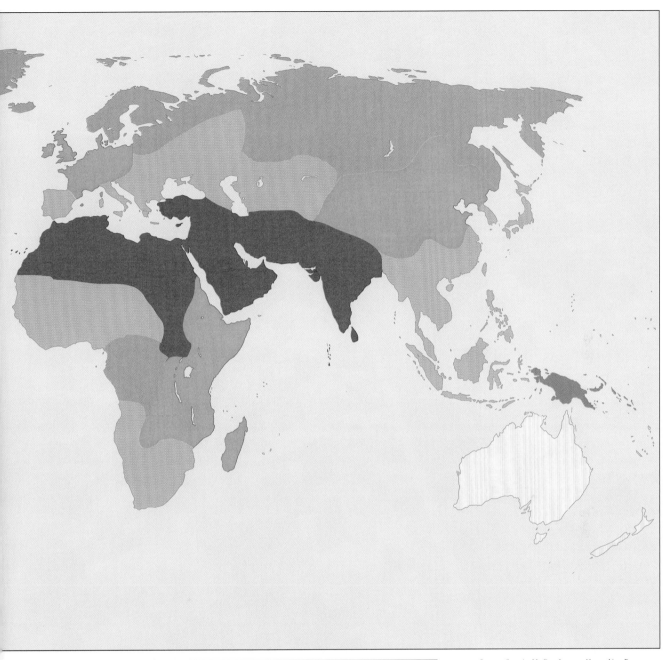

Source: *Sustainable Development Networking Programme,*
"International Year of Freshwater," www.sdnbd.org.

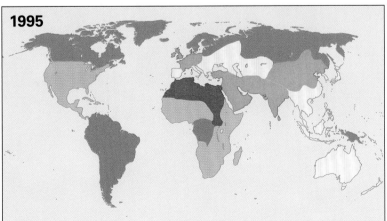

1995

Urban Sprawl in North America: Where Will It End?

5

5.1 Introduction

Would you be surprised if you brought a picnic to a place called Hickory Woods, and there were no woods? Or if you took a drive to Partridge Farms, and there were no farms? What if you went for a walk through the Meadowlands and discovered that there were no meadows?

You might be confused at first, but you would soon grasp what these places had in common: houses—lots and lots of houses. Hickory Woods, Partridge Farms, and the Meadowlands are all housing developments. Across North America, housing developments have been named after the types of land that were cleared in order to build new homes.

For many decades, urban development in the United States and Canada has been moving out from cities to **suburbs**. A suburb is an area of housing built at the edge of a city. Developers create suburbs by buying up farmland or forested areas outside a city. Developers replace this open space with mile upon mile of housing tracts, shopping centers, and office parks. Often the only way to get from place to place in a suburban area is by car on traffic-clogged roads.

The rapid and often poorly planned spread of cities and suburbs is known as **urban sprawl**. In this chapter, you will learn why urban sprawl happens and how it affects people and the environment. You will also find out how people in three North American cities have dealt with it.

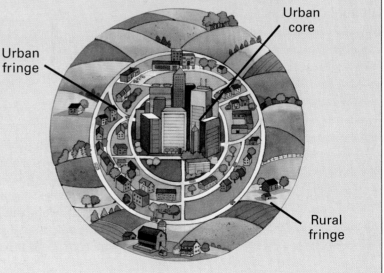

Essential Question

How does urban sprawl affect people and the planet?

Most cities begin as a small, compact urban core, as shown in the center ring of this diagram. As more people move to the city, development pushes outward to form an urban fringe. Beyond this is an area of rural, or open, land. This is called the rural fringe. Keep this diagram in mind as you try to answer the Essential Question.

Graphic Organizer

Urban core

Urban fringe

Rural fringe

◀ Housing development in Las Vegas, Nevada

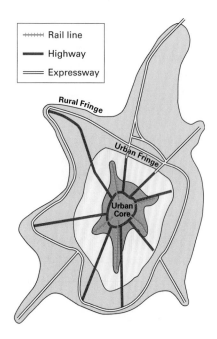

Stages of Urban Growth

This diagram shows how a city becomes a sprawling metropolitan area. The old "walking city" lies at the center. Over time, this urban core expands along rail lines and highways. The result is an urban fringe. Later growth pushes development out into the rural fringe.

5.2 The Geographic Setting

"Welcome to LA!" announce signs in the Los Angeles International Airport. Most people seeing these signs are visitors who have arrived in Los Angeles for business or to see the sights. Some people, though, have come to stay. The LA **metropolitan area** is growing by more than 200,000 new residents a year. A metropolitan area is a major city and its surrounding suburbs.

Today 8 out of 10 people in the United States and Canada live in a metropolitan area. In the United States, New York City ranks first with more than 20 million people. In Canada, Toronto leads the way with more than 5 million residents. These two metropolitan areas have followed a similar pattern of growth.

The Old Walking City: The Urban Core The oldest Canadian and American cities were founded during colonial times. At that time, cities were small enough for people to get around by horse or on foot. Homes and workplaces were in one compact geographic area. Because of the high cost of building materials, the front room of a home often served as the owner's workplace. Today that old "walking city" is a city's **urban core**. People often think of this urban core as their city's "downtown" or business district.

By the 1890s, many cities were bursting at their seams with residents. Around that time, electric streetcars and commuter rail lines were developed. People began to build homes near the rail lines, taking trains or streetcars into the city center to work and shop. As a result, the urban core began to bulge outward along rail lines.

Suburbs Around the City: The Urban Fringe By the 1920s, cars were becoming part of American life, and highway construction boomed as drivers, now in the millions, demanded paved roads. No longer did city dwellers have to live near a rail line to get to their jobs—they could buy a car and commute.

As cars became common, people began to build new housing areas farther away from the old urban core. In time, suburbs ringed most cities, forming a new **urban fringe**.

As people moved out of the urban core, some businesses moved out too. The loss of people and businesses led to decay in older city neighborhoods. Meanwhile, people in the suburbs built their own town centers. These new communities were complete with shops, businesses, theaters, and parks.

Where City Meets Country: The Rural Fringe Beyond the urban fringe lies an area with fewer people. Here small towns mix with farms and open space. These less-developed areas form a **rural fringe** around a metropolitan area but stay connected to the city by roads and highways.

As populations grow, more and more of the rural fringe is developed. New homes, schools, shopping centers, and business parks seem to spring up almost overnight. Some people see this growth as a sign of progress while others see it as harmful urban sprawl. In this chapter, you will explore both points of view.

▶ Geoterms

metropolitan area a major population center made up of a large city and the smaller suburbs and towns that surround it

rural fringe the small towns, farms, and open spaces that lie just beyond a city's suburbs

suburb a developed area at the edge of a city that is mainly homes. Many suburbs also have stores and businesses.

urban core the older part of a big city. Often the urban core serves as the downtown or central business district of a city.

urban fringe the ring of small towns and suburbs that surround a big city

urban sprawl the rapid, often poorly planned spread of development from an urban area outward into rural areas

Urban Sprawl in Two Countries
Metropolitan areas are found across the United States and Canada. Most people in both countries now live in cities and suburbs. As urban areas grow, they tend to sprawl outward.

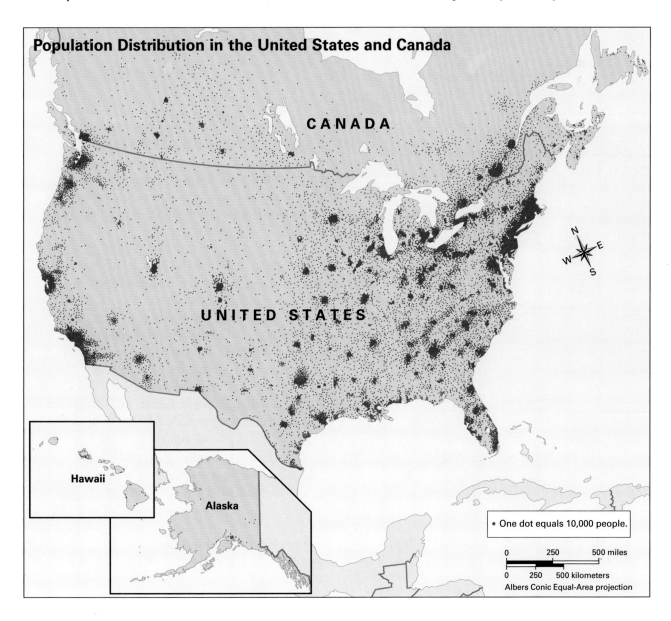

Population Distribution in the United States and Canada

CANADA

UNITED STATES

Hawaii

Alaska

• One dot equals 10,000 people.

0   250   500 miles

0   250   500 kilometers

Albers Conic Equal-Area projection

U.S. Farmland Converted to Developed Land, 1982–1997

UNITED STATES

Hawaii

Alaska

No data available for Alaska

Federally protected land

• One dot equals 1,000 acres of converted land.

7,970,500 total acres converted from cropland to developed land, 1982–1997.

Source: U.S. Department of Agriculture, Natural Resources Conservation Service.

Urban Sprawl and Farmland

Between 1982 and 1997, the United States lost almost 7 million acres of farmland to urban sprawl. This is an area about the size of Maryland. Only about a tenth of Earth's land is suitable for farming. If sprawl continues, will there be enough land left to feed Earth's growing population?

5.3 The Case for and Against Urban Growth

Suppose a developer wants to build a housing development at the edge of a city. In many cities, a planning commission would need to approve the project. This body is made up of citizens who are chosen to guide a city's growth. At public hearings, the commissioners listen to people who support and oppose a project. Here are some of the arguments that might be heard at such a meeting.

Urban Growth Creates Needed Homes Everyone knows that when populations grow, new homes are needed. The question is where and at what cost to families.

Those who favor growth argue that the best way to meet the need for new housing is to develop empty land outside a city. Land in rural areas is less expensive than city land. Building costs, too, are lower in the country than in the city. These factors keep new homes affordable. In addition, many people want homes outside of cities because they believe that suburbs are better places than cities to raise a family.

Pro-growth people say that urban growth has other benefits as well. New housing projects create jobs for construction workers. And as people move into new homes, they spend money for furniture, garden supplies, and other things. All of this spending is good for local stores. In addition, new homeowners pay taxes, which help fund roads, schools, and other city services.

Urban Sprawl Damages the Environment Everyone agrees that people need housing, say those who oppose urban sprawl. The question is where and at what cost to the environment.

These people argue that the worst way to meet the need for new housing is to develop open spaces outside a city. Open spaces are not empty land—they are **habitats** for plants and animals. When land is developed, that habitat is lost and with it the wildlife that lived there. The National Wildlife Foundation warns that more than a thousand animal and plant species are in danger of dying out because of habitat loss to urban sprawl.

Anti-sprawl proponents say that urban sprawl creates other problems as well. When housing is spread out, people rely on cars for transportation, and this creates traffic jams as well as air **pollution**. Urban sprawl can also be detrimental to people living in small towns. They often see their taxes rise when nearby land is developed. The extra tax money is needed to pay for roads, schools, and other services required when a small town suddenly grows.

5.4 Portland, Oregon, 1973

The Willamette Valley in Oregon is 120 miles long and 25 to 40 miles wide and has Oregon's richest farmland. More than 170 crops are grown there. Orchards produce pears, plums, apples, and nuts while fields of sweet corn and green beans mix with colorful flowerbeds and vineyards. The Willamette Valley is not all farmland, though. Oregon's largest city, Portland, is located at its northern edge.

Growth Threatens the Willamette Valley Portland is known as the "City of Roses" because of the fragrant rose bushes that fill its parks and gardens. Still, Portland is very much a big city, with a downtown and many businesses. Its attractions include colleges, museums, shopping areas, and a beautiful geographical setting. And, like all big cities, Portland has a lot of people.

It was Portland's growing population that first began to worry people in the 1960s and 1970s. They feared that urban sprawl would soon gobble up the farms and forests of the Willamette Valley.

A Difficult Decision: How Best to Grow? In 1973, Governor Tom McCall called on the state legislature to deal with the issue of population growth. "We are in dire need of a state land-use policy," McCall said. Oregon lawmakers agreed, but they weren't sure how best to control urban growth.

There were many options that the lawmakers might have considered. For example, one might have been to allow urban growth to continue, but with a condition: for each acre of land that was developed, the state government would require that another acre be set aside to be preserved as open space.

A second option might have been to create firm boundaries around cities. Once this was done, no new development would be allowed outside these boundaries.

A third option was to ban all development in some rural areas, such as the Willamette Valley. Growth could be allowed in other areas that did not seem so valuable.

Whatever lawmakers decided, one thing was clear. Their actions would affect the future of Oregon's people and environment.

Portland's Natural Setting
The city of Portland lies at the north end of the Willamette Valley. In the distance you can see Mt. Hood. As Portland grew in the 1960s and 1970s, its urban fringe gave way to housing. People began to fear that the rest of the valley would soon be paved with homes and shopping malls.

Smart Growth in Portland

Portland is known for its smart growth policies. One of these policies calls for mixed-use developments like those shown here overlooking South Waterfront Park. Mixed use combines housing and business in one area.

Getting Around on MAX

Portland's light rail system is called the Metropolitan Area Express, or MAX. In 1986, MAX had 15 miles of track. By 2005, it had 44 miles of track. MAX connects downtown Portland to three suburbs and Portland's airport.

5.5 Portland Plans for Smart Growth

In 1973, Oregon became the first state in the United States to create a set of **land use** planning laws. These laws promote an approach to land use planning known as *smart growth*. The basic idea of smart growth is to control sprawl by making better use of land that has already been developed.

Urban Growth Boundaries Limit Sprawl Smart growth in Oregon began with a law creating **urban growth boundaries**. An urban growth boundary is a legal border that separates urban land from rural land. New development is allowed inside the growth boundary but is not allowed on rural land outside the boundary.

An urban growth boundary was drawn around the Portland metropolitan area. It included not only the city of Portland, but also several suburbs. To control growth inside this boundary, voters created a new regional government called Metro. Its main job is to plan growth inside the growth boundary.

Mixed Use Helps Portland to Grow Up, Not Out Oregon's land use planning laws have worked well. Today Portland is a compact city with controlled growth. Its downtown area is friendly to pedestrians and has hundreds of beautiful parks and open spaces. Portland also has a well-planned **public transit system**. As a result, its buses and streetcars make it easy to get around without a car.

These improvements have attracted many new residents to Portland. To provide housing for more people, the city is developing up, not out. Older, run-down neighborhoods have been revived with new **mixed-use developments**. This is development that combines housing and businesses in one area, somewhat like cities founded during colonial times. For example, a building today might have shops and offices on the ground floor and apartments above.

Supporters of mixed-use development argue that it encourages people to live, work, and shop in one neighborhood. In addition, people can walk to jobs or shops instead of driving, and this reduces not only traffic, but also air pollution. Opponents, however, argue that mixed-use development limits the kind of new homes that can be built. People who want a big house on a large lot will not find their dream home in a city apartment over a business.

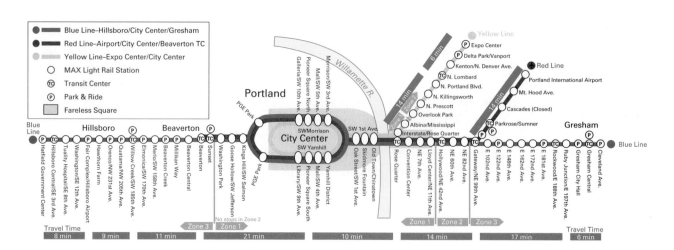

5.6 Toronto, Ontario, 1999

Toronto, Ontario, is Canada's largest metropolitan area as well as its primary business center. Toronto leads Canadian cities in printing and publishing. Television and movie production are important as well. With more than 5.5 million people, the city has been growing for decades. For a time, Toronto managed this growth by stretching up, but soon it began to sprawl out.

Building Up and Filling In Limits Sprawl Toronto has a long history. It began as a French fur-trading post in colonial times. Later, Americans who had been loyal to the British in the American Revolution and fled to Canada founded a city there. In the 1800s, Toronto became a factory town and later still it developed into a banking center. By the 1960s, though, its urban core was run down. Something had to be done to keep the downtown alive.

In 1965, Toronto announced a plan to renew its urban core. The plan encouraged **infill** over sprawl. Infill involves filling in empty or run-down parts of a city with new development. Building an apartment high-rise on an empty lot is an example of infill. So is building a shopping mall on the site of an old amusement park.

During the 1960s and 1970s, Toronto rebuilt its urban core. The new buildings included some of the world's tallest skyscrapers. These towers had offices, shops, museums, parking, and housing.

Rapid Growth on Toronto's Rural Fringe Toronto kept growing in the 1980s and 1990s. Instead of building up, though, it began to spread out. Urban sprawl took over farmland, forests, and wetlands. Traffic clogged suburban highways, increasing air pollution. Traffic and air quality both got worse as the years went by.

By 1999, officials in Toronto knew they had to do something to control sprawl. They considered many ideas. One was to reduce sprawl by encouraging smart growth ideas like mixed-use development. Another idea was to ban all growth in rural areas. A third was to allow a lot of growth in part of the city while limiting it in the rest. Whatever was decided would shape Toronto's future.

Urban Sprawl in Toronto
Toronto has been growing at a rapid pace for many years. By the late 1990s, urban sprawl stretched for miles and miles beyond the city limits.

5.7 Toronto Plans for 30 Years of Growth

On May 27, 2002, the mayor of Toronto gave a speech about urban growth. "Toronto is a great city, and we want it to stay that way," he said. "Where we go from here depends on all of us." Then he introduced a document known as the Official Plan. It contained a plan for controlling Toronto's growth for the next 30 years.

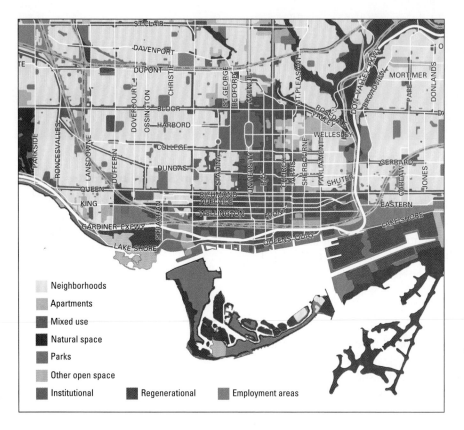

Neighborhoods
Apartments
Mixed use
Natural space
Parks
Other open space
Institutional   Regenerational   Employment areas

Future Land Use in Toronto

Toronto's Official Plan includes a map showing how land is to be used in the city. This part of the map shows the downtown area bordering Lake Ontario. Development will be limited in neighborhoods marked in yellow and orange. Mixed use is encouraged in red areas. Parks and open space are shown in green. The brown areas near the waterfront are marked for redevelopment.

Planning for Future Growth

The Official Plan took three years to complete. The effort was led by Toronto's city council, which wanted to hear what residents had to say about the plan. Town hall meetings were held around Toronto to give people an opportunity to express their thoughts. An invitation in French, Polish, Chinese, Portuguese, and English was published for people's suggestions and ideas. The council also received advice from land use experts from Toronto and elsewhere in the province. The result was a plan that allows some growth in some places.

The Official Plan allows growth to continue in 25 percent of the city. Most areas targeted for growth are in the urban core and include the old downtown and the waterfront area on Lake Ontario. Growth is also allowed in four "centers" in outlying parts of the city. Public transportation is to be expanded in order to link these growth areas together.

In the remaining 75 percent of the city, development is to be limited. This area includes the city's residential neighborhoods. It also includes waterways, parks, and open space.

The Official Plan also lays out what kind of growth Toronto should encourage. New developments are to be mainly infill and mixed-use projects. Such projects will bring new homes, shops, and businesses into the urban core.

Concerns About Infill Supporters of the Official Plan believe that it offers a sensible approach to controlling sprawl. But while infill sounds like a good idea, not everyone supports it. Developers raise concerns about its hidden costs, such as the extra time and money needed to clean up abandoned sites. This work must be done before new development can begin. And if a site is polluted with toxic chemicals, these costs can rise very quickly.

People living in neighborhoods marked for growth raise a different concern about infill. They worry that building new developments on empty lots will make the urban core more crowded.

5.8 Atlanta, Georgia, 1998

In 1996, Atlanta, Georgia, hosted the summer Olympic Games. People came from around the world to watch the events. They filled hotels and restaurants and cheered the athletes in new stadiums and arenas. Few visitors, however, traveled outside the city. Only those who did could see why Atlanta has been called "the fastest-spreading human settlement in history."

Rapid Growth Leads to Traffic Jams During the 1990s, the Atlanta metropolitan area boomed. Atlanta led the nation in new jobs, homes, and highways. It also led the nation in urban sprawl. Hundreds of acres of forest were cleared each week to make room for new residents. Without controls on development, housing tracts pushed deep into the rural fringe, destroying habitats for plants and animals.

The people who bought these new homes relied on cars to get around. Atlanta's commuters drove more miles every day than drivers anywhere else in the world. If you added up all the miles that Atlanta commuters drove in just one day, they would stretch all the way to the sun. There were traffic jams night and day.

Air Pollution Threatens Highway Funds All those vehicles traveling along Atlanta's roads also led to air pollution. The air became so polluted that it caused asthma attacks and made people suffering from other respiratory ailments much worse.

Atlanta's dirty air also violated the Clean Air Act. This is a federal, or national, law that sets limits on air pollution. In 1998, the federal government ordered Atlanta to meet the law's clean air standards. If it did not, Atlanta would lose federal highway funds, which the federal government gives to cities to improve roads.

Atlanta had to make a decision. One option was to do nothing to control growth, but this would mean giving up federal highway funds. Another was to continue growing but to create a regional transportation system. Such a system could cut pollution by getting people out of their cars. A third option was to limit sprawl in some areas while requiring mixed-use development in others. Over time, this option could also reduce car travel and air pollution.

Atlanta's Crowded Roads

Traffic jams are a daily event in the Atlanta area. All of this driving creates major air pollution problems. In 1998, 13 counties in the Atlanta region failed to meet the Clean Air Act. A plan was needed to cut pollution in the entire metropolitan area.

5.9 Atlanta Fights Pollution with Public Transit

In 1998, Roy Barnes was elected governor of Georgia. In his campaign, he promised to do something about the problems caused by sprawl. He made it clear, though, that he was not an enemy of development. "I'm no tree hugger," he said. "I'm a businessman who thinks you can't let your prosperity slip through your fingers."

A Regional Transportation Authority Is Born Governor Barnes wanted Atlanta to continue to grow. At the same time, he believed it was important for the city to meet Clean Air Act standards, so he focused on public transit.

Under Barnes' leadership, the state created the Georgia Regional Transportation Authority. This agency had three goals: First, reduce traffic jams. Second, reduce the amount of air pollution caused by cars. Third, reduce poorly planned development.

The Georgia Regional Transportation Authority works in conjunction with other government agencies to encourage people to get out of their cars. One approach has been to promote mixed-use development. As you read, in mixed-use neighborhoods, people can walk to shops and jobs. Another approach has been to encourage people to walk or bike instead of drive. New bike trails and walking paths have been constructed for just that purpose.

In addition, the region's public transit system had been expanded. The Metropolitan Atlanta Rapid Transit Authority (MARTA) is a system of trains and bus lines that serves the entire Atlanta region. New rail lines have been built, and a regional subway system has been expanded. New buses and bus routes have also been added. And the new buses don't pollute the air as much as older ones.

Atlanta Continues to Grow The growth of public transit has helped Atlanta meet federal air-quality standards. It has not slowed growth, though.

Urban sprawl remains a hot issue. Many people think the region should do more to control sprawl, which has increased pollution and has strained the water supply. In contrast, others say that Atlanta is doing just fine. They point out that there is new mixed-use development for those who want it. But they also think that people who want to buy new houses on the rural fringe should be allowed to do so.

Rails and Trails in Atlanta

Rather than slowing growth, Atlanta is trying to reduce air pollution with a better transit system. This map shows major rail lines. It also shows existing and future hiking and biking trails. As more people use rails and trails, traffic jams should decrease.

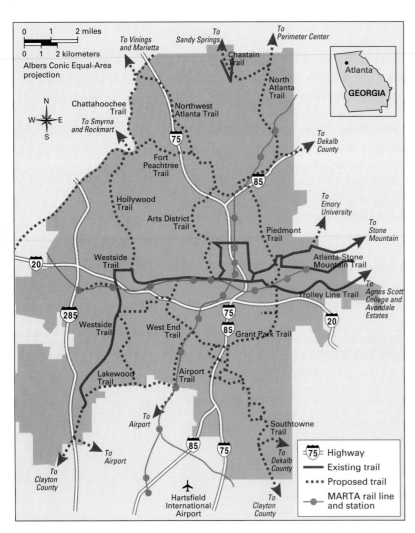

5.10 Beginning to Think Globally

In this chapter, you learned about urban sprawl. You learned that cities grow outward, expanding from the urban core to the urban fringe to the rural fringe. You also visited three metropolitan areas in the United States and Canada and saw how those areas are trying to deal with growth.

Cities Continue to Sprawl The United States and Canada are still growing. As their populations increase, so does their need for housing. Even though sprawl isn't good for the environment, development continues to push into the rural fringe.

As you have seen, sprawl continues for many reasons. Land and building costs are lower in the rural fringe than in the urban core. Some people prefer suburban homes to city apartments. And others simply don't like laws that limit where people can choose to live.

Sprawl Is a Worldwide Problem Cities around the world are struggling with the issue of urban sprawl. The Indian city of Mumbai (formerly known as Bombay) is a good example. In 1950, Mumbai had barely 3 million people. By 1995, the city's population had expanded to more than 14 million. All those people could no longer fit into the old urban core. By 2015, Mumbai's population is expected to rise to 22 million people. The only way the city will be able to house so many people is by sprawling outward.

Mumbai is not alone. Over the last century, the percentage of people living in urban areas around the world has risen rapidly. In 1900, about 14 percent of people worldwide made their homes in cities. By the year 2000, almost 47 percent of people around the world were living in urban areas. That's nearly half of the world's population. Think about these statistics as you examine the map of urban populations around the world in the next section.

Urban Sprawl in India
Urban sprawl looks different in different parts of the world. In the urban fringe of Mumbai, India, new high rises have sprung up to house the wealthy. Nearby are shantytowns where poor people live.

5.11 Global Connections

This map shows metropolitan areas around the world. Cities with more than 5 million people are marked with large black dots. The circle graphs show the change in percentages of urban and rural world populations over time. The bar graph shows how the populations of six cities have grown over time.

Why might some regions have more metropolitan areas than others? Wealthy regions tend to have more large cities than poor ones. That's because the majority of jobs in wealthy countries are found in cities. **Climate, landforms,** and **vegetation zones** also play a role. There aren't many big cities in extremely cold or **arid** regions. Nor are there many urban areas in mountains or rainforests.

Why are there so many cities with more than 5 million people in Asia? The simple answer is this: Asia has more people than any other continent. More than 3 billion people live in Asia. Together, China and India are home to 4 out of 10 of the world's people. Also, the economies of many Asian countries are shifting from farming to manufacturing and trade. Such **economic activity** generally takes place in urban settings. As a result, metropolitan areas are growing rapidly in Asia.

What special problems might urban sprawl create for poor countries? Poor countries often have little control over how their cities grow. People moving to a city simply build homes wherever they can find space. In addition, the governments of such countries lack funds to provide growing cities with basic services, such as clean water, sewers, paved roads, electricity, medical care, and schools.

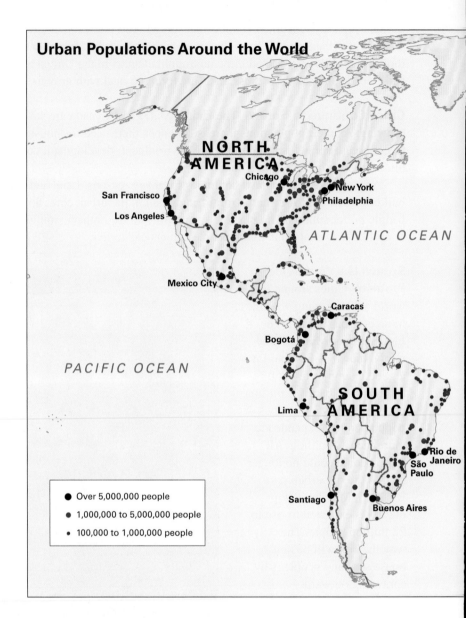

Urban Populations Around the World

● Over 5,000,000 people

● 1,000,000 to 5,000,000 people

· 100,000 to 1,000,000 people

Urban and Rural World Populations

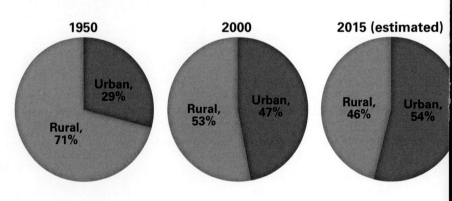

1950 — Urban, 29% / Rural, 71%

2000 — Rural, 53% / Urban, 47%

2015 (estimated) — Rural, 46% / Urban, 54%

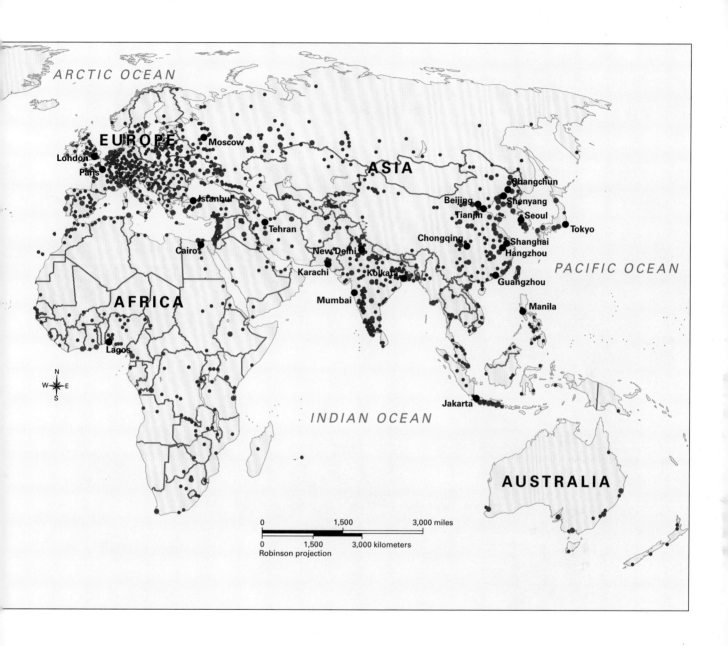

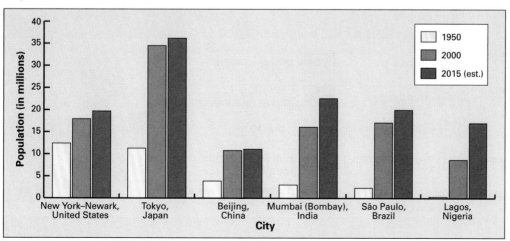

Populations in Six World Cities

Source: *United Nations Population Division*, "World Population Prospects: The 2004 Revision Population Database," esa.un.org/unpp/.

Topography of Grand Canyon National Park (detail)

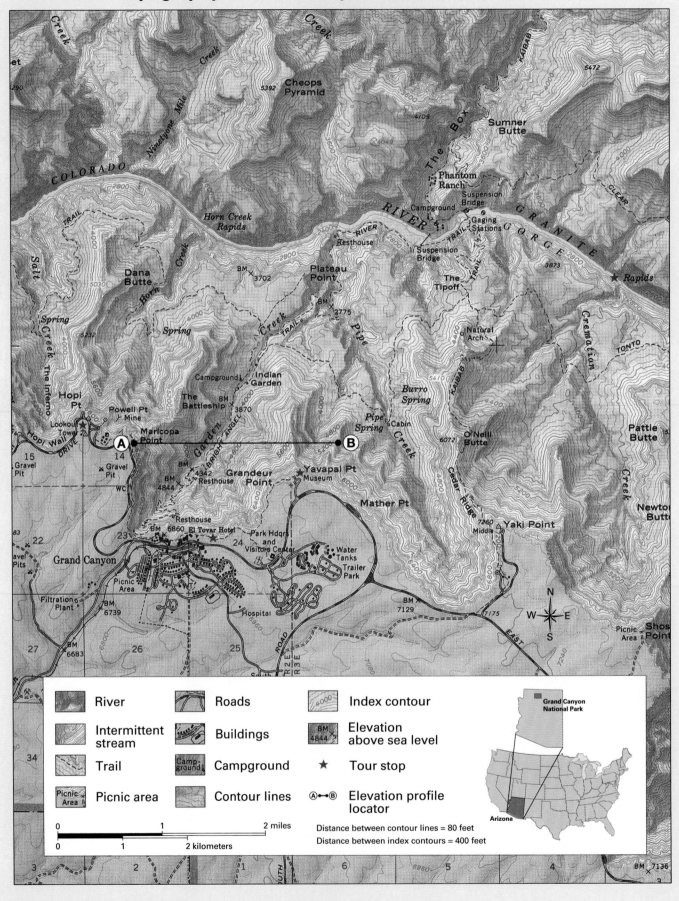

River	Roads	Index contour			
Intermittent stream	Buildings	Elevation above sea level			
Trail	Campground	★ Tour stop			
Picnic area	Contour lines	Ⓐ⤍Ⓑ Elevation profile locator			

Grand Canyon National Park

Arizona

0   1   2 miles

0   1   2 kilometers

Distance between contour lines = 80 feet
Distance between index contours = 400 feet

National Parks: Saving the Natural Heritage of the U.S. and Canada

6.1 Introduction

Imagine standing on the rim of the Grand Canyon and looking out at one of the world's most spectacular sights. The canyon is enormous — 18 miles across at its widest point. Its colorful walls look like an artist painted them in shades of red, orange, yellow, and green. A mile below, the Colorado River winds like a ribbon along the bottom of the canyon. How fortunate people must feel that this special place is open to anyone who wants to visit it.

The Grand Canyon is available to visit because it is a **national park**. National parks are large areas of land set aside by governments to preserve the land in its natural state. Today there are 55 national parks in the United States and 42 in Canada. Most of the parks were created to protect land and wildlife because of their rarity, beauty, or other qualities. Some parks preserve lands with historic interest as well.

Grand Canyon National Park is a good example of a single park that serves many purposes. Besides the majestic canyon, the park boasts abundant wildlife and plant life as well as ruins of ancient Native American pueblos, or villages.

In this chapter, you will explore some of North America's national parks. To do so, you will use **topographic maps**. These large-scale maps show the landforms and other surface features of an area, both physical and human. The maps will help you understand the special features of each park.

Essential Question

What features make national parks special and worth preserving?

This map legend is from a topographic map of a national park. This type of map shows a park's topography, or the features on the surface of the land. Some are natural features. Others are created by humans. Keep the symbols on this legend in mind as you try to answer the Essential Question.

Graphic Organizer

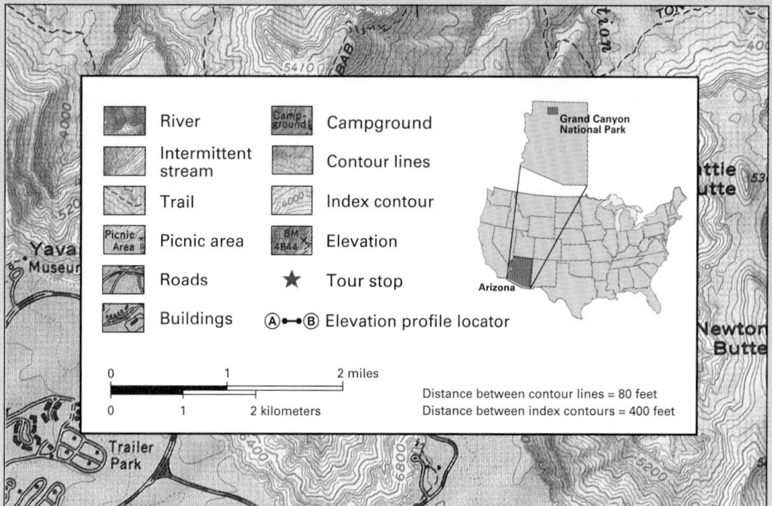

River		Campground	Grand Canyon National Park
Intermittent stream		Contour lines	
Trail		Index contour	
Picnic area		Elevation	
Roads	★	Tour stop	Arizona
Buildings	Ⓐ●➤Ⓑ	Elevation profile locator	

0   1   2 miles
0   1   2 kilometers

Distance between contour lines = 80 feet
Distance between index contours = 400 feet

◀ Topographic map of a section of Grand Canyon National Park

Flora in Yellowstone National Park

Fauna in Yellowstone National Park

6.2 The Geographic Setting

When American fur trappers explored the Rocky Mountains in the 1800s, they came across a remarkable place. They saw pools of water so hot that they were covered with clouds of steam. They found puddles of boiling mud that sputtered and spattered day and night. They also saw hot springs called **geysers** that threw jets of hot water up in the air. Some of the geysers erupted on regular schedules while others would suddenly blow sky high with no warning. The trappers called this strange landscape "the place where hell bubbles up." Today we know the area as Yellowstone National Park.

At first, people thought the trappers' stories of boiling springs were just "tall tales." In 1870, however, the government sent an expedition to explore the area, and it turned out that the tales were all true.

Yellowstone is a unique place. It has about 300 geysers—two thirds of all the geysers in the world. Some of those geysers on occasion erupt to 100 feet and beyond. Yellowstone also has more than 10,000 hot springs, mud pots, and steam vents.

Yellowstone Becomes the First National Park In the 1800s, more and more people moved west. As Americans turned wilderness into farms and ranches, some people began to talk about protecting the Yellowstone area as a public park.

The idea of a national park for the public was new. European cities had public gardens, but no country had ever set aside a large area of land for its citizens to visit and enjoy.

In 1872, Congress passed a law creating Yellowstone National Park out of federal land in what became the states of Montana, Idaho, and Wyoming. Yellowstone was the first national park in the world. Over time, Congress created many more national parks, and the national park movement eventually spread to Canada and other countries.

Parks Protect Special Places for Future Generations National parks have been created to protect many different places. Some parks preserve unique landforms and bodies of water. Others protect unusual **flora,** or plant life. Some provide homes for rare **fauna,** or animal life. And some preserve historic reminders of the past, such as national battlefields and national cemeteries.

The movement to set aside special places as parks was led by people called **conservationists**. Probably the best-known American conservationist is John Muir. Muir was born in Scotland, and his family relocated to the United States when he was 11. As a young man, he suffered an injury that left him temporarily blind. When his sight returned, he vowed to turn his eyes to nature. Muir walked across much of the American West. On that journey, he fell in love with the West's plains, mountains, and forests.

Muir spent most of his life trying to preserve beautiful wild places as parks. "Everybody needs beauty as well as bread," he wrote, "places to play in and pray in, where nature may heal and give strength to body and soul alike." Today many people remember him as "The Father of the National Parks." In this chapter, you will learn more about the special features of several national parks.

▶ Geoterms

conservationist someone who works to protect the beauty and natural resources of the environment from destruction or pollution

fauna all the animal life in a particular region

flora all the plant life in a particular region

topographic map a map that uses elevation lines and symbols to show a region's physical and human features. These features may include hills, valleys, rivers, lakes, roads, trails, and buildings.

Three Views of the Grand Canyon

This photograph looks out over the Grand Canyon from near Maricopa Point on the West Rim. The ship-shaped rock formation at its center is known as the Battleship. The section of topographic map below the photo shows this same feature. It also shows Bright Angel Trail, which leads down Garden Creek to the canyon floor. The elevation profile below the map shows this same area from a different point of view. It traces changes in elevation from Maricopa Point to a ridge near Pipe Spring.

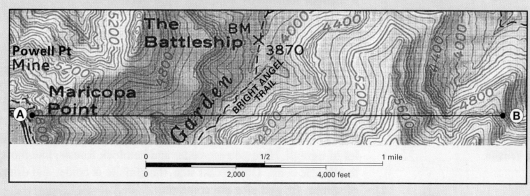

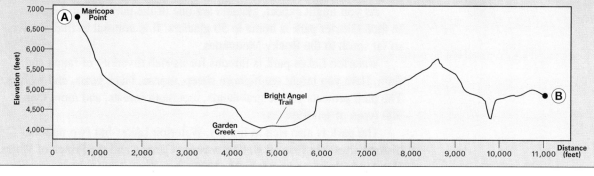

Sperry Glacier

Mountain goat

Lake Ellen Wilson

6.3 Waterton-Glacier International Peace Park

About 10,000 years ago, huge **glaciers** covered the tops of the Rocky Mountains and gradually slid down their slopes. A glacier is a large, slow-moving mass of ice. Because of their enormous size and weight, glaciers act like bulldozers, scraping and reshaping the land as they move. Almost everywhere you look in Waterton-Glacier International Peace Park, you can see strange and wonderful shapes carved by glaciers. Landforms created by glaciers are called **arêtes, cirques, hanging valleys, horns,** and **moraines**.

Two Parks into One Waterton-Glacier International Peace Park unites two parks, one on each side of the border separating the United States and Canada. The park's land was once home to Kootenai and Blackfoot Indians. Both tribes fished the mountain rivers and hunted herds of buffalo there. During the 1800s, European settlers arrived and began clearing land for farms and ranches. Miners searched for copper and gold, although no large deposits were ever found. In 1895, the Blackfoot sold their homeland to the United States.

By that time, many people in both the United States and Canada wanted to protect some wilderness areas as parks. In 1895, Canada set aside the Waterton Lakes area as a park. In 1910, the U.S. Congress created Glacier National Park. The two countries joined the parks in 1932 to create the world's first international park. It was called a peace park in honor of the long friendship between the two countries. The Blackfoot and Kootenai Indians were forced to live outside the park on reservations to the east and southwest of Glacier.

Natural Attractions and History Waterton-Glacier park is notable for a number of physical and human features. To begin with, the park straddles the **Continental Divide**. The Continental Divide is a ridgeline along a chain of mountains stretching from Mexico to Canada and Alaska. Rivers on the west side of the divide run toward the Pacific Ocean. Rivers on the east side flow toward the Atlantic Ocean and the Gulf of Mexico.

One of the most popular recreational activities in Glacier is to drive along Going-to-the-Sun Road. This highway links a valley on the east side of the divide and a valley on the west side. Along the drive, the road climbs through a spectacular mountain pass.

Driving the highway is a good way to experience the different **climates** on each side of the divide. On the west side, the weather is mild, with a lot of rainfall. Here you see cedar and hemlock forests, like those along the Pacific coast. On the east side, the climate is colder and drier. Forests of spruce, fir, and pine are common.

As you might expect, glaciers are one of the park's main features. In fact, Glacier park is home to 50 glaciers. It is unusual to find glaciers so far south in the Rocky Mountains.

Waterton Lakes park is famous for its rich diversity of fauna and flora. Here you might see bighorn sheep, moose, black bears, and wolves. The park protects prairie grasslands, mountain forests, and more than 900 types of wildflowers.

The park is also rich in history. Waterton Lakes has two national historic sites: the first oil well in western Canada and the Prince of Wales Hotel, which opened on July 25, 1927.

Topography of Waterton-Glacier International Peace Park (detail)

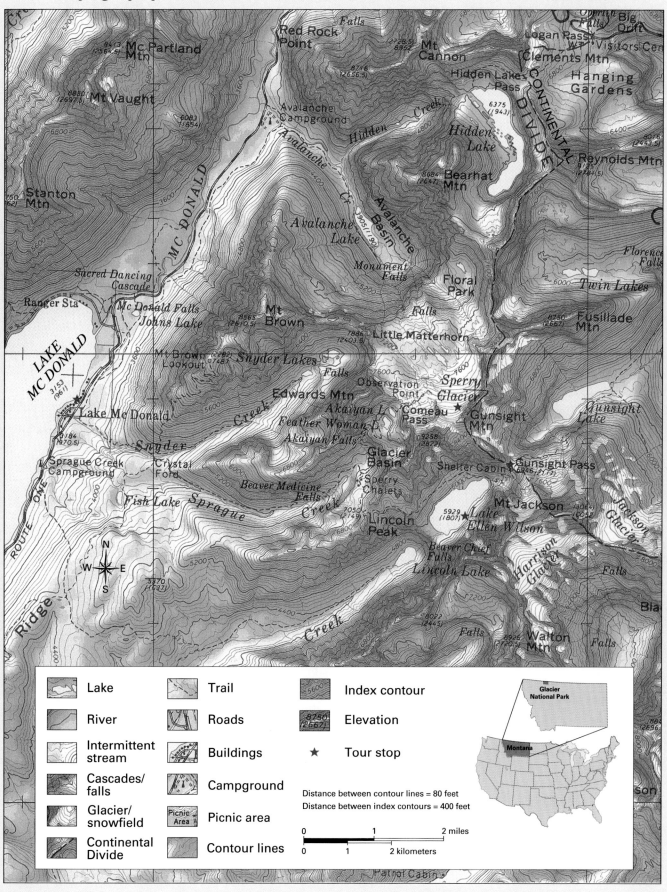

Lake

River

Intermittent stream

Cascades/falls

Glacier/snowfield

Continental Divide

Trail

Roads

Buildings

Campground

Picnic area

Contour lines

Index contour

Elevation

★ Tour stop

Glacier National Park

Montana

Distance between contour lines = 80 feet
Distance between index contours = 400 feet

0   1   2 miles
0   1   2 kilometers

Sand dunes

Green Gables house

Red sandstone cliffs

6.4 Prince Edward Island National Park

It was broad daylight when Anne awoke and sat up in bed....
For a moment she could not remember where she was. First came
a delightful thrill, as something very pleasant; then a horrible
remembrance. This was Green Gables and they didn't want her
because she wasn't a boy!

Maybe you recognize this scene from the novel *Anne of Green Gables*.
At about the age of 11, an orphan named Anne Shirley came to live with
an elderly couple on Prince Edward Island in Canada. The house they
lived in was called Green Gables.

The book's author, Lucy Maud Montgomery, knew the island well
because she had grown up there. A local farm gave her the inspiration
for Green Gables. Today, Green Gables house is just one of many attractions that bring visitors from all over the world to Prince Edward Island
National Park.

A Fragile Island Environment Prince Edward Island has a fragile
environment of beaches, sand dunes, and **wetland**. The forces of wind
and water and human activity over time have left their mark here. On
its north shore, ocean waves have carved steep cliffs into the red sandstone. While forests of beech, sugar maple, yellow birch, and red oak
once covered the island, today there are only evergreens such as fir,
spruce, and tamarack.

More than a thousand years before Europeans reached North America,
the Micmac Indians lived on Prince Edward Island. They called the island
Epekwitk, which means "resting on the waves."

Between about 1720 and 1911, French and then English settlers
made Prince Edward Island their home. In their eagerness to build homes
and make a living, the settlers cleared the forest from more than half the
island. They cut down trees for farming, timber exportation, and ship-
building. In 1937, the Canadian government created Prince Edward
Island National Park to protect and preserve the delicate environment
of a portion of the island.

Old Settlements and Moving Dunes Visitors come to Prince Edward
Island National Park to explore its natural and historical heritage. At Green
Gables they can see how people lived on the island in the late 1800s.
They can wander through old homes of early settlers.

Visitors to the park can explore the island's marshes, woods, and
sandy beaches. The park is an important **habitat** for many types of birds
and rare plants. Migrating sand dunes draw visitors to the park's north
shore. A dune is a hill of sand that has been piled up by the wind; a
migrating sand dune is one that is being pushed by the wind to a different
location. On Prince Edward Island, the winds are slowly driving the
dunes from the edge of the beach inland.

Seeing the dunes move over a period of months and years is similar
to watching nature playing a game of leapfrog. The island's migrating
dunes have covered up entire sections of forests, killing the trees. As
the dunes move on, they reveal a "skeleton forest" of trees that were
previously buried.

Topography of Prince Edward Island National Park

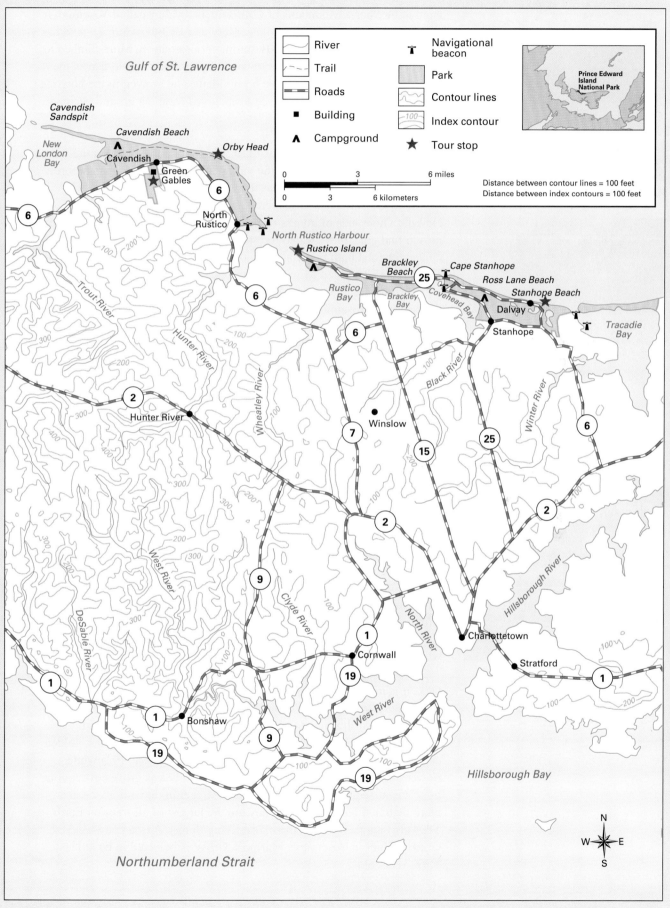

Legend:

- River
- Trail
- Roads
- ■ Building
- ⋀ Campground
- ⊤ Navigational beacon
- Park
- Contour lines
- —100— Index contour
- ★ Tour stop

0   3   6 miles
0   3   6 kilometers

Distance between contour lines = 100 feet
Distance between index contours = 100 feet

Prince Edward Island National Park

Gulf of St. Lawrence

Cavendish Sandspit
New London Bay
Cavendish Beach
Cavendish
Green Gables
Orby Head
North Rustico
North Rustico Harbour
Rustico Island
Brackley Beach
Cape Stanhope
Ross Lane Beach
Stanhope Beach
Dalvay
Stanhope
Tracadie Bay
Rustico Bay
Brackley Bay
Covehead Bay
Winter River
Black River

Trout River
Hunter River
Wheatley River
Winslow
Hunter River
West River
Clyde River
Charlottetown
Stratford
Cornwall
Bonshaw
DeSable River
North River
West River
Hillsborough River
Hillsborough Bay
Northumberland Strait

Half Dome

El Capitan

Yosemite Falls

6.5 Yosemite National Park

High in the Sierra Mountains of California is a valley called Yosemite. It was a favorite camping site of the conservationist John Muir. Legend has it that one night in the late 1800s, during a fierce storm, Muir climbed to the top of a tall Douglas fir tree to watch as lightning forked across the dark sky. Muir could easily have been killed as he swayed in the howling winds. Luckily, he survived to see his beloved camping ground become Yosemite National Park.

A Gold Rush, Miners, and Tourists The first people in Yosemite were Miwok Indians. They roamed the valley for thousands of years before Europeans arrived. The park was named after a Miwok tribe.

In 1849, Europeans discovered gold in the foothills of the Sierra Nevada. Thousands of miners rushed in, hoping to get rich. In their eagerness to find gold, they cleared forests and polluted streams and rivers. They hunted for food until many animal species were in danger of disappearing. The miners also killed Miwok who did not flee the area.

Meanwhile, writers, artists, and photographers spread the word about the beauty of Yosemite Valley. Tourists began arriving on foot, on horseback, and by stagecoach. People built hotels to accommodate these many visitors. Others planted orchards and provided supplies for the miners. All of this human activity encroached on the expanse of natural beauty in the valley.

Led by John Muir, conservationists appealed to Congress to protect the valley and the surrounding land. In 1890, Congress agreed to create Yosemite National Park. It was the nation's third national park.

Granite Domes and Giant Trees Rounded mountains and tall, pointy rock towers circle Yosemite Valley. Millions of years of glacial activity created these amazing rock walls.

One of the most famous features rising above the valley floor is called Half Dome. Once it was a huge granite mountain with a rounded top, but long, long ago, a moving glacier sliced the mountain in two. The ice left just half of the dome behind, with a sheer 2,200-foot cliff.

El Capitan—a favorite wall for experienced rock climbers—is a 3,600-foot-high block of granite that forms the north wall of the valley. Climbers from all over the world come to Yosemite to scale "The Captain." A few climb the incredibly steep cliff in less than 24 hours while others take a week or two to make their way to the top.

Yosemite Falls is one of the most photographed attractions in the park. It is really three connected waterfalls that, together, drop almost 2,500 feet from the valley's rim to its floor. Yosemite Falls is the highest waterfall in North America and the among the tallest in the world.

The park's fauna includes California bighorn sheep, coyotes, golden eagles, and black bears. Among its flora is the mariposa lily, a white flower that resembles a butterfly. The park also boasts groves of sequoia trees. Giant sequoias can measure up to 30 feet in circumference and more than 300 feet in height. They are the largest of all trees on Earth. They also number among the oldest living things. A tree known as Grizzly Giant in Yosemite's Mariposa Grove is believed to be at least 2,700 years old.

Topography of Yosemite National Park (detail)

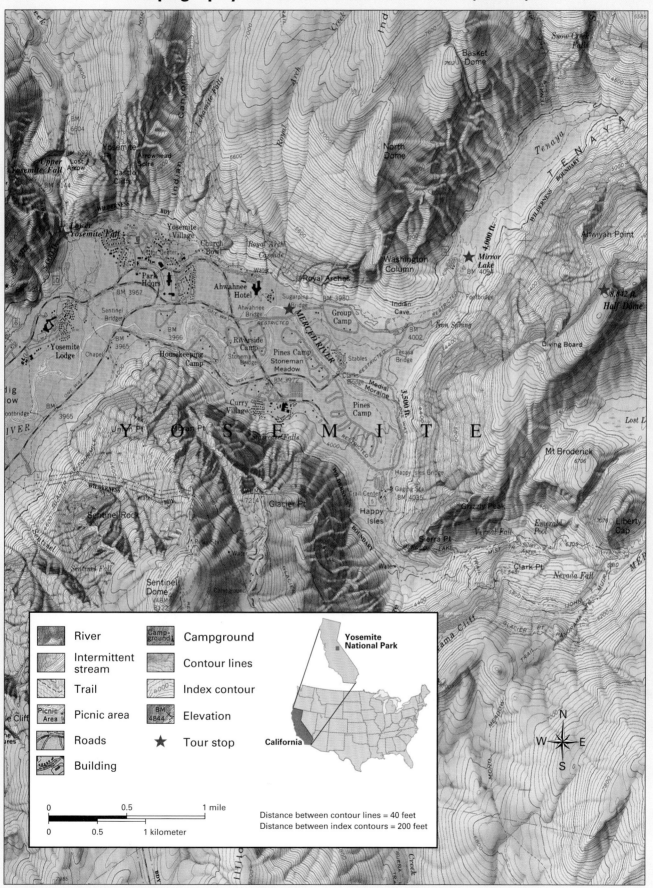

River
Intermittent stream
Trail
Picnic area
Roads
Building

Campground
Contour lines
Index contour
Elevation
Tour stop

Yosemite National Park

California

0   0.5   1 mile
0   0.5   1 kilometer

Distance between contour lines = 40 feet
Distance between index contours = 200 feet

Mt. McKinley

Polar bears at Wapusk Park

Alligator in Everglades Park

6.6 Peaks, Bears, and a Water Wilderness

You have read about two national parks and one international park in North America. There are many other parks to explore in the United States and Canada, each with its own special attractions. Here is a sampling of three quite different national parks.

Denali National Park Alaska's Denali National Park was established to protect its large mammals and is home to Mt. McKinley. At more than 20,000 feet, Mt. McKinley is the highest mountain in North America. The mountain was originally called Denali, an Indian word meaning "The Great One" or "The High One." It was renamed for President William McKinley in 1896.

Mt. McKinley is not the only mountain in Denali. The park includes other impressive mountains in the Alaska Range. Glaciers cover many of the tallest peaks. The park's **subarctic** climate is habitat to **mammals** such as grizzly bears, wolves, and moose.

Cars are not allowed in most of the park. Instead, visitors must explore on foot or by bicycle or bus. Park buses shuttle visitors to trails and campsites. Visitors can also board tour buses to view Denali. The bus drivers are very good at spotting wildlife. On a good summer day, visitors might even see caribou and bald eagles.

Wapusk National Park Wapusk National Park is Canada's 37th national park. The name Wapusk is a Cree Indian word that means "white bear." It's a good name for this park because Wapusk National Park was created to protect one of the world's largest known polar bear denning areas. A denning area is a place where mother bears give birth to their cubs each spring.

Wapusk is not an easy park to visit. It is located in northern Manitoba, bordering Hudson Bay and far from any road. Much of the park is **tundra,** meaning the ground freezes hard in winter and becomes a swamp in summer. The park also includes a **taiga** forest of stunted spruce, larch, and willows.

The park is home to beluga whales, hundreds of thousands of birds, and a wide variety of wildflowers. But its most important animals are bears. Every year, about 190 pregnant polar bears come to the park to dig dens in the damp earth and give birth to their cubs.

Everglades National Park A tall, long-necked bird called a great egret stands with one leg drawn up in the shallow water of a river. On the bank, an alligator is sunning itself. Nothing moves. Suddenly, with a flip of its tail, the alligator slides into the water and the egret flies off in a rush. Then everything is still again in Everglades National Park.

Everglades National Park spans the southern tip of the Florida peninsula. It is the only North American preserve with a **humid subtropical** climate. A preserve is an area where animals are protected from hunting. Summers here are hot and rainy, while winters are mild.

Everglades Park contains many different environments. It has ponds, rivers, and swamps as well as sawgrass prairies and pineland forests. These environments support a great variety of birds and other animals. The park is known for its large wading birds, like the spoonbill, the wood stork, the great blue heron, and the egret. It is also the only place in the world where alligators and crocodiles live near one another.

6.7 Beginning to Think Globally

As you have read, the United States was the first country in the world to set aside wilderness areas as national parks. The idea of protecting land in parks soon spread to Canada. People from all over the world come to both countries to visit national parks. Some of these parks are known for their scenic beauty while others are visited for their flora and fauna.

Threats to National Parks The United States has led the movement to preserve wilderness areas. However, putting land in a park does not guarantee that it will be preserved from harm.

Many parks face threats from outside their boundaries. Air pollution, for example, drifts into parks from other areas. Great Smoky Mountains National Park spans Tennessee and North Carolina. Air pollution from nearby power plants is harming plants and wildlife there. Exotic, or non-native, species are another threat to native plants and animals. Infestations of nonnative insects and diseases occur when changes in the environment reduce their usual predators.

Local development can also hurt parks. Water levels are dropping in the Everglades because canals, levees, and other water-control systems divert water away from the park. The water that does reach the park is often polluted with **sewage** and **toxic waste**.

Loving Parks to Death Popular parks are also in danger of being loved to death. Large numbers of visitors are hard on parks. Their cars cause pollution, and their feet wear away fragile soil. Careless campers sometimes litter areas with trash or start fires.

Parks rich in natural resources face other threats. People eager to use those resources may pressure governments to open parks to farming, logging, mining, or oil drilling.

Around the world, lands set aside for parks or wildlife face similar threats. Think about these threats as you examine preserved land around the world in the next section.

Air Quality in the Great Smokies

Air pollution is a major problem in many national parks. These images are of Great Smoky Mountains National Park on a clear and a polluted day. Factories and cars outside parks create pollution that is carried by wind over the parks. The resulting haze and smog can destroy the beautiful views that people come to see. Air pollution can also harm a park's flora and fauna.

6.8 Global Connections

The map shows amounts of land preserved for parks and wildlife around the world. Some of these areas are preserved as national parks. Some are protected as national forests or wilderness areas. Some are set aside as special preserves for rare or unique flora and fauna.

What problems make it hard for countries to set land aside for parks? In many countries, the cost of creating parks may be a preventive factor. Poor countries may decide they are better off spending their money on things their citizens need more than parks. If a country lacks schools, for instance, parks may look like an unaffordable luxury.

What challenges do countries face in managing lands already set aside? Often the greatest management challenge is finding the right balance between preserving and using land. Some people argue that preserved land should be closed to all uses. They believe that this is the best way to protect special places and environments. Others feel just as strongly that people should be able to use and enjoy protected lands. They believe that this is the best way to build public support for parks. Balancing these two opinions is not easy.

Has the world done a good job of setting aside unique lands for preservation? Thousands of special areas have been preserved around the world. Still, many people think we can and must do better. The world is growing more crowded year by year, they argue. Unless we act now to protect more land, many other special places may be lost forever.

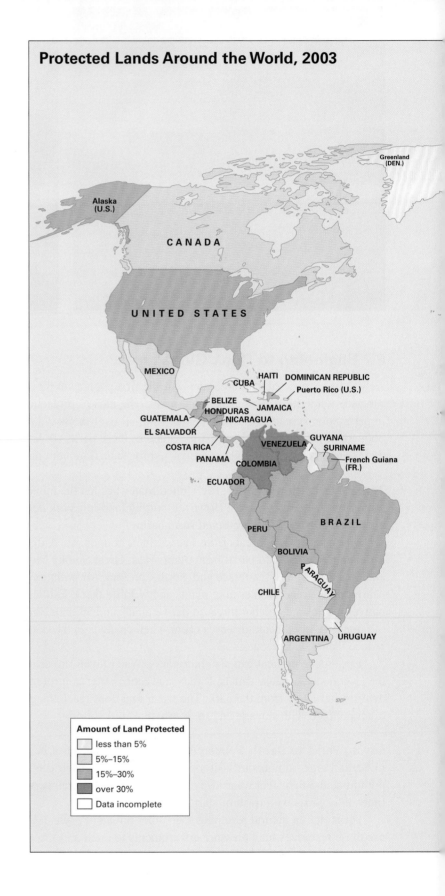

Protected Lands Around the World, 2003

Amount of Land Protected
- less than 5%
- 5%–15%
- 15%–30%
- over 30%
- Data incomplete

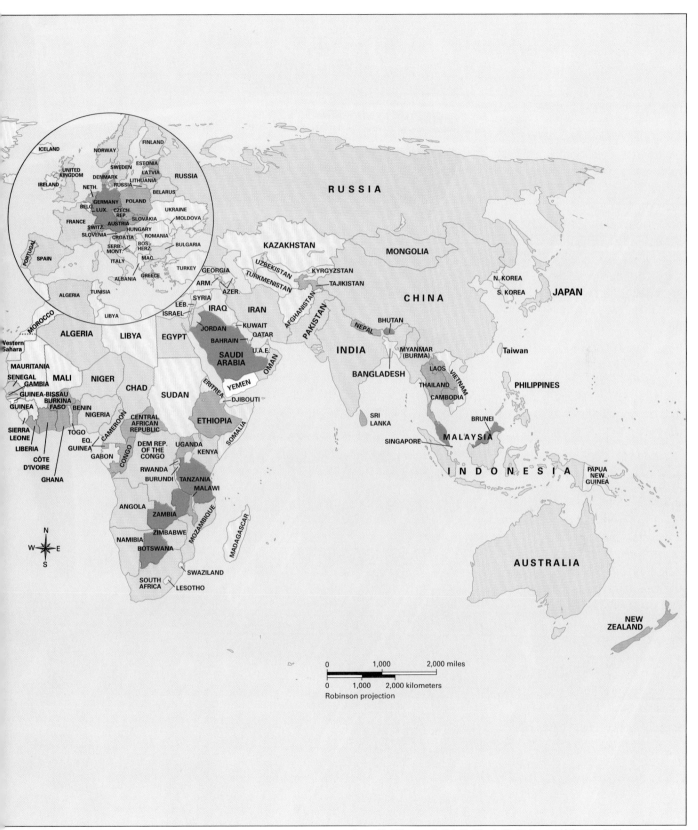

ICELAND · NORWAY · FINLAND · SWEDEN · ESTONIA · LATVIA · RUSSIA · UNITED KINGDOM · DENMARK · LITHUANIA · IRELAND · NETH. · RUSSIA · BELARUS · GERMANY · POLAND · BELG. · LUX. · CZECH REP. · UKRAINE · FRANCE · SLOVAKIA · MOLDOVA · SWITZ. · AUSTRIA · HUNGARY · SLOVENIA · CROATIA · ROMANIA · PORTUGAL · SERB.-MONT. · BOS.-HERZ. · BULGARIA · SPAIN · ITALY · MAC. · TURKEY · GEORGIA · ALBANIA · GREECE · ARM. · ALGERIA · TUNISIA · AZER. · LIBYA · SYRIA · LEB. · ISRAEL

RUSSIA

KAZAKHSTAN

MONGOLIA

UZBEKISTAN · KYRGYZSTAN · TURKMENISTAN · TAJIKISTAN

N. KOREA
S. KOREA
JAPAN

CHINA

AFGHANISTAN

BHUTAN

PAKISTAN

NEPAL

Taiwan

MOROCCO

ALGERIA · LIBYA · EGYPT

IRAQ · IRAN · JORDAN · KUWAIT · BAHRAIN · QATAR · SAUDI ARABIA · U.A.E. · OMAN

INDIA

MYANMAR (BURMA)

BANGLADESH

LAOS · VIETNAM · THAILAND · CAMBODIA

PHILIPPINES

Western Sahara

MAURITANIA · MALI · NIGER · CHAD · SUDAN · ERITREA · YEMEN · DJIBOUTI

SENEGAL · GAMBIA · GUINEA-BISSAU · BURKINA FASO · BENIN · NIGERIA · GUINEA · SIERRA LEONE · TOGO · EQ. GUINEA · LIBERIA · CÔTE D'IVOIRE · GHANA · CAMEROON · CONGO · GABON

CENTRAL AFRICAN REPUBLIC · DEM REP. OF THE CONGO · ETHIOPIA · SOMALIA

UGANDA · KENYA · RWANDA · BURUNDI · TANZANIA · MALAWI

SRI LANKA

SINGAPORE

BRUNEI

MALAYSIA

INDONESIA

PAPUA NEW GUINEA

ANGOLA · ZAMBIA · ZIMBABWE · MOZAMBIQUE · MADAGASCAR · NAMIBIA · BOTSWANA · SWAZILAND · SOUTH AFRICA · LESOTHO

N
W · E
S

AUSTRALIA

NEW ZEALAND

0 — 1,000 — 2,000 miles
0 — 1,000 — 2,000 kilometers
Robinson projection

Source: *World Resources Institute,* EarthTrends: The Environmental Information Portal, earthtrends.wri.org.

Consumption Patterns in the United States: The Impact of Living Well

7.1 Introduction

Americans are eager consumers. They buy and use a lot of goods and services. Shopping centers in the United States offer consumers a huge variety of products, and supermarkets are filled with foods for every taste. Stores large and small begin selling holiday merchandise months in advance to encourage shoppers to buy more. Car dealers tempt buyers with row upon row of shiny vehicles. Meanwhile, the Internet has turned the home computer into a virtual shopping mall.

Americans have made **consumption** a way of life. Consumption means the using up of goods or services. Some goods, like food, can be consumed only once. Others, like clothing, can be used again and again until they are worn out or go out of style.

The average American spends thousands of dollars each year on personal consumption. These purchases include spending on everything from food and clothes to gas and rent. This amount is typical for people living in **developed countries,** which are wealthy countries like the United States and Canada. But it is more than most people in **developing countries** earn in a year. Developing countries are poor countries like Mexico and India.

In this chapter, you will read about consumption patterns in the United States. You will discover how they compare with those of other countries, both developed and developing. And you will read about the impact of American consumption on the resources and environment of the planet.

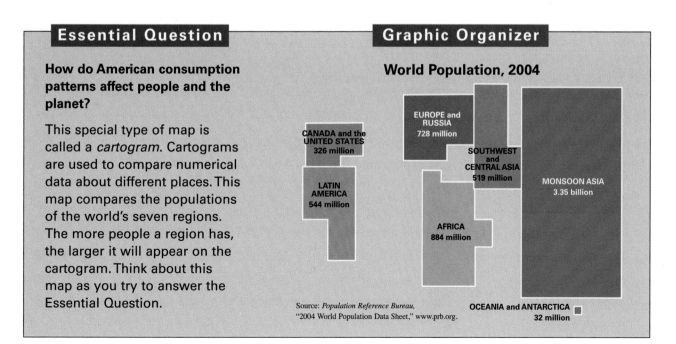

Essential Question

How do American consumption patterns affect people and the planet?

This special type of map is called a *cartogram.* Cartograms are used to compare numerical data about different places. This map compares the populations of the world's seven regions. The more people a region has, the larger it will appear on the cartogram. Think about this map as you try to answer the Essential Question.

Graphic Organizer

World Population, 2004

CANADA and the UNITED STATES
326 million

LATIN AMERICA
544 million

EUROPE and RUSSIA
728 million

SOUTHWEST and CENTRAL ASIA
519 million

MONSOON ASIA
3.35 billion

AFRICA
884 million

OCEANIA and ANTARCTICA
32 million

Source: *Population Reference Bureau,* "2004 World Population Data Sheet," www.prb.org.

◀ A crowded shopping mall in Syracuse, New York

7.2 The Geographic Setting

In 2005, the United States had a population of around 300 million people, which made it the third most populated country in the world. But in terms of population, the United States was still much smaller than the two largest countries, China and India. They each had a population of more than 1 billion people. Despite having fewer people, the United States consumed far more than did either China or India. This difference was the result of many factors. The most important factor, however, was the countries' different levels of development.

Consumption Depends on Levels of Development The United States is one of the world's developed, or wealthy, countries. Today there are about 30 developed countries around the world. Most countries in Western Europe belong to this group. So do Japan, South Korea, Canada, Australia, and New Zealand.

People in developed countries live well compared to most of the world. Most people in developed countries live in urban areas and work in factories or offices. Their governments provide them with many benefits. These benefits include public schools, fire protection, and safe drinking water. Most workers in developed countries earn good wages. They can afford to consume a lot of goods and services.

In contrast, there are more than 150 developing nations in the world today. These are countries that are still building their economies by improving agriculture, developing industries, and increasing trade. This group includes most of the countries in Asia, Africa, and Latin America. Most of these countries have too few industries to provide good jobs for their people, and many also lack a strong and stable government.

People in developing countries are more likely to live in rural areas and work on farms. Their governments provide them with only limited benefits. They may not have access to good schools or safe drinking water. Most of these people earn low wages. As a result, their consumption may be quite limited, their homes modest, and their possessions few.

Per Capita GDP Is One Measure of Development There are many ways to measure a country's level of development. One method of evaluation is to look at how many years of schooling people in the country have. Another gauge of development is to look at average **longevity,** or how long its people live.

The most common measure of development is based on a country's **gross domestic product, or GDP.** This is the total value of goods and services that a country produces in a year. Goods are things that are produced for sale or use. Food, clothing, and cars are all goods. Services are tasks done by some people for other people. Teaching is a service. So is repairing a car or a computer.

A country's level of development depends on its **per capita** GDP. Per capita means "per person." Per capita GDP is calculated by dividing a country's total GDP by its population. The result, the average production for one person, serves as a rough measure of how rich or poor a country is. The United States has a high per capita GDP. This means that it is a wealthy country. This fact strongly influences how much Americans consume year by year.

Gross Domestic Product in Six Countries, 2004

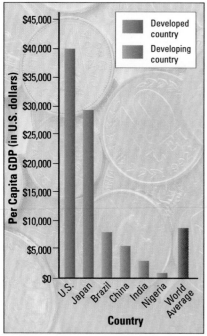

Source: *Central Intelligence Agency,* "CIA Factbook," www.cia.gov.

Levels of Development

This bar graph compares per capita GDP in six countries. Per capita GDP is the value of goods and services produced per person in a country in a year. Developed countries have a high per capita GDP. People in those countries have more money to spend on consumer goods. As a result, they consume more.

▶ Geoterms

consumption the using up of goods and services. This term is also used to describe the purchase and use of goods and services by consumers.

developed country a wealthy country with an advanced economy. Developed countries have many industries and provide a comfortable way of life for most of their people.

developing country a poorer country with a less advanced economy. In general, developing countries are trying to increase their industries and improve life for their people.

gross domestic product (GDP) the total value of goods and services produced in a country in a year

per capita by or for each person. A per capita figure is calculated by dividing the total amount of something by the number of people in a place.

Resources Help Development

As this map shows, the United States has many natural resources. It has fertile farmland and vast forests. It is rich in minerals and fossil fuels. Over time, Americans have used these resources to develop the United States into one of the world's richest countries.

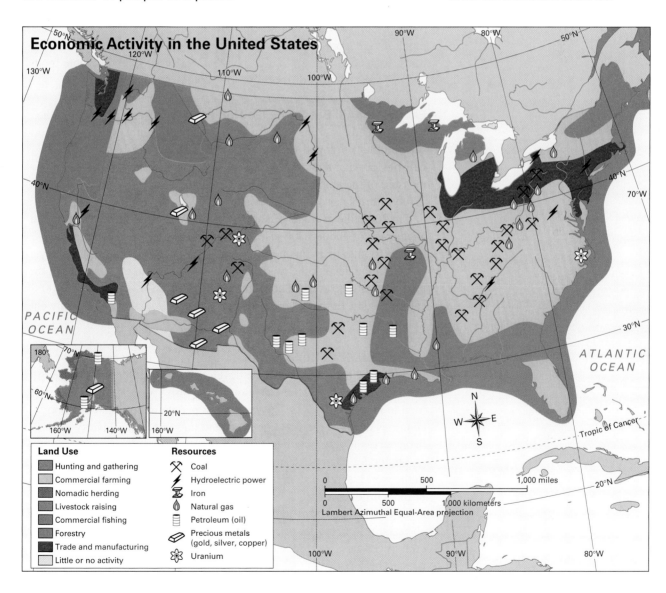

Economic Activity in the United States

Land Use
- Hunting and gathering
- Commercial farming
- Nomadic herding
- Livestock raising
- Commercial fishing
- Forestry
- Trade and manufacturing
- Little or no activity

Resources
- Coal
- Hydroelectric power
- Iron
- Natural gas
- Petroleum (oil)
- Precious metals (gold, silver, copper)
- Uranium

Lambert Azimuthal Equal-Area projection

More Than Enough Food

Food is plentiful in the United States. Supermarkets offer a wide range of foods from around the world.

7.3 Food Consumption Patterns

Imagine a wealthy diner sitting down to eat in a fancy restaurant. The table is set with fresh flowers and fine china. The food looks as good as it smells and tastes. Outside, however, a poor person clothed in rags is picking scraps of food from the restaurant's trash bin. These two people represent the world's rich and poor countries. As your mental image suggests, such countries are likely to have different ways to distribute food and different patterns of food consumption.

Enough for All, But Some Go Hungry There is enough food on the planet to feed everyone, but it is not distributed evenly. Much of the food stays in the developed world. People in rich countries consume more **calories** per day than people in the developing world. Calories are a measure of the amount of energy in food. On average, adults need about 2,700 calories per day to live healthy lives.

In 2002, the average person in many developed countries consumed an average of about 3,300 calories a day. This intake was more than enough food to meet one person's nutritional needs. Meanwhile, many people in the developing world did not get enough to eat. In some of the poorer countries, average consumption per person was less than 2,400 calories a day. In the poorest parts of Africa, half of the population went to bed hungry each night.

Poverty Leads to Hunger As you read, hunger is not caused by a worldwide shortage of food. The developed world produces more food than it can consume. Many developing countries also produce enough food to feed their people. However, poor people in both rich and poor countries may not earn enough money to buy that food. Poverty denies them access to adequate nutrition.

India, for example, has the largest number of people living in poverty in the world, and it also has the largest number of hungry people. Farmers in India produce enough food to feed the entire population, but many of them export their crops to other countries. When they sell their crops abroad, they get higher prices for them than they would at home. Higher crop prices are good for Indian farmers. However, they may mean that many other poor Indians have less to eat.

7.4 Oil Consumption Patterns

Picture morning rush hour in any city in the developed world, where the streets are filled with gas-guzzling cars, motorcycles, and buses. Now picture that same scene in a city in the developing world. You will still see lots of cars, buses, and motorcycles, but most people are riding bicycles or walking to work because they cannot afford the cost of using motorized transportation.

As these mental images suggest, oil, or petroleum, consumption follows a pattern similar to food consumption. Developed countries use more than developing countries. Oil is a **fossil fuel** that has many uses. It is refined into gasoline. It is used to make asphalt to cover roads. Petroleum is also used to make plastics, nylon, and other products.

Oil Fuels the Developed World Developed countries depend on oil to meet most of their energy needs. Their cars, trains, and planes burn fuels made from oil, and they use oil to heat buildings in the winter. Their power plants burn oil to generate electricity.

The United States leads the world in oil consumption. Americans make up just 5 percent of the world population, but they consume 25 percent of the oil pumped out of the ground each year. Most of the oil Americans consume is burned as gasoline.

Oil Use in the Developing World Is Growing As poor countries develop their economies, more of their people are able to afford luxuries like cars. Oil consumption is rising in many developing countries as a result.

China is a good example. In 1990, there were slightly more than 5 million cars in China; 10 years later, China had more than 16 million cars. By 2015, that number could rise to 50 million. To keep all those cars running, China will need far more oil than it uses today.

At present, there is enough oil to meet world demand. But oil will run out someday. Some experts expect oil production to peak around 2020. Others believe this peak could occur even earlier, after which oil production will begin to decline. If they are right, the world may face an oil shortage in the not-too-distant future.

U.S. Fuel Oil Uses, 2003

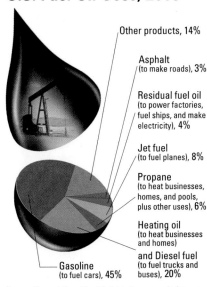

Other products, 14%

Asphalt (to make roads), 3%

Residual fuel oil (to power factories, fuel ships, and make electricity), 4%

Jet fuel (to fuel planes), 8%

Propane (to heat businesses, homes, and pools, plus other uses), 6%

Heating oil (to heat businesses and homes) and Diesel fuel (to fuel trucks and buses), 20%

Gasoline (to fuel cars), 45%

Source: *Energy Information Administration*, www.eia.doe.gov.

How Americans Use Oil

This circle graph shows the major ways oil is consumed in the United States. Notice how much oil is used to fuel motor vehicles and airplanes. A smaller share is used for heating. Think about how we might we might meet these various needs if the world ran out of oil.

Goods Made from Oil

Oil is the main ingredient in most goods made of plastic, nylon, or vinyl. This family in Ohio is shown with everything they own that was made from oil.

Computers Making Cars
Computers control the machines at work in this automobile assembly plant. Only the more developed countries have the technology to make cars this way.

7.5 Computer and Internet Use Patterns

Walk into almost any school in the United States today, and you will see students and teachers using computers. Walk into a school in a poor village in India, and you may not see a single computer. In fact, you may not even see a light bulb; many Indian villages do not yet have electricity.

Developed and developing countries differ in their access to **technology**. Technology is the creation and use of tools to meet practical needs. Most people in poor countries are limited to cheap and simple technologies such as water pumps and irrigation systems. People in wealthy countries have access to advanced technologies such as computers and the Internet.

Computers Are Everywhere in the Developed World It is hard to imagine life in developed countries without computers and the Internet. Governments and businesses use computers to store and manage information. Businesses also use the Internet to reach customers. Families use computer e-mail to stay in touch with relatives, and the Internet to buy goods, share photographs, and read late-breaking news.

Computers and the Internet were invented in the United States. Americans also lead the world in their use of this technology. By 2005, about 75 percent of American adults reported using a computer and the Internet. The majority of U.S. households also owned a computer.

Developing Countries Face a Digital Divide Access to computers is more limited in the developing world. By 2003, only 6 of every 100 people in China used the Internet. In India, the number of Internet users was less than 2 out of 100. This gap between people with access to computers and the Internet and those without is called the **digital divide**. Without computer and Internet access, it is becoming more and more difficult to participate in the modern economy and climb out of poverty.

Many poor countries are working to reduce this divide. India is an example. Today more than 1,150 colleges and universities in India offer computer classes to students. India is also bringing Internet access to thousands of schools across the country.

7.6 The World's Greatest Producers

You have read that the United States consumes more goods and services than many other countries—but it also produces more. The GDP of the United States is greater than that of China and India combined. Several factors contribute to this high GDP. They include abundant natural resources and advanced technologies. However, the greatest source of wealth for any country is its people.

An Educated Workforce The United States has a highly skilled workforce. It was one of the first countries to create a public education system. Today most young people in the United States complete high school. About half of these graduates continue on to some form of higher education after high school. Many adults return to school during their lifetime to learn new skills. All of this schooling helps to make American workers among the most productive in the world. Worker productivity is measured by the value of the work done per hour.

A Strong Work Ethic Education is not the only reason Americans are so productive. Another factor is the American work ethic, which is the belief in the moral value, or goodness, of hard work. Most Americans believe that working is good for people. They believe that work gives purpose to life and that it benefits families and communities.

This strong work ethic is tied to another belief. Most Americans grow up believing that they can be successful in life. Many of them view success as making a lot of money, while others see success as having work they love to do. In either case, Americans believe that hard work produces success.

Both the work ethic and the drive for success encourage Americans to work hard. On average, Americans work longer hours than workers in most developed countries. They also take less time off for vacation. All of this hard work helps Americans to produce more than workers elsewhere. And because Americans produce more, they have the money to consume more.

Average Hours Worked per Person per Year, 2003

Country	Hours Worked
United States	1,792
United Kingdom	1,673
Denmark	1,475
France	1,431
Netherlands	1,354
Norway	1,337

Source: *San Jose Mercury News,* Organization for Economic Co-operation and Development survey, March 22, 2005.

Hardworking Americans

This graph compares hours worked per year in six developed countries. Notice that Americans work the most hours. One reason may be Americans' strong work ethic and drive for success.

Educated Americans

In 1900, only about 1 in 10 Americans completed high school. Today more than four fifths of all students graduate from high school. One in 4 goes on to graduate from college. These students graduated from New York City's Baruch College in 2004. So many students graduated that year that Baruch held its ceremony in New York's famous sports and entertainment stadium, Madison Square Garden.

The Consumer Class, 2003

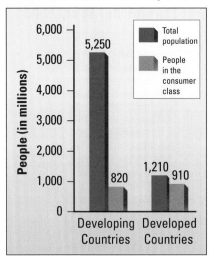

Source: Matthew Bentley, "Sustainable Consumption: Ethics, National Indices and International Relations" (Ph.D. dissertation, American Graduate School of International Relations and Diplomacy, Paris, 2003).

Growing Consumption

This graph compares the number of people in the consumer class in developed and developing countries. This growing class is made up of people who earn $7,000 or more a year. In 2002, the global consumer class was 1.7 billion people strong.

7.7 Beginning to Think Globally

In this chapter, you have read about patterns of consumption. You saw that consumption of food, oil, and computers varies in different parts of the world. Generally, developed countries consume more than developing countries. Developed countries like the United States can afford to consume more goods and services because they are more productive than developing countries.

The Growing Global Consumer Class Consumption, however, is growing worldwide. One reason is population growth in developing countries. More people means more consumers and greater demand for goods and services.

Another reason is the growth of the global consumer class. This class of consumers is made up of people who earn at least $7,000 a year. About 75 percent of people in developed countries belong to this group. Only about 16 percent of people in developing countries are members of the consumer class. Still, nearly half of the global consumer class lives in developing countries.

Income levels in the consumer class vary widely. A few people are very rich, though most people have more modest incomes. But even in developing countries, most members of the consumer class can afford televisions and telephones. Those with more money own cars, have computers, and use the Internet to shop.

Pressure on Resources and the Environment Wherever they live, most members of the consumer class would like to consume the way people in wealthy countries do. This level of consumption might create two kinds of problems. One is pressure on resources, and the other is harm to the environment.

Most resources in the world are limited. There is only so much fertile land, fresh water, and oil available to meet human needs. If current consumption patterns continue, there may not be enough of these resources to go around. The result could be shortages of food, water, or fuel, rising prices as supplies shrink, and greater competition for resources.

Increased consumption may also do great harm to the environment. China, for example, already has dirty air from burning coal in power plants. As China's consumption of gasoline to fuel its growing number of cars increases, air pollution is likely to get worse.

Increased consumption creates another problem for the environment. The more people consume, the more trash they produce. Most of what people buy is eventually thrown away. Surprising as it may sound, this statement is true for everything from milk cartons to cars.

Air pollution from burning fuels may affect people's health as well, especially the young and the elderly. Research groups study links between air pollution and diseases such as childhood asthma and heart disease to help understand the potential effects.

Much of what consumers throw out ends up in landfills or dumps, but many landfills are already overflowing with garbage. Worse yet, some of the trash in them is toxic, or poisonous. Old computers and cell phones, for example, are filled with toxic materials. Over time, these poisons can leak into water supplies. Tainted water can harm fish and contribute to increases in diseases among humans.

Living Well While Protecting the Planet Consumption is a part of life. People need food, clothing, and shelter to survive. Goods like cars and computers improve people's quality of life. Unlimited consumption, however, may be bad for the planet. Fortunately there are ways to live well while consuming less.

One way to promote the health of the planet is to cut back on waste. Most people buy more food than they can eat, leave lights on in unused rooms, and drive cars when they could walk. Buying less, using less electricity, and driving less would reduce such waste. Personal changes such as these would have only a small impact on how well a single individual lives, but multiplied by millions, these changes could have a significant impact on the life of the planet.

A second approach is find ways to do more with less. The first computers, for example, were large machines that filled an entire room. Over time, engineers found ways to make computers smaller. Today a thin laptop can do far more computing than the old giants and can do it much faster, while using far less material and energy to do the job.

A third way is to use cleaner resources. Most of the electricity we use today is generated by the burning of fossil fuels, but this process creates air pollution. However, new technologies are making it possible to use sun and wind power and even the force of ocean tides to generate electricity. None of these alternative energy sources adds air pollution to the environment. And the world is not about to run out of sunshine, wind, or oceans.

Still another way to help the planet is by **recycling**. Recycling turns used goods into materials that can be used to make new ones. Many people already recycle glass, plastic, paper, and metals. Other materials, from lumber scraps to computer parts, can also be recycled. Recycling saves resources and reduces trash. You will learn more about trash and recycling in the next section.

China's New Consumer Class

China has a huge population. And it is quickly becoming a country of consumers. Every year, the Chinese are buying more televisions, computers, and cars. If all Chinese owned cars, however, there wouldn't be enough oil in the world to keep them running.

7.8 Global Connections

The map shows how much municipal waste—garbage and trash collected from homes and businesses—various countries produce. The circle graph shows the makeup of municipal waste in the U.S. The bar graph shows what percentage of various materials was being recycled in 2003 in the U.S.

Which countries appear to produce the most waste? Developed countries appear to produce the most waste per person. People there may throw more things away because they consume more. Comparisons between rich and poor countries are difficult, however. Most developing countries do not have data on their waste production. Their governments may not provide trash-collection services. Or trash may be collected but not measured.

How effective is recycling as a way to reduce trash? Recycling can reduce trash in landfills. Between 1990 and 2000, waste per person in the U.S. dropped by about a third because of recycling. Government recycling programs are less common in poor countries; it costs money to build recycling centers, transport recycled materials, and construct factories to process the recycled products. But that doesn't mean that people in poor countries don't recycle. Poverty forces people to reuse everything they can rather than throw it away.

How can recycling help people and the planet? Recycling creates jobs, which is good for a nation's economy. And recycling saves resources, which reduces pressure on the planet to provide raw materials for industries. By 2005, for example, two thirds of all the steel produced in the U.S. was made from recycled scrap steel, and more than a third of the paper produced in the U.S. came from recycled paper.

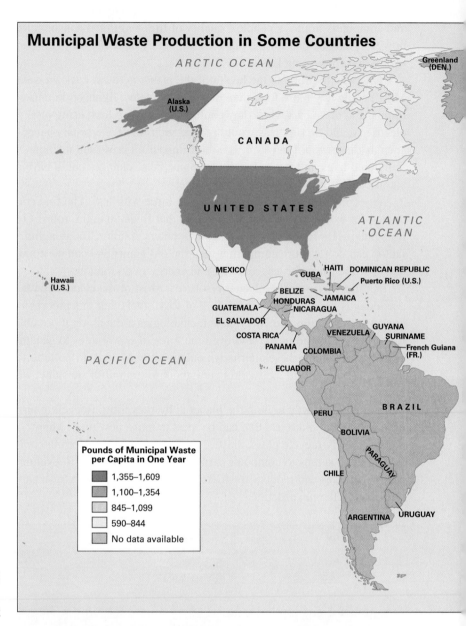

Municipal Waste Production in Some Countries

Pounds of Municipal Waste per Capita in One Year

- 1,355–1,609
- 1,100–1,354
- 845–1,099
- 590–844
- No data available

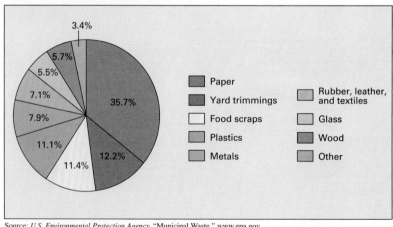

U.S. Municipal Waste, 2003

3.4%
5.7%
5.5%
7.1%
7.9%
11.1%
11.4%
12.2%
35.7%

- Paper
- Yard trimmings
- Food scraps
- Plastics
- Metals
- Rubber, leather, and textiles
- Glass
- Wood
- Other

Source: *U.S. Environmental Protection Agency,* "Municipal Waste," www.epa.gov.

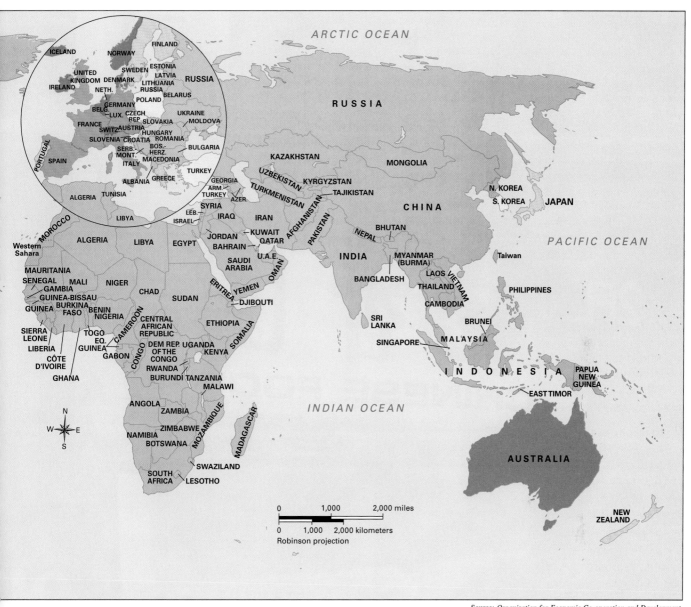

Source: *Organization for Economic Co-operation and Development,* "Environmental Data Compendium 2004," www.oecd.org.

Recycling Rates in the United States, 2003

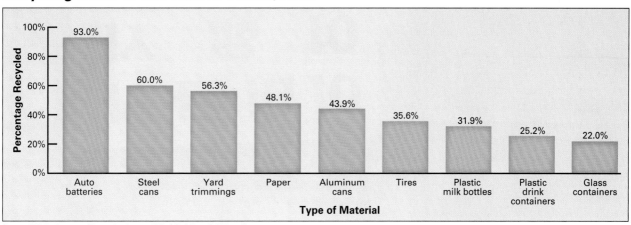

Source: *U.S. Environmental Protection Agency,* "Municipal Recycled Waste," www.epa.gov.

Migration to the United States: The Impact on People and Places

8

8.1 Introduction

Has your family moved recently? If so, was the move a big change or a small change? Many families change their neighborhood when they move to a new place, while others change their city or state. Some families change the country in which they live.

Making the decision to **emigrate,** or move away from one's home country, is never easy. It means leaving behind family and friends, and familiar places and customs. And yet millions of people around the world make this decision every year. Many come to the United States. Since the beginning of the country's history, the U.S. population has been made up of families who have come from other countries.

When people **immigrate,** or move to a new country, they experience many changes. They leave familiar things behind and arrive in a place where most things are new to them. Often they need to learn a new language and how to make a living in a strange place. These changes can be difficult to adjust to at first. People also bring their culture and traditions with them. Their different ways can sometimes be hard for their new neighbors to adjust to.

In this chapter, you will learn why people decide to emigrate from their home countries, and you will find out why people immigrate to the United States. You will also learn about the impact that different **migration streams,** or flows of immigrants, have had on this country. And you will see how migration affects the countries that people leave behind.

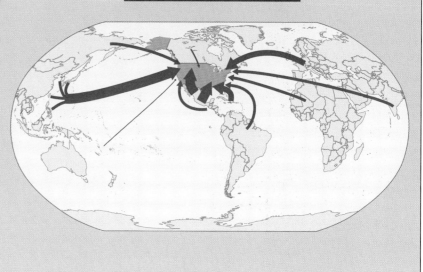

Essential Question

Graphic Organizer

How does migration affect the lives of people and the character of places?

This map shows the migration of people from around the world to the United States in 1998. Each arrow represents a migration stream. Each arrow's thickness reflects the number of people in that migration stream. Keep this map in mind as you try to answer the Essential Question.

◀ Street signs in an immigrant neighborhood in New York City

Top Ten Countries of Origin of U.S. Immigrants, 2002		
Country	Number of Immigrants	Percentage of All U.S. Immigrants
Mexico	115,864	16.4%
India	50,372	7.1%
Philippines	45,397	6.4%
China	40,659	5.8%
El Salvador	28,296	4.0%
Dominican Republic	26,205	3.7%
Vietnam	22,133	3.1%
Colombia	14,777	2.1%
Guatemala	14,415	2.0%
Russia	13,951	2.0%

Source: *2002 Yearbook of Immigration Statistics,* Department of Homeland Security, 2003.

Immigrants to the United States

The table shows where many migrants to the United States came from in 2002. Note that the largest numbers of people came from countries in Latin America and Asia.

A World of Immigrants

The map shows which countries attract the most immigrants. The United States leads the world, with more than 20 million immigrants.

8.2 The Geographic Setting

Both **push factors** and **pull factors** drive people to move to a new country. Push factors give people good reason to leave unpleasant circumstances in their home country. Such factors include war and poverty, **discrimination,** and **famine**. Pull factors attract people to a new place and encourage them to immigrate there. These factors include freedom and opportunities for a better life.

Push and pull factors have helped to drive one of the most dramatic migrations in history. Since 1820, more than 65 million people have come to the United States. This enormous migration came in three great waves.

Three Waves of Immigrants The first great wave of immigration began with the founding of the United States. These early immigrants came mostly from northern and western Europe. Many were escaping from poverty or hunger. Some settled in cities, and others found land to farm as the nation expanded westward.

In the late 1800s, a second wave of immigrants began to arrive from eastern and southern Europe. Many were **refugees** fleeing war or **persecution** because of their religious beliefs. Most found work in the growing cities of the United States and settled in neighborhoods with other immigrants from their home countries.

A third great wave of immigration began in the late 1960s and is still going on today. In 1965, the United States changed its immigration laws, allowing many more newcomers to enter. Between 1970 and 2003, about 24 million people moved to the United States. About 75 percent of them came from Latin America and Asia.

Many Asians found new homes on the West Coast. Most Mexican immigrants settled in the Southwest. Cubans flocked to Florida. New York City attracted people from other Caribbean islands. Over time, these immigrants have moved to communities throughout the country. Like earlier immigrants, they are both adjusting to and changing life in the United States.

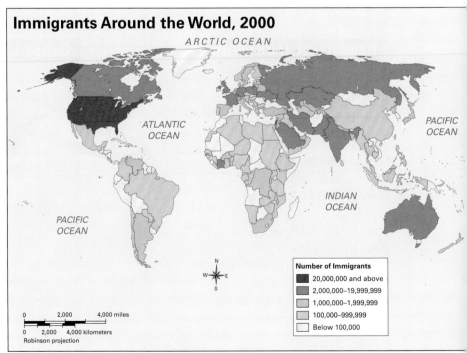

Immigrants Around the World, 2000

Number of Immigrants
- 20,000,000 and above
- 2,000,000–19,999,999
- 1,000,000–1,999,999
- 100,000–999,999
- Below 100,000

Source: United Nations Population Division, *International Migration 2002,* New York: United Nations, 2003.

▶ Geoterms

emigrate to move from a country. People who leave a country are called *emigrants*.

immigrate to move to a country. People who move to another country are called *immigrants*.

migration stream the constant flow of migrants from one country into another country. The largest migration stream into the United States today is from Mexico.

pull factor something that encourages people to move to a new place

push factor something that encourages people to leave a place behind

refugee someone who seeks safety by going to another country. Refugees may be escaping political unrest or war. Or they may fear being attacked because of their beliefs.

Origins of Immigrants

Since 1820, the United States census, or official count of the population, has tracked immigration to this country. The early waves came from Europe. More recently, most immigrants have come from Asia and Latin America. By the early 2000s, the United States was taking in about 1.5 million immigrants each year.

U.S. Immigration, 1820–2000

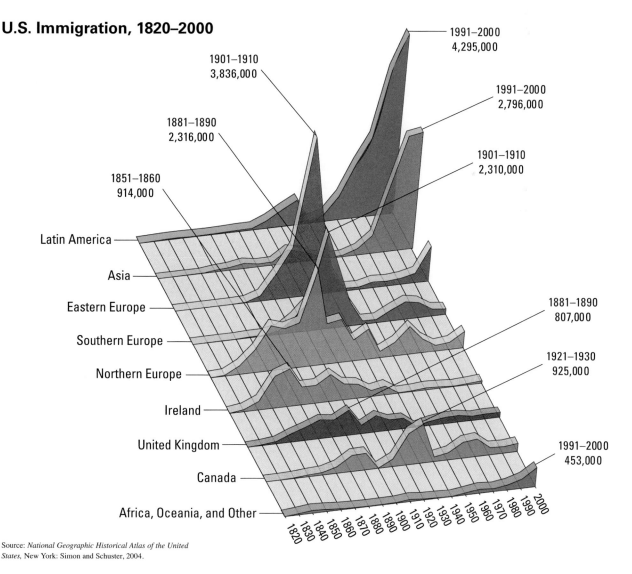

Source: *National Geographic Historical Atlas of the United States*, New York: Simon and Schuster, 2004.

The Push Factor of War

These refugees are fleeing a war in the country of Bosnia in 1996. Recent wars have caused millions of people to leave their homelands. Sometimes the refugees return home when the conflict ends. But often they stay in their new country.

8.3 What Push Factors Drive Emigration?

One night in the late 1980s, John Deng James awoke to the sound of gunfire. The terrified child ran barefoot into the nearby woods. There he found other frightened children. They were too young to know why their homeland, the African country of Sudan, was at war. But they did know that they had to escape the horror, even though they had no means of transportation. And so they began to walk.

John Deng James is part of a group of political refugees known as the "Lost Boys of Sudan." The Lost Boys, and other children who lost their parents in the war, walked for hundreds of miles in search of a safe place. Many died along the way of hunger and thirst. Those who survived finally reached a camp set up for refugees in the neighboring country of Kenya. The survivors were among the countless people around the world who have been pushed to emigrate because of war or violence.

Political Push Factors War is one of many political factors that can create refugees. Political refugees may flee a country because they fear its leaders. Or they may fear persecution. Persecution is unfair treatment of people because of who they are or what they believe.

These political push factors have one thing in common. They involve the way a government treats its people. People are not likely to flee a government that treats its citizens fairly. But a government that rules through fear is likely to create discontent among its people. Many of these people may become political refugees.

Many Cuban immigrants have come to the United States as political refugees. Cuba is an island in the Caribbean Sea, south of Florida. In 1959, a leader named Fidel Castro took over Cuba's government and quickly made himself a dictator. If Cubans spoke out against Castro or the way he ran Cuba, they risked being jailed. Faced with that threat, thousands of Cubans have fled to the United States.

Environmental Push Factors Changes in the environment, such as a long-term **drought,** can push people to emigrate. In the 1840s, a devastating plant disease struck Ireland. A fungus destroyed Ireland's most important crop, the potato. Potatoes had been the main food of the Irish. Without enough potatoes, people faced starvation. In response to this crisis, 1.5 million people left Ireland. A great many of these Irish emigrants came to the United States.

Other changes in the environment are the result of human activity. In 1986, an explosion rocked the Chernobyl nuclear power plant in what is now Ukraine. This accident left a large area of poisoned soil, air, and water around the power plant. Tens of thousands of people were forced to leave their homes and move to safer areas. You will read more about the Chernobyl accident in Chapter 16.

Economic Push Factors The most common push factors are economic. Most of the early immigrants to the United States were poor farmers or working people. They saw no way to improve their lives in Europe, so they chose to try their luck in a new country. In the United States, they found many kinds of economic opportunities.

These same economic push factors are still at work today. Many people around the world want a better future than they can see in their homeland. Some of them will seek that future in another country. Often that country is the United States.

8.4 What Pull Factors Draw Immigration?

In 2001, some of the "Lost Boys of Sudan" began another long journey. This one took them from a refugee camp in Africa to a new life in the United States. They arrived in the city of Boston, Massachusetts, in winter. "I was wearing very light clothes, and we'd never seen snow before," recalled John Deng James. "When we went outside, we couldn't feel our hands and our ears."

Like many refugees, the Sudanese teenagers looked forward to feeling safe, going to school, and getting jobs. These are just some of the "pull factors" that attract immigrants to the United States.

The Pull of Education
Free public schools are a strong pull factor for many immigrant families. This student from Mexico is taking a computer class in her middle school in Texas. Few Mexican schools are well equipped with computers.

Family Pull Factors Another powerful pull factor is the desire to unite divided families. Often young men are the first members of a family to immigrate to another country. Once they find jobs and a place to live, they send for their wives, children, and parents. Between 1965 and 1975, more than 142,000 Greeks came to the United States. Almost all of them were joining relatives who were already living here.

Education Pull Factors Education is a strong pull factor in immigration. Many families migrate so that their children can attend good schools. One of every 15 students in this country's schools was born in another country. Older students come to attend colleges and universities. In the 2003–2004 school year, there were more than 572,000 foreign college students in the United States. Many of these students will later decide to make the United States their permanent home.

A Refugee Finds Work

Peter "Nyarol" Dut, one of the "Lost Boys of Sudan," is seen here working at a new job in the United States. Like other U.S. workers, he pays taxes out of his earnings.

Workers in the U.S., 2003

U.S.-born workers, 86% (124,791,000 people)

Foreign-born workers, 14% (20,826,000 people)

Source: *U.S. Census Bureau, Population Division, Immigrant Statistics*, "Current Population Survey, Annual Social and Economic Supplement," 2003.

Immigrants in the Workforce

Today, about 14 percent of all U.S. workers are immigrants. Some hold low-paying jobs as farmworkers or household help. But others hold well-paid jobs as doctors, nurses, and engineers.

Quality-of-Life Pull Factors Most people, however, move hoping to improve the quality of their lives. In the United States, this hope is called the "American Dream." This is the belief that people here can create better lives for themselves and their children, thanks to the greater economic opportunity and political freedom this nation enjoys.

For many refugees, a better life begins with a sense of safety. For much of their history, Jews have been persecuted for their religious beliefs. In the United States, Jewish immigrants found freedom to worship without fear.

For other immigrants, a better life usually starts with a better job. Even low-wage jobs in the United States usually pay more than most immigrants could earn back home. With more money, immigrant families can afford better food, housing, and health care. They can also save up to bring other relatives to this country.

8.5 How Does Immigration Affect the U.S.?

For John Deng James and other "Lost Boys," adjusting to life in a new land was hard. At first they were terribly homesick. They were also hungry. They did not know how to shop for food in supermarkets. Nor did they know how to cook. They had never seen a stove or a microwave before. They had never even used a telephone.

Like millions of other immigrants, the Sudanese refugees found their way. Within six months, James had two jobs and was studying for college. These changes affected how James thought about life. "In the United States, you determine who you are," he told a reporter. "Now I have a vision of my future. I can go to school, I can work, and I can do what I want." At the same time, he and the other "Lost Boys" were starting to have an impact on their adopted country.

Economic Impacts: Jobs The United States has long depended on immigrants for labor. Early immigrants cleared large tracts of forests for farms. Later immigrants built roads and railroads across the continent. They filled jobs in mines and factories. And they helped fight this country's wars. Immigrants needed no special skills to do theses types of work. They were determined to succeed in their new land and became important builders of the nation.

Some of the immigrants entering the United States today arrive with few skills. As a result, they are often limited to low-paying jobs. Some work as farm laborers, planting and harvesting crops on large farms. Others find jobs as cab drivers, house cleaners, restaurant workers, or nannies. The work that these immigrants do helps to keep the economy of the United States going.

Not all immigrants take low-paying jobs. Some newcomers are highly educated and skilled. They contribute to the economy in many ways. They work as doctors, professors, and computer programmers. Some become famous athletes, musicians, or artists, while still others start new businesses. Those who succeed thus create jobs for immigrants and native-born workers alike.

Some native-born Americans resent having to compete with immigrants for work. They complain that immigrants are "taking our jobs." Often, however, the jobs that immigrants find are ones that native-born workers are not eager to fill.

Economic Impacts: Taxes Like native-born workers, immigrants who work pay taxes. Their taxes help support public schools, libraries, and health clinics. These public services are important to immigrants and native-born Americans alike.

At the same time, many immigrants also need services that are paid for with tax money. For example, immigrants who don't speak English may need language classes. Those who can't work may need public assistance or free health care.

In states with many immigrants, such as California and Texas, the cost of providing such welfare services is high. Some taxpayers resent these costs. Others believe the benefits that immigrants bring to their state outweigh the cost to taxpayers.

Cultural Impacts: Neighborhoods, Foods, and Holidays Immigrants create cultural as well as economic change. They introduce Americans to different ways of life from all over the world. This mixing of cultures sometimes leads to conflict. But it can also make life more varied and interesting.

Newcomers to the United States often live close to other people from their homeland. These immigrant neighborhoods sometimes have names like Chinatown or Little Italy. Here immigrants can speak their native language. They can find familiar foods and eat in restaurants that serve dishes they grew up eating. And they can hear news from their homeland. Such immigrant neighborhoods have made American cities more exciting places as immigrants share languages, foods, and customs with native-born residents.

Chinese New Year Celebration
The dragon dance is a colorful part of Chinese New Year celebrations. Once such events were limited to immigrant communities. Today they are enjoyed by Americans from many backgrounds.

Immigrants bring new foods to the United States. Some of these foods, such as potstickers, sushi, bagels, and tacos, have become very popular. They now seem almost as American as apple pie.

Immigrants have introduced new holidays to American life. Today people from many different backgrounds in cities all over the United States enjoy celebrating St. Patrick's Day, Chinese New Year, and Cinco de Mayo.

Newcomers to the United States bring their music, art forms, and stories with them as well. The result is a rich mixture of ideas, sights, and sounds.

Finally, immigrants help their new neighbors to learn more about the world. Many Americans knew very little about the country of Sudan before seeing news stories about John Deng James and his fellow Sudanese refugees. But once people read about the "Lost Boys," they could no longer ignore Sudan and its problems.

Top Countries with Brain Drain to the U.S., 2002

Country	Number of Immigrants
India	64,980
China	18,841
Canada	11,760
Philippines	9,295
United Kingdom	7,171
Korea	5,941
Japan	4,937
Taiwan	4,025
Pakistan	3,810
Colombia	3,320

Source: *2002 Yearbook of Immigration Statistics,* Department of Homeland Security, 2003.

Skilled Immigrants

A brain drain occurs when a country loses its most talented people to emigration. The table shows the number of highly skilled people coming to the United States from 10 countries in 2002. These people came to work for American companies that wanted their skills.

A Money Office in Mexico

The sign in this money office says "We send and receive money orders to and from the USA." Payments sent home by immigrants help support families left behind. By 2004, one of every 10 people in the world was either sending or receiving such payments.

8.6 How Does Emigration Affect the Homelands People Leave Behind?

When the "Lost Boys of Sudan" left their homeland, Sudan lost their talents and energy. Still, it may not have lost them forever. "I have a vision that I may be going back to Sudan," John Deng James told a reporter. "I want to make the economy stronger."

Economic Impacts: Brain Drain and Gain When people emigrate, they take with them whatever they might have contributed to life in their homeland. The economy of that country loses productive workers and consumers. When doctors or engineers leave, the homeland loses their skills and training as well. Experts call the loss of such well-educated people a **brain drain**. A country suffers from brain drain when its most talented people leave for better jobs in other countries.

As painful as these losses are, they may benefit the home country in some ways. The first is by bringing in needed money. Many immigrants send money back to their families. These payments are called **remittances**. In many countries, money sent by emigrants to their families is a very important source of income. Mexico, for example, receives more money from remittances than from anything else except tourism and the sale of its oil.

Brain drain can also turn into "brain gain." Not all emigrants permanently stay in their new countries. Sometimes people leave to attend school or to work and then return. The result is a gain in skills and experience for the home country.

Social Impacts: Divided Families and Community Improvements Emigration can have mixed social impacts as well. On the minus side, when young people leave to find jobs in another country, families are splintered. Family members may remain separated for years. Emigrants sometimes never return to their homelands.

On the plus side, the money that emigrants send home can have positive effects. Families may use remittances to care for aging parents or to send children to school. Some emigrants have sent enough money to help their home village build a well or a school. These improvements can make life better for the entire community.

Political Impacts: Working for Better Government Emigration can also have political impacts on the home country. Many refugees have come to the United States to flee political unrest. Once here, some refugees work hard to bring democracy to their homeland.

Valdas Adamkus is a good example of the difference that one person can make in society. He was born in Lithuania, a small country in northeastern Europe. He came to the United States after the Soviet Union took over Lithuania in the 1940s. Adamkus went to college in Illinois. Later he led efforts to clean up the Great Lakes. He also led an organization that worked to free Lithuania from Soviet rule.

Adamkus saw his dream of a free Lithuania come true in 1991. He then returned to his homeland to help shape its new government. In 1998, Adamkus was elected president of Lithuania. "Growing up in a western democracy you have a different outlook," he said on taking office. Lithuanians liked that outlook—so much so that they elected Adamkus to a second term in 2004.

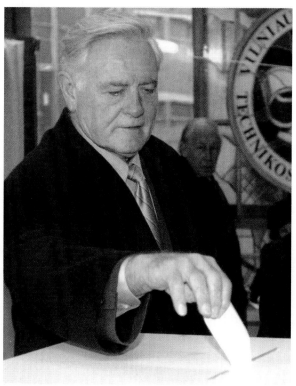

From Refugee to President
Here you see U.S. immigrant Valdas Adamkus voting in Lithuania. Adamkus left this small European country in the 1940s. He came to the United States as a political refugee. Adamkus returned in the 1990s to become president of Lithuania.

8.7 Beginning to Think Globally

In this chapter, you learned about migration. You explored some of the push factors, such as war, famine, and changes in the environment, that drive people to emigrate from their home countries. You also looked at some of the pull factors, such as opportunity, freedom, and the desire to reunite with family members, that lead people to immigrate to the United States. Combinations of these factors help to explain the growth of immigration.

Since its founding, the United States has attracted migration streams from around the world. Some immigrants have come as refugees. Others have come in search of better job and education opportunities. Many have come to join family members who emigrated earlier. Of course, the United States is not the only country with many immigrants. As you read in Chapter 3, Canada has also attracted large numbers of people from other countries.

Today countries in other **regions** are also attracting immigrants. Two examples are Spain in Europe and Australia in Oceania. Think about why people might be moving to these places as you examine migration streams around the world in the next section.

8.8 Global Connections

The map shows migration streams around the world. The color of each country reflects its wealth in terms of income per person. This is an average number. Some people make more than this, and some people make less. The starbursts show areas of armed conflict, or warfare, between 1990 and 2005.

Why might some regions "push" more migrants than they "pull"?
Two big push factors driving migration streams today are poverty and conflict. Both come together in Africa. In most of the world, poverty has decreased since 1990. However, in parts of Africa, it has grown worse. Africa has also experienced many wars in that time. These conditions have forced many Africans to flee their homeland. Some make their way to nearby refugee camps, where they stay until they can return home. Others emigrate to more peaceful countries.

Why might other regions "pull" more migrants than they "push"?
Migrants generally are attracted to developed regions. Here they can hope to find jobs, schools, health care, and safety. Often emigrants move to the developed region nearest their homeland. For North Africans, this is Europe. For Latin Americans, it is the United States or Canada. For Southeast Asians, the journey is to Australia.

How does migration change the places people leave and those they come to? The effects of migration are mixed. If too many people leave a place, its economy may suffer. Its traditional customs may fade away. It may even become abandoned. If too many people come to a place, it can become overcrowded. On the other hand, newcomers may enrich a place's social and cultural life. Either way, places will continue to change as long as people are on the move.

Migration Streams Around the World

Income per Person, 2000
- $10,000 and over
- $5,000–$9,999
- $4,999 and under
- No data

Areas of conflict
- ✳ Armed conflicts, 1990–2005

Annual Net Migration Streams
- 500,000 people
- 10,000 people

Net migration equals the flow of people into a region minus the flow out of the region.

Source: *The State of the World Atlas* by Dan Smith, London: Penguin Group, 1999.

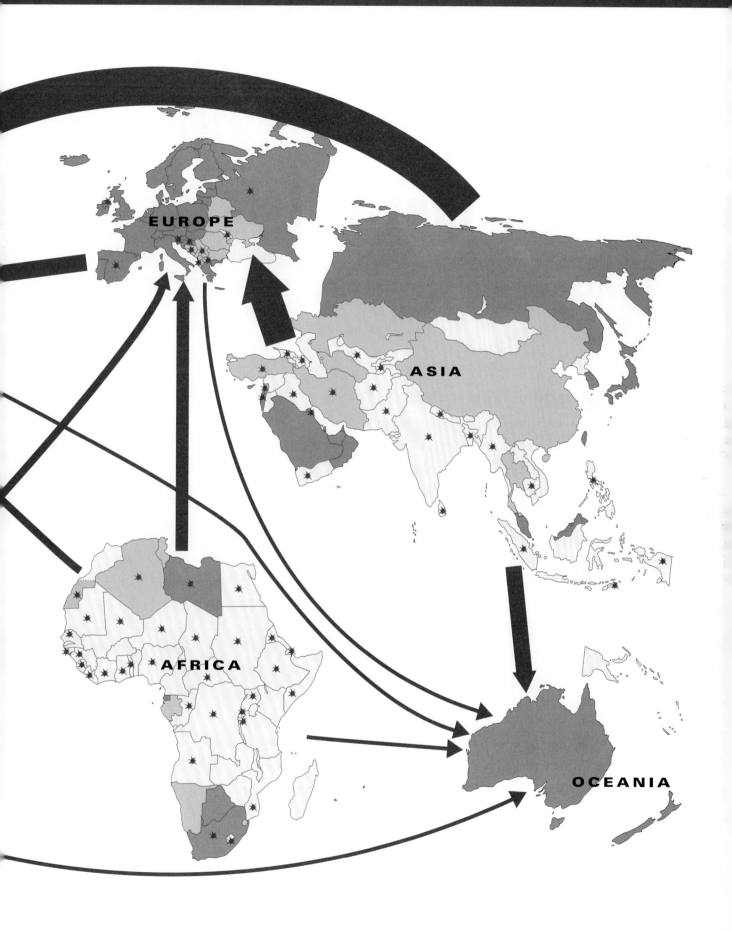

Latin America

Introducing the Region:
Physical and Human Geography

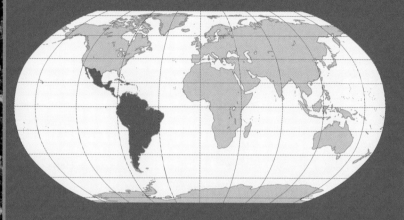

What do you see in this photograph?
See page 514 for details.

▼

Latin America includes all the countries in the Western Hemisphere, except the United States and Canada. It has three sub-regions: Mexico and Central America, the Caribbean islands, and South America.

To the north lies Mexico, which shares a border with the United States. Mexico is connected to South America by a 1,200-mile-long land bridge. This land bridge is known as Central America. East of Central America lie the many islands of the Caribbean Sea. South America is a long continent. Its hot northern lands span the equator. Its cool southern tip reaches toward the Antarctic Circle.

Physical Features of Latin America

Elevation

Feet	Meters
Over 10,000	Over 3,050
5,001–10,000	1,526–3,050
2,001–5,000	611–1,525
1,001–2,000	306–610
0–1,000	0–305
Below sea level	Below sea level

▲ Mountain peak

0   500   1,000 miles
0   500   1,000 kilometers
Lambert Azimuthal Equal-Area projection

Physical Features

Smoking **volcanoes,** dripping **rainforests,** and bone-dry **deserts**—Latin America has them all. Almost every physical feature on Earth is found in this vast **region**. But one feature runs from the north of Mexico to the tip of South America: mountains. For centuries, these mountains have kept the peoples of Latin America isolated from one another.

Mexico and Central America

On a map, Mexico and Central America look like a kite with a long tail. Baja California dangles off the top of the kite. The Yucatán Peninsula juts out from the bottom into the Gulf of Mexico.

Two great mountain ranges run north and south through Mexico. The Sierra Madre Occidental lines the west coast. The Sierra Madre Oriental lines the east coast. A high plain called the Mexican Plateau lies between the two ranges.

Mountains also run through Central America. Many of these mountains are active volcanoes. From Panama's highest peak, you can look down on two different oceans.

The Isthmus of Panama connects Central America to South America. An **isthmus** is a narrow strip of land that links two larger **landmasses**. The Panama Canal was built across this isthmus in the early 1900s. It allows ships to travel between the Atlantic and Pacific oceans without going around all of South America.

The Caribbean Islands

The Caribbean islands curve in an arc from the tip of Florida to the north coast of South America. There are at least 7,000 dots of land in this island group. A few of these islands support large populations. Others are too small to put on most maps.

Many of these islands are the tops of submerged mountains. **Volcanic islands** rise steeply from warm beaches to rugged peaks. Tiny sea creatures known as coral formed other islands. Coral islands are flat and sandy.

South America

South America is shaped like giant triangle. The Andes Mountains line the western side of the triangle. Plains and **plateaus** cover the rest. The vast Amazon **basin** covers much of the center of the continent. Further south lie grassy plains called the *Pampas*.

South America has many amazing physical features. They include these:

- the Amazon River—the world's second longest river. The Amazon carries more water than any other river in the world.
- Lake Titicaca—the highest lake in the world that can be used for boat travel. This large lake has more than 40 islands.
- the Atacama Desert—one of the driest places on Earth. Average rainfall in the Atacama is only half an inch a year.
- Angel Falls—the world's highest waterfall. The water drops down a rocky cliff for nearly two thirds of a mile.

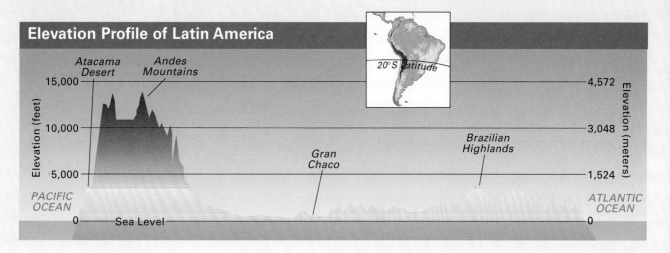

Elevation Profile of Latin America

20° S latitude

Atacama Desert — Andes Mountains

15,000 — 4,572

Elevation (feet) / Elevation (meters)

10,000 — 3,048

Brazilian Highlands

Gran Chaco

5,000 — 1,524

PACIFIC OCEAN

ATLANTIC OCEAN

0 — Sea Level — 0

Climate

Latin America is a region of many **climates**. One reason is that it spans a huge range of latitudes. As you read in Chapter 2, climate generally varies with latitude. Low latitudes, close to the equator, have a tropical year-round climate. High latitudes, near the poles, have short summers and long, cold winters. Between those two extremes lie the middle latitudes, which have more **temperate,** or mild, climates.

Another reason Latin America has such diverse climates is its wide range of altitudes. Altitude has much the same effect on climate as latitude. The higher the altitude, the colder the climate. At lower elevations, mountain climates may be tropical. At higher elevations, the climate can be very cold.

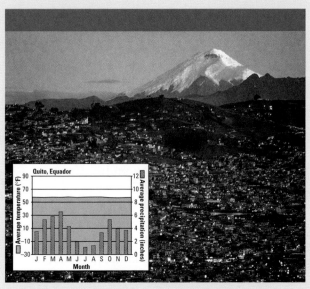

Quito, Ecuador, lies high in the Andes Mountains. Based on the climagraph, what would be the best month for a Quito family to go on a mountain hike?

Mexico and Central America

Mexico's climate ranges from **arid** in the north to tropical in the south. The Mexican Plateau is more temperate, with a **semiarid** climate. Closer to the coast, the climate becomes **tropical wet and dry**. Mexicans call this tropical area the "Tierra Caliente," or hot land.

The climate of Central America is tropical near the coast. The air becomes cooler in the mountains. The mountains of Costa Rica are home to a rare **ecosystem** known as a **cloud forest**. Low clouds hang over this forest all year round. Mist from the clouds collects on leaves and drips off the trees like rain. The result is a high-elevation rainforest.

The Caribbean Islands

Most of the Caribbean islands also have a tropical wet and dry climate. People from North America and Europe enjoy winter vacations on these tropical islands.

Huge storms called **hurricanes** are common during summer months. These huge swirling storms form over warm seas near the equator. Then they move toward the poles in a wide, destructive path. Hurricane winds can reach more than 150 miles per hour. At that speed, they can easily knock over trees and tear the roofs off houses.

South America

In South America, climate varies with both latitude and altitude. The northern half of the continent nearest the equator is mostly **tropical wet**. Further south, the climate becomes subtropical and even arid. The Andes Mountains have a **highlands** climate. This means that the climate varies by elevation, getting colder the higher one goes.

Vegetation

With so many climates, it is no surprise that Latin America is home to an incredible variety of plants. The most widespread type of vegetation is **broadleaf evergreen forest**. It occurs in both tropical wet and tropical wet and dry climate zones.

In a broadleaf evergreen forest, most or all of the trees have leaves rather than needles. But unlike broadleaf trees in cooler climates, these trees do not lose their leaves in winter. Instead they are green all year round. Rainforests and jungles are examples of broadleaf evergreen forests. So are the cloud forests of Central America.

Mexico and Central America

In Mexico, what plants grow where depends mainly on rainfall. **Desert scrub** covers the arid north. Cactus plants survive here with little water. Forest once covered the Mexican Plateau. Over time, most of the trees were cleared to make way for farms.

Southern Mexico and Central America are covered with broadleaf evergreen forest. Pine and oak trees are found in the high cloud forests. Along the coasts, palms, figs, vines, and Spanish moss create a dense rainforest.

Huge cactus plants grow with little rain in the deserts of northern Mexico.

The Caribbean Islands

The Caribbean islands have a mix of **tropical grasslands** and broadleaf evergreen forests. Black and red mangrove trees and coconut palms are typical trees. Underwater coral reefs circle many of the islands. These reefs are home to broad-leafed turtle grass, feathery green algae, and red algae that can make the coral look rusty.

South America

The largest **vegetation zone** in South America is the Amazon rainforest. This broadleaf evergreen forest is home to more kinds of plants than any other place on Earth. There are hardwood trees, such as mahogany and rosewood, which people use to make furniture. There are also Brazil nut and rubber trees. The **forest floor** is a tangle of plants, vines, and colorful orchids.

Tropical grasslands and **temperate grasslands** cover most of the rest of South America. Cacti and flowering plants bloom in desert scrub regions. The Atacama Desert is so dry that almost no plants survive there.

A unique ecosystem known as a cloud forest is found in the mountains of Central America.

Latin America is home to 33 countries and more than 500 million people. Brazil is the largest country in both area and population. About 180 million people lived in Brazil in 2000. This means that one Latin American out of three was a Brazilian. Brazil is the largest country in the world where Portuguese is the first language.

This region is called *Latin* America because most of its people speak Spanish or Portuguese. Both are modern languages based on Latin. This was a language spoken in the Roman Empire about 2,000 years ago. Languages based on Latin are called Romance languages because of their Roman roots.

Political Boundaries of Latin America

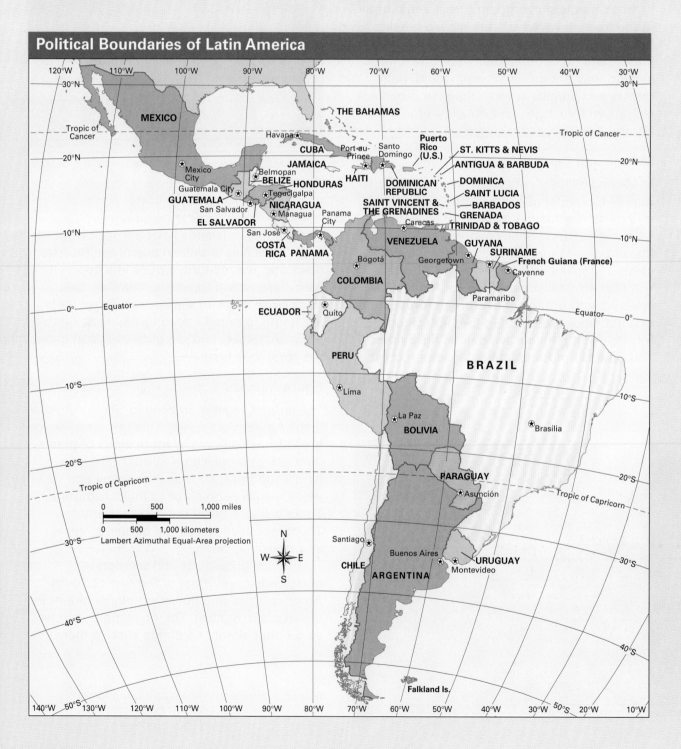

History

Over time, many peoples have come to Latin America. Each group has left its mark on the history of this region.

Early Times

The first Americans were probably hunter-gatherers from Asia. They may have followed animals they hunted across a land bridge that once connected Asia to Alaska. From Alaska, their descendents spread to the tip of South America.

Over time, some native peoples learned how to farm. Their most important crops were maize (corn) and the potato. Farming allowed native peoples to settle down in one place. It also led to the growth of civilizations.

The Maya created civilizations in Mexico and Central America. Four hundred years later, the Aztecs built their **empire** in Mexico. The Incas built a large empire that spread down the western coast of South America.

The Colonial Period

In 1492, a European explorer named Christopher Columbus landed on an island in the Caribbean. As news of his discovery spread, more Europeans came to the Americas. In the early 1500s, Spain conquered the Aztec and Inca empires.

These conquests began a long period of European colonization. Many native peoples died in wars against the colonists. But diseases brought by the Europeans proved even more deadly than war. As the native peoples died out, the Europeans brought Africans over to work as slaves.

Eventually, Spain and Portugal controlled most of Latin America. During the colonial period, Spanish and Portuguese replaced many Native American languages. At the same time, many native peoples became Christians.

In time, Latin Americans began to rebel against their European rulers. The wars for independence began with an uprising of slaves in Haiti in 1791. By 1825, most of Latin America had thrown off colonial rule. One of the first acts of the newly independent countries was to outlaw slavery. The exception was Brazil, which did not free its slaves until 1888.

The Modern Era

Independence did not bring democracy to Latin America as it had to the United States. From Mexico to Argentina, military leaders seized power and ruled as **dictators**. Most dictators were only interested in holding onto power. They cared little about the rights or welfare of their people.

By the 1980s, Latin Americans were weary of dictators. In one country after another, the people demanded the right to choose their leaders. Today, elected governments run most Latin American countries.

Democracy has not solved all of Latin America's problems. Poverty is widespread. Schools are poor. Governments are not stable. Living standards remain low. But for many Latin Americans, the right to vote has brought with it hope for a better future.

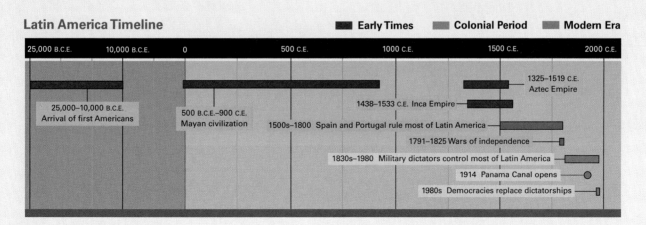

Latin America Timeline

■ **Early Times**   ■ **Colonial Period**   ■ **Modern Era**

25,000 B.C.E.   10,000 B.C.E.   0   500 C.E.   1000 C.E.   1500 C.E.   2000 C.E.

25,000–10,000 B.C.E. Arrival of first Americans

500 B.C.E.–900 C.E. Mayan civilization

1325–1519 C.E. Aztec Empire

1438–1533 C.E. Inca Empire

1500s–1800 Spain and Portugal rule most of Latin America

1791–1825 Wars of independence

1830s–1980 Military dictators control most of Latin America

1914 Panama Canal opens

1980s Democracies replace dictatorships

Population

Latin America includes more than 15 percent of the world's land area. But it is home to less than 9 percent of the world's people. Still, its population is growing fast. From 1950 to 2000, the number of Latin Americans more than tripled. Only Africa has a higher growth rate.

As the population grows, it is becoming more **urban**. In 1950, more than half of Latin Americans lived on farms. Today, three fourths live in urban areas. Most large cities are located on the coasts.

Most Latin Americans are Christian. This region is home to nearly half of the world's one billion Roman Catholics. However, other Christian churches are gaining members.

Some Latin Americans still follow indigenous religions. These are traditional beliefs held by native peoples. The *Other* category in the circle graph below includes several religious traditions. Some of these traditions were brought to the Americas long ago by Africans. Others were brought by more recent immigrants from Asia.

Latin America: Major Religions

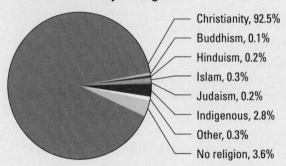

- Christianity, 92.5%
- Buddhism, 0.1%
- Hinduism, 0.2%
- Islam, 0.3%
- Judaism, 0.2%
- Indigenous, 2.8%
- Other, 0.3%
- No religion, 3.6%

Latin America: Urban and Rural Population, 2000

Urban, 75.7%

Rural, 24.3%

= 10% of the total population

Latin America: Population Growth, 1950–2050

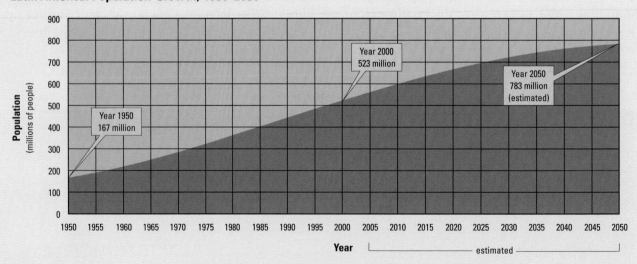

Year 1950 167 million

Year 2000 523 million

Year 2050 783 million (estimated)

Population (millions of people)

Year — estimated

Sources: *Population Division of the Department of Economic and Social Affairs of the United Nations Secretariat*, "World Population Prospects: The 2004 Revision" and "World Urbanization Prospects: The 2003 Revision," esa.un.org/unpp. "Religion," *Encyclopædia Britannica*, 2005, Encyclopædia Britannica Premium Service, www.britannica.com.

Economic Activity

Latin America has a wealth of **natural resources**. Those resources support a broad range of **economic activities**. The most widespread economic activities are **livestock raising** and **subsistence farming**.

Subsistence farmers usually grow only enough food to feed their families. Good weather may sometimes allow them to produce a crop surplus. They can then sell or **barter** their extra food for other things they need. But surpluses are rare. As a result, subsistence farmers are generally poor. The most important crops grown by subsistence farmers are corn, potatoes, and beans.

Resources

The Europeans who first came to Latin America wanted its mineral wealth. They were interested mainly in mining silver and gold. Later, people mined copper, uranium, and other minerals as well. Most of these metals are found in the Andes Mountains.

Today Latin America is better known for its energy resources. This region has about 12 percent of the world's petroleum, or oil supply. Large oil deposits have been found in Mexico and Venezuela.

Latin American rivers are another source of energy. Dams on rivers in Brazil and Paraguay produce large amounts of **hydroelectric power**.

A subsistence farmer in Mexico harvests corn. Subsistence farming is widespread in Latin America.

Land Use

Farming and ranching are important across Latin America. One of the most important **commercial farming** crops is coffee. Coffee beans are grown on large **plantations** in Brazil, Colombia, and Central America. Ranchers raise mostly cattle and sheep. The largest cattle ranches are found on the Pampas of Argentina.

Forestry is another major industry. Many types of trees are harvested from Latin American forests. This wood is used for building materials and fuel. It is also used to make products such as furniture and musical instruments.

Some areas in Latin American specialize in a particular activity. The most important industry in the Caribbean islands, for example, is **tourism**. Mexico, in contrast, is strong in manufacturing. Many of the cars you see on American roads were made in Mexico.

This dam supplies electricity to industries in northern Brazil.

Spatial Inequality in Mexico City: From Cardboard to Castles

9.1 Introduction

Anna Romero lives in a poor part of Mexico City. She and her family of six share a simple two-room house made of concrete blocks and scraps of wood and cardboard taken from the dump. There is no glass in the windows, and there is no running water. The Romeros must walk to a water tap they share with their neighbors.

Six days a week, Anna travels by bus to her job as a maid for the Alba family. The Albas live on the other side of Mexico City in a beautiful 15-room house with a large garden and swimming pool. To Anna, the Alba home seems like a castle. The Albas pay Anna $6 for a 12-hour day of cleaning, cooking, and doing laundry. At 7:00 P.M., as the Albas sit down to a big meal of chicken, meat, or fish, Anna heads home to cook rice and beans for her family.

The Albas and Romeros live just 15 miles apart in the same city, but in some ways they live in different worlds. The contrast between their two ways of life is an example of **spatial inequality**. This is an unequal distribution of wealth or resources over a geographic area. It means that some places within that area are richer or poorer than others. Mexico City offers many examples of spatial inequality.

In this chapter, you will learn about the growth of Mexico City as an **urban** area. You will read about the causes and effects of the city's rapid growth. You will also learn about the spatial inequality that has resulted from the city's expansion.

Essential Question

Why does spatial inequality exist in urban areas?

This map shows the Federal District of Mexico. This district is the capital of Mexico. Most of Mexico City is located here. The district is divided into areas called *delegaciones*. (shown here in different colors). Some neighborhoods are wealthy. Others are very poor. Keep this spatial inequality in mind as you try to answer the Essential Question.

Graphic Organizer

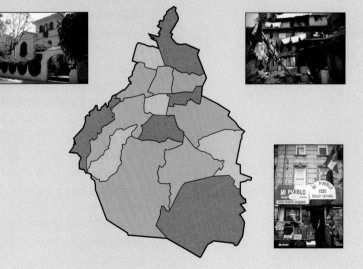

◀ An aerial view of Mexico City, Mexico

A Blend of Old and New
The Plaza of Three Cultures shows the mix of cultures that make up Mexico City today. The stone platforms in this photograph are Aztec ruins. The church was built by the Spanish. The office buildings represent modern Mexico.

9.2 The Geographic Setting

Mexico City is one of the world's largest cities in population. It sits in a highland **basin** called the Valley of Mexico at about 7,000 feet above sea level. The valley is surrounded by mountains and has a mild climate and rich soil. The Valley of Mexico has been an important place of settlement since ancient times.

A City of Wonders: The Aztec Capital of Tenochtitlán The first settlers in the Valley of Mexico arrived thousands of years ago. At the time, several large, shallow lakes covered the valley floor. Small cities later grew up around these lakes.

In 1325, a group known as the Aztecs settled on an island in Lake Texcoco and founded a city called Tenochtitlán. The Aztecs were great warriors, and by conquering other groups they created a mighty empire with Tenochtitlán as its capital. By the time the Spanish arrived in 1519, Tenochtitlán had become one of the greatest cities in the world, with a population of around 250,000 people. Up to a million people lived in the Valley of Mexico.

Tenochtitlán was a city of wonders. One Spaniard said it was like an "enchanted vision" from a fairy tale. Great pyramids and temples towered above the city. Fine palaces and homes lined its streets and **plazas**. Many canals crossed the island, and three causeways, or raised roads, connected the island to the shore. A huge market sold exotic goods from around the Aztec Empire.

The people of Tenochtitlán enjoyed a high **standard of living,** a term that refers to people's overall level of comfort and well-being. City residents had plenty of food from farming, fishing, and trade, and an **aqueduct** brought fresh water into the city from the surrounding hills. The houses in Tenochtitlán were well built, and people lived in clean, orderly neighborhoods.

A Bustling National Capital: Mexico City In 1521, Spain conquered the Aztec Empire, destroying Tenochtitlán and building a new city called Mexico City in its place. Over time, Mexico City became one of the most beautiful cities in the Americas.

Some 300 years later, in 1821, Mexico won its independence from Spain. Mexico City became the capital of the new country and continued to grow slowly. By the 1950s, the city was a blend of modern and historic buildings. Broad avenues and tree-filled parks made it a pleasant place to live.

Today Mexico City remains the center of Mexican life, but it is no longer the graceful city of old. In the past 50 years, **urbanization,** or city growth, has increased at a rapid rate. In 1970, the city had more than 8 million people. Ten years later, it had almost doubled in population. There are now at least 18 million people in Mexico City's **metropolitan area,** which includes the city and its **suburbs**.

A key factor in Mexico City's growth is migration from **rural** parts of the country to the city. Many people have relocated to the capital because of **rural decline,** or increasing poverty in the countryside. Life in rural areas is hard, but for many people, the city has become a difficult place to live too, as you will see.

▶ Geoterms

rural decline worsening economic conditions in the country-side, including rising unemployment and growing poverty. Rural decline drives migration to cities.

spatial inequality the unequal distribution of wealth or resources in a geographic area, so that some places are richer than others

standard of living the overall level of comfort and well-being of a group or a country. People in developed countries generally have a higher standard of living than people in developing countries.

urbanization the movement of people from rural to urban areas, resulting in the growth of urban areas

District, City, State
The Federal District is the capital of Mexico. Like the District of Columbia, where the U.S. national capital is located, it is not part of any state. You can see below how the urban area has spread from the Federal District into the state of Mexico.

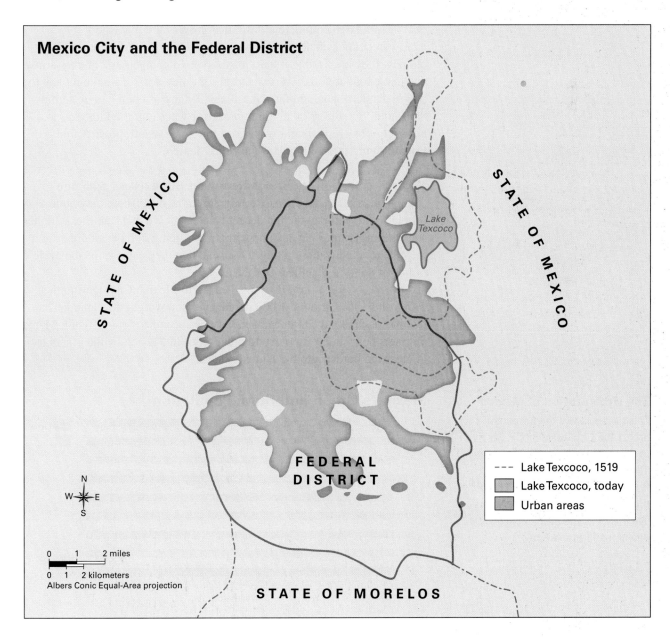

Mexico City and the Federal District

Lake Texcoco

STATE OF MEXICO

STATE OF MEXICO

FEDERAL DISTRICT

- - - Lake Texcoco, 1519
Lake Texcoco, today
Urban areas

N
W E
S

0   1   2 miles
0   1   2 kilometers
Albers Conic Equal-Area projection

STATE OF MORELOS

9.3 Rural Decline Causes Urban Migration

Juan Ortiz and his family live in a small village in central Mexico. Like his father and grandfather before him, Juan is a farmer. He grows corn, beans, and other vegetables on a few acres of land that his family owns. But conditions have declined in the countryside. Juan can no longer support his family by farming, and now he is forced to seek other work. Like many farmers, Juan plans to leave his village and move to the city, making him a part of the large urban migration caused by rural decline in Mexico.

Farmers Struggle in the Countryside Life for most Mexican farmers is tough. Only about 15 percent of the land in Mexico is suitable for farming, while the rest is too dry, rocky, or mountainous to grow crops. In addition, a small number of wealthy landowners own most of the best farmland in Mexico.

There are several types of farms in Mexico. One type is the small, privately owned farm. Another type is the larger farm held in common by groups of farmers. These **communal lands** are called *ejidos*. A third type of farm is a large commercial farm that grows food for export.

At one time, small farmers were the backbone of Mexican society, but now they are finding it hard to survive. To compete with large farms, they have to increase their production. But they don't have the money to buy seeds, fertilizer, and farm machinery. Many of them end up selling their land. Sometimes they go to work for wages on the large farms, but such jobs are few, and wages are low. As a result, poverty and **unemployment** have increased in rural Mexico.

Migration to the City Brings Renewed Hope Faced with rural decline, many farmers choose to migrate to the city. There they hope to find jobs that will pay them a decent wage and give their families a higher standard of living. They also hope their children will have an opportunity to get a good education in city schools so that they can escape the cycle of poverty and find skilled jobs later.

For years, most rural migrants headed to Mexico City. During the 1970s and 1980s, around 1,000 people a day moved to the capital. That rate has declined as life in Mexico City has become more difficult. Many migrants now choose to move to other cities in Mexico, while others try to cross the border into the United States.

The Urbanization of Mexico
This graph shows the percentage of urban and rural residents in Mexico over time. In 1950, more Mexicans lived in rural areas than in cities. But that had changed by 1960. Today, around 75 percent of all Mexicans live in cities. The graph also shows estimates for the future.

Mexico's Urban and Rural Population

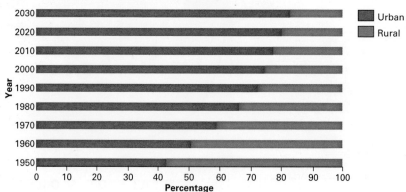

Source: "World Population Prospects: The 2002 Revision Population Database," *United Nations Population Division*, esa.un.org/unpp/.

Polluted City Air

Mexico City has some of the worst air pollution in the world. About 70 percent of this pollution comes from vehicles. The government tries to limit the number of vehicles on city streets. But there are still about 4 million cars in the city.

9.4 Urbanization Creates New Problems

Julio Cu is a professional diver. But he doesn't go diving in the ocean. Instead, he dives under the streets of Mexico City. On workdays, Julio puts on a special diving suit and swims into the city's giant sewer system. He clears trash and other objects from sewer pipes. Once he even found half a car. It's a nasty job, but someone has to do it. Mexico City's sewers are overloaded. This is just one of the problems caused by rapid urbanization.

Too Many People, Too Little Land You have read that rural migration is a key factor in Mexico City's growth. Large families have also played a part. In recent years, however, both migration from rural areas and the number of children in the average family have gone down. As a result, the city is not growing as fast as it once did.

In spite of this decreased growth rate, Mexico City is continuing to expand. Its suburbs are spreading up the sides of the mountains that surround the Valley of Mexico. Newcomers are also filling in areas that were once covered by the valley's lakes, which were drained long ago to allow for expansion. But there is still not enough land or housing for the city's growing population.

Urbanization and overcrowding have caused problems in Mexico City. Clean water is in short supply, making sanitation difficult and aiding the spread of disease. Roads are clogged with traffic, polluting the air and making it difficult for people to get from one place to another. Buses and subways are also packed. Mexico City is bursting at the seams.

Pollution, Poverty, and Crime Rapid growth has had a negative impact on Mexico City's environment. One of the city's worst problems is air **pollution**. Years ago, residents had a clear view of two great, snow-capped **volcanoes** that lie just east of the city, but now the mountains are rarely visible. A thick blanket of **smog** often hangs over the city, sometimes making it hard just to see across the street.

Because of poor **air quality,** many city residents suffer from asthma and other illnesses. On some days the air is so bad that schools are closed and people are warned to stay inside. Recent laws to limit pollution have helped, but the problem persists.

Social problems have also grown with urbanization. There are not enough jobs in the city to keep everyone employed, so poverty has increased. When poverty rises, so, too, does crime. Mexico City was once a relatively safe place to live, but now many residents fear for their safety.

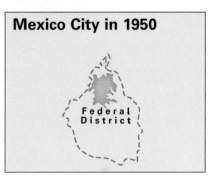
Mexico City in 1950

Federal District

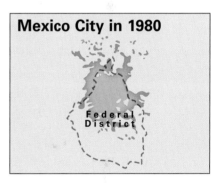
Mexico City in 1980

Federal District

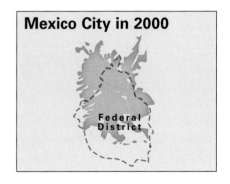
Mexico City in 2000

Federal District

The Growing City

These maps show the growth of Mexico City from 1950 to 2000. About one out of every five Mexicans lives in Mexico City. The urban area once lay entirely within the Federal District. It has since spread well beyond those boundaries. Much of this growth consists of poor neighborhoods.

9.5 A City of "Haves" and "Have Nots"

Sylvia Martinez lives in one of Mexico City's huge garbage dumps. She sorts through piles of trash to find bits of glass, metal, and other materials that she can recycle for cash. She is one of the millions of "have nots" in Mexico City.

The "have nots" are poor people who have little money and few possessions. They make up the majority of the city's population. In contrast, the "haves" are people with money and comfortable lives. The differences between these two groups reflect the spatial inequalities of Mexico City.

The "Have Nots" Struggle to Survive The poorest of the "have nots" are typically recent migrants to the city who often live in **slums** on the edge of town. Most houses in these slums are one-room shacks made of cardboard and other junk. Many of these houses lack electricity and running water. The streets of the slums are seldom paved and are often littered with trash. Many of the people who live in these slum areas have little or no work.

Migrants who have been in the city for a while may live in somewhat better conditions. Most have some kind of work. Many hold more than one job, often working as maids, dishwashers, cooks, construction workers, street vendors, or bus drivers. Still, even migrants who have found a job end up working long hours for little pay. To make things worse, they may have to travel for hours by public transportation to get to their jobs.

Recent arrivals are not the only people in Mexico City who are poor. Many city residents are "working poor," which means that they have jobs that are too low-paying to lift them out of poverty. Most working poor live in working-class neighborhoods that are usually closer to the center of the city than the slums. Some live in cinder-block homes with metal or tar-covered roofs, while others live in large **tenements,** or run-down apartment buildings.

Houses in working-class neighborhoods generally have electricity, but some lack running water. The streets are usually paved, though often in poor repair. While their lives are better than those of recent migrants, the working poor of Mexico City still face many struggles and uncertainties as they try to stay employed and provide for their families.

Cardboard Housing for "Have Nots"

Shacks like this one are located in slums on the outskirts of Mexico City. Houses are made of scrap materials like cardboard boxes and bits of wood and metal. The people who live in these slums are often recent migrants to the city. Many end up selling cheap goods on the street or begging for a living.

The "Haves" Live Well The "haves" are members of Mexico City's middle and upper classes. They make up approximately one fourth of the city's residents.

A very small percentage of the "haves" belong to the upper class. These extremely wealthy people are large landowners or leaders in business or government. They enjoy a luxurious standard of living, many living on large castle-like **estates** with high walls and security systems. They often hire the working poor to serve as their maids, gardeners, and drivers.

Members of the middle class live in houses or apartment buildings near the center of the city, or in modern suburbs farther away. Many work in business, education, or government. They can usually afford some luxuries, such as a telephone at home.

Life has become harder in recent years for many middle-class Mexicans because the Mexican economy has suffered hard times. Some middle-class families can no longer save money for the future or send their children to good private schools. They are struggling just to maintain their middle-class standard of living.

9.6 Beginning to Think Globally

In this chapter, you learned about spatial inequality in Mexico City. You read how rural decline has increased migration to the city and learned about problems that have come with rapid urbanization. You have also seen how rich and poor have very different standards of living. These differences are clear in housing, transportation, and many other aspects of city life.

Spatial inequality does not exist only in large cities, but also in any area where differences in wealth affect how people live. You can observe such differences in standard of living in small towns as well as in suburbs and cities.

Spatial inequality also exists on a global scale. Think about global spatial inequality as you examine the map on the following two pages. The map compares the standard of living—measured by **life expectancy,** level of education, and **per capita** GDP—of people in countries around the world.

The Good Life

This home is located in a wealthy area of Mexico City. Homes like this often have large gardens and many rooms. They may also have security systems to guard against crime. Only a tiny portion of the city's population can afford to live like this.

9.7 Global Connections

This map compares standards of living around the world. The rankings are based on a measure of living standards known as the Human Development Index. The HDI looks at how well countries are doing in three areas— life expectancy, education, and per capita GDP. You may recall that GDP is a measure of a country's economic production.

Why do some countries have a higher HDI rank than might be expected? The blue circles on the map indicate countries that rank higher in the HDI than their GDP alone might lead you to think. In these cases, other factors reflected in the HDI—life expectancy and education—might push their HDI rank higher. Often in these countries, the differences between rich and poor are not great. Also, many of these countries provide education and health care to all of their citizens.

Why do some countries have a lower HDI rank than might be expected? The countries marked by a red square rank lower in the HDI than you might expect from their GDP. In such countries, there is likely to be a large gap between rich and poor. While the rich live well, the poor have limited access to schools and health care.

How do patterns of spatial inequality change over time? Each year, the HDI ranks of some countries rise as living standards in these countries improve. At the same time, other nations drop in rank. Often such changes reflect government policies. In Zimbabwe, for example, decisions by the government have hurt the economy, and as a result living standards have declined. In Malaysia, government policies have helped raise living standards.

Standard of Living Around the World

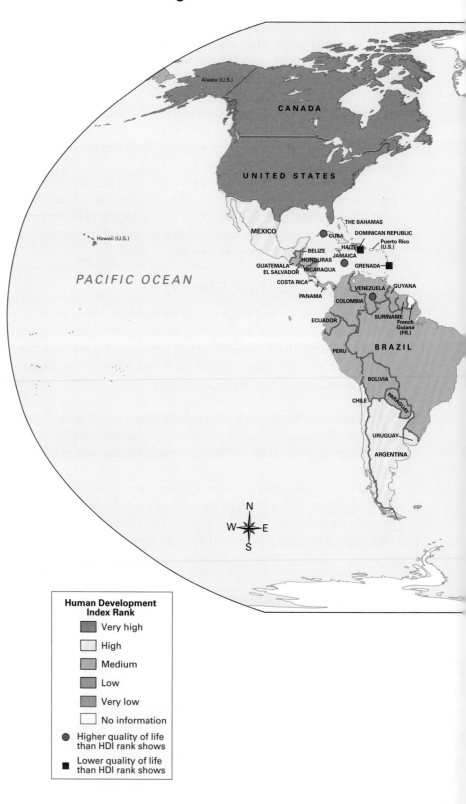

Human Development Index Rank

- Very high
- High
- Medium
- Low
- Very low
- No information
- ● Higher quality of life than HDI rank shows
- ■ Lower quality of life than HDI rank shows

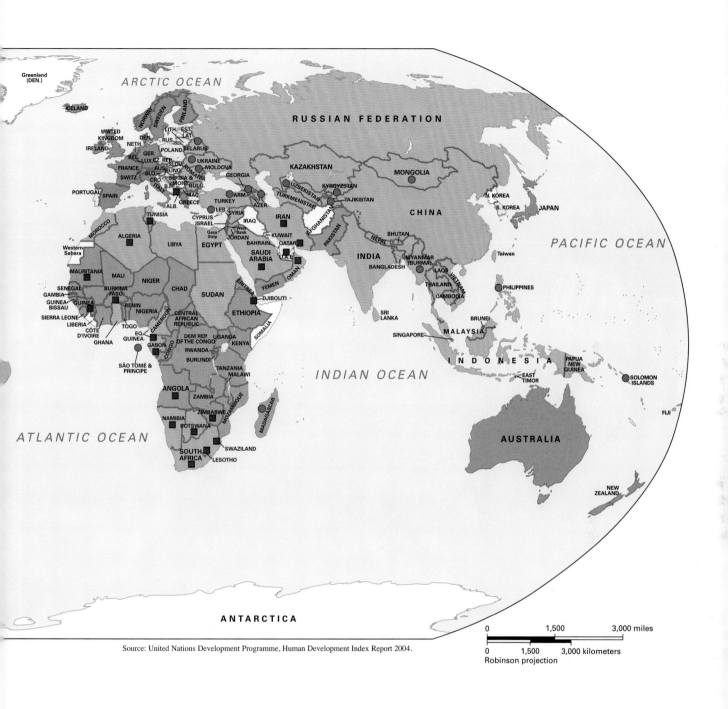

Greenland (DEN.)

ARCTIC OCEAN

ICELAND

RUSSIAN FEDERATION

NORWAY
SWEDEN
FINLAND

UNITED KINGDOM
IRELAND
NETH.
DEN.
RUS.
EST.
LITH.
LAT.
GER.
POLAND
BELARUS
BEL.
LUX.
CZ. REP.
FRANCE
AUS.
SLOV.
UKRAINE
MOLDOVA
SWITZ.
SLO.
HUNG.
ROMANIA
CRO.
B.H.
SERBIA & MONT.
GEORGIA
PORTUGAL
SPAIN
ALB.
MAC.
GREECE
BULG.
ARM.
AZER.
ITALY
TURKEY
LEB.
SYRIA
CYPRUS
ISRAEL
IRAQ
West Bank
JORDAN
Gaza Strip

KAZAKHSTAN

MONGOLIA

UZBEKISTAN
KYRGYZSTAN
TURKMENISTAN
TAJIKISTAN

CHINA

N. KOREA
S. KOREA
JAPAN

PACIFIC OCEAN

TUNISIA

MOROCCO

Western Sahara

ALGERIA

LIBYA

EGYPT

IRAN

AFGHANISTAN

PAKISTAN

NEPAL

BHUTAN

KUWAIT
BAHRAIN
QATAR
U.A.E.
SAUDI ARABIA

OMAN

INDIA

BANGLADESH

MYANMAR (BURMA)

Taiwan

MAURITANIA

MALI

NIGER

CHAD

SUDAN

ERITREA

YEMEN

DJIBOUTI

ETHIOPIA

SOMALIA

LAOS
THAILAND
VIETNAM
CAMBODIA

PHILIPPINES

SENEGAL
GAMBIA
GUINEA BISSAU
GUINEA
SIERRA LEONE
LIBERIA
CÔTE D'IVOIRE
GHANA
BURKINA FASO
BENIN
NIGERIA
TOGO
CAMEROON
CENTRAL AFRICAN REPUBLIC
EQ. GUINEA
GABON
CONGO
DEM. REP. OF THE CONGO
UGANDA
RWANDA
BURUNDI
KENYA

SRI LANKA

SINGAPORE

BRUNEI

MALAYSIA

SÃO TOMÉ & PRINCIPE

TANZANIA
MALAWI

INDONESIA

PAPUA NEW GUINEA

EAST TIMOR

SOLOMON ISLANDS

ANGOLA

ZAMBIA

ZIMBABWE

MOZAMBIQUE

MADAGASCAR

INDIAN OCEAN

FIJI

NAMIBIA
BOTSWANA

ATLANTIC OCEAN

SOUTH AFRICA

SWAZILAND

LESOTHO

AUSTRALIA

NEW ZEALAND

ANTARCTICA

Source: United Nations Development Programme, Human Development Index Report 2004.

0   1,500   3,000 miles

0   1,500   3,000 kilometers
Robinson projection

Indigenous Cultures: The Survival of the Maya of Mesoamerica

10.1 Introduction

You are traveling by bus through the **highlands** of Guatemala. The road winds through steep, misty mountains. It passes small mud-brick houses set in fields of corn. The bus is piled high with bags, bundles, and even a crate of live chickens.

Most of the passengers on your bus are Mayan Indians. The woman next to you is wearing a colorful headdress and a beautiful woven blouse called a *huipil*. As she gives her children a snack of corn tortillas, she talks to them in a language you don't recognize. You feel like you are a world away from everything familiar. Suddenly, you hear a ringing sound. The woman reaches into her bag, pulls out a cell phone, and begins speaking in Spanish.

You have just witnessed an example of how old and new cultures are blending together in the Mayan world. Mayan Indians are one of the largest groups of **indigenous peoples** in the Americas. Indigenous peoples are natives of an area who have been conquered or dominated by other people who came to the area later. Indigenous peoples often try to preserve their **traditional culture,** or the customs and ways of life handed down from their ancestors.

Mayan Indians still maintain much of their traditional culture, but they have also changed along with the world around them. In this chapter, you will learn how the Maya have both preserved their traditions and adapted to, or changed with, modern life.

Essential Question

How do indigenous peoples preserve their traditional culture while adapting to modern life?

This illustration shows where the highland Maya live. The Mayan highlands stretch from southern Mexico through Guatemala. Notice the photograph of a highland village. You will learn about key features of Mayan life in a village like this one. Keep this illustration in mind as you try to answer the Essential Question.

Graphic Organizer

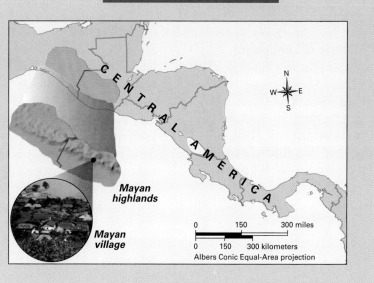

Mayan highlands

Mayan village

0   150   300 miles
0   150   300 kilometers
Albers Conic Equal-Area projection

◄ A Mayan family at home

10.2 The Geographic Setting

The Maya live in an ancient cultural region known as Mesoamerica. A cultural region is an area with a distinct culture or set of similar cultures. Mesoamerica stretches from central Mexico to the Isthmus of Panama, a **region** that includes hot jungle **lowlands,** dry **plateaus,** and cool mountain highlands.

The Maya Created an Advanced Civilization About 2,000 years ago, the Maya created a remarkable civilization in Mesoamerica. They built great stone cities with towering pyramids, some of which stand today. They developed a writing system and created the first books ever made in the Western Hemisphere. They also developed an advanced system of mathematics and combined their knowledge of math and astronomy to create one of the world's most accurate calendars.

Around 900 C.E., Mayan civilization collapsed. Scholars believe that **drought,** warfare, and other problems led to a sharp decline in population, and the Maya abandoned their cities. Then, in the 1500s, Spanish soldiers arrived and took over the region, which was later divided among several countries.

Geography Isolates the Maya from Modern Life Today there are around 6 million Maya. Some still live in the lowlands, especially Mexico's Yucatan Peninsula, but most live in the highlands of Guatemala and the Mexican state of Chiapas.

The Mayan highlands are a rugged **landscape** of steep mountains and deep valleys. Heavy clouds often hang over the mountains, and moisture from the clouds helps produce dense **cloud forests.** A line of great **volcanoes** rises up along the southern edge of the highlands. These volcanoes have erupted many times in the past, covering the land with **lava** and ash. Several of these volcanoes are still active.

Volcanic ash has enriched the soil in much of the highland region. As a result, the land is generally fertile and good for farming. Most Maya practice **subsistence farming,** which means they farm mainly to provide food for themselves and their families. In general, they sell very little of the food they grow.

The mountain geography of the highlands has helped isolate the Maya from the rest of the world. Few roads cross the highlands, and many Maya live in remote areas miles from the nearest town. This isolation has limited contact between the Maya and others, but it has also helped the Maya survive as a people and preserve their culture.

One People Speaking Many Languages Not only has the mountain geography separated the Maya from the outside world. It has also separated different Mayan groups from one another. Over time, the Maya in different areas have developed their own customs and languages. More than two dozen distinct Mayan groups now live scattered across Mesoamerica. Each speaks its own language and has its own special form of dress.

Despite these differences, the Maya are still a single **ethnic group,** meaning they share common physical features and a cultural identity. They also share the challenge of making **adaptations** to modern life. An adaptation is a change in a way of life to suit new conditions. As the story in the introduction shows, old and new are blending in the Mayan world.

Mayan Languages

A Mixture of Languages

There are as many as 31 Mayan languages. Each is spoken in a particular part of the Mayan region. Among the most widely spoken highland languages are Quiché, Cakchiquel, Tzotzil, and Tzeltal. Many Maya also speak Spanish.

▶ Geoterms

adaptation a change in a way of life to suit new conditions

indigenous peoples natives of an area who have been conquered or dominated by others who came later. Native American tribes, such as the Cherokee and Navajo, are indigenous peoples.

subsistence farming farming carried out mainly to provide food for farm families, with little surplus for sale to others

traditional culture customs and ways of life handed down from ancestors

The Highlands of Guatemala and Southern Mexico
The Mayan highlands isolate groups of Maya from one another and from the outside world. High peaks and deep valleys separate one mountain range from another. Some Mayan villages are perched on high mountain ridges. Many can be reached only on narrow paths.

10.3 A Strong Sense of Community

Several Mayan judges are seated at a table. Two men are standing before them. One man claims that the other killed and ate one of his chickens. The accused says the chicken entered his yard and ate his chicken feed. Finally, one of the judges speaks up. In the Quiché language, he says, "You will pay the man for his chicken by working for three days in his fields."

This story is an example of Mayan community justice. As you will see, this justice system is one part of the Maya's deep attachment to their local villages and their strong traditions of self-rule. These traditions are part of what enables the Maya to preserve their way of life while adapting to the influences of the modern world.

Local Government The highland Maya are citizens of either Mexico or Guatemala. Over time, their local communities have adapted to the demands of national life. For example, most highland towns have a mayor who governs the community according to national laws.

The Maya also have their own traditional forms of government. Many towns have a municipal council that follows Mayan customs. The council members are respected members of the community and make decisions based on traditional values.

Mayan towns also have religious brotherhoods. In Guatemala, the brotherhoods are called *cofradias*. In Chiapas, they are called *cargos*. These brotherhoods are responsible for guarding the images of Catholic saints and for organizing ceremonies and festivals. The heads of these brotherhoods are also important community leaders.

A Mayan Community

Mayan villages are a mix of old and new. The ancestral shrine (on the left) and sacred tree in this illustration are traditional. The tree connects heaven and earth in the ancient Mayan religion. The plaza, with its Spanish colonial buildings, is an adaptation to the outside world.

Meeting Community Challenges The Maya work hard to keep their communities together. One way they do this is through their justice system. Mayan judges rarely send offenders to jail, which would take those offenders away from their families and hurt the community. Instead, offenders usually pay for crimes through labor or community service, a traditional form of punishment known as *restitution*. At the same time, the Maya have adapted to national laws. For serious crimes such as murder, Mayan judges turn offenders over to the national courts.

In spite of their strong tradition of community problem solving, some Maya face challenges that prompt them to leave the community. Poverty and lack of jobs, schools, and good health care have caused some Maya to move to cities to find work or to get an education.

10.4 The Traditional Home and Family

Home and family are the foundation of Mayan life. Most Mayan families live in simple one-room dwellings constructed of wood or mud brick called **adobe**. But the Maya don't see a house as just an arrangement of building materials. Rather, they envision their dwelling as a living thing, with a soul like a person. In fact, the Maya believe that everything on Earth is alive. Before they build a house, they hold a ceremony to ask Earth's permission.

Weaving on a Belt Loom
This woman is weaving on a traditional belt loom. The loom is made of two wooden rods linked together with threads. One end is attached to a post or a tree. The other is attached to the weaver's belt. In the past, each village had its own designs. Today villages borrow designs from each other.

The Old and New at Home A traditional Mayan house is simple on the inside. The floors are made of packed earth, and there is little furniture. A family might own only hammocks for sleeping and a small wooden table and chairs. A cook fire typically sits in the middle of the floor, with a few clay pots by the side. Or there might be a small cookhouse next door to the main house. There is also a family altar for religious worship.

Like other aspects of Mayan life, the traditional Mayan home is changing. Some houses in larger towns now have electricity and running water, and some have a radio or a television. Metal and plastic cooking utensils are now common, and some homes even have gas stoves, blenders, and other appliances.

Men's and Women's Roles There is still a very clear division of labor between men and women in most Mayan communities. The men work in the fields, planting, weeding, and harvesting the crops, as well as doing occasional hunting. The women work mostly at home, caring for the children and weaving clothes for the family.

Women also cook the meals, consisting mainly of beans and tortillas, which most women make the traditional way. They pat the corn dough out by hand and fry it on a griddle. Some women, however, use a tortilla press made of metal.

Most children go to school, though many quit at an early age to help out at home. Parents teach their children traditional skills such as farming and weaving, as well as the old customs that children are expected to pass on to their own children. Still, many young Maya also adopt new ways. They may listen to popular music and wear jeans, T-shirts, and sneakers instead of traditional Mayan clothing.

10.5 Changing Ways of Work

Two farmers are heading to work in a highland Maya village, but they are heading in different directions. One is walking to his field on the slopes above town, where he will work to provide food for his family as his ancestors have done for hundreds of years. The other is catching a bus for the lowlands. This farmer works for cash on a modern **plantation**. While farming has always been central to the Mayan way of life, changing circumstances and new agricultural methods have altered the way farmers work.

Traditional Farming Most Maya are subsistence farmers, growing corn, beans, squash, and other vegetables on small plots called *milpas*. Each year these farmers hope to gather enough food at harvesttime to feed their families for the next year. The majority of what they harvest will be corn, the Maya's most important crop. In fact, corn is considered sacred to the Maya, who call it the "giver of life."

Traditionally, Mayan farmers cleared their land using the **slash-and-burn method**. They cut down the forest and burned the cut trees and shrubs after they dried out. Then, using simple wooden tools, the farmers dug the ash into the ground to fertilize the soil. Some also mixed in manure and other natural fertilizers to help their crops grow.

Some Maya still follow traditional farming methods, but in many parts of the highlands, much of the land has already been cleared. As a result, slash-and-burn agriculture is no longer as common as it once was among Mayan farmers. Many farmers have adapted by using chemical fertilizers to enrich the soil. Some Mayan farmers have developed new methods for growing crops in the shade of their own orchards.

Working for Wages Mayan farmers have adapted in other ways. Many spend part of the year working for wages on commercial farms, which now account for most of the land in Guatemala. This concentration of land on large farms dates back to when the Spanish colonized and took over the best land. Today about 2 percent of the population still owns 70 percent of the land. Most large landowners raise sugarcane, coffee, cotton, and other crops for export.

Large plantations depend on Mayan farmers who travel to the lowlands to work. These **migrant workers** spend weeks or even months away from their families. When they return, they usually have some money saved. But plantation wages are low, and many farm families still struggle to make a living.

Land Use in Guatemala

This map shows a mix of old and new in farming. Subsistence farming takes place mainly in the highlands, where most Maya live. Commercial farming takes place at lower elevations. Many Maya work on lowland plantations as migrant workers.

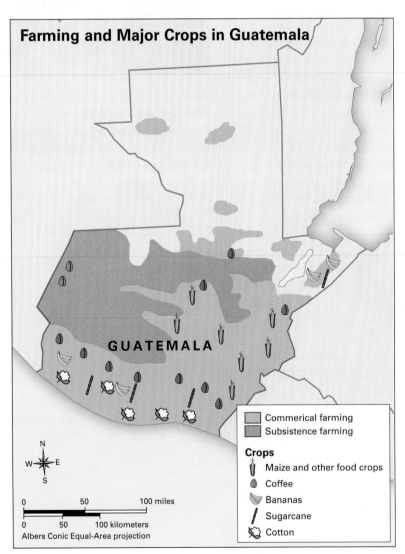

Farming and Major Crops in Guatemala

GUATEMALA

Commerical farming
Subsistence farming

Crops
Maize and other food crops
Coffee
Bananas
Sugarcane
Cotton

N W E S

0   50   100 miles

0   50   100 kilometers

Albers Conic Equal-Area projection

10.6 Making the Most of Market Day

It's market day in Chichicastenango, Guatemala. At 7:00 A.M. a chilly mist still hangs over the town, but already the plaza is jammed with people. Most are Maya from the surrounding countryside. They have come to buy and sell food, tools, and other goods. There are also many tourists from around the world who have come to experience one of the most famous markets in the Mayan region.

Market day is an important tradition in the Mayan highlands. Markets still offer a strong flavor of Mayan culture. They also reflect many changes taking place in the Mayan world.

Trading Goods and Services Mayan markets are held one or two days a week, with Sunday often the most popular choice for market day. A Mayan market typically spreads out from the central plaza into the surrounding streets. Stalls selling the same type of goods are usually grouped together; fruits and vegetables are found in one area, household goods in another, and so on. Markets also have food stalls to feed hungry shoppers. Merchants in some stalls offer such services as shoe repair, portrait photography, and money lending.

The Growing Tourist Trade Highland markets have changed as tourists have come to the highlands to see historic Mayan sites. In Chichicastenango, a large part of the market is devoted to tourist items. Some popular items are traditional Mayan products, like weavings and wood carvings. Other items, such as purses and baseball caps, are designed just for tourists.

The way merchants conduct trade in Mayan markets has also changed as a result of tourism. Many years ago, **barter** was a common way to obtain goods in these markets. For example, a Maya might exchange a basket of vegetables for a certain amount of salt or sugar. With so many outsiders visiting the markets, merchants today trade mostly with money.

Other recent changes in the Mayan marketplace also reflect modern influences. For instance, at one time merchants did most market trading in Mayan languages. Now that more people from outside the local community shop at the markets, Spanish has become the common tongue. In addition, certain goods in highland markets, such as radios and plastic toys, show adaptations to modern life.

Mayan Markets and Tourism
Mayan markets are colorful affairs. While many tourists come to Guatemala to see Mayan ruins, they also visit highland markets. Here they find traditional crafts, some of which are made especially for tourists.

10.7 Keeping Mayan Traditions Alive

On a hillside above Chichicastenango sits the Mayan shrine of Pascual Abaj. The Quiché Maya come to this shrine to worship their ancient gods, kneeling before a small, carved altar and burning candles and incense. They ask the gods to bring a good harvest and to cure the sick. Five hundred years after the Spanish conquest, the Maya still keep their ancient traditions alive.

Religion and Celebrations The ancient Maya worshiped many gods. These gods represented elements of the natural world, such as the sun, rain, and lightning. For the Maya, everything in the world, even rocks and water, had a spirit.

When the Spanish arrived in the 1500s, they sought to convert the Maya to Christianity. Spain was a Catholic country, and over time most Maya also became Catholics. But they also kept their ancient beliefs. In fact, they blended their old beliefs with Catholicism to form a new kind of religion.

The Maya saw little conflict between their old and their new beliefs. They felt that they could worship Catholic saints and still remain faithful to their own gods. Mayan representations of Catholic saints even took on features of the Mayan gods.

Today religious festivals throughout the Mayan highlands express this blended religion. Easter week and Christmas are major holidays, celebrated by attending Catholic mass and carrying images of the saints through the streets. The Maya also celebrate these occasions in Mayan fashion. They listen to traditional music played on Mayan instruments and watch traditional dances performed by masked dancers in Mayan costumes. They also pray to Mayan gods in **rituals** that date back thousands of years.

At festivals, the Maya dress in their finest traditional clothes. Women wear beautiful woven blouses, or *huipiles,* and colorful skirts, belts, and headdresses. Even men who usually wear modern clothing may dress in Mayan style for festivals. The designs in traditional clothing reflect the history and myths of the Mayan people, providing a living link to the Mayan past.

Marimba Players

Music plays a key role in Mayan celebrations. Musicians play traditional instruments such as drums, flutes, and the marimba. A marimba is a type of xylophone.

Mayan Healer
Mayan healers are experts in herbal medicine. They know how to use plants and other natural remedies to cure disease. They preserve other traditions, too, such as sacred rituals and the ancient calendar. But they are also familiar with modern medicine. They will send patients to modern doctors when necessary.

Traditional Medicine The Maya have also preserved their traditional medicine. They may go to modern doctors for major problems, but many still prefer to visit traditional healers.

Mayan healers have great knowledge of their natural environment, and they use medicinal plants to help cure disease. They know how to fix broken bones and heal snakebites. But Mayan healers don't treat only physical illness. The Maya believe that illness has both physical and spiritual causes. For this reason, healers also use rituals to treat the soul and mend the spirit.

The most skilled Mayan healers are also the wise men of their community. They may also become "daykeepers"—men who preserve knowledge of the ancient Mayan calendar, which was central to Mayan religion. Daykeepers perform rituals on key days to maintain harmony among people, the gods, and the natural world.

10.8 Beginning to Think Globally

In this chapter, you read about Mayan culture in the highlands of Guatemala and southern Mexico. You learned that the Maya have kept alive many of their ancient customs and beliefs while at the same time adapting to the modern world.

Other indigenous peoples have also tried to preserve their cultures while adapting to modern life. The Navajo people of the American Southwest are one such group. The Navajo still practice their traditional crafts and observe their ancient religious customs. At the same time, they drive cars, attend colleges all around the United States, and leave home to find work.

Indigenous peoples live all around the globe. In the next section, you will find out more about how they preserve their culture and yet adapt to the modern world.

10.9 Global Connections

The map shows some indigenous groups around the world. There are at least 250 million indigenous peoples spread across 70 countries. Note that some groups live in areas that span national borders. Why might this be?

What do indigenous peoples gain by adapting to modern life? The graphs below the map show that indigenous peoples are generally poorer than other people in their countries. They may benefit from adopting the language and customs of the majority population in order to give them access to better jobs, health care, and schools.

What is most often lost when indigenous peoples adapt to modern life? Indigenous peoples often lose their language, history, and customs when they join the dominant culture. Over time, children stop being taught about the things that make their culture special. As a result, they may lose some of their sense of identity as adults. When certain cultures are lost, the world as a whole loses some of its cultural **diversity**. Notice the number of languages listed in the table below the map. As indigenous people integrate into the dominant culture, many of those languages will disappear.

Can indigenous peoples preserve their traditional culture while adapting to modern life? Many are trying to do just that. The Maori of New Zealand, for example, turned to modern courts of law to win back their traditional lands and fishing areas. The Inuit of Canada now use rifles and snowmobiles for their traditional hunting activities. Like other indigenous peoples around the world, they are using new tools to preserve ancient ways.

Indigenous Populations Around the World

Arctic
1. **Arctic:** Inuit (Eskimo) in Alaska, Canada, Greenland, and Russia

North America
2. **Central Canada:** Innu, Cree
3. **Plains:** Crow, Cheyenne, Arapaho, Pawnee, Comanche, Oglala Sioux, Shoshone

Central America
4. **Mexico Mayan descendants:** Lacandon, Yucatec
   Aztec descendants: Huichol, Tarahumara, Nahua, Zapotec

South America
5. **Amazon Basin—Brazil:** Tukano, Xavante, Kayapo, Yanomami
   Amazon Basin—Ecuador, Bolivia, Peru, Colombia, Venezuela: Amarakaeri, Amuesha, Tukano, Panare, Quichua
6. **Argentina, Chile:** Mapuche

0   1,000   2,000 miles

0   1,000   2,000 kilometers
Robinson projection

Languages in Active Use

Country	Number of Languages
Indonesia	694
Nigeria	455
India	337
Cameroon	247
Australia	226
Mexico	188
United States	165
Brazil	150
Malaysia	128
Russia	90

Source: *Your Dictionary.com*, "Endangered Language Repository: Living Languages by Country," www.yourdictionary.com.

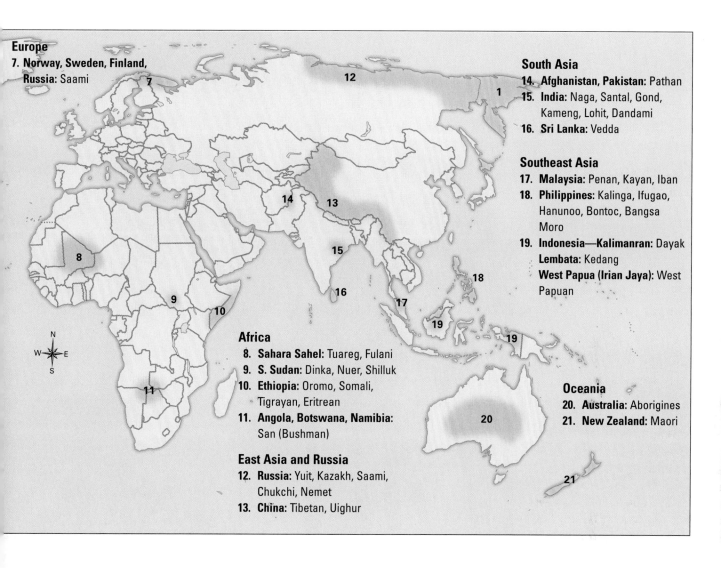

Europe
7. **Norway, Sweden, Finland, Russia:** Saami

South Asia
14. **Afghanistan, Pakistan:** Pathan
15. **India:** Naga, Santal, Gond, Kameng, Lohit, Dandami
16. **Sri Lanka:** Vedda

Southeast Asia
17. **Malaysia:** Penan, Kayan, Iban
18. **Philippines:** Kalinga, Ifugao, Hanunoo, Bontoc, Bangsa Moro
19. **Indonesia—Kalimanran:** Dayak **Lembata:** Kedang **West Papua (Irian Jaya):** West Papuan

Africa
8. **Sahara Sahel:** Tuareg, Fulani
9. **S. Sudan:** Dinka, Nuer, Shilluk
10. **Ethiopia:** Oromo, Somali, Tigrayan, Eritrean
11. **Angola, Botswana, Namibia:** San (Bushman)

East Asia and Russia
12. **Russia:** Yuit, Kazakh, Saami, Chukchi, Nemet
13. **China:** Tibetan, Uighur

Oceania
20. **Australia:** Aborigines
21. **New Zealand:** Maori

Poverty Among Indigenous and Non-indigenous Populations in Latin America

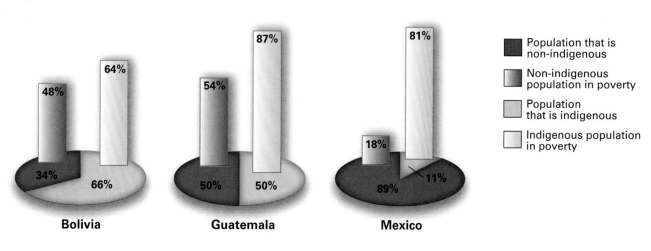

- Population that is non-indigenous
- Non-indigenous population in poverty
- Population that is indigenous
- Indigenous population in poverty

Bolivia
48% — 64%
34% — 66%

Guatemala
54% — 87%
50% — 50%

Mexico
18% — 81%
89% — 11%

Sources: *Indigenous People and Poverty in Latin America,* by George Psacharopoulos and Harry A. Patrinos, World Bank Group. *The Gaia Atlas of First Peoples,* by Julian Burger, London: Gaia Books, 1990.

Dealing with Extreme Weather: Hurricanes in the Caribbean

11.1 Introduction

On September 7, 2004, Hurricane Ivan slammed into the Caribbean island of Grenada. "It was absolutely terrifying," one resident said. "The winds were gusting over 145 miles per hour and just tearing off roofs." Ivan damaged just about every home on the island and destroyed almost half of them, and more than 30 people lost their lives in the storm. One woman whose roof was torn off spent the storm huddled under a mattress with her family. "I stared death in the face," she said. "What could be more scary than that?"

Hurricanes such as Ivan are an example of **extreme weather,** a term that refers to severe or unusual weather conditions. In addition to hurricanes, extreme weather includes **tornadoes,** blizzards, and even severe heat waves or cold spells.

Since extreme weather is often destructive, people may try to make preparations for these natural events. However, such preparations aren't always possible, because extreme weather can be difficult to predict or guard against. When great damage or loss of life occurs, an extreme weather event is called a **natural disaster**. Hurricanes often produce natural disasters.

In this chapter, you will learn about the hurricanes that strike the Caribbean **region**. You will examine the causes and effects of hurricanes, and you will discover the ways in which people in the region deal with this form of extreme weather.

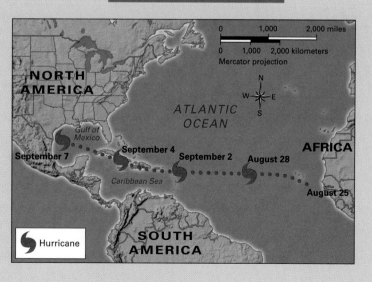

Essential Question

What causes extreme weather, and how do people deal with it?

This map shows the course of a hurricane from the coast of Africa to the Caribbean Sea. Notice that the storm passes through several locations in its journey. At each location, people must deal with the hurricane as a dangerous form of extreme weather. Keep this map in mind as you try to answer the Essential Question.

Graphic Organizer

◄ Hurricane Georges hit Puerto Rico in September 1998 with winds of 110 miles per hour.

11.2 The Geographic Setting

The Caribbean islands stretch in a gentle arc that extends from the tip of Florida to the northern coast of South America. Also known as the West Indies, these islands divide the Atlantic Ocean from the Caribbean Sea and the Gulf of Mexico. Thousands of islands make up this chain, with many being so tiny that only a few people live on them. However, some islands, such as Cuba and Hispaniola, are large enough to be home to millions of people.

Islands in the Sun The Caribbean islands lie within one of Earth's **tropical zones**. They have a warm to hot **climate** year-round, but regular sea breezes cool the islands and make the days pleasant.

These islands were first settled by small groups of Native Americans. The word *hurricane* comes from the language of one of these groups, the Taino, who believed that a storm god called Huracan controlled extreme weather events.

During the 1600s, European countries claimed the islands as colonies. The colonists set up **plantations,** or large farms, where they planted warm-weather crops such as tobacco and sugar. The planters tried to make native peoples work on their land, but in a short time the native peoples died out. Most of them were killed by diseases that were brought by Europeans to the Caribbean. After that, the European colonists brought large numbers of Africans to the Caribbean islands to work on their farms as slaves.

During the 1800s, almost all the Caribbean islands gained their independence. Slavery was also ended. However, independence brought new challenges, including the creation of stable governments and dealing with widespread poverty.

Today many Caribbean islands still base their economies on agriculture. Sugar remains a major **cash crop,** and bananas, coffee, and spices are also important. In recent years, **tourism** has become a key industry on many islands, and tourists flock to the Caribbean to enjoy the region's warm weather, beautiful beaches, and clear blue waters.

Extreme Weather Is a Part of Island Life Despite its pleasant climate, the Caribbean does get hit by extreme weather. Severe thunderstorms sometimes strike the islands, and heat waves and dry spells also occur.

The most extreme form of weather in the region is the **tropical cyclone**. In the Caribbean, tropical cyclones are called *hurricanes*. This is a powerful storm with winds of 74 miles per hour or more. From above, the storm looks like a giant pinwheel as it forms over warm water, and it produces heavy rain and high waves as it grows.

Our knowledge of tropical cyclones comes from **meteorology,** which is the scientific study of climate and weather. Meteorologists are scientists who study Earth's **atmosphere** and climate in an effort to understand weather patterns and the forces that cause them. The size and power of tropical cyclones make these storms especially challenging for meteorologists, who have nevertheless made progress in understanding these severe storms. Through their work, meteorologists are acquiring knowledge that can help to limit the damage and loss of life caused by these extreme weather events.

A Sun-Drenched Beach on the Island of Trinidad

Tourism is a key industry in the Caribbean. Tourists are attracted to the region by sunny beaches like this one in Trinidad. Tourist areas have sprung up to meet their needs. These areas have fine hotels, restaurants, and shops. Outside these areas, however, many people still live in poverty.

► Geoterms

El Niño a warm ocean current that flows off the west coast of South America every few years. An El Niño event changes weather patterns around the world. It may also cause extreme weather in some regions.

extreme weather severe or unusual weather conditions, such as hurricanes, tornadoes, and blizzards

meteorology the scientific study of climate and weather patterns

natural disaster great destruction or loss of life caused by natural forces rather than by human actions

tropical cyclone a severe storm with high winds that spiral around a calm center. Depending on where they form, tropical cyclones are called *hurricanes, typhoons,* or *cyclones.*

One Day's Weather

This map shows weather conditions in the Caribbean and surrounding areas on a specific day. Weather maps are important tools in meteorology. Scientists use them to analyze weather patterns. With this information, they can predict the weather for the next few hours or days.

Sample Weather Map

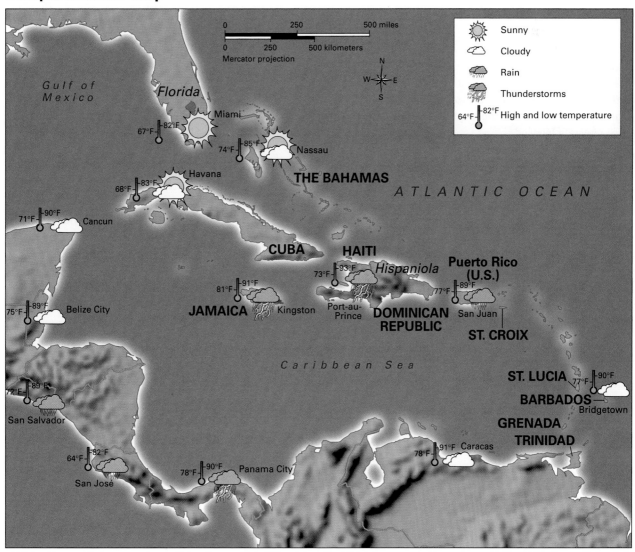

11.3 Understanding the Weather Machine

Weather doesn't just happen by itself. Instead, it is the product of natural forces working together like a machine. This "weather machine" takes energy from the sun, Earth, and the atmosphere and transforms it into rain, wind, and other types of weather.

Weather affects us every day, in large and small ways—and extreme weather, such as hurricanes, can have extreme effects. Storms with powerful winds can pick things up and drop them miles away. In 1997, toads rained down on the town of Villa Angel Flores in Mexico. A whirlwind had picked up the amphibians from a nearby body of water and then dropped them over the town.

The Sun Starts It All Weather is caused by interactions among heat, air, and water, with the sun acting as the "engine" that drives the weather machine. As you read in Chapters 1 and 2, the sun warms Earth's surface unevenly. Its rays fall most directly between the Tropic of Cancer and the Tropic of Capricorn, whereas higher latitudes receive less direct sunlight. That is why temperatures are generally warmer near the equator and cooler near the poles.

The sun's heat is distributed around Earth through a process known as **convection,** or heat transfer. This transfer of heat occurs in both gases and liquids, such as air and water. Warm air and warm water are less dense than cooler air and water. As a consequence, warm air has a tendency to rise in the atmosphere while, meanwhile, warm water rises in the oceans.

When warm air or water rises out of an area, cool air or water flows in to take its place. The steady movement of air or water due to convection is called a **current**.

Winds and Trade

This map shows the main prevailing winds around the globe. Notice the winds blowing toward the equator from higher latitudes to the north and south. They are known as *trade winds*. These winds were named for their ability to move trade goods across the seas in the days when sailing ships were powered by wind.

Prevailing Winds Around the World

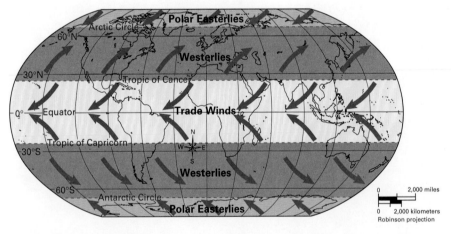

Prevailing winds
Lower latitudes
Middle latitudes
Higher latitudes

Air and Water Move in Predictable Patterns The movement of air and water around the globe occurs in regular patterns. In general, warm air and water currents flow from the equator toward the poles. At the same time, cool air and water currents flow from the poles toward the equator.

This predictable weather pattern creates **prevailing winds,** which are winds that predominantly blow in one direction for most of the year. If Earth didn't rotate, the prevailing winds would move in straight lines between the equator and the poles. Instead, Earth's rotation causes the wind currents to move in a curving pattern that is known as the **Coriolis effect**. You can examine the curvature of the paths of the prevailing winds on the map above. You can also see the names given to prevailing winds, depending on their locations.

Cyclones Around the World

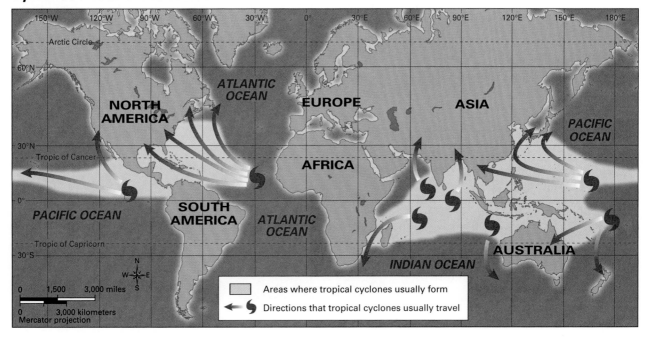

Small Changes Can Cause Extreme Weather Wind and ocean currents have an important influence on weather because they distribute heat and cold throughout the world. Even relatively minor changes in prevailing winds or ocean currents can result in significant changes in the weather.

A good example of this effect is the impact of an **El Niño,** which is a warm ocean current that sometimes flows along the west coast of South America. This warm current does not appear every year, but when it does develop, it usually shows up during the Christmas season. That is why the current is called El Niño, which is a nickname for "the Christ child" in Spanish.

In an El Niño year, the weather on the Pacific coast of North and South America gets warmer. As a result, rainfall increases and flooding is common. At the same time, weather on the other side of the Pacific becomes drier. During these dry spells, severe forest fires sometimes occur in Southeast Asia and Australia. The effects of an El Niño's appearance can be felt as far away as India and Africa.

Tropical Cyclones: The Most Violent Weather Events Throughout the tropics, the weather machine can be extremely powerful because in these regions there is more energy from the sun to warm the air and water. This solar energy produces tropical cyclones, which are the most violent storms on Earth.

Tropical cyclones occur only in areas where the ocean temperature reaches at least 80°F. A large amount of warm, moist air is needed to start these storms. That is why tropical cyclones usually occur during the warmer months of the year.

Tropical cyclones form in three oceans. In the Atlantic Ocean and the eastern Pacific, they are called *hurricanes*. In the western Pacific, they are usually called *typhoons*. In the Indian Ocean, these storms are called *cyclones*.

Tropical Cyclones

The word *cyclone* comes from a Greek word that means "moving in a circle." Tropical cyclones form over three oceans at different times of the year. In the Atlantic Ocean and the eastern Pacific, the season runs from June through November. In the western Pacific, the season lasts from April to December. In the Indian Ocean, the season is from December to April.

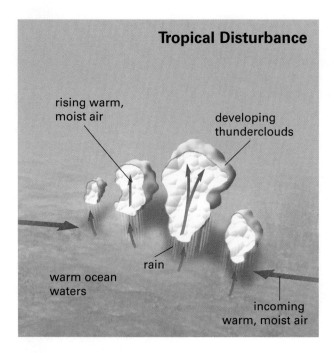

Tropical Disturbance

rising warm, moist air

developing thunderclouds

rain

warm ocean waters

incoming warm, moist air

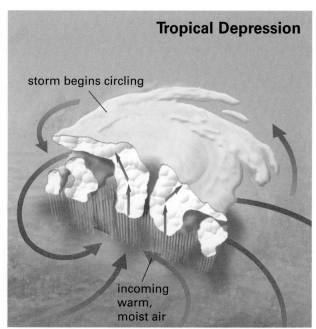

Tropical Depression

storm begins circling

incoming warm, moist air

Birth of a Hurricane

A hurricane develops in four main stages. First, various storms come together to form a tropical disturbance. Second, the disturbance grows into a tropical depression. Third, the depression becomes a tropical storm. Finally, the storm becomes a tropical cyclone, or hurricane. In each stage, wind speeds increase as the storm sucks in more air and moisture.

11.4 Extreme Weather: A Hurricane Is Born

Have you ever witnessed a thunderstorm approaching? The wind picks up and the temperature drops. As clouds roll in and the sky grows dark, a bolt of lightning pierces the sky, followed by a crack of thunder. Suddenly it's pouring rain. In some regions of the world, such a storm might be the first stage of a hurricane.

Tropical Thunderstorms Begin the Process Hurricanes in the Atlantic Ocean usually start out off the coast of Africa. In the summer, water temperatures in that part of the ocean rise to 80°F or more. The ocean releases warm, moist air into the atmosphere, and as the warm air rises, the moisture **condenses** to form clouds and rain. The result is a tropical thunderstorm.

Sometimes several thunderstorms come together to create a **tropical disturbance**. This is a cluster of thunderstorms that move together with the prevailing winds.

From a Tropical Disturbance to a Hurricane As a tropical disturbance grows, more warm, moist air rises from the ocean. In the Northern Hemisphere, this rising air begins to circle in a counterclockwise direction as a consequence of the Coriolis effect, which you read about earlier. When wind starts circling inside a tropical disturbance, the storm becomes a **tropical depression**.

When the weather conditions are right, a tropical depression will suck up even more warm air and moisture. When the wind speeds inside the storm reach 39 miles per hour, a tropical depression is known as a **tropical storm**.

Most tropical storms die out in time, but a few storms will continue to grow in size and wind speed. When the wind speeds reach 74 miles per hour, the storm becomes a tropical cyclone. A hurricane is born!

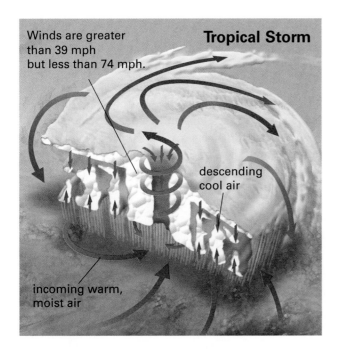

Tropical Storm

Winds are greater than 39 mph but less than 74 mph.

descending cool air

incoming warm, moist air

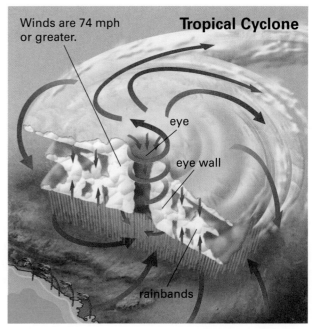

Tropical Cyclone

Winds are 74 mph or greater.

eye

eye wall

rainbands

11.5 Inside a Monster Storm

A hurricane is a massive, whirling storm, and it packs an extremely powerful punch. In just a single day, a hurricane releases more energy than 500,000 atomic bombs. If you could transform that amount of energy into electricity, it would be sufficient to satisfy the electrical needs of the United States for six months.

The Parts of a Hurricane A hurricane is made up of three key parts. The first part is the **eye,** which is a calm spot at the center of the storm. The winds of the hurricane swirl around the calm eye, which might be 20 to 40 miles across.

The second part of a hurricane is known as the **eye wall,** which is made up of thunderstorms that surround the eye. The eye wall, which can be anywhere from 5 to 30 miles thick, looks like a huge curtain of clouds when it is viewed from the center of the storm.

The third key part of a hurricane consists of **rainbands,** which are bands of dense clouds that swirl around the eye wall. Spiraling toward the center of the hurricane, the rainbands drop large amounts of rain as the storm travels across the ocean.

The Path of Hurricanes As you read, Atlantic hurricanes are born off the coast of Africa. When a monster storm develops, trade winds blow it from east to west across the Atlantic. The hurricane spins rapidly as it moves, like a giant top.

The exact track, or path, of a hurricane is unpredictable. A hurricane may change course with a shift in wind direction, and it may also speed up, slow down, or even stop for a while and build up strength. As long as a hurricane stays over warm water, it can continue to grow in both size and power. Severe storms can swell to 1,000 miles across in size while registering wind speeds of up to 200 miles per hour.

Getting Ready for a Hurricane

This Cuban is tying a tarp over his roof in preparation for a hurricane. People in this region know how to prepare for big storms. Hurricane survival kits typically include these things:

- Water: 1 gallon a day per person for 3 to 7 days
- Food: enough to feed people and pets for 3 to 7 days
- First aid kit and medicines
- Blankets and clothes
- Flashlight and batteries
- Battery-powered radio
- Tools for repairing storm damage

11.6 Tracking and Preparing for a Hurricane

"Hold on," the pilot says to his flight crew. "We're going in!" The plane shakes violently as it enters the storm's eye wall, but soon the shaking stops. The plane has reached the calm eye of the hurricane.

This plane and its crew are part of a special Air Force unit that is known as the Hurricane Hunters. The Hurricane Hunters fly into tropical storms in order to record weather data such as wind speed, wind direction, pressure, and temperature. The work is extremely dangerous, but the crews believe that what they are learning is well worth taking such risks. "The bottom line for all of us," says one of the pilots, "is that we do save lives."

Meteorologists Track and Name Hurricanes The Hurricane Hunters work with meteorologists to track the paths of tropical storms. The meteorologists use satellite images and data from the flight crews to predict a storm's movement and to decide when a storm has become a hurricane. At that point, they give the hurricane a name.

Meteorologists have alphabetical lists of male and female names to use in naming hurricanes each year. The name of the year's first hurricane always begins with the letter A. When a very destructive hurricane hits land, its name is retired and never used again. Since 1954, at least 40 hurricane names have been retired.

Preparing for a Hurricane When meteorologists have determined the track of a storm, they warn people who are in the storm's path. When a storm might hit land within 24 to 36 hours, they issue a *hurricane watch*. When the storm is less than 24 hours away, they issue a *hurricane warning*. These predictions are not always perfect, but they do give people a chance to prepare for the storm.

Meteorologists use the Saffir-Simpson scale to rate the strength of a hurricane. This scale rates hurricanes from 1 to 5; the higher the number, the more damage the storm can potentially cause. This hurricane-rating information helps people decide whether to board up their windows and stay home or to seek a safer shelter away from the coast. Storms often change ratings as they travel. In 2003, Hurricane Isabel stayed at level 5 for over 30 hours, which made it one of the longest-lasting Category 5 storms on record.

The Saffir-Simpson Scale

Scientists rate hurricanes using the Saffir-Simpson scale. Category 5 storms are the most dangerous. But less powerful storms can also be deadly.

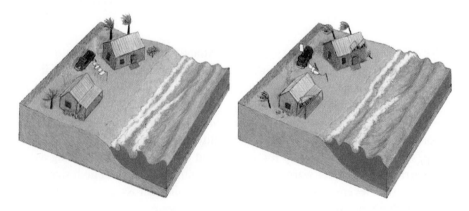

Category 1 hurricane   Category 2 hurricane

11.7 Landfall: A Natural Disaster Begins

When a hurricane hits land, its power is truly awesome. "The wind is at a ferocious roar and coming in powerful bursts," wrote a reporter who witnessed Hurricane Ivan's landfall in Jamaica in 2004. "Even stepping outside for a minute would mean serious injury or worse. Hurricane Ivan has arrived in all its fury and it's terrible indeed."

The Power of Wind and Rain When a hurricane strikes, it lashes everything in its path with wind and rain. The most powerful hurricanes carry winds with speeds as great as 200 miles per hour. Such fierce winds can uproot trees or snap them in half. The winds are also powerful enough to shatter windows, blow off roofs, flip over cars, and hurl boats through the air.

Heavy hurricane rains often cause terrible flooding. They can also loosen rocks and soil on hillsides. The result may be deadly mudslides that crush everything in their path. In 1998, a Category 5 hurricane called Mitch dropped more than 75 inches of rain on Honduras, a small Central American country bordering the Caribbean Sea. The rain caused floods and mudslides that killed about 11,000 people.

Storm Surge: The Most Dangerous Force of All The most destructive feature of a hurricane is the **storm surge,** which is a wall of water that is pushed ashore by a storm. A storm surge can rise as much as 33 feet above sea level, which is as high as a three-story building. When this wall of water hits land, it is capable of destroying everything in its path. Storm surges cause about 9 out of every 10 deaths that result from hurricanes.

The more powerful the hurricane, the higher the storm surge is likely to be. In 1999, a Category 4 storm named Lenny hit several Caribbean islands. In St. Croix, Lenny's 15-foot storm surge knocked over power poles, threw boats up on shore, and destroyed a ballpark. On the island of St. Lucia, dozens of people were left homeless when their homes were washed away. A Category 5 storm named Katrina tore through the Caribbean region in 2005. Katrina's storm surge flattened levees that protected the U.S. city of New Orleans from flooding. When the storm ended, much of New Orleans was under water. The storm damage was so widespread and serious that Katrina became the costliest Atlantic hurricane of all time.

Storm Surge from Hurricane Ivan
A storm surge is a hurricane's most deadly feature. When this wall of water hits land, it causes massive floods. In 2004, a storm surge from Hurricane Ivan flooded this beach home in Cuba. This monster storm killed about 70 people across the Caribbean.

Category 3 hurricane

Category 4 hurricane

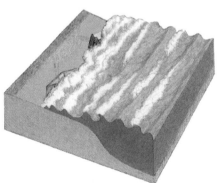

Category 5 hurricane

Rescuing Survivors of Jeanne

These people are being rescued from a flooded house in Puerto Rico after Hurricane Jeanne in 2004. The worst damage from this storm occurred in Haiti. About 3,000 Haitians died as a result of flooding and mudslides. Many Haitians may never fully recover from this disaster.

11.8 Cleaning Up After a Natural Disaster

A hurricane can have a very powerful impact, but the problems do not end when the storm moves on. Although the hurricane itself may be over, the effects of the natural disaster continue.

Hurricanes Lose Strength over Land Fortunately, hurricanes do not last forever. Hurricane John, which was the world's longest-running storm, lasted nearly a month and crossed approximately 5,000 miles of ocean. However, most hurricanes die out sooner than that, mainly as a result of encountering land.

Hurricanes die when they lose their main source of energy. Remember that these storms need warm ocean water to keep them going. When the storms hit land or cross over cool water, they begin to weaken. In the Caribbean region, hurricanes can cross an island and then pick up force on the other side. However, they lose steam when they encounter a large **landmass** such as the United States or Mexico, usually dying out within a few days.

Rebuilding After a Natural Disaster After a hurricane has passed, the people living in its path face the task of rebuilding, which is often an enormous challenge. A hurricane may destroy many of the homes on a hard-hit island. It may damage schools, hospitals, roads, bridges, and power lines. Many people may be left homeless, and hunger and disease may become serious problems.

The first task after a storm passes is to rescue the people who were caught in the wreckage. Relief agencies are set up to find and treat the injured, and relief workers supply food, water, shelter, and clothing to people in need.

The next task is cleaning up after the storm. The floodwaters have to be drained from the low-lying areas. The water and **sewage** lines have to be repaired in order to provide clean water and **sanitation**. The roads need to be cleared. Electrical power has to be restored. Damaged buildings must be knocked down. All of this work requires time and money, and it can take months or even years for a Caribbean island to fully recover from a severe hurricane.

11.9 Beginning to Think Globally

In this chapter, you learned about extreme weather in the Caribbean region. You learned how tropical cyclones get started and how they develop into deadly storms. You read about the methods meteorologists use to analyze and track tropical cyclones. You also learned how natural disasters caused by these storms affect people and communities throughout the Caribbean.

Few Places Escape Extreme Weather Tropical cyclones are tremendously destructive, but they are not the only example of extreme weather. Tornadoes, blizzards, and heavy rains can all do great harm as well.

Most parts of the world experience some form of extreme weather. In the United States, primarily in the midwestern and southern states, tornadoes rip through towns and destroy property every spring. During the winter months, blizzards can block roads, knock out power lines, and interrupt air travel.

The story is much the same on other continents. For instance, heavy rains often cause flooding in South Asia (see Chapter 27 for information on the **monsoon** season in this part of the world). Sandstorms in parts of Africa can destroy crops, fill wells with sand, and force people from their homes.

El Niño's Impact on Weather El Niño plays a key role in extreme weather. As you have learned, El Niño is a warm ocean current that flows from time to time along the Pacific coast of South America. When an El Niño occurs, it can trigger extreme weather in the Pacific region and in other parts of the world.

A major El Niño appeared off the coast of South America in 1997 and 1998. This warming of the ocean caused heavy rains and flooding in South America and produced tornadoes in Florida. At the same time, it caused dry spells that led to wildfires in Southeast Asia, Australia, and Central America.

Scientists are still trying to understand the role El Niño plays in extreme weather, but the effects are clear. You will look at El Niño's impact around the world in the next section.

Counting the Costs
This table shows effects of five recent hurricanes in the Caribbean. These estimates are rough. It is difficult to gather accurate information about the loss of lives and property caused by extreme weather events.

Five Destructive Hurricanes in the Caribbean, 1998–2004

Hurricane	Year	Major Areas Affected	Estimated Deaths	Estimated Damage
Jeanne	2004	U.S. Virgin Islands, Puerto Rico, Dominican Republic, Haiti, Bahamas, Florida	3,005	$6.9 billion
Ivan	2004	Grenada, Jamaica, Grand Cayman, Cuba, Alabama, Florida, Texas, Louisiana	92	$18 billion
Michelle	2001	Cuba, Honduras, Nicaragua, Jamaica, Cayman Islands	17	$28 million
Mitch	1998	Honduras, Nicaragua, El Salvador, Guatemala	11,000	$5 billion
Georges	1998	Puerto Rico, Dominican Republic, Haiti, Florida, Mississippi	602	$5.9 billion

Source: National Hurricane Center.

11.10 Global Connections

The small map shows the warmer-than-usual ocean currents that develop during an El Niño year. Notice that the warmest ocean area is located off the west coast of South America. The large map shows how different areas of the world are affected during a major El Niño year. The table includes data on some extreme weather events that occurred in the United States between 1990 and 2000.

What parts of the world are most affected by an El Niño?

As you might expect, the lands that are bordering the Pacific Ocean show the greatest effects from an El Niño. The west coasts of North and South America experience weather that is wetter than usual. The areas on the other side of the Pacific suffer from extremely dry weather.

What relationship do you see between an El Niño and extreme weather?

An El Niño can affect weather in ways that you might not expect. The years 1991, 1993, 1994, and 1997 were all considered to be El Niño years. As shown in the table of extreme weather events, there were fewer hurricanes in the Atlantic region during those years. Meanwhile, there were also fewer extreme temperature events in the United States than in an average year.

How can understanding an El Niño's effects help meteorologists to predict extreme weather?

Just how an El Niño shapes climate is not yet fully understood. But the more meteorologists learn about the factors that shape our climate, the better they will become at predicting extreme weather. This improvement in weather prediction, in turn, could help people to prepare for natural disasters that are caused by weather.

El Niño's Effects Around the World

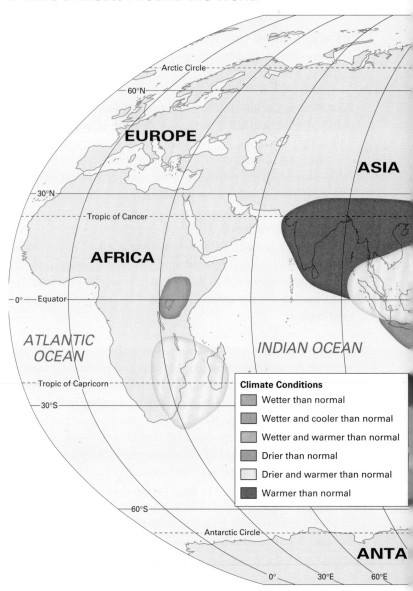

Climate Conditions
- Wetter than normal
- Wetter and cooler than normal
- Wetter and warmer than normal
- Drier than normal
- Drier and warmer than normal
- Warmer than normal

Sea Surface Temperatures in an El Niño Year

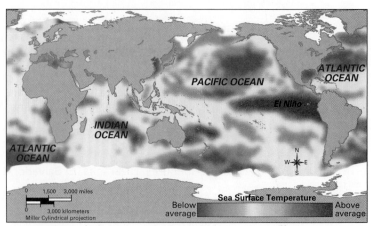

Sea Surface Temperature
Below average — Above average

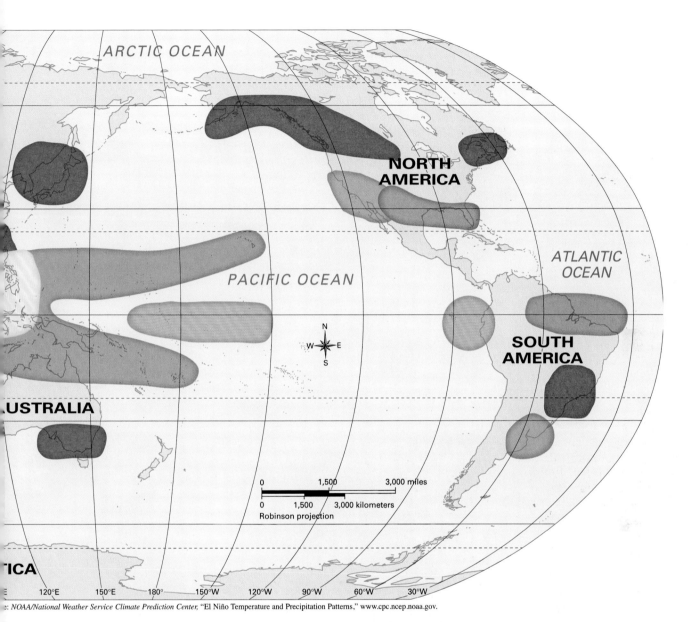

ARCTIC OCEAN

NORTH
AMERICA

PACIFIC OCEAN

ATLANTIC
OCEAN

SOUTH
AMERICA

AUSTRALIA

0   1,500   3,000 miles

0   1,500   3,000 kilometers
Robinson projection

120°E   150°E   180°   150°W   120°W   90°W   60°W   30°W

NOAA/National Weather Service Climate Prediction Center, "El Niño Temperature and Precipitation Patterns," www.cpc.ncep.noaa.gov.

Extreme Weather Events in the United States, 1990–2000

El Niño year	1990	1991	1992	1993	1994	1995	1996	1997	1998	1999	2000
Atlantic Hurricanes	8	3	4	4	3	11	9	3	10	8	8
Violent Tornadoes	50	12	32	5	6	14	4	10	14	18	3
Extreme Hail Events	56	84	134	38	48	110	99	65	100	73	71
Extreme Temperature Events	(no information available)			33	65	229	272	238	344	395	418

Sources: *National Oceanic and Atmospheric Administration,* www.noaa.gov. Jan Null, "El Niño and La Niña Years: A Consensus List," Oct. 2004,
Golden Gate Weather Services, ggweather.com. *Weather Underground,* "Hurricane Archive," www.wunderground.com.

Land Use Conflict in the Amazon Rainforest

12.1 Introduction

Picture yourself in a hot, steamy forest. It has just stopped raining, and everything around you is green and moist. Green vines wind around the slender trunks of trees that reach more than 100 feet into the air. High overhead, a tangle of vines, branches, and leaves nearly blocks out the sun. Except for the buzzing of insects, the forest is practically silent. Then you hear a strange barking sound coming from the treetops. You look up and get your first glimpse of a red howler monkey.

Welcome to the Amazon rainforest, an enormous **tropical rainforest** in South America. The rainforest seems timeless, yet it is changing rapidly. For thousands of years, small groups of **indigenous peoples** have made their home here, making a living by hunting and gathering. In more recent times, other groups have come to the rainforest, including rubber tappers, farmers, cattle ranchers, and loggers. In addition, the rainforest is of great interest to environmental groups, which are organizations that work to protect the natural world.

Each of these groups has its own ideas about the Amazon rainforest. The rubber tappers, farmers, cattle ranchers, and loggers want to use the rainforest to make a living. Indigenous peoples want to maintain their traditional way of life. Environmental groups want to preserve the rainforest in its natural state. These differences have led to **land use conflict,** or arguments about the best ways to use the land. In this chapter, you will learn what the various groups want and examine some possible solutions to land use conflict within the Amazon rainforest.

Essential Question   **Graphic Organizer**

How should the resources of rainforests be used and preserved?

This illustration shows six groups that are interested in the Amazon rainforest. Some want to use the resources of the rainforest to make a living. Others want to preserve the rainforest in its natural state. Keep the possible conflicts among these groups in mind as you try to answer the Essential Question.

Native Amazonians   Rubber Tappers   Loggers   Settlers   Cattle Ranchers   Environmentalists

---

◀ The Amazon rainforest (top), Brazilian family cutting wood (bottom)

The Amazon Basin

The World's Largest Rainforest

The Amazon basin covers much of northern Brazil and several other countries in South America. It contains the world's largest rainforest. It receives 80 to 115 inches of rain a year. The Amazon rainforest is home to more types of plants and animals than any other place on Earth.

12.2 The Geographic Setting

Tropical rainforests are a type of **broadleaf evergreen forest** found near the equator, where the **climate** is warm and wet all year. The Amazon rainforest is the largest tropical rainforest in the world, covering more than 2 million square miles. That is more than half the size of the United States. Most of this vast rainforest lies in Brazil. However, it also covers parts of Colombia, Ecuador, Peru, Bolivia, and Venezuela.

A Many-Layered Ecosystem A rainforest is a complex **ecosystem** that has several layers. The bottom, or ground, layer is called the **forest floor**. The thick layer consisting of overlapping tree branches at the very top of the forest is known as the **canopy**. Between the forest floor and the canopy are shrubs and smaller trees that form a layer known as the **lower story**.

An amazing variety of plants and animals live in the various layers of the rainforest. Rainforests cover only approximately 6 percent of Earth's surface, but they are home to about 50 percent of the world's living species.

Scientists use the term **biodiversity** to describe the variety of plant and animal species that live in a particular area. The great biodiversity of rainforests attracts scientists of different specialties who come to study the flora and fauna there.

Other groups of people have different reasons for coming to the rainforest. Some people come to clear land for farming and ranching, a process that results in **deforestation,** or the removal of trees from large areas. Other people are more interested in **sustainable development,** which means finding ways to use the resources of the rainforest without destroying it.

The Lungs of the Earth Many people around the world worry about the fate of the Amazon rainforest. A major reason for their concern is that tropical rainforests affect life far beyond their borders. The trees and other plants that grow in these dense forests have been called the "lungs of the Earth."

The nickname "lungs of the Earth" comes from the key role that rainforests play in Earth's **carbon-oxygen cycle**. The carbon-oxygen cycle consists of a series of events that turn a gas called *carbon dioxide,* or CO_2, into oxygen and then convert the oxygen back into CO_2. In this way, carbon and oxygen are "cycled" among the living things that need them to survive.

Here is how the carbon-oxygen cycle works. When people and other animals breathe, their bodies take in oxygen and breathe out CO_2. Cars and factories also produce CO_2 as a waste product when burning fuel. Trees and other plants absorb CO_2 from the air, using the carbon for their growth. Plants then release the oxygen back into the air as a waste product. When people and other animals breathe in this oxygen, the cycle begins again.

Because rainforests are rich in plant life, they are a major part of the carbon-oxygen cycle throughout Earth. Scientists believe that the Amazon rainforest alone creates about one quarter of Earth's oxygen. A rainforest tree may have produced the oxygen that you are breathing right now.

► Geoterms

biodiversity the variety of plants and animals living in one area. The term can also mean the great variety of all living things on Earth.

carbon-oxygen cycle the process by which carbon and oxygen cycle among plants, people and animals, and the environment

deforestation removing or clearing away the trees from a forest. Deforestation is often done to clear land for farming or ranching.

sustainable development using resources in ways that meet the needs of people today without hurting the ability of future generations to meet their own needs. This means finding ways to use resources without using them up.

tropical rainforest a broadleaf evergreen forest found in wet and hot regions near the equator

Canopy: 100–165 feet

Lower story: 3–100 feet

Forest floor: 0–3 feet

The Three Layers of a Rainforest

A tropical rainforest grows in three layers. Shade-loving mosses and ferns thrive on the dark forest floor. Small trees and vines fill in the lower story, or middle layer. Trees reaching for sunlight form a canopy of branches at the top of the forest. Some very tall trees even poke their heads above the canopy.

A Native Amazonian Hunter

Native peoples have lived in the rainforest for about 12,000 years. This man is using a traditional bow and arrow to hunt for game. In recent years, native Amazonians have lost much of their land to loggers, farmers, and ranchers.

12.3 What Native Amazonians Want

Once there were as many as 10 million native people living in the Amazon rainforest, but today the number of native Amazonians is much smaller. Those who remain want one thing above all: to continue their traditional way of life.

A Sustainable Way of Life Native people have lived in the rainforest for about 12,000 years. Most live as they always have, by hunting, fishing, and growing crops on small plots of land that they have cleared in the forest. When a field is no longer fertile, they clear a new field somewhere else. Over time, new forest covers the old field. This is a sustainable way of life that is using the resources of the Amazon rainforest without causing long-term damage.

In the 1960s, the government of Brazil decided that it would open the Amazon basin to development. The government began by building a highway, which farmers, ranchers, and loggers followed into the Amazon region.

The arrival of so many newcomers has hurt native Amazonians. Many of the native people have been driven from their homelands in order to make room for farms and ranches. Some of them have died from diseases brought by newcomers. Other native people have been killed or injured in land use conflicts.

Save the Forest to Save Us Today native Amazonians are fighting to save parts of the rainforest from development, arguing that they have a right to preserve themselves and their way of life. As native leader Davi Kopenawa has said, "I want to live where I really belong, on my own land."

In their struggle to survive, native Amazonians have had to learn new skills. One of these new skills is how to speak Portuguese, which is the official language of Brazil. Another skill is how to work with Brazil's government and legal system. Native groups have called on the Brazilian government to make them the legal owners of their homelands. Only through legal ownership will they be able to keep others from destroying their rainforest home.

12.4 What Rubber Tappers Want

Rubber tappers have lived in the Amazon basin for many generations. These workers "tap," or collect, the sap from rubber trees that grow in the rainforest. The sap is then dried to make rubber products such as erasers or tires for cars and bikes.

Rubber Tapping Does Not Hurt the Forest Rubber tappers first came to the Amazon region during the 1870s, when they were hired to work on rubber tree plantations in the rainforest. When the price of rubber dropped, most of the plantations were abandoned. However, some of the rubber tappers decided to stay in the region and continue making their living in the rainforest.

Rubber tappers remove sap from a rubber tree by making diagonal cuts in the bark and then collecting the sap in cups. Removing the sap in this way does not harm the tree, which makes rubber tapping a sustainable activity. Rubber tapping is one way to use the resources of the rainforest without harming the environment.

In the 1960s, the government of Brazil decided that there were better ways to use the rainforest. It encouraged people to clear the forest for farms and ranches. In the deforestation that followed, many rubber trees disappeared, leading to land use conflict between the rubber tappers and the newcomers.

Let Us Continue Our Sustainable Way of Life Since rubber tappers want to continue making a living from the rainforest, they need to stop the widespread clearing of trees. Therefore they have asked the government of Brazil to create protected **reserves** within the rainforest. These areas would be set aside for sustainable activities such as rubber tapping.

Rubber tappers believe that their right to the rainforest comes from having worked there for so long. They also argue that their way of life does not harm the rainforest. For this reason, they believe, the government should protect their activities.

Scoring a Rubber Tree

Rubber tappers collect sap from rubber trees without hurting them. One tapper, Chico Mendes, became a leader in the fight to preserve the rainforest. Eventually, because of his activities, he was murdered. His death brought world attention to the rubber tappers' cause.

12.5 What Loggers Want

Logging companies began moving into the Amazon basin during the 1960s. Loggers harvest trees from forests for use in wood products, which range from paper to fine furniture.

The Rainforest Is a Source of Valuable Hardwoods A great variety of trees grow throughout the Amazon rainforest. The most valuable tree species are the hardwood trees, such as mahogany and rosewood. Furniture manufacturers all over the world appreciate the beautiful wood from these trees.

Unfortunately, these valuable trees are scattered throughout the rainforest, making it difficult to find and cut only the hardwoods. Instead, loggers **clear-cut** whole patches of rainforest, which means that they cut down all of the trees in an area. After all of the trees have been removed, the loggers move on to another patch.

The logging companies argue that clear-cutting is the only way they can make money, but clear-cutting is also a major cause of deforestation. The larger the area that is stripped of its trees, the longer it takes for the rainforest to grow back.

Logging also leads to other types of development. Logging companies build roads deep into the rainforest so that they can transport logs by truck. Meanwhile, settlers who are looking for land follow these logging roads into the forest. Once there, the settlers claim land for farming and ranching.

We Need Trees to Help Brazil's Economy Many groups oppose the clear-cutting of the rainforest. Loggers reply that they are helping Brazil's economy grow by creating jobs for people in the **forestry** industry. In addition, logging provides wood for Brazil's furniture factories and paper mills.

Lumber companies also argue that they have made forestry a valuable **economic activity** for Brazil. In 2004, Brazil exported more than $5 billion worth of wood. The money earned from these sales is helping Brazil to pay off its debts to other countries and is improving the living conditions of many of its citizens.

Loggers Lead the Way in Developing the Rainforest

In the 1960s, loggers began building dirt roads into the rainforest. Other groups began to develop land near these roads. In time, some logging roads became paved highways.

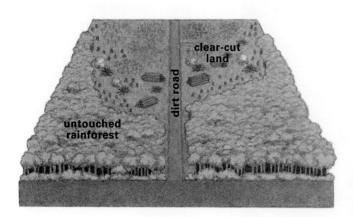

untouched rainforest · dirt road · clear-cut land

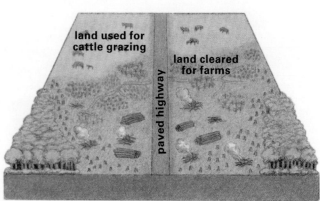

land used for cattle grazing · paved highway · land cleared for farms

Clearing Rainforest for Farming
Settlers who come to the rainforest clear the trees off their land to create farm fields. Farming in this environment is not easy. The constant rain washes away the soil's nutrients. Tropical insects also kill many crops.

12.6 What Settlers Want

Though Brazil has the eleventh largest economy in the world, almost one quarter of Brazilians are poor. In **rural** areas, an even greater proportion of the population is poor.

During the 1960s, the government of Brazil began to encourage poor people to move into the Amazon rainforest. These new settlers arrived in large numbers, looking for rainforest land to farm.

A Lot of Land, but Not for the Poor Brazil is a vast country, but it has limited areas of farmland. Furthermore, this farmland is not shared equally. A few wealthy families have long owned most of the best farmland, whereas millions of poor Brazilians own no land at all. For many families in Brazil, the prospect of owning a farm in the Amazon basin had seemed like a distant dream.

The Brazilian government did what it could to try to make this dream a reality. The government brought poor families to the rainforest, supplying them with money and free land to enable them to plant their first crops.

We Need Land to Feed Our Families Over time, however, the settlers' dream has become a nightmare for many farm families. As native Amazonians had learned long ago, farming in a rainforest is extremely difficult. The thin soil is surprisingly poor in **nutrients,** which are the substances that make a field fertile. Constant rainfall soon washes away whatever nutrients the soil once contained. As the soil loses its fertility, the amount of food it can produce shrinks. The native Amazonians solved this problem by clearing new fields every few years. Over time, their abandoned fields regained some fertility.

However, Brazilian settlers cannot relocate as easily as the native Amazonians. As more settlers have cleared land for farming, opposition to settlers has grown. Native Amazonians, rubber tappers, and ranchers all want the settlers to leave the rainforest. In response, the settlers argue that there is no land for them in other parts of Brazil. They say they must look to the rainforest for land to feed their families.

A Cattle Drive in the Rainforest

Cattle like these are a common sight in the Amazon basin. Cattle ranching is now one of the main causes of deforestation in the rainforest. Ranchers say they are raising food for the world. And many countries are happy to buy Brazilian beef.

12.7 What Cattle Ranchers Want

A rainforest may not seem like it could be cattle country, but since the 1960s parts of the Amazon basin have become just that. Although the Amazon cattle ranchers are a small group, they own large areas of rainforest land.

Cattle Need Grasslands to Graze Rainforest cattle graze primarily on grass. They consume the grass in an area all the way down to the dirt, and then they are moved to a new area with fresh grass to eat. Moving cattle from place to place gives grazed areas an opportunity to grow new grass, but this practice also uses up a lot of land.

Today cattle can be found grazing on vast areas of grassland throughout the Amazon basin. Loggers cleared some of this land, and farmers and ranchers cleared the rest. After large tracts of rainforest are cleared, the trees seldom grow back. Instead, the cleared areas become grasslands. This permanent deforestation upsets many people, but it is of great benefit to ranchers.

We Need Land to Feed the World Many people argue that cattle don't belong in a rainforest. Cattle ranchers strongly disagree, arguing that they are making good use of rainforest land by raising food for the world and earning income for Brazil.

Many countries import beef from Brazil. In fact, the United States is one of the biggest buyers of Brazilian beef. Some environmental groups are dissatisfied with this trade. They estimate that 55 square feet of rainforest have to be cleared for every hamburger that is sold in the United States.

Like logging, cattle ranching has become an important economic activity in Brazil. In 2003, the value of beef exported to other countries was in excess of $1.5 billion. The government of Brazil can use the money that is earned from beef sales to help pay its debts and to care for its citizens.

12.8 What Environmental Groups Want

Not all Brazilians want to see the Amazon basin developed. For example, environmental groups have worked for many years to attempt to slow the clearing of the rainforest. Their ideas have led to conflict with many other groups.

Protecting the Biodiversity of the Rainforest Scientists and **environmentalists** began coming to the rainforest in the 1970s. Some came to study rainforest plants, hoping to find plants that could cure diseases. Others came to study rainforest animals. Still others came to work with native peoples.

All of these groups want to protect the rainforest and its biodiversity. Scientists estimate that a 2.5-acre patch of rainforest contains about 750 species of trees and 1,500 species of flowering plants. The same patch is also home to approximately 125 species of mammals and 400 species of birds. And these numbers include only the plants and animals that scientists already know about. Countless unknown species also make their homes in the rainforest.

We Want Slower, Smarter Rainforest Development Environmental groups argue that all rainforest species have a right to exist, which means their rainforest home must be preserved. Environmentalists therefore want to slow down development of the rainforest. This would give scientists time to study the effects of new activities so that better decisions can be made for the future.

In 2000, environmental groups won a major victory against ranchers. The ranchers tried to get a law passed that would allow them to clear rainforest land without restriction. Environmental groups successfully blocked the law. Another victory came in 2004, when Brazil's government created two large rainforest reserves where only sustainable activities like rubber tapping are allowed. "We are extremely happy," said one environment leader, "with the government's decision to protect the planet's biggest tropical forest."

The Rainforest Is Home to Earth's Greatest Biodiversity

Experts estimate that we are losing over 100 plant, animal, and insect species every day to rainforest deforestation. Some of these species haven't even been discovered yet! Look closely at this illustration. Why are these plants and animals drawn in unusual sizes relative to one another?

Number of species

1,500
1,400
1,300
1,200
1,100
1,000
900
800
700
600
500
400
300
200
100

amphibian   reptile   mammal   butterfly   bird   tree   flowering plant

Source: The Nature Conservancy, nature.org

Ecotourism in the Rainforest

Ecotourism attracts people who like being close to nature. Visitors to the rainforest learn about its great variety of plants and animals. Meanwhile, the money they spend creates jobs.

12.9 Ideas for Reducing Land Use Conflict

Each of the groups that you have read about in this chapter has its own ideas for how best to use or preserve the resources of the Amazon rainforest. Often these differences have led to land use conflict. A few groups, however, are looking at ways to balance preservation and development. In this way, they hope to meet the needs of people while also reducing harm to the rainforest. Here are some of their ideas.

Promote Ecotourism Most countries encourage **tourism,** which is the business of organizing travel for pleasure. Attracting tourists supports a country's economy because tourists spend money on hotels, meals, services, and souvenirs.

Some tour companies are promoting a new type of tourism that is known as **ecotourism**. This kind of travel attracts people who would like to visit unique ecosystems, such as a rainforest. Boat tours of the Amazon rainforest are popular with ecotourists, who come from all over the world.

Ecotourism offers many benefits. It creates jobs for people in the tourist industry. It helps the economy by bringing in money. Most important, it gives people a reason to preserve the places that ecotourists come to experience. The great danger of ecotourism is overuse. If too many tourists visit a fragile area, they may help to destroy what they have come to see.

Encourage Sustainable Development Another way to balance development and preservation is to encourage sustainable development. In Brazil, sustainable development means finding ways to use the rainforest without destroying it. One way is by growing crops that don't require large areas of land to be cleared.

An example of such a crop is shade-grown coffee, a method of growing coffee that makes good use of rainforest trees. The coffee bushes are planted under a canopy of trees, a location that keeps the bushes from getting too much sun. Leaves from the coffee bushes enrich the soil. Meanwhile, the coffee bushes also provide **habitat** for birds, which in

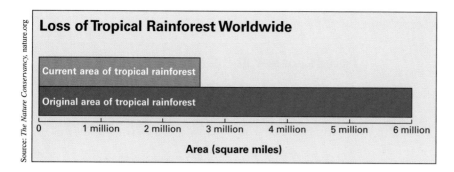

Source: The Nature Conservancy, nature.org

Loss of Tropical Rainforest Worldwide

Current area of tropical rainforest

Original area of tropical rainforest

| 0 | 1 million | 2 million | 3 million | 4 million | 5 million | 6 million |

Area (square miles)

turn eat insects that attack coffee plants. This type of farming requires the use of few or no chemicals, which is good not only for the coffee planters but also for coffee drinkers.

Another less harmful way of using the rainforest is strip logging. Instead of clear-cutting large areas, strip loggers clear long, narrow strips of forest. The forest grows back in these strips far more quickly than in large clear-cut areas.

Buy Products that Protect the Rainforest Consumers can help protect the rainforest by buying products that support sustainable development. Examples include ice creams and cereals made with Brazil nuts. The companies that make these products buy the nuts from native Amazonians, thereby helping native peoples make a living without damage to the rainforest.

Another step that consumers can take is to buy products made from wood that is harvested in a sustainable manner. Not all wood is harvested in the same way. Some wood is logged in ways that can destroy a forest, whereas other wood is harvested with care and respect for the forest.

Until recently, there was no way for people to know whether they were buying "good wood." Then, in the 1990s, logging companies and environmental groups created certification programs to help wood buyers. Under these programs, products from well-managed forests are certified, or labeled. The label tells a buyer that the product comes from "good wood." Consumers today can buy many certified "good wood" products from forests in Brazil, including lumber, charcoal, pencils, furniture, and musical instruments.

12.10 Beginning to Think Globally

In this chapter, you read about land use conflict in the Amazon rainforest. You learned that the rainforest is an important part of the carbon-oxygen cycle. The rainforest is also rich in biodiversity. However, since the 1960s, loggers, settlers, and ranchers have cleared large parts of the rainforest. Native Amazonians, rubber tappers, and environmental groups continue to oppose this deforestation. Still, the rainforest is shrinking year by year.

Not all countries are losing forests as rapidly as Brazil. Some are even gaining forests, a process that is known as **reforestation**. In some places, the process of reforestation is happening naturally. For example, forests in the eastern United States have taken over abandoned farm fields. In other parts of the world, people are planting trees to create new forests. In the next section, you will examine rates of deforestation and reforestation around the world.

Shrinking Rainforests
These satellite images show the same part of the Amazon rainforest in 1975 and 2001. The light green patches are areas of deforestation. Rainforests are shrinking worldwide. A few thousand years ago, they covered 12 percent of Earth's surface. Today only 5 percent of Earth is covered with rainforests.

12.11 Global Connections

The map shows deforestation and refor- estation in countries around the world. Notice that some countries have ex- perienced little forest loss during the 10-year period. This may be because these countries are doing a good job of protecting their forests. Or it may be because they have no remaining forest to lose.

What factors contribute to the loss of forest worldwide? There are many reasons why people cut down forests. One reason is population growth. As the number of people in the world increases, so does people's demand for farmland and wood prod- ucts. Another reason is poverty. Poor people in many countries depend on wood for cooking fuel, heating, and building materials. To meet these basic needs, they cut down trees.

Can deforestation be slowed or reversed? Some countries have been able to slow deforestation. Other coun- tries, such as Ireland, have begun refor- estation. For thousands of years, the Irish stripped their land of trees to cre- ate farmland. By 1900, less than 1 per- cent of Ireland remained forested. Since the 1950s, the government of Ireland has supported tree planting. The gov- ernment has also educated people about the importance of forests. Today about 8 percent of Ireland is forested.

What is the best way to use and preserve the world's forests? Each country has to find its own answer to this question. In recent years, defores- tation has slowed worldwide. This slow- ing trend suggests that some countries are doing more to preserve their forests. Still, both rich and poor countries are continuing to lose forests, and some of these forests may be gone forever.

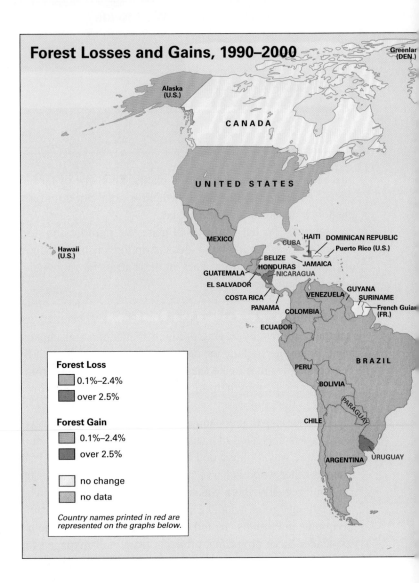

Forest Losses and Gains, 1990–2000

Forest Loss
- 0.1%–2.4%
- over 2.5%

Forest Gain
- 0.1%–2.4%
- over 2.5%

- no change
- no data

Country names printed in red are represented on the graphs below.

Per Capita GDP of Neighboring Countries with Different Rates of Forest Loss or Gain

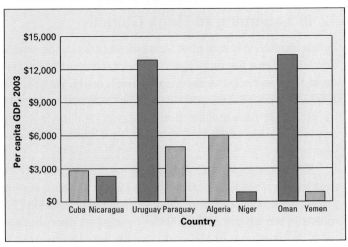

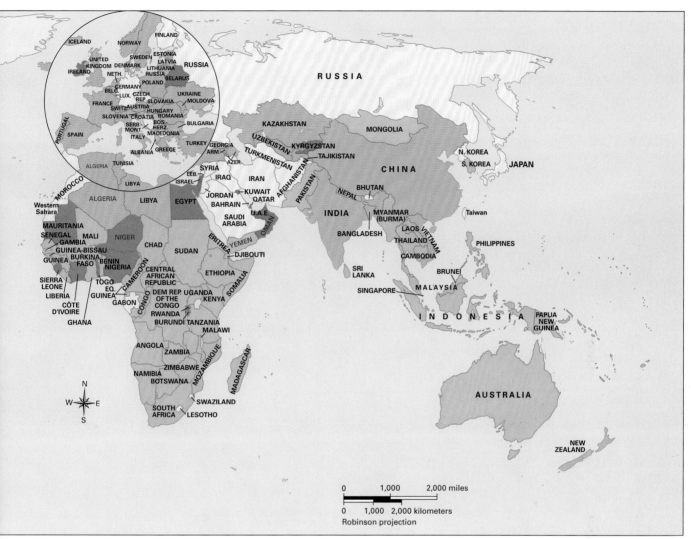

Source: *Penguin State of the World Atlas,* 7th ed., by Dan Smith, New York: Penguin Group, 2003.

Population Growth of Neighboring Countries with Different Rates of Forest Loss or Gain

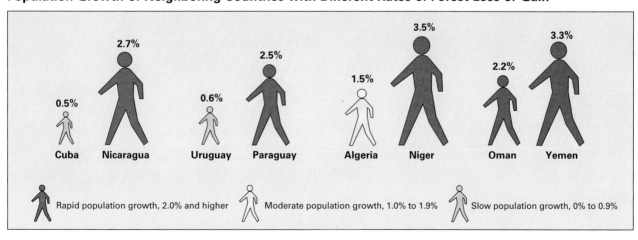

These two graphs show neighboring countries that have different rates of forest loss or gain. The color of each country on the bar graph matches its color on the map. What connections do you see between deforestation, poverty, and population growth?

Life in the Central Andes: Adapting to a Mountainous Region

13.1 Introduction

La Paz, Bolivia, is the highest big city in the world, sitting at 12,000 feet above sea level in the central Andes Mountains of South America. This high elevation can produce some odd effects. Golfers in La Paz can hit a golf ball much farther than they can at sea level. At a nearby ski resort, a skier may need to wear an oxygen tank to go skiing.

These effects are the result of thin air. The air is thinner at high elevations because the force of gravity pulls air downward, which means that there is less oxygen in the air at high elevations. This is why the skier in La Paz requires an oxygen tank. The thin air is also the reason a golf ball will travel farther at 12,000 feet. At that elevation, there is less air to cause friction on the ball and slow it down.

The people of La Paz are accustomed to living at high elevations. Like all of the people who live in the Andes Mountains, they have had to adapt to the effects of high elevation. The Andes include some of the highest mountain peaks in the world, with many of them rising much higher than La Paz. The various elevation levels in these mountains influence the way people live.

In this chapter, you will read about life in the central Andes. You will also learn about **altitudinal zonation,** a term that refers to the division of mountainous land into zones based on altitudes, or elevations. You will find out about the four main elevation zones in the Andes and how the people living there have adapted to each zone.

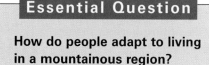

Essential Question

How do people adapt to living in a mountainous region?

This diagram represents the Andes Mountains of South America. Notice that the mountain is divided into four zones based on elevation. Each zone has its own range of temperatures. It also has its own distinct plant and animal life. The features of each zone influence how people live. Think about this diagram as you try to answer the Essential Question.

Graphic Organizer

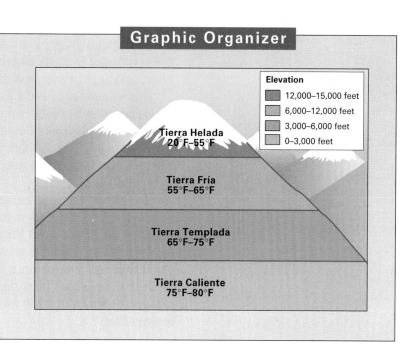

Elevation
- 12,000–15,000 feet
- 6,000–12,000 feet
- 3,000–6,000 feet
- 0–3,000 feet

Tierra Helada
20°F–55°F

Tierra Fría
55°F–65°F

Tierra Templada
65°F–75°F

Tierra Caliente
75°F–80°F

◄ A mountain valley and snow-covered volcano in Ecuador

A Mountain City

La Paz, Bolivia, is the highest big city in the world. It is located at 12,000 feet in the heart of the Andes Mountains. The Andes run the length of South America. The only higher mountains in the world are the Himalayas of Asia. The people of the Andes have had to adapt to life at high elevations.

13.2 The Geographic Setting

South America, the world's fourth largest continent, encompasses 12 countries and a wide range of environments. The continent has deserts, **tropical rainforests,** and several mountain ranges, with the greatest mountains being the Andes.

The Andes: Backbone of South America The Andes consist of several mountain ranges that are known in Spanish as *cordilleras*. These cordilleras form the longest chain of high mountains on Earth, stretching for approximately 4,500 miles from north to south, along the west coast of South America. The Andes have appropriately been nicknamed the backbone of South America.

The Andes Mountains pass through seven countries, featuring many different landscapes along the way. Some parts of the Andes are covered with dense forest, whereas other regions are rocky and bare. More than 50 mountains within the Andes reach elevations of more than 20,000 feet. These lofty peaks are always covered with snow and ice.

The Andes can be grouped in three sections. The northern Andes cross Venezuela and Colombia. The southern Andes run through Chile and Argentina. The central Andes cover Ecuador, Peru, and Bolivia. This chapter focuses on the central Andes.

The Four Elevation Zones of the Andes In the introduction, you read about altitudinal zonation, learning that there are four main elevation zones in the Andes. These elevation zones are also called **climate zones** because elevation helps determine **climate**. The four elevation zones are illustrated in the diagram on the facing page.

The elevation zones in the Andes are known by their Spanish names. The lowest zone is called *tierra caliente,* or hot country. Above that is a zone known as *tierra templada,* or cool country. Next comes *tierra fría,* or cold country. The highest elevation zone is known as *tierra helada,* which means frost country.

The link between climate and elevation is based on two factors. The first factor is **solar energy,** which is the heat and light emitted by the sun. This energy from the sun warms Earth's surface. Some solar energy is also reflected by Earth back into the **atmosphere,** with the air closest to the surface absorbing most of the reflected heat.

The second factor is the force of gravity. Gravity pulls air in the atmosphere down toward Earth. As a result of this process, the air becomes denser at lower elevations. The denser the air, the more heat it can absorb. As you move higher, the air becomes thinner and holds less heat. For every 1,000-foot rise in elevation, the temperature of the air drops by around 3.5°F.

The higher you go in the Andes Mountains, the cooler the temperature becomes. This is true even in regions that are near the equator. For example, both of Ecuador's two largest cities, Guayaquil and Quito, lie near the equator. Guayaquil has an annual average temperature of 77°F, but Quito's average temperature is much cooler, just 55°F. The reason for the difference is elevation. Guayaquil is located at sea level, whereas Quito sits at an elevation of 9,350 feet. One city lies in tierra caliente, the other in tierra fría.

▶ Geoterms

altitudinal zonation the division of land into zones based on elevation, which in turn helps determine climate and vegetation

snow line the lowest elevation on mountains where snow remains year-round

terracing the creation of flat areas on mountain slopes for the purpose of farming

tree line the highest elevation where trees grow on a mountain

vertical trade the trading of crops between lowland and highland areas

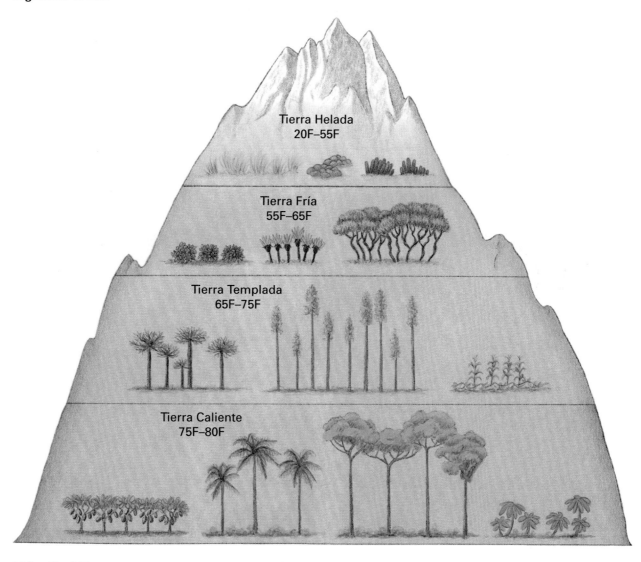

Tierra Helada
20F–55F

Tierra Fría
55F–65F

Tierra Templada
65F–75F

Tierra Caliente
75F–80F

Altitudinal Zonation in the Andes

This diagram shows the four elevation zones of the Andes. Notice how the climate cools the higher you go. That's because the air gets thinner and holds less heat.

13.3 The Tropical Lowlands: Tierra Caliente

A worker is picking bananas on a plantation in Ecuador. The temperature is high, so he stops frequently to wipe the sweat from his brow. He also must watch out for spiders because tarantulas often hide within banana stalks. A tarantula bite may not be deadly, but it is extremely painful.

This banana plantation is located in the tierra caliente. Consisting mostly of tropical lowlands, this elevation zone lies at the foot of the Andes on both the eastern and western sides. People who live in the tierra caliente must adapt to a hot year-round climate.

Physical Characteristics The tierra caliente is the lowest of the four elevation zones of the Andes, extending from sea level to approximately 3,000 feet. The climate of this zone is generally hot and humid, with the average temperature ranging from 75°F to 80°F.

Broadleaf evergreen forests cover the eastern slopes of the Andes Mountains heading into the Amazon River basin. On the western slopes of the Andes, the natural vegetation ranges from lush rainforests to **tropical grasslands**.

The Pacific coast of Peru is different. This area is also situated within the tropics, but it receives little rainfall. Here the land is mostly desert. Great sand dunes rise up in some places, whereas other parts are flat and rocky. Where there is water from rivers or streams, however, the vegetation is tropical.

**Tierra Caliente
75°F–80°F**

The Tierra Caliente

The tierra caliente is the lowest elevation zone in the central Andes. Conditions here are tropical. People dress in light clothing and live in houses open to the air. They also have to cope with tropical diseases like malaria.

Banana Plantation

Bananas thrive in the tierra caliente. They are grown on large plantations like this one. Many plantation workers are descended from Africans brought to South America as slaves.

Human Adaptations The tropical heat of the tierra caliente can make it an extremely difficult place to live. As a result, the area is less populated than the cooler, higher elevation zones. Some inhabitants are descended from the Africans who were brought by the Spanish to labor on large plantations as slaves. **Indigenous peoples** also live in some parts of the tropical rainforest.

People in this elevation zone have adapted to life within the tropics. Farmers plant crops that can do well in the heat, with some of the most common crops being bananas, rice, and sugarcane. People dress in light clothing, and they live in houses that are open to the cooling breezes. Their houses are often constructed of bamboo or wood, with palm-thatch roofs, and some houses have been raised on stilts to provide protection against flooding.

13.4 The Pleasant Uplands: Tierra Templada

In the rolling hills of Ecuador's tierra templada, gardeners are raising flowers, tending long rows of carnations, daisies, and roses. The flowers they grow will be shipped to buyers thousands of miles away. In fact, many of the roses enjoyed by Americans on Valentine's Day come from Ecuador because the mild weather of Ecuador provides the perfect climate for cultivating flowers.

Physical Characteristics The tierra templada is the second elevation zone of the Andes. It lies between approximately 3,000 and 6,000 feet above sea level. At these elevations, the climate is **temperate,** with temperatures ranging from 65°F to 75°F, with rarely any frost. This pleasant weather lasts throughout the year, which is why people often call the tierra templada "the Land of Eternal Spring."

In this zone, the types of vegetation change with elevation. At the lower elevations, tropical plants such as palms, bamboo, and jungle vines are quite common. At the higher elevations, broadleaf evergreen forests are typical.

Human Adaptations The mild climate of the tierra templada makes it a good place to live. As a result, this elevation zone is more populated than the tierra caliente. Many of the people who live here are *mestizos*. Mestizos are a mixture of indigenous and European peoples. European cultural influences are strong within the tierra templada.

Farmers in this zone choose their crops based on elevation. At lower levels, they grow heat-loving crops, like bananas and oranges. Higher up, they grow corn, beans, and other vegetables. They also grow flowers for export. However, the main commercial crop of the tierra templada is coffee because the conditions here are ideal for growing high-quality coffee beans. Most of the coffee is grown on small farms, but there are also large coffee plantations.

People who live in the tierra templada have adapted their housing and dress to the comfortable climate. They live in solid homes made of concrete brick or plaster and covered with tile roofs. More well-off residents may live on large estates called *haciendas*. During the heat of the day, people wear light clothing, but they switch to warmer clothing for the cool mornings and evenings.

The Tierra Templada
The tierra templada is the second elevation zone in the Andes. It has a pleasant, springlike climate year-round. This mild weather appealed to European settlers. Some of the largest cities in Latin America are found here.

Flower Growing
Flowers like these roses are an important crop in the tierra templada. Most flowers are shipped to Europe and the United States. Flower prices rise and fall depending on events in those distant markets. Flowers are one of the first things people stop buying in hard times.

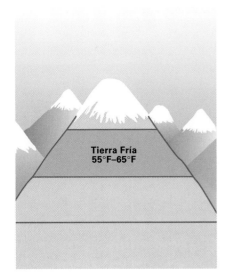

Tierra Fría
55°F–65°F

The Tierra Fría

The tierra fría reaches elevations of 12,000 feet. Many native peoples live in this zone. They have developed larger lungs to take in more oxygen from the thin air at these heights. Five hundred years ago, the centers of the Inca Empire were located here.

Market Day in Peru

The people at this market are wearing the dress of highland Indians. High-land markets are centers of vertical trade. Potatoes and wheat from the highlands are traded here for bananas and oranges from the lowlands.

13.5 The Cool Highlands: Tierra Fría

A woman rises early in the highland city of Cuzco, Peru. This is tierra fría, and the morning air is cold. The woman puts on a warm sweater and shawl and heads off to the market to buy food, walking down ancient stone streets built by her ancestors, the Incas. A light frost on the stones makes them slippery, so she steps carefully. She is accustomed to life in the highlands.

Physical Characteristics Covering much of the central Andes Mountains, the tierra fría elevation zone lies between 6,000 and 12,000 feet. The average temperatures within this zone vary from 55°F to 65°F, but the nights are colder. At higher elevations, the temperatures often dip below freezing.

Mountains and valleys are the main physical features of the tierra fría elevation zone. The mountains are steep and rugged, but flat **basins** and **plateaus** can be found among the peaks.

A high plateau called the Altiplano lies at an average elevation of over 11,000 feet between Peru and Bolivia. This plateau contains Lake Titicaca, the world's highest **navigable lake**. A navigable lake is one that is large and deep enough for large boats. Lake Titicaca is rumored to hold hidden treasure, according to legends that say the Incas threw gold into the lake to protect it from the Spanish invaders.

Vegetation within the tierra fría depends partly on the amount of rainfall. In some places, enough precipitation occurs to support dense forests of pines and other **conifers**. In other places the land is so dry that only shrubs and grasses can survive there.

Elevation is another factor that affects what grows where. The **tree line** in the central Andes lies between 10,000 and 12,000 feet. The tree line is the highest elevation at which trees will grow.

Human Adaptations Approximately half the population of the central Andes are indigenous peoples. Most of these people live in the tierra fría. The two main indigenous groups are the Quechua and the Aymara. Both of these groups were once part of the mighty Inca Empire.

Over the centuries, the native peoples of the Andes have adapted to life at high elevations. They wear warm woolen clothes to protect themselves from the cold. They also build thick-walled houses out of stone or **adobe** brick. Even their bodies have adapted to high elevations, as they have developed larger lungs that can draw more oxygen from the thin mountain air.

Farmers have adapted their practices to the highland environment. They grow crops that do well at high elevations. These crops include potatoes, wheat, barley, corn, apples, and pears.

Farmers also use **terracing** to carve fields out of steep hillsides, building walls on the slopes and filling them in with soil to create flat land for planting. They irrigate these terraces with mountain streams. This method of farming goes back many centuries. The Incas used terracing to build a great civilization.

Another sign of adaptation to life at high elevations is **vertical trade**. This is the trade of farm products between the higher and lower elevation zones of the Andes Mountains. Highland farmers cannot grow crops from the lower zones, such as bananas, oranges, and tomatoes. Therefore, traders bring those products up to the highland markets. The traders also take highland crops, such as potatoes and wheat, down to the lowland markets. Through vertical trade, people who live in one elevation zone can have access to foods grown in other elevation zones. In this way, they are able to achieve a more balanced and varied diet.

Making Freeze-Dried Potatoes
Long ago, Indians in the high Andes learned how to make chuño, or freeze-dried potatoes. They leave the potatoes out in the cold night air to freeze. The next day, they squeeze the water out of the thawing potatoes. They rinse them in the riverbed and then leave them out to dry. Chuño can be stored for years without spoiling.

The Tierra Helada

The tierra helada is the highest zone of the central Andes. Conditions here can be harsh. The climate is cold, and vegetation is sparse. People grow hardy crops like quinoa, a grain that is rich in protein. They also work in mines. The mines of Bolivia were once among the richest in the world.

13.6 The Icy High Elevations: Tierra Helada

Every year, many Quechua Indians hike to a shrine in the mountains high above the city of Cuzco. They travel there to worship the *apus,* or mountain gods. "We make offerings to the mountains," says one pilgrim, "asking them to send water for our crops and livestock."

The shrine above Cuzco is set in the tierra helada, the highest elevation zone of the Andes. The pilgrims who make this journey have to be careful to walk slowly because the air is very thin. If people move too quickly at this high elevation, they can experience altitude sickness from a lack of oxygen. Altitude sickness can cause headaches, fatigue, shortness of breath, and nausea.

Physical Characteristics The tierra helada lies between 12,000 and 15,000 feet, with average temperatures varying from 20°F to 55°F. This is an extreme environment. The climate is very cold and windy. It often freezes at night, and snow falls at the higher elevations. At the upper edge of this zone lies the **snow line,** which is the elevation at which permanent snow and ice begin. Above the snow line, snow remains on the ground year-round.

Most of the tierra helada lies above the tree line, which means that trees are very rare in this elevation zone. The most common forms of plant life are low-lying shrubs and hardy grasses, which are found in **alpine** meadows called *paramos* or *punas.*

Human Adaptations The tierra helada is a challenging environment for humans, which is why relatively few people live at these extreme elevations. Most of the people who live here are indigenous peoples like the Quechua and the Aymara.

Spinning Wool

These highland women are spinning wool from an alpaca into yarn. The yarn will then be woven into cloth. Alpaca wool is finer and straighter than sheep wool. It is one of the best fibers for making soft, warm garments.

People have adapted to life in the tierra helada in various ways. As in the tierra fría, they dress in warm clothing. They plant the few crops that will grow at high elevations, including a native grain called *quinoa,* along with certain types of potatoes. They also raise llamas and alpacas, two types of animals that are related to the camel. Llamas and alpacas produce thick wool for blankets, bags, and clothing. Llamas also make good pack animals for transporting heavy loads across the mountains.

Some of the people who live in this elevation zone work in mines. The high Andes have many mineral deposits, including tin, lead, copper, and silver. Working conditions in the mines are quite dangerous, with many miners contracting lung disease or getting injured on the job. However, mining does provide one of the few sources of cash income in this harsh environment.

Above the Snow Line The highest part of the Andes lies just above the tierra helada. This area extends from the snow line to the tops of the tallest mountain peaks. In this cold and rocky region, snow and ice cover much of the land.

This part of the Andes is generally not inhabited, but it still plays a key role in Andean life. The reason is **glaciers**. These large ice fields cover the highest peaks in the Andes, storing large amounts of water above the snow line. In the summer, water from melting glaciers flows down to people living at lower elevations. Streams fed by these glaciers form a crucial part of the water supply.

Glaciers are very sensitive to changes in climate. They can grow or shrink, depending on the changes in temperature and precipitation that occur over time. If glaciers melt too fast, the result can be disastrous for the people who are living below them. "Glaciers don't always behave nicely," said a scientist who studies them. "Some glaciers have a nasty habit of storing up large amounts of water and then releasing it suddenly in a massive melt…which may involve floods, landslides, or avalanches."

Shrinking Andes Glaciers

This satellite image shows a shrinking glacier in the Andes. There is still enough ice in this glacier to feed mountain streams year round. But if the glacier disappears, some of those streams may run dry part of the year.

13.7 Beginning to Think Globally

In this chapter, you read about the four elevation zones in the central Andes Mountains. Each of these elevation zones has its own climate and vegetation. You have also learned how people have adapted to the conditions in each zone.

In other parts of the world, people have made different adaptations to mountain living. In general, however, relatively few people in the world live at high elevations because the conditions of life there are just too difficult.

In the future, mountains may become more attractive to people as places to live. There are signs that the world's climate is getting warmer, and if this warming trend continues, life will change at higher elevations. For example, tree lines and snow lines are likely to rise. As mountains become warmer, more people may choose to live at higher elevations. At the same time, a warmer climate is likely to have a negative effect on mountain glaciers. Keep this in mind as you look at glaciers in the next section.

13.8 Global Connections

The map to the right shows glaciers around the world. There are about 160,000 glaciers worldwide today. Some of these glaciers are found in lowland cold areas such as Antarctica, whereas others have formed on high mountain peaks. Can you find examples of both lowland glaciers and mountain glaciers on the map?

What is happening to mountain glaciers around the world? Many mountain glaciers are retreating, or shrinking. Look at the image of the Gangotri Glacier, which is a mountain glacier that is located in the Himalayas. The lines on the photograph show how Gangotri Glacier has retreated over time. Not all glaciers are shrinking, however. Some are staying the same size or even expanding.

Why are some mountain glaciers retreating? Most scientists blame climate change for the shrinking of glaciers. These scientists say that Earth's climate has been slowly warming. These rising temperatures are causing glaciers to melt more than they have in the past. As their ice turns to water, the glaciers retreat.

What impact do retreating glaciers have on people living in mountainous regions? Approximately 75 percent of the world's fresh water is frozen inside glaciers. When glaciers melt, they provide water for people to use. For example, the glaciers near Quito, Ecuador, supply about 80 percent of this South American city's water. If Quito's glaciers continue to shrink, they will provide less and less water to the city. "It's kind of like a bank account," said one scientist. "When you've withdrawn all the water, there isn't any more."

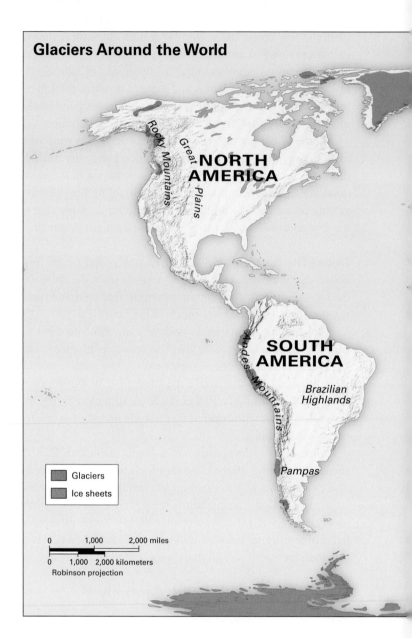

Glaciers Around the World

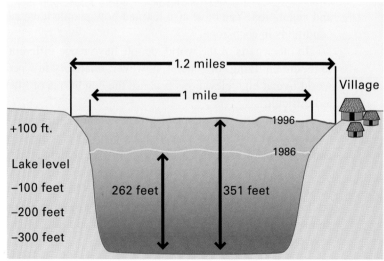

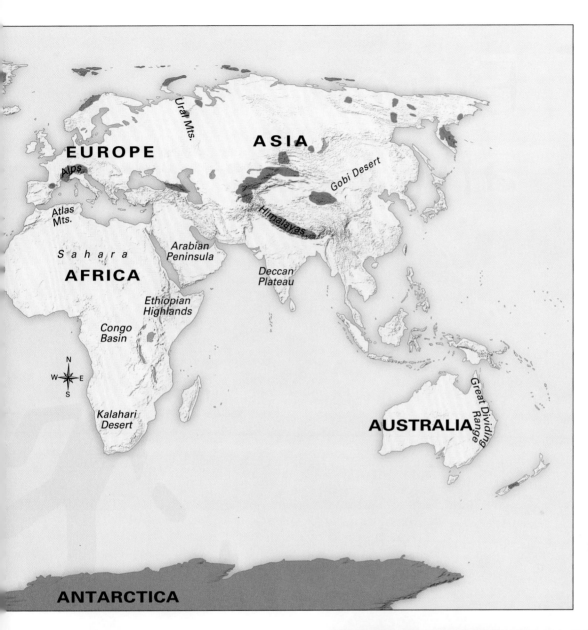

ASIA

EUROPE

Ural Mts.

Alps

Gobi Desert

Atlas
Mts.

Himalayas

Sahara

Arabian
Peninsula

AFRICA

Deccan
Plateau

Ethiopian
Highlands

Congo
Basin

N
W   E
S

Great Dividing Range

AUSTRALIA

Kalahari
Desert

ANTARCTICA

◄ **Lake Raphstreng Tsho**

This diagram shows changes in
Raphstreng Tsho, a glacial lake in the
Himalaya mountain range of Asia. As the
glaciers that feed the lake melt, its water
level rises. Between 1986 and 1996, the
lake's water level rose by 89 feet.

Gangotri Glacier ▶

This satellite image shows the Gangotri
Glacier in 2001. It is one of the largest
glaciers in the Himalayas. The lines added
to the image show how this glacier has
shrunk since 1780.

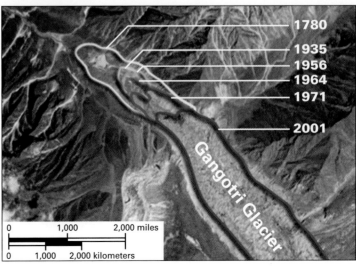

1780

1935
1956
1964
1971

2001

Gangotri Glacier

0   1,000   2,000 miles

0   1,000   2,000 kilometers

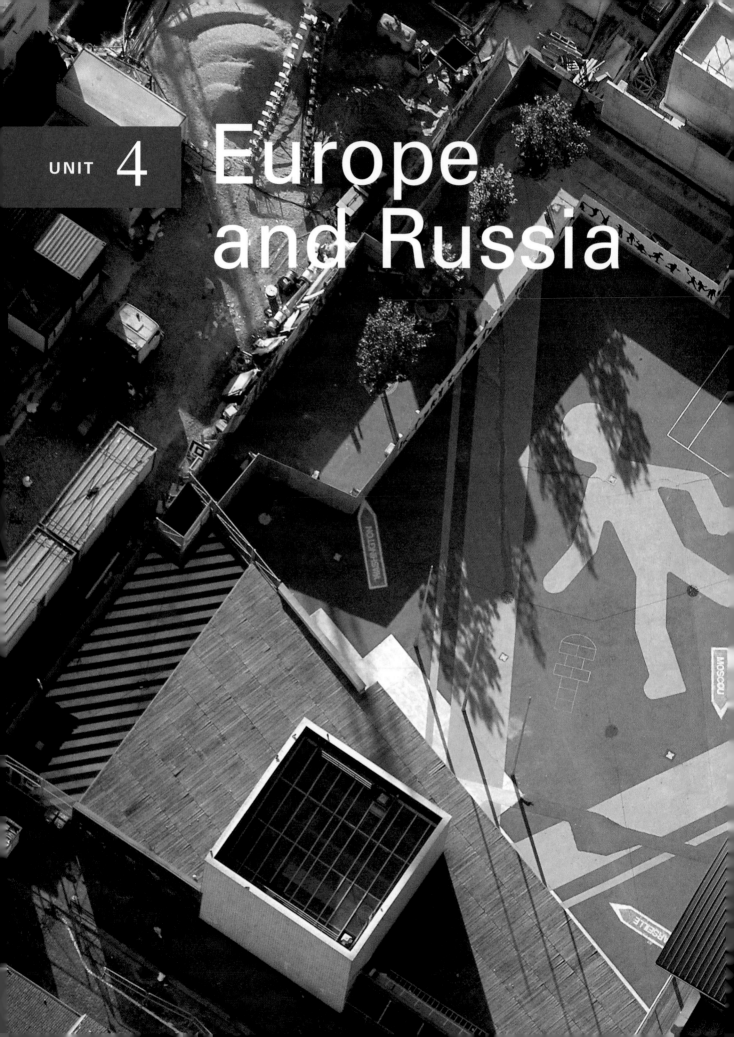

UNIT **4**

Europe
and Russia

Introducing the Region:
Physical and Human Geography

What do you see in this photograph?
See page 514 for details.

▼

Europe and Russia occupy part of the huge **landmass** called Eurasia. Eurasia reaches from the Atlantic to the Pacific Ocean. It is so large that geographers divide it into two continents, Europe and Asia.

Europe is the world's second smallest continent. Oceans and seas border Europe to the north, south, and west. Asia borders Europe on the east.

Russia is the world's largest country. It spreads over two continents. Western Russia lies on the continent of Europe. Eastern Russia stretches across Asia to the Pacific Ocean. The Ural Mountains, at 60°E longitude, mark the dividing line between Europe and Asia, and between western Russia and eastern Russia.

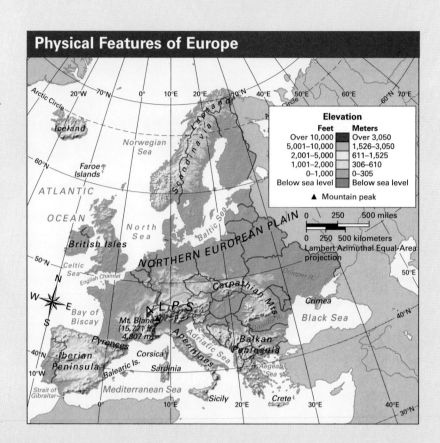

Physical Features of Europe

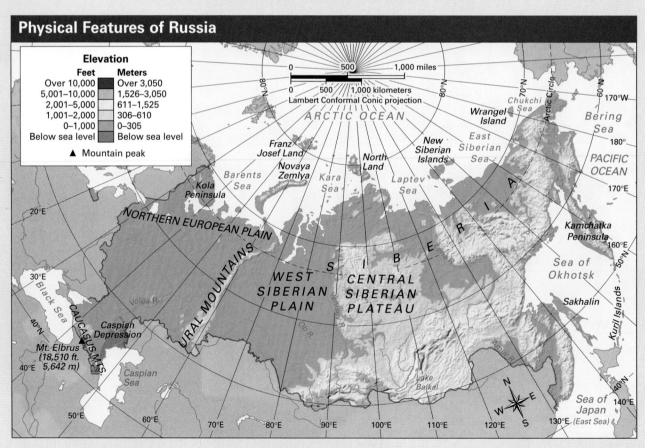

Physical Features of Russia

Physical Features

Europe and Russia share a **landscape** of sweeping plains and rugged mountains. Large rivers wander across the broad plains. These rivers drain into three of the world's four oceans—the Atlantic, the Pacific, and the Arctic oceans.

Europe

On a map, the European landmass looks like a giant **peninsula** attached to Eurasia. Smaller peninsulas jut out from all sides of Europe. They include the Balkan Peninsula, the Iberian Peninsula, Italy, and Scandinavia. Various seas, bays, and gulfs are tucked in between. Several big islands are also part of Europe.

Much of Europe lies on the Northern European Plain. This plain is one of the largest expanses of flat land on Earth. From east to west, it extends almost 2,500 miles. Several mountain ranges cut across Europe. The snowcapped Alps form a major barrier between central and southern Europe. The Pyrenees range separates France and Spain. The Apennines run through Italy.

Europe's large rivers serve as water highways. They are also a source of drinking water and of power for electricity. The Danube River flows through six countries, more than any other major river in the world.

Russia

Much of Russia also lies on broad plains. The western, or European, part of Russia shares the Northern European Plain. Western Russia

The Alps cut through France, Italy, Switzerland, Liechtenstein, Austria, and Slovenia.

extends to the Ural Mountains in the east and to the Caucasus Mountains in the south.

From the Ural Mountains, eastern Russia spreads across the full width of Asia. This area is called Siberia. The West Siberian Plain is a large area of flat land with many lakes and swamps. To the east lies the Central Siberian Plateau. Rivers have carved narrow canyons through this high, flat plateau.

Russia has thousands of lakes. The largest of these, Lake Baikal, is the oldest and deepest lake in the world. It holds one fifth of Earth's fresh water. In winter, the lake is frozen with ice up to three feet deep. In summer, Baikal is warm enough for swimming.

At the eastern edge of Russia, the Kamchatka Peninsula reaches out into the Pacific Ocean. More than 100 **volcanoes** rise from this finger of land. No roads or railroads connect the peninsula to Siberia. Everything must arrive by airplane or boat.

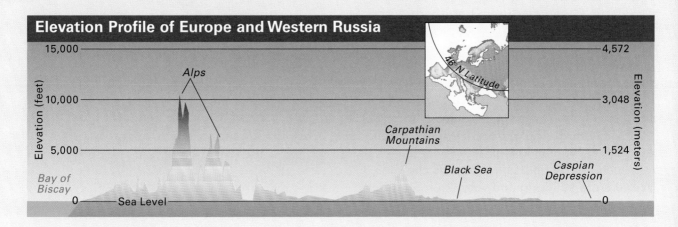

Elevation Profile of Europe and Western Russia

Alps — Carpathian Mountains — Black Sea — Caspian Depression — Bay of Biscay

Elevation (feet): 15,000 / 10,000 / 5,000 / Sea Level 0

Elevation (meters): 4,572 / 3,048 / 1,524 / 0

46° N Latitude

Climate

Two factors shape the climates of Europe. The first is latitude. Areas to the south of the Alps enjoy more **temperate** climates than those areas to the north.

The second factor is **relative location**. Areas near the ocean have a **marine climate**. *Marine* means found in or close to the sea. Ocean winds and warm ocean currents help keep temperatures about the same all year.

Inland areas far from the sea have a **continental climate**. *Continental* means influenced by a large landmass, like a continent. Cooling ocean breezes in summer and warming ocean currents in winter do not affect places with a continental climate. As a result, summers are usually hotter than near the sea, while winters are longer and colder.

Europe

Every year, crowds of tourists head to the Mediterranean Sea for vacation. Southern Europe has a **Mediterranean** climate. Its summers are longer, hotter, and drier than in northern Europe. Mediterranean winters are short and mild.

Most of northern Europe enjoys a **marine west coast** climate. A warm current that flows across the Atlantic Ocean from the Gulf of Mexico keeps winters from becoming too cold. Cool ocean breezes keep summers from becoming too hot. These same breezes bring year-round rain to northern Europe.

Russia

Russia is known for its long, harsh winters. The Arctic Ocean on Russia's northern border is frozen most of the year. As a result, it does not have a marine influence on Russia's climate. In some areas, snow covers the ground for eight or nine months of the year.

The most northern part of Russia has a **tundra** climate. The weather is so cold all year that the land is always frozen. Winter temperatures can drop as low as –90°F.

Much of Siberia has a **subarctic** climate. Winters are still long and very cold. Summers are too cool and short for farming.

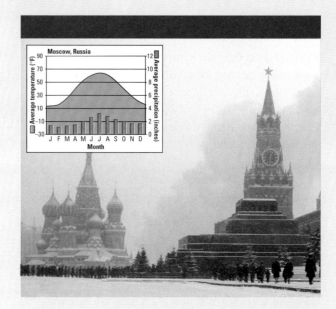

Moscow, the capital of Russia, has a humid continental climate. When are people living in Moscow likely to have very high heating bills?

Areas to the south and west have milder climates. Much of western Russia has a **humid continental** climate. Winters here are still freezing cold, but summers can be hot and steamy. The most southern parts of Russia have a **semiarid** climate. Here the hot summers and cool winters are both fairly dry. Most of Russia's crops are grown in these areas with longer growing seasons.

Vegetation

Europe and Russia have a mix of **vegetation zones,** but forests are the most common. The largest forest on Earth, the Russian **taiga,** stretches across most of the Eurasian landmass.

Three types of forests are found in this region—**deciduous, coniferous,** and **mixed forests**. All three are named for the types of trees that are found in them. Deciduous trees have broad, flat leaves that drop each fall. Coniferous trees have needle-like leaves that stay green all year. Mixed forests have both deciduous and coniferous trees.

Europe

All three types of forests once thrived in Europe. But over time, people cleared the forested areas to use the land for farming. Pockets of deciduous and mixed forests can still be found. Large coniferous forests survive in the far northern parts of the continent.

The coastal parts of Europe bordering the Mediterranean Sea are covered with **chaparral**. Here the small trees and bushes are well adapted to long, rainless summers. They send their roots deep into the soil to search for hidden water sources. Most have thick bark and small leaves that keep them

The Russian taiga accounts for about one fifth of Earth's total forested area.

from losing water during the dry season. Olive trees and cork trees are common in this vegetation zone.

Russia

In northern Russia, the **tundra** is treeless. Because the ground is always frozen under the surface, trees cannot send their roots down into the soil. During the short summer, the top layer of soil thaws. Then, for about two months, mosses, grasses, and scrubs cover the ground.

South of the tundra lies the taiga, a vast region of thick, dark forests. The taiga consists mainly of coniferous trees such as cedar, fir, pine, and spruce. Further south, the taiga becomes more mixed forest with the addition of aspen, birch, and other deciduous trees.

Far to the south lie the **steppes,** or grassy plains, of Russia. This region of **temperate grasslands** is too dry to support trees. The steppes have mostly been plowed for farms.

Summer sun thaws the surface of Siberia's tundra. With the return of winter, this boggy area will freeze solid.

The region of Europe and Russia is home to 43 countries. You've learned that Russia is the world's largest country. It covers about 6.6 million square miles. At the other extreme, Vatican City is the world's smallest country. It covers only 109 acres. It lies in the center of the city of Rome, Italy.

The people of Europe and Russia are linked together by language and culture. At least 50 languages are spoken here. Yet most of them belong to just three language families: Latin, Germanic, and Slavic. Europeans and Russians also share many elements of culture. These include art, music, and religion.

Political Boundaries of Russia

Political Boundaries of Europe and Western Russia

History

Europeans and Russians are also linked together by history. Over thousands of years, peoples and armies have moved back and forth across this region. Ideas and ways of life have moved with them.

Early Times

Two great civilizations appeared in Europe in ancient times. The first arose on the Greek peninsula in the 700s B.C.E. The Greeks created distinct styles of art and literature. They also invented the idea of democracy.

The second great civilization arose on the Italian peninsula. Around 500 B.C.E., the city of Rome began to grow. It would become a mighty **empire**. At its peak, the Roman Empire included most of Europe.

Roman rule collapsed in the late 400s. But the Romans left behind their language and ideas about law and government.

The Rise of Nations

After the fall of Rome, many small kingdoms appeared across Europe and Russia. A local chief or lord ruled each one.

In time, some rulers expanded the lands under their control. Sometimes this was done through marriage. In 1469, for example, Prince Ferdinand of Aragon married Princess Isabella of Castile. The union of Aragon and Castile led to the rise of the **nation** of Spain.

More often, nations were built through war. In 1533, a ruler known as Ivan the Terrible became the Grand Prince of Moscow. Ivan used his army to conquer vast lands south and east of Moscow. In 1547, he had himself crowned czar, or ruler, of all Russia.

As nations grew in power, their rulers looked for new lands to conquer. For the czars of Russia, this meant expanding east across Asia. For rulers in Europe, it meant founding colonies in the Americas, Africa, and Asia.

The Modern Era

Two kinds of revolutions shaped Europe and Russia in more recent times. The first was economic. The **Industrial Revolution** began in the 1700s. It moved the production of goods out of homes and into factories. Machines began to take over work that had been done by hand. European nations led this revolution. They became the world's first **developed countries**.

The second kind of revolution was political. Political revolutions led to changes in how countries were ruled. In some cases, they led to the rise of democratic governments. The Glorious Revolution of 1688–89 is an example. It limited the power of England's monarchs. This was a step toward democracy.

In other cases, political revolutions led to the rise of **dictators**. A dictator is a leader who rules a country with absolute power, and often with brutal force. In 1917, the Russian Revolution drove the last czar from power. A series of dictators then ruled for more than 70 years.

Today, elected governments rule most countries in this region.

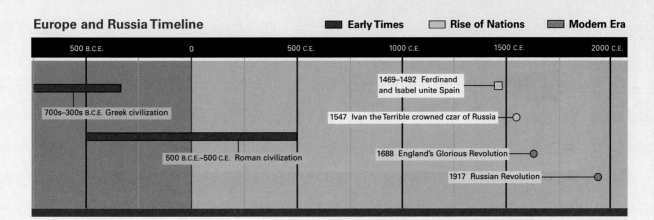

Europe and Russia Timeline ■ Early Times ▢ Rise of Nations ■ Modern Era

500 B.C.E. 0 500 C.E. 1000 C.E. 1500 C.E. 2000 C.E.

700s–300s B.C.E. Greek civilization

500 B.C.E.–500 C.E. Roman civilization

1469–1492 Ferdinand and Isabel unite Spain

1547 Ivan the Terrible crowned czar of Russia

1688 England's Glorious Revolution

1917 Russian Revolution

Population

Europe and Russia are home to one seventh of the world's people. In 2000, about 875 million people lived in this region. Most of them live west of the Urals.

Europe has long been very **urban**. Rome was the first city to reach 1 million people. That was 2,000 years ago. In 1810, London became the first modern city to reach a million people. Today, most Europeans and Russians live in towns and cities. **Rural** eastern Russia is thinly settled.

Most parts of the world have growing populations. But in parts of Europe and Russia, populations have stopped growing. Some are even shrinking. The main reason is a drop in the **birth rate,** or the number of births per 1,000 people.

Christianity is the most common religion in Europe and Russia. More than half of all Europeans belong to the Roman Catholic Church. Most Christians in Russia follow the Russian Orthodox faith. Islam is the second largest faith in this region.

Europe and Russia: Major Religions

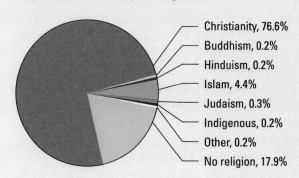

- Christianity, 76.6%
- Buddhism, 0.2%
- Hinduism, 0.2%
- Islam, 4.4%
- Judaism, 0.3%
- Indigenous, 0.2%
- Other, 0.2%
- No religion, 17.9%

Europe and Russia: Urban and Rural Population, 2000

Urban, 72.7%

Rural, 27.3%

= 10% of the total population

Europe and Russia: Population Growth, 1950–2050

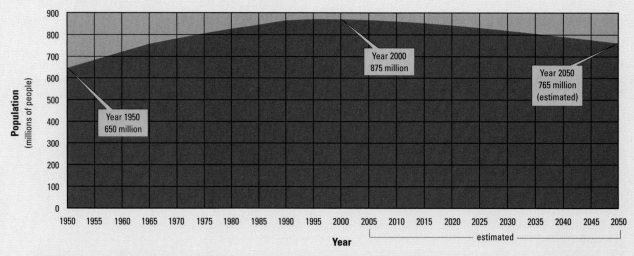

Year 2000
875 million

Year 2050
765 million
(estimated)

Year 1950
650 million

Population (millions of people)

Year

estimated

Sources: *Population Division of the Department of Economic and Social Affairs of the United Nations Secretariat,* "World Population Prospects: The 2004 Revision" and "World Urbanization Prospects: The 2003 Revision," esa.un.org/unpp. "Religion," *Encyclopædia Britannica,* 2005, Encyclopædia Britannica Premium Service, www.britannica.com.

In Poland, much of the land is used for commercial farming.

Economic Activity

Europe and Russia are both important industrial areas. Russian factories produce heavy machinery, such as tractors and electric motors. Factories in Denmark turn out stereos, furniture, dishes, and silverware. German factories produce steel, automobiles, and electronics. Swiss factories turn out watches, chocolate, and medicines. Global trade has made Europe and Russia one of the world's richest regions.

Resources

Europe and Russia are rich in **natural resources**. These include **fossil fuels** and minerals. About a third of the world's coal reserves are found in Siberia. In addition, Siberia has mines for gold, copper, lead, and diamonds.

In the North Sea and Russia, people drill for petroleum and **natural gas**. Russia is also a major producer of **hydroelectric power**. Most of this power comes from dams located along Russia's rivers.

Land Use

Outside of its cities, Europe is largely a land of farms. Commercial farms are spread along river valleys and across the Northern European Plain. In Western Europe, farmers use machines to produce large **cash crops**. In poorer parts of Eastern Europe, however, some families are limited to **subsistence farming** on small plots of land.

In Scandinavia, **forestry** and fishing are both big industries. Even though Norway is very far north, a warm ocean current keeps some ports free of ice. As a result, fishing can continue all year. Fishing is also the main industry of Iceland.

Manufacturing has become important to Russia over the last 75 years. But many Russians still use their land in more traditional ways. In southern Russia, farmers grow a wide variety of crops, from wheat to apples. Across the taiga, forestry is a major industry. On the northern tundra, people herd reindeer. Reindeer are a source of meat and hides.

Supranational Cooperation in the European Union

14

14.1 Introduction

Have you ever traveled from the United States to another country? If so, you know that crossing international borders isn't as easy as crossing state borders within the U.S. You probably had to stop and show identification. You might have had to trade your U.S. dollars for a different type of money.

Now imagine that you're in Europe, crossing the border between France and Germany. You don't have to stop to show your passport. You use the same money in both countries. The main difference you notice after crossing the border is a change in language—people here are speaking German instead of French.

People today travel easily between many European countries because of the **European Union,** or EU. The EU is a *supranational* organization. In 2004, it had 25 member countries. *Supra* is a Latin prefix that means "above" or "over." The government of the European Union stands above the governments of its members. Because it is supranational, the EU has been able to remove barriers that once made travel between European nations complicated. In addition to having "open" borders with each other, many EU nations use a common form of money.

While EU countries use **supranational cooperation** to work toward shared goals, they remain separate countries. These countries are united in certain ways, but divided in others. In this chapter, you will learn about the forces that work for and against supranational cooperation in the EU.

Essential Question

What forces work for and against supranational cooperation among nations?

These two maps show Europe. The highlighted countries are members of the European Union. The map on the left represents things that unite EU countries. The map on the right represents things that pull EU countries apart. Keep these maps in mind as you try to answer the Essential Question.

Graphic Organizer

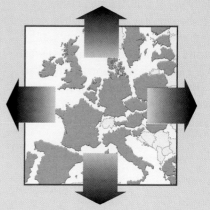

◀ European Union flag flying over a city in the Czech Republic

14.2 The Geographic Setting

Europe is a region made up of many peoples and countries. Throughout Europe's history, certain forces have brought its peoples together, while others have pulled them apart. The forces that bring things together, or unite them, are called **centripetal forces**. The forces that divide things, or move them away from one another, are called **centrifugal forces**. The European Union was formed to unite countries that had been torn apart by years of war.

A History of Bloody Conflict For much of its history, Europe has been a battleground. During the first half of the 20th century, European nations were torn apart by two devastating wars that also spread to other parts of the world. Both wars were so widespread that people now remember them as "world wars."

The First World War began in 1914. This bloody conflict lasted four long years and caused the deaths of over 21 million people. The Second World War broke out in 1939. On one side of the conflict were the Axis powers—Germany, Italy, Japan, and other countries. The Allies—Great Britain, the Soviet Union, the United States, and their allies—opposed the Axis.

World War II was even more deadly than World War I. It lasted six years and claimed the lives of 50 million people worldwide. The fighting left many European cities and farms in ruins. When the guns finally fell silent in 1945, Europeans wanted to make sure that such horrors never happened again.

Creating a Future of Peaceful Cooperation On May 9, 1950, a French leader named Robert Schuman made a famous speech. In his talk, he put forward ideas for bringing a lasting peace to Europe. These ideas led to what is now the European Union.

Schuman suggested that France, Germany, and other European countries work together to manage their coal and steel production. If these countries learned to cooperate, he said, they would not be so likely to make war on each other.

Six countries agreed with Schuman. By 1952, they had all ratified a treaty that formed the European Coal and Steel Community. This group created a **common market** for steel and coal products. In a common market, countries reduce or remove trade barriers, such as **tariffs**. Tariffs are taxes on goods that cross country borders. Belgium, France, West Germany, Italy, Luxembourg, and the Netherlands all became members of the community.

By 1958, the same six countries created the European Economic Community (EEC), which then removed trade barriers for all kinds of goods. The EEC came to be known as the Common Market. Over the years, more European countries joined the Common Market.

In 1993, twelve Common Market countries formed the European Union. The main goal of the EU is to promote peace and prosperity, which means economic well-being. The EU works toward this goal by seeking to create jobs, protect citizens' rights, and preserve the environment. It also has programs to promote freedom, security, and justice for its members. In 2004, the EU had 25 member countries spread across Europe, with several other countries hoping to join.

World War II Destruction

On May 14, 1940, German planes bombed the city of Rotterdam in the Netherlands. Much of the city was destroyed. Many other cities in Europe were also bombed during World War II. The EU was formed to make sure such horrors never happened again.

▶ Geoterms

centrifugal force a force that divides people and countries

centripetal force a force that unites people and countries

common market a group of countries that acts as a single market, without trade barriers between member countries

supranational cooperation a form of international cooperation in which countries give up some control of their affairs as they work together to achieve shared goals

The European Union, 2004

Legend:
- Original member countries, 1952
- Countries joining from 1973 to 1995
- Countries joining in 2004
- € Countries using the euro
- **1995** Date of admission

The Growth of the European Union

Before 2004, all of the European Union countries were in Western Europe. In 2004, ten new member countries put Central and Eastern Europe on the EU map. The European Union promotes cooperation among member countries.

14.3 Economic Cooperation in the EU

In the United States, people move freely across state borders. Some work in one state and live in another. In Europe before the EU, citizens did not have a similar freedom to move between countries. National laws made it hard for citizens of one country to live or work in a different country.

Before the EU, each European country had its own rules about who could live or find work within its borders. Each country had its own **currency,** or type of money. Individual countries also charged tariffs, or taxes, on goods imported from its neighbors, making these goods expensive for citizens to buy.

Today members of the EU work together toward shared economic goals. Many centripetal forces promote such economic cooperation. At the same time, centrifugal forces work against unity.

Economic Forces That Unite the EU The creation of a common market has been an important economic force uniting the EU. This single market benefits EU consumers in several ways. With goods moving freely across borders, people have more choices about what to buy. The elimination of tariffs on EU goods has lowered prices for EU consumers. The common market benefits workers as well. They are able to travel freely to other EU countries to find work.

The adoption of a common currency in 2002 has also helped unite the EU. The common currency is called the **euro,** and in many EU countries, it has replaced the national currency. No longer do Europeans change money when they cross most borders. The euro makes it easier to travel and trade across the EU.

By joining their economies, EU members have also created a powerful **trade bloc**. A trade bloc is a group of countries that act together to increase their influence over world trade. Hundreds of millions of consumers live in the EU trade bloc. As a result, outside nations are eager to do business in the EU. The size of its market has made the EU trade bloc an important force in the global economy.

EU countries share other economic goals. The EU works to create jobs, develop resources, and make improvements that encourage trade. For example, the EU has spent large sums to upgrade highways. It has also helped farmers modernize their operations.

The EU Trade Bloc

This graph compares the GDP of the EU to other large countries. GDP is the total value of goods and services produced in a place. By joining together, members of the EU trade bloc have far more economic power than they would have acting alone.

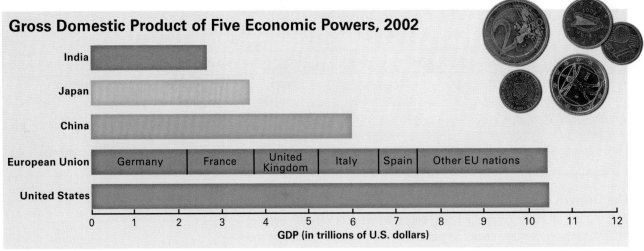

Gross Domestic Product of Five Economic Powers, 2002

		GDP (in trillions of U.S. dollars)
India		
Japan		
China		
European Union	Germany / France / United Kingdom / Italy / Spain / Other EU nations	
United States		

Source: *The World Factbook 2004*, Central Intelligence Agency.

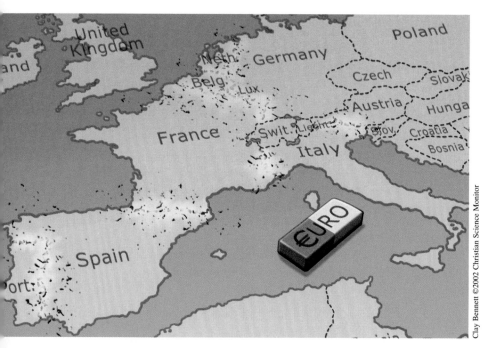

Erasing EU Borders
In January 2002, the euro became the currency in 12 EU countries. About 291 million people traded in their old money for euros. To prepare for this change, banks were stocked with 12.5 billion new bills and 76 billion coins. According to this cartoon, what effect has the euro had on Europe?

Economic Forces That Divide the EU Other forces work against economic cooperation. EU members don't always agree on the many issues they face. Nor do they always see eye to eye on how EU money should be spent.

In general, the Western European members of the EU are wealthier than those in Central and Eastern Europe. In an effort to bring all of its members up to the same level, the EU spends large sums of money on projects in its poorer nations. Some Western Europeans object to so much EU money being spent outside their own area.

Economic differences between EU members create other strains. Generally, workers in Western Europe are paid higher wages than those in Central and Eastern Europe. Living costs are higher in Western Europe as well. These factors have led some Western European businesses to move manufacturing to poorer EU countries. Costs are lower there, and they can pay workers less. As a result, workers in Western Europe worry about losing jobs to poorer EU countries.

Wage differences also encourage workers in poorer EU countries to move to richer ones in search of jobs. Workers in the wealthier countries often resent these immigrants. They also fear that too many newcomers from poor countries will drive down wages for everyone.

There are centrifugal forces at work in the use of the euro as well. Not all EU countries adopted the common currency in 2002. Three members decided to keep their own currency and make their own decisions about money. Other countries have not been allowed to adopt the euro. Before joining the euro zone, they must show that they have developed stable economies. (See the map in Section 14.2, which shows which countries use the euro.)

As you can see, both centripetal and centrifugal economic forces are at work in the European Union. But overall, EU member countries have decided that the economic benefits of supranational cooperation outweigh the costs.

14.4 Political Cooperation in the EU

Before the EU was formed, there were many political divisions among European countries. Each nation was independent, setting its own individual policies. Nations could choose to work together, but they did not have to. As you have read, political conflict was often more common than cooperation.

The EU encourages political cooperation among its members, in part through its common EU government. This government does not replace the governments of individual member countries. Rather, the EU government is supranational—it operates above the governments of its members. All member countries participate in the EU government.

How the EU Government Unites Europe The EU government works in two ways to unite Europe. First, it brings its members together to focus on issues they all share. For example, it tries to take a common approach to environmental problems.

Second, the EU encourages Europeans to think of themselves as citizens of Europe. European citizenship operates on top of citizenship of a home country, and gives individuals certain benefits. For example, citizens of member countries can live and work anywhere in the EU. They can also vote in EU elections. They have these rights no matter where they live in the EU.

The EU government has several important bodies. The Council of the European Union, the main decision-making body for the EU, is made up of national leaders from each member country. The council sets overall goals for the EU.

The European Commission, the executive body of the EU government, is made up of commissioners appointed by member governments. The commission proposes new laws to the Council and Parliament, and handles the day-to-day business of carrying out EU policies. It also makes sure members abide by EU treaties and laws, taking rule-breakers to the EU's judicial branch, the Court of Justice, if needed.

The European Parliament is the largest EU body, with 700 members directly elected by citizens of EU countries. The main job of Parliament is to pass European laws, a task it shares with the Council. Parliament and Council also share the job of approving the EU budget. Together they determine how money should be spent on various EU projects.

The EU government helps to unite Europe by speaking with one voice for all of its members. Within Europe, the EU focuses on shared issues, such as transportation and the environment. Outside of Europe, the EU works to strengthen Europe's role in the world. By working together, EU members have more power in world affairs than any one European country would have by itself. In these ways, the EU government acts as a centripetal force in Europe.

How the EU Government Divides Europe There are centrifugal forces at work as well in the EU government. When a country joins the European Union, it is expected to give up some power to the EU government. This means that the country must carry out EU decisions even if it does not agree with a given policy.

Giving up power has been a problem for many EU members. Some countries still want to make independent decisions in areas like defense

The EU Headquarters

The EU government works on issues shared by member countries. Its headquarters is in Brussels, Belgium. In 2004, this was the center of government for more than 450 million people in 25 countries. Because of this, some might call Brussels the "capital of Europe."

and foreign affairs—especially when they don't agree with EU decisions on these matters.

The growing size of the EU is also a centrifugal force. By 2004, the EU included more than 450 million people in 25 countries. As the size of the EU has increased, so have the differences among the EU's nations and peoples. With more countries and cultures, cooperation has become more difficult.

Finally, the idea of European citizenship has been hard for some Europeans to embrace. A recent poll of Europeans found that almost half would not mind if the EU simply disappeared. People who feel this way may fear that their national identity will get lost in the push for a more united Europe. For them, the advantages of political cooperation may not be worth the costs.

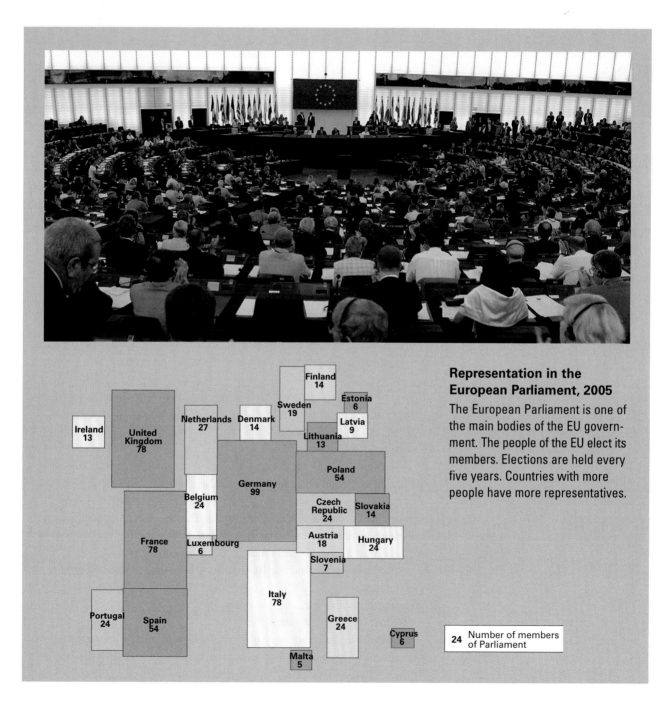

Representation in the European Parliament, 2005

The European Parliament is one of the main bodies of the EU government. The people of the EU elect its members. Elections are held every five years. Countries with more people have more representatives.

Ireland 13 · United Kingdom 78 · Netherlands 27 · Denmark 14 · Finland 14 · Estonia 6 · Sweden 19 · Latvia 9 · Lithuania 13 · Belgium 24 · Germany 99 · Poland 54 · Czech Republic 24 · Slovakia 14 · France 78 · Luxembourg 6 · Austria 18 · Hungary 24 · Slovenia 7 · Italy 78 · Portugal 24 · Spain 54 · Greece 24 · Cyprus 6 · Malta 5

24 Number of members of Parliament

Europe Day in the EU

Celebrations and symbols help create a cultural identity. Every year on May 9, people celebrate Europe Day. The day honors Europe's "birthday." It was on this day in 1950 that Robert Schuman proposed creating a more united Europe. Symbols like the EU flag add to the feeling of a shared culture.

14.5 Cultural Cooperation in the EU

In the year 2000, students across the European Union took part in a contest to create a motto for the EU. These students sent in more than 2,000 possible mottos. After considering the students' ideas, the EU announced its choice in 2003: "United in Diversity."

The words in this motto are important. The goal of the EU is to unite Europeans to form an "ever closer union." Since the EU began, it has worked toward a common European **cultural identity**. At the same time, the EU recognizes the **diversity** of its members, and sees diversity as a strength. The word *diversity* refers to all the ways in which people are different from one another. Areas of diversity may include language, religion, ethnicity, beliefs, traditions, and values. These aspects of culture are what make each member country of the EU unique.

How the EU Promotes a European Cultural Identity A common cultural identity is a centripetal force. To help make EU countries "United in Diversity," the EU has made it a goal to encourage a common European cultural identity.

One way the EU encourages a European cultural identity is through the use of common cultural symbols. The European flag, which shows a circle of 12 yellow stars on a blue background, symbolizes unity. It was originally created by the Council of Europe, which encouraged all European institutions to adopt the symbol. When the EU formed, it also used the flag as the official emblem of European unity.

Another symbol that the EU has adopted is the European anthem, which takes its melody from Ludwig van Beethoven's Ninth Symphony. When used as the anthem, it is always played without words, in the "universal language of music."

Europe Day is another symbol of European unity. Europeans celebrate Europe Day on May 9, the anniversary of the date in 1950 when Robert Schuman first proposed a supranational European organization.

Europe Day has become a time for Europeans to come together to share and celebrate their common culture.

The EU also supports cultural programs. One example is the European Union Youth Wind Orchestra. It brings together young musicians from across Europe. Also, each year the EU chooses one or two cities to be European Capitals of Culture. The EU pays for special shows and events that highlight that city and its culture.

As you have read, EU passports and the euro make travel easy within the EU. As Europeans visit other EU countries, they come to view Europe as a united region. The EU also encourages people, especially youth, to learn other European languages. Its long-term goal is for all Europeans to learn two languages in addition to their home language.

Forces Working Against a European Cultural Identity Sometimes cultural diversity can become a centrifugal force that the EU has to work to overcome. The EU celebrates the diversity of languages in Europe, yet those many languages can sometimes make communication hard. To overcome the communication barrier, the EU must translate all of its speeches and documents into 20 languages. In 2004 alone, the EU had to translate more than 2 million pages.

Other centrifugal forces work against a shared cultural identity. National pride is one of them, as countries have a hard time putting the interests of all of Europe above their national interests. Competition and rivalry between countries can make cooperation a challenge.

Cultural traditions sometimes clash even at EU headquarters. For example, traditional Czech foods are often cooked slowly, tasting even better the next day. Yet EU rules for their cafeteria state that cooked food can't be served if it is more than two hours old. One Czech citizen complained, "This will make many of our best dishes illegal!"

Cultural Clashes in the EU
Cultural traditions can divide EU members. For example, bullfighting is a cultural tradition in Spain. Every year, matadors kill thousands of bulls in bullfights. In other EU countries, bullfighting is seen as cruel. Many Europeans think that bullfights should be banned.

14.6 Beginning to Think Globally

In this chapter, you learned about the European Union. The EU is built on supranational cooperation. You read about centripetal forces that work toward such cooperation. You also read about centrifugal forces that work against unity.

The EU is the best example of supranational cooperation in the world today. It works because its member countries have been willing to give up some power. Just how much power remains an issue. Some Europeans want the EU to become a "United States of Europe." Others fear giving up any more power to the EU.

Cooperation among nations is not limited to Europe. Other countries also work together on problems they share. In the next section, you'll look at several examples of international cooperation around the world.

14.7 Global Connections

The map shows international organizations in the world today. The countries in these organizations work together on common issues. The most truly international organization is the United Nations (UN). Its members include almost every country in the world.

What kinds of international organizations do countries join?

Countries form many kinds of organizations. Some organizations work to promote the economic well-being of their members. The Free Trade Area of the Americas (FTAA) is a good example. Others bring nations together to defend themselves. The North Atlantic Treaty Organization (NATO) is a defense organization.

Are all international organizations like the EU?

The EU is the best example of a true supranational organization. Other organizations have more limited goals and powers. For example, NATO commits its members to defend one another. They promise to view an attack on one member as an attack on all. But NATO countries don't give up as much control of their individual affairs as EU nations do. The goal of NATO is defense more than unity.

What forces might work against supranational cooperation in the United Nations?

The United Nations is the world's largest international organization. Its 191 member countries range in size from a few thousand to more than a billion people. Each has its own interests. For such diverse countries to cooperate, they must agree to put the world's interests above their own. This is often difficult or impossible for UN members to do. Sometimes their national interests seem in conflict with the interests of other countries.

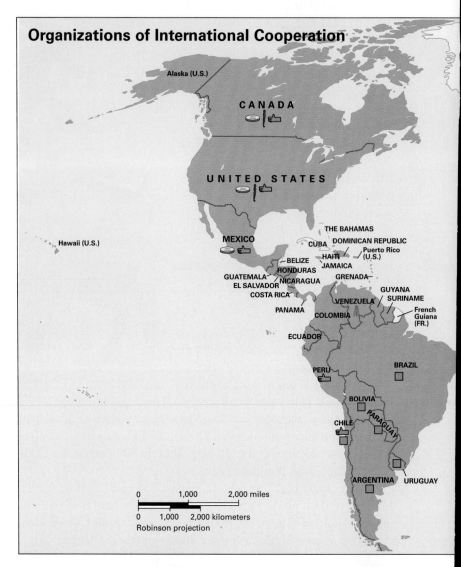

Organizations of International Cooperation

The UN Headquarters
The United Nations was founded in 1945. Its goal is to promote peace and cooperation among the countries of the world. Member countries meet at the UN headquarters in New York City to discuss world issues.

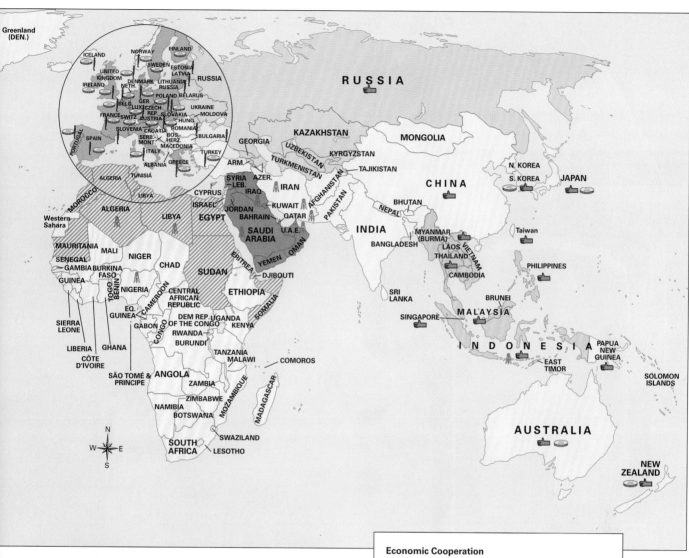

Greenland (DEN.)

ICELAND
NORWAY FINLAND
SWEDEN ESTONIA
UNITED DENMARK LATVIA
KINGDOM LITHUANIA RUSSIA
IRELAND NETH. RUSSIA
BELG. POLAND BELARUS
GER. CZECH UKRAINE
LUX. REP. SLOVAKIA MOLDOVA
FRANCE SWITZ. AUSTRIA HUNG.
SLOVENIA CROATIA ROMANIA
PORTUGAL SPAIN SERB. BOS. BULGARIA
MONT. HERZ. MACEDONIA
ITALY ALBANIA GREECE TURKEY

ALGERIA TUNISIA
LIBYA
MOROCCO CYPRUS
ISRAEL SYRIA AZER. IRAN
Western LEB. IRAQ
Sahara ALGERIA LIBYA JORDAN KUWAIT AFGHANISTAN
EGYPT BAHRAIN QATAR PAKISTAN
GEORGIA
ARM.
SAUDI U.A.E.
MAURITANIA MALI ARABIA OMAN
SENEGAL NIGER CHAD YEMEN
GAMBIA BURKINA DJIBOUTI
GUINEA FASO SUDAN ERITREA
NIGERIA CENTRAL
TOGO AFRICAN ETHIOPIA
BENIN REPUBLIC
SIERRA EQ. CAMEROON SOMALIA
LEONE GUINEA DEM. REP. UGANDA
GABON OF THE CONGO KENYA
LIBERIA CONGO RWANDA
GHANA BURUNDI
CÔTE TANZANIA
D'IVOIRE MALAWI COMOROS
SÃO TOMÉ &
PRINCIPE ANGOLA ZAMBIA
MOZAMBIQUE ZIMBABWE MADAGASCAR
NAMIBIA BOTSWANA
SOUTH SWAZILAND
AFRICA LESOTHO

N
W — E
S

RUSSIA

KAZAKHSTAN MONGOLIA
UZBEKISTAN KYRGYZSTAN
TURKMENISTAN TAJIKISTAN
N. KOREA
S. KOREA JAPAN
CHINA
BHUTAN
NEPAL Taiwan
INDIA MYANMAR
(BURMA)
BANGLADESH LAOS VIETNAM
THAILAND
CAMBODIA PHILIPPINES
SRI
LANKA BRUNEI
SINGAPORE MALAYSIA
INDONESIA PAPUA
NEW
GUINEA
EAST SOLOMON
TIMOR ISLANDS

AUSTRALIA

NEW
ZEALAND

The United Nations Flag

The UN flag shows a world map centered on the North Pole. Two olive branches frame the map. The world map represents all the people of the world, while the olive branch is a symbol for peace.

Economic Cooperation

- Asia-Pacific Economic Cooperation (APEC)
- Association of Southeast Asian Nations (ASEAN)
- Commonwealth of Independent States (CIS)
- Organization of American States (OAS)
- Organization of Economic Cooperaton and Development (OECD)
- Organization of the Petroleum Exporting Countries (OPEC)
- Southern Cone Common Market

Economic and Political Cooperation

- African Union

Political Cooperation

- North Atlantic Treaty Organization (NATO)

Political and Cultural Cooperation

- League of Arab States

Economic, Political, and Cultural Cooperation

- European Union (EU)

Population Dilemmas in Europe

15.1 Introduction

You are driving in the south of Italy on a hot summer day. As you wind your way through dry, brown hills, you decide to stop for a cold drink. You park your car in the tiny village of Cersosimo. As you begin to walk through the old narrow streets, you notice something strange. Cersosimo is filled with elderly people! In fact, for every three faces you see, two of them are over 65 years old. Looking in at the village school, you see that children of all ages are studying together in just one small class.

Finally you find a shop where you can buy your cold drink. You ask the shopkeeper why there are so many elderly people and so few children in Cersosimo. He replies that families here just aren't having babies these days. A few years ago, the village tried to change this trend by offering to pay mothers a "birth bonus" for every baby born in Cersosimo. Even with the birth bonus, though, little had changed. Villagers still chose to have small families.

The story of Cersosimo is the story of Italy. Scientists who do research in **demography** say that it is also the story of Europe. Demography is the study of human populations and how they change over time. Demographers look at **birth rates** and **death rates** and human migration. These measures help them track population trends, or the general direction in which population numbers are moving. In Europe, for example, they are tracking a trend toward smaller families.

In this chapter, you will learn about population trends in Europe. You will see some of the problems created by shrinking family sizes. And you will explore how European countries are trying to address these problems.

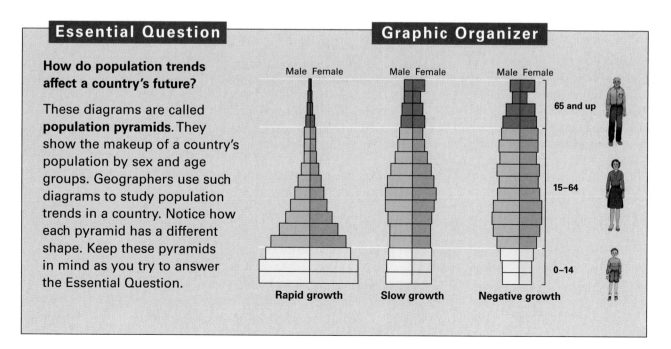

Essential Question

How do population trends affect a country's future?

These diagrams are called **population pyramids.** They show the makeup of a country's population by sex and age groups. Geographers use such diagrams to study population trends in a country. Notice how each pyramid has a different shape. Keep these pyramids in mind as you try to answer the Essential Question.

Graphic Organizer

Male Female   Male Female   Male Female

65 and up

15–64

0–14

Rapid growth   Slow growth   Negative growth

◀ A small town in Italy

Europe, 2000

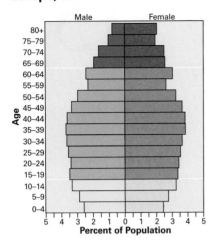

Male   Female

Age / Percent of Population

Europe, 2025 (Estimated)

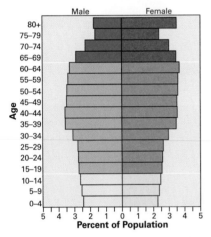

Male   Female

Age / Percent of Population

Source for population pyramid data: *United Nations Population Division,* "World Population Prospects: The 2004 Revision Population Database," esa.un.org/unpp/.

Population Trends in Europe

A population pyramid is made up of two back-to-back bar graphs. One shows the number of males in different age groups. The other shows the number of females. The first of these pyramids graphs Europe's population in 2000. The second reveals how that makeup is likely to change by 2025.

15.2 The Geographic Setting

Europe is one of the smallest continents in size, yet about an eighth of the world's people live there. This high population density may not hold steady much longer for two reasons. First, Europe has the oldest population of any continent. Second, it has the lowest birth rate, or number of births per 1,000 people, of any continent. As a result, its population is shrinking.

Population Change: Births, Deaths, and Migration The study of population trends focuses on three factors: births, deaths, and migration. Whether a population grows or shrinks depends on the trends of these three factors.

Children are born every day in Europe, but the average number of babies born to each woman is low. This average number of births is called the **total fertility rate,** or TFR. In 2000, for example, the TFR in Italy was just over one baby per woman.

If the TFR remains this low, Italy's population will continue to shrink. To stop this trend, the TFR would need to rise to the **replacement rate**. This rise will occur when enough babies are born to replace the people who die each year. In Italy, the replacement rate is just over two babies per woman.

People also die every day in Europe, but they don't die as young as they used to. Over the past century, **life expectancy,** or the number of years a person can expect to live, has increased in Europe. In 2004, the average person in France could expect to live about 80 years. A century earlier, life expectancy in France was only 50 years.

People move into and out of Europe every day as well. In the past, most migration was out of Europe, as people left to escape wars and poverty. Today more people are migrating into Europe than are leaving it. Still, there are not enough immigrants arriving to keep Europe's population stable.

Population Pyramids Show Growth Trends Geographers use graphs shaped like pyramids to study population. These graphs show the ages and sexes in a population, with the youngest ages shown at the bottom and the oldest at the top.

The shape of a population pyramid shows how a country's population is growing. A pyramid that is wide at the bottom shows rapid population growth. More babies are being born each year than the number of people who die. A pyramid with straight sides shows slow population growth, with births and deaths nearly equal in that country. A pyramid that is narrow at the bottom shows negative population growth. More people are dying each year than are being born.

Population growth affects a country's **dependency ratio**. This ratio compares the number of people too young or old to work with the country's working-age population. In Europe, most young people under the age of 16 don't work, and most people over the age of 64 are retired. Both groups depend on other people to support them. A low dependency ratio means that workers have few dependents to support. A high dependency ratio means just the opposite—that there are a lot of young or old people for workers to support. Later you will see how Europe's high dependency ratio has posed problems for its economy.

► Geoterms

demography the study of human populations, including how they change due to births, deaths, aging, and migration

dependency ratio the number of old and young dependents who don't work compared with the working-age population. The higher the ratio, the more young and old people the workers have to support.

life expectancy the average age that a person in a given population can expect to live to. Life expectancy varies from one country to another.

replacement rate the total fertility rate needed for a population to replace itself. This number varies by country, but is about 2.1 in most developed countries.

total fertility rate (TFR) the average number of children a woman in a given population will have in her lifetime. This number is different in different countries.

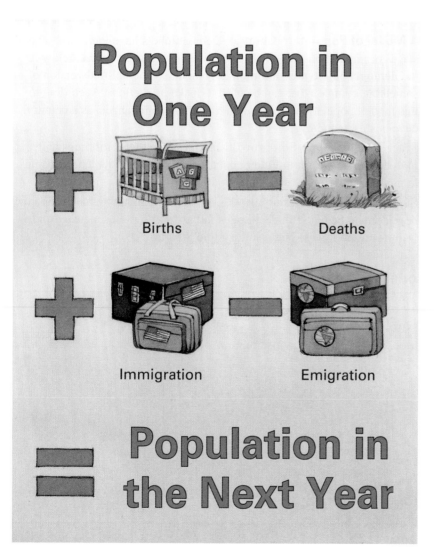

Factors That Cause Population Change

This diagram shows the factors that cause population change. Births and immigration cause growth. Deaths and emigration cause a population to shrink.

15.3 Population Change in Europe

In 1840, Queen Victoria of England married Prince Albert. The couple had nine children, which kept Victoria so busy that Albert had to take over many of her royal duties. In those days, such large families were common in Europe. Today, as you have read, families of that size are very rare in Europe. In fact, Europe has gone from a growing population to one that is stable or shrinking.

From Slow to Fast to No Growth Before the 1750s, the population of Europe rose and fell over time. In bad years, plagues, famines, and wars killed huge numbers of people. In good years, there was enough food to support large families. Overall, there were slightly more births than deaths, keeping population growth low.

In the 1750s, Europe entered a long period of accelerated population growth. Improvements in sanitation and health care caused death rates to drop. Food supplies increased, making it possible for the population in Europe to grow.

After 1900, most Europeans moved from farms to cities. As a result, they no longer needed large families to help with the farming. Birth rates began to fall. By 2000, Europe had entered a period of no, or even negative, population growth.

A Model of Population Change Demographers have identified several stages of population growth. The four major stages are shown below in the **demographic transition model**. A model is a simplified version of something complex that can be used to make predictions. According to this model, populations go through transitions, or changes, as a country develops its economy.

Stage 1: Low population growth. In this stage, high birth rates and high death rates result in little population change. All populations begin at this stage.

Stage 2: Rapid population growth. Birth rates remain high as economic development begins. But death rates fall as food supplies increase and health care improves. The result is rapid growth.

A Large Royal Family

In the 1800s, Queen Victoria and Prince Albert had nine children. A century later, Prince Charles and Princess Diana had two children.

Populations in Transition

The demographic transition model shows population change over time. The word *transition* means change. There is no fixed time for each stage. Some countries may pass through all four stages as they develop. Others may not.

The Demographic Transition Model

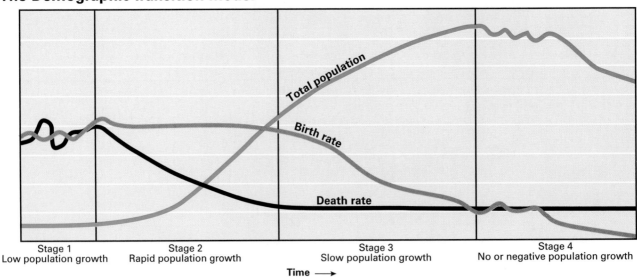

Total population

Birth rate

Death rate

| Stage 1 | Stage 2 | Stage 3 | Stage 4 |
| Low population growth | Rapid population growth | Slow population growth | No or negative population growth |

Time →

Stage 3: Slow population growth. As the economy improves, birth rates drop. Death rates stay low, and population growth begins to slow down.

Stage 4: No or negative population growth. In **developed countries,** both birth rates and death rates drop to low levels. As a result, there is little or no population growth. Over time, birth rates may fall behind death rates, resulting in a shrinking population.

15.4 Dilemma One: A Shrinking Population

Between 2005 and 2050, Italy's population is expected to shrink from 58 million to about 50 million people. This dramatic plunge in population could have far-reaching effects on the country. Looking ahead, Italy might see empty schools, vacant apartments, and closed businesses.

Causes of Negative Population Growth A country's total fertility rate is an important factor in determining its future population. By 2004, Italy's TFR had fallen well below the replacement rate of 2.1 children per woman. And Italy was not alone. Across Europe, total fertility rates were on the decline.

There are many reasons for Europe's low birth rates. More European women are putting off having children so that they can pursue their education and careers. Women who wait until they are older to start having babies tend to have fewer children. And access to family-planning methods in Europe makes it possible for women to control the number of children they have.

Family finances play a part in how many children people choose to have. The high cost of living in much of Europe makes people concerned about being able to support a family. Because housing costs are high, young couples often need two incomes to buy a home. As a result, young women sometimes put off having children in order to work.

Working couples who want children face the issue of childcare. In the past, mothers cared for their children at home. When both parents work, however, they need help to care for their children during the day. Quality childcare can be expensive and hard to find, discouraging couples from having large families.

Problems Caused by Negative Growth Many problems arise when populations shrink. Fewer children need fewer schools and teachers. Over time, declining enrollment means that schools may have to close and teachers may lose their jobs. Other people who work with children may also find themselves out of work. And businesses geared toward children, such as toy stores and children's clothing stores, could go out of business.

Declining population can have a serious effect on a country's economy. Babies grow up to be workers, so, down the line, low birth rates can lead to labor shortages. When businesses cannot find enough workers, they sometimes move to countries that have a better labor supply. This change could hurt Europe's economy.

Negative growth also means fewer people to serve in military forces. As a result, European countries may lose some of their power and influence in the world.

Italy, 2000

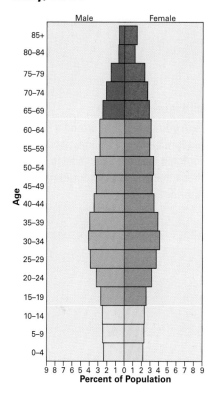

A Shrinking Population in Italy

This pyramid shows the population of Italy in 2000. Notice how narrow the graph is at the base. This is a sign of a shrinking population.

Childcare in France

These young children attend a childcare center in France. Good, affordable childcare is a must in nations that want to encourage higher birth rates.

15.5 Responses to Negative Growth

In the past, the Italian government encouraged large families as part of Italy's culture. Even so, many couples did not choose to have lots of children. In 2003, the government tried something new. If families with at least one child had another baby, it would pay them a "birth bonus" of 1,000 euros, or about $1,000.

Cash and Benefits for Having Babies It may seem strange to pay families for having babies. Yet Italy is not the only country in Europe to offer a cash incentive for larger families. France, for example, gives a birth bonus for every child born in the country. A family with three or more children receives additional benefits, such as reduced rents and lower taxes. It's not yet clear whether paying cash for having babies works well over time. Sometimes birth rates will rise for a few years and then drop again.

Other countries don't believe in paying families to have babies. Instead, some try to lower the costs of having children. One example is Sweden, which offers government assistance to help parents pay for daycare for small children.

Family-Friendly Policies for Parents European governments recognize that the difficulty of balancing work and family life discourages many couples from having children. Quality childcare is one prevalent issue. Another is job security. Working parents often want to take time off work to care for their children. But they fear that if they do so, they may lose their jobs.

Many European governments have responded to this fear with family-friendly policies to help working parents. One policy allows a new parent to stay home with a baby without losing his or her job. This time away from the job is called a *leave*. During the leave, the parent is still paid. When the leave ends, the parent returns to work. Other policies include flexible work hours and the right to work part-time. Governments hope that policies like these will help remove some of the barriers to having children and to staying in the workforce.

15.6 Dilemma Two: An Aging Population

Europe is sometimes called "the old continent" because of its aging population. By 2050, the average age of a person in Spain will be 50 years, making the population of Spain the oldest in the world. This aging population will also mean more old people for Spain to care for.

In the past, most old people in Spain lived in their own homes or with relatives. With people living longer today, Spain needs new living arrangements to accommodate its elderly population. To illustrate this point, consider the example of a home for seniors near Madrid, the capital of Spain. The home is large, with space for 600 people. Not only is the home filled, but also there are 20,000 people on a waiting list who would like to move in! The demand for retirement housing will only grow as Spain's elderly population grows.

Causes of an Aging Population A population ages for two reasons. The first is a rise in life expectancy. The second is a drop in the birth rate. Both trends are taking place across Europe today. The result is that there are more old people and fewer young people than in the past—an aging population.

Europe will age even more rapidly in the years ahead because of a **baby boom** from 1945 to the 1960s. A baby boom is a sudden increase in the birth rate. Europe's baby boom began not long after World War II ended. During the 1950s and 1960s, women had a lot of babies. This means that there is a large population of Europeans born in these years. In the 1970s, birth rates began to fall.

By the year 2000, the first people born during Europe's baby boom were entering their 50s. In the next decade or two, many of these baby boomers will retire, swelling the elderly population of Europe.

Problems Caused by an Aging Population Most people would agree that having longer, healthier lives is a good thing. Yet an aging population also creates problems for a society. The two biggest concerns are **pensions** and health care.

A pension is a fixed amount of money paid to a retired person by a government or former employer. A pension is usually paid from the time a person retires until he or she dies.

Health care is of concern because as people age, their need for health care increases. Older people are more likely than young people to suffer from such diseases as cancer, diabetes, and arthritis. They are more likely to need expensive surgeries and costly medicines. Some need special care available only in nursing homes. All of these needs cost money.

Most European governments provide pensions and health care for senior citizens. The money to pay for both comes from taxes paid by working people. This system works as long as the dependency ratio is low. But the combination of a growing elderly population and fewer young people joining the workforce is causing the dependency ratio to rise. In other words, an ever-smaller workforce is supporting an ever-larger elderly population.

The simplest solution to rising costs is for governments to budget more money for pensions and health care, which most governments have done. To do this, though, governments must collect more tax revenue. And there are limits to how much workers are willing to be taxed.

Spain's Elderly Population

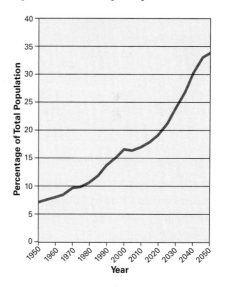

Population Aging in Spain
This line graph shows how the percentage of people aged 65 and over is increasing in Spain. One reason for the change is a steady rise in life expectancy.

Spain, 2025 (Estimated)

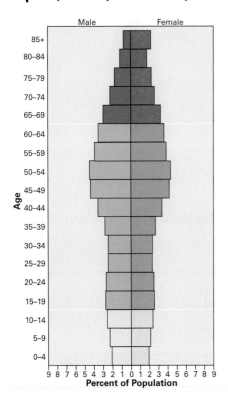

Spain's Baby Boom "Bulge"

Note the "bulge" in this population pyramid. It represents Spain's baby boomers. Over time, the bulge will move up the pyramid. At this happens, the number of pensioners in Spain will increase.

15.7 Responses to an Aging Population

In 2002, Spain hosted the United Nations Second World Assembly on Ageing. Kofi Annan, the United Nation's secretary-general, opened the meeting. For the first time in history, he reported, older people will soon outnumber young people. Borrowing a line from a song by the English band the Beatles, Annan asked the assembly, "Will you still need me, will you still feed me, when I'm 64?" Then he added, "I trust the answer is yes."

Dealing with Pension Costs One of the issues discussed at the UN assembly was how to solve the problem of rising pension costs. With more retired people in Europe than ever before—who are also living longer than in the past—European countries face the challenge of how to support their seniors.

One way to reduce pension costs is to cut the amount of money each worker receives. But cutting pensions too much seems unfair to people who depend on this income to live.

Another approach is to raise the retirement age. Keeping people in the workforce longer will shorten the time during which they will need government pensions. Germany, Italy, and the United Kingdom have all increased the age at which pensions begin. Other countries give bonuses to people who delay their retirement. Spanish workers get a higher pension if they put off retirement until after age 66.

Providing Health Care Governments are also searching for smarter ways to provide health care for their elderly citizens. For example, two relevant principles guide health care policies for Germany's elderly population. The first principle is that preventing health problems is better than treating them. The second is that home care is preferable to care in a nursing home.

Many countries are looking at ways to encourage family members to care for older relatives at home. Home care costs less and is often preferred by older people. Italy provides special health services to families who care for relatives. Austria pays pensions to people who give up jobs to care for family members.

Lining Up for Pension Checks

These Italians are waiting for their pension checks. Like most older Europeans, they live on monthly payments from their government.

Changes in Germany's Population and Labor Supply

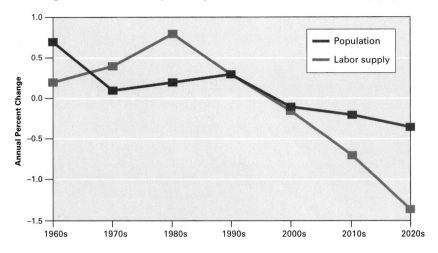

Germany's shrinking population creates problems for business. One problem is fewer customers. Another is a shortage of skilled workers. This will get worse as baby boomers retire. Look at the percentage of change for each decade.

15.8 Dilemma Three: A Declining Workforce

In 2004, a German museum opened an exhibit called "Shrinking Cities." It showed what happens when a city like Leipzig, Germany, loses most of its workforce. Leipzig's problems began with a drop in the birth rate which, in turn, meant an eventual drop in the city's workforce. Faced with a shortage of workers, businesses left the city. Workers left as well in search of better jobs. Now Leipzig is mainly a city of elderly citizens and unemployed workers.

Causes of Workforce Decline The main cause of workforce decline across Europe is simple. More workers retire each year than join the workforce. This decline will only grow worse as baby boomers start to retire. The number of workers in Germany, for example, will likely fall from 42 million to 30 million over the next 50 years.

Workforce decline leads to changes in the dependency ratio—the ratio of dependents to workers—as more and more people are dependent on fewer and fewer workers. In Germany there were 87 dependents for every 100 workers in the year 2000. By 2030, however, estimates show that 100 workers will be supporting 121 dependents. That's a rise of 39 percent in Germany's dependency ratio.

Problems Caused by Workforce Decline In many European countries, young people have trouble finding jobs. To them, a shrinking workforce looks like a good thing. As older workers retire, there will be more jobs for young workers.

For a business, however, workforce decline can be a problem. By the year 2050, the number of highly skilled German workers will decline by about 2 million people. Faced with a shortage of skilled workers, some businesses may choose to leave Germany. Others may shrink their operations or close their doors altogether. The German economy may start to shrink as well.

Not only does workforce decline cause problems for businesses, but it also poses a big problem for the government. Workers pay most of the taxes that support government programs. Fewer workers will mean less tax money just at a time when the dependency ratio is rising.

Germany, 2000

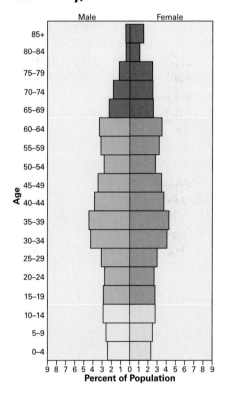

Germany's Working-Age Population in 2000

Germany's working-age population is shown in medium colors in the middle part of this graph. People too young to work are shown in light colors at the bottom. People too old to work are in dark colors at the top. In 2000, working-age people outnumbered these dependents. By 2030, just the opposite will be true.

Making Cars in Germany
These workers are assembling a car in a German factory. As the workforce shrinks, this factory may be moved to another country.

15.9 Responses to a Declining Workforce

In 2004, about 75,000 jobs in Germany went unfilled. Employers could not find enough skilled German workers to fill these positions. Then the government passed a new immigration law making it easier for companies to hire skilled workers from other countries. The government hoped that this change would slow Germany's workforce decline.

Finding More Workers in Europe Many countries in Europe are trying to slow workforce decline. One approach is to keep older workers working longer. Germany, for example, retrains its older workers and gives aid to companies that hire older workers. Other countries encourage older people to work part-time or at home.

Another approach to slowing workforce decline is to encourage more women to join and then stay in the workforce. In the past, a woman often left the workforce after having her first child because she found it difficult to balance work and family life. Women also made less money than men, a further disincentive to work.

Now European governments are realizing how crucial family-friendly work policies are to retaining women in the workforce. You read earlier about such policies as giving parents paid time off work when they have a baby, allowing flexible work schedules, and ensuring quality childcare. By helping women balance work and family, governments hope to make staying in the workforce appealing.

Looking for Workers Outside of Europe Another way to address the problem of workforce decline is to look for workers outside of Europe. One way to find those workers is to move jobs once done in Europe to other parts of the world. For example, the German company Volkswagen no longer makes all of its cars in Germany, but has factories in Brazil, Mexico, South Africa, and other countries.

A second way to find additional workers is to encourage immigration to Europe. Not all Europeans, however, welcome this idea. They worry that immigration may cause more problems than it solves.

15.10 Beginning to Think Globally

In this chapter, you learned about demography, the study of human populations and how they change. You learned how a type of graph called a *population pyramid* shows the population makeup of a country. These graphs show whether a particular population is likely to grow, stay the same, or decline.

Negative Growth in Europe You also learned that most countries in Europe face negative population growth. This happens because the total fertility rate has dropped below the replacement rate. In other words, women are not having enough babies to replace the people who die each year. At the same time, Europe's population is aging. This is because life expectancy is rising.

Negative population growth in Europe has posed several problems, including an increase in dependency ratios. Most retired Europeans depend on their governments for pensions and health care. Governments, in turn, depend on taxes paid by working people to pay for these benefits. But with declining populations, there are fewer workers each year to pay those taxes at the same time that there are more old people depending on those taxes for support.

Global Population Trends Europe is not the only place with an aging population. Developed countries in other world regions are seeing the same population trends. Japan, for example, is aging as rapidly as Europe.

Many developing countries are seeing different population trends than developed countries. In developing countries, total fertility rates are dropping more slowly, and life expectancy is rising slowly as well. For example, in Nigeria the total fertility rate in 2004 was over five children per woman. Life expectancy for a child born that year was about 50 years. As a result, Nigeria's population is young. It is also still growing.

As you look at the next section, think about these population trends in developed and developing countries around the world.

A Young Population in Nigeria
Nigeria has a much higher birth rate than Italy. As a result, 43 percent of its population is under the age of 15. Only 14 percent of all Italians are under the age of 15.

15.11 Global Connections

This map divides the world into developed (rich) and developing (poor) countries. Most rich countries have industrial economies and a high per capita GDP. Most poor countries have an agricultural economy and a low per capita GDP. The pyramids compare the populations of rich and poor countries in 2000 and in 2025.

Why do developed countries have lower birth rates than developing countries? People in all countries want children. But in developed countries, children usually aren't needed to support a family or aging parents. Instead, the cost of raising children is seen as an expense. Also, family-planning methods are more available to help couples choose the size of their families.

Why do developing countries have higher birth rates than developed countries? In poorer countries, poverty plays a role in family size. Children often help support their families by working, and also often support their parents in old age, since the government often does not. As a result, a large family is seen as a benefit, not an expense. In addition, many poor countries have a high infant mortality rate. Couples sometimes choose to have many children, fearing that some may die early in life. Finally, a lack of access to family-planning methods means that women sometimes have little control over the number of children they have.

How might high birth rates affect a country's future? Countries with high birth rates have more young than old people. They may not have enough schools to educate their children or enough jobs to employ their young adults. Anger over the lack of such opportunities may lead to widespread frustration and unrest.

The Developed and Developing World

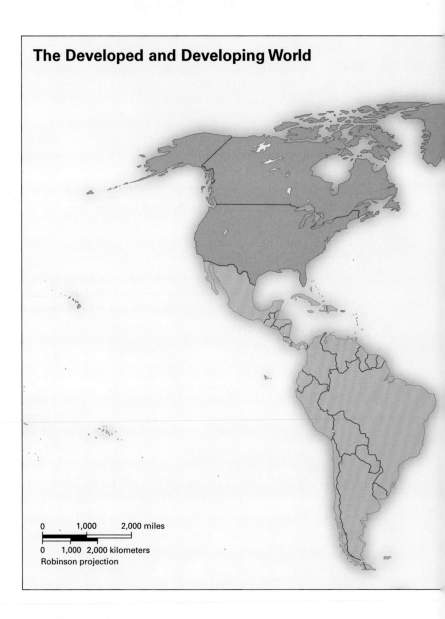

0   1,000   2,000 miles

0   1,000 2,000 kilometers
Robinson projection

World Population, 2000

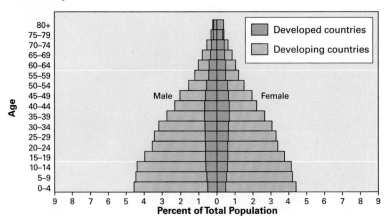

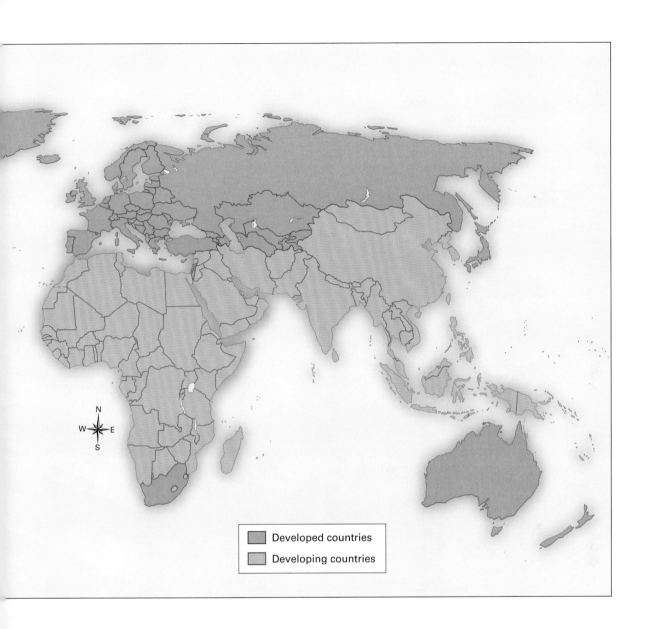

Developed countries

Developing countries

World Population, 2025 (Estimated)

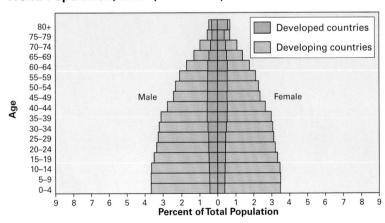

Developed countries

Developing countries

Age

80+
75–79
70–74
65–69
60–64
55–59
50–54
45–49
40–44
35–39
30–34
25–29
20–24
15–19
10–14
5–9
0–4

Male   Female

9 8 7 6 5 4 3 2 1 0 1 2 3 4 5 6 7 8 9
Percent of Total Population

Invisible Borders: Transboundary Pollution in Europe

16.1 Introduction

On April 28, 1986, scientists at a nuclear power plant in Sweden listened in horror as their computers began to beep. The beeps meant that there were high levels of **nuclear radiation** in the air. This form of energy, produced by nuclear power plants, is deadly to living things when present in large amounts. The signals that the Swedish scientists were receiving indicated a radiation leak—a sign that something had gone very wrong in a power plant.

The scientists searched their plant for a leak, but they soon discovered that the radiation was not from the Swedish plant. In fact, the source of the radiation was not even anywhere in Sweden. Instead, winds had carried the radiation to Sweden from the Soviet Union. Eventually the world learned that there had been an accident at a Soviet nuclear power plant called Chernobyl.

The Chernobyl accident is an example of **transboundary pollution**. As you know, **pollution** is damage to the environment that is caused by harmful substances. The word *transboundary* means "across country boundaries." Transboundary pollution starts in one country and then spreads to other countries.

In this chapter, you will learn about several cases of transboundary pollution in Europe. You will find out how different kinds of pollution begin and how that pollution can then easily cross borders between countries. You'll also learn about people's efforts to reduce transboundary pollution.

Essential Question

How can one country's pollution become another country's problem?

This illustration shows parts of Europe and Russia. It also shows one source of transboundary pollution in this region. Notice how this pollution spreads across borders. Keep this illustration in mind as you try to answer the Essential Question.

Graphic Organizer

◀ Destruction after an explosion at the Chernobyl nuclear power plant in 1986

16.2 The Geographic Setting

Beginning in the 1700s, Europe went through a great change known as the **Industrial Revolution**. More and more goods were produced by machines instead of by hand. As a result, work moved from homes into factories. This shift created great benefits for many people. It also created big problems for the environment.

From Handmade to Machine-Made Goods Before the Industrial Revolution, people made almost everything they needed using simple hand tools. Most work was done at home or in small workshops. Goods were costly because they took so long to make.

The entire process of producing goods changed with the Industrial Revolution. The change began in the textile industry. The invention of machines to spin cotton and wool into thread and to weave thread into cloth revolutionized the way cloth was made. The new machines produced cloth much faster than people could with hand looms. Over time, people invented machines to produce everything in the modern home, from clocks to computers.

The Industrial Revolution has made life better for people in many ways. Machine-made goods are usually cheaper than those made by hand. As a result, many people today can afford to buy goods that only the rich could buy in the past. However, this revolution has also created big environmental problems. As factories churn out their goods, they also produce pollution.

Water Pollution Then

This 1858 illustration shows the River Thames in England during the Industrial Revolution. The figure in the rowboat is a symbol of death. The artist used it to represent the poisoning of the Thames by pollution.

The Granger Collection

How Pollution Occurs and Spreads

Pollution occurs when dangerous substances, such as certain chemicals, are added to the air, water, or soil. Pollution sometimes has a natural cause. A volcano, for example, may pollute the air with poisonous gases. More often, however, pollution is the result of human activity.

People create two kinds of pollution. One kind is **accidental pollution,** or pollution that occurs as the result of an accident. For example, when an oil tanker spills oil into the sea, the spill can pollute vast areas of ocean and coastline, killing fish and seabirds.

The other kind of pollution is **general pollution,** which is caused by everyday activities. One example of general pollution is the smoke that comes from burning coal to produce electricity. The smoke from coal-burning power plants pollutes the air and also contributes to **acid rain**. This is rain that has been turned slightly acid, like vinegar, by pollution in the air. Acid rain can harm plants, fish and other animals, and even buildings.

Pollution is an even bigger problem when it spreads. Wind currents can quickly spread pollution into the atmosphere. Water currents can spread it almost as rapidly through a river system. A **river system** includes a river and all the streams that flow into it. Pollution in one country can quickly become another country's problem.

▶ Geoterms

acid rain rain that can damage the environment because it contains acid from factory smoke and car exhaust. Acid rain can damage plants, fish, animals, and even buildings.

nuclear radiation a form of energy that comes from nuclear reactions. Radiation has no smell or taste, but it can be very harmful to living things. Materials polluted with nuclear radiation are said to be radioactive.

river system a river and all the streams that flow into it. The streams that flow into a river are called *tributaries*.

transboundary pollution pollution that starts in one country and crosses boundaries into other countries. Generally, transboundary pollution is carried by wind or water.

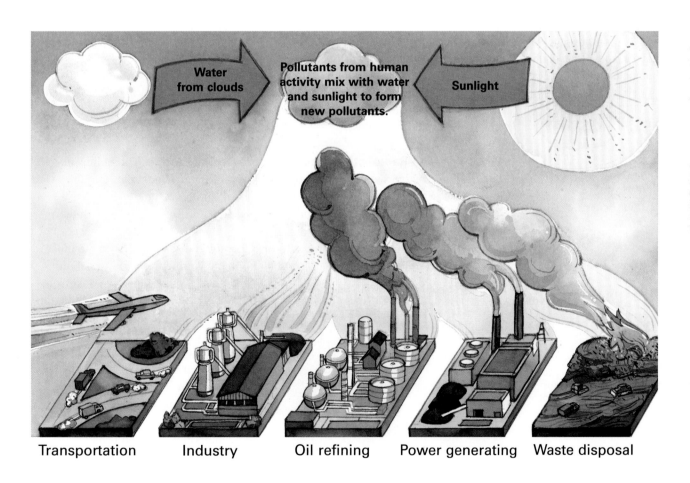

Water from clouds

Pollutants from human activity mix with water and sunlight to form new pollutants.

Sunlight

Transportation Industry Oil refining Power generating Waste disposal

Air Pollution Has Many Causes

There are many sources of air pollution. Most air pollution is caused by the burning of fossil fuels. Fossil fuels include coal, oil, and natural gas. Burning fossil fuels releases energy for heating, running motors, and making electricity. It also releases harmful chemicals into the air.

16.3 The Chernobyl Radiation Accident

At 1:24 A.M. on April 25, 1986, an explosion rocked the Chernobyl nuclear power plant. A fireball of radioactive dust rose three miles into the air. Soon the radioactive cloud rode the winds to places thousands of miles away. A terrible accident at a single power plant became a matter of concern for the entire world.

Human Error Creates a Deadly Radiation Leak The Chernobyl nuclear plant lies near the city of Kiev in Ukraine, which at that time was part of the Soviet Union. Ukraine later became independent, after the breakup of the Soviet Union into 15 separate countries.

Chernobyl was one of hundreds of nuclear power plants operating in about 30 countries around the world. These plants use uranium for fuel. The uranium is mined from the ground, like coal or copper, and then put in a special container called a *nuclear reactor*. Inside the reactor, the uranium gives off energy in the form of heat, which is used to boil water. The boiling water creates steam, which in turn powers a turbine to produce electricity.

During the Chernobyl accident, one of the reactors got too hot to control. This accident did not just "happen." It occurred when workers doing a routine check failed to follow their own safety rules. As a result, an explosion blasted through the reactor.

The explosion started a fire that quickly raged out of control. But the biggest problem was not the fire. It was the huge cloud that formed over Chernobyl after the explosion. This cloud was made up of deadly radioactive dust.

The Radioactive Cloud Spreads Across Europe The radioactive cloud did not remain over Chernobyl for long. Winds sent it north toward Sweden and then south toward Central Europe. Radiation also moved east across Asia. It eventually crossed the Pacific Ocean to reach the United States.

The countries closest to the Chernobyl disaster suffered the most. Hardest hit was Belarus, which borders Ukraine to the north. About 70 percent of the radioactive dust from Chernobyl fell on Belarus, contaminating its soil and water. As a result, the people of Belarus eat, drink, and breathe radiation every day. This exposure to radiation has led to higher rates of cancer in Belarus than in other countries.

The people of Lapland also suffered as a result of the accidental pollution from Chernobyl. Lapland is an area in the far north of Europe, including part of Sweden. Many people in Lapland fish or raise herds of reindeer for a living. After the Chernobyl accident, radiation polluted their fishing grounds and reindeer herds, killing large numbers of fish and reindeer. Those that survived were not safe to eat.

A Deadly Explosion at Chernobyl
The explosion at the Chernobyl nuclear power plant left a pile of rubble on the ground. It also spread radioactive pollution over a wide area. Children who were exposed to this radiation have a higher than normal risk of getting cancer.

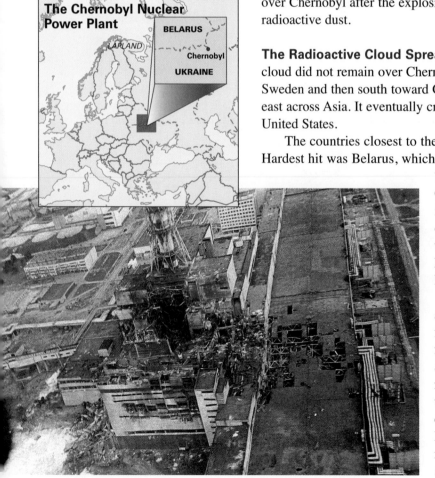

The Chernobyl Nuclear Power Plant

BELARUS

LAPLAND

Chernobyl

UKRAINE

Radiation Spread from Chernobyl

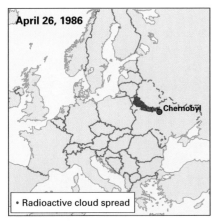

April 26, 1986

• Radioactive cloud spread — Chernobyl

April 30, 1986 — Chernobyl

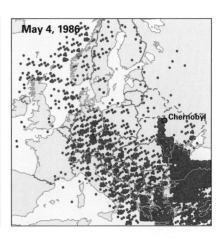

May 4, 1986 — Chernobyl

Efforts to Reduce Radioactive Pollution At first, the Soviet government denied that there had been an accident. But Swedish scientists sounded alarms about the rising radiation levels. Finally, the Soviets made an announcement on television.

An accident has taken place at the Chernobyl power station, and one of the reactors was damaged. Measures are being taken to eliminate the consequences of the accident. Those affected by it are being given assistance.

The Soviet government sent an army of engineers into Chernobyl. Over the next few weeks, they built a huge concrete box around the damaged reactor. This giant tomb will have to remain in place until the reactor is no longer dangerously radioactive—a process that will take hundreds of years.

In addition to securing the reactor, the Soviet government relocated people living closest to the plant to safer areas. About 135,000 people had to leave their homes, in many cases without prior warning. Rescue workers would suddenly appear at their homes, looking like spacemen in their protective clothes, and hurry residents onto buses. Workers also destroyed contaminated crops, food, and animals. Despite these efforts, an estimated 8,000 people have died in Ukraine from health problems caused by radiation.

Chernobyl was the world's worst nuclear accident. Since then, world leaders have paid greater attention to improving safety at nuclear power plants. Changes in reactors make them less likely to overheat and make it easier to shut the reactors down in an emergency. These efforts reduce the chances that accidents at power plants will cause major radiation pollution in the future.

A Deadly Cloud
These maps show how quickly winds spread radiation released by the Chernobyl explosion.

Checking for Radiation
This inspector is checking a train in Germany for radiation after the Chernobyl accident. He is using a Geiger counter. This device clicks when it measures radiation nearby. The more radiation there is, the faster a Geiger counter clicks.

The Black Triangle Region

A Region of Dying Trees

A "black triangle" of factories and power plants spreads across Central Europe. Air pollution in this region is killing forests and fish.

16.4 The "Black Triangle" and Acid Rain

Tourists flock to Europe each year to visit its famous stone monuments. Some of these monuments, such as ancient Greek temples and Roman bridges, are more than 2,000 years old. They have survived wars, floods, and fires. But they may not survive modern pollution. Acid rain is slowly eating away at these precious relics.

Soot from Factories Creates Acid Rain As you read, acid rain is caused by pollution of the air. People cause most air pollution by burning things. A century ago, when many people burned coal to heat their homes, thick clouds of soot hung over many cities. Today exhaust from factories and cars are the main sources of air pollution and, in turn, acid rain.

Air pollution is a problem in many places, but some areas create more pollution than others. One major source of air pollution, and acid rain, is the "triangle" where Germany, Poland, and the Czech Republic meet. Many factories and power plants are located here, and most of them burn lignite, a soft brown coal, as their main fuel. Because soot from the burning coal blackens the air, this area is often called the "Black Triangle."

When lignite burns, it gives off two chemicals, sulfur dioxide and nitrogen oxides. When these two chemicals react with water, they form acids. Acids have a sour taste. You can taste acid in lemon juice or vinegar. Acids are also corrosive, which means they will slowly eat away at something until it is destroyed.

Acid rain results from sulfur dioxide and nitrogen oxides mixing with water in the air. When acid rain or snow falls on lakes, it can turn the lake water acidic. In some lakes, high acid levels have killed fish. Acid rain can also harm forests, weakening trees by eating away at their leaves or needles.

The Sudety Mountains are on the border between Poland and the Czech Republic, just east of the Black Triangle. That means they are **downwind,** or in the direction the wind is blowing, of some of the worst pollution in Europe. If you go there, you will see many sick trees without leaves.

Air Pollution Brings Acid Rain to Other Countries Ever since people began burning coal as a fuel, acid rain has been a problem. But in the past the problem was more severe in cities, where most factories were located and large numbers of people lived.

Beginning in the 1950s, however, acid rain was no longer mostly an **urban** problem. Around that time, coal-burning factories and power plants began constructing very high chimneys. The smoke coming out of these chimneys was carried away by high winds. These new, taller chimneys improved the air quality in industrial cities, but led to the spread of air pollution over much wider areas.

Today air pollution from the Black Triangle results in acid rain and snow falling on many countries. In Sweden and Finland, a great majority of the pollution that causes acid rain originates in other countries, especially Germany and Poland. Naturally, these countries are very concerned about reducing acid rain and the air pollution that causes it. They recognize that such an undertaking, however, involves the cooperative effort of many countries.

Efforts to Reduce Acid Rain The countries of Europe are trying to reduce acid rain in many ways. One approach is to offer rewards to companies that reduce pollution. Some governments propose doing this by allowing companies that pollute less to pay lower taxes.

Another approach is to promote new technologies that result in less pollution. For example, many factories and power plants that burn coal have begun installing devices called *smokestack scrubbers*. These scrubbers chemically remove the sulfur dioxide from the gases leaving the smokestack; as a result, less pollution enters the air. Another technology that reduces air pollution is the catalytic converter that is required equipment on most cars manufactured today. The converter works in a similar way to the smokestack scrubber to reduce the emissions of nitrogen oxides from exhaust pipes. Other pollution-reducing technologies have been created that are specific to certain appliances and businesses.

A third approach to reducing acid rain is to decrease the use of coal as a fuel for power plants and factories. Scientists today are looking for new ways to harness the power of the wind, water, and sun. Using wind, water, and sun to generate electricity does not pollute the air or cause acid rain. You will learn more about these alternative energy sources in Chapter 24.

The Impact of Acid Rain
Acid rain is rain that pollution has turned acidic. When acid rain falls on forests, leaves and needles turn brown. Acid rain also dissolves nutrients in the soil. The nutrients then wash away before plants can use them.

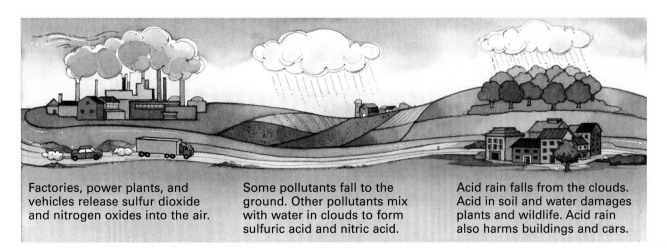

Factories, power plants, and vehicles release sulfur dioxide and nitrogen oxides into the air.

Some pollutants fall to the ground. Other pollutants mix with water in clouds to form sulfuric acid and nitric acid.

Acid rain falls from the clouds. Acid in soil and water damages plants and wildlife. Acid rain also harms buildings and cars.

16.5 The Tisza-Danube Cyanide Spill

On January 30, 2000, a large amount of cyanide spilled into a river in Central Europe. Cyanide is a **toxic chemical** that is used in mining and other industries. This accidental spill triggered the worst environmental disaster in Europe since Chernobyl. In fact, many people called the spill the "water Chernobyl." Central European countries are still seeing the effects of this disaster.

The Tisza-Danube River System

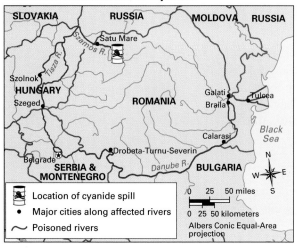

Poisoned from Source to Sea

The Tisza-Danube river system was poisoned in 2000. The source of the poison was a cyanide spill in Romania. Rivers carried the poison all the way to Black Sea.

A Burst Dam Releases Deadly Chemicals The accident took place at a mining operation in Romania, one of 13 Central European countries in the Danube river system. The mining company used cyanide to separate gold from less valuable rock. The cyanide was then stored in a pond formed behind a small dam.

On the night of the spill, a driving rain swelled the pond, causing the water to reach a dangerous level. Suddenly, the dam burst. About 100,000 cubic meters of water laced with cyanide spilled out of the pond and into a river. This surge of **toxic waste** was enough to fill about 30 Olympic-size swimming pools.

Cyanide Flows into the Danube River System The cyanide spilled first into the Szamos River in Romania. The Szamos carried the toxic waste across Hungary, where it entered the Tisza River. The Tisza then emptied into the Danube River, which carried the toxic spill across Serbia and Montenegro and Bulgaria. Finally, the cyanide emptied into the Black Sea.

The first sign of this transboundary pollution was dead fish. The cyanide killed some 200 tons of fish as it washed down the Tisza River. Otters living in all three rivers died by the hundreds after eating the poisoned fish, and the rivers' bird population, especially fish-eating species, was also affected.

The toxic spill also affected the water supply of some 2.5 million people along the Danube river system. Fearing the pollution, towns along the Tisza and Danube shut down their water systems. People near the rivers flew black banners and posted warning signs for people to stay away from the water. Many tourists canceled their trips to the area, fearing the contamination.

Sources of Water Pollution

Water pollution comes from both urban and rural areas. Factories and farms create waste that pollutes water. Garbage and sewage from towns and cities add to the problem. Acid rain pollutes water as well.

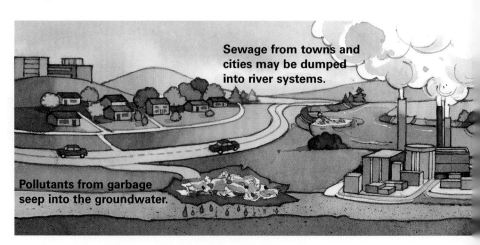

Efforts to Reduce Water Pollution As deadly as the cyanide was, its effects did not last long, since cyanide breaks down in sunlight. By the time the spill reached the Danube, it was no longer toxic to fish. Even so, scientists do not know how long it will take for the river to recover completely. Most agree that it could take many years.

The spill did have one positive outcome. It focused people's attention on pollution in the waterways that make up the Danube river system. Mining accidents are only one source of pollution. The runoff from farms adds chemicals and fertilizers to the river water, and transport boats pollute it with oil and lead. Factories also pollute the rivers, and many towns dump untreated **sewage** into these waterways as well.

The United Nations Environment Program and the European Union, as well as other environmental organizations, have all committed to helping solve the Danube's environmental problems. In addition, the International Commission for the Protection of the Danube River was established in 1998. The members of the commission represent the 13 countries that share the Danube river system. They are working together to find ways to reduce transboundary pollution in this region.

On June 29, 2004, the commission held its first "Danube Day." On that day, millions of people gathered along the banks of the Danube. They came together to celebrate the river's past and to think about its future. Each country held different events, but they all began with this simple truth: "Everybody lives downstream."

16.6 Beginning to Think Globally

In this chapter, you read about transboundary pollution in Europe. Pollution has many causes. Sometimes pollution occurs naturally, but more often, people cause pollution. Radioactive pollution, like that released from the Chernobyl power plant, is usually the result of an accident. Acid rain, which comes from air pollution, is an example of general pollution.

You also saw how easily pollution can be spread by wind and water. The Tisza-Danube cyanide spill showed how an accident in one country can affect an entire river system.

Transboundary pollution is not only a problem in Europe. Wind currents can carry pollution across oceans and continents. As a result, one country's pollution can create problems in countries halfway around the world. Consider this idea as you look at the map of global wind patterns in the next section.

Acid rain runs off into lakes and rivers.

Fertilizers and pesticides run off into waterways.

Chemicals are released into rivers.

16.7 Global Connections

The map at the bottom of this page shows the locations of two different levels of acid rain around the world. One category is "acid rain detected," which means that acid rain has already been discovered to be a serious problem in these areas. The other category is "acid rain potential," which means that in these places acid rain is not yet a problem, but may be in the future. The diagram of wind currents on the facing page illustrates how winds can carry the chemicals that cause acid rain over vast distances.

Why do North America and Europe have the highest acid rain levels? North America and Europe are highly industrialized, which means they have more factories, cars, and other polluting machines than other parts of the world. As you have learned, the pollution created in industrialized areas is the cause of acid rain.

What changes in Asia are raising the acid rain potential there? China, India, and other countries in Asia are developing at a rapid rate. These countries are building more and more factories and power plants, and the number of cars is rising quickly as well. One likely result of rapid industrialization is an equally rapid increase in air pollution and, therefore, in acid rain.

Why must acid rain be tackled as a global problem? As you have seen, pollution is not always a local issue. Wind and water can carry toxic waste great distances. For this reason, a country that creates pollution may not have to live with all of its effects. Only by working together will countries be able to tackle problems that may begin halfway around the world.

Pollution Patrol Plane
This airplane is used to study air pollution. The pods on the end of its wings contain scientific instruments. These devices detect chemicals in the air.

Acid Rain Around the World

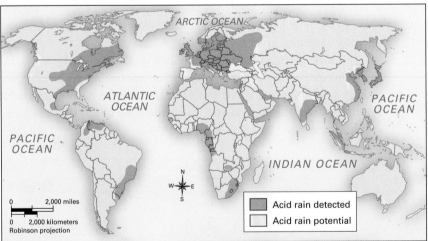

Source: Charles Novosad, ed., *Nystrom Desk Atlas*, Chicago: Nystrom, 1994.

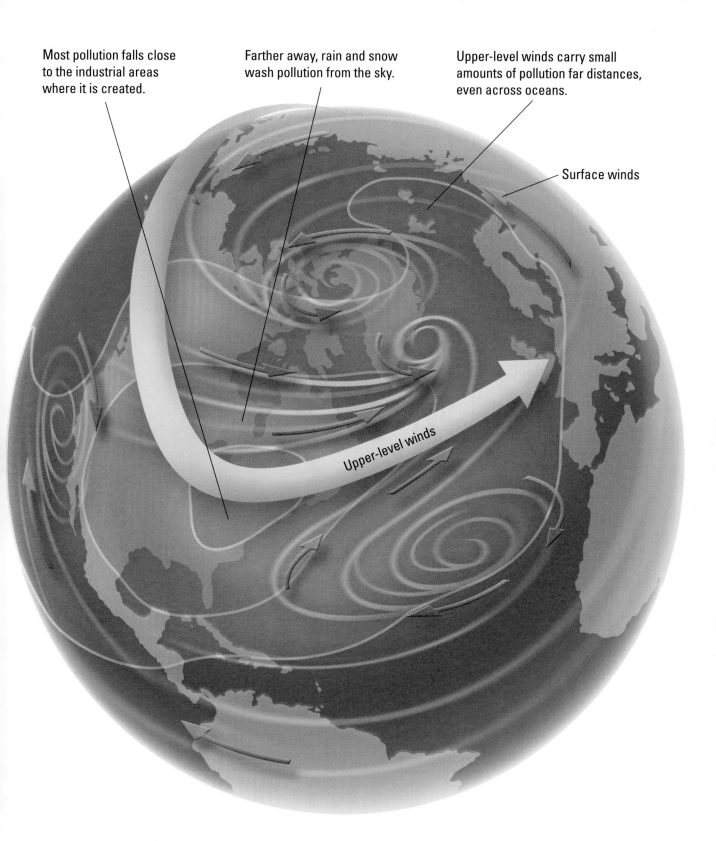

Most pollution falls close to the industrial areas where it is created.

Farther away, rain and snow wash pollution from the sky.

Upper-level winds carry small amounts of pollution far distances, even across oceans.

Surface winds

Upper-level winds

The Spread of Pollution from North America

Most air pollution falls close to where it is produced. But winds high above Earth, or upper-level winds, can also carry pollution over great distances.

Russia's Varied Landscape: Physical Processes at Work

17.1 Introduction

In 1687, an English scientist named Isaac Newton proposed an amazing idea. He suggested that humans could launch a craft into space. This artificial satellite would orbit Earth, just as the moon does. Almost 300 years later, Newton's idea finally came to pass when, in 1972, Russian scientists launched a satellite known as Sputnik. Since then, a number of countries have launched more than 5,000 satellites into space. Cameras and other instruments carried by satellites have given humans a new view of Earth from space.

Geographers use these **satellite images** to study Earth. Among other things, these views of Earth from space show how landscapes develop and change over time. It may seem like mountains and valleys have always been where they are and always will be, but actually, Earth's surface is forever changing. **Physical processes,** or natural forces, are always at work on the landscape. Some physical processes build up land into mountains. Others wear down land into valleys and plains. Satellite images help scientists study the forces of change that shape these physical features.

In this chapter, you will learn about four physical processes that shape our Earth. You will also learn how those processes have changed Russia's landscape. Russia is the largest country in the world, covering almost one eighth of the world's land surface. Because of its great size, Russia has a large variety of landscapes to explore, and scientists are able to see many physical forces at work.

Essential Question

How do physical processes shape Earth's landscape?

The map at the center shows the physical landscape of Russia. The four drawings around the map represent physical processes that have shaped the Russian landscape. Two have built up the landscape. Two have worn it down. Keep this illustration in mind as you try to answer the Essential Question.

Graphic Organizer

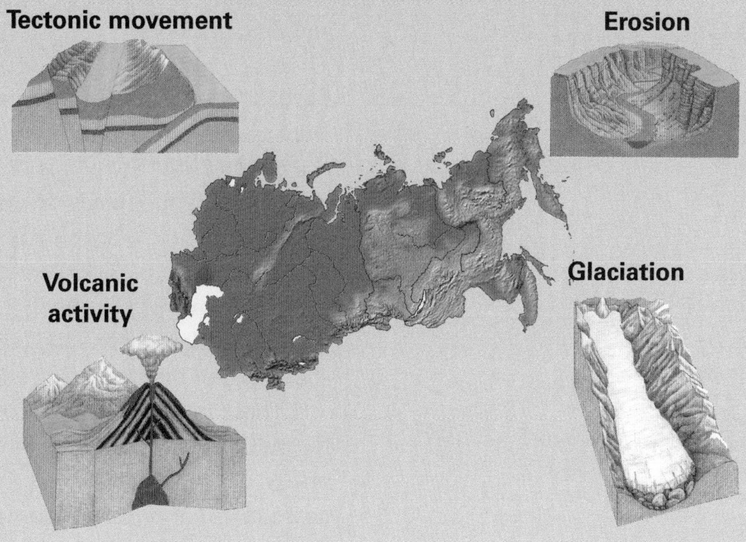

Tectonic movement

Erosion

Volcanic activity

Glaciation

◀ Satellite image of Lake Baikal in southeastern Russia

17.2 The Geographic Setting

Russia is a giant country that covers almost 7 million square miles, including large parts of Europe and Asia. It is so big that it includes 11 of Earth's 24 **time zones**. In contrast, the continental United States has only 4 time zones.

The western part of Russia is one large plain. At the eastern edge of this plain are the Ural Mountains, which separate Europe from Asia. East of the Urals lies Siberia, another vast plain that is part of Russia. High plateaus, icy mountains, and deep valleys surround Siberia. Physical processes have shaped this varied landscape. These processes begin deep inside our planet.

Inside Planet Earth The planet Earth was once a liquid fireball. While Earth has been cooling for more than 4 billion years, temperatures are still so high deep inside the planet that in some places rock and metals are a fiery liquid.

At the center of Earth lies its **core**. The core has two parts: the inner core, made up of solid iron, and the outer core, made up of liquid iron. Earth's core is the hottest part of the planet, with temperatures that may reach over 10,000 degrees Fahrenheit.

The next layer out from the core is called the **mantle**. The mantle is made up of molten, or liquid, rock called **magma** and accounts for about two thirds of Earth's mass.

The outermost part of Earth is called the **lithosphere**. The lithosphere includes a layer of solid rock and, above that, the **crust**. The crust is the only cool layer of Earth. It is where we live.

Forces Below the Crust Build Up Land Two physical processes build and shape land from below the crust. These two processes are **tectonic movement** and **volcanic activity**.

Tectonic is a Greek word that means "builder." Tectonic movement is movement inside Earth that results in changes on the planet's surface. Over millions of years, tectonic movement builds up mountains. It also triggers earthquakes.

Volcanic activity includes the formation and eruption of **volcanoes**. Like tectonic movement, volcanic activity also begins below Earth's crust. When volcanoes erupt, they can change the landscape suddenly and dramatically.

Forces Above the Crust Wear Down Land Two physical processes work above Earth's crust to reshape landscapes. These forces are **erosion** and **glaciation**. Erosion is the wearing away of Earth's surface, most commonly by the forces of wind or moving water, but also by the force of ice or gravity. Glaciation is the formation of large, thick masses of ice called **glaciers**. The weight of the ice exerts pressure that causes the glaciers to move very slowly across the land. This movement can gouge out deep valleys, carve and polish mountains, and push piles of rock and soil ahead of them. Erosion and glaciation create change very slowly.

These four physical processes have been changing Russia's landscape for millions of years. They have built its mountains and worn down its plains, canyons, and valleys. In this chapter, you will find out more about how these four physical processes have shaped not only Russia, but also the rest of our Earth.

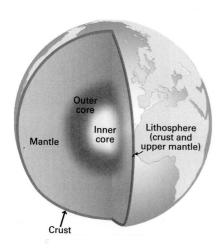

A Cutaway View of Earth

Earth may seem cool on the surface. But deep inside lies a hot liquid core. Earth's crust "floats" on this molten core. Cracks in the crust may result in volcanic activity or tectonic movement.

▶ Geoterms

erosion the gradual wearing away of Earth's surface by the action of wind, water, ice, and gravity

glaciation the creation and movement of glaciers

physical processes natural forces that change Earth's physical features, including forces that build up and wear down Earth's surface

tectonic movement the movement of plates below Earth's surface

volcanic activity the formation and eruption of volcanoes

Physical Features of Russia

The World's Largest Country

Russia stretches from Europe across Asia to the Pacific Ocean. Tectonic activity and volcanoes have created its mountains. Erosion and glaciation have shaped its vast plains and plateaus.

17.3 How Tectonic Movement Shapes Earth

Early in the morning of April 18, 1906, a terrifying earthquake shook the city of San Francisco, California, causing massive devastation. "Trolley lines snapped like threads" and buildings "crumbled like card houses," wrote one eyewitness. "The cobblestones danced like corn in a popper." Hundreds, and perhaps thousands, of people lost their lives, and hundreds of thousands more were left homeless. No one at that time understood how or why earthquakes happen. Today we know that they are caused by tectonic movement.

The Continents and Oceans Rest on Plates Scientists solved the mystery of earthquakes in the 1960s. They discovered that the lithosphere is broken into huge pieces called **tectonic plates**. Earth's lands and seas rest on these plates, which lie below the surface of the planet. The plates float like rafts on Earth's liquid mantle.

Tectonic plates move in three ways. They can move away from each other, they can move toward each other, or they can scrape sideways past each other. When two tectonic plates collide, one plate usually slides under the other.

Tectonic plates are incredibly heavy. When they meet, friction can lock them into place for long periods, allowing enormous pressure to build up below Earth's crust. When the pressure gets too great, the plates come unstuck and move with tremendous energy. We feel this sudden movement as an earthquake.

Earth's Tectonic Plates

A Crust of Moving Plates

Earth's solid crust is made up of tectonic plates. These plates float on the liquid rock that makes up the middle layer of Earth. There are at least 14 plates, some very large in area, some smaller.

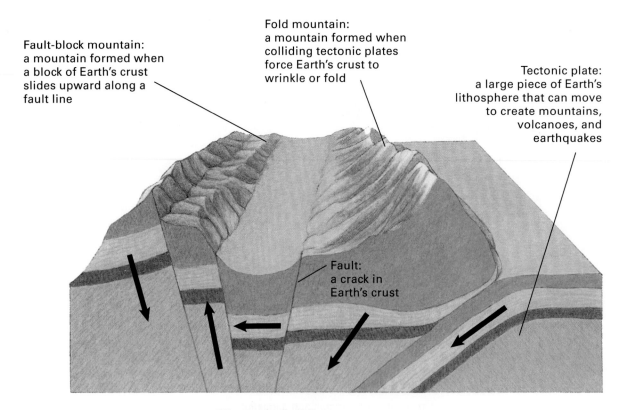

Fault-block mountain: a mountain formed when a block of Earth's crust slides upward along a fault line

Fold mountain: a mountain formed when colliding tectonic plates force Earth's crust to wrinkle or fold

Tectonic plate: a large piece of Earth's lithosphere that can move to create mountains, volcanoes, and earthquakes

Fault: a crack in Earth's crust

Mountain Building

Over millions of years, the slow movement of tectonic plates has created mountains. When plates collide, they push rock upward to form mountains.

The Movement of the Plates Creates Mountains When tectonic plates collide head-on, they can build mountains in two ways. The first way is when the pressure of colliding plates forces Earth's crust to fold, or wrinkle, without breaking. The resulting folds form mountains. The Appalachian Mountains in the United States and the Ural Mountains in Russia are examples of **fold mountains**.

The second way in which colliding plates create mountains is when their collision causes the crust to crack into huge blocks. The cracks between the blocks are called **faults**. As pressure builds up, the blocks of crust tilt and tip. Then some tilted blocks slide upward along **fault lines** to form mountains. The Sierra Nevada mountain range in California is made up of **fault-block mountains,** as is the West Sayan range in Russia.

17.4 Signs of Tectonic Movement in Russia

Russia covers a large part of both Europe and Asia and includes several mountain ranges. These mountain ranges tell the story of how tectonic movement can shape a landscape.

The Ural Mountains in western Russia are considered the dividing line between Europe and Asia. Even though Europe and Asia form one huge **landmass,** this division into two continents makes good geographic sense. The Urals mark the place where two tectonic plates meet beneath Earth's crust. Over millions of years, pressure from these two colliding plates has pushed the crust upward to create the Urals.

Ural Mountains The Urals slice through Russia from north to south. This long chain of mountains separates the Northern European Plain to the west from the West Siberian Plain to the east.

The Urals are fold mountains, formed as the two underlying plates caused Earth's crust to wrinkle. In some places, erosion has worn these mountains down into rolling hills. Other parts of these mountains still have rugged peaks. Mount Manaraga in the northern Ural Mountains is sometimes called Bear's Paw because of its jagged ridge.

Caucasus Mountains The Caucasus Mountains are in southwestern Russia. They run west to east on a narrow strip of land between the Black Sea and the Caspian Sea, marking a southern dividing line between Europe and Asia.

Like the Urals, the Caucasus Mountains are fold mountains. They also include volcanic formations and glaciers, which still carve the jagged landscape. Mount Elbrus, the highest peak in the Caucasus range, stands at 18,510 feet and is an extinct volcano.

West Sayan Mountains The West Sayan Mountains are in southern Siberia, just west of Lake Baikal. Around Lake Baikal, major faults separate high mountains and plateaus from deep valleys and basins.

The West Sayan Mountains are fault-block mountains. In this range, erosion has worn away loose soil and rocks from the peaks. This process has left behind steep ridges and exposed layers of rock on the upper slopes of the mountains.

Snowy Caucasus Ridges
The Caucasus Mountains mark the southeastern edge of Europe. This mountain range was formed by moving plates around 25 million years ago.

Volcanic Activity

Inside Earth is a layer of liquid rock called *magma*. When magma reaches the surface, it creates a volcano. Volcanic eruptions can be quite violent. Lava flows and falling ash can change the surrounding landscape. Eruptions can also build up and reshape mountains.

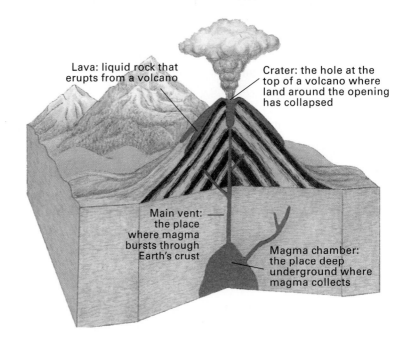

Lava: liquid rock that erupts from a volcano

Crater: the hole at the top of a volcano where land around the opening has collapsed

Main vent: the place where magma bursts through Earth's crust

Magma chamber: the place deep underground where magma collects

17.5 How Volcanic Activity Shapes Earth

Like earthquakes, volcanoes can reshape the landscape with awesome force. In 1883, an erupting volcano destroyed most of Krakatau, an island in Indonesia. People heard the explosion more than 2,000 miles away. Clouds of ash flew 20 miles or more into the air, and dust from the eruption created colorful sunsets around the world. In the end, two thirds of Krakatau disappeared into a hole under the sea.

Volcanoes Form Below Earth's Surface As you read earlier, hot liquid rock called *magma* lies beneath Earth's crust. This molten rock is always moving and sometimes pushes its way to the surface through cracks in the crust. Scientists call the place where magma reaches Earth's surface a *volcano*. When magma erupts from a volcano, scientists call the liquid rock **lava**.

Volcanoes often occur along the edges of tectonic plates. The hot magma rises through the cracks between two plates. Magma can also rise at "hot spots," or weak points, in Earth's crust. Either way, the result might be a single volcano, or it could be a whole chain of volcanoes. The Hawaiian Islands are an example of a chain of volcanoes.

Volcanic Explosions Alter the Landscape Some volcanic eruptions are relatively quiet, with lava oozing out or spraying like a fountain. At other times, volcanoes can explode with enormous force, literally blowing their tops off. In 1980, a huge volcanic eruption shook Mount St. Helens in the state of Washington. Afterward Mount St. Helens was at least 1,300 feet shorter than it had been before the eruption.

Volcanoes alter the landscape in another way. Violent eruptions hurl tiny bits of rock and volcanic ash into the air in an enormous cloud. Eventually that hot ash falls to Earth, where it can dramatically change the surrounding region. If thick enough, the ash can bury vegetation and even people and buildings. Sometimes ash mixes with steam to create a fast-moving mudslide, capable of burying everything in its path. After a violent eruption, the land around a volcano may collapse, creating a large **crater,** or hole.

17.6 Signs of Volcanic Activity in Russia

Two immense tectonic plates meet under the easternmost edge of Russia. As a result, this area is one of the world's most active earthquake zones. It is also the location of several volcanoes, most of which are on the Kamchatka Peninsula.

Some of the volcanoes in this region are dormant, or inactive, meaning that they have not erupted for a very long time. Others remain active. When these volcanoes do erupt, they can change the landscape for miles around through lava flows, mudslides, and deposits of ash. They can cause numerous deaths and destroy entire cities. Some eruptions also change the shape of the volcanoes themselves.

The Kliuchevskoi Volcano The Kliuchevskoi Volcano rises to a height of 15,584 feet out of the northern part of the Kamchatka Peninsula. It is the highest volcano in Russia and also the most active, with smoke continuously billowing from its crater.

In 1994, Kliuchevskoi erupted with tremendous force. Rivers of lava flowed down the sides of the volcano, and a cloud of gray ash rose almost 12 miles into the air. Still more ash combined with melting snow to trigger major mudflows.

The Maly Semyachik Volcano The Maly Semyachik Volcano rises out of the center of the Kamchatka Peninsula. It is characterized by a large crater at the top called Troitsky Crater, which is filled with warm, bright blue water.

The Krenitsyn Volcano The Krenitsyn Volcano is on Onekotan Island, which is part of the Kuril Island chain. During one of its eruptions, part of the volcano collapsed, leaving a large hole at the base of the volcano. Once the mountain cooled, the hole filled with water, creating a lake known today as Ring Lake.

Russia's Karymsky Volcano
The Karymsky Volcano is one of 160 volcanoes located on Russia's Kamchatka Peninsula. Of these, 29 are still active. Karymsky has erupted 29 times since 1771.

17.7 How Erosion Shapes the Landscape

Landslide! A hill starts to move, sending dirt, rocks, and trees tumbling down its slope. If you lived in the house at the bottom of the hill, you would probably see this event as a terrible disaster. A geographer, however, would also see it as an example of how erosion can reshape the surface of Earth.

Wind, Water, Ice, and Gravity Cause Erosion Erosion takes place everywhere on Earth through natural forces. Wind, moving water and ice, and gravity can all wear down the land around us.

Wind erodes land by picking up tiny grains of dirt and carrying them to distant places. This process wears away the layer of soil that covers Earth's crust. Wind can also grind away rocks and hills by blasting them with gritty sand and dirt.

Moving water also shapes the land. Rivers can carve away at the surrounding land to create deep **V-shaped valleys**. The faster a river flows, the more soil it can wash away and carry downstream. Along coastlines, ocean waves can wear away the shoreline to create steep banks and cliffs. Waves can also erode soil at the base of cliffs, causing the land above to collapse. When this happens, homes built on the cliffs may slide down into the sea.

Glaciers are another force of nature that reshapes the landscape. The weight of these enormous masses of ice exerts pressure that causes the glaciers to travel slowly downhill. As they move, glaciers gradually carve out valleys and create new landforms by depositing rock and soil. Over time, glaciers can transport huge quantities of rocks and soil debris over great distances.

Sources of Erosion

Wind, water, ice, and gravity all cause erosion. Wind moves soil from one place to another. Moving water and ice create cliffs and valleys. Gravity pulls land downhill in landslides and mudslides. Erosion caused by wind and water created the Grand Canyon.

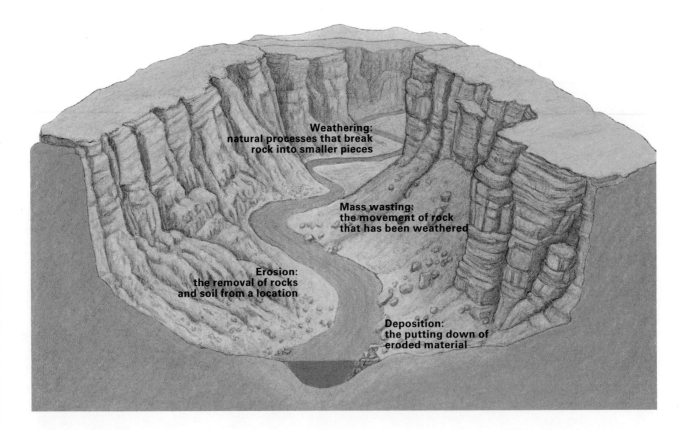

Weathering: natural processes that break rock into smaller pieces

Mass wasting: the movement of rock that has been weathered

Erosion: the removal of rocks and soil from a location

Deposition: the putting down of eroded material

Gravity is a constant force on the landscape. Anything that is not well rooted or attached to the ground will eventually give in to the force of gravity and move downhill. This downhill movement can occur so slowly that we may not even be aware of it, or it can occur quickly, as in a landslide or mudslide.

Floods Build Up Land On flat plains, water can build up as well as wear away land. After heavy rains, rivers overflow their banks and flood the surrounding plain. When the river returns to its banks, soil carried by the floodwater is left behind on the **floodplain**. This fresh layer of soil makes floodplains good places to farm, but the floods that create floodplains also make them dangerous places to live.

17.8 Signs of Erosion in Russia

Much of Russia is made up of vast plains. On the west side of the Ural Mountains is the Northern European Plain, and on the east side of the Urals are the West and Central Siberian plains. Over millions of years, wind, water, ice, and gravity have worn away any high ground on these plains. The flat or gently rolling land of the plains today is the result of this erosion.

The Volga River Many major rivers crisscross Russia's plains. One of them, the Volga, is Europe's longest river.

The Volga wanders south across the Northern European Plain, carrying along many tons of **sediment,** or soil and sand. When it floods, the Volga leaves some of the sediment on the surrounding land, a process known as *sedimentation*. Eventually the Volga deposits any remaining sediment into the Caspian Sea, turning its waters a cloudy green.

The Volga flows through the agricultural and industrial heartland of Russia. Almost half of the Russian population lives in the Volga River basin, relying on the river for power, transportation, and irrigation. No wonder Russians call the Volga "Matushka," which means "Mother."

The Amur River The Amur River flows from the mountains of northeast China and through eastern Siberia to empty into the Sea of Okhotsk. This sea is a large arm of the Pacific Ocean on the eastern boundary of Russia. For about 1,000 miles, the Amur River forms a natural boundary between Russia and China.

Like the Volga, the Amur River has become an important part of Russia's economy. Frequent springtime floods have created flat and fertile floodplains along the river's banks, making the plains a rich agricultural area. The Amur is also a source of transportation, with large boats traveling most of its length from April to November.

The Lena River The Lena River flows northward through Siberia into the Arctic Ocean. From above, this river looks like a black snake winding its way across the plains. In late spring, ice blocks the flow of water at the mouth of the Lena, causing water to back up and flood the land.

The Lena River Delta
This land along the Lena River shows signs of both flooding and erosion. Flooding built up the land that forms the Lena's banks. Erosion has worn it away.

17.9 How Glaciation Shapes the Landscape

In the coldest places on Earth, large fields of winter snow turn into ice that stays frozen all year. These masses of ice are called *glaciers*. Glaciers form over thousands of years as each new snowfall compresses the snow beneath it into a dense ice mass.

About 20,000 years ago, during the last ice age, glaciers covered one third of Earth's land surface. Most of North America was covered by ice. Gradually the glaciers retreated, changing the landscape as they moved. Today glaciers cover only one tenth of Earth's surface, but they can still shape the landscape in dramatic ways.

Two Kinds of Glaciers Geographers have identified two kinds of glaciers. **Continental glaciers** form in huge, thick sheets in areas with extremely cold climates, such as the two polar regions. Much of Antarctica, for instance, is buried under continental glaciers. The weight of the ice sheet eventually forces the edges of the glacier to push outward in all directions. Scientists call this movement *creeping*.

A second type of glacier, the **alpine glacier,** forms in high mountain valleys where snowfall is plentiful and temperatures are low. Instead of creeping outward, these rivers of ice slide downhill As the weight of new snow and ice grows, the glacier is pulled down the mountain by the force of gravity.

Glaciers Reshape the Land as They Move Glaciers move very slowly, but they have enormous power. They can grind the hardest rock into fine soil and push great loads of rock and dirt over long distances.

Continental glaciers erode land as they spread outward. They pick up rocks and soil as they creep, and pile them into mounds called **moraines**. Sometimes they leave behind finger-shaped holes in the land that, when the glaciers melt, become lakes. The Great Lakes of North America are an example of lakes formed by the movement of continental glaciers during the last ice age.

Alpine glaciers reshape the land as they travel downhill. Sometimes they scrape away whole hillsides, turning rounded mountaintops into pointed peaks that are called **horns**. As they move down canyons, alpine glaciers carve narrow V-shaped river valleys into broad **U-shaped valleys**. California's famous Yosemite Valley was reshaped in this way by an alpine glacier.

17.10 Signs of Glaciation in Russia

Earth has seen several long cold periods when glaciers covered vast regions. During the last of these ice ages, continental glaciers covered parts of Russia. As the climate warmed, those glaciers melted, but alpine glaciers still exist in the high mountains. Both types of glaciers have left their mark on Russia's landscape.

The Kolka Glacier The Kolka Glacier of the Caucasus Mountains is located on Mount Kazbek, one of the highest peaks in the range. In 2002, ice from a glacier overhanging the Kolka fell, triggering an **avalanche** that slid more than 11 miles. The glacial debris dammed rivers, creating several new lakes.

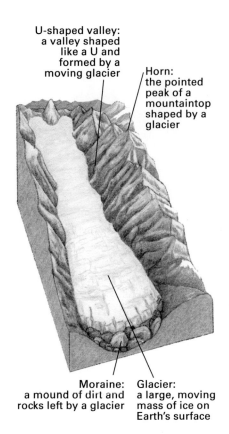

U-shaped valley: a valley shaped like a U and formed by a moving glacier

Horn: the pointed peak of a mountaintop shaped by a glacier

Moraine: a mound of dirt and rocks left by a glacier

Glacier: a large, moving mass of ice on Earth's surface

A Landscape Carved by Glaciers

Continental glaciers are large ice sheets that form over land with extremely cold weather. Their weight forces them to spread outward. Alpine glaciers form at the top of some mountains. Gravity pulls them downhill. Glaciers act like bulldozers, grinding and pushing land as they move. Glaciers can move between two inches and two feet a day.

The Amanauzsky Glacier The Amanauzsky Glacier is located in the western Caucasus Mountains. As this glacier slides downward, it is creating a large valley between two jagged mountain ridges.

The Glaciated Yamal Peninsula The Yamal Peninsula juts into the Arctic Ocean in northwestern Siberia. Continental glaciers once scraped across this peninsula, but today summers are just warm enough to melt each winter's snowfall. The melted water then fills the holes left behind by the glaciers, creating glacial lakes.

Glaciers in the Caucasus
Glaciers have covered the Caucasus Mountains since the last ice age. But over the last century, many have been melting. Curiously, as glaciers shrink, their numbers increase. This happens when big glaciers break up into smaller ones.

17.11 Beginning to Think Globally

In this chapter, you learned how four physical processes—tectonic movement, volcanic activity, erosion, and glaciation—shape our Earth. You read about how each process is at work on the varied landscape of Russia.

Tectonic movement is the slowest of these natural processes. Over time, however, tectonic movement has reshaped Earth's surface. Scientists believe that about 200 million years ago, all of Earth's land formed one huge continent. In time, this supercontinent broke apart into tectonic plates. Scientists have studied how the movement of these lithospheric plates formed the continents we know today.

Tectonic movement is still a powerful force at work on Earth's landscape. We feel the immediate effects every time an earthquake rattles windows or a volcano starts to smoke. Over time, these events will continue to reshape Earth's surface. Keep this idea in mind as you examine tectonic plates around the world in the next section.

17.12 Global Connections

The map shows the boundaries of the world's tectonic plates as well as active volcanic and earthquake zones. Notice how many volcanoes are located around the rim, or edge, of the Pacific Ocean. Scientists call this zone of volcanic activity the Ring of Fire.

Why is the Ring of Fire located around the Pacific Rim? A vast tectonic plate called the Pacific Plate lies under the Pacific Ocean and stretches from Asia to North America. When it moves against plates around the Pacific Rim, one plate is forced under the other. As one plate sinks, friction and the Earth's heat cause part of the plate to melt and rise to the surface, forming a volcano.

Why isn't there a Ring of Fire around the edge of the Atlantic Ocean? Look closely at edges of the Atlantic Ocean in North America and Europe, and notice that there are no plate boundaries there. The North American Plate and the Eurasian Plate meet in the middle of the Atlantic Ocean. As a result, there are no colliding plates around the edge of the Atlantic—and no Ring of Fire along those coastal areas.

How has tectonic movement shaped human life on Earth? Imagine our world without tectonic movement. All humankind might be living together on one flat supercontinent. Tectonic movement not only broke up the supercontinent into the continents we know today, but also built up most of Earth's mountains. In the past, both the oceans between continents and the high mountains that were hard to cross kept people isolated from one another. As a result, many individual human cultures developed over time in different landscapes.

Volcanoes and Earthquakes Around the World

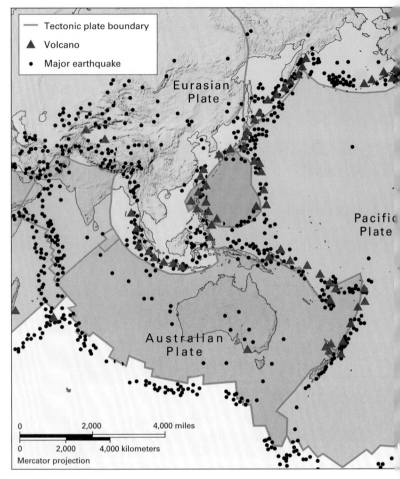

The Largest Earthquakes of the Twentieth Century

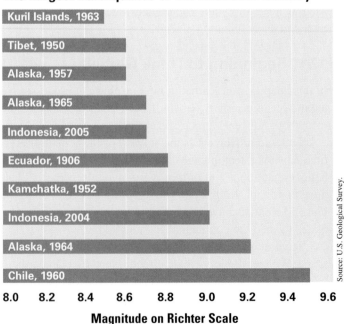

Source: U.S. Geological Survey.

Magnitude on Richter Scale

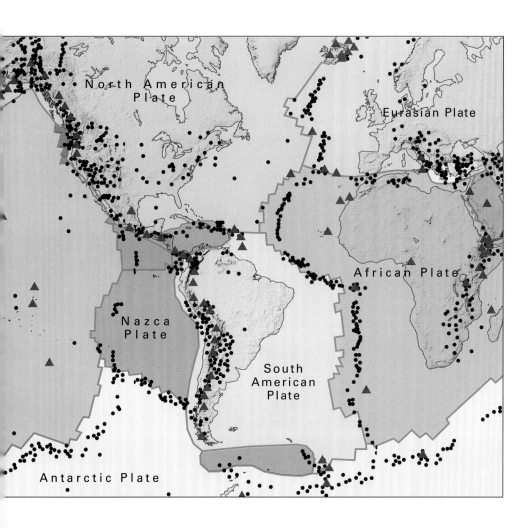

North American Plate

Eurasian Plate

African Plate

Nazca Plate

South American Plate

Antarctic Plate

Lava flow in Hawaii Volcanoes National Park

New Nation-States from the Old Soviet Empire: Will They Succeed?

18.1 Introduction

"Iron Felix" Dzerzhinsky was a brutal man. Under his direction, hundreds of thousands of people were killed in the Russian Revolution of 1917. The revolution destroyed the czarist **empire** of Russia. In its place, leaders created a new state called the Union of Soviet Socialist Republics, or Soviet Union, in 1922.

The new government controlled the 15 separate republics that made up the Soviet Union, and chose Iron Felix to set up a secret police force tasked with the job of destroying all opposition. The secret police arrested millions of people who were suspected of being disloyal. A statue of Dzerzhinsky in a Moscow square reminded people that the police were always watching.

In the 1980s, the Soviet government faced serious challenges to its authority. By 1991, people had had enough. An angry crowd attacked the statue of Iron Felix, cheering wildly as the symbol of fear tumbled. By year's end, the government had fallen as well. The Soviet Union was no more.

Fifteen new **nation-states** were formed out of the ruins of the Soviet empire. The term *nation-state* combines two ideas. The first, **nation,** refers to a group of people who share a common history and culture. Another term for people with such a shared identity is **ethnic group**. The second, **state,** refers to a political unit that controls a fixed territory. A nation-state is a country whose people mostly share a common identity.

In this chapter, you will read about the Soviet Union and five of the new nation-states that replaced it. And you will find out what makes a new nation-state likely to succeed or fail.

Essential Question

What factors contribute to the success or failure of new nation-states?

This illustration names 5 of the 15 new nation-states that came out of the old Soviet Union. Their success will depend on both economic and political factors. Keep this illustration in mind as you try to answer the Essential Question.

Graphic Organizer

LITHUANIA
BELARUS
RUSSIA
KAZAKHSTAN
AZERBAIJAN

◀ Statue of "Iron Felix" Dzerzhinsky in Moscow (top), Russian protesters toppling the statue in 1991 (bottom)

Voting in a New Nation-State

Every year an organization called Freedom House rates countries on how free they are. Freedom House looks at how well a country protects two kinds of rights. The first is political rights, such as the right to vote or run for office. The second is civil rights, including the right to speak and worship freely. Freedom House rates a country as free, partly free, or not free.

18.2 The Geographic Setting

The Soviet Union was a vast country, covering more than half of Europe and nearly two fifths of Asia. In area it was almost two and a half times the size of the United States. It had the third largest population in the world, behind China and India.

From Superpower to Failed State From 1945 to 1990, the Soviet Union was one of the world's two great **superpowers**. (The United States was the other.) Its armed forces were the largest in the world, and it possessed a fearsome nuclear arsenal. The Soviet Union also took the lead in space exploration for much of this period in history.

In 1991, however, this superpower collapsed. That year, the Soviet Union became the world's largest **failed state**. The question is why. One way to answer this question is to compare the Soviet Union with a successful nation-state.

Features of Successful Nation-States Many factors affect the success of a nation-state, but five are critical. Those factors are security, political freedom, economic growth, quality of life, and national unity.

The most important job of a nation-state is to keep its people safe. A successful state is strong enough to protect its people from foreign enemies, and its police work to keep people safe from crime. While the Soviet Union had a powerful army for defense, its secret police made people feel less, not more, secure.

A successful nation-state also protects the rights and freedoms of its citizens. In a free country, people choose their leaders by honest and fair elections, voting freely without fear of arrest. Elected leaders usually have the authority that comes from strong public support. In contrast, the Soviet Union was ruled by **dictators**—leaders who governed by force without the people's consent.

Another key to the success of a nation-state is economic growth, with the state using its resources and location to promote a healthy economy. Its **gross domestic product** (GDP)—the total value of goods and services produced in the country—rises over time. As GDP rises, incomes rise, and as incomes rise, poverty declines. In the Soviet Union, GDP rose slowly or not at all.

A successful nation-state also tries to improve its people's quality of life. The government works to ensure that its citizens have adequate and safe food, clean water, and good medical care. As people live healthier lives, **life expectancy** increases and **infant mortality rates** decrease. In the Soviet Union, however, quality of life was not improving for many people.

Successful nation-states inspire patriotism, or love of country, in their people, encouraging citizens to work to make the country succeed. Successful nation-states also inspire **nationalism**—feelings of pride and loyalty toward one's nation. In countries like the Soviet Union that have many ethnic groups, nationalism can create a sense of unity.

However, ethnic group nationalism can sometimes work against national unity. By 1991, ethnic loyalty in the Soviet Union had more support than loyalty to country. At that point, many ethnic groups decided that they would be better off as independent nation-states than as part of a failing Soviet Union.

▶ Geoterms

ethnic group a group of people in a country who share a unique culture and identity

nation a large group of people who share a common history and culture. Not all nations have their own government or control a territory. But in common use, the word *nation* often means a country or nation-state.

nationalism feelings of loyalty and pride toward one's nation or ethnic group. Nationalism sometimes includes the belief that one's nation or group is better than all others.

nation-state an independent state, or country, whose people mostly share a common identity

state a political unit that controls a particular territory

A Diverse Region

More than 100 ethnic groups lived in the Soviet Union at the time of its collapse. This map shows the major ethnic groups that were in various areas. Conflicts among ethnic groups helped bring about the collapse of this state.

Major Ethnic Groups in the Soviet Union

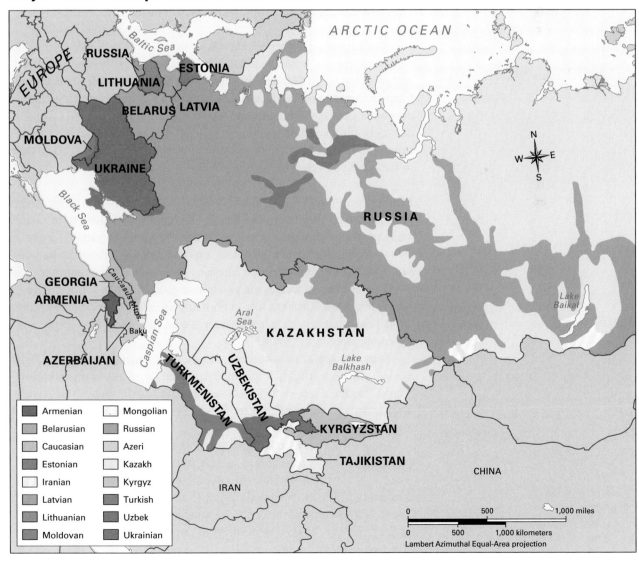

A Kazakh Herdsman

For centuries, the Kazakhs were mainly nomads, people who move from place to place. They raised sheep, goats, cattle, and horses for meat, wool, and hides. They traveled hundreds of miles each year in search of pasture for their herds. A few Kazakhs still follow this ancient way of life.

KAZAKHSTAN

18.3 Kazakhstan: A Central Asian Giant

The nation-state of Kazakhstan is a Central Asian giant surrounded by other giants. To the southeast lies China. To the north lies Russia. To the west lies the Caspian Sea.

An Arid Land with Many Resources While much of Kazakhstan is too **arid** for agriculture, the northern region and some irrigated areas in the south yield abundant crops. Kazakhs also raise cattle, goats, poultry, pigs, and sheep.

Kazakhstan's greatest resource is its minerals. It has large deposits of coal, lead, copper, iron, and zinc. But Kazakhstan's most significant mineral resource is oil. Some of the world's largest oil reserves lie under the Caspian Sea, and oil production has become a major part of the country's economy. Because of Kazakhstan's prime location between the Caspian Sea and China, oil production promises to be even more important in the future. Construction of pipelines across Kazakhstan will allow oil to flow to the rapidly developing cities of China.

Ethnic Conflicts Create a Split The Kazakhs are the main ethnic group in Kazakhstan, making up about half of the nation's population. Russians, many of whom **immigrated** to Kazakhstan during the Soviet era, make up about a third of the population. Religious and cultural differences between Muslim Kazakhs and Christian Russians often divide the two groups.

To make things worse, the two ethnic groups have a serious north-south split. Most Russians live in northern Kazakhstan, where they work in the heavy industry developed under Soviet rule. Most Kazakhs live in the countryside in the south.

Meanwhile, Kazakhstan faces serious environmental problems. Under Soviet rule, poor irrigation methods damaged farmland, and **pesticides** seeped into the water supply. Factories released **toxic waste**. The Soviets also carried out secret nuclear testing, and many people still suffer serious health problems as a result.

Looking ahead, Kazakhstan's survival will depend on several factors. One factor is using its resources wisely to promote economic growth. Another is solving its environmental problems and therefore improving the quality of life of its citizens. A third factor crucial to the success of Kazakhstan is calming the conflict among ethnic groups that divides the country. If it can succeed at meeting all three challenges, Kazakhstan may face a bright future.

18.4 Azerbaijan: Where Europe Meets Asia

Together, the new nation-states of Armenia, Georgia, and Azerbaijan are known as the Caucasus because of the steep Caucasus Mountains that tower over them. This region is one of the world's great crossroads, where Europe meets Asia. Azerbaijan's location and resources hold the keys to its future.

A Country Rich in Oil Azerbaijan's huge deposits of oil are its greatest source of wealth and its number one export. In fact, Azerbaijan was the birthplace of the oil-refining industry. Today the capital city of Baku, with the finest harbor on the Caspian Sea, is the center of Azerbaijan's oil industry.

During Soviet rule, oil pipelines sent all of Azerbaijan's oil to neighboring Russia. When the Soviet Union collapsed, however, so did its hold on Azerbaijan. The new country was then free to sell its oil anywhere in the world.

Since 1991, Azerbaijan has signed agreements with many foreign oil companies. Construction of new pipelines will enable Azerbaijan to move its oil to customers outside of Russia. Working with foreign oil companies is not easy, but Azerbaijan's economic success depends on opening new markets for its oil.

Ethnic Warfare Clouds the Future Ethnic conflicts between groups in Azerbaijan and neighboring Armenia have been a major obstacle to progress for the new nation-state. The Azeris are the main ethnic group in Azerbaijan, making up over 90 percent of the population. Most Azeris are Muslim. About 2 percent of the population in Azerbaijan is Armenian, and most Armenians are Christians. The Azeris and the Armenians have a long history of conflict.

Nagorno-Karabakh is a region within Azerbaijan that is primarily Armenian. The people of this region want to be independent from Azerbaijan and, in 1992, war broke out between the two groups. Thousands of people were killed, and almost a million people fled from the fighting. Though a cease-fire was called in 1994, the problem was not solved. Violence continues to this day and threatens the stability of Azerbaijan.

A Wealth of Oil

Oil is Azerbaijan's most important resource. It has enough oil to fill more than 200 billion barrels. One barrel of oil produces about 19 gallons of gasoline.

18.5 Belarus: Between Europe and Russia

The word Belarus means "white Russia." No one knows for sure why the color is part of the country's name. It might refer to the snow that often covers the land. It might describe the white bark of the birch trees in its forests. The "rus" part of Belarus reflects its location next to Russia on its eastern border. On the west, Belarus borders Europe.

A Landlocked Country of Many Lakes This nation of rolling plains and dense forests is **landlocked**. In other words, it is surrounded entirely by land, with no access to the sea. Long ago, glaciers scraped across its plains, creating the 11,000 lakes that dot the Belarus landscape.

In the past, the economy of Belarus was based on agriculture and logging. While both activities are still important today, now about a fifth of Belarusian farmland and forestland can no longer be used. Tragically, this land was poisoned when the nearby Chernobyl nuclear power plant exploded in 1986. Much of this large area will never be safe for farming or logging again.

Belarus Looks East to Russia Russian influence is strong in Belarus, though the population of the country is approximately 81 percent Belarusian and only 11 percent Russian. During Soviet rule, Russian workers and government officials did much to develop Belarus. They cleared and drained its land to create farms managed by the government. They also brought manufacturing and industry to Belarusian cities. The Russians also shaped the Belarusian political system and influenced its culture.

Today Belarus still has close ties to Russia. Most of its foreign trade is with Russia, and it depends on Russian gas and oil to run its industries. The two countries have signed agreements to work together closely in the future.

However, relations between Belarus and Russia are not always smooth. The two countries disagree about labor and trade issues and have different ideas about how much power the government should have over its citizens and industries. Although the economy of Belarus is growing, there are many challenges ahead.

A Belarus Tractor Factory

Making farm machines is a large industry in Belarus. These tractors were built in Minsk, the capital of Belarus.

18.6 Lithuania: One of Three Baltic States

Three former republics of the Soviet Union—Lithuania, Latvia, and Estonia—are known as the Baltic States. They line the eastern shore of the Baltic Sea. Lithuania can look either east or west for political ties. More and more, it looks west.

An Economy Based on Soil and the Sea The fertile soil of Lithuania produces good crops. Farmers grow potatoes, sugar beets, and flax for cloth. Fields of grain cross the central plains. Dairy farms are everywhere, and cattle, sheep, pigs, and poultry provide meat and eggs. The Baltic Sea provides a rich source of food as well, with its fishing grounds and fish farms.

Lithuania has limited mineral resources. The Lithuanians mine limestone, gravel, sand, and clay to make cement, glass, and ceramics. But fossil fuels and metals are in short supply.

Lithuania Looks West to Europe Lithuania has a long history of unity, having come together as a nation around 1200. With a strong sense of nationalism, Lithuania was the first republic of the Soviet Union to declare its independence as a nation-state in 1990.

Since their independence from Soviet rule, the Lithuanian people have reformed their political system. They have looked toward Europe for their models, and today they have a democratic government with leaders chosen in free and fair elections.

Lithuania has sought to join the European community economically as well. In 2004, Lithuania became a member of the **European Union,** or EU. Chapter 14 explores the EU in detail. Lithuania receives monetary support from the EU to help develop its economy.

Lithuania has also joined the North Atlantic Treaty Organization, or NATO. Members of NATO promise to defend each other if attacked by another country. By joining NATO and the EU, Lithuanians hope to create a future of peace and prosperity.

RUSSIA

18.7 Russia: The Largest Nation on Earth

Imagine observing from space as your country breaks apart and then ceases to exist. That's what Soviet astronaut Sergei Krikalev did in 1991. He flew up to the Mir space station as a citizen of the Soviet Union. While he circled Earth 16 times a day, the Soviet Union collapsed. When he finally set foot on land, he was still a citizen of the largest nation on Earth. But that nation was now Russia.

Rich Resources in a Vast Land Although Russia is not as large as the Soviet Union was, it's still huge. It has vast forests and large deposits of coal and minerals, with its most important resources being oil and natural gas. Because of its cold **climate,** however, less than 8 percent of Russia's land is suitable for farming.

During Soviet rule, the government owned and operated this vast country's farms, factories, and businesses. When Soviet rule ended, the government sold these factories and businesses. But these sales did not help the Russian people. Powerful political leaders grabbed the best businesses for themselves.

Today most Russian businesses are privately run, but not always well run. Many of the factories the government sold were old, run down, and in need of modernization, but often the new owners had no money to make the changes. Other businesses made goods of such poor quality that no one wanted to buy them. As a result, many businesses failed.

In spite of all its challenges, Russia's economy has been growing every year. Oil exports are a big reason for this growth.

St. Basil's Cathedral

Ivan the Terrible, the first czar of all Russia, built St. Basil's Cathedral. Legend says that when the church was finished, Ivan ordered its architect to be blinded. This, the czar hoped, would prevent him from ever creating anything so beautiful again. However, the architect did go on to design another cathedral.

The Challenges Facing Russians Today Life is not easy in Russia. The crime rate is high. Housing is very costly, and many people have to crowd in with relatives. Alcohol abuse and pollution are also big concerns that threaten people's health.

Ethnic nationalism and religious divisions have caused problems in Russia as well. Russia's 150 million people come from dozens of ethnic groups, not all of which are pleased to still be a part of Russia. In addition, most Russians belong to the Russian Orthodox Church, but Russia also has minority religious groups such as Muslim, Jewish, Buddhist, and non-Orthodox Christian. The law limits the activities of some religious groups. For example, some of them are not allowed to print religious literature or operate religious schools.

In an area of southwest Russia known as Chechnya, opposition to Russian rule has led to outright rebellion. During the collapse of the Soviet Union in 1991, a group of Chechen leaders declared independence from Russia. But in 1994, Russian tanks rolled into Chechnya to crush the independence movement. More than 100,000 Chechens died in the war that followed. Though a cease-fire brought an official peace to Chechnya in 1996, the conflict continues. Battles, bombings, and terrorist attacks have killed thousands of people on both sides of the conflict.

18.8 Beginning to Think Globally

In this chapter, you learned about five factors that affect whether a new nation-state will succeed or fail. These factors are security, political freedom, economic growth, quality of life, and national unity. You have seen the power of nationalism to unite a country. You have also seen how conflict among ethnic groups can tear a country apart.

Each of the 15 nation-states that arose from the former Soviet Union has its own story, and only time will tell whether each will succeed. The same could have been said about the United States in its early years, as its future also looked uncertain. It won its war of independence only with outside help. Its people felt more loyal to their states than to a new country called the United States, and they distrusted the federal government. The country's economy was weak. And its first government could not seem to hold the new nation together.

The world is always changing, with empires rising and collapsing and new nations starting and failing. Think about these changes as you look at the map showing the rise of new nations in the next section. Which nations will succeed? And which are likely to fail?

Air Pollution in Russia
During Soviet rule, new factories were built across Russia. But little attention was paid to pollution. In 84 of Russia's largest cities, air pollution is still 10 times the level that is considered safe.

18.9 Global Connections

The map shows new nations that have arisen since 1945, and the table gives data about three nations that have gained their independence since 1990. Think about what the information in the table might reveal about each nation's chance of success.

What were these new nations before they gained their independence? Most of the new nations formed since 1945 were once colonies ruled by other nations. This history of colonial rule is especially true for the new nations of Africa and Asia. Namibia, for example, was once a German colony in Africa. Other new nations were parts of dying empires or failed states. Croatia, for instance, was once a part of the failed state of Yugoslavia. Still other new nations were parts of nations that still exist. East Timor, for example, was part of Indonesia from 1976 until 1999, when it won its independence.

How did these new nations gain their independence? Most new nations gain their independence through violent struggle. Namibia, Croatia, and East Timor all had to fight to become independent nations. Some new nations, however, have a peaceful start. When the Soviet Union collapsed in 1991, its 15 republics peacefully gained their independence.

Which of these new nations are most likely to succeed? The answer, as you have learned, depends on many factors. Namibia, for example, is rich in mineral resources, but its black majority is divided among many ethnic groups. Neither East Timor nor Croatia is so divided, but both are struggling to rebuild economies devastated by years of war.

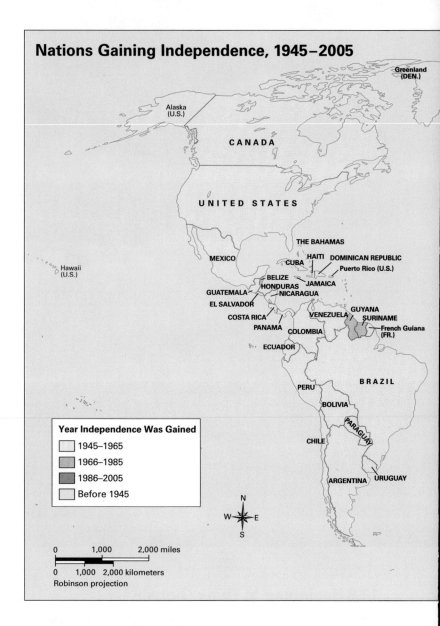

Nations Gaining Independence, 1945–2005

Year Independence Was Gained
- 1945–1965
- 1966–1985
- 1986–2005
- Before 1945

Information About Three New Nations

Nation	Life Expectancy (years)	GDP per Capita	Population Below Poverty Line
Namibia	41	$7,200	50%
Croatia	74	$10,600	under 10%
East Timor	66	$500	42%

Infant Mortality (deaths per 1,000 births)	Ethnic Diversity	Freedom Index Ranking*	Year of Independence
70	black 88%, white 6%, mixed 6%	political rights, 2 civil liberties, 3	1990
7	Croatian 90%, Serb 4%, other 6%	political rights, 2 civil liberties, 2	1992
49	Austronesian, Papuan, small Chinese minority	political rights, 3 civil liberties, 3	2002

*On this scale, 1 represents the highest degree of freedom, and 7 the lowest.

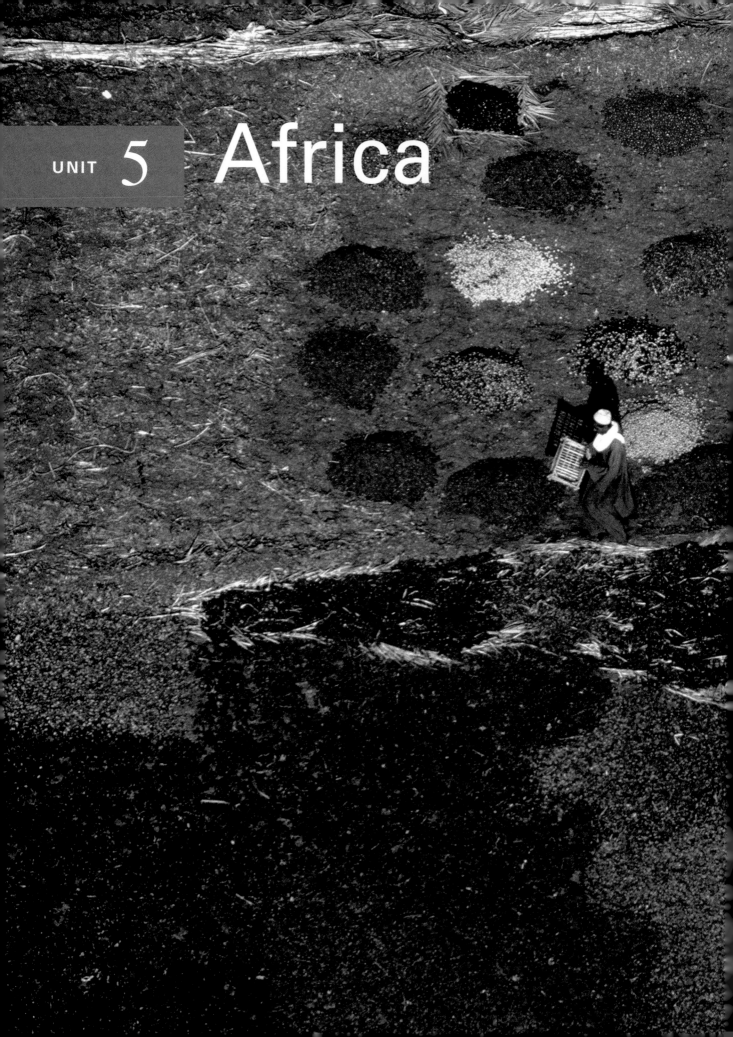

UNIT **5** Africa

Introducing the Region:
Physical and Human Geography

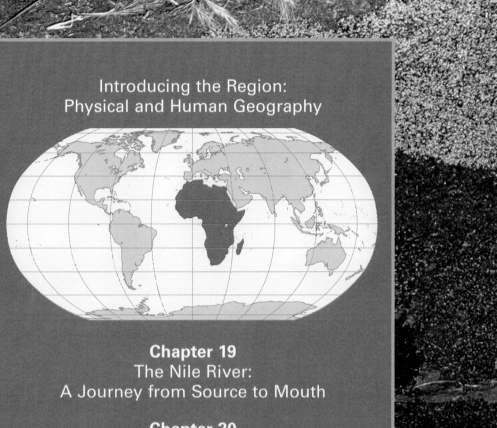

What do you see in this photograph?
See page 514 for details.

▼

Introducing the Region: Physical Geography

Africa is the second largest continent. The Atlantic Ocean lies to the west. The Indian Ocean lies to the east. The Mediterranean Sea and Red Sea lie to the north. A small piece of land in the northeast corner connects Africa to Asia. There are 47 countries on the continent of Africa. Six island **nations** are also part of the **region**. The largest of these islands is Madagascar.

Africa is made up of four subregions. The subregions of North Africa, East Africa, and West Africa occupy the northern half of the continent. The southern half is one large subregion called Central and Southern Africa.

Physical Features of Africa

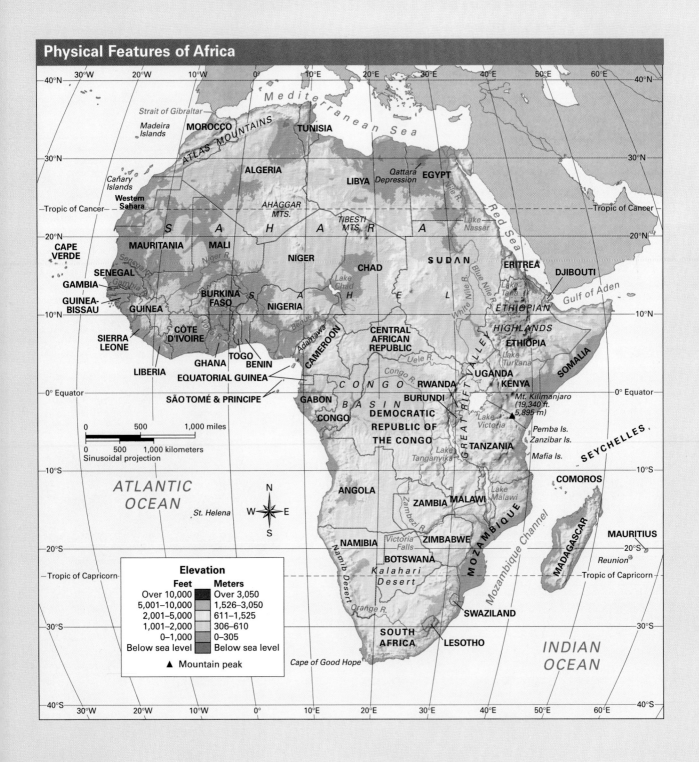

Physical Features

Africa is often called the "plateau continent." The land is shaped like an upside-down pie plate. Much of the center is a high, dry **plateau**. At the edges of the continent, this plateau sometimes slopes to a coastal plain. In other places, it drops sharply into the sea.

There are huge, low-lying areas called **basins** in several places on this plateau. Four mighty rivers flow from these basins to the sea. Sometimes the land falls steeply as the rivers flow downstream. As a result, ships are not able to sail very far up these rivers into Africa's interior.

North Africa

The Sahara is the main **physical feature** in North Africa. It is the world's largest **desert**. The Sahara has sand dunes, bare rock, gravel plains, and mountains. The Nile, Africa's longest river, runs through this desert and empties into the Mediterranean Sea. The Atlas Mountains stretch across the northwestern part of this region. They are part of the same mountain system as the Alps in Europe.

West Africa

South of the Sahara lies the Sahel region. The plains of the Sahel are mostly dry grassland. The Niger River runs through the western Sahel. This is the third longest river in Africa. Also in the Sahel is a large lake called Lake Chad. This lake shrinks and grows depending on the season. In general, it has been getting smaller for many years.

Mount Kilimanjaro towers over the grasslands in East Africa.

East Africa

Three large lakes lie in or near the Great Rift Valley. Lake Tanganyika is the longest **freshwater** lake in the world. Lake Victoria is the world's second largest freshwater lake, and Lake Malawi is the ninth largest.

To the east of Lake Victoria, Mount Kilimanjaro rises from the plains. At 19,340 feet, this peak is the highest point in Africa.

The Ethiopian Highlands lie to the north of the lake. This rugged area covers two thirds of the country of Ethiopia.

Central and Southern Africa

The Congo basin is a major physical feature of Central and Southern Africa. This large, low-lying area sits at the center of the continent. The Congo River loops through this basin and empties into the Atlantic Ocean. Farther south lies the Zambezi River. This river has many waterfalls. The largest of these is the beautiful Victoria Falls. Two deserts, the Namib and Kalahari, make up much of the southern part of this region.

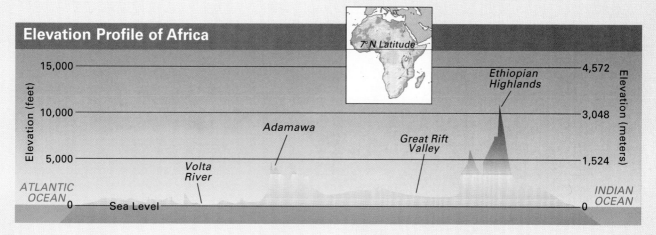

Elevation Profile of Africa

7° N Latitude

Elevation (feet)		Elevation (meters)
15,000	Ethiopian Highlands	4,572
10,000		3,048
5,000	Adamawa / Great Rift Valley	1,524
0 Sea Level	Volta River	0

ATLANTIC OCEAN

INDIAN OCEAN

Climate

The equator runs through the middle of Africa. As a result, the **climate** in most of Africa is warm all year. However, some regions are very wet and others very dry.

As you read in Chapter 2, places near the equator are warm because the sun is almost directly overhead all year. As the air over the equator warms, it expands and rises. Once it rises, the air begins to cool. If the air is wet, it drops moisture in the form of rain as it cools. In Africa, this rain falls in a wide band north and south of the equator.

After rising, this air begins to move toward the North or South poles. But by this time, it is quite dry. As a result, little or no rain falls on parts of Africa farther away from the equator. This lack of rainfall has created vast deserts in northern and southern Africa.

North Africa

Most of North Africa is very dry. Some places in the Sahara can go for six or seven years without rain. Areas of North Africa near the Mediterranean Sea enjoy a **Mediterranean** climate. Here it is warm all year with dry summers and short, rainy winters.

West Africa

The climate of West Africa varies widely from north to south. The northern part is **arid** and **semiarid**. Moving south, the climate changes to **tropical wet and dry**. This area is hot all year with rainy and dry seasons. Closer to the equator, coastal areas have a **tropical wet** climate. This means it is hot and rainy all year. Some coastal areas get an average of more than 120 inches of rain a year.

East Africa

The parts of East Africa that lie in or close to the Sahara have an arid or semiarid climate. But the Ethiopian Highlands and Mount Kilimanjaro have a **highlands** climate. In these areas, the higher land is cooler and wetter. The lower land is warmer and drier. The southern part of East Africa has a tropical wet and dry climate.

Boats sail on the Nile River near the city of Aswan, Egypt. Would you ever need an umbrella in Aswan?

Central and Southern Africa

In this large subregion, the land nearest the equator has a tropical wet climate. Farther south, the climate shifts to tropical wet and dry, and finally to arid or semiarid.

The climate shifts again in the southernmost part of this subregion. Some coastal areas along the Indian Ocean have a **marine west coast** climate. People there enjoy warm summers, cool winters, and rainfall year-round. Other coastal areas have a **humid subtropical** climate. Summers are hot with heavy rains. Winters are mild with some rain.

The large island of Madagascar has three **climate zones**. The eastern half has a tropical wet climate. The northwestern and central area has a tropical wet and dry climate. The southwestern part has a semiarid climate.

Vegetation

About two fifths of Africa's land is **tropical grassland**. Another name for this vegetation zone is **savanna**. In addition to short and tall grasses, shrubs and trees are scattered over this rolling grassland. Both the grasses and trees are adapted to a tropical wet and dry climate. Many trees drop their leaves in the long dry season. Some have trunks that can store water. The grasses have long roots that reach for water deep in the earth.

North Africa

Desert and **desert scrub** cover most of North Africa. Few plants grow in the desert. Small trees, bushes, and other plants adapted to a dry climate make up desert scrub.

The land along the Mediterranean Sea is covered with **chaparral** plants. The small trees and bushes of this area are adapted to long, dry summers. A narrow strip of **broadleaf evergreen forest** runs along the Nile River through Egypt. Tropical grasslands cover the southern edge of the Sahara.

West Africa

Tropical grassland blankets much of West Africa. But over the years, some of this grassland has become desert. This has happened partly because of long dry periods with very little rain.

The southern part of West Africa is a broadleaf evergreen forest. This is also called **rainforest**. Many trees grow to 100 feet or taller. The shady floor of this forest zone gets little direct sunlight. As a result, few bushes or grasses grow there.

Heavy rain makes travel difficult in the tropical rainforests of the Congo basin.

East Africa

Tropical grassland also covers most of East Africa. Some coastal lands are broadleaf evergreen forests. Much of Ethiopia lies in a **highlands** vegetation zone. There, the kinds of plants change with the altitude. Bamboo, cedar trees, and tree ferns grow in lower areas. On the higher slopes are meadows covered in grasses and flowers. Mosses and lichen grow near the mountaintops.

Central and Southern Africa

Broadleaf evergreen forest covers the Congo basin, which lies on the equator. Hundreds of kinds of trees live in this forest. South of this basin, most of the land is tropical grassland.

The Namib and most of the Kalahari have desert and desert scrub vegetation. The eastern Kalahari has tropical grassland. Mountain ranges in Southern Africa have highlands vegetation. The southern tip of this region is blanketed in chaparral.

Zebras thrive on the tropical grasslands in East Africa.

Africa is home to 53 countries. The largest one is Sudan. It covers almost 1 million square miles. The smallest African country is Seychelles. This is a group of about 115 small islands scattered over the Indian Ocean, north of Madagascar. Together these islands have a land area of only about 176 square miles.

Africa is a region of many cultural and language groups. By some estimates, Africans speak at least 2,000 languages. Some of these, such as Arabic and Swahili, are widely used. Others are spoken only by small groups. Despite their differences, all Africans share a long history.

Political Boundaries of Africa

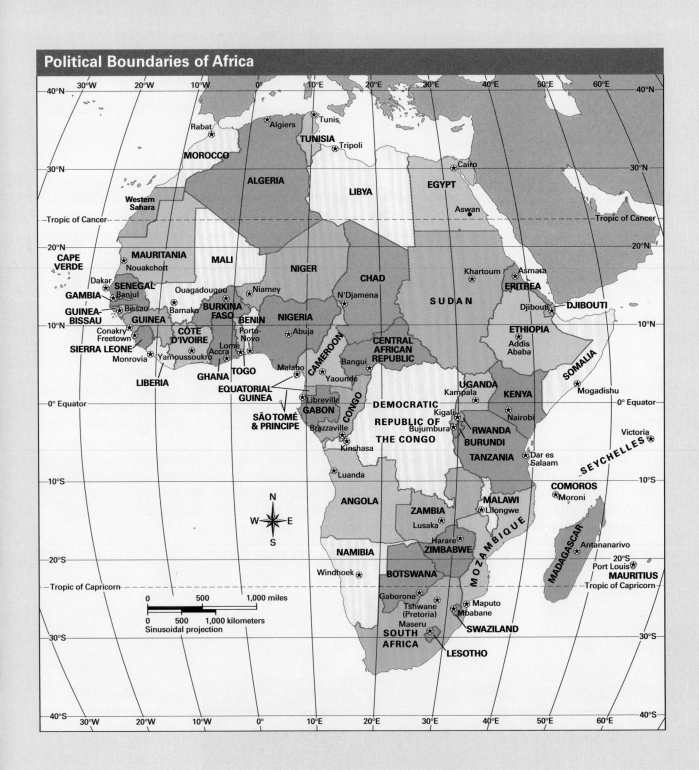

History

Scientists have found the bones of human-like species who lived in Africa millions of years ago. For this reason, people call Africa the birthplace of the human race.

Early Times

Early African people were hunters and gatherers. Learning to farm changed the way people lived. By 5000 B.C.E., Africans were raising animals and growing crops.

The Nile River valley was home to one of the world's earliest civilizations. The Egyptian civilization lasted for more than 2,000 years. The ancient Egyptians invented a kind of paper and a form of picture writing. They learned how to preserve the bodies of the dead as mummies. They also built the Egyptian pyramids, which still stand today.

Kingdoms and Colonies

Beginning around 300 C.E., three great kingdoms arose in West Africa. The first one, Ghana, ruled until the mid–11th century. After the fall of Ghana, the kingdom of Mali rose to power. The last of the three, the Songhai **empire**, rose and fell between 1400 and 1600.

The wealth of these kingdoms came from their control of trade across the Sahara. Arab traders from North Africa brought salt and copper from mines in the Sahara to West African markets. They traded these goods for gold, ivory, and slaves. The traders carried their faith with them. They spread the religion of Islam across much of Africa.

Europeans began to explore Africa in the 1400s. The Portuguese set up trading posts along the west coast of Africa. At first they were interested in gold. But they soon began to ship Africans to Europe as slaves.

The slave trade expanded after Europeans set up colonies in the Americas. The European colonists needed workers to help them raise crops like sugar and tobacco. To meet that need, millions of Africans were captured and shipped across the Atlantic Ocean as slaves. The Atlantic slave trade did not end until around 1850.

In the 1700s and 1800s, Europeans began setting up colonies in Africa. The Belgians took control of the Congo basin. France gained control of Algeria and Tunisia. Great Britain took over Egypt. By 1914, European countries had divided up most of Africa.

The Modern Era

In 1957, Ghana became the first black African colony to gain its independence. Over the next 10 years, most of Africa threw off colonial rule.

Few of the new countries were prepared for self-rule. Since gaining their independence, they have struggled to create stable governments. Tensions between **ethnic groups** have led to unrest in many countries.

In 2002, most African countries came together to form the African Union. The African Union helps its members work together for the benefit of all Africans. It promotes peace and human rights. It also works to improve public health.

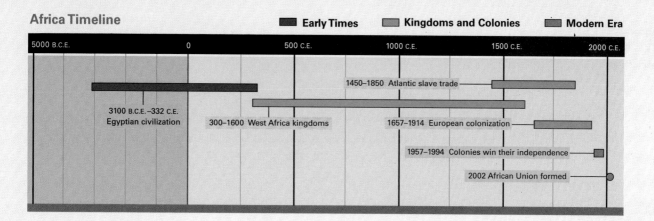

Africa Timeline   ■ Early Times   ■ Kingdoms and Colonies   ■ Modern Era

| 5000 B.C.E. | 0 | 500 C.E. | 1000 C.E. | 1500 C.E. | 2000 C.E. |

1450–1850 Atlantic slave trade

3100 B.C.E.–332 C.E. Egyptian civilization

300–1600 West Africa kingdoms

1657–1914 European colonization

1957–1994 Colonies win their independence

2002 African Union formed

Population

As of 2005, about 906 million people live in Africa. This is one seventh of the world's people. Only Asia has more people. Africa has the fastest growing population in the world.

About three fifths of Africans live in **rural** areas. Most of them live in small villages, much as their ancestors did. In recent years, however, a growing number of Africans have been moving to cities.

People in Africa follow many different religious traditions. About 4 out of 10 Africans are Muslims. Most Muslims live in North and West Africa. Christians just slightly outnumber Muslims. The majority of Christians live in West, East, and Central and Southern Africa.

Over 100 million people practice indigenous religions. There are hundreds of these local faiths. But they have many features in common. Like most other religions, they explain how the universe was created. They teach what is right and wrong. And they help people know how to live a good life.

Africa: Major Religions

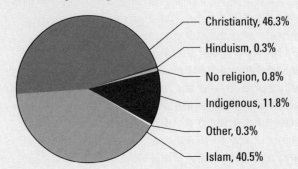

Christianity, 46.3%
Hinduism, 0.3%
No religion, 0.8%
Indigenous, 11.8%
Other, 0.3%
Islam, 40.5%

Africa: Urban and Rural Population, 2000

Urban, 37.1%

Rural, 62.9%

= 10% of the total population

Africa: Population Growth, 1950–2050

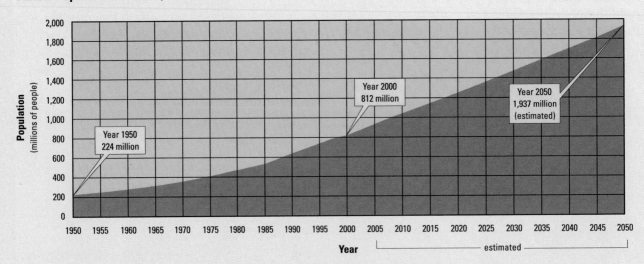

Year 1950
224 million

Year 2000
812 million

Year 2050
1,937 million
(estimated)

Population (millions of people)

Year — estimated

Sources: Population Division of the Department of Economic and Social Affairs of the United Nations Secretariat, "World Population Prospects: The 2004 Revision" and "World Urbanization Prospects: The 2003 Revision," esa.un.org/unpp. "Religion," *Encyclopædia Britannica*, 2005, Encyclopædia Britannica Premium Service, www.britannica.com.

Economic Activity

Mining is an important **economic activity** in Africa. Mining is the process of digging minerals and coal out of the ground. Mining most likely began in Africa thousands of years ago. Today half of the value of Africa's exports is from mining.

There are many methods of mining. Each depends on where a mineral deposit is located. When the deposit is near the surface, mining can be done in large, open pits. When the deposit is deep underground, miners must dig tunnels to reach it. Both open pit and underground mines are used in Africa to get at its mineral wealth.

Resources

Oil is a key resource in parts of North and West Africa. Most of the oil imported into Europe comes from this region.

Central and Southern Africa are a center for diamond mines. In fact, Africa produces almost three fourths of the world's diamonds.

Gold is another important resource. More gold is mined in Central and Southern Africa than in any other region of the world.

Land Use

The grasslands of North and East Africa are used for **nomadic herding**. Herders move from place to place to find food and water for their animals.

A herder in Senegal gives his goats water from a well. Senegal lies in the arid western Sahel.

More than half of Africa's farmland is used for **subsistence farming**. This means that the farmers are raising just enough food to feed their families.

In recent years, many Africans have turned to **commercial farming**. Egyptian farmers raise cotton along the Nile River and in the Nile Delta. Large groves of date palms grow around **oases** in the Sahara. The rainforests of West Africa produce cocoa beans. These are used to make chocolate.

Most trade and manufacturing takes place in South Africa. This country produces about two fifths of Africa's manufactured goods, including cars, clothing, steel, and electronics. Many other nations across Africa are working to promote the growth of industry.

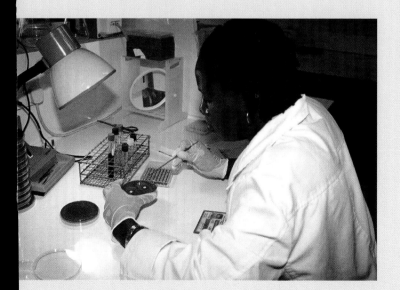

As African countries continue to develop, the importance of trade and manufacturing will increase. There will be more jobs for highly skilled workers like this lab scientist in Nairobi, Kenya.

The Nile River: A Journey from Source to Mouth

19

19.1 Introduction

Thousands of years ago, the Nile River gave rise to one of the world's first civilizations. The ancient Egyptians built great cities, temples, and pyramids along the river. They grew crops on the river's banks and sailed boats on its waters. The Egyptians wrote songs and poems in praise of the river. The Nile gave life to ancient Egypt, and today it remains a key part of Egyptian life.

However, the Nile is not just an Egyptian river. The river begins its long journey far to the south of Egypt in the **highlands** of East Africa. Along its way to the Mediterranean Sea, the Nile River crosses mountains, **plateaus,** plains, and **deserts**. The **river basin** of this great waterway encompasses an area of more than 1 million square miles, which is approximately one tenth of the African continent. A river basin is the area that is drained by a river and the smaller streams that flow into that river. The Nile River basin includes portions of 10 African countries. Forty percent of all Africans live in these 10 countries.

In this chapter, you will follow the course of the Nile River, discovering how the river changes during its lengthy journey from the highlands of East Africa to the Mediterranean Sea. You will read about the origins of the Nile and about the explorers who traced the great river to its sources. You will also learn about the impact of the river on the people and environment of the Nile River basin.

Essential Question

How do rivers change as they flow across Earth's surface?

This map shows the course of the Nile River on its journey from its sources to the sea. The Nile flows through several countries. It also crosses several parallels of latitude, including the equator and the Tropic of Cancer. During its long journey, the Nile changes in many ways. Keep this map in mind as you try to answer the Essential Question.

Graphic Organizer

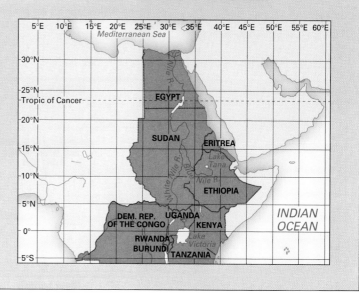

◀ Ancient mosaic of life on the Nile River

19.2 The Geographic Setting

Since most of Egypt is a barren, sandy desert, the ancient Egyptians could not have survived without the life-giving waters of the Nile River. For that reason, the ancient Greek scholar Herodotus referred to Egypt as the "gift of the Nile." Despite the river's great importance, the ancient Egyptians never knew just where it came from. In fact, the sources of the Nile would remain a mystery for thousands of years.

The World's Longest River The Nile River has two main branches, the White Nile and the Blue Nile. The White Nile is the river's longest branch, running north for about 4,160 miles from its most distant **tributary** in the highlands of Burundi. This great length, which is more than twice the distance from Chicago to Los Angeles, makes the Nile the world's longest river.

Every year, the waters of the Nile rise and fall with the seasons. These changes in the river level are tied to the water cycle that brings rain to the highlands of Africa. The **water cycle** is the constant movement of water from Earth's surface to the **atmosphere** and back again. After the rainy season, the rising water will often flood the land that lies along the Nile's banks.

The Gifts of Water, Transportation, and Power The Nile has long been essential to the people who live and work along its banks. These people rely on the river water not only for drinking, washing, and cooking, but also for raising crops. During ancient times, the seasonal flooding of the Nile left large deposits of rich **silt** on farmlands near the river. Farmers planted their crops in this fine, dark soil, and they used the floodwaters to help irrigate their fields. Later on, farmers developed **perennial irrigation,** which is a system that distributes water to farm fields throughout the year.

The Nile is also useful for transportation and energy. People living near the Nile have long used the river as a water highway that carries goods and people by boat from place to place. Furthermore, the Nile has great **hydroelectric potential,** which means that the power of the flowing water can be used to generate electrical power. Cities along the Nile depend on **hydroelectric power** to meet their energy needs.

Two Views of the Nile

The satellite image above shows the path of the Nile River after the White and Blue Niles join. The diagram below shows the change in the Nile's elevation as the river flows from its source in the highlands of Burundi to the Mediterranean Sea. From its source to the sea, the Nile drops more than a mile in elevation.

Elevation Profile of the Nile

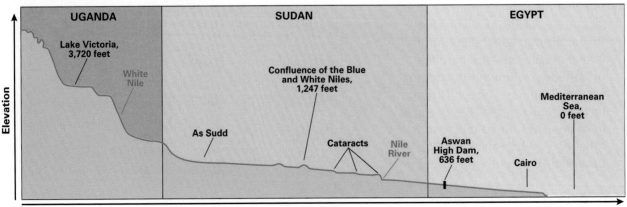

▶ Geoterms

hydroelectric potential the electrical power that can be generated from flowing water

perennial irrigation a system that allows for the year-round watering of crops

river basin the area drained by a river and its tributaries. These tributaries are the smaller streams that flow into the main river. Rain falling anywhere in a river basin will eventually flow into the main river.

water cycle the movement of water from the surface of Earth to the atmosphere and back again. During this cycle, water evaporates from rivers, lakes, and oceans, rises and condenses into clouds, and then falls back to Earth as rain, hail, sleet, or snow. This process is also known as the *hydrologic cycle*.

Two Branches, Ten Countries

The Nile, with its two main branches and many tributaries, travels through ten countries: Congo, Tanzania, Burundi, Rwanda, Uganda, Kenya, Ethiopia, Sudan, Eritrea, and Egypt. The Nile River basin covers around one tenth of the African continent.

The Nile River Basin

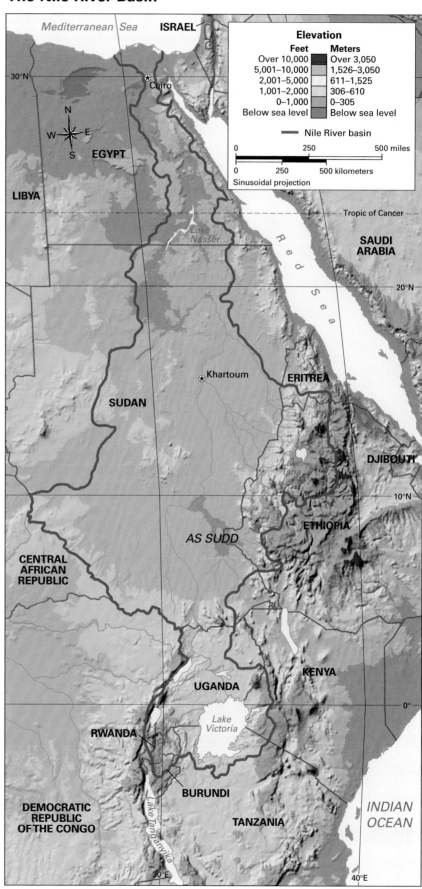

19.3 The Beginnings of the Nile

The ancient Egyptians believed that the Nile River sprang forth from an underground lake in southern Egypt. The ancient Romans later tried to locate the source of the Nile but were unsuccessful. It was only in more recent times, within the last 200 years, that explorers finally discovered the origins of the Nile. Like all rivers, however, the Nile actually begins with the water cycle.

From Rainwater to Rivers: The Water Cycle As you read earlier, the water cycle is the process that recycles water from the surface of Earth to the atmosphere and back again. This never-ending process moves water through the environment, with some of the water ending up in rivers like the Nile.

The water cycle begins with the **evaporation** of water from oceans, lakes, and rivers. This evaporation occurs when the sun heats the water. When water evaporates, it becomes **water vapor**. Steam is a visible form of water vapor.

As water vapor rises into the atmosphere, it cools down. This cooling process then causes the water vapor to **condense** into tiny water droplets, which will come together to form clouds. Under certain conditions, the water droplets become too large and heavy to remain in the atmosphere. At this point, the droplets fall to Earth as **precipitation,** which can take a variety of forms, including rain, snow, sleet, and hail.

Several things can happen to precipitation after it hits the ground. Some precipitation gets stored as snow and ice within glaciers. Some soaks into the ground in a process known as **infiltration**. Some runs off the ground to form streams. In areas that have extensive **runoff,** streams come together to form rivers. Most rivers eventually flow into the sea, where the water cycle begins again.

The Water Cycle

This diagram shows how nature recycles water. The water cycle is a "closed system." No water is ever lost. However, some water may collect unseen under the ground. This water can be tapped for human use.

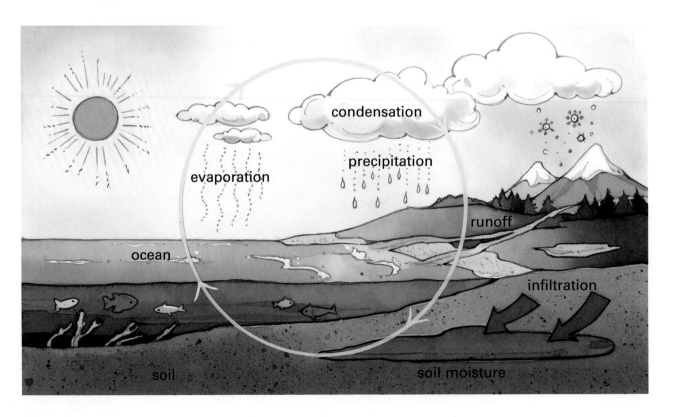

Lake Tana: Source of the Blue Nile Both main branches of the Nile, the Blue and the White, are fed by rainfall and runoff in the East African highlands. In the lush, forested hills of Ethiopia, this runoff flows into Lake Tana, which is considered to be the main source of the Blue Nile. The **headwaters** of the Blue Nile, however, are found above Lake Tana. Headwaters are the stream or streams that make up the beginnings of a river.

The Blue Nile is a fast and extremely powerful river. Fed by heavy summer rains, it roars down from Lake Tana through deep canyons to the plains below. Along its route, the river picks up lots of dark soil. Most of the silt that is deposited on flooded farmlands downstream comes from the Blue Nile.

The source of the Blue Nile remained a mystery to outsiders until the 1600s. Around 1615, a Spanish priest named Pedro Paéz made his way to Lake Tana, finding the outlet where the river leaves the lake. In the late 1700s, the Scottish explorer James Bruce also reached the source of the Blue Nile. He later published a book about his travels and took credit for the discovery.

Lake Victoria: Source of the White Nile The other main branch of the Nile starts farther to the south. As you may recall, the White Nile's headwaters consist of its most distant tributary, a stream that flows out of the mountains of Burundi. However, the main source of the White Nile is really Lake Victoria, a large, shallow lake located in the country of Uganda.

For years, however, the origins of the White Nile remained as mysterious as those of the Blue Nile. Various explorers attempted to follow the river from Egypt to its source, but they lost their way in swamps or were turned back by river rapids.

Then, in the 1850s, the English explorer John Hanning Speke reached Lake Victoria. Convinced that this body of water was the White Nile's source, he returned to the lake a few years later. In 1862, he found a river flowing out of the lake's northern side. After following the river for a distance, he returned to England to announce that he had discovered the source of the White Nile.

At first, many scholars doubted Speke's claim, thinking that he had not explored the area around Lake Victoria well enough. However, later expeditions confirmed that Lake Victoria was indeed the main source of the White Nile. In 1937, a German explorer named Bruckhart Waldekker traced the White Nile's headwaters farther south, into Burundi.

Just as the Blue Nile exits Lake Tana, the White Nile flows out of Lake Victoria as a rushing torrent. It passes through two more lakes and over a large waterfall before reaching the flat plains of Sudan, where it slows down. Along the way, the White Nile becomes a muddy gray color, from which the river gets its name.

Murchison Falls

North of Lake Victoria, the White Nile thunders over Murchison Falls. This is one of the most dramatic spots on the Nile's long journey to the sea. Today, these falls are part of a national park in Uganda. Park wildlife includes elephants and giraffes. Hippos and crocodiles are often found in these waters.

Watered by Two Niles

Al Jazirah, a state in Sudan, lies between the White and Blue Niles. Irrigation canals begun in the 1920s turned this state into a cotton-growing center. Today wheat is Al Jazirah's most important crop.

19.4 Two Niles Meet: Confluence and Cataracts

After leaving the highlands of Burundi, the White Nile crosses the plains of Sudan. Along the way, the river passes through a huge swamp known as the As Sudd, where it spreads out into many small channels that are clogged with **vegetation** and extremely difficult to navigate. In the first century C.E., a Roman expedition that was sent out to find the source of the Nile got lost in this swamp.

The White and Blue Niles Meet at Khartoum Beyond the As Sudd, the White Nile continues its sluggish journey north. Just to the east, the Blue Nile also flows northward from the Ethiopian highlands. In north-central Sudan, the two branches of the Nile finally meet. This **confluence,** or coming together, takes place at the city of Khartoum, the capital of Sudan.

At the confluence of the White Nile and the Blue Nile, the Nile becomes a much larger river, particularly during the summer rainy season. Although the flow of the White Nile remains essentially the same throughout the year, the Blue Nile grows much larger as a result of the summer rains. It is this rise in the level of the Blue Nile that causes most of the flooding downstream.

At first, the waters of the White and Blue Niles do not mix. The gray flow of the White Nile runs alongside the darker waters of the Blue Nile. After a few miles, however, the two rivers do blend, and finally the Nile truly becomes one river.

Rough Waters Slow River Travel North of Khartoum, the Nile rolls on for another 800 miles before reaching the southern border of Egypt. During this stage of its long journey, the river makes a wide turn to the south and west, a turn that is known as the "great bend." The Nile also passes over six **cataracts,** which are rapids or low waterfalls where the water cascades over rock outcroppings.

The Nile cataracts have been famous throughout history as a barrier to river travel and trade. Although boats can sail on stretches of water between the cataracts, the rapids are far too dangerous for river travel. In ancient times, river traders had to unload their boats and move their goods by land around these rough waters.

19.5 Through the Desert: Wadis and Dams

North of the city of Khartoum, the Nile flows through one of the harshest landscapes in the world. Rain is scarce here, but when it does fall, it can cause a flash flood. During a storm, rainwater rapidly fills the normally dry riverbeds, which are called **wadis**. If you are in a wadi when a storm hits, you had better move fast, or you may find yourself swept away by a wall of water.

An Arid Landscape In northern Sudan, the Nile enters a vast desert that continues northward through Egypt. Here the land on both sides of the river is sunbaked and desolate. The largest desert in the world, the Sahara, stretches to the west for thousands of miles across northern Africa. To the east, between the Nile River and the Red Sea, lies the Nubian Desert, a land full of rocky hills, sand dunes, and wadis. Few people live here.

The Nile provides relief from this **arid** landscape. Here and there, trees grow up along the banks of the river, and in some places people have settled down and irrigated small plots of land for farming. Farther to the north, in Egypt, there is more extensive farming and settlement along the banks of the Nile. The land along the river as it winds its way through Egypt looks like a ribbon of green stretched across the red-brown sands of the desert.

Controlling the Nile: The Aswan High Dam After winding for hundreds of miles through Sudan, the Nile finally reaches Lake Nasser, which straddles the border between Sudan and Egypt. Lake Nasser is not a natural lake, however, but a **reservoir**. Formed in 1970 by the construction of the Aswan High Dam in Egypt, Lake Nasser is one of the largest reservoirs in the world.

The Aswan High Dam was built for two main reasons. One purpose was to develop the Nile's hydroelectric potential. The power plant at the dam generates an enormous amount of electricity, which has helped both Egypt and Sudan to develop their cities and start new industry.

The second reason for building the dam was to control the river's flow. As you know, in the past the Nile flooded its banks nearly every year. Although those floods benefited Egypt, they also destroyed villages along the river. In the years when rainfall in the mountains was light and floods didn't occur, Egypt lacked water.

The Aswan High Dam holds back the floodwaters that had caused problems. Instead, the dam releases water in a more steady flow from Lake Nasser, thereby providing a reliable, year-round supply of water for Egyptian farms and cities. The steady flow of water also makes navigating the river easier.

Along with these benefits, the Aswan High Dam has also brought some negative effects. At the time that Lake Nasser was formed, thousands of people were forced to relocate because their homes had been covered by water. In addition, the dam traps most of the rich silt that had previously flowed down to Egyptian farmlands. That silt now sits at the bottom of the lake. As a result, farmlands downstream have become less fertile, and farmers must now buy artificial fertilizers to enrich the soil.

The Aswan High Dam
This photograph, taken from the space shuttle, shows the Aswan High Dam and its reservoir, Lake Nasser. The dam is enormous. Enough rock was used in its construction to build 17 pyramids the size of the Great Pyramid at Giza, Egypt. The lake is huge, too. It stretches for 300 miles from Egypt into Sudan.

Aswan High Dam

19.6 Across Egypt: Floodplains and Delta

For most of its journey through Egypt, the Nile flows through a narrow valley. In this Nile River valley, **floodplains** lie between the banks of the river and low cliffs on either side. Near the river's end, the Nile fans out to form a large **delta**. Together, the floodplains and delta make up just 3 percent of Egypt's land area, but these lands are home to most of the country's people. In fact, approximately 95 percent of all Egyptians live along the Nile.

A Narrow Strip of Farmland Lines the River The floodplains of the Nile River valley have served as farmland for thousands of years. Although in most places the floodplains are merely a few miles wide, the ancient Egyptians used them to produce bountiful harvests of wheat, barley, and other crops. These harvests enabled the Egyptians to create one of the greatest early civilizations.

Until recent times, farmers along the Nile depended on the annual floods to water and add fertile soil to their fields. The farmers also used traditional irrigation techniques to bring water from the river. They built canals and transported water with simple machines like the *shaduf,* a pole with a bucket at one end and a weight at the other. The pole is attached to a brace so that it can be moved up and down. The farmer dips the bucket into the water and, once it is filled, allows the weight to pull it out again.

The construction of the Aswan High Dam has brought major changes to farming along the Nile River. Lake Nasser now supplies water for a large system of perennial irrigation. With this water, farmers have been able to expand the amount of land under their cultivation. As a result, Egyptian harvests have increased, with cotton in particular becoming a major export crop.

Water for Rapidly Growing Cairo About 600 miles from the Aswan High Dam, the Nile reaches Cairo, the capital of Egypt. The river flows through the center of the city, with broad, tree-lined avenues and modern skyscrapers lining its banks. In the evening, people stroll along the Nile or relax with their friends in cafes over-looking the water.

With more than 10 million people, Cairo is one of the largest cities in the world. Like the rest of Egypt, Cairo gets most of its water from the Nile. This reliance on river water has worked well in the past, but with the rapid growth of the city, water needs are increasing as well. At the same time, Cairo is discharging **sewage** and industrial waste into the river. These two factors—population growth and pollution—are putting pressure on the water supply. Cairo will have to plan carefully to avoid water problems in the future.

Old and New Irrigation

As in ancient times, some Egyptian farmers still rely on oxen to draw water from the Nile for their crops. Today, many farmers use electric pumps to irrigate their fields. With a steady water supply, Egypt has increased its farmland by almost 50 percent.

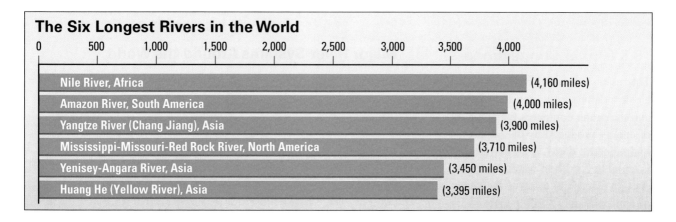

The Six Longest Rivers in the World

Nile River, Africa	(4,160 miles)
Amazon River, South America	(4,000 miles)
Yangtze River (Chang Jiang), Asia	(3,900 miles)
Mississippi-Missouri-Red Rock River, North America	(3,710 miles)
Yenisey-Angara River, Asia	(3,450 miles)
Huang He (Yellow River), Asia	(3,395 miles)

The River's Final Gift: The Nile Delta North of Cairo, the Nile travels another 100 miles before emptying into the Mediterranean Sea. In this area, the floodplains of the Nile spread out into a broad, triangular-shaped delta. At its widest point, on the coast, this fan-shaped delta measures about 155 miles across, creating a fertile area where much of Egypt's food is produced.

The Nile Delta began forming many thousands of years ago. When the river reached the coastal plain, it slowed down and divided into several branches. As the Nile slowed, it deposited the remainder of the load of silt it brought down from the highlands. Over time, this silt built up into a thick layer of soil. The Nile Delta became the richest farmland in Africa, and some of the richest in the world.

In ancient times, the Nile split into seven channels while crossing the delta. Over time, silt has filled some of those channels, so that today only two channels remain. At the end of its long journey, the Nile pours from two mouths into the Mediterranean Sea.

19.7 Beginning to Think Globally

In this chapter, you read about the long journey of the Nile River from its sources in the highlands to the Mediterranean Sea. You also read about the water cycle and how this recycling of water between Earth's surface and the atmosphere gives rise to rivers such as the Nile. You learned where the Nile River basin is located and how the Nile changes as it flows downstream. You also learned that hydroelectric potential and water for perennial irrigation are major benefits that the Nile brings to the people who live along its banks.

The Nile is one of many great rivers in the world. Another is the Amazon River, which drains a larger area than even the Nile. Starting in the snowy Andes Mountains of South America, the Amazon flows east through the world's largest **tropical rainforest** to the Atlantic Ocean. The Ohio, Missouri, and Mississippi rivers also form a mighty river system, which stretches from the Appalachians west to the Rocky Mountains. This river system drains a large part of the North American continent into the Gulf of Mexico.

All rivers change as they flow across the surface of Earth. Some changes are natural, whereas others are the consequence of human activity. Think about this as you look at the impact of hydroelectric dams on rivers around the world.

From Tributary to Mouth

The length of each of these six rivers is measured from its most distant tributary. It's hard to measure rivers, though, and experts sometimes disagree. For example, some geographers believe that the Amazon is longer than the Nile.

19.8 Global Connections

This map shows major rivers and hydroelectric dams throughout the world, and the graph compares the amounts of energy produced by the largest hydroelectric dams. A megawatt (MW) is equal to 1 million watts, which is enough electricity to serve the needs of approximately 1,000 people. A large hydroelectric dam can produce about 1,000 MW of electrical energy. The diagram at the bottom of this page shows how a hydroelectric dam works to generate all of this electrical power.

What are the main benefits of building hydroelectric dams?

Hydroelectric dams produce clean energy. Unlike power plants that burn **fossil fuels,** hydroelectric dams do not contribute to air pollution. Furthermore, these dams do not produce radioactive waste products the way nuclear power plants do. The dams control flooding and provide water for farms and cities. They also create lakes that can be used for recreation.

What are the main costs of building hydroelectric dams?

Giant hydroelectric dams can cost billions of dollars to construct. The dams have environmental costs as well, such as when the lakes that form behind them flood large areas. Towns, farms, and forests may be submerged by the rising water, forcing many people to move. Wildlife may suffer as well from loss of **habitat**.

Do the benefits of damming rivers outweigh the costs?

There are clear benefits to building hydroelectric dams. However, these benefits must be weighed against the potential harm. All rivers change as they flow across Earth's surface, but large hydroelectric dams change rivers in ways that can have a major impact on people and the environment.

Major River Systems Around the World

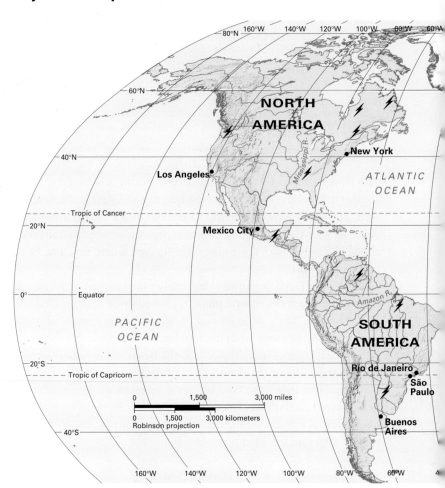

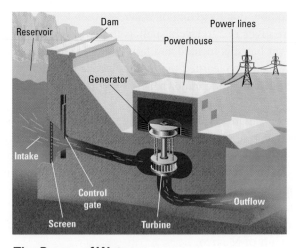

The Power of Water

A hydroelectric dam turns waterpower into electric power. Water flowing through the dam turns the blades of a turbine. The spinning turbine creates an electric current inside a generator. This current travels over power lines to distant towns and cities.

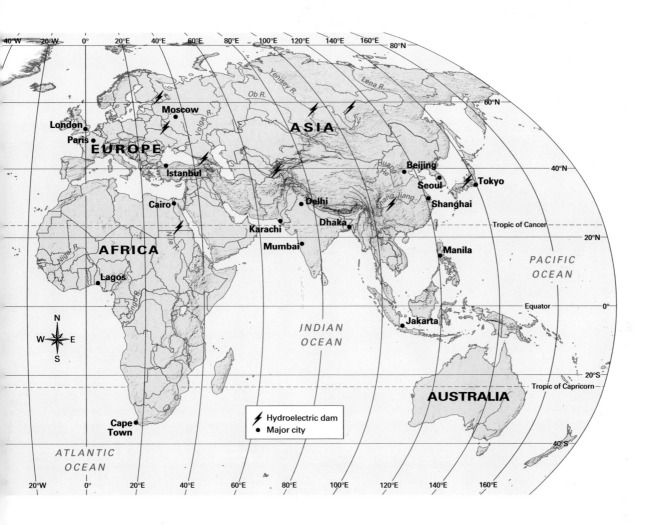

Ten Major Power-Generating Hydroelectric Dams

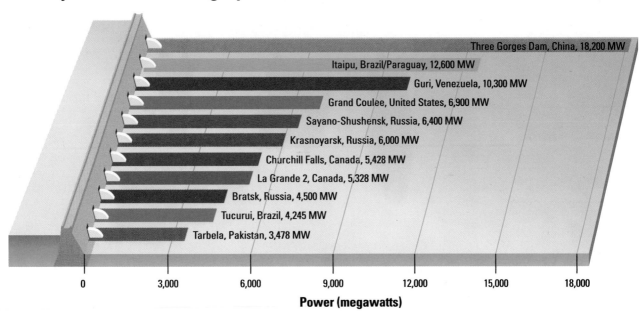

Three Gorges Dam, China, 18,200 MW
Itaipu, Brazil/Paraguay, 12,600 MW
Guri, Venezuela, 10,300 MW
Grand Coulee, United States, 6,900 MW
Sayano-Shushensk, Russia, 6,400 MW
Krasnoyarsk, Russia, 6,000 MW
Churchill Falls, Canada, 5,428 MW
La Grande 2, Canada, 5,328 MW
Bratsk, Russia, 4,500 MW
Tucurui, Brazil, 4,245 MW
Tarbela, Pakistan, 3,478 MW

0   3,000   6,000   9,000   12,000   15,000   18,000

Power (megawatts)

Life in the Sahara and the Sahel: Adapting to a Desert Region

20.1 Introduction

The Saharan **region** is filled with the unexpected. Just ask someone who has survived the Dakar Rally, a competition in which cars, trucks, and motorcycles race not only against each other but also against the wind, sand, and heat of this **desert**. With few roads, the drivers speed over shifting dunes, rocky plains, and dry grasslands. They cross parched riverbeds that have not seen water in years, and they struggle through sandstorms and scorching heat. If driving across the Sahara is this difficult, think how much harder it must be to live there.

The Sahara is one of the harshest environments on Earth. Through the years, however, people have adapted to living in this hot, **arid** region. Most people live near a desert **oasis,** which is an isolated location where water is found in a desert.

The Sahel is a semiarid grassland that is located along the Sahara's southern edge. Although its environment is not quite as harsh as the Sahara, the Sahel often suffers from **drought,** or long periods with very little or no rain. This decrease in rainfall has made life in the Sahel even more challenging.

In this chapter, you will read about the **physical features** of the Sahara and the Sahel. You will find out how the environments of these two regions have been shaped by changes in **climate.** You will also learn how people have adapted—and still are adapting—to the environments of these arid lands.

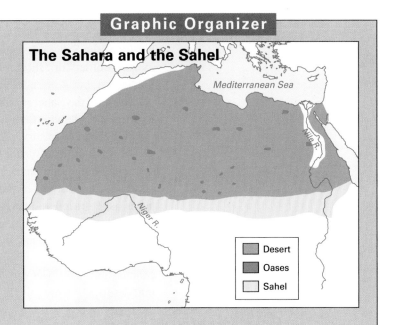

Essential Question

How do people adapt to living in a desert region?

This map shows the vast Saharan region, which includes the Sahara and the Sahel. The Sahara is the world's largest desert. The Sahel is a wide belt of semiarid lands to the south of the desert. Over many centuries, people have found ways to survive in both of these dry landscapes. Keep this map in mind as you try to answer the Essential Question.

Graphic Organizer

The Sahara and the Sahel

Mediterranean Sea

Nile R.

Niger R.

- Desert
- Oases
- Sahel

◀ A camel caravan carries trade goods across the Sahara.

Shrinking Lake Chad

Lake Chad is a large, shallow lake in the Sahel. The lake shrinks or grows depending on the amount of rainfall. But its overall size is slowly shrinking.

20.2 The Geographic Setting

The Sahara stretches across most of North Africa, covering approximately 3.5 million square miles, an area roughly equal to that of the United States. This huge desert region is bordered on the east by the Red Sea and on the west by the Atlantic Ocean. To the north, the Sahara begins at the Atlas Mountains. From those mountains, the desert sweeps south for more than 1,000 miles, eventually merging with the semiarid Sahel. Together, the Sahara and Sahel regions include all or parts of 15 African countries.

The World's Largest Desert The Sahara is the largest desert in the world. Its name is derived from the Arabic word *sahra,* which means "desert." The region's climate is very hot and very dry. In fact, the world's highest known daytime temperature, 136°F, was recorded in the Sahara in 1922. Average rainfall is less than five inches a year.

The Sahara has not always been so dry. Many thousands of years ago, the region had a much wetter climate. Rivers and lakes were filled with fish, and elephants and other animals roamed through grasslands and forests. People settled throughout the region and survived by hunting and fishing.

About 6,000 years ago, the climate of North Africa began to change, as year by year less rain fell. Eventually the Saharan region began its transformation into a desert. Ever since then, the desert has gradually been expanding.

Trade winds blowing across North Africa help to keep the region dry. These winds begin in northern latitudes and blow south toward the equator. As trade winds pass over the Sahara, they pick up any moisture from the ground below, leaving so little moisture that few clouds form over the Sahara. With no clouds to provide shade, the sun beats down on the land, making it even drier.

Parts of the Sahara are so arid that nothing lives there, but in other areas an oasis makes life possible. Most of the plants and animals that live in the Sahara are found near its oases.

The Sahel: On the Sahara's Edge The Sahel lies on the southern border of the Sahara. Its name comes from the Arabic word *sahel,* which means "border" or "shore." This region receives more **precipitation** than the Sahara, but it often suffers from long periods of drought.

Most of the Sahel is **marginal land,** land that is not well suited for farming. People who farm marginal land may harvest barely enough food for their families to survive.

For thousands of years, **pastoral nomads** have adapted to life on the Sahel's marginal lands. Pastoral nomads are herders who wander endlessly in search of water and grazing land for their animals. Once their herds have grazed an area, the nomads move on. This gives marginal grazing land a chance to recover.

In more recent years, the Sahel region has been undergoing **desertification,** a process in which an area becomes increasingly dry. In this chapter, you will discover why parts of the Sahel are being transformed into desert and what this desertification means for the people who live in the region.

▶ Geoterms

desertification the process by which land becomes more and more dry until it turns into desert. This may be caused by climate change, human activities, or both.

drought an unusually long period in which little or no rain falls

marginal land land that is not well suited for growing crops

pastoral nomads groups of herders who move with their animals from place to place in search of pasture and water

North Africa

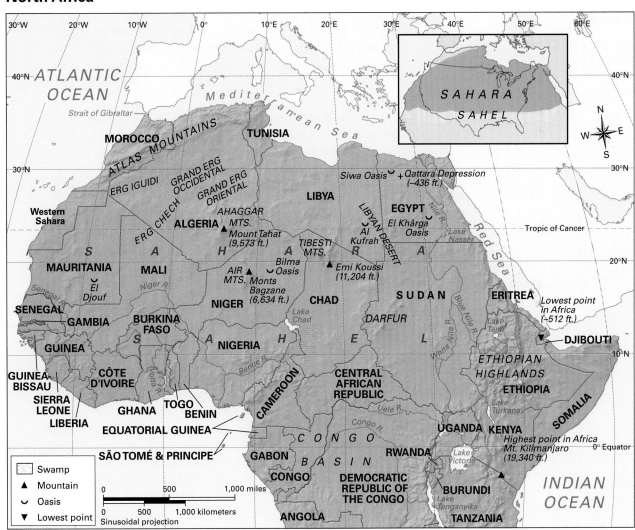

A Vast Desert Region

The Sahara and Sahel stretch across most of North Africa. You can see how large this region is by looking at the inset map, which compares it to the size of the United States. The mountainous parts of this region receive the most rainfall. The water seeps into underground streams that flow down to the desert below. In low areas, it may bubble up to the surface and create an oasis.

The Sahara's Sea of Sand

Ergs, or vast expanses of sand, cover about 13 percent of the Sahara's land area. Sand dunes move like slow-breaking waves through these "seas of sand." Little grows on the dunes, and in some places the sand is so soft that camels sink halfway to their knees in it.

20.3 The Desert Environment

A line of 500 camels stretches for a mile across the desert. This camel caravan is traveling to retrieve blocks of salt from a distant mine, enduring a difficult 400-mile round trip that will take 30 days. Along the way, the caravan will pass camel bones and abandoned trucks, grim evidence that travel is not easy in the Sahara.

The Desert Landscape: More Than Just Sand Many people picture the Sahara as a sea of burning sand, but its **landscape** is actually far more diverse. In just a single afternoon, a traveler in the Sahara saw "pink and yellow dunes, blue craggy cliffs, black volcanic rubble... an eroded gulch, two dry rivers, a cone, a canyon, [and] many badlands [barren hills]."

The Sahara has three principal types of **landforms:** ergs, regs, and hammadas. **Ergs** are great seas of sand with tall sand dunes that can reach heights of over 400 feet. Most dunes are slowly blown across the desert by the wind. **Regs** are gravel-covered plains. **Hammadas** are high, rock-covered flatlands, some of which are so tall that maps indicate their locations as mountains.

Only two rivers flow through the Sahara: the Nile and the Niger, with the water in both rivers coming from mountains beyond the desert. There are also dry riverbeds called **wadis** that can turn into raging rivers after a rain and then quickly dry up again.

The Harsh Desert Climate Temperatures can vary greatly in the desert, often soaring above 100°F during the day and sometimes dropping below freezing at night. According to an old saying, "Nighttime is the winter of the desert."

Sandstorms can begin when strong winds stir up enormous dark clouds of dust and sand from the desert floor. A severe desert sandstorm can reduce visibility to practically nothing while also getting sand into everything.

Rain is extremely unpredictable throughout the desert. During a desert rainstorm, it may rain three inches in one spot, while nearby no rain falls. When rain does come to a parched area, the water may quickly fill the wadis, resulting in flash floods that can carry away rocks, people, and even trucks.

Plants are able to adapt to these changing conditions in several ways. Some plants sprout rapidly after a rain and then set seed and die. The seeds then lie in wait, sometimes for years, until the next rain. Other plants send roots deep into the ground to find water. Deep roots anchor these plants in place during sandstorms and flash floods. Most desert trees and shrubs have small, waxy leaves that lose little moisture. During long periods of drought, they may shed their leaves, further reducing water loss.

20.4 Adaptations to Life in the Desert

About a third of the people who live in the desert are pastoral nomads. Many desert nomads belong to a group known as the Tuareg. The Tuareg live in six countries in the southern Sahara and the Sahel.

The Wandering Tuareg The nomadic Tuareg raise camels, goats, cattle, or sheep. When the pasture in one area has been exhausted, or used up, the Tuareg move their animals to a fresh grazing area.

The Tuareg are known as the "Blue Men of the Desert" because of their flowing blue robes. Their long, loose clothing protects them from the scorching sun. Men also wear blue cloth wrapped around their heads and across their faces. Some Tuareg men never remove this face cover, even in the presence of close family members.

Tuareg nomads live in family groups of fewer than 100 people. Always prepared to move, a Tuareg family needs only two hours to disassemble the tents that are their homes and pack up their belongings. All of a family's possessions will fit on one camel or two donkeys. When the nomads reach an oasis, they trade meat, cheese, or milk for grain, vegetables, fruit, and water.

Tuareg traders lead camel caravans across the desert. Camels can walk long distances over sandy ground with little food or water, making them well suited for desert travel. It is easy for travelers to get lost in the Sahara, but the Tuareg know the local landmarks. They also know how to use the stars to find their way, enabling them to travel at night when the air is cooler.

Technology Makes Life Easier Modern **technology** has improved life for many desert dwellers. Pastoral nomads have found many uses for lightweight plastic and metal containers. Meanwhile, some desert traders can afford satellite phones to keep in touch with their customers.

Technology has even created new oases. Drilling machines cut through rock to locate underground water, and electric pumps then draw this water to the surface.

Trucks and planes have improved desert transportation. Trucks are replacing camels for hauling heavy loads, and small planes are used to fly people and goods between oases.

Nomads Tend Their Herds
Tuareg nomads move their herds to find water or better pasture. The Tuareg depend upon their animals for milk. They trade milk, cheese, and some meat for the goods they cannot make or grow themselves.

Trucks Replace Camels
Trucks are gradually replacing camels in the Sahara. There are not many roads, though, so trucks are built to deal with the rough and sandy desert. The owner of this truck has to clear away the sand that has piled up overnight before beginning the day's work.

20.5 The Oasis Environment

The Sahara region holds many surprises, including a variety of life. In a hidden canyon oasis, crocodiles feed on fish and on animals that come to drink. At a larger oasis, thousands of date palms provide shade for other fruit trees, and wild gazelles graze nearby. In the arid Sahara, where there is water there is life.

Islands of Water Surrounded by Desert For weary, thirsty travelers trekking across the Sahara, no sight is more welcome than the appearance of a distant palm tree, a sign that they are approaching an oasis. Each oasis is an island of fresh water in a sea of dry sand and rock.

Some oases are formed by natural processes. Many are created by springs that bubble up to the surface from streams that flow beneath the ground. Other oases appear in low spots, where the land dips down to meet an underground stream.

Humans have also created some oases. In the past, people constructed oases by digging wells by hand. As you read earlier, drilling machines are now being used to dig deep into the ground to locate hidden water.

Large and Small Centers of Life The Sahara has approximately 90 large oases. Each large oasis can supply enough water to support a village and small farms. In addition, there are many small oases, with some supporting only one or two families.

Many species of plants and animals can be found at a desert oasis. Acacia and baobab trees mix with smaller shrubs. Gazelles and other animals drink in the pools, while butterflies, crickets, and other insects flit through oasis gardens.

Date palms are by far the most important and common oasis plant. Every part of the date palm is useful. Its fruit, the date, is eaten fresh or dried. Its trunk and leaves are used as building materials, and the fiber from its bark is twisted together to make rope. Date pits, or seeds, are burned as fuel or fed to animals. A visitor to the Sahara once wrote,

Those magnificent palm groves are the blood and bone of the desert; life in the Sahara would be unthinkable without them.... The size of an oasis is reckoned by the number of trees it contains, not by the number of square miles it covers.

Desert Oases

An oasis is a place in the desert where water is found. Some oases are natural. Others have been created by people. However they came to be, all oases are precious. They allow life to exist in one of the world's harshest environments.

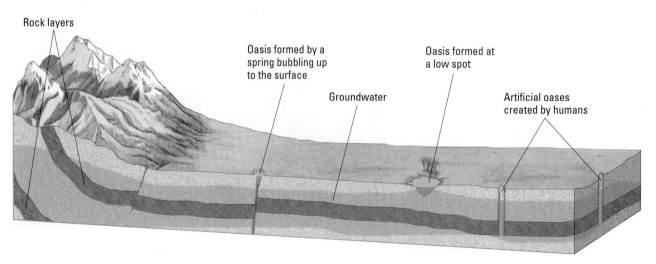

Rock layers

Oasis formed by a spring bubbling up to the surface

Oasis formed at a low spot

Groundwater

Artificial oases created by humans

20.6 Adaptations to Life in the Oases

Most oasis settlements are relatively small, accommodating fewer than 2,000 people. The largest oases may support thousands of date palms, but in an oasis that has little water, several families may have to share a single date palm.

The Traditional Ways of Oasis Settlers

Trading and farming are the major **economic activities** at an oasis. Most people are subsistence farmers, but others grow **cash crops** such as dates, wheat, barley, and vegetables. Farmers exchange their produce for goods brought in by camel, truck, and plane, while visiting nomads trade their meat, milk, and cheese for water and food. Caravans and trucks stop to trade and to fill their containers with water.

Most homes within an oasis town are constructed from mud bricks; in order to keep out the heat, the homes have few windows. Little work is done during the hottest part of the day. In the cool of the evening, men gather to discuss the day's news.

An oasis farmer is always struggling against the harsh desert environment. Blowing sand and creeping dunes will rapidly cover crops unless the plants are protected by **windbreaks,** which are walls or hedges that break the force of the wind. Windbreaks can also prevent sand from piling up on farm fields.

Water Problems Limit the Growth of Oasis Towns

Oasis settlements come in a variety of sizes. Most are small villages, but a few settlements are growing into towns and cities. As an oasis settlement expands, its water problems increase as well.

People move to an oasis for many reasons. Some may be looking for jobs on date farms or in date-processing factories that prepare dates for export. Nomads sometimes settle at an oasis when they can no longer find pasture for their animals. Refugees from drought or wars may move to an oasis in search of water, food, and safety.

Growing oasis settlements face two kinds of water problems. The first challenge is how to transport water to people as the town expands. New housing areas and camps that are established to shelter refugees often lack wells or piped water. If the residents of these settlements cannot walk to water sources, water may have to be brought to them by truck.

Water shortages are the second problem facing oasis towns. In some oases, palm groves have been expanded into the surrounding desert. The new palm trees are kept alive with water that is pumped out of the ground. However, if too much water is pumped out, the underground streams that create an oasis could run dry.

Palms Produce a Cash Crop
Date palms produce the desert's most valuable cash crop. Other fruit trees are often planted in the shade of date palms.

Cattle in the Sahel

Overgrazing by cattle is a major cause of desertification in the Sahel. When too many cattle graze in an area, they destroy its cover of plants. Without this protective cover, the soil is eroded by wind or water.

20.7 The Sahel Environment

A television advertisement in southern Niger begins by panning slowly across a desert landscape. The next scene focuses on camels, donkeys, and trucks carrying firewood into towns. A quick cut shows a coal-mining operation. The advertisement ends by showing a woman cooking with coal in her smoke-free kitchen. The purpose of the advertisement is to persuade people in Niger to switch from using wood to coal for cooking, in the process helping to preserve Niger's trees and perhaps, in the long run, to prevent desertification.

The southern area of Niger is part of the Sahel. Other areas of the Sahel include Gambia and parts of Senegal, Mauritania, Mali, Burkina Faso, Nigeria, Chad, and Sudan. In good years, just enough rain falls in the Sahel to grow crops. During years of drought, life in the Sahel region becomes very difficult.

A Landscape Threatened by Drought and Desertification The Sahel region begins at the Sahara's edge. The land here is marginal for farming because the soil is not fertile and water is scarce most of the year. The natural **vegetation** of the Sahel is a mixture of grasslands, acacia trees, baobab trees, and small bushes. Farther south, where rain is more plentiful, there is a greater variety of vegetation.

Drought is a fact of life throughout the Sahel. One severe drought began in 1968, and very little rain fell during the next six years. Since then, there has been some rain, but not enough for the land to recover completely.

As the drought continued, desertification began. In areas with little rain, few plants grew. Without vegetation to anchor the dry soil in place, desert winds picked up the soil and carried it away. When this happened, marginal lands were transformed into desert. Experts aren't sure whether desertification in the Sahel is a short-term problem or whether these marginal lands will be lost forever to an expanding Sahara.

20.8 Adaptations to Life in the Sahel

Most people in the Sahel are farmers or herders. In the past, these people have adapted to the challenge of farming and herding on marginal land in many ways.

One **adaptation** was to plant crops such as millet and sorghum, which are grains that will flourish in dry places. Another adaptation was to use a farming system known as **shifting agriculture**. In this method, a farmer first cleared a field and planted it with crops for a year or two. Then the farmer moved on to a new field. Herders used a similar system to feed their animals, moving their herds from one grazing area to another throughout the year. Both of these systems provided worn-out fields with an opportunity to rest.

Human Causes of Desertification The changing ways of life in the Sahel may be contributing to desertification. Some farmers, for example, have begun to raise cash crops, like peanuts, which often wear out the soil faster than traditional crops. After the soil has been depleted, or worn out, it may blow away before it can recover its fertility.

Similarly, some nomads have increased the size of their herds so that they have surplus animals to sell for cash. The result is too many animals on limited grazing land. Loss of vegetation from overgrazing may also contribute to desertification.

Yet another problem is **deforestation**. Most people in the Sahel rely on wood as their fuel for cooking. In their search for firewood, the people cut down trees. When the trees are gone, soil **erosion** increases, which is why the government of Niger has been promoting coal as a cooking fuel. "I think that with coal, our sparse forests could be saved," says a forestry expert in Niger.

Cooking with coal is only one of the changes that people are making to counteract desertification. In addition, farmers are testing new agricultural methods that can conserve water and reduce soil erosion. Many farmers are working to keep desert sand from burying their fields by building windbreaks of trees and brush.

No one can say how successful this war against the desert will be. However, for the people of the Sahel, this struggle against desertification is a fight they cannot afford to lose.

20.9 Beginning to Think Globally

In this chapter, you learned how people have adapted to living in the Sahara and the Sahel. Pastoral nomads survive by staying on the move. Farmers adapt by settling around oases that serve as farming and trading centers in this arid land. You found out how people have learned to raise crops and animals on the marginal lands of the Sahel. In addition, you explored the effects of drought and desertification on the Sahel region.

The Sahel is not the only area in the world that continues to be threatened by desertification. About one third of Earth's land is arid or semiarid, and some of these desert regions are expanding. In China, for example, the capital city of Beijing is sometimes blasted by sandstorms. This blowing sand comes from parts of China that are undergoing desertification. Think about the causes of desertification as you examine the world map of arid regions in the next section.

Sahel Sandstorm
Sandstorms like this one in Mali are made worse by desertification. Winds pick up loose soil from worn-out land and blow it away. Dust from the Sahel is sometimes carried across the Atlantic Ocean. When this dust reaches Florida, it creates reddish sunsets.

20.10 Global Connections

This map shows the world's deserts and areas that are threatened by desertification. The diagram below the map illustrates one set of human activities that may lead to desertification. There may be other contributing factors, such as many years of drought.

Are the world's deserts growing or shrinking? Many areas of marginal land are now being threatened by desertification. These places could eventually become new deserts. Climate change is a critical factor in this process. In some areas, droughts may speed desertification, whereas in other areas unusually wet weather may help to slow the process.

What human activities contribute to desertification? The ways people use marginal lands may lead to desertification. Poor farming methods can wear out thin soil, while overgrazing can strip areas of their protective plant cover. Nonnative plants can crowd out native plant species that are better suited to a dry climate. Deforestation can leave marginal lands exposed to erosion. All of these factors can contribute to the spread of deserts in arid regions.

How might people adapt to living in areas threatened by desertification? People deal with desertification in many ways. Villagers in China are learning new methods of farming, with the goal of reducing soil erosion. To keep fire from destroying forests and grasslands, the Australian government has developed new programs aimed at preventing wildfires. Many developing countries, however, cannot afford such projects and must look to other countries and the United Nations for help in keeping their deserts from spreading.

Desert Regions Around the World

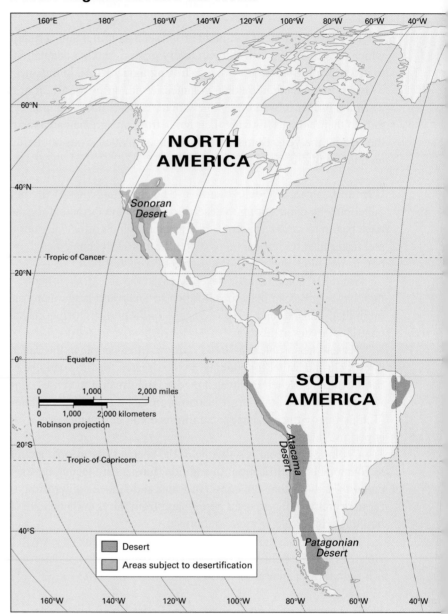

A Problem with Many Causes ▶

As this diagram shows, desertification is a problem with many causes. Long periods of drought can kill off the vegetation that holds soil in place. Farming and grazing on marginal lands can also leave soil without a protective cover of plants. Without such a cover, soil is easily eroded by wind and rain. The result is an arid wasteland of sand and rock in which little will grow.

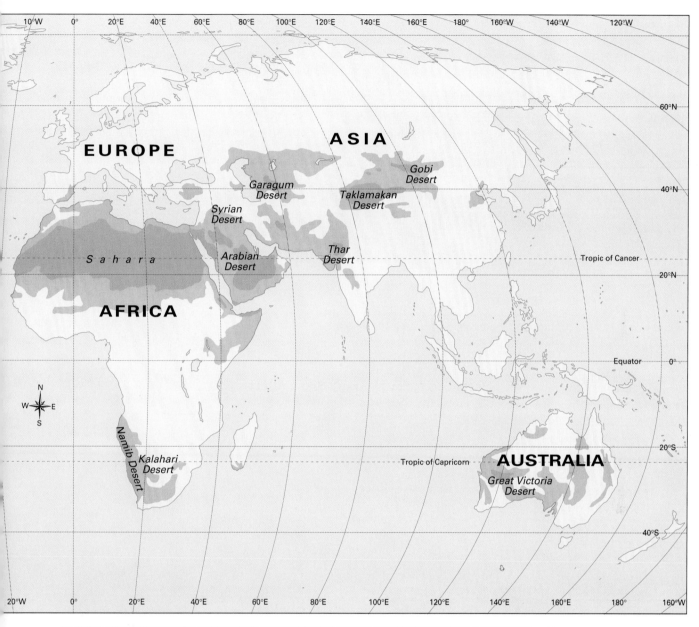

EUROPE

ASIA

Garagum
Desert

Syrian
Desert

S a h a r a

Arabian
Desert

AFRICA

N
W   E
S

Namib Desert

Kalahari
Desert

Taklamakan
Desert

Gobi
Desert

Thar
Desert

Tropic of Cancer

Equator

Tropic of Capricorn

AUSTRALIA

Great Victoria
Desert

10°W · 0° · 20°E · 40°E · 60°E · 80°E · 100°E · 120°E · 140°E · 160°E · 180° · 160°W · 140°W · 120°W

60°N

40°N

20°N

0°

20°S

40°S

20°W · 0° · 20°E · 40°E · 60°E · 80°E · 100°E · 120°E · 140°E · 160°E · 180° · 160°W

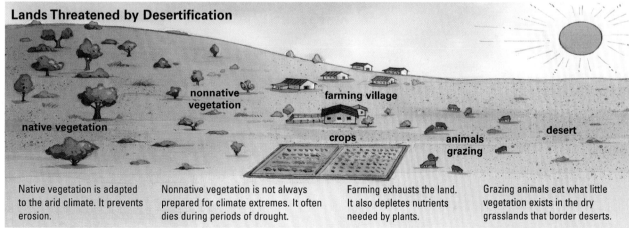

Lands Threatened by Desertification

native vegetation

nonnative
vegetation

farming village

crops

animals
grazing

desert

Native vegetation is adapted
to the arid climate. It prevents
erosion.

Nonnative vegetation is not always
prepared for climate extremes. It often
dies during periods of drought.

Farming exhausts the land.
It also depletes nutrients
needed by plants.

Grazing animals eat what little
vegetation exists in the dry
grasslands that border deserts.

Micro-entrepreneurs: Women's Role in the Development of Africa

21.1 Introduction

Hassana, a widow with five children, lived in a small village in West Africa. With so many mouths to feed, Hassana often lacked money to buy clothes and school supplies for her children. She had no money saved in the event that someone got sick, and sometimes even buying food for the family was difficult.

However, Hassana had an idea for starting a small business, or **micro-enterprise**. She wanted to bake bread and sell it in the local street market. Hassana borrowed money from an organization that had been established to help women start businesses. She used the money to buy an oven, and later she was able to repay the loan with her earnings from selling bread. She was also able to slowly grow her business and take better care of her family.

Small business owners like Hassana are called **micro-entrepreneurs**. Entrepreneurs are people who start businesses, and *micro* means tiny, so micro-entrepreneurs are people who start very small businesses. Hassana's business may be tiny, but the effect that micro-entrepreneurs are having in developing countries is not so small. Hassana's story is one of many about women in Africa who are making life better by starting new businesses.

In this chapter, you will learn about some of the challenges faced by poor women in Africa. You will read how some women are pulling themselves out of poverty by becoming micro-entrepreneurs. And you will find out how these women, by helping themselves, are changing their communities.

Essential Question

How are women micro-entrepreneurs in developing countries changing their communities?

Pictured in this outline of the continent of Africa is a micro-entrepreneur. She is one of many African women who have started their own businesses. These women are playing a growing role in the development of Africa. Keep this image in mind as you try to answer the Essential Question.

Graphic Organizer

◀ Selling bread in an African street market

Women Carry a Heavy Load
There is a traditional division of labor in Africa between men and women. Men hunt, herd, or work for wages. Women take care of the family. This often involves hauling firewood and water over long distances.

21.2 The Geographic Setting

In this chapter, you will visit three countries in Africa. All three of these countries are south of the Sahara. Mali is in West Africa. Uganda is in East Africa. Botswana lies in the center of Southern Africa.

A Developing Country Most of Africa is made up of **developing countries**. Twenty-one of the world's 30 poorest countries are found in Africa. Nearly half of the Africans in these countries survive on less than $1 per day.

Poverty makes survival a daily challenge. In 2004, an estimated 200 million Africans were **undernourished,** which means they did not get enough food to lead a healthy life. Lack of food has stunted, or slowed, the growth of about a third of all African children.

Disease remains a serious challenge throughout much of the continent. Malaria, for example, affects people in many parts of Africa. Mosquitoes spread the parasite that causes this illness, which can be deadly, especially to children. Health experts estimate that every 30 seconds a child in Africa dies from malaria.

Natural disasters have created other challenges. In recent years, **drought** has struck many African countries. The lack of rain has resulted in crop failures for many farmers. For **pastoral nomads,** drought has caused the death of their animal herds. The loss of crops and livestock has led to severe food shortages.

War is another serious challenge. Many countries in Africa, such as Rwanda, Liberia, and Angola, have been torn apart by **civil war**. A civil war is a war between groups that are living in the same country. Each of these conflicts has resulted in the deaths of hundreds of thousands of people.

Women Face Added Challenges The challenges of poverty, disease, natural disasters, and wars affect most Africans, but they often weigh heaviest on women. One reason for this is Africa's traditional **gender-based division of labor**. This is the division of work in a society based on a person's sex, or gender.

Traditionally, men in Africa are the money earners, raising cash crops or working for wages. Meanwhile, women have been responsible for the care of the family. This responsibility often includes growing food on small plots of land to feed their families. As important as this work is, it does not earn money.

Poor women who need to earn money face added challenges. One is a lack of education. In 2002, nearly half of all African women over the age of 15 could not read, which left few jobs open to them.

Often the only place poor women can find to make money is in the **informal economy**. People in the informal economy exchange goods and services without much government control. They might, for instance, sell food in a street market or trade childcare for firewood. They do not have a license for their business, and they do not pay taxes on any money they might earn.

For many African women, the informal economy has become an area of opportunity in which they can start a new business without a lot of money. In this chapter, you will get to know some of these women micro-entrepreneurs.

▶ Geoterms

gender-based division of labor the division of work into two categories based on sex, or gender. The result is that men and women do different kinds of work.

informal economy the part of the economy in which goods and services are exchanged outside of government control. People who work in the informal economy often sell goods on the street or in a street market.

micro-enterprise a very small business with few or no employees

micro-entrepreneur a person who starts and runs a very small business

Gender Differences in Africa

This map compares the relative condition of men and women in Africa. It is based on a ranking system called the Gender Development Index (GDI). This index rates countries by comparing men and women in three areas: education, income, and life expectancy. In all three areas, women fare worse than men in Africa. As a result, the GDI rankings of African countries are low.

Gender Equality in Africa, 2000

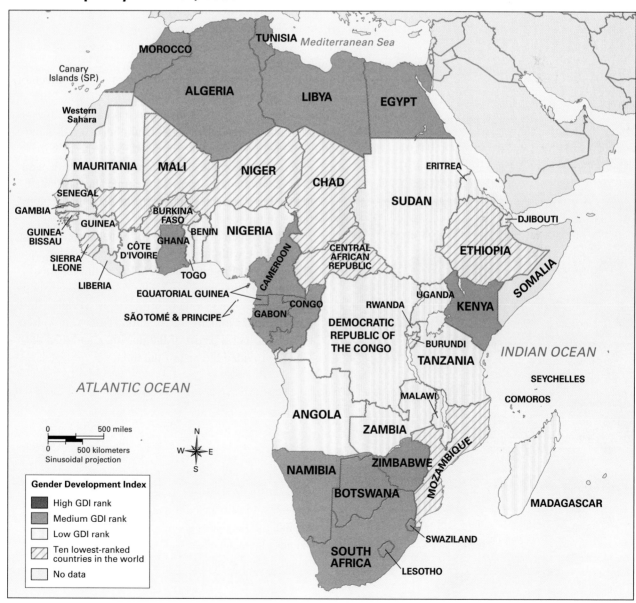

Source: *The Penguin Atlas of Women in the World,* by Joni Seager, New York: Penguin, 2003.

The Country of Mali

Mali is a large country in West Africa. The Sahara covers the northern half of Mali. Grasslands spread across most of the southern half.

21.3 Grinding Peanuts in Rural Mali

The sound of wood hitting wood is common in many villages in Mali. It is the sound of women preparing two of Mali's most common foods for cooking: grains and peanuts. It takes a lot of energy to grind these crops to the point that they can be made into meals.

Mali is one of the poorest countries in the world. Much of its population lives in rural villages. Women work especially hard, but things are changing in some villages in Mali—and women micro-entrepreneurs are leading the way.

A Machine Changes the Way Women Work In the small village of Sanankoroni in Mali, a machine grinds peanuts so the village women do not have to pound them by hand. The machine grinds the peanuts much faster and also does a better job.

Grinding peanuts is just one of the things that this machine, called a *multifunctional platform,* is capable of doing. The multifunctional platform is a simple, sturdy machine that can be used in many ways. Its heart is a small engine that runs either on diesel fuel or on oil from plants. Rubber belts connect this engine to different tools. The people of Sanankoroni connect their engine to a grinding tool that grinds their peanuts into peanut butter.

The multifunctional platform was the brainchild of a Swiss inventor, who believed that the machine would make women's lives easier and change entire villages. He was right. His invention has changed how women like Biutou Doumbia spend their time. Doumbia used to spend three days grinding 100 pounds of peanuts by hand. Now the machine grinds that amount of peanuts in a little more than an hour. Doumbia uses some of the time she has gained to grind extra peanuts, and then she sells this peanut butter in the local market.

The women of the village of Sanankoroni bought the machine with the help of the United Nations Development Programme (UNDP), an international organization that works to reduce poverty in developing countries. The women formed a group called the Sanankoroni Women's Association. This group raised $2,000, or half the cost of the machine, and then the UNDP provided the rest of the money.

A Machine with Many Functions

The multifunctional platform is built around a simple engine. But the things it can do are anything but simple. The machine can be attached to different tools. Depending on the tool, it can grind grains, pump water, generate electricity for lights, charge batteries, and much more.

Earning While Learning New Skills The Sanankoroni Women's Association has started a peanut-grinding business with their multifunctional platform. Customers from Sanankoroni and nearby villages pay a fee to use the machine to grind peanuts. The women earn money by running the machine for their customers.

The new business owners have learned many new skills. They have learned how to run the machine and keep it in good repair. They have learned how to set up schedules for their workers and customers. And they have learned how to handle the money they earn so that they have enough funds to buy fuel and to pay their workers.

Improving the Quality of Life In Mali, 300 villages now have their own multifunctional platform. This machine has improved the quality of life in these communities. For example, families in Sanankoroni have more time together now that the women do not spend all day grinding peanuts by hand.

Another improvement in these villages is that attitudes toward education have changed. Before the machine's arrival, only 9 women in Sanankoroni, a village of 460 people, could read and write. A year after the machine arrived, more than 40 women were attending classes to learn how to read. Girls who used to stay home to help with chores are now going to school.

The machine has improved the lives of men as well. The Sanankoroni Women's Association hired several men to work in their business as mechanics, maintaining and repairing the machine. "It's better than farming," says one mechanic.

In the village of Mountougoula, women purchased an electrical generator to connect to their machine. A generator is used to produce electricity. They also set up a lighting system in their village to use electricity produced by their generator. The lights have made the village safer at night, and storeowners are making more money now that people can shop after dark.

One man in the village is teaching his daughters to read at night. He has seen for himself that women can change the world. All they need is education and encouragement.

Grinding Peanuts

This woman is grinding peanuts using a multifunctional platform. Despite their name, peanuts are not true nuts. They grow in the ground rather than on a tree. For this reason, they are often called *groundnuts*. Peanuts are raised both to eat and to press for their oil.

A Machine Brings Change

The multifunctional platform has changed the lives of many people in Mali. More girls are attending school because they no longer need to stay home and help with chores like grinding. Women are hiring men to repair and run the machines. Families have more time to be together.

The Country of Uganda

Uganda is a densely populated country in East Africa. Its capital, Kampala, lies on the shores of Lake Victoria. This is Africa's largest freshwater lake.

Open-Air Markets Are Popular

Much of the buying and selling in Uganda goes on in outdoor markets like this one. Some micro-entrepreneurs build stalls. Others sell their goods and services in the open. Such markets are part of Africa's informal economy.

21.4 Selling in Uganda's "Poor Man's Market"

Kalerwe market in Uganda is an amazing place to visit. From the center of the market, stalls stretch as far as the eye can see. Buyers roam the muddy, crowded lanes between the stalls. Sellers shout information about the food, goods, and services they have to sell. Kalerwe is known as the "poor man's market," but it attracts all kinds of people from nearby Kampala, the capital of Uganda. They are drawn to the market by its bargain prices.

Markets like Kalerwe are quite common in Uganda and most other African countries. Such markets are part of the informal economy. They provide opportunities for people to sell goods and services without having to obtain a business license, and often the sellers can pocket the money they make without having to pay taxes. Many successful women micro-entrepreneurs got their start in these markets. Margaret Saajjabi is one of them.

Soap and Drinks Fund a Micro-enterprise Margaret Saajjabi runs several profitable micro-enterprises in Uganda. She owns a quarter acre of land in Kalerwe market and rents 27 market spaces to other people. Some of her tenants have built stalls in the space, while others sell their goods and services in the open air. Her tenants include hairdressers, electricians, vegetable sellers, and cooks.

Born into a very large family, Saajjabi was studying in high school when her father told her that there was no longer enough money for her to continue her education. Saajjabi then left high school and worked for the police and later as a telephone operator, but she longed to start her own business.

She got her start by selling laundry soap and bottled soft drinks. Because she had no money to buy goods, she talked sellers into letting her sell their products. She received a small percentage of the money she took in from customers. Slowly she saved the money she earned and eventually had enough to buy land in Kalerwe market.

An Outdoor Beauty Shop
Some of Africa's most successful micro-enterprises can be found in local markets. Many are owned by women. With the money they earn, women can send their children to school or build homes for their families.

Saajjabi has found many ways to use this land. In addition to renting out market spaces, she has set up a water-selling business there, selling water in large cans to local people. She also created a parking lot that can accommodate 50 cars. People who come to Kalerwe pay to park there.

Saajjabi found that women face special challenges in business. One challenge is getting the money necessary to start or expand a business. Men in Uganda are able to borrow start-up money from other men, but few men will loan money to women. To get around this problem, Saajjabi created a savings club with several other women. The women in the club help one another save their money, and when they need a loan, they borrow from other women in the club.

Supporting an Extended Family Margaret Saajjabi is a good example of how one woman's success can benefit many others. In her case, the people who have benefited the most from her success are the members of her large family. Saajjabi supports 6 children of her own and is also helping to raise 19 nieces and nephews.

Most of these children are going to school. Saajjabi believes that it is very important for both girls and boys to receive a good education and that all children should learn to respect the value of work. Her children, nieces, and nephews have all come to Kalerwe market to work during their school holidays.

Creating New Economic Opportunities Saajjabi's success has rippled outward from her extended family and has helped other people in her community. She has hired six guards for her parking business. She has plans to build more shops and to hire young women to work for her. In addition, the people who rent market space from her now have a way to make money for their families.

Saajjabi encourages other women to start their own businesses. "You have to be confident," she says when asked for advice. "Develop the skills of your trade. Don't beg off and say, 'I'm just a woman.'" If Saajjabi had thought that way, she might still be selling someone else's soap and soft drinks.

A Micro-entrepreneur at Work
Margaret Saajjabi has built a successful business from very small beginnings. She once sold soap and soda. Now she rents out space to other micro-entrepreneurs.

The Country of Botswana

Botswana is a thinly populated country in the center of Southern Africa. Gabarone is its capital and largest city. The city is located on the border between Botswana and South Africa.

21.5 Cooking Up Comfort Food in Botswana

Kgosi lives and works in Gabarone, the busy capital of Botswana, a country in southern Africa. But Kgosi grew up in a rural village. At lunchtime, he used to long for a hot dish of *stampa* (shredded beef) or *papa* (mixed corn and beans). These are "comfort foods" that he grew up with, but the only restaurants near his workplace in Gabarone were fast-food chains.

One day Kgosi looked down the street and saw a colorfully painted caravan, or trailer, with a sign above it proclaiming "Mama's Fast Food." From the wonderful smells drifting out of the caravan, Kgosi knew at once that the foods of his childhood were cooking inside.

A Used Trailer Becomes a Street-Side Restaurant Kgosi is typical of many people who live and work in the city of Gabarone. They grew up in the country and then moved to the capital to find work. Most eat breakfast and lunch near their workplaces. This has created an opportunity for many women micro-entrepreneurs to open restaurants in caravans, which are similar to vacation trailers that families in the United States might use to go camping.

A woman must do several things to open such a restaurant. First she needs to buy a caravan. Most are purchased in neighboring South Africa. Because of the cost of the caravans, women often have to borrow money from parents or family members, and some have to save money for years before they can afford one.

The caravan must then be converted into a restaurant. Most caravans come with a small stove and a cooler already installed. The women hire someone to build shelves for dishes and racks to hold the gas tanks needed to fuel the stove.

Caravans Dish Up Popular Food

Most street-side restaurants seat people outside. Some caravans are big enough to seat people inside. Here diners can enjoy a tasty meal of "comfort food."

Finally, a woman must find a place to park her caravan. Any place where many people work and shop is a good location. After choosing a good spot, the owner removes the caravan's wheels, creating an instant street-side restaurant. At most caravans, people eat outside under a canvas canopy, sitting on plastic chairs at plastic patio tables to enjoy a meal that reminds them of home.

Creating Jobs Along with Food Successful caravan owners can make enough money to repay their loans and then expand their business. Some save up enough money to buy a small truck, making it easier to purchase supplies in South Africa, where prices are usually lower.

As their businesses grow, some women who own caravans are able to hire workers, usually family members who help cook, clean, and transport supplies. Some of these micro-entrepreneurs also create opportunities for other women who want to start their own businesses. For example, a restaurant owner might prepare "box lunches" for another woman to sell in a different part of the city. This financial arrangement benefits both women.

The families of these micro-entrepreneurs receive many benefits. Some of the relatives get jobs. Many of the women use the money they make to send their children to school. Some have been able to purchase land and build a home.

The people of Botswana also benefit from the restaurants run by these micro-entrepreneurs. Street-side restaurants allow them to buy a traditional meal for a low price anywhere in the capital. As one customer explained, "They are dishing up African culture for city folks who like to eat what they grew up with."

Open for Business
Many women in Botswana have set up restaurants like this one. Often these restaurants are parked illegally on public streets.

21.6 Beginning to Think Globally

In this chapter, you learned that women in Africa face many challenges. Poverty is widespread, and the gender-based division of labor has made it difficult for African women to earn money. You met some of the micro-entrepreneurs who have started small businesses as part of the informal economy. Through their micro-enterprises, these resourceful women have been helping to pull their families and communities out of poverty.

Women micro-entrepreneurs can be found in every country. Most of them face similar problems. One of these challenges is finding the money needed to start a small business. Although the loan amounts needed by these women are often small, banks are generally unwilling to make loans to the poor.

As a result, many groups have been formed in order to make small business loans to poor people. The average loan amount is typically less than $100. Because the amounts of the loans are so small, these groups are known as *micro-credit organizations*.

Micro-credit organizations will often make small loans to groups of women. In these arrangements, no member of a group of women will be eligible to take out another loan until everyone's first loan is repaid. With this requirement, the group makes sure that each woman repays her loan. As you examine the map of micro-credit organizations in the next section, think about how these loans can change lives.

21.7 Global Connections

This map shows where micro-credit organizations make the most loans worldwide. You can learn more about these loans by examining the information in the table under the map.

In what parts of the world are micro-credit organizations most active? Why might this be so?
Micro-credit organizations are most active in Africa, Asia, and Latin America. Since most banks in these regions will not make loans to poor people, micro-credit organizations have stepped in to help poor people get start-up loans for businesses. More than 500 million people in developing countries own small businesses, and many of these micro-entrepreneurs got their start with a small business loan.

Which gender gets the most micro-loans? Why might this be so? More than 80 percent of small business loans are made to women micro-entrepreneurs. Part of the reason for this is that it is women who need the most help. The majority of people living in poverty are women and their children. Also, micro-credit organizations have learned that women are a good risk. Ninety-five percent of the women who receive small loans will repay the money. In addition, women are more likely than men to invest the earnings in their families and communities.

How do micro-credit organizations help women change their communities? Micro-credit organizations help people help themselves. When women begin to earn money, they can send their children to school. They create jobs and opportunities for other people in their communities. In some countries, more than half the people who receive micro-credit loans are able to rise out of poverty within 10 years.

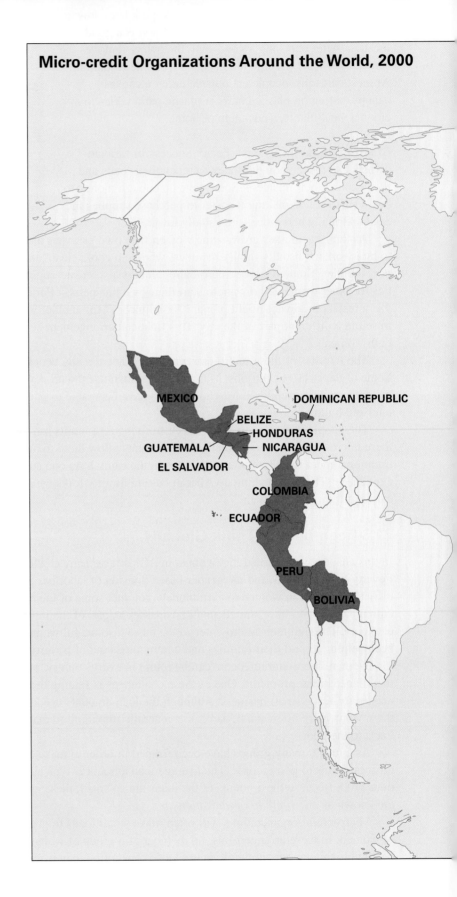

Micro-credit Organizations Around the World, 2000

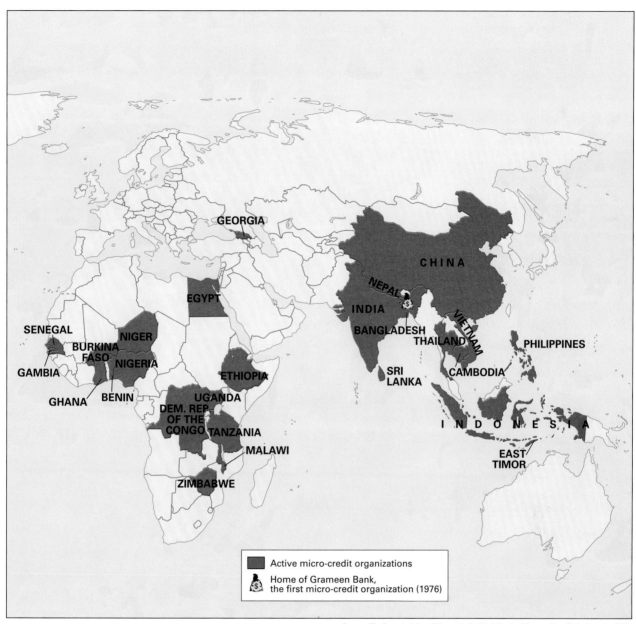

Source: *The Penguin Atlas of Women in the World,* by Joni Seager, New York: Penguin, 2003.

Fast Facts About Micro-credit
More than 500 million people in developing countries run micro-enterprises.
Less than 3% of micro-entrepreneurs obtain loans from banks.
About 3,000 micro-credit organizations served 80 million clients in 2003.
More than 95% of micro-entrepreneurs who get loans pay them back.
More than 80% of micro-loans are made to women.
More than 90% of the income earned by women from micro-loans is used to support their families.
About 40% of the income earned by men from micro-loans is used to support their families.
In some countries, more than 50% of micro-credit clients rise out of poverty within 10 years.

Nigeria: A Country of Many Cultures

22.1 Introduction

Long ago, people from many parts of the African continent met to trade in the land now known as Nigeria. **Nomads** from the **desert** came to trade with the forest people, exchanging salt, cloth, and weapons for slaves, ivory, and kola nuts.

Over time, many different **ethnic groups** settled in this area. An ethnic group is a group of people who share a common culture. Each of these various ethnic groups retained its own identity and way of life.

Today the country of Nigeria has more than 250 ethnic groups living within its borders. Each of these groups has its own name and speaks its own distinct language. Together these groups have created great **ethnic diversity** within Nigeria. No other country in Africa is home to such a wide variety of people, each group having its own culture.

With such ethnic diversity, Nigeria can be a confusing place to study. To help examine such a diverse area, geographers often divide it into **regions**. In Chapter 2, you learned that a region is an area defined by one or more characteristics that set it apart from other areas. One way to understand Nigeria is to divide it into **cultural regions,** each set apart by the way of life of the people who live there.

In this chapter, you will explore the three main cultural regions of the country of Nigeria. You will learn about the **physical features** of each region, meet the largest ethnic group living there, and learn about the region's culture and economy.

Essential Question

How can dividing a diverse country into regions make it easier to understand?

This map shows the African country of Nigeria. Notice that it is divided into three regions: northern, western, and eastern. Each region is home to one of Nigeria's three largest ethnic groups. Keep the map in mind as you try to answer the Essential Question.

Graphic Organizer

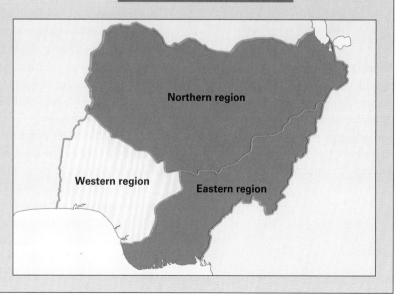

◀ A street market in Lagos, the largest city in Nigeria

Abuja: A New Capital City
The city of Lagos in western Nigeria was the country's first capital. In 1991, the capital moved to Abuja. The new capital is in the center of the country. Many people hoped the move would help to unite this diverse country.

Ethnic Groups of Nigeria

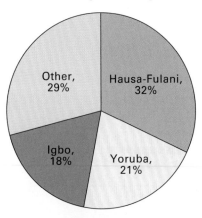

Other, 29%

Hausa-Fulani, 32%

Igbo, 18%

Yoruba, 21%

Nigeria's Diversity
Nigeria has hundreds of ethnic groups, some large and some small. Within an ethnic group, more than one language may be spoken. As a result, there are more than 450 linguistic groups in this country.

22.2 The Geographic Setting

To locate Nigeria on a map of Africa, follow the Atlantic coastline of the continent until you reach the Gulf of Guinea. The country of Nigeria lies beside this large inlet of the sea. Two rivers form a Y inside Nigeria, naturally dividing the country into three regions. The Benue River forms the right arm of the Y, flowing from east to west across the country. The Niger River forms the left arm and the stem of the Y, flowing from west to east to meet the Benue River. After the two rivers meet, the Niger turns south to the sea.

From Many Ethnic Groups to One Country For most of its history, the area around the Niger River has been home to many peoples. Its hundreds of ethnic groups are further divided into **linguistic groups,** groups of people who share a distinct language.

During the mid-1800s, **colonialism** came to West Africa. Colonialism is a system of government in which one country rules other places as colonies, with the ruling country controlling trade with its colonies for its own benefit.

During this time, Great Britain took over areas of West Africa. In 1914, it joined parts of these areas to form the colony of Nigeria. As the ruling country, Britain gained control of Nigeria's **natural resources,** with the most valuable resources being oil, tin, and gold. At the same time, Nigeria became a new market for many goods that were produced by British factories.

Under British rule, some groups of people were more willing to cooperate with their colonial rulers. As a result, they were treated better than other groups, receiving more education and the best jobs. Other groups resented the favored groups—and they resented their British rulers as well.

Resentment finally brought about demands for self-rule, with protestors marching in the streets and refusing to work. As the protests grew, Britain found it harder to control Nigeria. On October 1, 1960, Nigeria became an independent country.

Ethnic and Religious Tensions Divide Nigeria After independence, Nigerians adopted a federal system of government, but conflict between ethnic groups made governing the country very difficult. A more stable government was finally elected in 1999. Today Nigeria is divided into 36 states, each with its own local laws. An elected president heads Nigeria's national government.

Cultural differences still divide Nigeria's various ethnic groups. Language is just one way in which these groups differ. The national government has made English the country's official language, and English is taught in schools throughout Nigeria. However, each group still speaks its own language at home.

The people are also divided by their religious beliefs. Almost half of Nigerians follow the religion of Islam. Around two fifths are Christians. Many Nigerians also follow traditional beliefs. One of these beliefs is that all natural objects, such as trees and clouds, have spirits. Another belief is that the deceased live on as spirits to guide and help the living in their journey through life.

▶ Geoterms

colonialism a system in which one country rules another area as a colony. The ruling country controls trade with its colony for its own benefit.

cultural region an area that is set apart from other places by the way of life of the people who live there

ethnic diversity a variety of people from different ethnic groups

linguistic group a group of people who share a common language

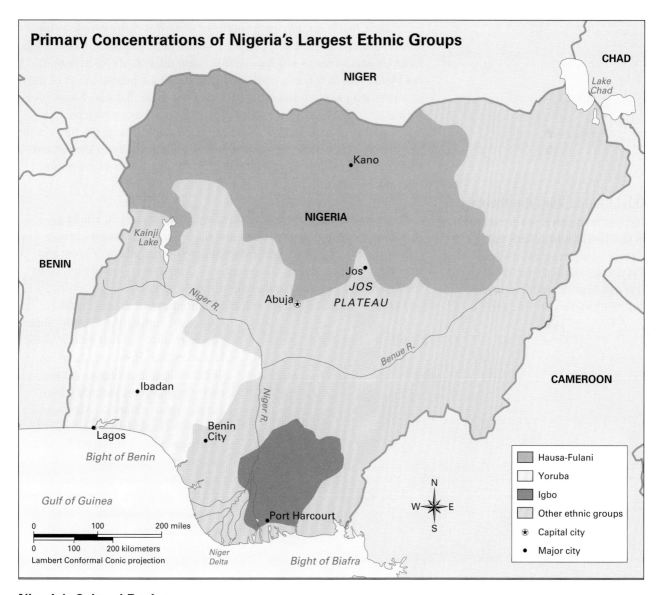

Primary Concentrations of Nigeria's Largest Ethnic Groups

Legend:
- Hausa-Fulani
- Yoruba
- Igbo
- Other ethnic groups
- ⊛ Capital city
- • Major city

0 100 200 miles
0 100 200 kilometers
Lambert Conformal Conic projection

Nigeria's Cultural Regions

This map shows the primary cultural regions of Nigeria's three largest ethnic groups. Members of each group also live in other parts of the country. About 29 percent of Nigerians belong to hundreds of smaller ethnic groups.

22.3 Life in Northern Nigeria

One of the first things a geographer notices about northern Nigeria is how dry the region is. In many places, women have to walk for miles each day in order to get water. During the six-month dry season, very little rain falls. Some rivers dry up completely, and lakes shrink so dramatically that a 5-mile walk for water in the wet season can become a 10-mile walk in the dry season.

Physical Environment: A Land of Little Water Much of northern Nigeria consists of high, flat plains. Grasses and thorn trees covered these plains before people cleared the land in order to start farming. Rising up out of the plains is the Jos Plateau. Many people live and farm on this high ground because the weather on the plateau is cooler and wetter than on the plains below.

Lake Chad is an important source of water for many people in the region, but over the last 40 years the lake has been shrinking. In the 1960s, Lake Chad covered as much as 4,000 square miles in its driest season, but by the year 2000, as a result of **drought** and the increased use of its water for irrigation, the lake was less than one tenth that size. Some geographers fear that Lake Chad could eventually dry up completely.

A powerful wind known as the *harmattan* also affects life throughout northern Nigeria. Blowing south from the Sahara between October and March, the harmattan brings large clouds of dust that coat everything with fine, gritty sand.

Dust Clouds from the Harmattan

October to March is the dry season in northern Nigeria. Winds from the Sahara blow hot across the land. People call this wind the *harmattan*. It brings huge dust storms to the northern region.

Ethnic Groups: The Hausa and Fulani The two largest ethnic groups in northern Nigeria are the Hausa and the Fulani. The Hausa came to this region about 1,000 years ago, establishing villages that later grew into important trading centers and, eventually, kingdoms. During the 1200s, the Fulani also began to settle in northern Nigeria.

Over time, people from both ethnic groups married and created a connected culture. As a result, some people refer to the two groups as the Hausa-Fulani. However, there are distinct differences between these two ethnic groups, including language. About a third of Nigerians speak the Hausa language, whereas traditional Fulani speak Fulfulde, a less common language.

The two ethnic groups also differ in where they live. The Hausa people tend to be more **urban**. In contrast, most of the Fulani people still live in **rural** areas, traveling with their cattle herds during the dry season to search for grazing land. During the rainy season, the Fulani live in villages and plant crops.

The Hausa and the Fulani are united by their faith because both groups are Muslim. However, many

other ethnic groups in Nigeria are Christian, and tension between Muslims and Christians has increased in recent years. One reason for this is that some states have chosen to make **shari'a,** or traditional Islamic laws, the basis of their legal system. These laws cover many aspects of daily life, like marriage and divorce. Non-Muslims often resent having to live under laws that do not agree with their religious beliefs.

Culture: Thatched Roofs and Kalangu Drums Northern Nigeria's hot **climate** affects the kinds of homes people build. In the city, most houses have flat roofs, and people sometimes sleep outside on their roofs on hot nights. In the country, people build round homes out of mud and cover them with roofs woven from reeds or palm leaves, materials that provide good shelter from the sun.

Northern Nigerians favor loose clothes that protect them from the sun. Men wear baggy cotton pants and floor-length robes, with the front of the robes often heavily embroidered. They also wear an Arab-style hat called a *fez*. Women also wear robes that cover the entire body. Some women wear a cloth headdress. Muslim women wear a *hijab*, or headscarf, that covers the hair and neck, and some also wear a veil that hides most of the face.

A popular traditional musical instrument is the tension drum, which is made from wood with an animal skin stretched tight over the drum's top. The Hausa tension drum, called a *kalangu*, makes sounds like those heard in Hausa speech.

Economy: Farming, Herding, and Trading Many of the people in northern Nigeria make their living as farmers and herders. Hausa farmers grow crops such as corn and millet, which is a kind of grain. These farmers eat some of the crops that they produce and sell the rest in local village markets. Fulani herders make their living by selling milk or products that are made from milk, like butter, to villagers. The herders rarely kill cows to sell as meat.

The Hausa have traditionally made beautiful cloth and leather goods. People once traveled from all over Africa to buy Hausa crafts. Some Hausa also work as traders and merchants, selling traditional crafts and factory-made goods to local people and tourists.

Traditional Hausa Dress
The Hausa people have long been known for their richly embroidered robes. Until recent times, the embroidery was done by men. Today women also do this work. Some Hausa women sell their robes to buyers in the United States.

A "Go-Slow" in Lagos
Many cities in Nigeria are famous for their traffic jams. Cars, buses, trucks, and bicycles crowd the streets during rush hour. These "go-slows" create a marketplace for thousands of street vendors. They weave through stopped cars and trucks selling drinks, nuts, sweets, and other goods.

22.4 Life in Western Nigeria

It is rush hour in Lagos, the largest city in Africa. The bustling streets are packed with cars, buses, trucks, and bicycles. The city has become famous for its "go-slows," or traffic jams. Young boys crowd around the stopped vehicles to sell a great variety of goods, everything from smoked fish to brushes. Girls also sell things, while balancing bags of water on their heads. They offer drinks, nuts, candy, and even watches and makeup to the frustrated drivers.

The Physical Environment: Rainforest to Savanna
Western Nigeria sits on the Gulf of Guinea beside a wide bay called the Bight of Benin. The Niger River forms the northern and eastern borders of this part of Nigeria.

Before people settled in western Nigeria, a **tropical rainforest** developed along the coastline. Over time, most of this rainforest was cleared for farming or was cut down to sell as timber. Much of western Nigeria is a **savanna,** a broad, flat land covered with tall grasses and scattered trees.

Twenty years ago, almost everyone in western Nigeria lived in villages, but since then many people have moved to cities to seek work. By 2005, about half of all Nigerians lived in cities. About a fifth of these city dwellers lived in western Nigeria's two largest cities, Lagos and Ibadan.

Ethnic Groups: The Yoruba The Yoruba make up the largest ethnic group in western Nigeria. Many Yoruba are Christian, although some follow Islam or traditional beliefs.

The Yoruba people first came to Nigeria around 100 B.C.E. They lived in villages that later grew into kingdoms. Each one of the Yoruba kingdoms had its own king and its own **dialect**. A dialect is a version of a language that is spoken in a specific area. A person from one Yoruba kingdom might not easily understand the dialect spoken in another kingdom. However, in recent years the various Yoruba dialects have become more similar. Today about one fifth of the people in Nigeria speak forms of Yoruba.

Culture: Tin Roofs, Beadwork, and Royal Statues Many of the Yoruba people have relocated from the countryside to one of western Nigeria's cities. Those who are well-off live in one-story houses or in apartments. The poor, on the other hand, live in shacks that are clustered on the outskirts of the cities. The shacks are often put together with such materials as scrap wood, metal, and cardboard. These **shantytowns** lack electricity, running water, and garbage service.

In the countryside, the Yoruba live in houses that are made of mud bricks and usually topped with a steeply sloped roof of tin or iron. During hot weather, the overhanging roof provides shelter from the sun. During the wet season, people put buckets under the edge of their roofs to collect rainwater.

The Yoruba are known for their colorful cloth and beadwork. The cloth is woven by Yoruba women and sold at markets in the cities. Yoruba kings wear beautiful robes covered with beads. In fact, every object made for a king is beaded, from his shoes to his crown. Yoruba crowns have beaded birds perched on them, looking as if they were suddenly going to fly away. Yoruba crowns have a beaded fringe to conceal the identity of the king.

Much of Yoruba art has been made to honor their long line of kings. Yoruba artists create fancy wood masks for their kings, and they make bronze or clay statues to represent kings who have died.

Like the Hausa, the Yoruba are also known for their drums. One type of tension drum, called a *dundun,* is shaped like an hourglass, wide at the top and bottom and narrow in the middle. This tension drum imitates some of the sounds of the Yoruba's spoken language, which is why it is sometimes called a *talking drum.*

Economy: Farms, Factories, and Markets Those Yoruba who live in cities hold a variety of jobs. Some work in factories. Others work in offices. Still others are teachers, engineers, or doctors.

Some urban Yoruba commute back to the country to work on small family farms. This is the reverse of what many Nigerians do, which is to commute from the country to the city.

Yoruba women often make money by selling goods in street markets. They sell produce, such as yams and corn, from their farms, and they sell homemade cloth, baskets, and other traditional goods that tourists might want to purchase.

Yoruba Beadwork
This Yoruba crown is covered with beadwork. In earlier times, colorful glass beads were very valuable.

Waiting for a Ride
These Yoruba women are waiting for a ride to take them to the market where they will sell their yams. Yams, like potatoes, are a root crop. They are an important part of the Yoruba diet.

22.5 Life in Eastern Nigeria

For centuries, the Niger River had served as an important source of fish for the people of eastern Nigeria. Then oil was found in the Niger River's **delta**. Today **pollution** from oil spills has killed most of the fish in the delta. For all of the wealth that oil brings to the country, oil pollution has made life difficult for eastern Nigerians who used to depend on the river for water and food.

Physical Environment: Rivers and Rich Resources Eastern Nigeria sits on the Gulf of Guinea beside a second bay known as the Bight of Biafra. The Benue River forms the northern edge of the region, and the Niger River forms the western edge.

This region receives more rainfall than other parts of Nigeria. Long ago, there were rainforests here, but people have cut down most of the trees to sell as timber. Today swamps line the coast.

The Niger River has built up a large delta where it enters the Gulf of Guinea. The Niger Delta is one of the world's largest **wetlands** and also contains Nigeria's large oil deposits.

Ethnic Conflict in Nigeria

These people are celebrating the end of Nigeria's civil war. The war began when the Igbo tried to leave Nigeria in 1967 to form their own country. Their rebellion ended 31 months later. More than a million Nigerians died as a result of fighting, hunger, and disease brought about by this conflict.

Ethnic Groups: The Igbo The Igbo (pronounced *ee-bo*) are the largest ethnic group in eastern Nigeria. This group of people first settled here thousands of years ago. Unlike the Yoruba, the Igbo did not develop kingdoms, but instead lived in villages, with each village ruled by a council of elders.

Each village spoke its own dialect of the Igbo language. There are more than 300 Igbo dialects, but some may soon disappear. Although about 18 percent of Nigerians are Igbo, the majority of Nigerians speak English as their primary language.

During colonial times, the Igbo worked with British missionaries and officials. Most became Christian, and many were educated at church schools. The British rewarded them with positions in business and government throughout the colony.

After Nigeria became independent, things did not go well for the Igbo people. Other ethnic groups in Nigeria resented their power. Igbo who had migrated to other regions of the country were killed by the thousands. At least one million more Igbo fled in terror back to their home region, where they remained deeply suspicious of their neighbors to the north and west.

In 1967, the Igbo tried to break away from Nigeria. Their goal was to form a country of their own called Biafra. The Nigerian government sent troops to the region to stop the breakaway, and hundreds of thousands of people died as a result of the war that followed. In 1970, Nigeria was once more united as a country, but the memories of the war are still fresh in the minds of many Igbo.

Culture: Houses on Stilts, Colorful Wraps, and Masked Dancers

In the cities, the Igbo build houses using mud bricks, with metal roofs protecting the houses from heavy rains. In swampy areas, people build their houses on stilts. During the rainy season, they paddle canoes to their homes and climb ladders to get inside.

Igbo wrap themselves in colorful cloths. Igbo women wear one cloth wrapped around the lower body and another around the head. The men also wrap a cloth around the lower body. The traditional hat for men is a small cap.

Across Africa, people create masks for rituals, ceremonies, and festivals. Masked dancing is popular among the Igbo, who make masks of wood or leather and decorate them with teeth, hair, fur, and other materials. The Igbo design their masks in secret and keep them hidden until they wear them, thereby allowing the masks to remain mysterious and important.

Economy: Oil and Education

Farming used to be the Igbo's main economic activity, but today it is oil. Most of Nigeria's wealth comes from selling oil to other countries.

Foreign oil companies are in charge of the country's oil industry. In the past, these oil companies brought in foreign workers instead of hiring local people. Nigeria's government has worked hard to change that practice, and today many Igbo work in the oil industry.

The Igbo have used education to change their lives. During colonial times, many of them were able to attend college. Today their children and grandchildren are serving Nigeria as doctors, lawyers, and teachers.

Cleaning Up After an Oil Spill
These workers are cleaning up after an oil spill in the Niger Delta. More than 4,000 spills have occurred in this region since oil production began in 1950s.

22.6 Beginning to Think Globally

In this chapter, you learned about Nigeria and its ethnic diversity. You explored the country's three main cultural regions: northern, western, and eastern Nigeria. In addition, you read about some of the problems that face a country with so many different ethnic and linguistic groups.

Ethnic conflict is a problem in many parts of the world. In Africa, ethnic tensions were made worse by colonialism. The colonial powers established most of Africa's present-day national boundaries, but they gave little thought to how well the groups within a country might get along. Think about this as you examine the map of African ethnic groups in the next section.

22.7 Global Connections

The small map shows how Africa was divided into colonies in 1914. The large map shows Africa today. The red lines indicate where people of various ethnic groups live, and the black lines represent country borders.

Why do most African countries have so many cultural regions?

In Africa, it is rare for ethnic boundaries and political boundaries to match. Most African countries were created during colonial times. European countries divided Africa into colonies to suit their own needs, without giving much consideration to tensions that might arise between ethnic groups living in the same colony.

What problems do countries with many cultural regions face?

Countries with many cultural regions have found it difficult to choose a national language because each group wants its own language to be chosen. To prevent conflict, many of the former colonies that were ruled by Britain or France have chosen English or French as their common language. Ethnic conflict has been another serious problem. Some ethnic groups have a long history of disagreements, and often old hatreds have erupted in war.

What are some ways governments might reduce cultural conflicts?

One way of reducing cultural conflict is to promote a common identity for everyone. In Nigeria, this means persuading people to think of themselves as Nigerians first, and as part of an ethnic group second. Another way is to give local governments more power so that each group can shape the laws in its own area to suit its way of life.

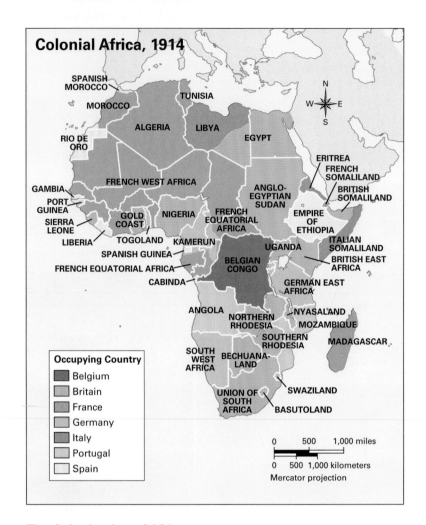

Colonial Africa, 1914

Occupying Country
- Belgium
- Britain
- France
- Germany
- Italy
- Portugal
- Spain

0 500 1,000 miles
0 500 1,000 kilometers
Mercator projection

The Colonization of Africa

Around 1500, European countries began setting up trading posts in Africa. By the 1800s, Europeans were competing fiercely for control of Africa and its resources. They divided most of Africa into the colonies shown on this map. Resistance to colonial rule grew over time. Between 1950 and 1980, 47 African colonies gained their independence.

Ethnic and Political Divisions in Africa

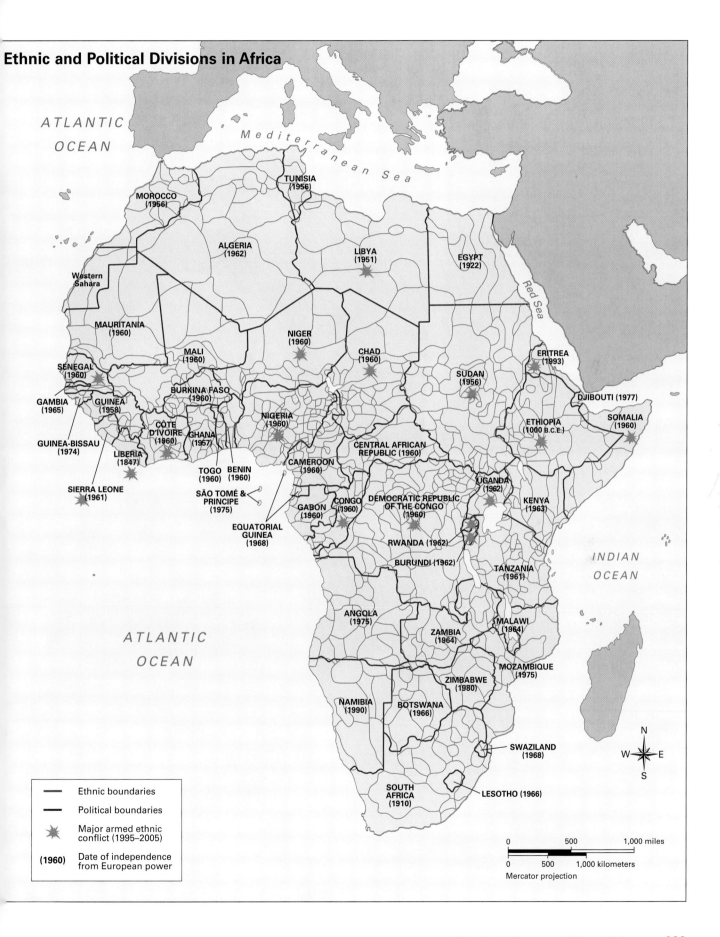

ATLANTIC OCEAN

Mediterranean Sea

TUNISIA (1956)

MOROCCO (1956)

ALGERIA (1962)

LIBYA (1951)

EGYPT (1922)

Western Sahara

Red Sea

MAURITANIA (1960)

NIGER (1960)

CHAD (1960)

SUDAN (1956)

ERITREA (1993)

MALI (1960)

DJIBOUTI (1977)

SENEGAL (1960)

ETHIOPIA (1000 B.C.E.)

SOMALIA (1960)

GAMBIA (1965)

GUINEA (1958)

BURKINA FASO (1960)

NIGERIA (1960)

GUINEA-BISSAU (1974)

CÔTE D'IVOIRE (1960)

GHANA (1957)

CENTRAL AFRICAN REPUBLIC (1960)

LIBERIA (1847)

TOGO (1960)

BENIN (1960)

CAMEROON (1960)

UGANDA (1962)

KENYA (1963)

SIERRA LEONE (1961)

SÃO TOMÉ & PRINCIPE (1975)

GABON (1960)

CONGO (1960)

DEMOCRATIC REPUBLIC OF THE CONGO (1960)

EQUATORIAL GUINEA (1968)

RWANDA (1962)

BURUNDI (1962)

TANZANIA (1961)

ATLANTIC OCEAN

ANGOLA (1975)

ZAMBIA (1964)

MALAWI (1964)

INDIAN OCEAN

MOZAMBIQUE (1975)

ZIMBABWE (1980)

NAMIBIA (1990)

BOTSWANA (1966)

SWAZILAND (1968)

SOUTH AFRICA (1910)

LESOTHO (1966)

N
W   E
S

— Ethnic boundaries

— Political boundaries

✳ Major armed ethnic conflict (1995–2005)

(1960) Date of independence from European power

0   500   1,000 miles

0   500   1,000 kilometers

Mercator projection

Resources and Power in Post-apartheid South Africa

23.1 Introduction

The tall, gray-haired man approached the ballot box. At 76 years of age, he appeared strong, fit, and determined. With a warm smile, he pushed his ballot into the box. Like other blacks throughout South Africa, he was being allowed to vote in an election for the first time. This elderly man was not just anyone, however. He was Nelson Mandela, and when all the votes had been tallied, Mandela would become the newly elected president of South Africa.

South Africa is a **multiracial** society, which is a society that is made up of many **ethnic groups**. South Africa has four major ethnic groups. South Africans call the four groups blacks, whites, coloreds, and Asians. Before that historic election day in 1994, it was illegal for black South Africans to vote or to hold office.

For nearly 50 years, whites had ruled South Africa under a policy called **apartheid,** a word that means "separateness." Under apartheid, whites and nonwhites lived apart from each other. This policy of racial **segregation** hurt nonwhite ethnic groups. They had fewer economic resources than whites, and they also had less political power.

In this chapter, you will learn about life in South Africa under the policy of apartheid. You will discover how the **distribution,** or division, of power and resources changed after the end of apartheid. Finally, you will read about some of the challenges facing the people of South Africa today.

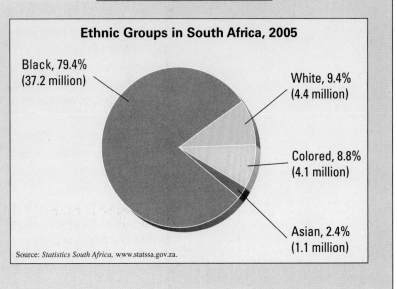

Essential Question

How might ethnic group differences affect who controls resources and power in a society?

This circle graph shows the four main ethnic groups in South Africa in 2005. Note the size of the white ethnic group. Until 1994, this group controlled most of the nation's wealth and power. Keep this graph in mind as you try to answer the Essential Question.

Graphic Organizer

Ethnic Groups in South Africa, 2005

Black, 79.4% (37.2 million)

White, 9.4% (4.4 million)

Colored, 8.8% (4.1 million)

Asian, 2.4% (1.1 million)

Source: *Statistics South Africa*, www.statssa.gov.za.

◀ "Whites Only" signs were common under apartheid.

Farming in South Africa
South Africa has two main types of farming. White farmers raise cash crops on large modern farms. Black farm families produce food mainly for their own needs on small plots of land.

23.2 The Geographic Setting

South Africa is located at the southern tip of Africa. Compared with many other African countries, it is small in land area, but it is the most developed African country. Although only about 5 percent of Africans live in South Africa, the country produces two fifths of Africa's factory goods and about half of its minerals. South Africa also produces about a fifth of the continent's farm products.

A Land Rich in Natural Resources Much of South Africa's wealth has been built on the export of mineral resources, including large deposits of gold, copper, and other valuable minerals. The development of these mineral resources has transformed the country of South Africa into an economic powerhouse.

South Africa's mild **climate** and rich soil are also valuable resources. Many **cash crops** grow well here, including corn, wheat, and sugarcane. Cattle, sheep, and goats graze on vast ranch lands.

South Africa has a great variety of **wildlife**. In the past, these animals were important for groups of people who lived by hunting. In recent years, however, wildlife has become a tourist attraction. Visitors arrive from all over the world to see elephants, lions, zebras, and other animals in their natural **habitats**.

The Development of a Multiracial Society People have lived in what is now South Africa for a very long time. The ancestors of most South African blacks came from Central Africa, probably migrating south approximately 2,000 years ago. South African blacks form a large ethnic group that is made up of many smaller groups, each with its own language and culture.

Europeans began to settle in Southern Africa in 1652. The first to arrive were Dutch colonists who were known as Boers, which is the Dutch word for "farmers." Their settlement was called Cape Colony. In time, settlers from other parts of Europe joined the Boers. Dutch remained the language of the colonists, with the addition of many words picked up from other settlers and from black Africans. The result was a new language called Afrikaans. The white colonists who spoke this language came to be known as Afrikaners.

Settlers from Great Britain began to arrive in Cape Colony around 1820. Most of these British settlers were farmers. In 1867, a rich diamond field was discovered within the colony. A few years later, gold was found. These discoveries of diamonds and gold attracted more colonists. Descendents of the first Afrikaners and British colonists make up South Africa's white ethnic group.

Over time, some blacks and whites in Cape Colony married and had families. The children from these mixed marriages were described as colored. Today their descendents form South Africa's third major ethnic group, the coloreds.

Asians first came to South Africa in the 1860s. Most were from India, which was then a British colony. The Asians came to work for British colonists on their sugarcane plantations. Their descendents in South Africa are still called Asians, and they form the last major ethnic group in this multiracial society.

► Geoterms

apartheid the former official South African policy of separating people according to race. Apartheid gave most of the political and economic power to whites.

distribution the way people or things are spread out over an area or space. This term can also refer to the way resources, power, or goods are divided among people or groups.

multiracial made up of people from several ethnic groups

segregation the separation of one group of people from another, such as by race. Segregation can involve laws or customs that require different groups to use different facilities and live in separate areas.

Mines, Farms, and Factories

South Africa is Africa's most developed country. Its mines produce more gold than any other country. Its farms grow enough food to feed its people. Its factories produce everything from clothing to cars. This wealth is not, however, evenly distributed among its four main ethnic groups.

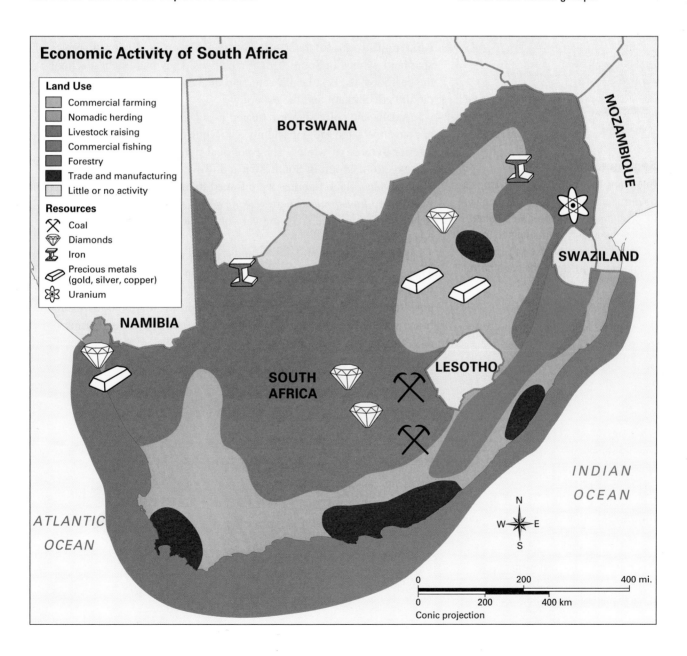

Economic Activity of South Africa

23.3 South Africa During Apartheid

South Africa's colonial period ended in 1910, which was the year that the Union of South Africa became an independent country. The new country's constitution awarded whites complete control over the national government.

Apartheid Makes Segregation an Official Policy Segregation became a way of life throughout South Africa after independence. Then, in 1948, the ruling whites took this practice a step further by making apartheid an official government policy.

Under the new apartheid laws, South Africans were classified by race. Whites and nonwhites were kept separate from one another. They lived in segregated neighborhoods. They went to different schools, hospitals, movie theaters, and restaurants. They were separated on trains and buses. Signs appeared on public beaches and in parks announcing "For White Persons Only."

Apartheid Treats Each Ethnic Group Differently Under the policy of apartheid, whites in South Africa lived well. They had the best schools, the best jobs, the best health care, and the best living conditions. They ran the government and the economy.

Asians and coloreds were treated as second-class citizens. They did not have the same job opportunities as whites, and their schools were inferior to those of whites. Their political rights were limited as well.

No ethnic group in South Africa, however, was treated as poorly as blacks. Many black families were forced to move to poor **rural** areas that were called *homelands*. There were few jobs or resources in these areas. Schools in the homelands were very poor, and there was little access to health care.

Blacks were not allowed to move freely throughout the country. They could leave their homelands to work in distant cities. However, blacks who worked in the cities were forced to live in **townships** that consisted of **slums** located just outside the cities. A typical township home was a shack that lacked running water and electricity. During the day, black workers went to their jobs in the "white" cities, and at night they had to return to the townships.

Homelands in South Africa During Apartheid

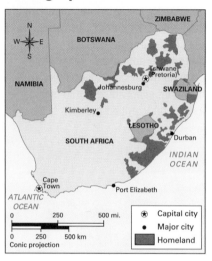

Segregated Homelands

Beginning in the 1960s, South Africa's government forced more than 4 million blacks to move to segregated homelands. The government claimed the move was to give blacks self-rule. But for the most part, the lands were barren.

Soweto: A Black Township

Soweto is the largest black township in South Africa. It is located near Johannesburg, the country's most important city. Today housing in Soweto ranges from shacks to mansions. During apartheid, the township was a center of protest.

23.4 Protests Lead to Political Change

Long before apartheid became an official government policy, blacks had formed groups to protest unfair treatment by whites. The most important group, the African National Congress (ANC), was established in 1912. "The white people of this country have formed what is known as the Union of South Africa," said one of the group's founders, "a union in which we have no voice in the making of the laws." It would take the ANC decades of protest to gain that voice for blacks.

The Fight Against Apartheid The African National Congress led the struggle against apartheid. In 1952, the organization began its "Campaign for the Defiance of Unjust Laws." An ANC lawyer named Nelson Mandela took charge of this fight to end apartheid laws. In 1962, Mandela was jailed for his protest activities, and he would remain in prison for the next 27 years.

The struggle continued, at times turning deadly. The worst violence began in the township of Soweto on a June morning in 1976, when 10,000 students gathered for a protest march against apartheid. When the police tried to break up the crowd, some of the students threw rocks in response. The police reacted by opening fire on the protesters. By the end of the day, 172 protesters lay dead. The protests quickly spread to other townships. Nearly 600 people had died by the time the demonstrations were finally crushed.

Some whites, coloreds, and Asians in South Africa joined the struggle. People around the world protested as well. Many countries refused to trade with South Africa until it ended apartheid. Mandela became the world's most famous prisoner, and the United Nations formally called for his release from jail.

Apartheid Ends and Blacks Gain Political Power In 1989, an Afrikaner named F. W. de Klerk became the president of South Africa. In the past, de Klerk had supported segregation, but later he decided that South Africa would never be at peace until apartheid was abolished. He quickly freed Mandela and other political prisoners. By 1991, South Africa's apartheid laws had been ended.

In 1993, de Klerk and Mandela were awarded the Nobel Peace Prize, an award given each year to those who have done the most to bring peace to the world. These two South Africans were honored for their work to end apartheid.

A year later, all South Africans could both vote and run for political office. As a result, the distribution of political power in the country shifted. The ANC became South Africa's most powerful political party, and the party's leader, Nelson Mandela, was elected as the country's first black president.

Under Mandela's leadership, South Africa established the Truth and Reconciliation Commission. *Reconciliation* means the ending of conflict between groups. This commission investigated many unjust acts that had taken place under apartheid. South Africans saw this as a necessary step toward healing the wounds left by those acts. As Bishop Desmond Tutu, the head of the commission, explained, "You cannot forgive what you do not know."

Waiting to Vote

These people are waiting to vote South Africa's 1994 election. This event was the first time people of all colors could vote for their national leaders. Some new voters walked for miles and stood in line for hours to cast their first ballot.

Voter Turnout in South Africa

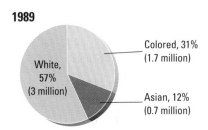

1989

White, 57% (3 million)
Colored, 31% (1.7 million)
Asian, 12% (0.7 million)

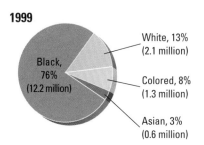

1999

Black, 76% (12.2 million)
White, 13% (2.1 million)
Colored, 8% (1.3 million)
Asian, 3% (0.6 million)

Sources: *Election '99: South Africa from Mandela to Mbeki,* Andrew Reynolds, ed., New York: St. Martin's Press, 1999. *South African Institute of Race Relations,* http://www.sairr.org.za/.

Changes in Voting

These graphs show who voted during and after apartheid. In 1989, whites made up more than half of all voters. This gave them control of the government. By 1999, all South Africans were voting. With this change, political power shifted to black South Africans.

Unemployed South Africans

1987

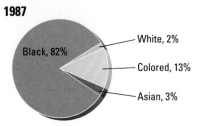

Black, 82%
White, 2%
Colored, 13%
Asian, 3%

2001

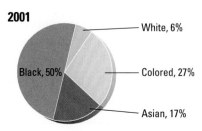

Black, 50%
White, 6%
Colored, 27%
Asian, 17%

Sources: *South Africa, 1989–1990: Official Yearbook of the Republic of South Africa*, 15th ed., Pretoria: Bureau of Information, 1990. *PBS*, "Wideangle," www.pbs.org.

Out of Work

South Africa has suffered from years of slow economic growth. This has caused a rise in unemployment, or joblessness. These circle graphs show unemployment by ethnic groups during and after apartheid. What changes do you see?

Poverty Comes in All Colors

This white family is part of South Africa's growing number of people living in poverty. Some South Africans, both white and nonwhite, have done very well since the end of apartheid. But the poor seem worse off than ever.

23.5 South Africa Today: Job Opportunities

In 2001, for the first time ever, blacks took home more than half of all the income that was earned by South Africans. Before then, whites had always earned the majority of the money. Yet this fact does not tell the whole story of the distribution of wealth within the country. As you know, there are far more blacks than whites in South Africa, which means that blacks still earned far less **per capita** than whites.

Government Programs Open Up Job Opportunities During apartheid, whites received the best jobs, and they also earned the most money. When apartheid ended, the ANC-led government took steps to change the distribution of job opportunities. One step was to help blacks start businesses. By 2010, the government wants 25 percent of businesses in the country to be headed by blacks.

In 1998, the government also passed the Employment Equity Act, which opens job opportunities to all South Africans. This law identifies groups that have been unfairly denied jobs in the past, including blacks, coloreds, Asians, women, and the disabled. The act requires businesses to hire people from these groups when filling jobs and also to pay all workers fairly.

The Employment Equity Act has opened to all groups jobs that were once limited to whites. At the same time, the law has caused resentment among white job seekers, who argue that it is unfair to deny them jobs just because they are white.

Slow Economic Growth Hurts All Ethnic Groups Despite these changes, many South Africans still lack jobs. One reason for this has been the slow growth of the economy. Not enough jobs are being created each year to hire everyone who wants to work. In 2005, four out of 10 job seekers could not find work. Some of these job seekers were whites, but blacks, coloreds, and Asians are still more likely to be out of work than white South Africans.

Slow economic growth has also led to an increase in poverty. By the year 2005, half of all South Africans did not make enough money to take care of their basic needs. Many of the poorest people were struggling just to survive.

23.6 South Africa Today: Education

Any students attending a public school in South Africa today will learn not only to read and to write but also to do math and science. However, this was not always the case. During apartheid, there were separate schools for each ethnic group. Students who were attending a black school were not taught much about science or math. This lack of education was not accidental. The government knew that people with math and science skills would be able to get higher-paying jobs. By not teaching those skills to blacks, the government ensured that South Africa had a supply of cheap labor.

The Link Between Education and Opportunity In general, the more years of school that a person has completed, the more money he or she will make as an adult. In South Africa, more than half of the adults with no education are poor, while only 5 percent of South Africans who have gone to college are poor.

During apartheid, nonwhites had limited educational opportunities. Their schools were poorly built, and their teachers were undertrained and not well paid. Although children were supposed to attend school from the ages of 7 to 16, this requirement was not enforced. In fact, more than 10 million nonwhite adults never went to high school, and over 4 million received no schooling at all.

Schools Are Now Open to All Ethnic Groups The end of apartheid brought important changes to the educational system. The amount of money the government spends on schools has risen sharply. Also, students of all ethnic groups now attend the same public schools.

Schools in South Africa today are teaching the skills that all students will need to get good jobs, with a strong focus on science and math. Students of all ethnic groups are being strongly encouraged to remain in school. As a result, the percentage of students who finish high school has risen in every ethnic group.

The number of nonwhites going to college has increased as well. This increase has occurred in spite of the fact that total college enrollment has declined because of slow economic growth. As more and more non-white children receive college educations, their opportunities for good jobs will improve.

High School Graduates in South Africa

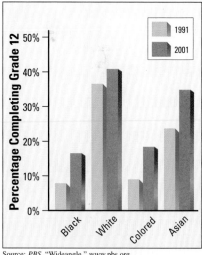

Source: *PBS*, "Wideangle," www.pbs.org.

Staying in School
More South Africans than ever are finishing high school. This graph shows the percentage of each ethnic group that graduated from high school in 1991 and 2001. For blacks and coloreds, the percentages more than doubled.

23.7 South Africa Today: Living Conditions

Under the policy of apartheid, most whites in South Africa lived well. They owned nice homes in the cities. In contrast with houses in the black townships, these houses had electricity and running water, and many had swimming pools. Today most South African whites still have those comforts. However, they also have something they did not have during apartheid: neighbors who are not white. A few nonwhites now live in the nice neighborhoods of South African cities.

Cities Are Becoming Less Segregated During apartheid, many South African cities were "whites only." Blacks were allowed to work in these cities during the day, but they had to leave at night. After apartheid, however, people could live wherever they could afford to buy housing. Some formerly "whites only" cities have become racially mixed as nonwhites have moved in.

Most nonwhites, though, cannot afford to live in nice city neighborhoods. Instead, the poor often settle in slums around the cities, typically living in homes constructed from scrap metal or wood. Even today, few of these houses have running water or electricity. Often these slum areas become a breeding ground for crime.

Housing Conditions Are Improving South Africa's constitution guarantees decent housing to all of the country's citizens. In the first decade following the end of apartheid, the government provided approximately 1.6 million homes to poor South Africans. Efforts to create more housing for the poor are continuing.

The government is also working to improve **urban** slums. Streets have been paved in some poor areas, and water systems have been constructed to provide safe water. Streetlamps have been installed to help combat crime. The government is starting to replace shacks with improved housing. It is also beginning to build schools, police stations, and health clinics in poor neighborhoods.

Health Care Remains Limited In addition to improving housing, the government must face the challenge of providing better health care. During apartheid, most doctors and hospitals were located in "white" cities, and people living in rural areas had a difficult time finding health care. Although the cities are no longer segregated, 9 out of 10 doctors in South Africa still work in urban areas.

Today South Africa is making a strong effort to bring health care to all citizens. By 2005, the government had built more than 500 health clinics in rural areas. Meanwhile, new doctors are being asked to work for a year in a rural clinic in order to help reduce the shortage of doctors outside cities. Pregnant women and children under six are entitled to free health care.

The need for health care has risen sharply as a result of the spread of HIV/AIDS throughout South Africa. The human immunodeficiency virus (HIV) attacks the body's ability to fight disease. Acquired immune deficiency syndrome (AIDS) is the medical condition that results from an HIV infection. Victims of AIDS slowly grow weak and lose weight. Eventually, most will die. There is no cure for the disease, but treatment can help people infected with the virus to live longer.

South African Households with Electricity

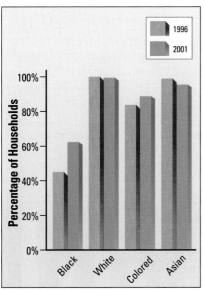

Source: *Statistics South Africa*, http://www.statssa.gov.za/.

Power to Homes

As this graph shows, housing conditions are improving in South Africa. By 2001, more than 60 percent of blacks had electricity in their homes. Many blacks, however, still live in shacks on the edges of cities.

South Africa has the highest number of people living with HIV/AIDS in the world. By 2003, about 5 million South Africans had become victims of this disease. Around 370,000 died from HIV/AIDS in that one year alone. The loss of so many people presents a huge challenge to South Africa's hope for a better future.

23.8 Beginning to Think Globally

In this chapter, you learned about life in South Africa before, during, and after apartheid. You saw how segregation divided a multiracial society. You learned how the distribution of power and resources in the society changed over time, and you read about some of the challenges that face South Africa today.

One of those challenges is the continued spread of HIV/AIDS. When this disease first appeared in humans, no one knew how the virus was spread. Today we know that the virus is found in the blood and other body fluids. The virus is passed through the transfer of blood or other body fluids from person to person. It can also be passed from mother to child during pregnancy and birth.

South Africa is not the only country facing the challenge of HIV/AIDS. The disease has become a global health threat. In 2004, about 40 million people worldwide were living with HIV/AIDS. During that one year alone, about 5 million people were newly infected with the virus, and approximately 3 million people died from the disease. Think about this as you examine the map of HIV/AIDS infection rates around the world in the next section.

Mobile Health Care
This mobile clinic brings health care to people living outside South African cities. Despite government efforts, health care remains poor in many areas. Because of the country's high rate of HIV infection, life expectancy in 2005 was just over 43 years.

23.9 Global Connections

This map shows the percentages of adults who have been infected with the HIV/AIDS virus in various areas worldwide. Note the areas with no color. These are the places where no one has collected information on HIV/AIDS. People there may or may not be free of the disease.

Why has Africa been more affected by HIV/AIDS than other regions?
Scientists think the disease may have begun in Africa in the 1950s, which means the virus has been infecting people in this **region** for longer than in other parts of the world. Poverty has also contributed to the spread of the disease in Africa because poor countries lack money for education programs that might slow the spread of the virus.

What factors have contributed to the global spread of HIV/AIDS?
Unlike many diseases, AIDS develops slowly. The virus that causes the disease can hide in the body for years without the person knowing it. As a result, victims can transmit the infection without knowing they have it. Improved transportation is also a factor, as people today travel easily from country to country. As they do so, they transport the disease with them.

How might HIV/AIDS hurt the countries that are most severely affected? Most victims of the disease are working-age adults. The loss of these adults hurts a country in many ways. As people sicken and die, they leave the **workforce**. This can hurt a country's economy. They also leave children behind. Caring for many orphans is a burden for a poor country. If too many working-age people die, a country may be left with a population consisting of the very old and very young.

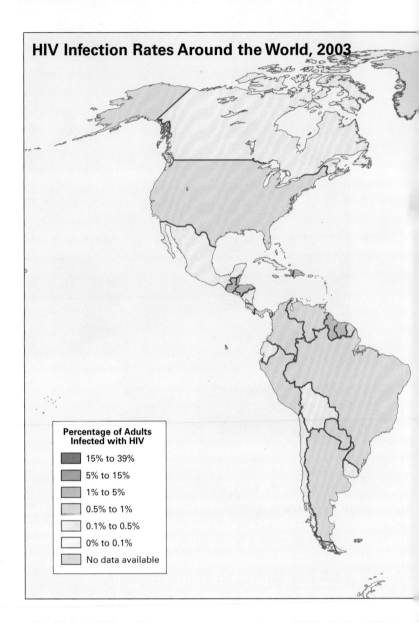

HIV Infection Rates Around the World, 2003

Percentage of Adults Infected with HIV

- 15% to 39%
- 5% to 15%
- 1% to 5%
- 0.5% to 1%
- 0.1% to 0.5%
- 0% to 0.1%
- No data available

An AIDS march in South Africa

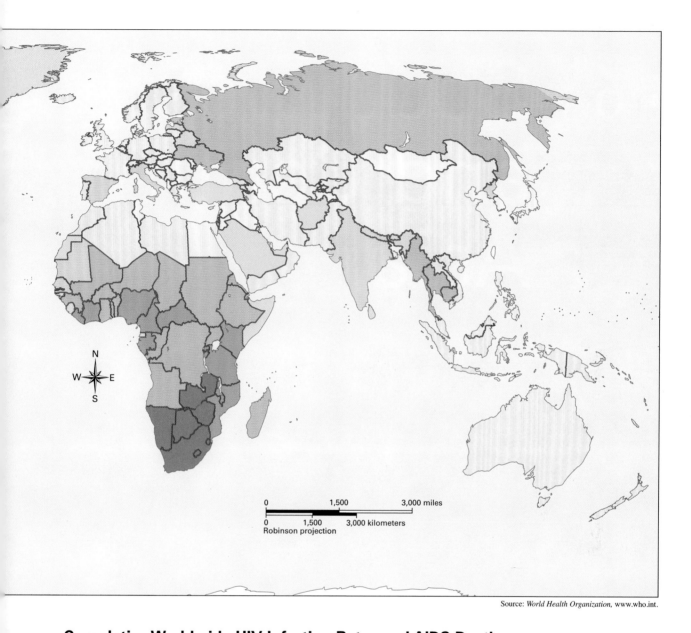

Source: *World Health Organization*, www.who.int.

Cumulative Worldwide HIV Infection Rates and AIDS Deaths

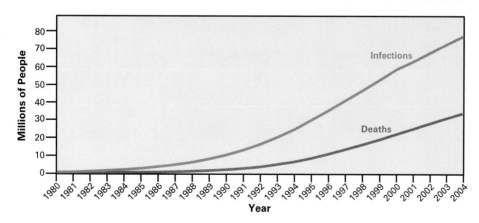

Source: Joint United Nations Programme on HIV/AIDS.

The Impact of HIV/AIDS

This line graph shows the cumulative effect of HIV/AIDS. *Cumulative* means becoming larger with each addition. Since 1980, the cumulative number of people infected with HIV has risen as new cases are added each year. So has the cumulative number of people who have died from AIDS.

Southwest and Central Asia

Introducing the Region:
Physical and Human Geography

What do you see in this photograph?
See page 514 for details.

▼

Introducing the Region: Physical Geography

Southwest and Central Asia are spread across one large section of the Eurasian **landmass**. The **region** is surrounded by seas, plains, and mountains.

Southwest Asia lies at the crossroads of Africa, Europe, and Asia. All three continents meet here at the Mediterranean Sea. Central Asia occupies the lonely center of the Eurasian landmass. Central Asia is a region of treeless plains and **deserts**.

Southwest Asia is bordered by several seas. The Mediterranean and Black seas mark the northwestern border. The Red Sea runs along the western side of the region. The Arabian Sea cradles the southern border.

Central Asia's northern border looks over the plains of Siberia. Rugged mountains rise along the southern and eastern borders. These mountains include the Hindu Kush, one of the highest ranges in the world.

Physical Features of Southwest and Central Asia

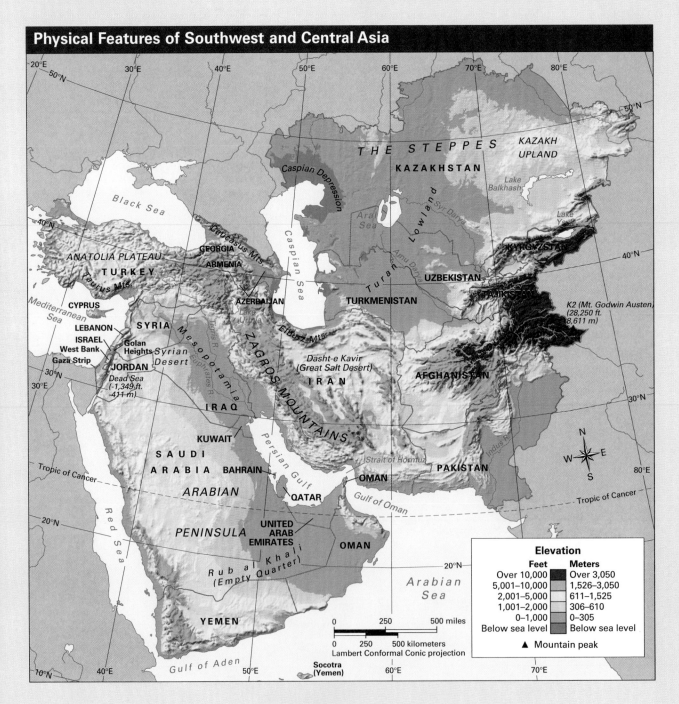

Physical Features

The physical landscape of Southwest and Central Asia is marked by great contrasts. This region includes both the lowest spot on Earth and some of the highest peaks. Dusty deserts cover much of the region. Yet there are also large bodies of water, such as the Persian Gulf. A **gulf** is an arm of the sea that is partly surrounded by land. The Persian Gulf is about 600 miles long. It averages almost 125 miles in width.

Southwest and Central Asia also have several **inland seas**. These are large bodies of salt water with little or no connection to the ocean. The Caspian Sea is the world's largest inland body of water. Its waters are salty, but not as salty as the ocean. As a result, this inland sea is home to both **freshwater** and saltwater fish.

Southwest Asia

Southwest Asia is a land of **peninsulas** and **plateaus**. The Arabian Peninsula occupies the southern part of the region. Covering more than 1 million square miles, it is the largest peninsula in the world.

Farther north lies the Anatolia Plateau. This rugged region stretches across much of modern Turkey. The center of the plateau has **landscapes** that are often described as "moonscapes." **Erosion** by wind and water has carved the hills in this volcanic region into caves, cones, and strange shapes called "fairy chimneys."

This satellite photograph shows two gulfs in Southwest Asia. You can see the Gulf of Oman at the bottom and the Persian Gulf at the top.

Southwest Asia has other interesting features, including

- the Arabian Sea—a shipping route known as a "hurricane alley" because of the violent storms that develop there.
- the Tigris-Euphrates Valley—one of the most fertile river valleys of the ancient world.
- the Dead Sea—an inland sea between Israel and Jordan. At about 1,349 feet below sea level, it is the lowest place on Earth. The Dead Sea is nine times as salty as the ocean. This is so salty that almost nothing can live in its waters.

Central Asia

Central Asia also varies greatly in elevation. The Caspian Sea lies below sea level. But Hindu Kush peaks rise over 25,000 feet.

Central Asia boasts some of Earth's largest inland seas. The Black Sea covers an area larger than the state of California. The Aral Sea was another large inland sea, but it is rapidly shrinking in size.

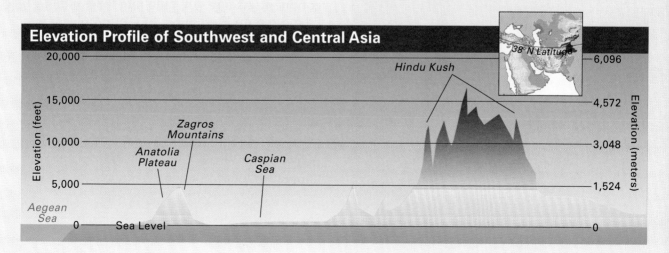

Elevation Profile of Southwest and Central Asia

38° N Latitude

Elevation (feet): 20,000 — 15,000 — 10,000 — 5,000 — 0 Sea Level

Elevation (meters): 6,096 — 4,572 — 3,048 — 1,524 — 0

Hindu Kush

Zagros Mountains

Anatolia Plateau

Caspian Sea

Aegean Sea

Climate

Despite the many seas in this area, Southwest and Central Asia is a region of arid and semiarid **climate zones**. Areas with an **arid** climate zone receive less than 10 inches of **precipitation** a year. But that is an average. An arid area may receive no rainfall for several years. Then, large amounts of rain might fall in a few hours. Areas with a **semiarid** climate have some rain now and then.

Arid and semiarid climate zones are often the hottest places on Earth. Summer temperatures may reach 100°F or higher during the day. Winters are usually mild. There are, however, cold deserts. Some are cold because they lie at a high altitude. Others are cold because they are far from the equator. Still others are chilled by cold winds.

Southwest Asia

Temperatures inland on the arid Arabian Peninsula can climb to 115°F in the summer. There is little moisture in the air, so the air cools rapidly at night. Temperatures can drop sharply in just a few hours.

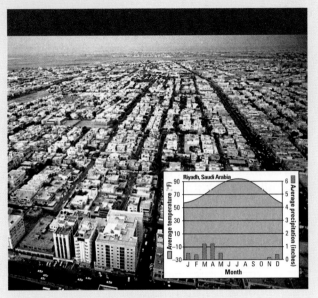

Riyadh is a city near the center of the Arabian Peninsula. When are air conditioners in Riyadh likely to work the hardest?

In coastal areas, the seas create a more moderate climate. For example, coastal Turkey enjoys a **Mediterranean** climate. The same climate zone extends south along the seacoast into Israel. Summers here are warm and dry. Winters are mild and rainy.

The climate varies more in the mountainous parts of this region. In general, temperatures drop as one goes up in elevation.

Central Asia

The tall mountains that bound Central Asia prevent storms that form over the Indian Ocean from reaching the center of the continent. As a result, little rain falls in this inland region. Thus most of Central Asia has arid and semiarid climates.

Two large deserts cover much of the Turan Lowland. North of this arid plain lie the **steppes**. Precipitation on these rolling plains is less than 15 inches a year.

The mountains of Central Asia have varied climates, depending on elevation. The highest peaks of the Hindu Kush are covered with snow throughout the year.

Enough rain falls in the foothills of the Hindu Kush to support farming.

Vegetation

Vegetation in Southwest and Central Asia is limited by the dry climate. **Desert scrub** covers much of the region. Desert scrub is mostly small trees and shrubs that can survive long periods without rain.

Plants adapt to arid conditions in many ways. For example, desert plants rarely grow close together. By being spread out, each plant can pull water from a larger area.

Some plants obtain water from deep beneath the ground. The roots of the acacia tree may reach as much as 100 feet underground in search of water. Other plants store precious rainwater in their leaves, roots, or stems. For example, the aloe plant stores water in its long, thick leaves. Aloe leaves have a waxy surface that limits water loss.

Many other desert plants also survive by reducing water loss through their leaves. The leaves of desert bushes tend to be small and sparse. During very dry periods, plants may shed their leaves altogether.

Desert scrub blankets much of the region, as seen here in southwest Jordan.

Southwest Asia

Southwest Asia has a mixture of **vegetation zones**. The type of plants growing in a particular place depends mostly on the temperature and rainfall.

Patches of **temperate grassland** appear on the central Anatolia Plateau. These grasses are adapted to the cooler climate found in this highland area.

Hills and river valleys are covered with **mixed forests**. Both deciduous and coniferous trees grow in these areas. At higher elevations, only coniferous trees grow.

The Mediterranean coastline supports **chaparral**. The small trees and bushes of this area are well adapted to a Mediterranean climate.

Desert scrub covers the deserts in southern Israel and much of the Arabian Peninsula. The more arid parts of this peninsula are too dry to support much plant life.

Central Asia

Temperate grasslands cover the steppes that stretch across the northern part of Central Asia. Steppes are broad, treeless plains that are usually covered with grasses.

Farther south, much of the region is covered in desert scrub. In the spring, the desert grasses and shrubs burst into bloom. Later on, the heat of summer dries them out.

Trees grow in areas with adequate water. The saxaul tree grows only in Central Asia. For thousands of years, people have relied on saxaul for firewood. The region is also known for its walnut trees. **Deciduous** and **coniferous forests** grow in highland areas.

In the eastern part of Central Asia, the mountains are very high. This small **ice cap** zone is too cold to support any plant life.

The Southwest and Central Asia region has 25 countries. Pakistan has by far the largest population. More than 162 million people live there. The largest country in area is Kazakhstan. The United Arab Emirates is the wealthiest country on a **per capita** basis. It is also one of the smaller countries in this region.

Southwest and Central Asia have long been linked by trade. Camel caravans carried trade goods from Southwest Asia across Central Asia to China and back as far back as 2,000 years ago. The two parts of this region are also linked to each other by a common faith. Most people in this region follow the religion of Islam.

Political Boundaries of Southwest and Central Asia

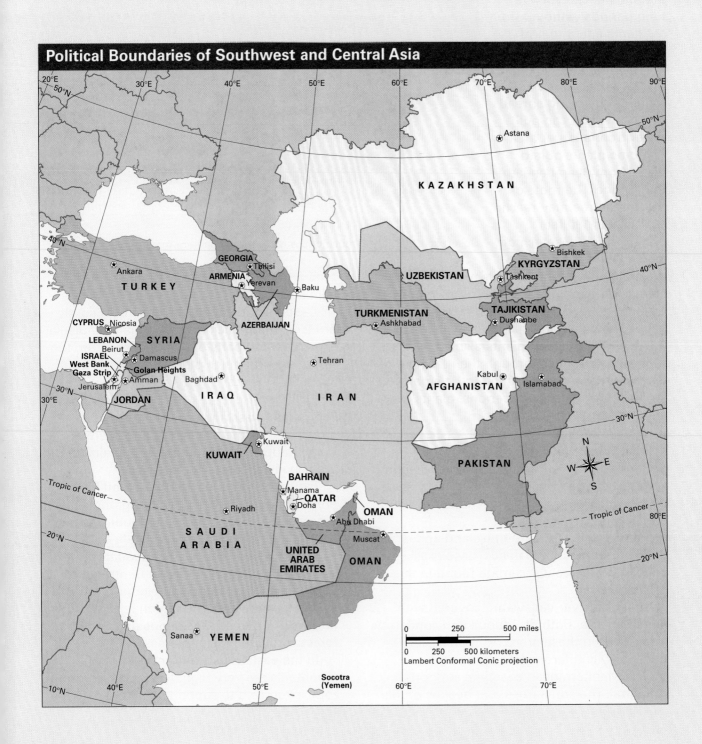

History

Southwest Asia is known as the "cradle of civilization." Farming began here. The world's first cities arose here. This region is also the birthplace of three major religions. All three share the belief that there is only one God. Each religion began with a single person. And each has its own sacred writings, or holy book.

Early Times

According to the Torah, or Jewish holy book, Judaism was founded by a man named Abraham. God told Abraham to leave his home on the Euphrates River. Abraham obeyed and moved his family to the land now known as Israel. God promised Abraham that this land would belong to him and his descendents if they would set the example of how God wants people to live. Abraham's descendents are known as Jews.

Christianity began with a Jew named Jesus about 2,000 years ago. The Gospels, part of the Christian Bible, or holy book, say that Jesus became a preacher in Israel. His words attracted many followers. They also created enemies powerful enough to have him killed. The Gospels say Jesus rose from the dead and appeared to his followers. Those who follow the teachings of Jesus are known as Christians.

Islam was founded on the Arabian Peninsula by a prophet named Muhammad. In 610 C.E., Muhammad told his family that he had seen an angel sent by God. The angel came many times, bringing Muhammad messages from God. These messages were later collected in the Qur'an, the holy book of Islam. Those who follow the teachings of the Qur'an are known as Muslims.

Conquest and Colonies

After his death, Muhammad's followers spread Islam across Southwest Asia, North Africa, and Spain. In the 800s, this Islamic Empire was the center of a brilliant culture.

Later, Turks from Central Asia established the Ottoman Empire in this same region. Islam was the empire's official religion. But Ottoman rulers allowed people of other faiths to live in peace in their empire.

The Ottoman Empire collapsed in 1922. Its territory was carved up into a patchwork of countries and colonies. The Soviet Union took over parts of Central Asia. Britain and France created colonies in Southwest Asia.

The Modern Era

In time, most countries in Southwest and Central Asia threw off colonial rule. Iraq became independent in 1932. Israel was founded as a Jewish state in 1948. The countries of Central Asia broke away from the Soviet Union after its collapse in 1991.

Today, deep conflicts divide this region. Many stem from religious differences. In many parts of Southwest Asia, Muslims oppose the existence of the Jewish state of Israel. In some Muslim countries, there is conflict between the two main branches of Islam—Sunnis and Shi'ites. In Central Asia, Christians sometimes clash with Muslims.

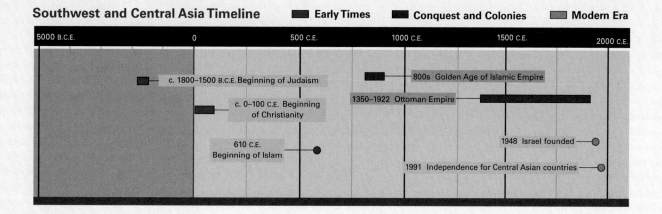

Southwest and Central Asia Timeline ■ Early Times ■ Conquest and Colonies ■ Modern Era

5000 B.C.E. | 0 | 500 C.E. | 1000 C.E. | 1500 C.E. | 2000 C.E.

c. 1800–1500 B.C.E. Beginning of Judaism

c. 0–100 C.E. Beginning of Christianity

610 C.E. Beginning of Islam

800s Golden Age of Islamic Empire

1350–1922 Ottoman Empire

1948 Israel founded

1991 Independence for Central Asian countries

Population

About 400 million people live in Southwest and Central Asia. They make up only 10 percent of the world's population. People are not spread evenly across the region. A few places have a **population density** of well over 250 people per square mile. Many more places have less than 2 people per square mile.

This region is still mostly **rural**. Yet the population has become more **urban** in recent years. In Saudi Arabia, for example, only one Saudi in four lived in a city in 1970. By 1990, three out of four Saudis lived in urban areas.

The Southwest and Central Asia region has one of the fastest-growing populations in the world. It also has one of the youngest populations. The majority of its people are younger than 25.

Most people in this region are Muslim. About 85 to 90 percent of these are Sunni Muslims. Only about 10 to 15 percent are Shi'ites. The region is also home to smaller numbers of Jews and Christians. Jerusalem, the capital of Israel, has holy sites sacred to each of these three religions.

Southwest and Central Asia: Major Religions

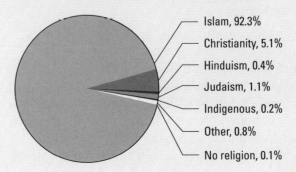

- Islam, 92.3%
- Christianity, 5.1%
- Hinduism, 0.4%
- Judaism, 1.1%
- Indigenous, 0.2%
- Other, 0.8%
- No religion, 0.1%

Southwest and Central Asia: Urban and Rural Population, 2000

Urban, 50.2%

Rural, 49.8%

= 10% of the total population

Southwest and Central Asia: Population Growth, 1950–2050

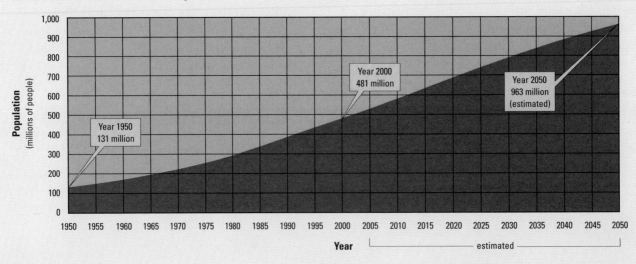

Year 1950
131 million

Year 2000
481 million

Year 2050
963 million
(estimated)

Population (millions of people)

Year — estimated

Sources: *Population Division of the Department of Economic and Social Affairs of the United Nations Secretariat,* "World Population Prospects: The 2004 Revision" and "World Urbanization Prospects: The 2003 Revision," esa.un.org/unpp. "Religion," *Encyclopædia Britannica,* 2005, Encyclopædia Britannica Premium Service, www.britannica.com.

Economic Activity

Two resources shape **economic activity** in Southwest and Central Asia. The first is petroleum, or oil. The second is water. Oil is important because the region is rich in it. Water is important for the opposite reason—because the region has so little of it.

As in other arid places, a lack of water limits commercial farming and livestock raising. In many areas, there is not enough water to grow large crops.

Nomadic herding, however, is still important in this region. Nomadic herders move around to find food and water for their herds. Their camels, sheep, and goats graze on the wild grasses in one area. Then, when the grass is gone, the herders move their animals to a fresh grazing area. Herders depend on their animals to meet most of their needs. They use and sell their animals' milk and meat. They also make tents and clothing from their animals' skin and wool.

Resources

Fossil fuels are key resources in this region. Southwest Asia has the world's largest known oil deposits. Because refined oil is used to fuel cars, trucks, and planes, it is in great demand worldwide. Countries with large oil deposits have grown rich meeting this demand.

Onions grow in the Negev Desert of Israel, watered with salt water and drip irrigation.

In Central Asia, coal is an important fossil fuel. Coal is used for heating and for generating electricity. It is plentiful in Kazakhstan and Afghanistan. Pakistan has large natural gas fields.

Land Use

Commercial farming is an important economic activity in some parts of this region. Olives, wheat, and fruit grow well along the Mediterranean coast. Dates grow in Saudi Arabia, Yemen, and Iran. Cotton is an important crop in Iran and Central Asia.

In some very dry areas, farmers have worked hard to make the most of their scarce water. Israel, for example, is more than half desert, yet it produces 95 percent of the food its people need.

Large cities are centers of trade and manufacturing. In Israel, many companies develop computer software and other advanced products. Israel also has a diamond cutting industry. In Pakistan, factories turn out cotton cloth and clothing for export. Industries in Iran produce building materials, leather goods, and tools.

These desert herders are using a truck to bring water to their flocks.

Oil in Southwest Asia: How "Black Gold" Has Shaped a Region

24.1 Introduction

A lot can change in 50 years. Fifty years ago in the United States, there were no computers, no cell phones, and no Internet. Television was just starting to appear in American homes. However, some parts of the world, such as Southwest Asia, have changed even more dramatically.

Look at the two photographs of the port city of Dubai on the facing page. Originally a small fishing village, Dubai is one of the seven **states** that make up the United Arab Emirates. Fifty years ago it was a small town, and electricity had only recently been introduced. Bedouin **nomads** roamed the **desert** nearby. Today Dubai is a modern, prosperous city with one of the world's largest human-made harbors.

Dubai, like much of Southwest Asia, has been transformed by oil. Southwest Asia provides much of the oil that is used in the world today. This **region** has the world's largest known **oil reserves**. This term refers to underground oil, or petroleum, that has been discovered but remains unused. There are also large reserves of **natural gas,** which is gas found within Earth's **crust,** or outer layer. Money from the sale of oil and natural gas has been used to pave roads and construct modern buildings throughout Southwest Asia. In addition, the money has provided medical care that will help people live longer.

In this chapter, you will learn how vast oil and natural gas reserves have affected Southwest Asia's economic development. You will also discover how these resources have changed the lives of many people in the region.

Essential Question

How might having a valuable natural resource affect a region?

This diagram shows 10 oil-rich countries in Southwest Asia. Together they export millions of barrels of oil each year. The sale of this valuable natural resource has changed life in these countries. Keep this map in mind as you try to answer the Essential Question.

Graphic Organizer

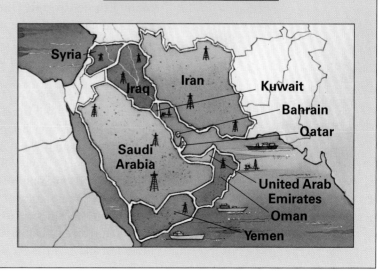

◀ The port city of Dubai in the early 1950s and in 2004

Oil in the Desert

The Arabian Desert covers an area of about a million square miles. Most of this region is too arid to farm. However, beneath the sandy wastes lie vast reserves of oil and natural gas. Oil rigs like this one bring that oil to the surface.

24.2 The Geographic Setting

Southwest Asia lies at the crossroads of three continents: Europe, Africa, and Asia. During ancient times, this location brought traders from distant lands to this region. Most traveled by land over dusty caravan routes. Traders from all over the world still come to Southwest Asia today. However, now many of them arrive in huge tanker ships and are looking for only one product: oil.

Oil: Southwest Asia's Hidden Treasure On the surface, Southwest Asia doesn't look very welcoming. Much of the region is hot and dry. The Arabian Desert is so barren that some people call it "the place where no one comes out." However, hidden beneath the region's deserts are vast reserves of oil and natural gas.

More than half of the world's proven crude oil reserves lie under Southwest Asia. **Crude oil** is another name for petroleum as it is found in the ground. Proven crude oil reserves are known deposits that can be pumped to the surface at a reasonable cost.

Worldwide demand is high for oil and natural gas. **Developed countries** depend on these fuels to meet most of their energy needs. Modern forms of transportation run mainly on oil. Power plants burn oil and natural gas to generate electricity. Oil is also a raw material that is used to make plastics, medicines, and other goods. Some of the countries in Southwest Asia have grown rich meeting the world's ever-growing demand for oil.

Although Southwest Asia has large oil reserves, it lacks other resources. Fresh water, for example, is in short supply throughout the region. Moreover, oil is a **nonrenewable resource**. In other words, there is only a limited amount of it. Once the world's supply of oil is used up, it can't be replaced.

When the supply of oil is gone, the world will have to rely on **renewable resources**. This term refers to resources that will not run out or resources that can be replaced. Three examples of renewable energy resources are sunlight, wind, and **geothermal energy,** which is heat energy drawn from inside Earth. Waterpower and trees are two other renewable resources.

Many Ethnic Groups, One Major Religion Most of the people who live in Southwest Asia are Arabs, people who speak Arabic. Other major **ethnic groups** include the Kurds and the Persians. The Kurds live in parts of Turkey, Syria, Iraq, and Iran, whereas the great majority of Persians live in Iran.

Islam is the most important religion in Southwest Asia. Only one country in the region, Israel, does not have a Muslim majority. There are, however, several branches of Islam. Conflict among different ethnic and religious groups has led to unrest and violence.

In this chapter, you will look at how oil has shaped the development of 10 countries in Southwest Asia. These countries differ in area and population, but each of them has large oil reserves, and each has used oil in different ways to meet its people's needs. These countries are Bahrain, Iran, Iraq, Kuwait, Oman, Qatar, Saudi Arabia, Syria, United Arab Emirates, and Yemen.

▶ Geoterms

crude oil petroleum as it comes out of the ground and before it has been refined or processed into useful products

nonrenewable resource a resource that takes so long to form that it can't be replaced. Oil, which takes millions of years to form, is such a resource.

oil reserves oil that has been discovered but remains unused in the ground

renewable resource a resource that can't be used up or that can be replaced quickly as it is used up. Sunlight is a renewable resource that cannot be used up. Wood is a renewable resource that can be replaced by planting more trees.

Major Oil-Producing Countries

The 10 countries labeled in bold type have the largest oil reserves in Southwest Asia. Combined, they possess about half of the world's known oil reserves. Notice that many of these countries border the Persian Gulf.

Southwest Asia

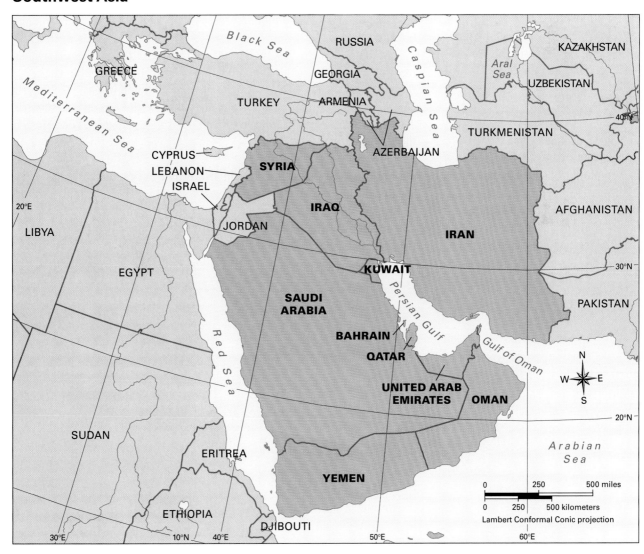

24.3 The Geology and Geography of Oil

For most Americans, oil comes from a gas station, which is where they typically purchase oil to lubricate their car engines. To power those engines, they also buy gasoline made from oil. In some regions of the United States, people also heat their homes by burning oil. The oil that Americans burn in their cars and homes took a long time to form, and more often than not, that oil has traveled a very long distance to reach this country.

Oil Was Formed Millions of Years Ago The oil that is pumped out of the ground today was formed a very long time ago. It began as tiny plants and animals that lived and died in the oceans. After they died, these creatures sank to the ocean floor. Over time, most of their remains were transformed into rock. Layer after layer of rock was formed in this manner. However, some of these plant and animal remains did not turn into rock. The weight of the water, heat from Earth's core, and chemical changes combined to transform some of the remains of these creatures into oil and natural gas.

Over time, the oil and natural gas seeped into pores, or tiny holes, within the layers of rock. These pores may be too small to see, but they are large enough to hold oil and gas, in much the same way that a sponge holds water.

At times, some of this oil or gas has risen to Earth's surface. However, most of it remains trapped underneath a layer of **impermeable rock**. *Impermeable* means "preventing the passage of liquid or gas." Geologists call this layer a cap rock because it functions like the cap on a container. This cap rock keeps most of the oil and natural gas contained deep inside the Earth.

Oil Is Found in Pockets Deep in the Earth A great amount of the world's oil lies buried under Southwest Asia. One reason for these large deposits is that millions of years ago this area was under water. The sea that covered the region contained the tiny plants and animals that began the process of making oil.

From Sea Creatures to Crude Oil

The oil we use today was formed millions of years ago. It began as tiny creatures that sank to the bottom of the sea. As the creatures decayed, parts of their remains slowly turned into oil. Because oil formation is so slow, oil is a nonrenewable resource.

Long ago, the remains of tiny plants and animals fell to the ocean floor.

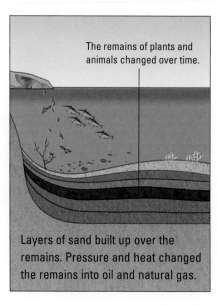

Layers of sand built up over the remains. Pressure and heat changed the remains into oil and natural gas.

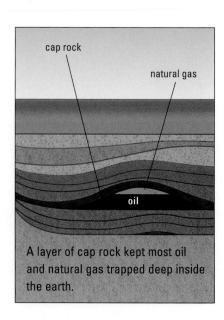

A layer of cap rock kept most oil and natural gas trapped deep inside the earth.

Another reason that oil formed underneath Southwest Asia has to do with the movement of Earth's crust. You read in Chapter 17 that Earth's crust is broken into giant sections called **tectonic plates**. These plates have continued to drift very slowly over the surface of Earth. When two tectonic plates collide, they may create pockets where oil can form. This is what happened in Southwest Asia very long ago. The Iranian Plate and the Arabian Plate bumped up against each other, creating spaces where oil and gas were formed and trapped.

It takes extensive effort to get oil out of underground pores and pockets. Oil companies must drill through the cap rock to get at the oil underneath. Then they pump the oil up to the surface. However, sometimes this pumping process is not successful. When that happens, petroleum engineers inject water or gases into the well, creating added pressure to force the oil out of the rocks.

The oil that reaches Earth's surface doesn't look much like the gasoline or oil that people purchase at their local gas station. Crude oil is usually combined with water and natural gas when it comes out of the ground. Oil companies have to refine this crude oil to make it into gasoline and other useful products. Some other petroleum products are asphalt, plastics, and the wax used to make candles.

Oil Is Not Distributed Equally Since very specific conditions were necessary for the production of oil, it is not surprising that these conditions existed in some places but not in others. Southwest Asia was one of the regions where an enormous amount of oil formed long ago.

Within Southwest Asia, however, the **distribution** of oil is uneven. Saudi Arabia is the largest country in this region, and it also has the most oil. In fact, approximately one quarter of the world's proven oil reserves lie under its desert sand.

Kuwait, in contrast, is a tiny country. Saudi Arabia could contain 125 Kuwaits and still have space left over, but little Kuwait holds almost a tenth of the world's known oil reserves. Other countries in Southwest Asia, such as Syria and Yemen, have less oil, but they still have more oil than most other countries in the world.

The Top Ten Oil Reserves in Southwest Asia, 2004

Rank	Country	Proven Oil Reserves (in millions of barrels)
1	Saudi Arabia	261,700
2	Iran	130,800
3	Iraq	112,500
4	United Arab Emirates	97,800
5	Kuwait	96,500
6	Qatar	16,000
7	Oman	5,500
8	Yemen	4,000
9	Syria	2,500
10	Bahrain	126

Source: *The World Factbook 2004*, Central Intelligence Agency, www.cia.gov.

Who Has the Oil?

The table lists the proven oil reserves of 10 Southwest Asian countries. *Proven reserves* are deposits that oil companies know they can pump to the surface at a reasonable cost.

Today, oil companies drill through the cap rock and pump crude oil to the surface.

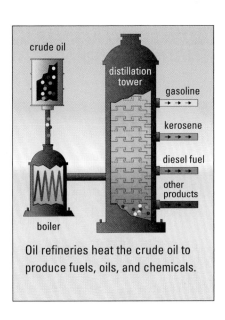

Oil refineries heat the crude oil to produce fuels, oils, and chemicals.

Products made from oil include gasoline, plastics, and materials used throughout our homes.

Per Capita GDP of Southwest Asian Oil Countries, 2001

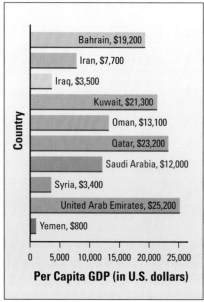

Per Capita GDP of Southwest Asian Oil Countries, 2001

Bahrain, $19,200
Iran, $7,700
Iraq, $3,500
Kuwait, $21,300
Oman, $13,100
Qatar, $23,200
Saudi Arabia, $12,000
Syria, $3,400
United Arab Emirates, $25,200
Yemen, $800

Country (vertical axis)

0   5,000 10,000 15,000 20,000 25,000

Per Capita GDP (in U.S. dollars)

Source: *The World Factbook 2004*, Central Intelligence Agency, www.cia.gov.

Wealth from Oil

This bar graph compares the per capita GDP of 10 Southwest Asian countries. Per capita GDP shows how rich one country is compared to another. But it does not show whether a country's wealth is being divided evenly among its people.

Rich and Poor

Oil has brought great wealth to some people in Southwest Asia. But as these images show, that wealth is not distributed evenly. Some people are fabulously rich. Others are desperately poor.

24.4 Oil Wealth and People's Well-Being

Oil has made the royal family of Saudi Arabia extremely wealthy. Consider the expensive vacation the royal family took in 2002. King Fahd and about 3,000 guests visited the town of Marbella, which is on the southern coast of Spain. The royal family spent about $185 million preparing a palace in Marbella for the vacation. Among the expenses was the cost of hiring hundreds of attendants. After the king arrived, he requested daily flower deliveries, with each delivery running approximately $1,500.

Few people in Saudi Arabia have such a luxurious lifestyle. Just as some countries have more oil reserves than others, some of the people living in oil-rich countries have much more wealth than others.

Oil Has Made Many People Better Off In general, oil money has improved the lives of many people in Southwest Asia. In 2002, researchers from the United Nations studied changes in the region over the past 30 years. These researchers determined that **life expectancy** has increased by 15 years and that the number of infants who die in their first year of life, or the **infant mortality rate,** has fallen by two thirds.

There is no doubt that oil has made some countries rich, but just how rich? There are two common methods to measure a country's wealth. The first method is to examine a country's **gross domestic product,** or GDP. As you read in Chapter 8, GDP is a measure of all the goods and services produced by a country each year. The second method of determining a country's wealth is to look at the **per capita** GDP, which measures the average income of the people in a country. To calculate this per-person GDP figure, divide the total GDP by the number of people in the country.

Per capita GDP varies extensively from country to country for many reasons. The United Arab Emirates and Kuwait, for example, both have a high GDP from selling oil. Since both of these countries also have small populations, they both have a per capita GDP that is relatively high. Countries with larger populations, such as Saudi Arabia and Iran, have to divide their GDP among many more people, thereby resulting in a lower per capita GDP.

Bahrain, in contrast, has far smaller oil reserves than the other oil-rich countries of Southwest Asia. Nevertheless, its per capita GDP is quite high because the country earns much of its GDP by processing, instead of pumping, crude oil. Bahrain's wealth has also increased as a result of the country's development into an international banking center.

Per Capita GDP Does Not Tell the Whole Story Per capita GDP is an average, which assumes that a country's wealth is divided equally among its citizens. In reality, however, some people may be extremely rich, whereas many of their fellow citizens remain quite poor. Accordingly, per capita GDP doesn't always reflect the general well-being of the people of a country.

Another method of measuring how well people are living in a country is the United Nations' Human Development Index (HDI). As you read in Chapter 9, the HDI examines a country's per capita GDP along with other factors that reflect the general quality of life. One of these factors is life expectancy. Another significant factor is education. How many of the people are literate—that is, how many know how to read? How many of the children have received a high school education? When these numbers are evaluated, countries are ranked from best to worst, with 1 being best.

Based on the HDI, Bahrain leads Southwest Asia in terms of living well. Although Bahrain does not have the most oil or the highest per capita GDP in Southwest Asia, the country does use its wealth to educate its population. Almost all of its young people, both boys and girls, attend school. Bahrain also invests in health care. The infant mortality rate in Bahrain is one of the lowest in Southwest Asia. As you have read, the infant mortality rate is the number of deaths of babies under age one that occur for every 1,000 births in a year.

Oil Has Not Improved Life for All Money from selling oil hasn't eliminated poverty in Southwest Asia. Yemen, for example, remains one of the 20 poorest countries in the world. Although its population is approximately 80 percent as large as Saudi Arabia's, its oil reserves are only about 1 percent the size of those in Saudi Arabia. The amount of oil produced by Yemen each year has not been sufficient to pull its people out of poverty.

Other Southwest Asian countries have made considerable money from oil, but they have not used that money to improve people's lives. For example, Iraq has the second-largest oil reserves in the region, but from 1979 to 2003, a dictator named Saddam Hussein controlled Iraq's oil income. He spent most of Iraq's oil wealth building an army, buying weapons, and fighting wars. Very little of the money went to make life better for ordinary Iraqis.

HDI Ranks in Southwest Asia, 2002

Southwest Asia Rank	Country	World Rank
1	Bahrain	40
2	Kuwait	44
3	Qatar	47
4	United Arab Emirates	49
5	Oman	74
6	Saudi Arabia	77
7	Iran	101
8	Syria	106
9	Yemen	149

Source: *HDR 2004,* "Human Development Reports," hdr.undp.org.

Measuring Well-Being

The Human Development Index measures the well-being of a country's people. This table shows the ranks of most of the oil-rich countries in Southwest Asia. Note that Bahrain ranks highest in this region but 40th in the world. Iraq is missing from this list because of the lack of data needed to rank it.

Oil Flows from Southwest Asia

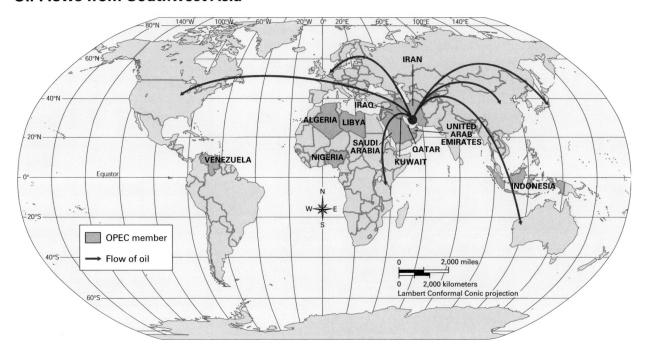

OPEC and Oil Flow

This map shows the members of OPEC, the Organization of the Petroleum Exporting Countries. It also shows where the oil-exporting countries of Southwest Asia send their oil. The United States alone uses one quarter of the world's oil. That's an average of three gallons of oil per person every day.

24.5 The Price and Flow of Oil

Thick black smoke filled the sky, darkening what had been a bright, sunny day. Kuwait's oil fields were on fire. The year was 1991, and Iraq had invaded Kuwait in an effort to take over its oil reserves. This invasion led to a conflict known as the Persian Gulf War. When the war ended, retreating Iraqi troops torched some of Kuwait's oil wells.

The Persian Gulf War was one of many conflicts over oil in Southwest Asia. These conflicts have involved both oil-exporting countries and oil-importing countries.

Oil-Exporting Countries: Working to Control the Price of Oil Most oil-exporting countries depend on oil sales to support their economies. Therefore, one their goals is to have a steady supply of oil flowing out of their countries. In return for their oil, they expect a steady flow of money to come back into their countries.

To ensure a steady supply of oil and a steady income, several oil-exporting countries formed the Organization of the Petroleum Exporting Countries (OPEC) in 1960. Today, OPEC has expanded to 11 members. Six members are Southwest Asian countries, but the organization also includes five oil producers from outside the region: Venezuela, Algeria, Nigeria, Libya, and Indonesia. Meanwhile, not all of the Southwest Asian oil producers belong to OPEC. Bahrain, Yemen, Oman, and Syria have not joined the organization.

OPEC wants oil prices to be steady—not too high and not too low. If too much oil is offered for sale, there will be less competition among buyers to purchase the oil they need. As a result, prices will drop too low. On the other hand, if too little oil is offered for sale, there will be more competition between buyers, causing prices to rise too high. In order to keep prices steady, OPEC members have agreed to regulate how much oil they will sell.

However, two realities limit OPEC's ability to control oil prices. First, OPEC cannot control all of the world's oil sales because its members export less than half of the world's crude oil. The rest of the crude oil comes from non-OPEC countries such as Russia and Mexico. Second, even OPEC members don't always act as a united group. For example, sometimes some members refuse to follow OPEC decisions on how much oil to sell.

Oil-Importing Countries: Working to Protect the Flow of Oil Other countries depend on the flow of oil from Southwest Asia to fuel their economies. The United States, Japan, and many countries in Europe are huge oil importers and therefore have a strong interest in protecting the flow of oil around the world.

As you have read, in 1990 Saddam Hussein, the dictator of Iraq, ordered his military to invade neighboring Kuwait. This invasion gave Saddam Hussein control of Kuwait's oil fields. Fears grew that the dictator would target Saudi Arabia next. If Iraq took over Saudi Arabia, Saddam would control much of the world's oil supply. If he then decided to cut off oil sales, many oil-importing countries would suffer severe energy shortages.

The United States and many other countries formed a coalition, or alliance, to drive Iraq out of Kuwait. Some members of the coalition were oil-importing countries that did not want their oil supplies threatened by Iraq. Others were oil-exporting countries that feared losing control of their oil reserves to Iraq.

The coalition went to war in 1991 to drive Iraqi forces out of Kuwait. The Persian Gulf War lasted just a few weeks. In that time, Kuwait was freed from Iraqi control. The coalition victory sent the world a clear message: as long as oil is the world's main source of energy, countries that import oil will work to keep it flowing.

24.6 Beginning to Think Globally

In this chapter, you learned that crude oil forms deep within Earth. Much of Earth's oil lies under Southwest Asia. However, oil reserves are not distributed evenly among the region's countries, nor is the wealth from oil sales distributed evenly among the citizens of oil-rich countries.

You also learned that oil is a nonrenewable resource. Eventually the world will run out of oil. Some countries are already developing their renewable resources to meet some of their energy needs. One example is solar energy, which is energy from the sun that can be converted into heat or electricity. As oil runs out, other countries will have to follow their example. Think about this as you examine the map of solar energy in the next section.

Oil Fields in Flames

Oil is so valuable that countries have gone to war over it. In 1990, Iraq invaded Kuwait to get control of Kuwait's oil reserves. A coalition of countries drove Iraq's forces out of Kuwait. But they were not able to prevent Iraqi soldiers from setting more than 730 oil wells in Kuwait on fire. It took eight months to put out these raging fires.

Top Contributors to Persian Gulf War Costs

Country
United States
Saudi Arabia
Kuwait
United Arab Emirates
Japan
Germany
United Kingdom
South Korea

Sharing the Cost of War

Many countries shared the costs of the 1991 Persian Gulf War. About two thirds of the money came from oil-exporting countries. They wanted to protect their oil reserves. The rest came from oil-importing countries. They wanted to protect the flow of oil into their countries.

24.7 Global Connections

This map shows the distribution of one renewable energy resource, sunlight. The circle graphs show energy produced by renewable and nonrenewable resources in two years. Renewable resources include sunlight, wind, and the power of moving water. They also include plants that can become fuel. Corn, for example, is used to produce a fuel called *ethanol,* which is mixed with gasoline to burn in cars and trucks that have been designed to run on this alternative fuel.

What energy sources is the world using to meet most of its energy needs? What do they have in common? The world is relying mainly on nonrenewable resources to meet its energy needs. All of these energy sources will someday run out.

Why isn't the world getting more of its energy from renewable resources? In the past, generating energy from renewable resources has cost more than burning oil or gas. Hydroelectric power was the only renewable resource that could compete with **fossil fuels**. However, building hydroelectric dams on rivers has been costly and can also harm the environment. Recently the cost of generating electricity from wind has dropped. As a result, many countries are now using wind power to meet some of their energy needs.

How might having renewable energy resources affect a region in the future? In the future, sunlight and wind may become key resources. Regions that have daily sunshine or steady winds could become major energy producers. Deserts in the U.S. Southwest are already home to solar power plants. Wind farms are sprouting up across the breezy Great Plains. On these farms, large windmills generate electricity as their blades spin in the wind.

Solar Energy Availability Around the World, 2002

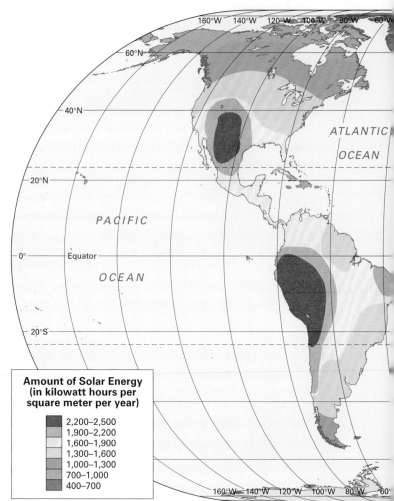

One kilowatt hour is enough energy to power sixteen 60-watt lightbulbs for one hour.

Solar energy power plant in California

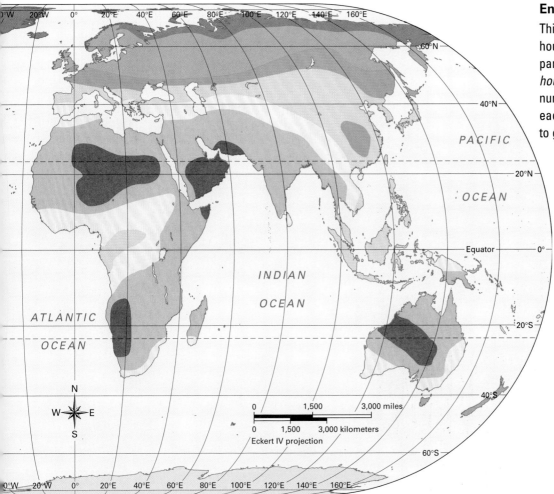

Energy from the Sun

This map shows peak sun hours per day in different parts of the world. *Peak sun hours* refers to the average number of hours of full sun each day that can be used to generate electricity.

Source: *Association for Science Education*, www.ase.org.uk.

World Energy Production

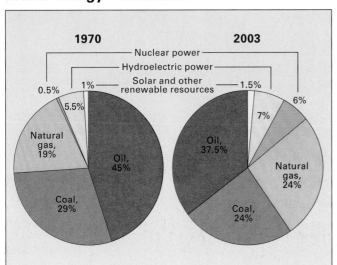

Source: *Energy Information Administration*, www.eia.doe.gov.

The Cost of Five Energy Sources, 2005

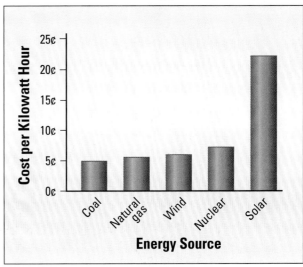

Oil in Southwest Asia: How "Black Gold" Has Shaped a Region   **367**

Istanbul: A Primate City Throughout History

25.1 Introduction

Meryem lives in Istanbul, the largest city in Turkey. It is early morning, and she is riding a ferryboat to get to work. The crowded ferry carries passengers across the Bosporus Strait, the narrow waterway that connects the Black Sea to the Mediterranean Sea.

Looking ahead to the west, Meryem sees the domes and spires of Istanbul's ancient mosques. The city's business district rises up among these old landmarks. Behind her, to the east, the sun is rising over the high-rise apartment building where she lives.

Every day, thousands of Turks like Meryem commute back and forth across the Bosporus Strait. In the morning, they leave their homes in Asia to travel to jobs in Europe. At night, they return to Asia. In the course of their commute, they have never left Istanbul. That's because the city spans two continents: the eastern part of Istanbul lies in Asia, and the western part is located in Europe.

Istanbul's unique location has helped to make its population more than twice the size of the next largest city in Turkey. Many other countries also have a dominant city that is by far the largest and most important one. Geographers have a name for such an **urban** area: they call it a **primate city**. The word *primate* means "highest ranking."

In this chapter, you will read about the traits of primate cities. You will also discover how geography, history, and culture have come together to make Istanbul a primate city.

Essential Question

Where are primate cities located, and why are they important?

This map shows where some of Turkey's cities, towns, and villages are located. The size of each dot represents the number of people living there. Istanbul is Turkey's primate city. Compare its location and size with other cities and towns. Keep this map in mind as you try to answer the Essential Question.

Graphic Organizer

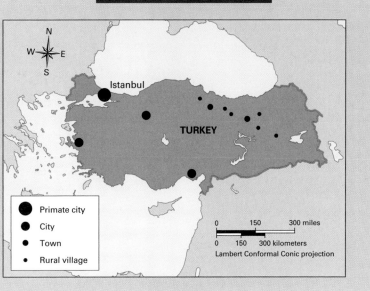

Legend:
- Primate city
- City
- Town
- Rural village

◄ Ancient Hagia Sophia and modern buildings in Istanbul

The Site of Constantinople

This illustration, made in the 1400s, shows the site of Constantinople. The city is located on the tip of a peninsula. This location made it easy to wall off the city for protection from invasion by land. In times of danger, the city also put a chain across the Bosporus Strait. The chain helped protect against invasion by sea.

25.2 The Geographic Setting

Founded more than 2,500 years ago, the city now known as Istanbul has been called by three names during the course of its long history. The ancient Greeks who first settled there called their city Byzantium. Later the Romans changed the name to Constantinople, and later still the Turks renamed the city Istanbul. Under each name, the city has thrived as a center of trade, government, and culture. Throughout much of its history, it was also a primate city.

Istanbul's Favorable Site and Situation The city has survived for so long because of its favorable location. Geographers describe a place's location in two ways. First, they look at its **site,** which is the natural setting of a place. Second, they look at its **situation,** which is the position of a place in relation to its surrounding area.

The site of this city was well chosen—the city was built at the tip of a **peninsula** with a natural harbor. Having water on three sides helped to protect the city from overland attack. And the peninsula is flat, fertile, and well watered, which makes it productive for farming.

The city's situation was equally well chosen. The city was built on the Bosporus Strait, the narrow waterway that links the Black Sea to the Sea of Marmara. The strait is part of a waterway that flows from the Black Sea to the Mediterranean Sea. The Bosporus Strait also marks the dividing line between Europe and Asia. In ancient times, trade routes from three continents—Europe, Asia, and Africa—met at this point, with trade goods flowing into the city from as far away as China, Russia, and East Africa.

The Capital of Three Empires The Greeks were the first to appreciate Istanbul's location, but they would not be the last. Over time, the city would eventually serve as the capital of three great empires.

Byzantium became part of the Roman Empire in 196 C.E. Almost four centuries later, a Roman emperor named Constantine moved his government there, and in 330 C.E., he made Byzantium the new **capital city** of the Roman Empire. A capital city is the center of government for a state, country, or empire. The new capital was renamed Constantinople after the emperor.

The western part of the Roman Empire fell in the late 400s, but the eastern part survived and became the Byzantine Empire. That empire grew to include much of Southwest Asia and parts of Eastern Europe. The Byzantine Empire lasted for the next 1,000 years, with Constantinople as its capital. During this time, the city's wealth attracted attackers, but the strong city walls kept them back.

By 1300, a group of Turks called the Ottomans began to conquer Southwest Asia. In 1453, the Ottomans took over Constantinople as well. They renamed the city Istanbul and made it the capital of the growing Ottoman Empire.

In 1922, the Ottoman Empire fell apart. Istanbul became part of the modern country of Turkey, but it did not become Turkey's capital city. That honor went to the much smaller city of Ankara. Even so, Istanbul remains one of the world's great primate cities.

► Geoterms

capital city a city that is the governmental center of a country or region. Sometimes a capital city is also a primate city.

primate city the largest and most important city in a country. A primate city has at least twice the population of the next largest city. It is a center of economic power and national culture.

site the specific place where something is located, including its physical setting

situation the way a place is positioned in relation to its wider surroundings

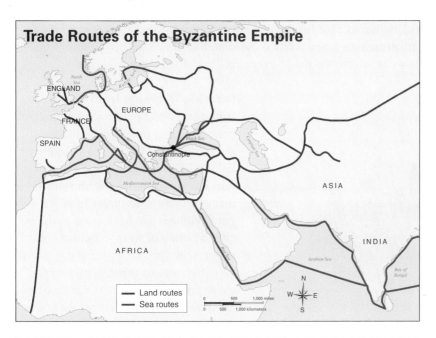

Trade Routes of the Byzantine Empire

The Situation of Constantinople

Constantinople was situated between Asia and Europe. Trade goods came from Asia by land and by sea. Other goods came from Africa and Europe. By 1000 B.C.E., trade had helped Constantinople become one of the world's largest cities.

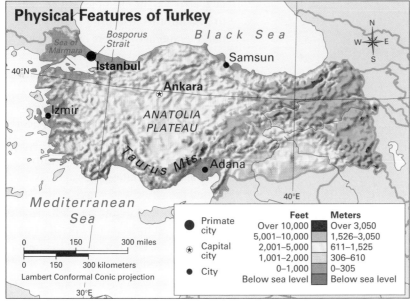

Physical Features of Turkey

Istanbul's Site and Situation

Istanbul has outgrown its original site on a peninsula. Its situation, however, remains the same. The city has access by water to two seas. It is surrounded by fertile farmland. All of these factors have contributed to its becoming a primate city.

25.3 A Country's Largest City by Far

Mustafa moved to Istanbul to make money so that he could afford to marry his girlfriend. He is a barber and works in the heart of the city. Before coming to Istanbul, Mustafa lived in a small town where he knew everyone. However, in Istanbul he walks among crowds of strangers. Mustafa's story is similar to the experiences of countless people living in this busy primate city.

The Urban Hierarchy

This diagram shows the ranking of urban places in terms of size and importance. Primate cities stand at the top of the urban hierarchy. A primate city has at least twice as many people as any other city in that country. People are drawn to a primate city because it has more opportunities than smaller areas.

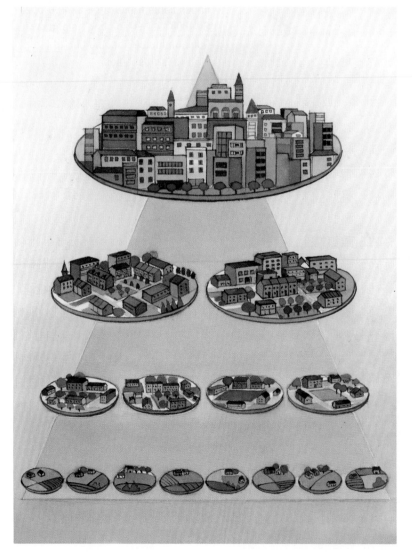

At the Top of the Urban Hierarchy Primate cities stand at the top of the **urban hierarchy**. A hierarchy is a ranking system, and an urban hierarchy ranks cities based on their size and the services they offer. A primate city is by far a country's highest-ranking city in terms of size, having at least twice as many people as the next largest city in the country. A primate city also ranks first in terms of just about anything else that might attract people, from schools and jobs to shopping and sports.

Istanbul is Turkey's largest city by a wide margin. In 2000, about 9.5 million people lived there. By comparison, Turkey's second-largest urban area, the capital city of Ankara, had only 3 million people. Istanbul is so large that one out of every six Turks lives there.

Drawing Migrants from Rural Villages Primate cities act like magnets, attracting people from many of the surrounding towns and villages. Each year, more than 400,000 people relocate to Istanbul. Like Mustafa, many of these newcomers have left **rural** villages and have come to the big city in search of work, education, and excitement.

This rural-to-urban migration can cause problems, as some primate cities are growing too fast to meet the needs of their residents. Many of Istanbul's new arrivals, for example, are unable to find affordable housing. Instead they build temporary shelters on open land on the city's outskirts. Turks call these **shantytowns** *gecekondus,* a Turkish word that means "built overnight." These neighborhoods may lack such basic services as running water, electricity, and garbage collection.

Istanbul also suffers from traffic jams and air pollution. Sewage has dirtied the city's waterways, and many homes have bad plumbing. Still, people keep moving to Istanbul. For all of its problems, the city remains at the top of Turkey's urban hierarchy.

25.4 A Center of Economic Power

Large ships rest in Istanbul's harbor, holding huge containers that are filled with goods that are coming into or leaving Turkey. All day long, gigantic cranes lift the containers and place them on ship decks or truck beds. For many centuries, Istanbul's symbols have been the domes of its many mosques. Today the cranes are also symbolic of this bustling city.

A Hub of Business, Trade, and Travel Istanbul is the economic center of Turkey, with almost two thirds of the country's industry being located there. Nearly half of all goods bought and sold in Turkey pass through the city, and it is also Turkey's banking center.

Istanbul's busy port welcomes ships from all over the world. The ships arrive carrying machinery, oil, metals, medicines, plastics, and chemicals, and they leave loaded with textiles, clothing, steel products, foods, and minerals.

The city connects Turkey to the rest of the world and has been a railroad center since the early days of train travel. Rail passengers took the famous Orient Express from Paris to Istanbul, and from there they boarded the Baghdad Railway to travel into Southwest Asia. Today visitors arrive by air and ship as well. Most people who travel to Turkey start or end their visit in Istanbul.

No Longer the Capital City Many primate cities are also capital cities. Government buildings and offices are housed there, and legislatures assemble in these cities to make laws.

As you read, Istanbul was once both a primate city and a capital city. However, it lost its place as a capital city in 1923, the year the Republic of Turkey was formed. The president of the new country, Kemal Ataturk, wanted Turkey to have a capital that had not been the center of ancient empires. By choosing Ankara as the capital city, he hoped to show the world that Turkey was a very modern place. Still, Istanbul remains Turkey's primate city.

Ships on the Bosporus Strait

Every year, tens of thousands of ships move through Turkey's Bosporus Strait. All of this shipping makes the Bosporus the world's most crowded waterway. Its narrow passages and tricky turns also make it one of the most dangerous.

25.5 A Center of National Life and Culture

Every day, almost half a million people come to shop in Istanbul's Grand Bazaar. A bazaar is somewhat like a shopping mall. Instead of stores, however, a bazaar has stalls, and instead of hired salespeople, it has traders who are selling their goods. With more than 60 streets and about 3,000 shops—all under one roof—the Grand Bazaar is one of the many attractions drawing people to this primate city.

The Grand Bazaar: A Reflection of Turkish Culture There are no price tags at the Grand Bazaar. Instead, buyers bargain with sellers. As a general rule, sellers may name a price that is 10 times what the object is worth. Buyers counter with a price that may be one tenth what the item is worth, and so the haggling begins.

Travelers from all over Turkey and from around the world come to explore the Grand Bazaar, where they can shop for a variety of pottery, jewelry, metalwork, and other items that reflect Turkey's culture. Buyers can also browse Turkey's famous carpets. Carpet weaving is an ancient and honored art throughout Turkey, with each village boasting its own traditional designs.

A Cultural and Sports Center Although Istanbul is not Turkey's capital city, it is still the country's cultural and sports center. The most important Turkish museums are found in this primate city, along with art galleries and concert halls. Musical events range from opera to jazz and rock concerts. Nightclubs offer more traditional entertainment such as Turkish songs and dance.

Istanbul has been a sports center for approximately 2,000 years. In fact, visitors can still view the ruins of the Hippodrome, an ancient Roman sports stadium that could hold 100,000 people. Romans gathered in the Hippodrome for horse races, chariot racing, and other athletic events. Turks still gather in Istanbul's sports stadiums, but today they come to watch soccer.

Historic Sites and Cultural Symbols The city draws tourists from all over the world. Its historic structures are cultural symbols of Turkey as well as tourist attractions.

One of the most visited historic buildings is the beautiful Hagia Sophia. Its name means "Holy Wisdom." The Byzantines built Hagia Sophia as a Christian church in the 500s. In the 1400s, the Ottomans turned the building into an Islamic mosque. Today the Hagia Sophia is a museum and also a reminder to visitors of how long Istanbul has been a major meeting place of many cultures and peoples. The city's history includes both Christian and Muslim ways of life.

The Topkapi Palace has become a lasting symbol of Turkey's Ottoman heritage. The palace is a sprawling mix of buildings and gardens and was once home to the rulers of the Ottoman Empire. Visitors can see great wealth on display at Topkapi, including one famous object known as the Topkapi dagger. Made during the 1700s, it is a sword covered with diamonds and emeralds.

The Blue Mosque is another important symbol of Turkey's Ottoman past. This mosque takes its name from the 20,000 blue tiles that line

Istanbul's Grand Bazaar

The Grand Bazaar reflects Turkish culture in its displays of arts and crafts. Its stalls present a colorful mix of rugs, pottery, jewelry, and clothing. There are workshops where skilled workers beat copper, brass, and silver into useful objects. This craft has been passed down from one generation to the next for hundreds of years.

its inside walls. Built during the 1600s, it is famous for its many domes and minarets. A minaret is a tall, slender tower that is attached to a mosque.

No visit to Istanbul would be complete without a trip to one of the city's famous public baths, called *hamam*. Turks go to these baths to wash, have massages, and visit with friends. Some of the baths date back more than 500 years. In this ancient primate city, however, that is not very old.

25.6 Beginning to Think Globally

In this chapter, you learned that Istanbul is a primate city. It has more than twice the population of the next largest city in Turkey. It is also the country's business and cultural center. Its site and situation have attracted people for more than 2,500 years. Today Ankara is Turkey's capital city, but Istanbul still stands out as by far the country's largest and most important city.

Although some countries have primate cities, others do not. France is one example of a country with a primate city. Its capital city, Paris, has more than twice the number of people as the next largest city in France, which is Marseille. Paris is also France's economic and cultural center. Bangkok, the capital city of Thailand, is another primate city. Bangkok draws people and resources from throughout the country. In contrast, China and Canada are two countries that do not have a primate city. That is, these two countries do not have one city that stands out as the center of the country's population, economic power, and culture.

Primate cities are like magnets, attracting people, trade, culture, and ideas. Think about this as you examine the map of primate cities around the world in the next section.

Hagia Sophia, "Holy Wisdom"

This immense church was built in just five years. When it was completed in 537 C.E., a writer described its effect on visitors. "No one ever became weary of this spectacle, but those who are in the church delight in what they see." Today it reminds visitors that Istanbul has long been a meeting place of religions and cultures.

25.7 Global Connections

This physical features map shows primate cities around the world. Note that some countries do not have a primate city.

What role do site and situation play in the development of primate cities? As you can see on the map, many primate cities are found along a coastline. Such cities often enjoy a mild **climate,** which makes them good places to live. Primate cities located away from a coast are usually situated along a river. Being next to an ocean or a river has helped many cities to become important trading centers. Their location by bodies of water may also have helped to protect them from attack.

What relationship do you see between primate cities and capital cities? Most primate cities are also capital cities. This is not surprising, because many countries choose their largest and wealthiest city to be their capital. However, not all capital cities have twice the population of the next largest city in the country. Some capital cities, including Washington, D.C., and Ottawa, Canada, just don't measure up. Other capital cities, such as Ankara, Turkey, or Canberra, Australia, have been chosen as capitals precisely because they were not their country's largest cities. This is a way of spreading power more evenly throughout a country.

What might explain why some countries do not have a primate city? Countries that do not have primate cities usually have many large cities, but no city is by far the largest and most important in the country. This is most likely to be true of very large countries such as India and the United States. In such countries, there are often several very large cities with substantial economic power and culture.

Primate Cities Around the World

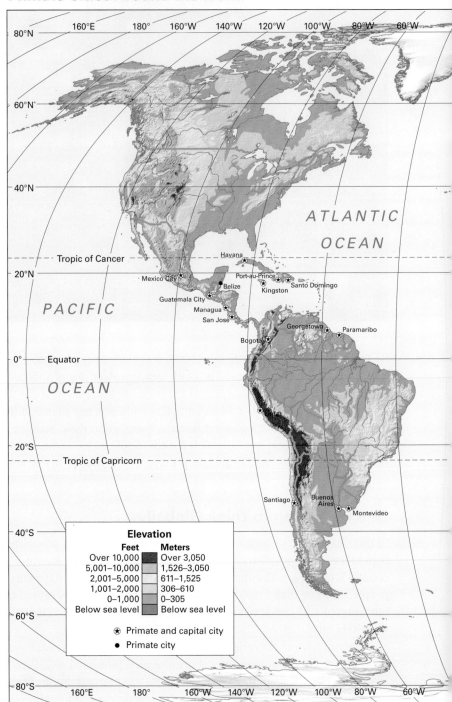

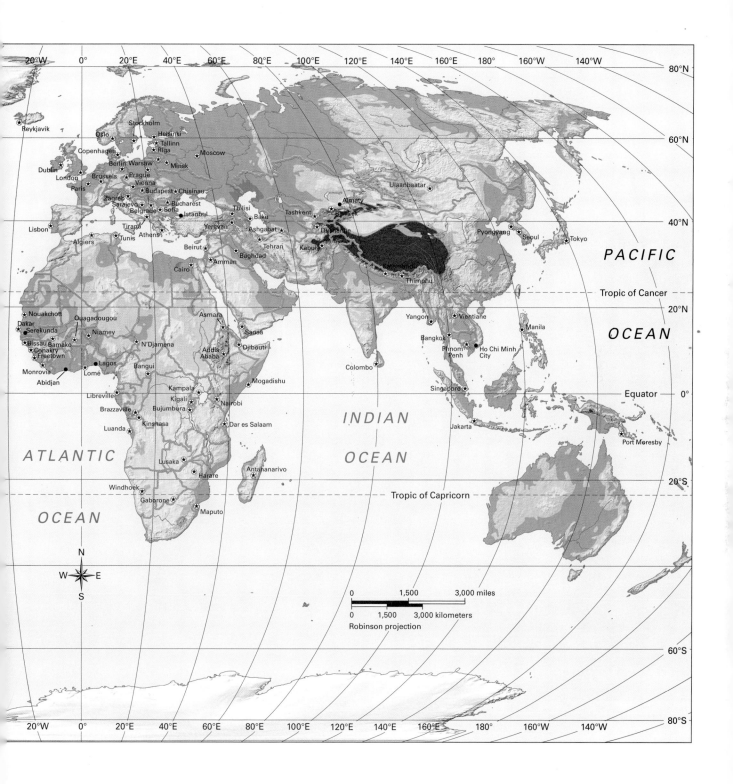

The Aral Sea: Central Asia's Shrinking Water Source

26.1 Introduction

In 1960, Moynaq was a fishing town in the Soviet Union. The town was nearly surrounded by the Aral Sea, a large lake in the Soviet republics of Uzbekistan and Kazakhstan. Visitors to Moynaq in 1960 saw fishing boats bobbing at its docks. At that time, Moynaq had a population of about 40,000 people. Most of these people made a living by farming, fishing, or working in the city's fish canneries.

All of that has changed. If you visited Moynaq today, you would find it surrounded by dust. Although a 20-foot welcome sign depicts a fish and a seagull, you wouldn't see the Aral Sea anywhere. The shoreline of this **inland sea** has withdrawn, and not just a small amount. The water's edge is now nearly 90 miles from Moynaq.

Moynaq and the surrounding area suffer from **water stress,** which occurs when an area requires more water than it has. As the Aral Sea has shrunk, water stress has increased in this **region**. The area also suffers from **environmental degradation**. To *degrade* something means to damage it or wear it down. In the Aral Sea region, the environment has been degraded by misuse of what little water there is.

In this chapter, you will find out what caused the shrinking of the Aral Sea. You will learn about environmental degradation in the surrounding region, and you will see how damage to the environment has affected farming, fishing, and quality of life in this region.

Essential Question

How are humans affected by changes they make to their physical environment?

This illustration shows the Aral Sea at two different times. Note how much smaller it is in 2005 than in 1964. The arrows represent three aspects of life that have been affected by the shrinking of the sea. Keep this illustration in mind as you try to answer the Essential Question.

Graphic Organizer

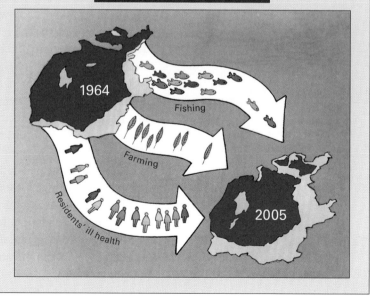

◀ This captain's boat was abandoned as the Aral Sea dried up.

The Aral Sea Region

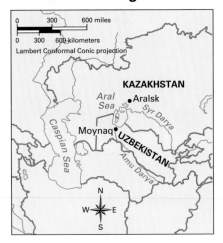

A Central Asian Sea

The Aral Sea lies in two countries, Uzbekistan and Kazakhstan. The Amu and Syr rivers feed this inland sea. It was once a large, freshwater lake. Today it is a shrunken, salty sea.

26.2 The Geographic Setting

The Aral Sea is located in Central Asia, lying in two countries, Uzbekistan and Kazakhstan. Before 1991, these two countries were part of the Soviet Union. Until the 1960s, when irrigation projects began, two rivers fed the Aral Sea: the Syr Darya from the northeast and the Amu Darya from the south. (In the Persian language, *darya* means "river.")

From Freshwater Lake to Inland Sea The Aral Sea was first called a sea only because of its great size, not because it was salty. It was really a large lake containing fresh water.

Until the 1960s, the water in the Aral Sea was **potable,** which means that it was drinkable. Potable water can also be used for the irrigation of crops. However, even **freshwater** lakes and rivers contain a small amount of salt. This salt is washed out of the surrounding soil by the flowing water. If the amount of salt in water is very low, the water is still considered to be fresh. The term *salt water* refers only to water that is too salty to drink.

Although the Aral Sea's water used to be fresh, now it has become **saline,** which means salty. *Salt* and *saline* are both derived from the Latin word *sal*, which means "salt." Today the Aral Sea is too salty to drink and too salty for watering crops.

Salinization Affects Water and Land **Salinization,** the process in which water or land becomes salty or saltier, can affect a body of water, such as the Great Salt Lake in the state of Utah. The process of salinization can also affect **groundwater,** which is water that lies deep underground and supplies wells and springs.

To understand salinization, think first about what happens to rainwater. Pure rain falls from the sky as fresh water. As rainwater seeps into the ground or runs off into streams, it picks up some salt from the soil. Most of that salt is carried by rivers to the ocean, which is why oceans are saline.

However, not all rivers flow directly into the ocean. Some of them end in lakes and inland seas. If water is flowing both into and out of a lake, the water that is flowing out of the lake carries some of this salt to the ocean. If no water flows out of a lake, the salt has nowhere to go. Therefore, when water evaporates from a lake, the salt is left behind. The lake grows more and more saline over time, eventually becoming an inland sea.

Salinization of land happens in a different way. When farmers irrigate their crops, they bring water from lakes and rivers to their fields. Often this fresh water contains a little salt. When the water evaporates, it leaves the salt behind on the surface of the soil. There might not be enough salt on the surface to damage plants, at least at first. However, if people don't wash the salt away, the soil becomes saltier as the years pass. Very few plants can grow in salty soil.

Both the water and the land in the region surrounding the Aral Sea have been degraded by salinization. The Aral Sea used to be Earth's fourth-largest freshwater lake. Now it is less than half that size, and it is as salty as any ocean. Meanwhile, much of the land around the sea is too salty to grow crops.

▶ Geoterms

environmental degradation damage to or destruction of the natural environment. When such damage occurs, habitats are destroyed, biodiversity is lost, or natural resources are used up.

groundwater water lying deep under the ground that supplies wells and springs. Over half the people in the world depend on groundwater for their drinking water.

salinization the buildup of salt in soil or water

water stress the condition that occurs when people don't have enough clean fresh water to meet their everyday needs

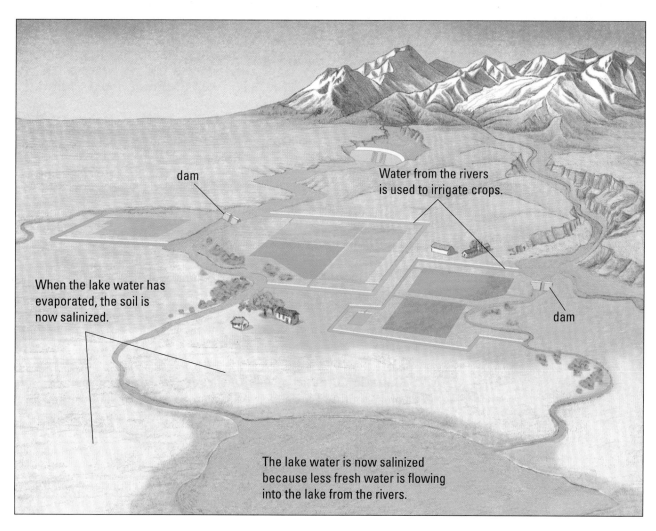

dam

Water from the rivers is used to irrigate crops.

When the lake water has evaporated, the soil is now salinized.

dam

The lake water is now salinized because less fresh water is flowing into the lake from the rivers.

Salinization of Inland Seas

A lake with no outlet to the ocean is likely to grow saltier over time. When water evaporates from a lake, any salt that was dissolved in that water is left behind. Over time, salt builds up in the lake. This process happens faster when water from the rivers that feed into a lake is used for irrigation. With less water coming in, the lake shrinks. At the same time, the concentration of salt in the lake water increases.

The Power of Cotton

Growing cotton in the desert meant more money for the people who lived there. The "white gold" crop became a central focus of life in desert communities. The city of Tashkent, Uzbekistan's capital, called its soccer team the Cotton Pickers.

26.3 The Shrinking Sea and Farming

Cotton is sometimes called "white gold." It's a **cash crop** that earns farmers a good income, but cotton needs a long, warm growing season and lots of water in order to thrive.

For the government of the former Soviet Union, finding a place to grow cotton posed a problem. Some of the areas had enough rain but were too cold. Other areas were warm enough but too dry. The solution was to plant cotton in a **desert** region of Central Asia, where the crops would be irrigated with water diverted, or taken, from two rivers.

From Desert to Cotton Kingdom The Soviet government provided water to cotton farms by building dams on the Amu and Syr rivers. The water stored behind the dams was used to irrigate large areas. Large amounts of chemical fertilizers and **pesticides** were used to increase production in this new cotton kingdom. At first, irrigating a desert to grow cotton seemed to work well, and the new crop provided jobs for local people.

Salinization Creates a New Desert An unplanned effect of the damming of the Amu and Syr rivers was the degradation of the Aral Sea. Approximately 90 percent of the rivers' water was stored behind the dams, and therefore only 10 percent of the water reached the Aral Sea. As water evaporated from the Aral, the sea began to shrink, resulting in large areas of dry seabed becoming a salty wasteland.

The shrinking of the sea affected the region's **climate**. When the sea was full, the Aral had cooled the surrounding land in summer and warmed it in winter. As the sea shrank, summers became hotter and winters became colder. The growing season decreased from the 200 days per year needed for cotton crops to only 170 days. As the climate cooled, some farmers turned from cotton to rice because rice has a shorter growing season. Like cotton, however, rice needs a lot of water.

The use of river water for irrigation also degraded the land. Year by year, salt carried by the rivers built up on farm fields. Some areas became too salty to grow crops, and many farmers were left with nothing but salty desert.

26.4 The Shrinking Sea and Fishing

A shocked visitor to Moynaq in 2001 described a spooky sight. Rusting hulks of fishing boats lay scattered across a desert. These abandoned boats were surrounded by junk, with fiberglass, metal, rusty springs, and cigarette butts littering the ground. A boat's propeller lay half-buried in the sand. The sight was so strange that the visitor almost expected to discover that space aliens had abandoned the boats there. Instead, the boats are reminders of a time when the Aral Sea was home to many productive fisheries. A **fishery** is a place where fish are caught, processed, and sold.

A Sea Once Rich in Fish Until about 1980, many of these fishing boats had docked at Moynaq. Before the Aral Sea began to shrink, its water was abundant in fish. About 95 million pounds of fish were harvested from the lake each year. The fish canneries in Moynaq produced 20 million cans of seafood a year, and this thriving industry supported about 35,000 workers.

The Collapse of the Aral Sea Fishing Industry The shrinking of the Aral Sea destroyed the fishing industry. As the sea began to withdraw, the fisheries were left high and dry. Today the town of Moynaq is some 90 miles from the water's edge.

The small amount of water that remains in the Aral Sea is extremely salty. Very few organisms can live in such saline conditions. In fact, most of the 100 species of fish that were once plentiful in the sea have disappeared. Commercial fishing ended in 1982, and as a result the fishing crews and cannery workers lost their jobs.

Most of these former fishing-industry workers have been unable to find other employment nearby. The highest level of joblessness in Kazakhstan is in the Aral Sea region. Thousands of people have left the region to seek work elsewhere. Often men **migrate** alone, leaving their families behind in the dying towns. The women and children must then survive on whatever money the men are able to send home. Of the 40,000 people who once lived in Moynaq, only a scant 3,000 remain.

The Aral Sea's Dying Industry
Fresh water used to cover the seabed in this photograph. As the sea has shrunk, the fish that once lived here have disappeared. Thousands of people who once worked in fisheries around the sea have lost their jobs as result. Many have left the region to look for work.

Searching for Fresh Water
Today the Aral Sea is too salty to drink. People in the region have turned to other water sources, such as rivers and groundwater. This woman relies on groundwater from her well. Unfortunately, that water may be polluted and unsafe to drink.

26.5 The Shrinking Sea and Quality of Life

Strong winds pick up sand that used to be at the bottom of the Aral Sea. The resulting dust storms, which the local people refer to as "black blizzards," have become a sign of the declining quality of life in the Aral Sea region.

From Plentiful Fresh Water to Water Stress Before the 1960s, the Aral Sea provided water for nearby towns. There was enough water for household use and to irrigate the crops raised on small farms.

Today the Aral Sea region faces severe water stress. Because the water in the Aral Sea is too salty to drink, people have turned to rivers and groundwater to try to meet their water needs. However, much of that water is unfit to drink because it has been polluted by salt, **sewage,** and **toxic chemicals** used on farms.

Pollution Damages the Health of Residents Many people living around the Aral Sea have become ill from drinking polluted water. Stomach problems and liver disease are common.

Air pollution poses another threat to health because the region's "black blizzards" carry toxic chemicals along with dust. People who breathe in these chemicals develop health problems ranging from throat cancer to deadly lung diseases like tuberculosis.

Widespread poverty only makes these health problems worse. Nearly all pregnant women in the Aral Sea region suffer from anemia, a disease caused by poor nutrition. Many babies are born sick, and a large number of them die before their first birthday.

An Uncertain Future Many scientific reports and news stories have been written about the Aral Sea region, but this reporting has done little to help the people who live there. As one Moynaq resident said, "If every scientist and journalist who visited the Aral Sea brought with them a bucket of water, the sea would be filled again."

All who study the Aral Sea region agree that repairing the environmental degradation will require expensive changes. First, they suggest, less water should be removed from the Amu and Syr rivers for irrigation. This would allow for increased water flow into the Aral Sea.

In addition, farming practices will need to change. With less water available for irrigation, farmers will have to plant crops that require less water. They will also need to be more careful in their use of fertilizers and pesticides.

Finally, governments will need to improve their water management. They need to construct water systems to provide safe drinking water to residents. Governments also need to build water treatment plants, which will treat sewage and **wastewater** to reduce water pollution.

These changes will cost many billions of dollars. This is a far greater expense than any country in the region can afford—but there is hope. International agencies like the United Nations and the World Bank are working to assist the Aral Sea region. Also, this part of Central Asia has large reserves of oil. In the future, the countries around the Aral Sea may be able to use money earned by selling oil to improve the quality of life in this region.

Infant Death Rates

Number of Deaths (before age 1 per 1,000 births)

Legend: Kazakhstan, Uzbekistan

Year: 1970, 1980, 1990, 2000, 2004

Source: *Central Intelligence Agency,* "CIA World Factbook," www.cia.gov/cia/publications/factbook/.

A Poor Place to Be Born

Infant mortality in the Aral Sea region rose as environmental degradation increased. New mothers are no longer advised to nurse their babies. Toxic chemicals in the air and water have polluted their milk.

26.6 Beginning to Think Globally

In this chapter, you learned about environmental degradation in the Aral Sea region. You discovered how dams on the Amu and Syr rivers have reduced the amount of water flowing into the Aral Sea. As a result, the sea has shrunk significantly. It has also grown very salty. Increased irrigation with river water has caused widespread soil salinization, and vegetation cannot grow in soil that is too salty. Air and water pollution have increased as well. These changes have created an environmental disaster around the Aral Sea.

The Aral Sea region is not the only part of the world facing water stress. Wherever people live, they require water. Many locations, however, don't receive enough rainfall to meet people's water needs, so people must turn to other water sources such as rivers and groundwater. Egypt, for example, is a desert country. For thousands of years, Egyptians have depended on the Nile River to meet all their water needs. Without the Nile, life would be impossible in Egypt. To meet their water requirements, some countries turn to desalinization, a costly process in which salt water is converted to fresh water.

Water stress results when a region's need for water becomes greater than its supply. Think about this as you examine irrigation around the world in the next section.

Women Sick with Tuberculosis

These women in Uzbekistan are suffering from a lung disease known as tuberculosis, or TB. TB used to be one of the most common causes of death in the world. Today it is found mainly in developing countries. TB usually strikes people whose health has been weakened by bad water, dirty air, or poor nutrition.

26.7 Global Connections

This map shows regions of the world that rely on irrigation to grow crops. The colors indicate the percentage of land in each area that is irrigated. Symbols for four crops that are heavy water users are shown in the countries where the majority of the total world production of each crop is grown.

What factors might affect how much water a region uses for irrigating crops? One factor affecting how much water a region uses for irrigation is population density. The more people who live in a particular region, the more food local farmers must grow to feed those people. Another factor affecting water use is climate. Areas with relatively high year-round rainfall need little irrigation. In contrast, areas with little **precipitation** depend on irrigation. A third factor is the type of crop being grown, as some crops are significantly thirstier than others.

What areas are most likely to experience water stress? Areas with dry climates and high population densities are most likely to face water stress. Most of California, for example, is **arid**. Farmers there must rely on irrigation to grow large amounts of cotton, fruits, and vegetables. As California's **urban** population continues to increase, farmers have to compete with cities for limited water supplies.

What choices can people make to reduce water stress? The best way to reduce water stress is to reduce water needs. For farmers in arid regions, this means growing less thirsty crops. Switching from cotton to wheat, for example, can cut water use by more than half. For families, this means using less water for daily living. For example, repairing one dripping faucet can save 3,000 gallons of water per year.

Irrigated Lands Around the World

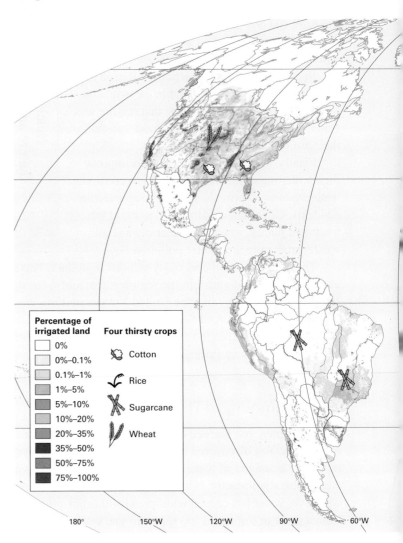

Percentage of irrigated land

- 0%
- 0%–0.1%
- 0.1%–1%
- 1%–5%
- 5%–10%
- 10%–20%
- 20%–35%
- 35%–50%
- 50%–75%
- 75%–100%

Four thirsty crops

- Cotton
- Rice
- Sugarcane
- Wheat

Irrigation of a rice field

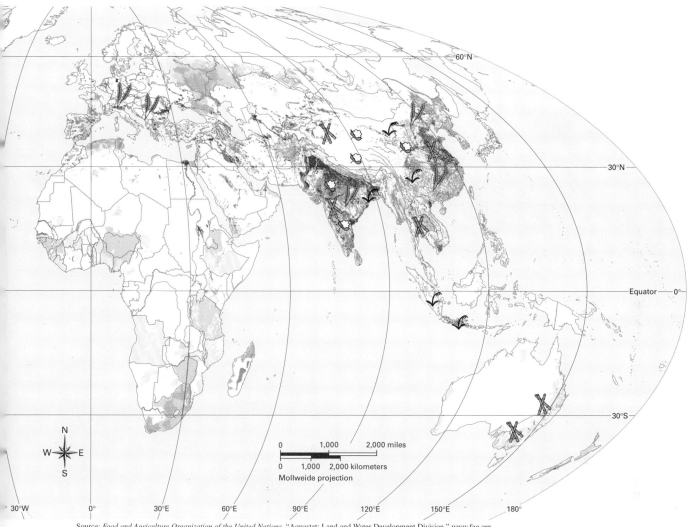

Source: *Food and Agriculture Organization of the United Nations,* "Aquastat: Land and Water Development Division," www.fao.org.

Four Thirsty Crops

Crop	Symbol	Water Needed to Grow 1 Pound of Crop	Major World Producers
Cotton		840–3,500 gallons	China, United States, India
Rice		360–600 gallons	China, India, Indonesia
Sugarcane		180–360 gallons	India, Brazil, Thailand, Australia, China
Wheat		110 gallons	China, India, United States, Europe

Source: *World Wildlife Fund,* www.wwf.org.uk.

UNIT 7 Monsoon Asia

Introducing the Region:
Physical and Human Geography

What do you see in this photograph?
See page 514 for details.

▼

Monsoon Asia begins at the western border of India. From there, it reaches east to the Pacific Ocean. In the north, it spreads across China to the Korean Peninsula. A large **peninsula** south of China includes Vietnam, Laos, Cambodia, and Thailand. This peninsula is ringed by the South China Sea, the Gulf of Thailand, and the Bay of Bengal.

This **region** has several countries made up of many islands. They include Japan, the Philippines, and Indonesia. Sri Lanka, Brunei, and East Timor are other island **nations**.

The countries of Monsoon Asia are often grouped into three subregions. These smaller regions are South Asia, East Asia, and Southeast Asia.

Physical Features of Monsoon Asia

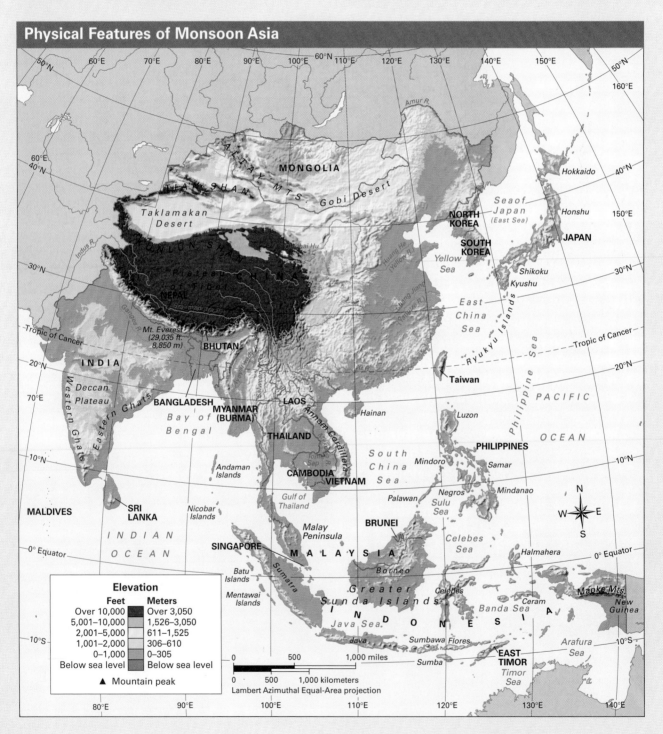

Elevation

Feet	Meters
Over 10,000	Over 3,050
5,001–10,000	1,526–3,050
2,001–5,000	611–1,525
1,001–2,000	306–610
0–1,000	0–305
Below sea level	Below sea level

▲ Mountain peak

0   500   1,000 miles

0   500   1,000 kilometers
Lambert Azimuthal Equal-Area projection

Physical Features

Mountains are the most commanding feature of Monsoon Asia's **landscape**. The rugged Himalayas form India's northern border. They include Mount Everest, the world's highest mountain. Like other mountains, the Himalayas were formed when sections of Earth's **crust,** called *plates,* collided. The two plates that came together to create the Himalayas are still colliding. As a result, the mountains are getting higher. But mountain building is a slow process. Mount Everest grows about half an inch a year.

The Himalayas are the world's highest mountain chain.

South Asia

India makes up most of South Asia. Many people call India a *subcontinent*. Mountains and ocean separate India from the rest of Asia, so it is almost like a small continent.

Three important rivers begin in the Himalayas. They are the Indus, the Ganges, and the Brahmaputra. The Ganges and Brahmaputra meet to form one of the world's largest river **deltas**. Then they empty into the Bay of Bengal.

The Ghats are another mountain range in India. The Eastern and Western Ghats run parallel to India's coasts. Between them lies the Deccan Plateau. The Deccan Plateau covers most of southern India's interior.

East Asia

East Asia's landscape is diverse. Mountains surround the Plateau of Tibet. The Huang He begins on this **plateau**. So does the Chang Jiang (Yangtze), the third longest river in the world. Both rivers run east across China before emptying into the Pacific.

North of the Tibetan Plateau lie the Taklamakan and Gobi **deserts**. The Gobi is one of the world's largest deserts. According to legend, an angry Mongolian chief created it. He turned the land to desert when Chinese warriors forced him to leave this area.

The hilly Korean Peninsula and the chain of islands that make up Japan are also part of East Asia. Japan's islands were formed by **volcanoes**.

Southeast Asia

Southeast Asia is not one big **landmass**. Instead, it is made up of peninsulas and islands. For example, the Malay Peninsula juts out into the South China Sea.

Thousands of islands dot the seas of Southeast Asia. Some, like Borneo, are fairly large. Others are so small that they just look like specks on a map.

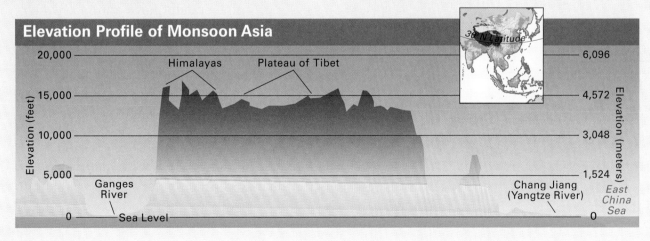

Elevation Profile of Monsoon Asia

Elevation (feet)		Elevation (meters)
20,000	Himalayas — Plateau of Tibet	6,096
15,000		4,572
10,000		3,048
5,000		1,524
0 — Sea Level	Ganges River / Chang Jiang (Yangtze River) / East China Sea	0

36°N Latitude

Climate

As the name of this region suggests, the **climate** of much of Asia is shaped by **monsoons**. Monsoons are strong winds that create the rainfall patterns in this region. In summer, monsoons blow from the ocean toward the land, bringing clouds that are heavy with rain.

In areas affected by monsoons, summers are very wet and winters fairly dry. Mumbai, India, for example, has a monsoon climate. It gets more than 70 inches of rain between June and September. But the same city gets little or no rain from December to April.

South Asia

South Asia's climate ranges from **arid** to tropical. The northwest part of the subcontinent is dry. So is part of the Deccan Plateau in central India.

The Himalayas have a **highlands** climate. In a highlands zone, the climate gets colder as elevation increases. The Himalayas are very high and very cold. Snow covers the higher peaks throughout the year. In fact, the word Himalaya means "House of Snow."

Tropical climates dominate the rest of South Asia. A **tropical wet** climate makes the west coast hot and rainy all year long. Much of interior South Asia is **tropical wet and dry**. The area has one rainy season and one dry season. Temperatures remain fairly high year-round. Finally, north central India has a **humid subtropical** climate, with hot, humid summers and mild winters.

Hats and parasols protect people in Bangkok from the tropical sun. In what month are these people likely to trade their paper parasols for umbrellas?

East Asia

Like South Asia, East Asia has a variety of climates. A highlands climate is found in the Plateau of Tibet. Arid and semiarid areas border this **landform**. They include the Gobi and Taklamakan deserts.

The Korean Peninsula has a **humid continental** climate. People there endure hot, steamy summers. Then they face very cold winters. Parts of Japan and eastern China experience a humid subtropical climate. They have hot, steamy summers and mild winters. Rain falls fairly evenly throughout the year.

Southeast Asia

Southeast Asia is tropical. Most areas nearest the equator have a tropical wet climate. It is hot and rainy all year in the Philippines, Singapore, and most of Malaysia and Indonesia. Other parts of Southeast Asia have a tropical wet and dry climate. The weather is hot all year with both rainy and dry seasons in most of Thailand, Cambodia, and southern Vietnam.

The mountain regions of Japan have severe winters with heavy snow.

Vegetation

The **vegetation** in Monsoon Asia varies as much as the region's climate does. In the drier parts of the region, only **desert scrub** survives. But in the tropical zones, lush plants thrive and form thick **rainforests**.

Elevation also has a big effect on Monsoon Asia's plant life. Remember that in a highlands climate, temperature varies with elevation. Vegetation varies with elevation as well. The region's highest mountains are so cold that they are covered by ice and snow. Very little can grow in this **ice cap** vegetation zone.

South Asia

The plant life of South Asia varies with the climates and the altitude. The driest land supports only desert scrub. **Tropical grassland** covers much of central India. **Mixed forest** appears on the lower slopes of the Himalayas. In the tropical climate zones, **broadleaf evergreen forest** is common.

East Asia

Because East Asia has so many **climate zones,** this subregion supports many different types of plant life.

The Plateau of Tibet and mountainous parts of China support **highlands** vegetation. The large deserts are home to **desert** and desert scrub vegetation. Much of the northern part of this subregion is too dry for trees. But grasses grow well there.

The warmer and wetter areas of East Asia support forests. Northeast China, the Korean Peninsula, and Japan are covered with mixed and **deciduous forest**. Many pines grow on Japan's mountains and along its seashores.

Much of southeastern China has a humid subtropical climate. Broadleaf evergreen forests thrive where it is warm and rainy.

Southeast Asia

Just about all of Southeast Asia is warm and wet. Rainforests and tropical grassland cover most of this region. Over time, much of the rainforest has been cleared to raise crops that do well in the tropics. People grow rice, sugarcane, tea, and rubber.

Many types of bamboo grow well here. Bamboo is a grass. But unlike most grasses, it can grow to huge sizes. Some types of bamboo may reach over 100 feet high and have stems a foot in diameter. Bamboo stems are made into everything from houses to tools. Bamboo probably has more uses than any other plant in tropical areas.

Tibet is often called the "Roof of the World." Yaks graze in the highland meadows on the Plateau of Tibet, which lies more than 10,000 feet above sea level.

There are 23 countries in Monsoon Asia. Some, like China, are very old. Others, like East Timor, are quite new.

Much of Monsoon Asia is densely settled. China is the world's most populous country. It has more than 1.3 billion people. India is a close second with more than a billion people.

With so many people, it is no surprise that some of the world's largest and most crowded cities are found in Monsoon Asia. They include Calcutta and Mumbai, India; Dhaka, Bangladesh; Shanghai, China; Seoul, South Korea; Tokyo, Japan; Manila, Philippines; and Jakarta, Indonesia.

Political Boundaries of Monsoon Asia

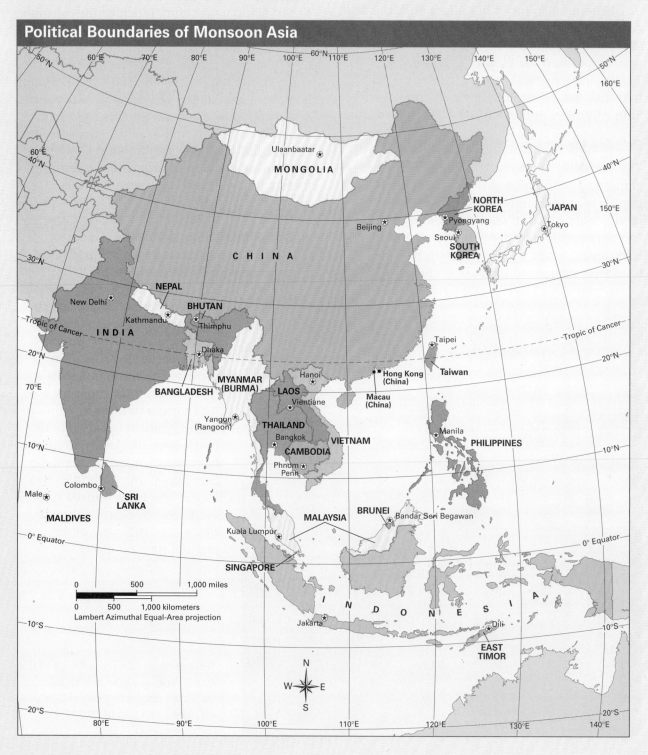

History

Some of the world's earliest civilizations arose in Monsoon Asia. At different times, rulers united parts of the region into **empires**. Later, European countries colonized much of the region. In modern times, most Asian peoples have gained their independence.

Early Times

East Asia's first civilization took root in the Huang He valley. China was split into many kingdoms early in its history.

In 221 B.C.E., one of these kingdoms, the Qin, united China. The name China comes from the word Qin. The first ruler of this empire, the Emperor Qin, built China's first Great Wall. From the first emperor until modern times, China was ruled by a series of dynasties, or ruling families. When one family lost power, another rose to take its place.

South Asia's first civilization arose in the Indus River valley around 2500 B.C.E. One of its main cities was Mohenjo-daro. As many as 40,000 people lived there. The people of Mohenjo-daro enjoyed comforts that were very advanced for that time. Their homes had indoor bathrooms that drained into a city sewer system.

No one knows how the Indus Valley civilization ended. But by 1700 B.C.E., it had vanished. For centuries after that, South Asia was a land of small kingdoms.

In the 320s B.C.E., a powerful family called the Mauryas saw how weak these kingdoms were. The Mauryas conquered most of them and united India into one empire. The Mauryan Empire lasted for about 130 years.

Conquests and Colonies

After the Mauryan Empire fell, India once more broke apart. Then in 1526, invaders from Central Asia conquered India. The invaders, called Mughals, united India as a new empire. The Mughals ruled India into the early 1700s.

Starting in the late 1400s, Europeans colonized many parts of Monsoon Asia. The Spanish set up trading posts in the Philippines. The Dutch started colonies in Indonesia. The British began businesses in India. By the late 1700s, the British ruled most of India.

In the 1800s, France joined the race for colonies. The French took over much of Southeast Asia. They controlled the area that is now Vietnam, Laos, and Cambodia.

The Modern Era

In the last half-century, most colonies in Monsoon Asia freed themselves from European control. India gained its independence from Great Britain in 1947. The French left Southeast Asia in the 1950s.

Parts of Monsoon Asia have prospered in recent years. Japan is now one of the world's leading industrial countries. Other areas, such as South Korea, Taiwan, and Singapore, have also developed modern industrial economies.

However, Monsoon Asia has developed unevenly. Some people live very well. But in many parts of the region, most people still live in poverty.

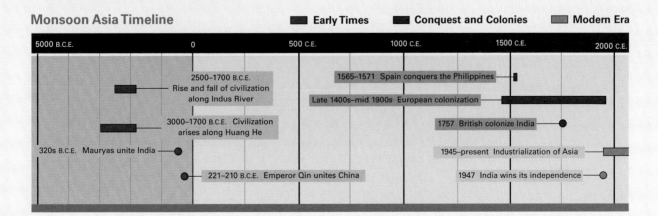

Monsoon Asia Timeline   ■ Early Times   ■ Conquest and Colonies   ■ Modern Era

5000 B.C.E.   0   500 C.E.   1000 C.E.   1500 C.E.   2000 C.E.

2500–1700 B.C.E. Rise and fall of civilization along Indus River

3000–1700 B.C.E. Civilization arises along Huang He

320s B.C.E. Mauryas unite India

221–210 B.C.E. Emperor Qin unites China

1565–1571 Spain conquers the Philippines

Late 1400s–mid 1900s European colonization

1757 British colonize India

1945–present Industrialization of Asia

1947 India wins its independence

Population

About 3.7 billion people live in Monsoon Asia. That is more than half the world's people. China, India, and Indonesia are three of the world's five most populous countries.

Monsoon Asia is mostly **rural**. However, cities are growing quickly. Every year, large numbers of people leave the countryside to look for work in cities. As a result, many cities suffer from overcrowding. The people who live there are often unemployed and poor.

Monsoon Asia is a region with many religious traditions. In India and Nepal, most people are Hindu. Islam also has many followers in Monsoon Asia. In fact, Indonesia has the world's largest Muslim population. Nine out of ten people there are Muslim.

Buddhism is the main religion in Southeast Asia. Most people in Japan practice Shinto or Buddhism. Confucianism began in China about 2,500 years ago. Its influence is still felt today. Christianity also has followers in Monsoon Asia, especially in the Philippines.

Monsoon Asia: Major Religions

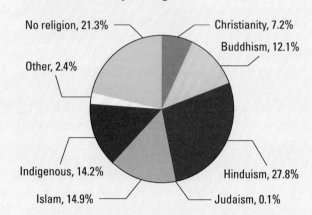

No religion, 21.3%
Christianity, 7.2%
Buddhism, 12.1%
Other, 2.4%
Indigenous, 14.2%
Islam, 14.9%
Hinduism, 27.8%
Judaism, 0.1%

Monsoon Asia: Urban and Rural Population, 2000

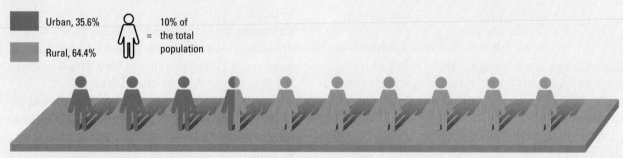

Urban, 35.6%
Rural, 64.4%
= 10% of the total population

Monsoon Asia: Population Growth, 1950–2050

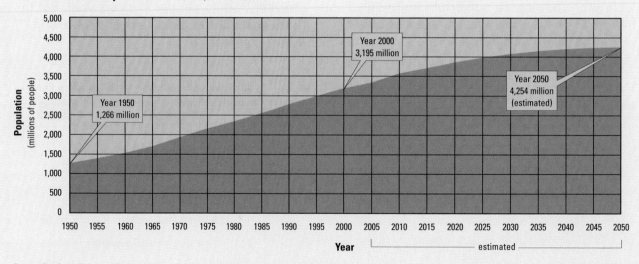

Year 1950
1,266 million

Year 2000
3,195 million

Year 2050
4,254 million
(estimated)

Population (millions of people)

Year   estimated

Sources: *Population Division of the Department of Economic and Social Affairs of the United Nations Secretariat*, "World Population Prospects: The 2004 Revision" and "World Urbanization Prospects: The 2003 Revision," esa.un.org/unpp. "Religion," *Encyclopædia Britannica*, 2005, Encyclopædia Britannica Premium Service, www.britannica.com.

Economic Activity

The economy of Monsoon Asia is a mix of old and new. Most people still work to feed themselves by farming and fishing. At the same time, parts of the region have become important centers for industry and finance.

The many people of Monsoon Asia who live near the seacoast have always fished for food. But fishing has also become a big business in Asia. **Commercial fishing** is different from traditional small-scale fishing. Commercial fishing boats can gather huge amounts of fish in their nets. Most of what they catch is processed, packaged, and sent all over the world.

Resources

Monsoon Asia is rich in resources. Northern China has large coal deposits. It produces more coal than any other country on Earth. Southeast Asia has much of the world's tin. Petroleum reserves lie beneath Indonesia. In addition, the region's many rivers are well suited for **hydroelectric power**.

An Indian villager watches over his fishing nets. Fishing is a major part of Monsoon Asia's economy.

Land Use

Most people in Monsoon Asia still live off the land. Some are subsistence farmers. They grow enough to feed their families. Rice is the staple for many of them. Others are commercial farmers. They grow crops for export, including tea, cotton, spices, and tobacco.

More than 90 percent of the world's rubber is produced in Southeast Asia. Rubber comes from the sap of the rubber tree. To get the sap, a rubber tapper cuts a diagonal shaving of bark from the tree. A metal spout and cup are attached to the bottom of this cut. Sap oozes from the cut and drips into the cup. Tappers collect about a teacup of sap each time they tap a tree.

China's commercial fishing industry is among the world's largest. Indonesia exports large amounts of shrimp and tuna. India, Japan, and South Korea also have large fishing industries.

Nomadic herders live in some remote parts of Monsoon Asia. Their lives are similar to their ancestors' lives. They herd cattle, goats, sheep, and yaks. Other parts of Monsoon Asia, however, have booming modern economies. International trade is strong in Taiwan, Singapore, Hong Kong, and South Korea. China makes machinery, as well as consumer goods. Japan is a world leader in the production of cars and electronics.

The Three Gorges Dam in China will be completed in 2009. It will produce more hydroelectric power than any other dam in the world. This power will support the growth of industry across China.

Waiting for the Rains: The Effects of Monsoons in South Asia

27.1 Introduction

Every June, all of India looks to the sky. When the rains come late, people begin to worry. Indian astrologers call this time of the year *rohini*—a time when hot, dry winds swirl dust across the parched plains. Women might have to walk for miles in 115°F heat to the nearest water source, sometimes collapsing from heat exhaustion.

As one blazing day follows another, farmers throughout India pray for help from the Hindu rain god Indra. In one area of the country, people catch frogs, hoping that the amphibians' loud croaking will call down rain clouds from the sky. Even the giant crocodiles of northern India wait eagerly for the rains because without flooded, moist riverbanks, they will have nowhere to lay their eggs.

When the skies finally darken, expectation builds: the **monsoons** have arrived. These strong and violent seasonal winds blow in from the ocean each summer, carrying with them clouds heavy with moisture. Almost all of the rain that South Asia receives each year is a product of these summer storms. All of India celebrates as sheets of rain pound the dry, thirsty land below.

In this chapter, you will find out why the monsoons blow across South Asia each year, and you will explore how monsoons affect the **climate** of four cities in this **region**. Finally, you will discover how people in these cities adapt to a lifetime spent waiting for the rains.

Essential Question

How does climate influence human activity in a region?

This climagraph shows average monthly temperatures and precipitation in the city of Mumbai, India. Notice the bars. They show the average precipitation for each month. Also notice the line. It shows average monthly temperatures for this city. Keep this climagraph in mind as you try to answer the Essential Question.

Graphic Organizer

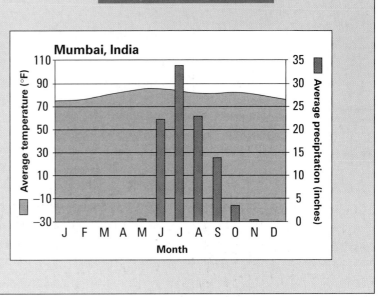

Mumbai, India

◀ A rickshaw traveling through the flooded streets of Dhaka, Bangladesh

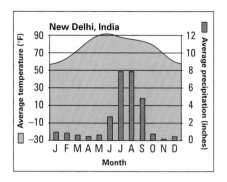

New Delhi's Monsoon Climate
Monsoon winds affect the climate of New Delhi, the capital of India. The city sits on the edge of the Thar Desert in northern India. From October to May, it stays mostly cold and dry. But during the summer monsoon months, rain can drench the city.

27.2 The Geographic Setting

South Asia juts out into the Indian Ocean like a giant triangle, forming a very large **peninsula** that is also known as the Indian subcontinent. The Himalaya mountain range cuts this subcontinent off from the rest of Central Asia. One out of every five people on Earth lives in South Asia. Most of them are farmers who both look forward to and fear the coming of the monsoons.

Changes in Atmospheric Pressure Create Monsoons Have you ever heard a weather forecaster talk about an area of high pressure or an area of low pressure? These terms are references to high or low **atmospheric pressure,** which is the weight of the **atmosphere** pressing down upon the surface of Earth. Falling cool air creates areas of high pressure, while rising warm air creates areas of low pressure.

In a high-pressure area, cool air from the upper atmosphere presses down toward Earth's surface and, in the process, causes atmospheric pressure to increase. With all of this downward pressure, very little surface air can rise into the upper atmosphere to form clouds. High pressure generally means sunny days and no rain. The opposite happens within a low-pressure area, in which warm surface air moves easily into the upper atmosphere. If this air is moist, it forms clouds that bring rain.

Air from high-pressure areas will naturally flow into low-pressure areas. This movement of air creates wind. During the spring and summer months, the air over the peninsula of South Asia warms up faster than the air over the Indian Ocean. As this hot air rises, it creates a low-pressure area. As a result, the cool, moist air that is over the Indian Ocean flows into the area of low pressure. This movement of air creates the summer monsoons.

During the fall and winter months, however, the air over South Asia cools down and then sinks, forming an area of high pressure. This high-pressure area keeps the moist air that blew in with the summer monsoons far out to sea. From October to March, only a small amount of rain falls throughout South Asia. During this long dry period, South Asians must deal with dusty fields and dwindling water sources.

Mountain Ranges Create Rain Shadows Mountains affect where summer storms will drop their moisture. A mountain slope facing **upwind,** or against the direction of the monsoon winds, generally receives a large amount of rain. In contrast, a slope facing **downwind,** or in the same direction the wind is blowing, will receive far less rain. Geographers call the impact that mountains have on rainfall patterns the **orographic effect**.

The orographic effect works this way. When clouds blow up against mountains, the moist air rises up along the slopes of the mountains. As the air rises, it gradually cools. Since cooling air cannot hold as much moisture as warm air, the clouds release their moisture as **precipitation** — either rain or snow.

By the time the clouds have crossed over the mountains, little moisture remains in them. As a consequence, people living on the downwind side of the mountains receive very little rainfall. That dry area is called a **rain shadow**. People living in a rain shadow have to adapt to life with little rain.

▶ Geoterms

atmospheric pressure the weight of the atmosphere pressing down on any point of the surface of Earth. Air sinks in high-pressure areas, and few clouds form. Air rises in low-pressure areas to form clouds that produce rain.

monsoon a seasonal wind. Summer monsoon winds in South Asia usually bring rain to that region.

orographic effect the precipitation that occurs when moist air rises up the side of a mountain. As the air rises, it cools down and releases most of its moisture as rain or snow.

rain shadow a dry area on the downwind side of a mountain

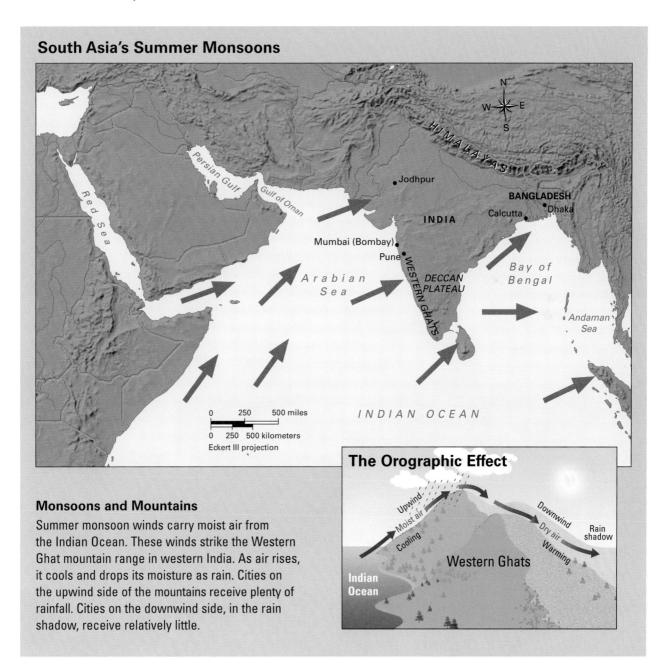

South Asia's Summer Monsoons

The Orographic Effect

Monsoons and Mountains

Summer monsoon winds carry moist air from the Indian Ocean. These winds strike the Western Ghat mountain range in western India. As air rises, it cools and drops its moisture as rain. Cities on the upwind side of the mountains receive plenty of rainfall. Cities on the downwind side, in the rain shadow, receive relatively little.

27.3 The Wet Months in Dhaka, Bangladesh

Ten million people live in Dhaka, the **capital city** of Bangladesh. For the residents of Dhaka, July can be a difficult month. In July 1996, the homes of approximately 3 million people were flooded. Two years later, about 1,500 people perished during July floods. Their deaths were blamed on everything from drowning to disease. In July 2004, rains left much of Dhaka under water.

One of the World's Wettest Capitals Most of Bangladesh lies on a river **delta** that seldom rises more than 30 feet above sea level. Rice, a crop that grows best in warm, shallow water, thrives here. In July, however, the monsoon rains often raise the rivers to dangerously high levels. When the rivers flood, even rice finds it difficult to survive.

Dhaka, which is located in the center of Bangladesh, has one of the wettest climates on Earth. Up to 80 inches of rain falls there each year, with most of this rain coming during the summer months. From November to April, the weather is dry.

Flooding is not Dhaka's only problem. In addition, Bangladesh is often pounded by **tropical cyclones**. Tropical cyclone is another name for hurricane. Because Dhaka is situated at sea level, the city is often lashed by high winds and waves during these violent storms.

Life Depends on the Rains Bangladesh's economy depends on agriculture. Nearly three out of every five people farm the country's rich delta soil, relying on the monsoon rains to water their fields. When the summer rains are late, crops such as rice, sugarcane, tea, and tobacco will suffer. Sometimes the monsoons bring too much rain too rapidly, flooding the fields. The deep water makes it impossible to plant and harvest the crops.

Dhaka also suffers from too much rain. When the streets flood, car and bus traffic comes to a halt. Schools and businesses close down because no one can get to work. Meanwhile, floodwaters pollute the city's drinking water supply, creating conditions in which disease spreads rapidly. Children growing up in Dhaka learn early that the rains that bring life to local fields can also end life in the city.

Preparing for the Rain

The people of Dhaka have come to expect flooding when the summer rains arrive. One way they have adapted is to raise their homes up on stilts. A raised home is not convenient most of the year, when everything has to be carried up and down stairs or ladders. In times of flood, however, it can be a lifesaver.

The Blue City Beneath the Fort
The Mehrangarh Fort was built in 1459. It sits on a tall hill overlooking Jodhpur. Because the buildings of this city are painted blue, Jodhpur has earned the nickname the Blue City.

27.4 The Dry Months of Jodhpur, India

The Mehrangarh Fort rises out of the **desert** like a towering giant, looking down on the "Blue City" of Jodhpur, India. The city gets its nickname from the fact that most of the houses are painted blue. Some people say that this color is used to keep away mosquitoes. In July 2002, nearly half of Jodhpur's crops could not be planted because the summer monsoons were late. The worst **drought** in more than 40 years had begun.

A City on the Edge of a Desert Jodhpur sits at the eastern edge of the Thar Desert in northern India. This region is a leading producer of cattle, spices, and grains. It has a typical **semiarid** climate, with hot, dry weather throughout most of the year.

The people living in and around Jodhpur are accustomed to their semiarid climate. In most years, the city receives only about 14 inches of rain. The average temperatures do not drop below 60°F, even in the winter. Summer monsoons bring much-needed rains from June to September.

Water Is a Critical Resource Approximately 80 percent of the people living around Jodhpur are farmers, but farming is difficult in this dry region. The desert soil requires a great amount of water to produce crops, and farmers depend on the monsoons for that water. How much rain will come and when will it arrive are questions people here ask every year.

The rains come late in some years. Sometimes too little rain falls, resulting in crop failures and shortages of drinking water. Families that run out of food sometimes survive by eating *samas,* a wild grass. As people grow weak from hunger, disease spreads more easily.

The people of Jodhpur have learned to adapt to their semiarid climate. In addition to growing crops, many farmers raise livestock, which can survive on native plants when crops fail. To conserve water, some farmers have begun to use drip irrigation, in which water drips directly onto a plant's roots. With the use of this irrigation method, little water is wasted as **runoff** or to **evaporation**. This careful use of water makes sense in Jodhpur, where every drop counts.

The Dry Plains Near Jodhpur
Water is a luxury in the area around Jodhpur. Women must sometimes walk miles in scorching heat to fetch drinking water for their families. Wind can pick up the thin dust on the arid plains. These dust storms are common before the summer monsoons.

Life Continues Despite Floods

Monsoon rains often fill the streets of Calcutta. Buses and cars can't drive through flooded streets. But rickshaws can. A rickshaw is a small cart with two or three wheels. It is pulled by someone who walks or bicycles in front of it. Rickshaw drivers are highly valued during the summer monsoon season.

27.5 Waiting for the Rains in Calcutta, India

Calcutta is a city of contrasts that has been described as both the "City of Joy" and the "Dying City." Its modern skyscrapers tower over the muddy Hooghly River, which is a branch of the Ganges River. When the monsoons come during the month of June, the river floods. After a rain shower or two, Calcutta finds itself knee-deep, or even neck-deep, in water.

Wet Summers and Dry Winters Approximately 15 million people call Calcutta home. About a third of the city's residents live in **slums**.

The city's winters are dry and pleasant, with moderate winds blowing in from the north. From June to September, the winds shift directions, as the moist monsoon air blows in from the Indian Ocean. The monsoons can dump nearly 50 inches of rain on the city in only four months, and temperatures can soar to 100°F. Clearly these summer rains present a great challenge to the people of Calcutta.

Monsoon Rains Begin and End Life Calcutta floods easily. The city's old canals overflow quickly when rainwater fills the streets, and buses and taxis can't navigate the flooded roads. Children must wade to school through waist-high water and spend the day in wet clothing. Nevertheless, the monsoon rains are welcome because the farmers need the rain to water their crops. The rains also provide relief from the sticky summer heat.

Calcutta has had to find ways to deal with the summer floods. In the past, a system of canals drained floodwater out of the city. This system was later abandoned in favor of modern streets and sewers, but when too much rain falls, garbage clogs the old canals. Standing water in the flooded streets breeds mosquitoes. Diseases that are carried by mosquitoes, such as malaria, then spread quickly, causing people to sicken and die.

Today officials in Calcutta are looking at rebuilding the city's antiquated canals to help with the flooding. Meanwhile, sewer lines are being repaired so that they can carry more water during storms. The city is also working to keep the river clear of debris so that more water can drain downstream during heavy rains.

27.6 Living in the Rain Shadow: Pune, India

The city of Pune, located on the Deccan Plateau in western India, is only 115 miles from Mumbai—a short two-hour drive. Yet Mumbai receives at least 70 inches of rain during the summer monsoons; in contrast, precipitation in Pune totals only 29 inches for the entire year.

A Year-Round Dry Climate Between Mumbai and Pune lies a mountain range known as the Western Ghats. As the monsoon winds rise up the slopes of these mountains, the air cools and releases its moisture. By the time the monsoon winds reach the downwind side of the mountains, the air retains very little moisture.

Pune sits in a rain shadow on the opposite side of the Western Ghats from Mumbai. While the coastal city of Mumbai must brace for heavy rain, Pune is spared from flooding. For most of the year, the air is dry and pleasant, and the monsoons bring welcome rains from about June to September.

Limited Rainfall Makes Water Precious The people of Pune have learned to survive with little water. In the past, farmers here raised sugarcane, a crop that requires large quantities of water. Today they plant crops that are more drought resistant, such as sugar beets.

Pune has also tried to increase its rainfall with **cloud seeding,** a process that involves scattering chemicals into clouds in order to bring about rain. Rain falls when the water vapor in clouds condenses into droplets, which form around tiny specks of ice in the air. Under the appropriate conditions, clouds can be seeded to encourage this condensation to occur. Usually this seeding is accomplished by spraying the clouds from the air with tiny amounts of either silver iodide or dry ice. The hope is that water droplets will form around these "seeds."

It is hard to determine just how effective cloud seeding has been in Pune because no one knows how much rain might have fallen if there had been no seeding. However, for people living in a rain shadow, the chance of more rain makes seeding seem worth the expense.

Living in a Rain Shadow
Pune lies in a rain shadow. Farmers in the area can grow crops like rice only if monsoon rains are plentiful.

27.7 Beginning to Think Globally

In this chapter, you learned how monsoons affect the climate of South Asia. The differences in atmospheric pressure between the land and sea cause the summer monsoons, and these winds bring both welcome rain and deadly floods to coastal cities. The orographic effect also shapes the climate of this region. Cities on the downwind sides of mountains often lie in a rain shadow. Unlike their coastal cousins, the people in these cities must adapt to limited rainfall.

Other regions also have monsoons. From November to April, for example, northern Australia braces for its monsoon season. Monsoons hit the West African coast from May to July. In Arizona, monsoon rains arrive in the middle of summer, as moist air from the Gulf of Mexico blows inland.

Wherever people live, the climate will affect their activities. Think about this as you examine the variety of climates around the world in the next section.

27.8 Global Connections

The map shows climate zones around the world. The three climagraphs show the average monthly temperatures and precipitation in three cities.

How might climate affect the type of housing people build? In hot and humid tropical climates, people build homes that will allow the breezes to flow through. In dry desert climates, builders of homes make windows small to keep out the sunlight. In very wet climates, people build houses that are elevated on stilts; the raised houses will stay dry when the land below floods. In regions with **tundra** climates, houses are also raised off the ground, thereby allowing cold air to flow underneath the buildings. Otherwise, the warmth of a house could melt the **permafrost,** or the permanently frozen ground, below. If the permafrost were to melt, the house might sink into the mud.

How might climate affect the type of clothing people wear? People who live in regions with arid climates often wear loose-fitting, flowing clothes. They want to cover up most of their skin to avoid being too exposed to the sun. People who reside in more temperate places like London have come to expect daily downpours, so they keep umbrellas and raincoats handy.

How might climate affect what people do for fun? In Alaska, dog sledding and ice fishing are common cold-climate sports. Surfing is popular in Hawaii. North Africans enjoy camel racing. In Namibia, people gather at the dunes in the Namib Desert to sandboard. Much like snowboarding, sandboarding involves sliding down a slippery slope of sand on a wooden board.

Climate Zones Around the World

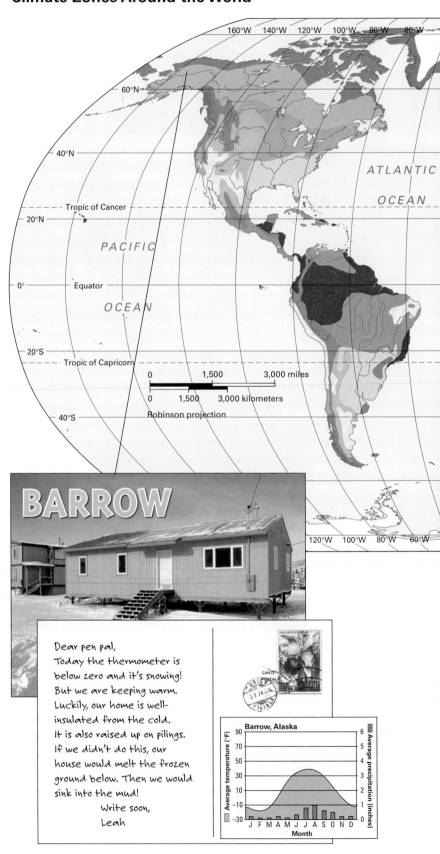

BARROW

Dear pen pal,
Today the thermometer is below zero and it's snowing! But we are keeping warm. Luckily, our home is well-insulated from the cold. It is also raised up on pilings. If we didn't do this, our house would melt the frozen ground below. Then we would sink into the mud!
Write soon,
Leah

Barrow, Alaska

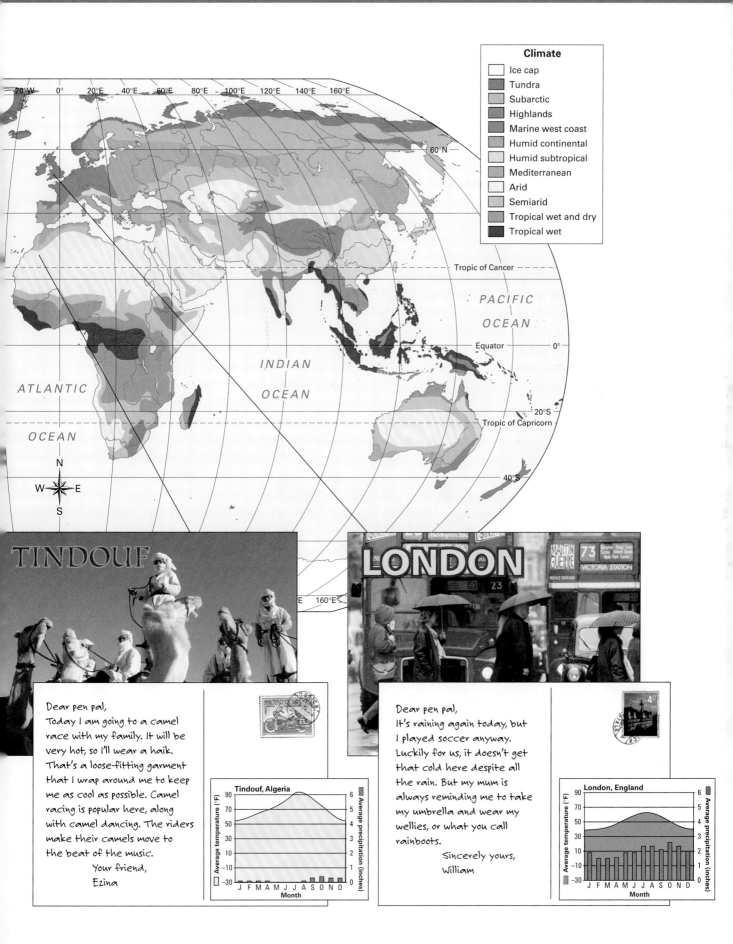

Climate

☐ Ice cap
■ Tundra
■ Subarctic
■ Highlands
■ Marine west coast
■ Humid continental
□ Humid subtropical
■ Mediterranean
□ Arid
■ Semiarid
■ Tropical wet and dry
■ Tropical wet

TINDOUF

Dear pen pal,
Today I am going to a camel
race with my family. It will be
very hot, so I'll wear a haik.
That's a loose-fitting garment
that I wrap around me to keep
me as cool as possible. Camel
racing is popular here, along
with camel dancing. The riders
make their camels move to
the beat of the music.
　　　　　Your friend,
　　　　　Ezina

Tindouf, Algeria

LONDON

Dear pen pal,
It's raining again today, but
I played soccer anyway.
Luckily for us, it doesn't get
that cold here despite all
the rain. But my mum is
always reminding me to take
my umbrella and wear my
wellies, or what you call
rainboots.
　　　　Sincerely yours,
　　　　William

London, England

Tech Workers and Time Zones: India's Comparative Advantage

CHAPTER
28

28.1 Introduction

When people lose their credit cards or have trouble with their computers, they need help fast. Usually they phone a call center. Such a place handles large numbers of phone calls for a business. Often the callers do not realize that the call center might be halfway around the world.

Call centers have become a big business in India. They are part of a global revolution in **information technology (IT),** the use of technology to move, record, and process information. Computers, satellites, cell phones, and the Internet are all part of IT. This technology allows us to talk by phone to people almost anywhere on Earth. It also allows computers to move data around the world in an instant.

IT makes it possible for companies to **outsource** call center jobs. To outsource means to hire someone outside a company to do work that was once done inside the company. In recent years, American companies have outsourced many jobs to India. Indian workers now prepare tax returns, review medical records, and tutor students for U.S. companies.

India attracts these jobs because it has a **comparative advantage** over many other countries. This means that India can offer some services more cheaply or effectively than competing countries. As a result, companies often look to India when they want to outsource jobs. In this chapter, you will learn about some of the factors that give India this comparative advantage.

Essential Question

What factors give some countries a comparative advantage in the global IT revolution?

This illustration shows a customer in the United States communicating with a worker in India. Both are part of the global IT revolution. Information technology, such as communications satellites, allows data to move quickly and cheaply around the world. This helps people in distant countries to work together. Keep this illustration in mind as you try to answer the Essential Question.

Graphic Organizer

◄ An information technology call center in Bangalore, India

An IT Worker in India

India is one of the world's poorest countries. But its economy is growing rapidly, in part thanks to the IT revolution. IT jobs like the one shown here are attractive to people because they pay more than most other work.

India's Major IT Centers

Information Technology Centers

India's IT centers attract jobs from around the globe. The main hub of IT work is the city of Bangalore. More than 5 million people live in this bustling IT center.

28.2 The Geographic Setting

India is a large and varied country in South Asia. In addition to great mountains, **rainforests,** and **deserts,** it has many large cities. India is about one third the size of the United States, but its population is more than three times as large. With over one billion people, India is the second most populous country in the world, with only China having a larger population.

The World's Largest Democracy India is ruled by an elected government. This makes the country the largest democracy in the world. Under India's constitution, all Indians are equal. However, Indians are not always treated equally in Indian society.

For thousands of years, Indian society has been divided into many groups called *castes*. The caste system was rooted in ancient beliefs. People were born into the same caste as their parents. The system fixed what jobs each caste could do. Upper caste people, consisting of priests and warriors, held the political and economic power in India. Lower caste people worked as farmers and laborers. Today the caste system is beginning to change, as members of the lower castes are improving their position. Still, the caste system remains a powerful force within Indian society.

India is also divided by religion, with the two main faiths being Hinduism and Islam. More than three fourths of Indians are Hindus, but Muslims form a large minority. The two groups disagree on many issues, and at times these religious conflicts lead to violence.

A Fast-Growing Economy Economic problems also trouble India. It is one of the world's poorest countries, with more than a fourth of all Indians living below the poverty line. Many of the poorest people survive on less than a dollar a day.

At the same time, India's economy is growing rapidly. One reason for this growth has been the global information technology revolution. Indian businesses have been quick to adopt this technology. They are offering IT services at low prices. As a result, Indian IT businesses have attracted jobs from many foreign companies.

Another attraction for American companies is India's location on the other side of the world. There is a time difference of 10 or more hours between India and the United States. These differences in **time zones** mean that Indians are at work while Americans are sleeping. A time zone is an area that uses the same clock time.

American companies take advantage of these time differences by setting up night call centers in India. During the day, customers' calls may be answered by call centers in the United States. At night, they are answered by call centers in India. In this way, a U.S. company can have workers answering calls around the clock without hiring a night shift in either country.

India's IT industry is spread across the country, but its main hub is the city of Bangalore in southern India. Like Silicon Valley, California's IT center, Bangalore attracts highly skilled people who are interested in new ways to get work done.

▶ Geoterms

comparative advantage the ability of one country to produce a good or provide a service at a lower cost or more effectively than another country

information technology (IT) the use of technology to move, record, and process information. IT includes computers, communication satellites, cell phones, and the Internet.

outsource to hire someone outside a company to do work that was once done inside the company. Information technology has made it possible to outsource jobs to businesses in other countries.

time zone an area that uses the same clock time. Earth is divided into 24 standard time zones. Each zone has its clocks set to the same hour and minute.

Time Zones Around the World

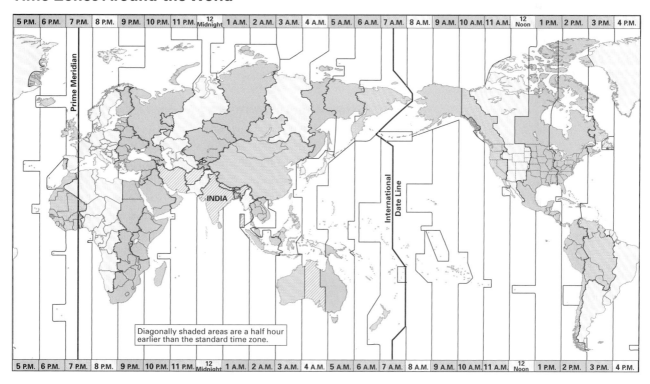

Diagonally shaded areas are a half hour earlier than the standard time zone.

Earth's Many Time Zones

The world has been divided into 24 standard time zones. Each zone covers about 15 degrees of longitude and represents 1 hour of the 24-hour day. The United States has six standard time zones. India has a nonstandard time zone. It is a half-hour off standard time. Note the International Date Line running through the middle of the Pacific Ocean. Travelers who cross that line going west toward Asia jump ahead one day on the calendar. When they cross the line heading east to the Americas, they lose a day.

28.3 Advantage Factor One: Low Wages

In 2003, a call center worker at a U.S. airline made $46,000 a year. Sangita Ray did the same job in India, earning merely $6,000. This tremendous difference in pay is one of the reasons why India attracts so many information technology jobs. American companies that outsource work to India can save money.

A Large, Fast-Growing Workforce India has a large and rapidly growing **workforce**. In 2003, there were more people working in India than the entire population of the United States. By 2020, India is expected to have the largest workforce in the world.

Labor costs in India are among the lowest worldwide, giving India a comparative advantage in attracting IT jobs. American companies have found that they can cut their wage costs in half by shifting some of their work to India.

Several factors affect how much workers in India earn. One factor is the size of its workforce. With so many people searching for work, competition for jobs can be fierce. As a result, Indians often accept lower pay than workers in other countries.

Another factor that affects earnings is the low **cost of living** in India. Basic goods like food and clothing cost much less than in many other countries. The city of Bangalore, in particular, is known for its low cost of living. This low cost of living makes it possible for many Indians to enjoy a high **standard of living** despite compensation, or pay, that may seem low to American workers.

Indian Workers Want IT Jobs Good pay and good working conditions make IT jobs attractive to Indians. In 2003, the average Indian worker earned $530 a year. In contrast, a computer programmer might be paid $10,000 or more. Call center jobs may pay half that much.

Many IT company workplaces look like college campuses, featuring modern buildings in parklike settings. Some have stores, swimming pools, and gyms for their employees. A pleasant work environment helps attract Indians to IT jobs. Of the thousands of Indians who apply for call center jobs, only about 5 percent are hired, and most of those are college graduates.

IT Worker Salaries, 2003

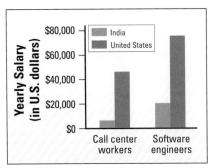

Sources: *Information Week,* www.informationweek.com. *International Herald Tribune,* www.iht.com.

Who Earns What

This graph looks at the average pay of American and Indian IT workers in 2003. Software engineers make more in both countries.

An IT Campus in Bangalore

IT companies offer workers attractive workplaces. More than 13,000 people work at this company campus in Bangalore. The company provides them with food courts, a large gym, and a small golf course.

28.4 Advantage Factor Two: English Speakers

A teacher is leading a class in American English. The students are call center workers who are learning to speak like Americans. They watch U.S. movies and television programs to pick up American accents, expressions, and slang words. Their skill in English is a second factor that drives India's success in the IT business.

English Is Widely Spoken in India People in India speak more than 1,000 languages and **dialects**. A dialect is a version of a language that is spoken in a specific geographic area. Hindi is India's national language. More than two fifths of Indians speak Hindi at home, but almost all educated Indians speak English as well.

Traders brought the English language to India during the 1600s. Great Britain later took over India and made it into a colony. British officials set up schools where Indians were instructed in English. These schools helped train Indians to work in government jobs. The British also hoped the use of English would help to unite India's many **linguistic groups**.

India gained its independence in 1947. By that time, English was widely spoken throughout India. Today it remains the main language of business and is also used in government business. In cities, many parents send their children to schools that teach classes in English. Many college classes are also taught in English.

English Skills Are a Key Advantage About a third of all Indians speak some English. This gives India a comparative advantage in attracting U.S. companies. India can provide IT services in English more effectively than countries where little English is spoken.

Because of India's colonial past, Indians tend to speak English with a British accent. That is why some companies are teaching workers how to talk with American accents. They hope that the training in American English will help workers communicate more effectively with callers and clients in the United States.

Homegrown Technology

Indian IT companies do a lot of out-sourced work. But they also create products for use at home. This man is holding an Indian invention. It is a small, affordable computer with Internet access. Devices like this may help bring the benefits of the global IT revolution to poor Indians.

28.5 Advantage Factor Three: Trained Workers

Sixteen-year-old Rajiv Johri wants to study computer science at a top university in India, but first he must pass the college entrance exam. To prepare, Rajiv attends a test prep class every day after school. He studies late into the night, and each morning he rises early to attend another test prep session before school.

Rajiv is not alone. Millions of Indians see education as their ticket to a good job. This educated workforce is a third factor in India's comparative advantage over countries with less skilled workers. American companies send work to India because they know it will be done by well-trained workers.

India Is a Leader in Technical Education India's educated workforce is no accident; the country invests a lot of money in higher education. In 2003, more than 3 million Indians graduated from college, many of them with training in such technical fields as math, engineering, and science. By 2010, the number of Indians with college degrees is expected to double.

India has made special efforts to promote technical education. In 1951, the Indian Institute of Technology, or IIT, was founded. Today IIT has seven campuses and is ranked among the best technical universities in the world. Some of the world's top scientists and engineers are educated there.

Not All Indians Have Equal Access to Education Indian law says that all children up to the age of 14 are required to go to school. However, only about half of India's children actually attend school to that age. As a result, about a third of the country's population is **illiterate**. In other words, there are about 350 million people in India who are unable to read and write.

Why don't more children go to school? One reason is poverty. Many poor children have no time or energy for school because they have to work to help support their families.

Another reason is the effect of the caste system. Many Indians still link education to caste. People expect children who are born into high castes to be well educated. However, they don't expect this for children born into low castes.

It is difficult enough for many Indians to receive a basic education, and it is even harder to go on to college. In 2005, only about 6 percent of the young people in India were able to attend college. And only a small fraction of these students will graduate with a degree in math, science, or engineering.

Technical Education in India

This graph shows the growth of engineering and IT programs in India over eight years. During this time, the number of people enrolled in these technical programs more than doubled, and the number of graduates nearly doubled.

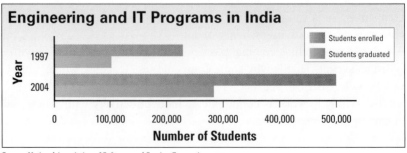

Engineering and IT Programs in India

Students enrolled
Students graduated

Year

1997
2004

Number of Students
0   100,000   200,000   300,000   400,000   500,000

Source: *National Association of Software and Service Companies*, www.nasscom.org.

India's Brain Drain and Brain Gain In the past, many students with technical degrees could not find the jobs they wanted near their homes. Some of these highly educated students left India to work in more developed countries, including the United States. The result was a serious **brain drain** for India.

This trend began to change when the IT industry took off in India. New opportunities for people with technical degrees opened up. Many Indians who were working outside of the country returned to join the boom. These IT professionals brought with them valuable business experience as well as special skills. For the companies they joined, the brain drain turned into a brain gain.

Some Indians also returned home with money to invest in new companies. This investment has helped the Indian IT industry to expand. In fact, some Indian companies have grown so fast that they now outsource jobs to IT workers in China.

28.6 Beginning to Think Globally

In this chapter, you read how India has become part of the global information technology revolution. You learned about three factors that give India a comparative advantage over some other countries in attracting IT jobs from the United States. Those factors are low wages, English speakers, and an educated workforce. In addition, India is located in a time zone halfway around the world from the United States; Indians work while Americans sleep. All three of these factors have led U.S. companies to outsource work to India.

Outsourcing is only one way that companies do business in another country. Another way is through **foreign investment,** or investment by a person or company based in another country. Many people and businesses around the world invest money in the United States. This money is used to purchase U.S. companies. It is also used to start new businesses in the United States.

In the next section, you will read more about foreign-owned companies in the United States. You will also explore this country's comparative advantages in attracting business from around the world.

Computers for Kids

These students are learning about computers at an IT exhibition in Bangalore. Not all Indian children get a good education. One project in Bangalore is helping poor children learn how to read and use computers. The project is paid for by some of the city's leading IT companies.

28.7 Global Connections

The United States loses jobs when they are outsourced to other countries, but gains jobs when foreign companies invest here. The map shows where companies owned by foreign investors were doing business in the U.S. in 2001. The graph shows foreign investment in the U.S. between 1994 and 2004. The U.S. attracts so much foreign investment because of its many comparative advantages.

Is the number of Americans working for foreign companies rising or falling? In 1987, about 2.6 million Americans worked for foreign-owned companies. Since then, the number has more than doubled to over 5 million. The new jobs created by foreign investment help to compensate for jobs that have been lost to outsourcing.

What kinds of jobs are created by foreign-owned companies in the U.S.? Americans working for foreign-owned companies do all kinds of jobs. They build cars, airplanes, and medical equipment. They conduct research and develop new technologies. In general, they earn more than people who work for U.S. businesses.

What gives the U.S. a comparative advantage in attracting foreign businesses? The U.S. is a highly developed country with many skilled workers. It has highly educated IT professionals, engineers, researchers, and businesspeople. Foreign companies invest here to take advantage of this talented workforce. The U.S. also has a very high per capita GDP. And many foreign companies start businesses in the U.S. to be close to its nearly 300 million consumers.

Foreign-Company Jobs in the United States, 2001

Three Foreign-Owned Companies in the U.S.

	Dassault Falcon Jet Corporation
Location of Parent Company	France
U.S. Locations	Arkansas, Delaware, New Jersey
Business Activities	• manufacturing jet airplanes • sales and service
Why Parent Company Invested in the United States	• skilled workers • talented engineers • close to customers in the Americas

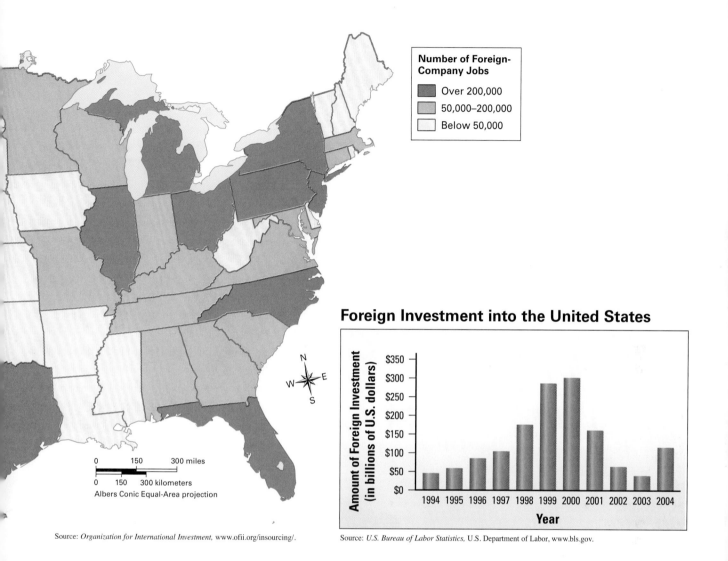

Source: *Organization for International Investment*, www.ofii.org/insourcing/.

Foreign Investment into the United States

Source: *U.S. Bureau of Labor Statistics*, U.S. Department of Labor, www.bls.gov.

Phillips Medical Systems	American Honda Motor Company
Netherlands	Japan
Massachusetts	Alabama, California, Colorado, Georgia, Michigan, North Carolina, Ohio, South Carolina, Texas
• manufacturing medical equipment • research and development of new products • sales and services	• manufacturing cars, motorcycles, ATVs, boats, engines • research and development of new products • safety education • sales
• skilled workers • talented engineers and medical researchers • close to North American customers	• skilled workers • talented engineers and designers • close to North American customers

Mount Everest: Climbing the World's Tallest Physical Feature

29.1 Introduction

On the afternoon of May 10, 1996, more than a dozen climbers were near the summit, or top, of Mount Everest. Suddenly a storm blew in, lashing the climbers with gale-force winds and driving snow. Later one of the climbers recalled, "At times you couldn't even see your own feet." Some climbers managed to survive the blizzard and make it down the mountain. Others didn't. In the end, nine of the climbers died. Later that month, another three climbers lost their lives on the mountain. It was the deadliest climbing season ever on Mount Everest.

Mount Everest is an amazing place. At over 29,000 feet, it is the tallest mountain in the world. It lies within Nepal's Sagarmatha National Park, which in 1979 was named a **World Heritage site**. These sites are places that are of great natural or cultural value to the world. **UNESCO,** which is a branch of the United Nations, identifies such places on its World Heritage List. UNESCO also assists countries in preserving and protecting World Heritage sites.

Climbing Mount Everest is an extremely difficult feat. Even so, more and more people come to Nepal each year to attempt the ascent. In this chapter, you will read about the challenges these climbers encounter on their way to the summit. In addition, you will see how **tourism** to Mount Everest is affecting Nepal and its people, and you will discover what is being done to protect this very special place from overuse.

Essential Question

How can people both experience and protect the world's special places?

This diagram shows one of the main climbing routes up Mount Everest. Notice that there are several camps along the route. Each lies at a different elevation. Moving from camp to camp, climbers face tough physical challenges. Keep this diagram in mind as you try to answer the Essential Question.

Graphic Organizer

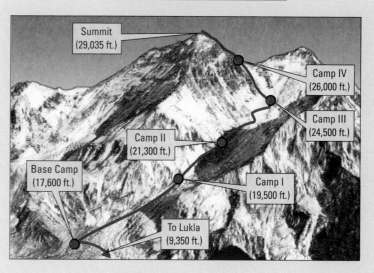

Summit (29,035 ft.)

Camp IV (26,000 ft.)

Camp III (24,500 ft.)

Camp II (21,300 ft.)

Camp I (19,500 ft.)

Base Camp (17,600 ft.)

To Lukla (9,350 ft.)

◀ The summit of Mount Everest, the world's tallest mountain

First to the Top

In 1953, Edmund Hillary and Tenzing Norgay became the first climbers to reach the top of Mount Everest. Their success has inspired many others to make the ascent. These climbers all want to stand at the top of the world's highest mountain.

29.2 The Geographic Setting

Mount Everest is located in the Himalaya Mountains of southern Asia, lying along the border between Nepal and the Chinese region of Tibet. In 1999, scientists measured the summit's height as 29,035 feet. In the future, this number may change as measuring methods become more accurate. Whatever its exact elevation, Mount Everest is more than five miles high. The mountain was named Everest for a British official in India. In Nepal, it is known as Sagarmatha, which means "forehead in the sky," and in Tibet the mountain is called Chomolungma, or "mother of the world."

Many Ways to the Top The first successful ascent of Mount Everest was achieved on May 29, 1953, the day that Edmund Hillary of New Zealand and Tenzing Norgay of Nepal reached the mountain's summit. "My first sensation was one of relief—relief that the long grind was over," Hillary later wrote. "I turned and looked at Tenzing. Even beneath his oxygen mask and the icicles hanging from his hair, I could see his infectious grin of sheer delight." Since then, a few thousand people have attempted to climb the mountain. About 2,000 of them have succeeded, but 180 or more have died while ascending or descending Everest's slopes.

There are many routes to the top, with the two main approaches being the southeast ridge from Nepal and the northwest ridge from Tibet. Most climbers take the first route, climbing in stages stretching over a period of weeks. At each stage, they stop at camps on the side of the mountain. These stops allow climbers to **acclimatize,** or adjust to the high elevation, as they go. If climbers didn't acclimatize, they would risk getting ill from the lack of oxygen at high elevations.

Another problem for climbers is **exposure,** or being unprotected against extreme weather conditions, such as freezing temperatures and high winds, which can cause injuries or even death. Most summit attempts occur during April and May, when the weather is at its best. Even then, the temperature never rises above freezing at the summit, and weather conditions can still be deadly, as they were during the climbing season of 1996.

Protecting the Future of Mount Everest As the popularity of climbing Mount Everest has grown, so have the problems caused by overuse. One problem is trash. In the past, many climbers left their trash on the mountain, dumping cans, bottles, and garbage at camps along the route. Most of this trash has now been picked up, but keeping the mountain clean remains a concern.

Another problem is overcrowding. During the climbing season, the camps become small villages, with dozens of people. More than 30 climbers might reach the summit in a day, and sometimes lines form as climbers slowly make their way to the top.

The growing number of climbers raises questions about the mountain's **carrying capacity,** a term that refers to the number of people or animals that a particular area can support. When a population grows too large, the area is likely to be damaged, which is one reason why Sagarmatha National Park was declared a World Heritage site. By drawing attention to the region, UNESCO hopes to protect it for future generations.

▶ Geoterms

acclimatize the process of adjusting to lower oxygen levels at high elevation. Climbers adjust through exercise and rest as they gradually move higher.

carrying capacity the number of people or animals the environment of an area can support. A place's carrying capacity depends on the environment.

exposure the harmful effects of cold, wind, or other extreme weather conditions

World Heritage site a place of great natural or cultural value that has been placed on UNESCO's World Heritage List. UNESCO helps countries preserve these sites for future generations.

The Mount Everest Region

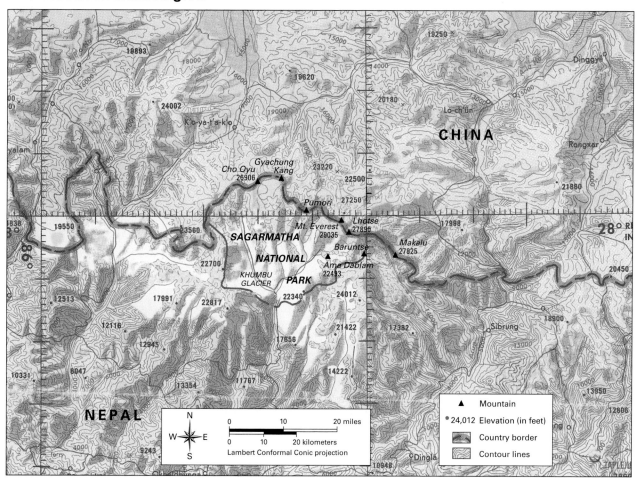

A Rugged Landscape

A topographic map uses elevation lines and symbols to show physical and human features in an area. Mount Everest lies in a very rugged region of the Himalaya mountain range. Climbers hike for days just to get to Base Camp. Then they face a nearly 12,000-foot climb to reach the summit.

The Effects of Tourism

This sign advertises one of the many tourist hotels in Nepal. Tourism has brought lots of money to Nepal. Climbing groups have also funded schools and medical clinics. Some Nepalese have benefited from tourism, but most are still very poor.

The High Cost of Climbing

Climbing Mount Everest has become a big business. Private guide services charge as much as $60,000 per person. A typical climber may spend another $8,000 to $20,000 on personal gear and airfare.

29.3 From Lukla to Base Camp

Expeditions to Mount Everest begin with a trek to Base Camp. Along the way, climbers can observe Everest in the distance. "I stared at the peak for perhaps 30 minutes," recalled one climber. "The summit looked so cold, so high, so impossibly far away. I felt as though I might as well be on an expedition to the moon."

A Slow Start Helps Climbers Acclimatize For most people, the quest to climb Mount Everest begins in Kathmandu, the capital of Nepal. From there the adventurers fly to the town of Lukla, at 9,350 feet above sea level, where they begin their hike to Base Camp. This trek, which typically takes from six to eight days, helps hikers to acclimatize to the thinning air. By the time they reach Base Camp, they are at an elevation of 17,600 feet.

Base Camp is set up every climbing season at the edge of the Khumbu Glacier. Consisting of dozens or even hundreds of tents, this "tent city" includes kitchens, dining halls, and even solar-powered lights. Most climbers will spend several weeks at Base Camp to adjust to breathing the thin air.

Climbers who do not acclimatize successfully may begin exhibiting symptoms of altitude sickness while they are at Base Camp. This illness is also called Acute Mountain Sickness, or AMS. Common symptoms of the sickness include nausea and headaches. In severe cases, AMS can cause fluid accumulation in the lungs, swelling of the brain, and even death.

The Impact of Tourism Climbing expeditions, and tourism in general, have had major effects on the people and environment of Nepal, which is a poor **developing country**. On the positive side, tourism brings in money, as tourists pay for food, lodging, and supplies. Villagers also earn wages as porters, carrying heavy loads of equipment and supplies for climbers. The porters often use yaks, a kind of longhaired ox, to help them transport goods.

At the same time, tourism has resulted in harmful effects. Porters, for example, are sometimes overworked and mistreated. Also, some of the villages have cut down trees in the process of constructing lodging for the tourist trade. More trees may have been cut to provide fuel for cooking and heating for tourists. This loss of trees has led to **deforestation** and soil erosion in the Everest region.

What Does It Cost to Climb Everest?

Item	Cost for a Team of Seven Climbers
Crew (includes guides, cooks, and doctor)	$98,000
Transportation and lodging en route to Base Camp	$41,000
Permits and fees	$79,000
Supplies (includes fuel, oxygen, batteries, tents, medical supplies, and climbing gear)	$49,000

29.4 From Base Camp to Camp I

Just above Base Camp lies the Khumbu Icefall, which consists of giant chunks of ice known as *seracs*. "Imagine trying to hopscotch uphill through a field of ice boulders the size of houses and weighing some 30 tons, each of which could shift at any moment without warning," wrote a climber about the icefall. "It's like a jigsaw puzzle of giant blue ice puzzle pieces."

Surviving the Khumbu Icefall Climbers reach the Khumbu Icefall on the second stage of their journey, a stage that takes them from Base Camp at 17,600 feet to Camp I at an elevation of 19,500 feet. It usually takes one to three weeks to set up Camp I, as climbers move up and down the icefall each day, transporting supplies to the higher camp. This process also helps them to acclimatize.

The Khumbu Icefall is the most dangerous section of the climb, with more climbers dying here than on any other part of the mountain. Some climbers have been crushed by shifting seracs. Others died after falling into a crevasse, or deep crack in the ice. Still others were swept down the mountain by an **avalanche**.

Climbers try to reduce the risks by starting out their hikes before dawn. Their objective is to get through the Khumbu Icefall before the sun melts the ice. That is because the ice starts to shift when it melts, becoming more dangerous.

Everest's Expert Climbers: The Sherpas On expeditions to climb Mount Everest, much of the work is done by a Himalayan people known as Sherpas. Tenzing Norgay, one of the first two climbers to reach the summit, was a Sherpa. Many of the great climbers on Everest, including a few women, have been Sherpas.

Sherpas play a critical role on Everest expeditions. They function as guides, cooks, and porters, setting up the camps and carrying most of the supplies. They go through the Khumbu Icefall before other climbers in order to set up ladders and ropes for safe passage. Many Sherpas have died doing this hazardous work.

Every climbing expedition has a head Sherpa, called a *sirdar,* who has authority over the other Sherpas. In some cases, an expedition will include two sirdars, with one remaining in Base Camp while the other makes the climb to the summit.

Climbing the Khumbu Icefall
The Khumbu Icefall is the riskiest section of the Everest ascent. Climbers must cross deep crevasses on shaky ladders. They have to beware of falling blocks of ice. One mountain climbing guide warns that "everything you stand or climb on can fall any minute without warning."

Sherpas Play a Key Role
Few Everest climbs would succeed without Sherpas. These natives of the Everest region work as guides and porters on most expeditions. One of the most famous Sherpa climbers was Babu Chiri Sherpa. He reached the summit 10 times and once spent 21 hours at the top. He died in an accident on Everest in 2001.

The Long Climb

Scaling Everest requires great skill and endurance. The risks of climbing are much greater at such high elevations. The lack of oxygen makes it hard to function. As people's thinking gets fuzzy, it is easy to make mistakes. And even a small mistake can prove fatal.

29.5 From Camp I to Camp IV

The third stage of the climb takes climbers from Camp I at 19,500 feet to three more camps. The highest is Camp IV, perched at an elevation of 26,000 feet. One of the most difficult parts of the climb is the Lhotse Face, a steep rock wall covered in ice. "The wind kicked up huge swirling waves of powder snow," a climber recalled of his climb up Lhotse. "Ice formed over my goggles, making it difficult to see. I began to lose feeling in my feet. My fingers turned to wood. It seemed increasingly unsafe to keep going."

Through the Valley of Silence When climbers depart from Camp I, they enter a long valley called the Western Cwm (pronounced *koom*). The Western Cwm is also known as the "Valley of Silence," because the ridges on either side of the valley block the wind. As a result, the most common sounds that climbers hear are their own labored breathing and the crunch of boots on ice and snow.

The hike through the Western Cwm is a long, gradual climb. On a sunny day, the valley can become extremely hot, which surprises most climbers because they expect to find freezing conditions throughout the expedition. "You literally pray for a puff of wind or a cloud to cover the sun," one climber recalled.

Crampons and Rocks: Ascending to Camp IV Camp II lies at the base of the Lhotse Face. To ascend this ice-covered wall, which rises up 3,700 feet, climbers use crampons and ropes attached to the ice. Crampons are spikes that attach to a climber's boots. Climbers kick the crampons into the ice to get a foothold and then pull themselves up on the rope.

Camp III is perched on a narrow ledge halfway up the Lhotse Face. On a clear day, the view is astounding. "I sat with my feet hanging over the abyss, staring across at the clouds, looking down at the tops of 22,000-foot peaks," wrote one climber. "At long last, it seemed as though I was really nearing the roof of the world."

From Camp III, climbers ascend another 1,500 feet to the South Col. This saddle between the Lhotse Face and the summit of Mount Everest is the location of Camp IV. A saddle is a low point on a ridge that connects two peaks.

At 26,000 feet, Camp IV is in the "Death Zone." At this elevation, it is difficult for humans to breathe. The lack of oxygen puts tremendous stress on the body, and climbers are at great risk of experiencing altitude sickness. With so little oxygen reaching their brains, they are also more likely to make fatal mistakes. Most climbers breathe bottled oxygen to survive, but even then it is hard to remain at this altitude for more than two or three days. If the weather turns bad, most climbers are forced to turn back.

Cleaning Up the World's Highest Junkyard Camp IV is the final camp before the summit. In the past, it was also a major dumping ground, littered with empty oxygen bottles, used climbing equipment, and human waste. Even dead bodies were abandoned on the mountain. All of this dumping led to the South Col being nicknamed "the world's highest junkyard."

Between 1953 and the mid-1990s, climbers discarded an estimated 50 tons of glass, plastic, and metal on the slopes of Mount Everest. In recent years, however, groups of climbers have scaled the mountain to bring down the trash. One Japanese team returned with 2.6 tons of garbage, including old tents, fuel bottles, and plastic. As a result of these efforts, the mountain is now much cleaner than it once was. As one climber commented, "If you want to find garbage on Everest now, you have to go looking for it."

To keep Everest clean, the government of Nepal charges climbers a fee to use the mountain. Part of this money helps pay for waste cleanup. Climbing groups are also required to leave a $4,000 "garbage deposit" with the government. If the climbers don't carry their trash off the mountain, they lose their deposit.

Nepal's government is also working to reduce deforestation, which is a significant environmental problem in this country. Mountain climbers must now bring their own fuel with them to Everest, and cutting down trees for fires is prohibited. Tree-planting programs have been organized in many parts of Nepal, with new forests being planted and protected from overuse.

Empty Oxygen Cylinders

Piles of trash were once a common sight on Everest. In recent years, climbing groups have cleaned up the mountain. Here Appa Sherpa, who climbed Mt. Everest 11 times, inspects oxygen bottles collected from the mountain. Climbers use bottled oxygen to help them breathe at very high altitudes.

29.6 From Camp IV to the Summit

After resting a few hours at Camp IV, climbers set out for the summit. They are now in the Death Zone, the most grueling stage of the climb.

Climbing in the Death Zone is a time-consuming physical test. "At those altitudes you're going quite slowly. You take a step and you breathe six to eight times and then you take another step and then you breathe six or eight times," a climber recalled. "You can't look at the whole ascent. You have to break it down into small sections and into tiny little steps. That's how you eventually chew your way to the summit."

Climbing in the Death Zone It's only about 3,000 vertical feet from Camp IV at 26,000 feet to the summit at 29,035 feet, but each step takes tremendous effort. Deep snow, steep drop-offs, and exposure to harsh weather make this part of the climb even more difficult.

It takes about 12 hours for climbers to reach the summit from Camp IV, and an additional 4 hours to make the descent back to the camp. Most climbers begin the final ascent in darkness at around 11 P.M., which usually gives them sufficient time to reach the top and return to Camp IV before the end of the following day.

Climbers first set their sights on the South Summit, a small dome of snow and ice just below the summit. To get here, they must ascend a long, steep ridge that is covered in unstable snow. "It took an age to climb that ridge, hour after hour," a climber later wrote. "Each step was a monumental effort of will, requiring a kick, and another kick, to secure a footing and ensure you didn't slide with the soft snow down again to where you had started."

From the South Summit, climbers have only 300 feet to go. However, they have to climb along a terrifying knife-edge ridge, where one slip can mean a fall of thousands of feet and certain death.

Climbers must also get over the Hillary Step, a rock cliff 40 feet high that lies just below the summit. The Hillary Step is one of the toughest obstacles that climbers face on Everest.

On Top of the World When climbers reach the summit, they are greeted by an extraordinary view. They see Tibet to the north and Nepal to the south. Surrounding them on all sides are other giant peaks of the Himalayas. They are truly on top of the world.

The summit itself, which is about the size of a picnic table, is covered with an assortment of flags, photographs, and other offerings from previous visitors, as well as used oxygen bottles and other trash. Climbers typically don't stay at the top for long because they have to head back down before it grows dark or the weather changes.

By the time they reach the summit, climbers are exhausted. This fatigue makes the return to Camp IV extremely dangerous because even a small mistake can cause them to lose their footing and plummet down the mountain. If the weather turns bad, the mistakes can multiply.

Summit Gear
Climbers who reach the top of Everest today wear special gear designed for high altitudes. Earlier climbers made the ascent with far less equipment. They wore wool sweaters, scarves, and jackets. They had heavy oxygen tanks but no radios. Note the flags left on the summit by earlier climbers.

Seeking Even Greater Challenges Over the years, climbers have sought new challenges on Mount Everest. Some make the ascent without oxygen. Others do it very rapidly. In 2004, a Sherpa set a speed record by climbing from Base Camp to the summit in just over 8 hours. In 2001, an American became the first blind person to scale Everest. And in 2003, a 70-year-old Japanese climber became the oldest person to reach the top.

Some people come down the mountain in challenging ways. A few have skied down or descended on snowboards. One man performed his descent with the use of a paraglider, which is a device like a large kite.

For still others, the adventure of climbing Mount Everest is part of a greater challenge called the Seven Summits. To meet that challenge, a climber must scale the tallest mountains on all seven continents. Whatever a climber's goals may be, reaching the summit of Mount Everest is an amazing feat.

29.7 Beginning to Think Globally

In this chapter, you read about the challenges that climbers experience on the world's highest mountain. You learned that climbers must acclimatize as they ascend Mount Everest, and you read about the danger of exposure to extreme weather conditions. In addition, you discovered some of the effects of tourism on the Mount Everest region and saw that tourism raises questions about the carrying capacity of the mountain environment.

People come to Mount Everest because it is a very special place. However, Everest is only one of the world's many wonders. Keep this in mind as you look at more World Heritage sites in the next section.

Seven Summits Challenge

Mountain (Continent)	Elevation
Denali (N. America)	20,320 ft.
Aconcagua (S. America)	22,840 ft.
Elbrus (Europe)	18,481 ft.
Kilimanjaro (Africa)	19,339 ft.
Everest (Asia)	29,035 ft.
Kosciusko* (Australia)	7,310 ft.
Vinson Massif (Antarctica)	16,067 ft.

* Some sources list Carstensz Pyramid (16,023 ft.) instead.

The Lure of Summits

The Himalayas contain 9 of the world's 10 tallest mountains. Some are visible in the photograph below, as are some climbers along the ridge. But every continent has its highest peaks. Taken together, they make up the Seven Summits Challenge. The challenge is to climb the highest mountain on each of the world's seven continents.

29.8 Global Connections

The map shows the location of many World Heritage sites. There are hundreds of these sites spread across the globe.

How does a place become a World Heritage site? Countries can nominate special places to be included on the World Heritage List. A committee at UNESCO votes on the nominations. There are three types of World Heritage sites: natural, cultural, and mixed. Natural sites are areas with unique physical features, such as the Grand Canyon in Arizona. Cultural sites have great historic, artistic, or scientific value. They may be monuments, groups of buildings, or an old city. India's Taj Mahal is a cultural World Heritage site. Mixed sites combine natural and cultural features. The Mayan ruin of Tikal in the rainforest of Guatemala is a mixed site.

What risks do World Heritage sites face today? Many World Heritage sites are at risk of being damaged or lost entirely. Some are threatened by ethnic conflict or war, whereas others are endangered by pollution or development. Often the greatest risk is overuse, which happens when more people visit a site than its carrying capacity allows. A World Heritage site that is overused may be in danger of being "loved to death."

Why should World Heritage sites be protected? World Heritage sites are among the greatest treasures in the world because they represent the wonders of nature or the finest expressions of human culture. People visit them to enjoy their beauty or to learn more about the history and achievements of humankind. By protecting these special places, we are preserving them not only for ourselves but also for future generations to enjoy.

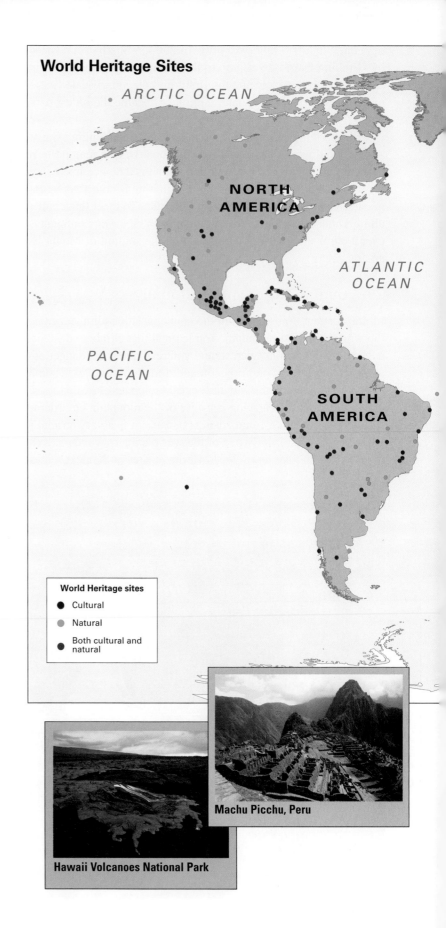

World Heritage Sites

World Heritage sites
- Cultural
- Natural
- Both cultural and natural

Machu Picchu, Peru

Hawaii Volcanoes National Park

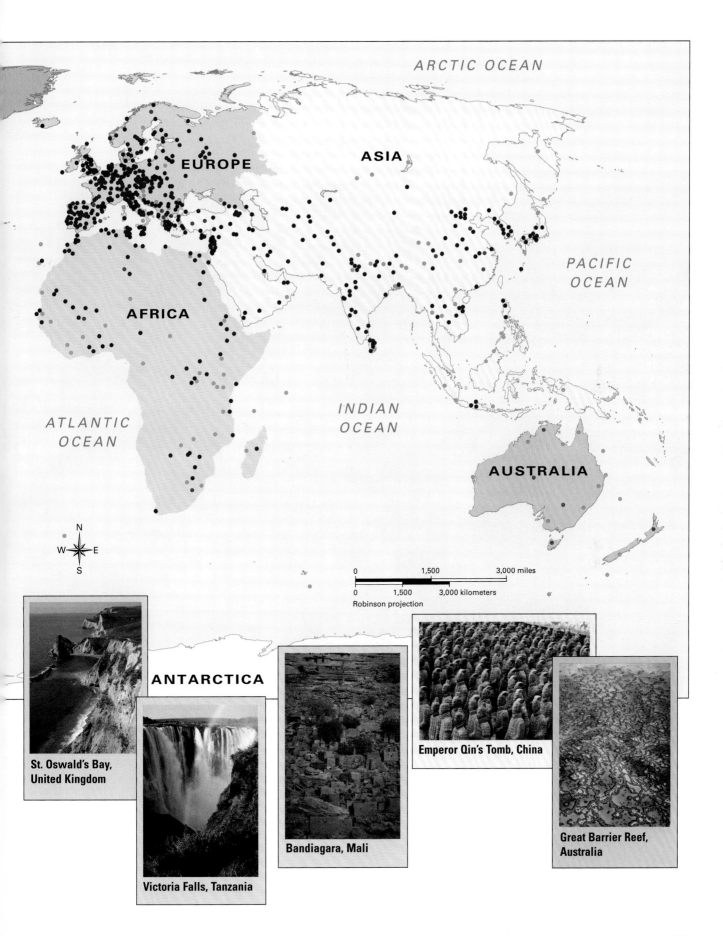

ARCTIC OCEAN

EUROPE

ASIA

AFRICA

PACIFIC OCEAN

ATLANTIC OCEAN

INDIAN OCEAN

AUSTRALIA

N
W E
S

0   1,500   3,000 miles
0   1,500   3,000 kilometers
Robinson projection

ANTARCTICA

St. Oswald's Bay, United Kingdom

Victoria Falls, Tanzania

Bandiagara, Mali

Emperor Qin's Tomb, China

Great Barrier Reef, Australia

China: The World's Most Populous Country

30.1 Introduction

During the 1870s, a **drought** of terrible magnitude occurred throughout China. As crops failed and many people began to starve, one witness to the suffering wrote,

> *They wait for death in their houses, stripped of everything.*
> *The cold winds pierce through their bones. They have no rice*
> *to cook, and the cravings of hunger are most painful.*

This was not the first time that the people of China had faced a terrible **famine,** for there had been severe food shortages many times before. However, this famine was made worse by a rise in China's population. By the time the famine was over, it had claimed almost 10 million lives.

This story of population growth and famine is, in some ways, the story of China because since ancient times China has experienced both. Despite hard times, China today is the world's most populous country, home to one out of every five of the world's 6 billion people.

Feeding such an immense population is a tremendous challenge. To help meet that challenge, China is working to achieve **zero population growth,** a condition that is met when a country's population stops growing. With zero population growth in a country, the number of people who are born each year roughly equals the number who die. In this chapter, you will learn how China is addressing the challenges created by its enormous and still growing population.

Essential Question

How does a country meet the challenges created by a large and growing population?

This graph shows the population of China from 1950 to 2050. The numbers after 2000 are estimates. Note how fast China's population grew between 1950 and 1990. Today, China has more than 1.3 billion people. Keep this graph in mind as you try to answer the Essential Question.

Graphic Organizer

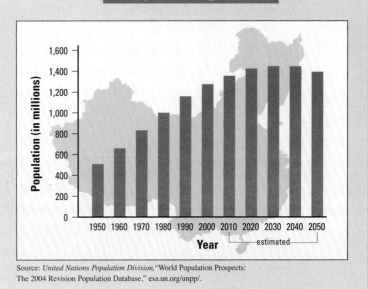

Source: *United Nations Population Division,* "World Population Prospects: The 2004 Revision Population Database," esa.un.org/unpp/.

◀ Crowds of Chinese tourists on the Great Wall of China

Natural Increase and Doubling Time

Rate of Natural Increase	Doubling Time (years)
3%	23
2%	35
1%	70
0%	no doubling time

Population Math

This table shows the relationship between the rate of natural increase and doubling time. A rate of natural increase that is greater than 2 percent a year is considered high. At that rate, a country's population will double in 35 years. The rate of natural increase varies widely around the world.

Population Growth in China

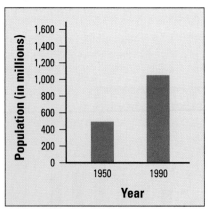

China's Doubling Time

As this bar graph shows, China's population more than doubled between 1950 and 1990. For a population to grow so rapidly, it must have a rate of natural increase above 2 percent.

30.2 The Geographic Setting

The ancient Chinese believed that China stood at the center of the world. They did not think there were any other civilized societies on Earth. This idea was understandable, because China was geographically isolated from the rest of the world. To the west, **deserts** and mountains cut China off from the rest of Asia, and to the east lies the vast Pacific Ocean. Even today, the Chinese people refer to their country as Zhong Guo, "the Middle Kingdom."

A Diverse Landscape If China could be picked up and placed on top of the United States, the two countries would match up pretty well. They are nearly equal in shape and size, although China is slightly larger. China's **landscape,** however, is very different.

Geographers sometimes describe China as a giant slope that stretches from the towering mountains of Central Asia in the west to the Pacific Ocean in the east. If you stood at the top of the slope, you would look down on the mountains, **plateaus,** and **basins** that make up western China. If you took a giant step down the slope, you would be in central China, where you would find lower mountains, hills, and plateaus. You would also find the Gobi Desert.

A final giant step down would take you to eastern China. Here you would find low hills, fertile river valleys, and plains. You would see vast **floodplains** covered with rice fields. Eastern China is where most of the country's 1.3 billion residents live.

The First Billion-Person Country China has been the world's most populous country for hundreds of years. In the 1980s, it became the first country to reach a population of 1 billion people.

A population grows when its **birth rate** each year is higher than its **death rate.** These rates are determined by the average number of births or deaths per 1,000 people. Birth and death rates are often shown as a percentage. To calculate a country's birth rate, for example, start with the number of births in the country for every 1,000 people. If there are 30 births for every 1,000 people in a year, the birth rate is calculated as 3 percent. Similarly, if there are 20 deaths per 1,000 people, the death rate would be 2 percent.

To find out how fast a country's population is growing, subtract the death rate from the birth rate. In the example just described, a 3 percent birth rate minus a 2 percent death rate equals a 1 percent growth rate. This means that the population of that country is growing by 1 percent each year. This annual growth rate is also referred to as the **rate of natural increase**.

China's population grew substantially during the second half of the 20th century. In 1950, China had about 550 million people. Only 40 years later, in 1990, it had twice as many people. The population had doubled to about 1.1 billion. The time it takes for a population to double like this is called its **doubling time**.

The rate of natural increase and the doubling time are tied to each other. The higher the rate of natural increase, the shorter the doubling time. Looking ahead from 1990, the Chinese could anticipate that if nothing changed, their population would likely double again in just another 40 years.

▶ Geoterms

doubling time the length of time it takes for a population to double

famine a severe shortage of food that results in widespread hunger

rate of natural increase the annual rate of population growth. This percentage is calculated by subtracting the death rate from the birth rate. It does not include people moving into or out of a country.

zero population growth a condition in which the population of a country does not grow but remains stable. This condition comes about when the birth rate plus immigration equals the death rate plus emigration.

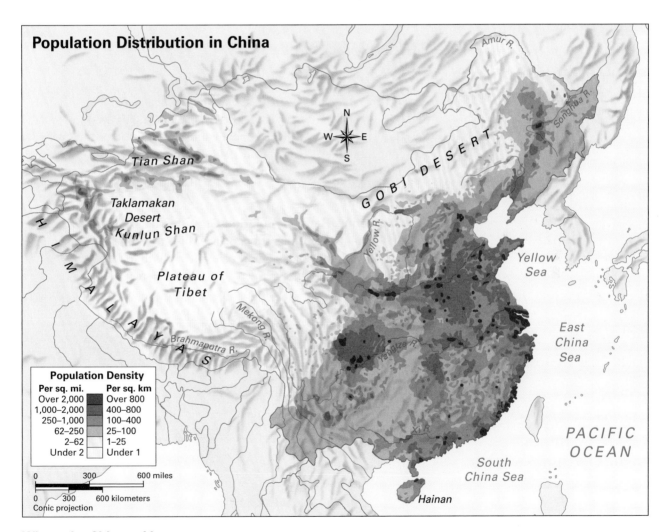

Population Distribution in China

Population Density

Per sq. mi.	Per sq. km
Over 2,000	Over 800
1,000–2,000	400–800
250–1,000	100–400
62–250	25–100
2–62	1–25
Under 2	Under 1

0   300   600 miles
0   300   600 kilometers
Conic projection

Where the Chinese Live

The purple areas on this map indicate a population density of more than 2,000 people per square mile. Notice that the majority of Chinese live in the eastern part of the country. Rivers flowing across this lowland region provide fish for food and water for irrigation. They are also used as transportation routes.

为四化一对夫妇只生一个孩

The Use of Posters in China

China uses posters to promote government policies. This poster supports the one-child policy. Traditionally, boys are favored. The government, however, is trying to change this way of thinking. This poster shows parents who are happy with their one daughter.

30.3 Plan One: Slow Population Growth

Great Teacher. Great Leader. Great Supreme Commander. Great Helmsman. These names were used to describe one of China's most important leaders, Mao Zedong. Mao led a revolution that brought a communist government to power in China in 1949. During his long rule of the new People's Republic of China until his death in 1976, Mao brought considerable change to China.

The Challenge: Rapid Population Growth Mao believed that large families would make China strong. Under his rule, China's population grew rapidly. With women, on average, giving birth to four or five children, the natural rate of increase rose to about 3 percent.

In 1958, Mao launched a program called the Great Leap Forward, which was a plan to help China become a modern industrial country. In other countries, such modernization has been achieved through the use of new **technology,** such as factory machines and computers. However, Mao thought that China could "leap forward" by getting more work out of its huge population.

One goal of the Great Leap Forward was to increase the production of steel. Across the country, small "backyard furnaces" were set up, and people were told to melt down their metal possessions. Bicycles, cooking pans, iron bed frames, and even doorknobs were melted to make steel. Another goal was to increase food production, and small farms were lumped together to create large factory farms.

Despite people's hard work, the Great Leap Forward did not turn China into an industrial giant. Production did not increase as Mao had anticipated. At the same time, there were severe droughts across China, resulting in famine. More than 20 million people died of starvation between 1958 and 1962. Those deaths were a tragic reminder that China could no longer support its rapidly growing population.

The Proposed Solution: The One-Child Policy After Mao's death in 1976, the Chinese government took steps to control population growth. In 1979, the government began a family-planning program known as the *one-child policy*. This program limited each married couple to just one child. The government rewarded couples who followed the policy and punished those who did not.

The one-child policy is still in effect in China, but there have been changes. The focus now is on rewards rather than punishments. Families receive benefits, including cash, for having just one child. In some **rural** areas, couples are allowed to have a second child. Furthermore, punishments for having more children than allowed are less severe than in the past. Overall, though, Chinese families still must strictly limit the number of children they have.

The Benefits: Slower Population Growth China has not yet reached zero population growth, but the one-child policy has been effective in moving the country toward that goal. A majority of Chinese families today have only one child. China's population is still growing, but at a much slower rate.

Slower population growth has had many benefits for China. It has reduced the strain on food and water supplies, and it has lessened the problem of having too many workers for too few jobs.

Families have benefited in other ways. Mothers and babies tend to be healthier in small families. With fewer children to support, parents have more money to spend on other things. With fewer children to care for, women have more time for a career.

The Costs: Less Choice and an Aging Population The one-child policy has not been completely successful. Many people don't want to be told how many children they can have, especially in rural areas where large families are a tradition. Economically, large families make sense in rural regions because for a farming family, more children mean more workers to help with farmwork.

The one-child policy has also clashed with ancient cultural traditions. Chinese families prefer having sons because the family name is passed on to sons, and sons are expected to care for aging parents. In contrast, daughters leave their parents to become a part of their husband's family. For these reasons, many people desperately prefer a son if they can have only one child.

Modern medicine makes it easy to determine the sex of a baby before it is born. Rather than give birth to a girl, some couples choose to end a pregnancy and try again for a boy. This practice is illegal. But still, boys are preferred over girls. Today about 120 boys are born for every 100 girls in China, and boys already outnumber girls in most classrooms. In the future, this difference may lead to a shortage of wives for young men in China.

There is another cost as well. In the past, old people in China were cared for by their children, especially their sons. One of the consequences of the one-child policy is that there are fewer children to care for older family members. As a result, China will need to find new ways to take care of a large and aging population.

China, 2000

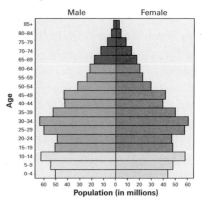

China, 2050 (Estimated)

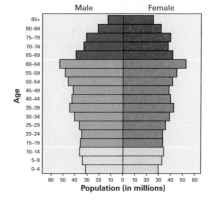

Source: *United Nations Population Division,* "World Population Prospects: The 2004 Revision Population Database," esa.un.org/unpp/.

Population Changes in China

The one-child policy has changed the population distribution in China. Compare the two population pyramids. If slow growth continues, China's population distribution will eventually look like the pyramid on the bottom.

The Three Gorges Dam in 2003

The Three Gorges Dam was not complete when this photograph was taken, but it was already generating clean energy. As the lake behind the dam fills, much of the beautiful scenery in the Three Gorges area will be lost.

30.4 Plan Two: Provide More Clean Energy

Huge populations require huge amounts of energy. Most of the electricity the Chinese people need is supplied by power plants that burn coal. Smoke containing **toxic chemicals** such as mercury and sulfur dioxide pours out of China's power plants, and high winds transport the poisonous plumes around the world. In the United States, mercury **pollution** from China has been discovered from California to New England.

The Challenge: Meeting Rising Energy Demands China has the second-largest **consumption** of energy in the world, exceeded only by energy consumption in the United States. China uses coal to meet 65 percent of its energy needs, burning more coal than any other country.

As its population grows, China's energy needs will expand. The country possesses large deposits of coal, but coal is not a clean fuel. When burned, it pollutes the air, and diseases related to air pollution have become leading causes of death in China. One way to reduce air pollution is to install equipment at power plants to clean the smoke, but this equipment is very expensive.

The Proposed Solution: Generate More Hydroelectric Power To meet its growing energy needs without increasing pollution, China has looked for cleaner sources of energy. One of the cleanest sources is **hydroelectric power,** which is power that is generated by water flowing through power plants in dams.

In 1993, China began construction of the world's largest dam. When it is completed, the immense dam will span the Yangtze River, the longest river in Asia. Flowing more than 3,700 miles through China, the Yangtze has been relied on for thousands of years to transport people and cargo and to provide fresh water for homes and crops. After the dam is finished in 2009, it will provide as much as one ninth of China's electricity as well.

The dam across the Yangtze is being built in a beautiful canyon area called the Three Gorges. When complete, the Three Gorges Dam will be over 600 feet high and more than 1.3 miles wide. The **reservoir** behind the dam will stretch upstream for about 400 miles.

The Benefits: Clean Energy, Flood Control, and Shipping Hydro-electric dams provide many benefits to the countries that build them. One is clean energy from a **renewable resource**. The power plant at the Three Gorges Dam will have 26 electric generators, which will produce more electricity than any other hydroelectric plant in the world. And they will do so without polluting the air.

A second benefit is flood control. Historically, the Yangtze River has flooded about every 10 years, and these floods have resulted in wide-spread death and destruction. The dam will reduce flooding by holding back the extra water that flows downstream when there are heavy rains. This will improve life for the people who are living near the river below the dam.

In addition, the dam will help river shipping. Before the dam was built, the Three Gorges area was difficult to navigate by boat. The lake forming behind the dam will be much safer for river travel. Locks will lift boats from the river below the dam up to the level of the lake. After the completion of the dam and the locks, shipping on the river is expected to increase rapidly, and at the same time shipping costs should drop by about a third.

The Costs: Lost Cities and Habitat While the Three Gorges Dam will surely benefit China, there are costs as well. The Three Gorges area contains hundreds of ancient settlement **sites**. When water backs up behind the dam, these archeological sites will disappear, and all that they could have revealed to historians about China's distant past will be lost.

The reservoir will cover up more than history. It will drown 13 cities, 140 towns, and hundreds of villages. Tens of thousands of acres of farmland will be submerged as well. More than a million people are being forced to relocate as their homes disappear under water. The Chinese government has promised to help these people start new lives elsewhere, but such assurances won't make up for what they have lost.

The dam will also alter the Yangtze River **ecosystem**. As the lake fills, hundreds of plant and animal species will lose their **habitats**. The Chinese river dolphin and the Chinese paddlefish are two threatened species that live only in the Yangtze River. The damming of the river may put their survival even more at risk.

Finally, the dam sits along an earthquake **fault**. Some scientists worry that the weight of the dam and the water it holds may make a major earthquake more likely to occur. If such a quake damaged the dam, a wall of water from the reservoir could rush downstream, causing a disaster worse than any previous Yangtze flood.

Lost Cities and Historic Sites

The damming of the Yangtze will affect the landscape for hundreds of miles along the river. Because of this, some people have called the dam project "China's new Great Wall." This map shows the cities and historic sites that will be lost under the reservoir's waters. Some of these sites date back to before 2000 B.C.E.

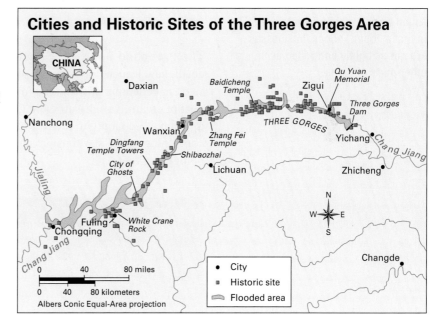

Cities and Historic Sites of the Three Gorges Area

Special Economic Zones

China's "Open" Areas

The map shows some of China's special economic zones (SEZs) along with their capital cities. It also shows "open cities," which operate like SEZs. In these "open" zones, businesses are not as tightly controlled as in other parts of China.

From Farmland to SEZ

Before 1990, Pudong was boggy farmland. Today, the Pudong New Area is a booming special economic zone. Like other SEZs, Pudong has attracted many foreign businesses.

30.5 Plan Three: Promote Economic Growth

A fish tank that cleans itself. A cellular phone that resembles a tube of lipstick. A belt that can be inflated into a life jacket in a mere five seconds. These were just a few of the inventions displayed in 2004 at the China Hi-Tech Fair in the city of Shenzhen. This fair is held every year to promote Chinese technology to visitors from around the world. This is just one way China is working to promote economic growth.

The Challenge: Increasing Jobs and Wealth China was not always open to interactions with businesspeople from other countries. Under the rule of Mao Zedong, the country had looked inward because Mao's goal was to make China economically self-sufficient. His government controlled the economy, with government officials deciding what goods should be produced and at what price. The government also controlled who should do what job and for what pay.

You have read about the failure of the Great Leap Forward, Mao's effort to transform China into a modern industrialized country. Just as China's economy began to recover from that experiment, Mao launched a new one. In 1966, he called for a "cultural revolution," with the goal of creating a new society in China. In this society, everyone would follow his ideas and would work for the common good.

Like the Great Leap Forward, the Cultural Revolution was a disaster. Many people who were suspected of not being loyal to Mao were sent to prison. Schools were closed as students joined the revolution. Meanwhile, factory and farm production dropped because there weren't enough workers. The country was in chaos.

The Proposed Solution: Special Economic Zones After Mao's death, new leaders took control of China. These leaders were more interested in economic growth than in changing society, and they gave up the goal of creating a self-sufficient China. Instead, they made plans to open up China's economy to the rest of the world. They hoped that foreign companies would start businesses, create jobs, and bring modern technology to China.

There was just one problem with this new policy. Foreigners were not willing to come to China if the government planned to control their businesses. Foreign companies demanded far more freedom than the government was willing to give to Chinese businesses.

China addressed this problem by setting up special economic zones (SEZs). These special areas have laws that are different from those in the rest of the country. In China's SEZs, businesses have the freedom to decide what goods to produce and at what prices to sell them. Most of the goods that are produced in special economic zones are for export to other countries.

The first four special economic zones opened on China's south coast in 1979 and 1980. Shenzhen is the capital of one of them. Many more SEZs have been added since.

The Benefits: More Jobs and Better Standard of Living Special economic zones have brought economic growth to China. In 1980, Shenzhen was a sleepy town of perhaps 20,000 people. Today it has been transformed into an international trade center with over 3 million people. Other SEZs have experienced similar growth.

China's SEZs have created millions of new jobs. These jobs are often filled by **migrant workers** from rural areas. Although wages are not high, most SEZ factory workers earn more than they could in their home villages. Many of these migrant workers are making enough money both to support themselves and to send some money back home to their families. With this extra money, their families are able to improve their own **standard of living**.

The Costs: Income Gaps and Crime Special economic zones have created problems as well. One problem is a widening income gap between rich and poor. China's booming SEZs have created a lot of wealth, but that wealth has not been spread evenly throughout the country. Much of China remains very poor, and the income gap between rich and poor may lead to unrest if it continues to widen.

Another problem has been the creation of a "floating population" of rootless migrant workers who drift back and forth between their villages and the SEZs. These migrant workers often find only low-paying, part-time jobs, and are sometimes unable to find work at all. Some turn to crime in order to survive.

30.6 Beginning to Think Globally

In this chapter, you read about the most populous country on Earth. You learned about the roles that population growth and famine have played in China's history. You discovered how a population's rate of natural increase and doubling time are related. You also looked at how China is working to achieve three goals: zero population growth, clean energy, and economic growth.

China is not the only country attempting to deal with population growth. By 2050, the number of people in the world is expected to increase by over 2.5 billion. Most of that population growth will happen in **developing countries**. Think about the problems these countries will face as you examine rates of natural increase in the next section.

HDI Rank by Province

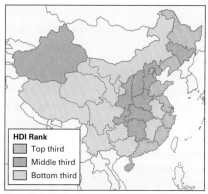

HDI Rank
- Top third
- Middle third
- Bottom third

Source: *United Nations Development Programme*, "China Human Development Report 2002," hdr.undp.org.

Varied Living Standards

The Human Development Index (HDI) measures the well-being of a people. Rankings are based on per capita GDP, education levels, and life expectancy. As this map shows, some parts of China rank higher than others on this index. The top-ranked provinces are home to most of China's special economic zones.

30.7 Global Connections

The map shows rates of natural increase in countries around the world. At these rates, the populations of the 50 poorest countries will more than double by the year 2050. The tables display information about education for women and spending on health care in countries with various rates of growth.

How might money spent on health care affect a country's rate of natural increase? With better health care, a country's **infant mortality rate** will decline, while **life expectancy** will rise. Parents will worry less that their children will not survive childhood, and as a result they may have fewer children. Better health care also means improved access to modern family-planning methods, which will help couples plan how many children they will have.

How might money spent on educating women affect a country's rate of natural increase? Women who are educated generally have more control over the number of children they have. In addition, educated women often marry later in life and may put off having children to focus first on a career. When these women do have children, they usually have fewer than women who lack an education.

How might a country with rapid population growth benefit by slowing its rate of natural increase? Countries that are able to slow their rates of natural increase will generally grow wealthier. With fewer children, they are better able to educate each child. These countries also have more money to spend on providing health care. A healthy, educated population will attract increased trade and business, often leading to economic growth and thus a rise in living standards.

Rate of Natural Increase Around the World, 2004

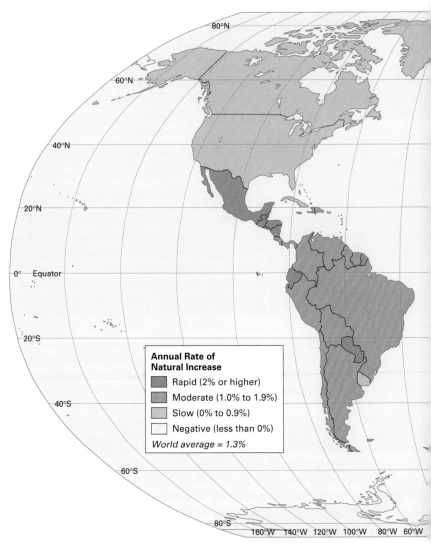

Annual Rate of Natural Increase
- Rapid (2% or higher)
- Moderate (1.0% to 1.9%)
- Slow (0% to 0.9%)
- Negative (less than 0%)

World average = 1.3%

Females Enrolled in Secondary Schools, 2004

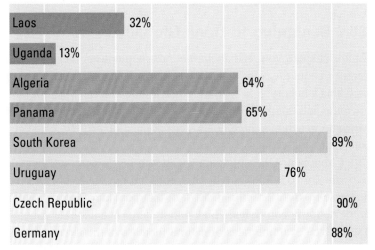

Country	Percent
Laos	32%
Uganda	13%
Algeria	64%
Panama	65%
South Korea	89%
Uruguay	76%
Czech Republic	90%
Germany	88%

Source: *United Nations Development Programme,* "Human Development Reports," hdr.undp.org.
*Data are for the appropriate age group (for example, 14 to 18 years of age).

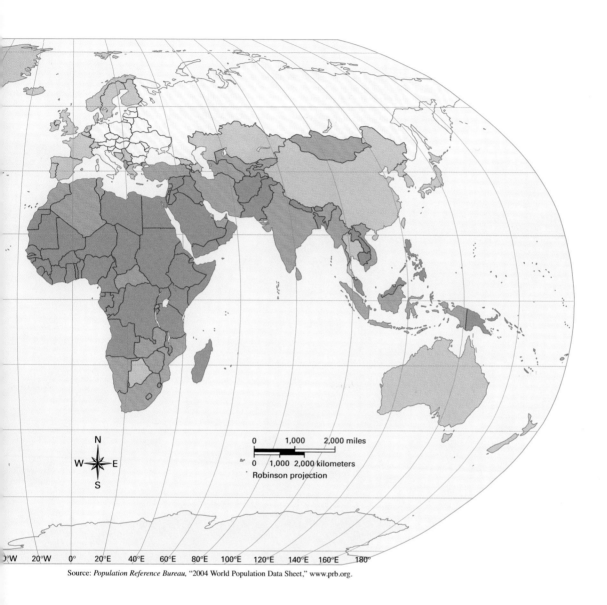

Source: *Population Reference Bureau*, "2004 World Population Data Sheet," www.prb.org.

Health Care Spending and GDP in Eight Countries, 2004

	Rate of Natural Increase							
	Rapid		Moderate		Slow		Negative	
Country, Rate	Laos, 2.4%	Uganda, 3.0%	Algeria, 1.5%	Panama, 1.8%	South Korea, 0.5%	Uruguay, 0.6%	Czech Republic, −0.2%	Germany, −0.2%
Per Person Spending on Health Care*	$49	$57	$169	$458	$948	$948	$1,129	$2,820
Per Capita GDP*	$1,759	$1,390	$5,740	$6,170	$16,950	$7,830	$15,780	$27,100

Source: *United Nations Development Programme*, "Human Development Reports," hdr.undp.org.
*Data computed in U.S. dollars.

Population Density in Japan: Life in a Crowded Country

31.1 Introduction

Imagine standing on a subway platform in Tokyo, Japan, during rush hour. The station is so crammed with people that you can barely move. Your train thunders into the station and lurches to a stop. As the car doors open, the crowd on the platform surges forward. In the crush, the person behind you steps on your heel and your shoe comes off. You reach down to pick it up, but there are too many people even to bend over. You are swept into the train without your shoe. Luckily, a station attendant will pick up your shoe and hold it for you to claim on your return trip. This is hardly the first time people have lost shoes during the Tokyo rush hour. And it will not be the last.

Tokyo is one of the world's most crowded **urban** centers. It is also the capital of the densely populated country of Japan. A country's population density is the average number of persons in a unit of area, such as a square mile or square kilometer. **Population density** is calculated by dividing the total number of people in a country by its total land area. The higher the result of that calculation, the more crowded the country.

In 2004, the population density of Japan was 880 persons per square mile. In comparison, the United States had a population density of 83 persons per square mile. This means that Japan is almost 11 times as densely populated as the United States. In this chapter, you will learn how Japan's high population density affects how people live and die in that crowded country.

Essential Question

How does population density affect the way people live?

The map in the center of this diagram shows where people live in Japan. The areas in red are the most densely populated parts of the country. Around the map are four symbols. They represent aspects of life that are affected by population density. Keep this diagram in mind as you try to answer the Essential Question.

Graphic Organizer

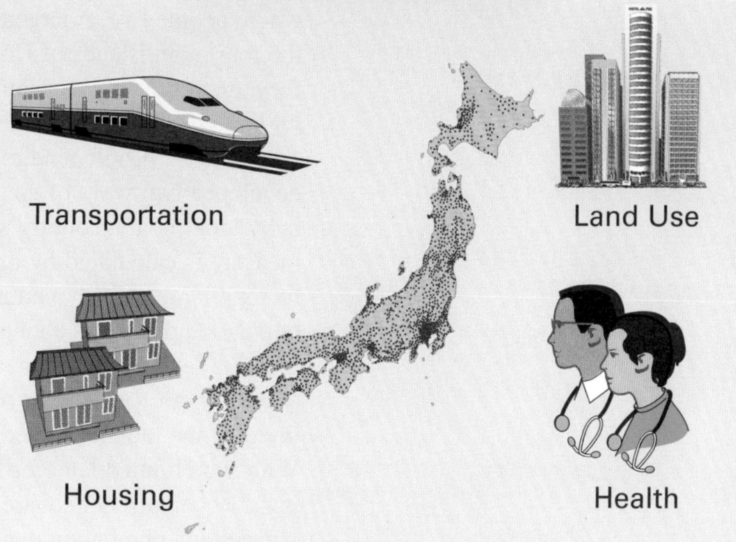

Transportation

Land Use

Housing

Health

◀ Swimming pool in Tokyo

Mount Fuji over Tokyo Bay
Japan's mountains limit the amount of land that is suitable for living. Many of these mountains, like Mount Fuji, are volcanoes. Mount Fuji was once thought to be a sacred place. Today this beautiful volcano attracts weekend hikers eager to escape crowded cities.

31.2 The Geographic Setting

Japan occupies an **archipelago,** or chain of islands, that lies off the East Asian mainland. On a map, the Japanese archipelago forms the shape of a thin crescent moon. The land area of Japan consists of four large islands and about 3,900 smaller ones. Taken together, these islands form a country about the size of the state of Montana. To the west, the Sea of Japan (East Sea) separates Japan from its nearest neighbors, Korea and China. To the east lies the vast Pacific Ocean.

Japan enjoys a **temperate climate,** with warm, humid summers and relatively mild winters. Heavy snowfall is limited to high elevations and the most northern of Japan's islands. Abundant summer rainfall makes Japan an ideal place for growing rice and other crops.

A Mountainous Landscape The Japanese archipelago was formed millions of years ago by mountains welling up from the sea. The mountains arose when **tectonic plates** collided deep beneath the Pacific Ocean. **Volcanoes** welled up in the cracks between the plates. Over millions of years, liquid rock flowing from the volcanoes built up into mountains that eventually emerged from the sea.

Today a chain of volcanic mountains forms the backbone of Japan. Many volcanoes are still active, although no one knows just when they might erupt again. The highest and most famous Japanese volcano is Mount Fuji, whose snowcapped cone towers above the city of Tokyo.

The tectonic plates that gave birth to Japan are still grinding against each other beneath the sea. Occasionally one of them slips, causing an earthquake to rattle the islands. Small tremors occur on an almost daily basis in Japan. Major earthquakes are less frequent but can cause extensive damage and loss of life. Undersea earthquakes can also trigger huge sea waves known as **tsunamis.** When one of these destructive waves hits the Japanese coast, entire villages can be washed out to sea.

Limited Land for Living Only about an eighth of Japan is **arable land,** or land suitable for agriculture. The remaining land is too steep to plow and plant. Much is also too mountainous to support large towns and cities.

The amount of arable land affects **population distribution,** or where people live. A large majority of Japan's 127 million people live on the four main islands of Hokkaido, Honshu, Shikoku, and Kyushu. But they are not evenly distributed across these islands. About 80 percent live on limited flat land near the coast or in narrow river valleys.

Because people tend to clump on arable land, geographers have developed two ways of measuring how crowded a country is. The first is by looking at a country's **arithmetic population density**. This measure is calculated by dividing the number of people in a country by its total land area. As you read in the introduction, Japan's arithmetic population density is about 880 persons per square mile.

The second way of measuring crowding is by looking at a country's **physiologic population density**. This measure is calculated by dividing the number of people in a country by the amount of *arable* land. With such limited land for living, Japan's physiologic population density is 7,219 persons per square mile. The United States, in comparison, has a physiologic population density of 433 persons per square mile. Both population density measures tell us that Japan is a crowded country.

▶ Geoterms

arable land land suitable for growing crops

arithmetic population density the population of a country divided by its total land area

physiologic population density the population of a country divided by its arable land area

population distribution where people live in a country, whether crowded together in cities or spread out across the countryside

Earthquakes in Japan

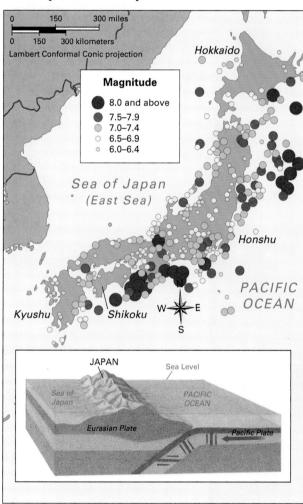

Physical Features of Japan

When Two Plates Collide

Earth's crust below the Pacific Ocean is called the Pacific Plate. It slides under the Eurasian Plate, which is Earth's crust below the continents of Europe and Asia. When these two tectonic plates rub against each other, Japan is hit with an earthquake.

A Mountainous Landscape

About 70 percent of Japan is covered with mountains. The rivers flowing out of these mountains are too short and steep for boat travel. But they do provide hydroelectric power to Japan.

31.3 How Population Density Affects Transportation

What happens when millions of people, living together in a densely populated **megalopolis,** all head out for work at about the same time in the morning? It takes most of them a very long time to get there! The average **commute time** in Tokyo is an hour and a half each day. This adds up to a whopping 400 hours or more a year, which is enough time to watch 160 movies or take 40 flights from Tokyo to San Francisco.

Public Transportation The Japanese have adapted to busy rush hours by creating an extensive and efficient **public transit system**. Underground subways whisk commuters from one part of a city to another, while passenger trains rush travelers from town to town. Japanese subways and trains run often and are almost always on time—to the minute. You can set your watch by them.

Rush hour in a Tokyo subway station is an amazing sight. Mobs of commuters bound for work mix with large groups of uniformed students heading for school. White-gloved subway workers called *pushers* stand on subway platforms waiting for the trains to roll in. Their job is to shove as many passengers as possible into the cars before the doors close.

The Japanese have developed some of the fastest passenger trains in the world. Bullet trains—so named for their shape and speed—called Shinkansen travel between many cities. The Shinkansen race across the Japanese countryside at speeds of up to 180 miles per hour. That's more than three times as fast as cars, which travel about 60 miles per hour on highways in those rare moments when there is no traffic congestion.

Subway Pusher in Tokyo

Tokyo's high density means that rush hours are crowded. Workers wearing white gloves push people into subway cars so that the doors will close. Some people spend two to three hours traveling to and from work each day.

Private Cars and Parking Problems Despite their excellent public transit system, many Japanese own their own cars and love to drive them. As car ownership has increased, traffic congestion has become part of daily life in Japan.

Cars create problems even when they are not moving. Finding a place to park in Tokyo is such a headache that the city has instituted strict regulations about car ownership. Residents of the city cannot own a car unless they can prove they have a place off the street to park it. With parking space so limited, Tokyo has pioneered the use of high-rise parking lots that look something like giant shoe cabinets. These garages use computer-controlled elevators to stack cars on top of one another in narrow parking slots.

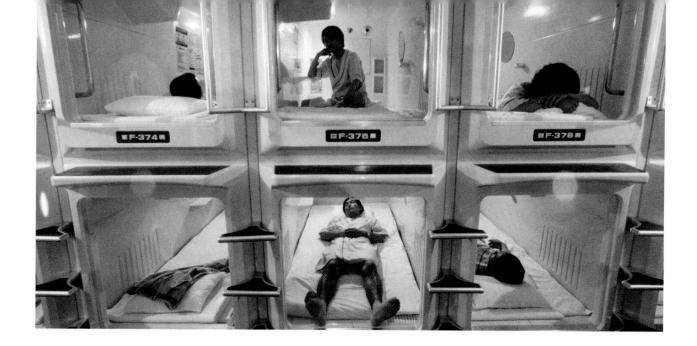

31.4 How Population Density Affects Housing

Because flat land for building is scarce in Japan, housing is expensive. Most homes in Japan are smaller than those in the United States. Many Japanese families live in apartments that are no larger than the typical family room in an American home.

From the Country to the City The Japanese did not always live crowded into small homes. Fifty years ago, when Japan was largely **rural,** most people lived in spacious one-story homes. They also lived in **extended families,** with grandparents, parents, and children together under one roof.

In the 1950s, this pattern began to change. Many Japanese left the countryside to pursue educational or job opportunities in Japan's growing cities. The houses and apartments available in urban areas were cramped compared to rural homes. With space so tight, the number of people living in extended families began to shrink. Today a majority of Japanese live in **nuclear families,** or families with just parents and their children.

Making the Most of Limited Space The Japanese have developed a number of clever ways to make the most of their limited living space. One is to use rooms for more than one purpose. Many homes in Japan do not have separate bedrooms. At bedtime, mattresses called *futons* are taken from closets and spread on the floor of living rooms. In the morning, the futons are put away again.

The Japanese also make good use of limited space by shrinking almost everything that goes into a home. Japanese appliance makers produce small stoves and refrigerators to fit in tiny apartment kitchens. Gardeners who lack garden plots grow tiny trees called *bonsai* in shallow pots on windowsills. A 10-year-old bonsai tree might be only a few inches tall.

Japan's population density even affects where people rest after death. Most cemeteries in Japan are a jumble of family graves filling every inch of available space. "Unless we try something new," warns a Buddhist temple leader, "all of Japan will turn into a graveyard." To prevent this, many people are choosing to have their bodies cremated after death. A box of ashes requires much less space than a coffin.

Capsule Hotel in Japan
Hotels that rent sleeping capsules make good use of space in crowded Japanese cities. Each capsule has a mattress, a television with headphones, and a clock. Guests can spend time in the hotel's restaurants and public areas until they are ready for bed.

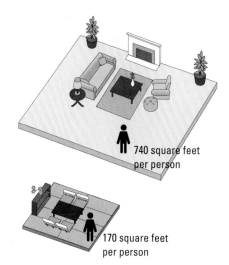

740 square feet per person

170 square feet per person

Homes in the U.S. and Japan
Japanese homes are smaller than those in the United States. A typical person in Tokyo has about 170 square feet of living space. A typical person in Washington, D.C., has about 740 square feet of living space.

31.5 How Population Density Affects Land Use

While land use may seem like a dull topic to most people, it's a vital issue for the neighbors of Tokyo's bustling Narita Airport. For years, plans to expand Narita were blocked by local homeowners. When the government offered to relocate the homeowners to another area, neighbors threatened to burn down the new home of anybody who agreed to move.

Conflicts over land use are common in Japan because there is simply not enough land to meet everyone's needs. This has forced the Japanese to find better ways to use the land they have and to create new land.

Building Up and Down One way to make more efficient use of land is to construct taller buildings. But building skyward creates severe construction challenges in an active **earthquake zone**. Until 1965, building heights were limited in Japan for safety reasons.

The development of **earthquake-resistant construction techniques** has allowed the Japanese to raise that height limit. Using these techniques, the Japanese are able to erect lofty towers that can withstand severe shaking. So many skyscrapers have gone up in recent years that some people call the construction crane Japan's national bird.

Another way to make more efficient use of land is to build underground. Under many Japanese cities lie **subterranean** shopping centers filled with shops and restaurants. A large underground center in the city of Osaka includes a park, an art museum, a Buddhist temple, and even a zoo.

Creating New Land The Japanese have created new land by filling in shallow **wetlands** with dirt and rubble. Much of Tokyo, for example, is built on filled-in bays and marshes. Filling wetlands saves precious farmland from urban development. At the same time, it destroys valuable fish and wildlife **habitat**.

Filled land is also unstable in earthquakes. In 1995, a massive earthquake hit the port city of Kobe, killing some 6,400 people and damaging $100 billion worth of property. Much of that property was on filled land.

Like the Incas of South America, the Japanese have created new land for farming by cutting terraces into hillsides. **Terracing** has made it possible to grow rice—Japan's most important crop—on the islands' mountain slopes.

Terraced Rice Fields in Japan
The Japanese have claimed new land for farming by building terraces into hillsides. Working these rice fields on steep slopes is hard work.

Land Use in a Japanese City

By building both up and down, the Japanese make efficient use of limited city land.

31.6 How Population Density Affects Health

Japanese cookies may be the best-packaged treats in the world. Each cookie is wrapped in an individual cellophane packet. The packets are placed in a box, which is then wrapped in paper. When sold, the box may be wrapped once more before being sent home in a paper bag. All of this packaging adds up. The average Tokyo resident creates 2 to 3 pounds of trash a day. Multiply this by 12 million people, and you get a mountain of garbage that can turn into breeding grounds for rats, flies, and disease.

Pollution Problems Garbage is not the only waste product that builds up as population density increases. Whenever people crowd into cities, **pollution** problems follow. Emissions from factories and cars pollute the air and cause breathing problems for many people. **Sewage** and **waste-water** poison rivers and streams, killing fish and threatening drinking water supplies.

No country seems cleaner than Japan with its daily-swept streets. However, like most other industrial countries, Japan has faced severe pollution problems. One growing problem is **acid rain,** which can poison lakes, kill trees, and corrode human structures.

The Japanese have also had serious water pollution problems. In the past, **toxic chemicals,** such as cadmium and mercury, were dumped into oceans, lakes, and streams. Such chemicals can poison fish and the people and other animals that consume contaminated fish.

One of the most severe pollution problems came to light in the 1950s when people living on Minamata Bay began coming down with a "strange disease." The disease was caused by mercury dumped into the bay by local factories. People who ate fish contaminated with mercury suffered slurred speech, seizures, and blurred vision. Mothers gave birth to babies with twisted limbs. Cats who ate the fish turned from placid pets into screeching monsters. More than a thousand people eventually died from mercury poisoning before Minamata Bay was finally cleaned up.

Long Life Spans

The Japanese enjoy the world's longest life expectancy. A person born in Japan can expect to live to be more than 80 years old.

Long Lives High population density can impact people's health in still other ways. Automobile accidents are more likely to occur on city streets than rural roads. Disease spreads more quickly in crowded cities than in the countryside. Even so, the Japanese enjoy a **life expectancy** that is among the highest in the world. In 2004, the life expectancy at birth for a Japanese person was 81 years.

The Japanese have clearly found ways to overcome the health hazards of crowding. Stand on any street corner in Tokyo and you'll see one of them. People who are sick wear face masks to avoid spreading disease. More important, the Japanese have passed some of the world's strictest environmental laws to clean up the air and water. As a result, the air is safer to breathe, and fish from the sea no longer poison people and their pets.

Garbage, however, remains a problem. In 1972, Tokyo opened a huge trash dump on an island in Tokyo Bay. It filled up in just eight years. Another nearby dump is filling up just as fast. "We are full up," reports a city official. "We can only survive by reducing." In an effort to reduce the daily avalanche of trash, Tokyo has turned to **recycling**. Tokyo residents today recycle everything from cans and bottles to cookie wrappers.

31.7 Beginning to Think Globally

In this chapter, you have seen how population density affects several aspects of life in Japan, including transportation, housing, land use, and health. You learned that despite their crowded cities and pollution problems, the Japanese enjoy long and healthy lives. Japan today enjoys a high life expectancy, in part due to strict environmental regulations.

Japan, however, is a wealthy, industrialized country. It can afford to build tall, earthquake-proof apartment and office buildings that make efficient use of limited city land. It can maintain an efficient public transit system to move people around quickly. It can also fund the costs of cleaning up dirty air and polluted water.

Other densely populated countries are not so fortunate. India, for example, has almost the same population density as Japan. It has more than four times as much arable land and is far richer in **natural resources** such as coal, minerals, and natural gas. Even so, India is a much poorer country. Life expectancy there is just 64 years compared to 81 years in Japan. Think about this contrast as you examine population density around the world in the next section.

Life Expectancy in Japan and the United States

	Japan	United States
Women	85	80
Men	78	75

A Crowded Street in Tokyo
The Japanese in this street scene appear well dressed and well fed. People in other densely populated nations are not so fortunate. In many countries, crowding may add to people's misery.

31.8 Global Connections

How does population density affect the way people live around the world? The map shows how people are spread out across Earth. As you study the map, look for population patterns. One thing you may notice is that people are not evenly distributed around the world. Nine out of 10 people live north of the equator, while about one out of two lives in an urban area. You might also notice that people tend to live in temperate **climate zones** and relatively near coastlines. Why might this be so?

Can a place have too many people?

The answer is yes and no. Consider Bangladesh, for example. This southeastern nation is about three times as densely populated as Japan. Most of its people are poor farmers with a life expectancy of barely 60 years. In contrast, nearby Singapore is almost 20 times as densely populated as Japan. Its people are relatively well-off city dwellers. Life expectancy in Singapore is almost as high as in Japan.

What other factors contribute to the well-being of crowded countries?

Resources and location are both important factors. The Netherlands, for example, is a small, densely populated country in Western Europe. It has no significant mineral or energy resources. But Netherlanders have learned to make the most of their fertile soil and coastal location. They produce high-quality agricultural and industrial products, which they then trade around the world for resources they lack.

How does population density affect a nation?

A high population density alone does not make a nation rich or poor. Nor do natural resources alone. How a people use their resources is as important as what they have.

Population Density Around the World

Arithmetic Population Density

Country	People per Square Mile of Land
Australia	7
Bangladesh	2,734
Colombia	103
Egypt	198
Japan	880
Netherlands	1,247
Nigeria	390
Singapore	16,492
United States	83

Sources: *The World Factbook 2004*, Central Intelligence Agency, and The World Bank Group.

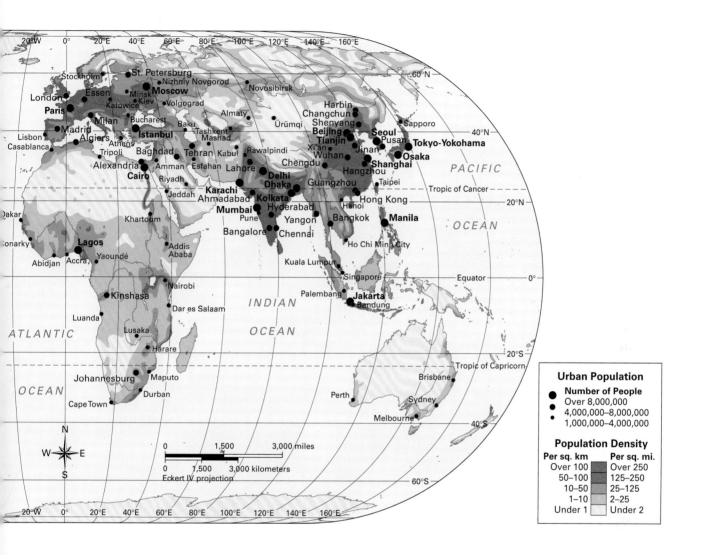

Urban Population

Number of People
- Over 8,000,000
- 4,000,000–8,000,000
- 1,000,000–4,000,000

Population Density

Per sq. km	Per sq. mi.
Over 100	Over 250
50–100	125–250
10–50	25–125
1–10	2–25
Under 1	Under 2

Life Expectancy

Country	Average Life Expectancy (years)
Australia	80
Bangladesh	62
Colombia	71
Egypt	71
Japan	81
Netherlands	79
Nigeria	50
Singapore	82
United States	77

Per Capita Income

Country	Average Income per Person*
Australia	$21,650
Bangladesh	400
Colombia	1,810
Egypt	1,390
Japan	34,510
Netherlands	26,310
Nigeria	320
Singapore	21,230
United States	37,610

*Amounts are in U.S. dollars.

The Global Sneaker: From Asia to Everywhere

32.1 Introduction

We live in a global marketplace, with many of the things that we wear or use or eat every day coming from other countries. Our cell phones might be manufactured in China. Our clothes might be produced in Malaysia, Mexico, or Madagascar. The gas in our cars might have been refined from oil pumped in Saudi Arabia or Venezuela. Americans drink coffee from Colombia and tea grown in Kenya. The grapes we eat in winter may have traveled to us from Chile. The shrimp in a seafood salad might have been raised in Thailand or Vietnam.

Americans buy goods from all over the world because of **globalization,** which means the development of a global, or worldwide, society. In a global society, people, money, information, and goods flow fairly freely across national borders.

It wasn't always like this. Most of the products that your grandparents used when they were growing up were probably made in their own country. However, a boom in world trade has changed all of that. The globalization of the world economy has had an enormous impact on workers, consumers, business, and the environment.

In this chapter, you will look at one common manufactured product that has become globalized: the sneaker. Historically, the sneakers on the feet of most Americans were produced in the United States, but today most sneakers are made in Asia. You will read about the steps that go into the making of a sneaker, and you will learn how the globalization of the sneaker affects people and places around the world.

Essential Question

What is globalization, and how does it affect people and places?

The sneaker is a good example of the growth and impact of globalization. The making of a pair of sneakers involves several steps and various countries. The map shows some of the places that have a role in sneaker production. Keep this map in mind as you try to answer the Essential Question.

Graphic Organizer

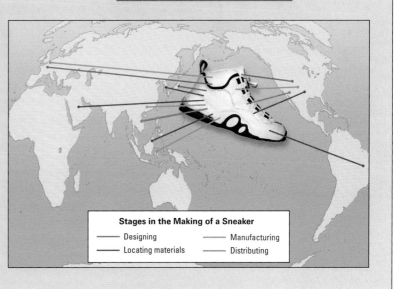

Stages in the Making of a Sneaker

- Designing
- Locating materials
- Manufacturing
- Distributing

◀ Shipping containers stacked on docks in Singapore

32.2 The Geographic Setting

Globalization affects every country in the world, but no **region** has been more involved than Asia. Countries such as China, South Korea, and Japan have played a major role in the global spread of manufacturing and trade. These and other Asian countries continue to be key players in the global economy.

The Growth of Globalization Globalization is the result of a number of factors. Advances in communication and transportation have played a major role. Another important factor is the movement toward **free trade,** the flow of goods and services across national borders with few controls by governments.

Support for free trade has grown over the past 60 years. In 1947, the United States and 22 other countries signed the General Agreement on Tariffs and Trade (GATT). These countries agreed to reduce **tariffs** and other barriers to trade. A tariff is a tax on goods imported from another country. The agreement led to the creation of the World Trade Organization (WTO), which works to reduce trade barriers. By 2005, the WTO had 148 member countries.

Globalization has also been helped by the rise of **multinational corporations,** which are large firms that operate in more than one country. Multinational corporations have become key players within the global economy, producing and selling goods and services throughout the world.

Globalization has brought economic growth to many **developing countries,** resulting in the creation of jobs for millions of people. This economic growth has also increased the **economic interdependence** among countries, as countries rely on one another for resources, technology, and trade.

Trade between China and the United States is a good example of economic interdependence. Factories in China produce a wide variety of goods for export to the United States. When the U.S. economy is booming, Americans have plenty of money to spend on Chinese products. When the economy is not doing so well, Americans spend less on goods. Therefore the jobs of many factory workers in China depend on the economic health of the United States.

What's the Difference?

One of the shoes above was made in the United States. In 2001, however, the last pair of these shoes came off an assembly line in North Carolina. Now they are made in Asia. Look carefully at the labels to tell which is which.

Athletic Shoe Production: Sneaking Away from the U.S. The history of sneaker production shows globalization at work. For years, the sneakers that Americans wore were made in the United States. Over time, however, most companies moved their production to Asia. By doing so, they were able to spend less on labor and materials. This reduction in production costs made it possible for the companies to sell sneakers for lower prices and still make a profit.

Look at your own shoes. The label probably says "Made in China" or another Asian country. This is true even for a famous American sneaker: the Converse Chuck Taylor All Star. This shoe's label once read "Made in U.S.A." But now these shoes, too, are made in Asia.

Behind every sneaker is a complex process that involves design, raw materials, manufacturing, and **distribution**. In this chapter, you will see what is done where and why.

▶ Geoterms

economic interdependence a condition in which countries have strong economic ties and depend on each other for resources, technology, trade, and investment

free trade the flow of goods and services across national borders, with little or no government control

globalization the development of a global, or worldwide, society in which people, money, information, and goods flow fairly freely across national borders

multinational corporation a large company that has operations in more than one country

Locations of a Multinational Corporation

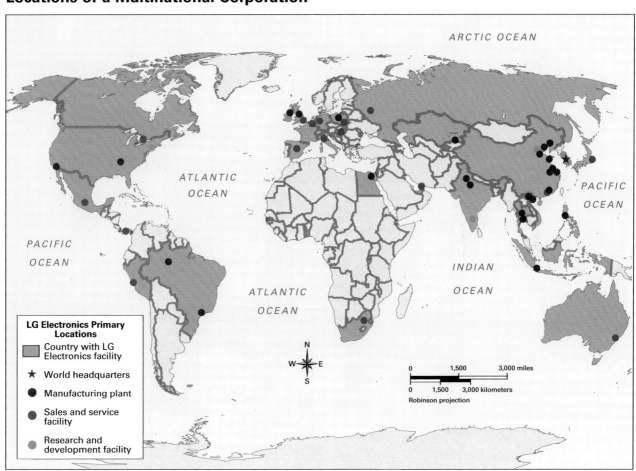

From South Korea to the World

Most multinational corporations are based in Western Europe or the United States. But Asia has its share, too. LG Electronics is a large company based in South Korea. It makes televisions, computers, and other products. It began to expand overseas in the 1970s. The countries shown in color on this map all have LG Electronics facilities today.

Shoes for All Kinds of Feet

Designing shoes for all kinds of feet and activities is a complicated process. Designers get help from scientists who study foot motion and materials. They also talk to athletes. Using their imaginations, they make drawings and models. Sample shoes are then tested in the lab and on the street. If the design works, the shoe goes into production.

New Looks Begin Here

This map shows where most sneakers are designed. Much of this work takes place in the United States. Designers often work closely with the sports stars who will wear and promote the shoes that they design.

32.3 Designing a Global Sneaker

In Britain, they are called trainers. In Australia, they're known as sand shoes. Their most common name, though, is sneakers. This name came from an American who noticed how quietly people walked when they wore them. Until the late 1960s, sneakers were relatively simple shoes. Today they are far from simple.

Design Then: A Simple Sports Shoe Sneakers were first made during the mid-1800s. They were used for sports like tennis, croquet, and running. Later they became popular for basketball.

For the next one hundred years, the designs of sneakers changed very little. The upper part of the shoe was fashioned from cotton canvas, and the sole was made of rubber. Buyers could choose from only a few brands and styles. There were high tops or low cuts, usually available only in black or white. Most consumers thought of sneakers only as athletic shoes.

In the 1950s, though, people began to change their view of sneakers. The shoes were not just for sports any more. They became casual shoes for everyday use. Men, women, and children began wearing them as fashion items.

Design Now: A Complex Fashion Statement Today's sneakers are designed for a wide variety of purposes. Athletes still wear them, of course, but so does just about everyone else. There are sneakers for all types of activities, from running and rock climbing to playing tennis or just walking around.

Sneaker companies have come up with innovative new designs and materials for their shoes, resulting in improvements in both performance and comfort. Today companies compete with each other to design the "latest and greatest" sneaker.

New designs and colors have also given sneakers more fashion appeal. To increase that appeal, athletic shoe companies often hire athletes and musicians to promote their sneakers as "cool." They know that many people will pay more to wear the articles of clothing that their favorite stars are wearing.

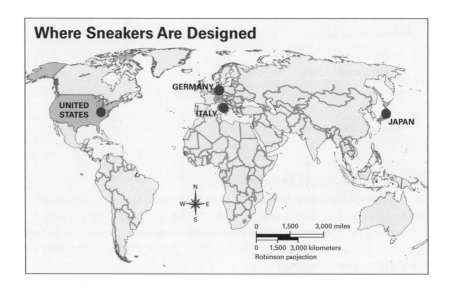

Where Sneakers Are Designed

32.4 Locating Global Sneaker Materials

Look at the soles of your sneakers. They're made of rubber. But sneakers are made of many other materials, too. Some of these materials are found in only a few places in the world. All of the materials come together at factories to create a shoe with three main parts: the upper, the midsole, and the outer sole.

The Complex Upper: Mesh Fabric, Leather, and More The upper is the top part of a sneaker. Some uppers are made of natural materials, such as cotton or leather. The leather comes from the hides of cattle that are raised in Texas, Venezuela, and other livestock centers. The cowhides are usually shipped to South Korea, where they are made ready for use in manufacturing.

Other uppers are made of synthetic, or human-made, materials such as nylon. Nylon fabric is light and dries easily.

The Squishy Midsole: Foam Padding and Air Bags The midsole is the part of the shoe that cushions the bottom of your foot. It is made of plastic and foam padding, which are materials that are produced from oil found in Saudi Arabia and other oil-rich countries.

The foam used in many sneakers may be produced in South Korean factories. Chemicals are poured into molds and then baked. In the process, these chemicals form millions of tiny gas bubbles that give the foam a cushiony feel. Some midsoles also contain small "air bags" filled with pressurized gas.

The Tough Outer Sole: Synthetic and Natural Rubber Treads The tread, or sole, of a sneaker needs to be tough but also flexible enough to put a spring in your step. All types of sneakers used to be manufactured with natural rubber soles. The rubber came from the sap of rubber trees that are grown in such tropical countries as Brazil, Indonesia, Thailand, and Malaysia.

Today most soles are formed from synthetic rubber, which is made from coal and oil. Much of the synthetic rubber used in sneaker production comes from factories on the island of Taiwan.

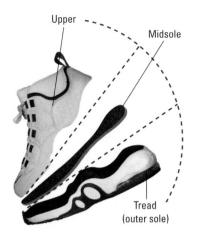

Inside the Sneaker
The three main parts of a sneaker are the upper, the midsole, and the tread. Many of the materials in each part are synthetic. They are made from oil and coal.

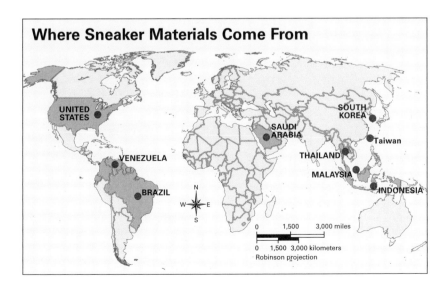

Where Sneaker Materials Come From

Global Sources
The materials used to make sneakers come from countries around the world. This map shows some of the sources of those materials. Some places supply raw materials, such as leather and oil. Others supply manufactured parts, like nylon and foam padding.

32.5 Manufacturing the Global Sneaker

By now you know that sneakers are not simple shoes. A lot of labor goes into creating their designs and materials. But that's not all. Manufacturing sneakers is also a complex job. A single sneaker may have more than 50 pieces. It can require the work of 120 people to put together one pair of shoes.

What Happened to "Made in U.S.A."? Most sneakers used to be made in the countries where they were sold. In the 1960s, simple canvas and rubber sneakers were still being produced in the United States, Britain, and Germany.

In the 1970s, however, sneakers became more complicated. The number of styles increased, and the designs became more complex. As a result, more labor was needed to assemble these shoes, and production costs began to rise. Eventually it became too expensive to make shoes in high-wage countries like the United States.

Production Moves to Low-Wage Countries Faced with high costs, sneaker companies began to move production offshore, or to other countries. At first, sneaker production moved mainly to South Korea, which offered a number of advantages. This country had a large pool of low-wage workers, and it had factories that could be used to make shoes. In addition, South Korea had ports for shipping raw materials into the country and finished sneakers out.

Over time, however, wages in South Korea rose. As a result, manufacturing shoes there became less profitable. In the 1990s, production shifted again, this time to China, Indonesia, and Vietnam. All three of these countries offered the same advantages that were once found in South Korea.

In fact, many of the sneaker factories in these countries were set up and run by South Korean shoe companies. Rising labor costs at home had led the South Korean companies to move their production offshore. This was just what American and European companies had done 20 years earlier—and for the same reasons.

South Korean Production

In the 1980s, South Korean workers made many of the world's sneakers. They worked for low wages and were very productive. However, wages went up over time. South Korean companies moved production to countries where pay was still low. Now they "offshore" their work the same way American companies do.

Moving Offshore

This map shows how sneaker production has moved over time. In the 1970s, it went from the United States and Europe to South Korea, Taiwan, and Japan. By the 1990s, production shifted to China and Southeast Asia. Lower labor costs have been the reason for these moves. Sneaker production may move again, perhaps to low-wage Africa.

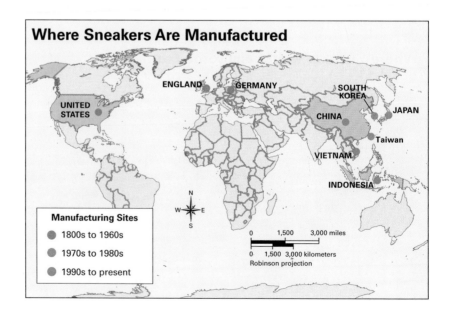

Where Sneakers Are Manufactured

Manufacturing Sites
- 1800s to 1960s
- 1970s to 1980s
- 1990s to present

0   1,500   3,000 miles
0 1,500 3,000 kilometers
Robinson projection

A Container Ship
Sneakers travel from Asia in shipping containers. These containers are a very efficient way to move goods. They can be transferred easily from ships to trains to trucks. By lowering the cost of shipping, containers have become a key factor in globalization.

32.6 Distributing the Global Sneaker

In 1990, a ship carrying sneakers from South Korea to the United States was hit by a fierce storm. Eighty thousand pairs of shoes spilled into the Pacific Ocean. A year later, the shoes were still washing up on American shores. Normally, though, sneakers have a smoother journey from Asia. Companies use several methods of transportation to move their shoes from the factory to the store.

Across the Globe by Ship Typically, sneakers are transported by container ship from Asia. This is the least expensive way to move goods over such long distances.

The trip to the United States takes about two weeks. The sneakers make this journey in freight containers, which are large, weatherproof steel boxes that are easy to stack on the deck of a ship. Huge container ships can accommodate 8,000 of these boxes.

Across the Country by Train and Truck When a ship arrives on the west coast of the United States, the containers are unloaded onto trains or trucks. In some ports, train tracks run right up to the docks to make unloading easier.

Train or truck transport across the United States can take a week or longer. Most of the sneakers end up in Memphis, Tennessee, which is a major distribution center where rail lines and highways meet. The sneakers are stored in warehouses in Memphis and then delivered by truck to retail stores around the country. A truck leaving Memphis in the morning can reach approximately 75 percent of the nation's population by the following day.

From the Store to Your Home Sneakers are distributed to approximately 18,000 stores throughout the United States. You probably shop at some of them. By the time a pair of sneakers makes the trek from an Asian factory to your home, it may have traveled more than 7,000 miles.

In 2000, Americans bought about 405 million pairs of sneakers. That is approximately one and a half pairs for every man, woman, and child in the United States. Sneaker sales totaled $15 billion—and that amount doesn't count sales in the rest of the world. Obviously, the global sneaker is a booming business.

Travel Time Around the World, 1500–2000

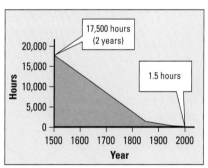

Our Shrinking World
This graph shows the time it took to travel around the world at different points in history. Around 1500, it took a sailing ship two, and sometimes three, years to circle the globe. Jet planes shrank that time to two days. A space shuttle can do it in less than two hours. As travel time has decreased, our world has seemed to shrink.

32.7 Beginning to Think Globally

In this chapter, you read about globalization and the making of the global sneaker. You learned that free trade plays a major role in the global economy. You read how shoe companies have been transformed into multinational corporations. In addition, you have seen how the production of global sneakers has increased the economic interdependence among several countries.

Globalization is changing the world. These changes may be either good or bad, depending on your point of view.

The Case for Globalization Globalization has benefits for both rich and poor countries. When companies in wealthy countries set up factories in poor countries, they create new jobs. The workers who fill these jobs often improve their standard of living, and the money they earn helps bring economic growth to their countries.

Companies that move production offshore do so to keep their costs low. Lower production costs help them keep their prices low as well. Low prices benefit consumers in both rich and poor countries. Many working people today can buy products that were once considered luxuries only the rich could afford.

Globalization has other benefits. Countries that trade with one another want to maintain good relations. As a result, they may be less likely to go to war against each other. In this way, economic interdependence may contribute to creating a more peaceful world.

A global society also brings the world's people together in ways that were never before possible. It gives us a glimpse into how people live and work in other lands. Furthermore, it allows us to share and exchange ideas, technology, music, and art across vast distances. As we learn more about one another, we can grow to understand and respect other ways of life.

Closed Factories, Lost Jobs

Globalization has brought new factories and jobs to developing countries. But as production has moved overseas, some U.S. factories have closed their doors. Factory closings are hard on workers who lose their jobs. Towns suffer as well from the loss of jobs and business.

The Case Against Globalization
Increased global trade can bring harm as well as good. Some developing countries lack laws to protect the environment. Factories that are set up in such countries often dump **toxic waste** into rivers and streams and release deadly fumes into the air. Such polluting practices would be illegal in **developed countries**.

Many poor countries also lack worker protection laws. Without such laws, factories can require workers to work long hours for low wages. For example, a sneaker factory worker in a developing country in Asia might earn just $2 for a 12-hour workday. A factory might even hire children, who are paid even less. Factories that abuse workers are called *sweatshops*. Working conditions in sweatshops are often unsafe or unhealthy.

Globalization can be harmful to workers in developed countries as well. When companies send work offshore, they often close factories at home. Many Americans have lost their jobs because of factory closings. Towns and cities may also suffer when unemployed residents move to other places to find work.

Finally, globalization can upset traditional ways of life. When foreign fast-food chains move into a country, they may crowd out traditional food sellers. A similar problem can occur when a country is flooded with foreign movies, television shows, and music. Traditional arts may be lost. Many people may welcome the arrival of global culture, but they may also lose traditions that have made their way of life unique or special.

The Future of Globalization People often disagree about the impact of globalization. Some observers think that its benefits outweigh its drawbacks. Other people believe that it is doing more harm than good. In any case, one thing seems certain: globalization is here to stay. And it is likely to increase.

One reason for the increase in globalization is that many developing countries see it as a path out of poverty. These poor countries have observed how countries like South Korea and Singapore have prospered from global trade. Both countries welcomed foreign companies, and both saw their economies grow rapidly as a result. Now other countries want to follow their example.

Another reason for the increase in globalization is that money now moves freely around the world. Money coming into a country from investors in another country is called **foreign investment**. Every year, billions of dollars of foreign investment move around the world. This money is used to build new factories or to invest in businesses. Think about this as you examine the map and graphs of foreign investment in the next section.

Fast Food in the Philippines
Globalization sometimes kills off local businesses. But some businesses survive by copying foreign ideas. This fast-food restaurant in the Philippines looks like an American chain. But it's owned by a local company. It now competes successfully with large fast-food chains.

32.8 Global Connections

Foreign investment is an important factor in globalization. It is the main way that multinational corporations expand offshore. The line and circle graphs show changes in foreign investment between 1914 and 1998. The map shows foreign investment flowing to the developing world in 2002.

How has foreign investment changed since 1914? Foreign investment has gone up since 1914. Most of this increase came in the years following 1960. This was a period of rapid growth throughout the global economy. The first circle graph shows that in 1914, most of the foreign investment went to countries in Latin America and Asia. The second graph shows that by 1998, the percentages going to these regions had decreased. Even so, the total dollar amount was much greater in 1998 than in 1914.

Which developing country attracted the most investment money in 2002? How might this investment have affected life there? China received more foreign investment than any other developing country in 2002. Most of this money was used to start new businesses in **urban** areas. These businesses attracted workers from **rural** areas. As a result, China is growing more urban year by year.

Which parts of the world attracted the least investment money? How might this affect the people living there? Most countries in Africa, Southwest Asia, and Central Asia attracted little investment. As a result, their economies have grown slowly or not at all. Most of their people still depend on agriculture to make a living. Other job opportunities are frequently quite limited.

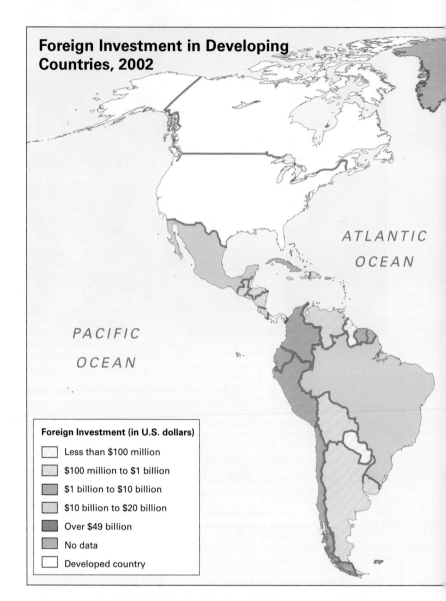

Foreign Investment in Developing Countries, 2002

Foreign Investment (in U.S. dollars)

- Less than $100 million
- $100 million to $1 billion
- $1 billion to $10 billion
- $10 billion to $20 billion
- Over $49 billion
- No data
- Developed country

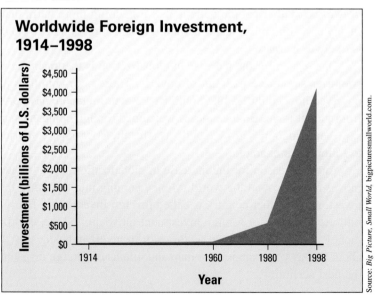

Worldwide Foreign Investment, 1914–1998

Source: *Big Picture, Small World.* bigpicturesmallworld.com.

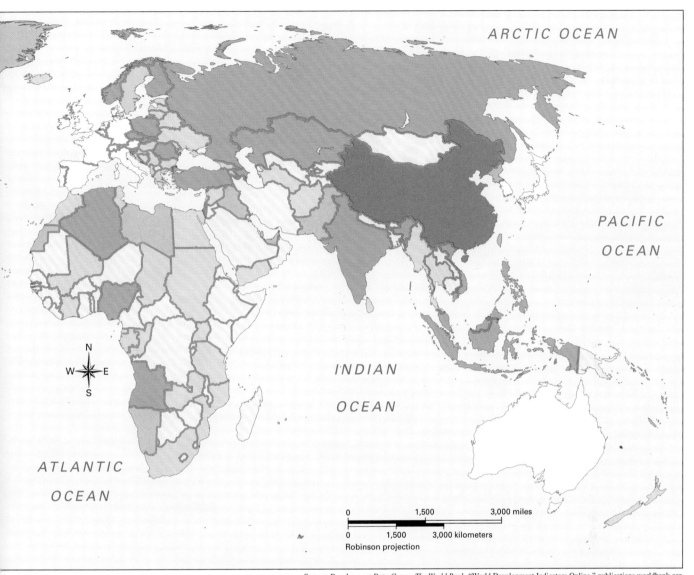

Source: *Development Data Group, The World Bank,* "World Development Indicators Online," publications.worldbank.org.

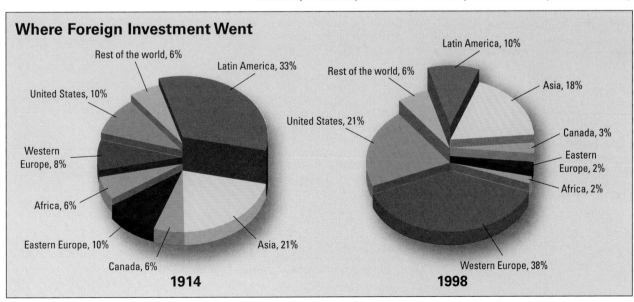

Where Foreign Investment Went

Rest of the world, 6%

Latin America, 33%

United States, 10%

Western Europe, 8%

Africa, 6%

Eastern Europe, 10%

Canada, 6%

Asia, 21%

1914

Latin America, 10%

Rest of the world, 6%

United States, 21%

Asia, 18%

Canada, 3%

Eastern Europe, 2%

Africa, 2%

Western Europe, 38%

1998

UNIT 8 Oceania and Antarctica

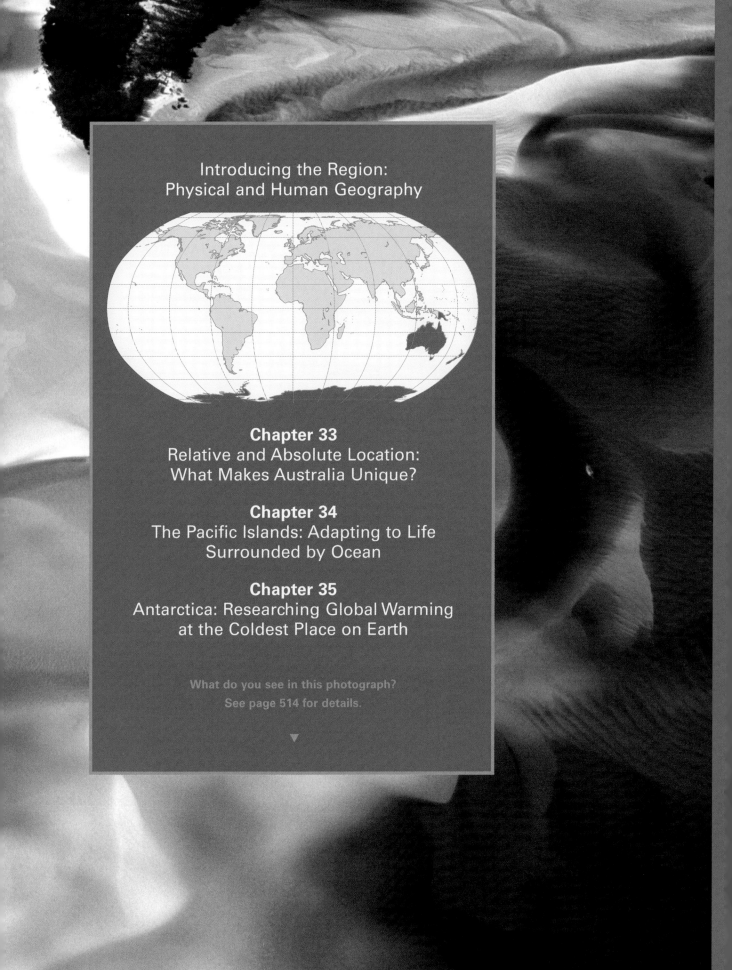

Introducing the Region:
Physical and Human Geography

Chapter 33
Relative and Absolute Location:
What Makes Australia Unique?

Chapter 34
The Pacific Islands: Adapting to Life
Surrounded by Ocean

Chapter 35
Antarctica: Researching Global Warming
at the Coldest Place on Earth

What do you see in this photograph?
See page 514 for details.

▼

Oceania is a vast **region** in the South Pacific Ocean. It includes the continent of Australia and the large islands of New Zealand and Papua New Guinea. There are thousands of smaller islands as well. They are scattered across hundreds of square miles of ocean. The Pacific Islands form three major groups called Melanesia, Micronesia, and Polynesia.

The continent of Antarctica lies to the south of Oceania. On some world maps, you see Antarctica as a narrow strip of land along the bottom. In fact, Antarctica is the fifth largest continent in the world. Near the center of this frozen **landmass** is the South Pole. The stormy waters of the Pacific and Indian oceans isolate Antarctica from the other lands in this region.

Physical Features of Antarctica

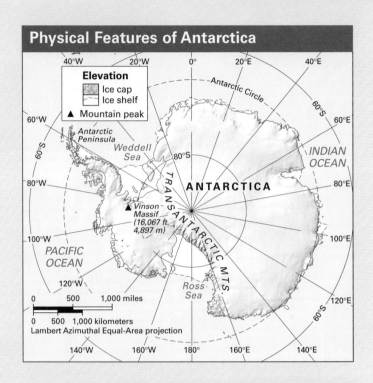

Physical Features of Oceania

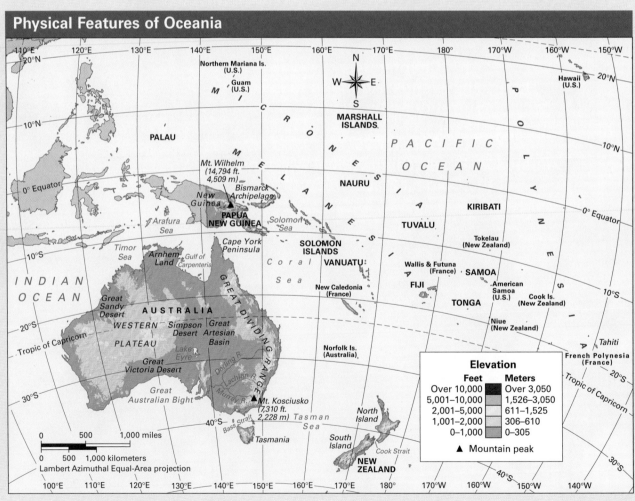

Physical Features

The landmasses in this region include both continents and islands. An island is a body of land surrounded by water. But most continents are also surrounded by water. What is the difference between an island and a continent? To a geographer, the main difference is size. Islands tend to be small, and continents are large. Australia is the smallest continent. But it is still over three times as large as Greenland, the largest island on Earth.

No one knows the exact number of islands in Oceania. Geographers estimate that between 20,000 and 30,000 islands dot this region. Some of them are large, such as the North and South Islands of New Zealand. Other islands are tiny specks in the sea.

Oceania

Australia is the largest landmass in Oceania. Most of the country is low-lying and very flat. One major mountain range, Great Dividing Range, runs along the eastern edge. The interior of Australia, called the *outback,* is a series of low **plateaus** and plains. The Western Plateau covers a great part of the continent.

Three **deserts** ring the Western Plateau. The Simpson Desert is famous for its red sand dunes. Row upon row of dunes, as much as 200 miles long, ripple across the land. The Great Victoria and Great Sandy deserts also have hills of red sand.

The rest of Oceania consists entirely of islands. The cluster north and east of Australia is called Melanesia. This name means

No one lives on this Polynesian island chain, which lies off the coast of New Zealand's North Island.

"black islands." It refers to the dark skin of the people who first settled there. The islands of Melanesia lie south of the equator.

North of Melanesia are the more than 2,000 islands of Micronesia. This name means "tiny islands." Most of the islands of Micronesia are low-lying coral islands. They are scattered on both sides of the equator.

The third island area, Polynesia, is the largest of the three. This name means "many islands." Polynesia includes New Zealand, Tahiti, Samoa, and Hawaii, as well as islands too small to map. The islands of Polynesia are separated by hundreds of miles of sea.

Antarctica

Most of Antarctica is covered by ice sheets. This ice ranges from one to three miles deep. Beneath all this ice, Antarctica has mountains and valleys like other continents.

The Transantarctic Mountains wind across the continent. They divide it into East and West Antarctica. The South Pole lies in East Antarctica. The Antarctic Peninsula juts out from West Antarctica like a tail. To the east of this **peninsula** is the Weddell Sea.

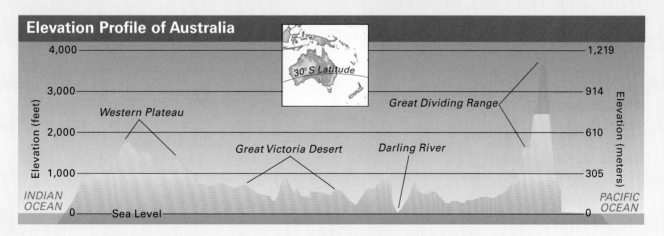

Elevation Profile of Australia

30° S Latitude

Elevation (feet)		Elevation (meters)
4,000		1,219
3,000	Great Dividing Range	914
2,000	Western Plateau	610
1,000	Great Victoria Desert — Darling River	305
0 Sea Level		0

INDIAN OCEAN

PACIFIC OCEAN

Climate

This geographic region covers a large part of Earth. It stretches from north of the equator all the way to the South Pole. Because there are such differences in latitude, every **climate zone** is represented.

These contrasts in **climate** result in part from the amount of sunlight each climate zone receives year round. The solar energy at the equator is the strongest. It also varies little throughout the seasons. The solar energy at the poles is the weakest. In Antarctica, the sun disappears completely in winter.

Antarctica has an **ice cap** climate zone. It is very cold all year. The snow and ice are permanent. In contrast, some places nearer the equator have a **tropical wet** climate. It is hot and rainy all year round.

Oceania

Australia has been called a "desert continent with green edges." Its center has an **arid** and **semiarid** climate.

Australia's coastal areas are not so dry. The northern coast has a **tropical wet and dry** climate. It is hot all year with rainy and dry seasons. Part of the eastern coast has a **humid subtropical** climate. Hot, rainy summers follow mild winters with some rain.

Farther south, the eastern coast has a **marine west coast** climate. Summers are warm, winters are cold, and there is rainfall year-round. Australia's southern coast has a **Mediterranean** climate. It is warm all year with dry summers and short, rainy winters.

New Zealand has a mild, marine west coast climate. Most of the other islands of Polynesia, Melanesia, and Micronesia have a tropical wet climate.

But opposite sides of some islands can have different weather. In the South Pacific, the **trade winds** near the equator blow from east to west. So when the wind hits an island's east, or **windward**, side, it stirs up rough surf near the shore.

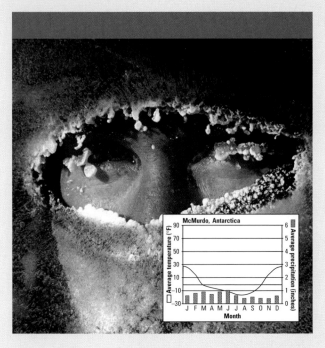

Scientists learn to live with the cold at McMurdo, a research station on Antarctica run by the United States. Which months would be the most comfortable there?

If there are **highlands** on an island, the air will rise as the wind moves up the windward slope. As air rises, it cools. The cooler air drops any moisture it might be carrying, so this side of the island gets rain.

By the time the wind reaches the **downwind,** or western, slope of the island, it has lost both moisture and strength. As a result, the downwind side of an island is usually drier than the windward side. The water on the downwind coast is calmer as well.

Antarctica

Antarctica is the coldest place on Earth. The lowest temperature ever recorded, −129°F, was at Vostok Station in Antarctica in 1983. But even this freezing ice cap climate has some variety. It is drier and colder on the inland plateau. On the coastline, there are slightly warmer, wetter conditions. At McMurdo Station, summer temperatures may rise above freezing, to 40°F or even 50°F.

Vegetation

The many climate zones in this region result in a great variety of plants. Australia alone has eight different vegetation areas. One such area, **chaparral**, is found in southern Australia.

Chaparral is a major plant community in many parts of the world. It is found on the west coast of the United States and around the Mediterranean Sea.

Areas with chaparral have cool, wet winters and hot, dry summers. The most common plants are shrubs and small trees. Most have small, leathery leaves that hold in moisture. Some chaparral plants have shallow roots that spread out to catch water as rain falls. Others send roots deep into the ground to search for **groundwater**.

Because summers are so hot and dry, fires are common in chaparral zones. But chaparral plants are adapted to fire. Some plants resist fires or grow back quickly after a blaze. Fires clear the ground, making new growth possible. The seeds of some chaparral plants will sprout only after being heated in fire.

Fires are so common in the chaparral that the driest months in Australia are called "bushfire season."

Oceania

Desert and **desert scrub** cover the dry, central part of Australia. Most of northern Australia is covered in **tropical grassland**. The grasses and scattered trees are adapted to the tropical wet and dry climate. **Broadleaf evergreen forest** grows on Australia's northeastern coast. The southeastern coast is blanketed by **mixed forests**. In the mountains of southeastern Australia, a small area of **highlands** vegetation is found.

The islands of Melanesia, Micronesia, and Polynesia mostly have broadleaf evergreen forests. New Zealand is an exception. It lies farther south in a milder area. New Zealand's North Island is covered in mixed forests. The South Island has a mix of **temperate grassland,** highlands, and mixed forests.

Antarctica

Few plants can survive in Antarctica's cold climate. Some mosses grow in rocky areas of the coast. Two kinds of flowering plants grow on the Antarctic Peninsula. Lichens grow on the coast and in inland valleys.

Tropical rainforests cover many islands in the South Pacific. Ferns and other broadleaf evergreen plants surround this waterfall on the Samoa Islands.

Oceania and Antarctica **471**

Oceania may not look much like the rest of the world. Still, it has 14 independent countries. The smallest country is Nauru. This island of less than nine square miles has a population of more than 10,000. Australia is the largest country, in both area and population. It is home to more than 20 million people.

Antarctica has no permanent population. It is not a nation. Many countries have agreed to share this unusual continent for scientific research. The population of visitors ranges from about 4,000 in the summer to 1,000 in the winter.

The countries of Oceania are loosely linked by their location in the vast Pacific. Still, great distances separate them. For most of their history, the peoples of this region lived in isolated groups and developed their own cultures.

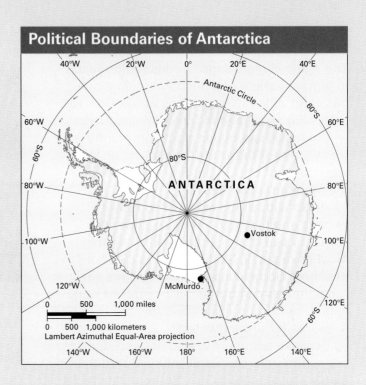

Political Boundaries of Antarctica

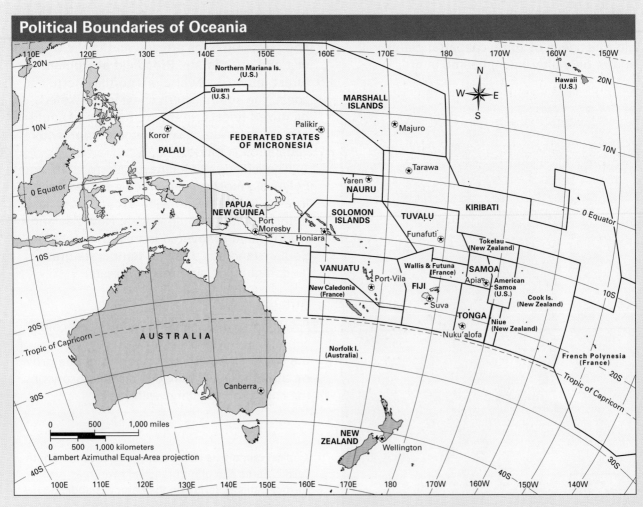

Political Boundaries of Oceania

History

For thousands of years, the first inhabitants of Oceania were sheltered from the rest of the world. Then European explorers came to these islands. Their arrival brought major changes to Oceania.

Early Times

Historians think that Oceania's first people came from Southeast Asia thousands of years ago. They followed land bridges from place to place when possible. They traveled by water, too, using rafts and canoes. Polynesia was the last of the island groups to be settled. The Polynesian islands are farther apart and could be reached only by long voyages.

As people settled on the islands, they built villages and a way of life that centered on the sea. Most people lived in family groups known as tribes. They ate fish and tropical fruits such as coconuts. They also grew root crops such as yams and taro.

The first people to live in Australia are called Aborigines. They were nomads who traveled in bands. They hunted and gathered their food. Aborigines lived in Australia for at least 50,000 years before Europeans came.

The Colonial Period

In the 1500s, Europeans began to explore the region. The first regular visitors to the region were whalers. People in Europe and the Americas burned whale oil in their lamps in the 1800s. Whalers came to Oceania in search of these giant sea mammals.

In time, European colonists began to settle in the region. At first, they traded with the people who lived there. Later, they established large farms and ranches. The colonists raised fruits, sugarcane, and livestock. By 1900, most South Pacific islands were colonies of European countries.

Australia has a different history from the rest of the region. In 1788, Great Britain turned Australia into a prison colony. People convicted of crimes were shipped to Australia to serve their prison terms. This practice ended by 1868. Gold was discovered in Australia in 1851. This news brought many new settlers to the colony.

The coming of Europeans was a disaster for most of the region's **indigenous peoples**. Often they lost most of their land. Many died of sickness brought by the Europeans. Some died fighting the Europeans over control of their homelands.

The Modern Era

The 1900s brought independence to much of Oceania. Australia became independent in 1901. New Zealand followed in 1907.

Since the 1960s, other South Pacific island groups have gained their freedom as well. Samoa was the first, in 1962. Fiji and Tonga followed in 1970. Palau, the newest country in the region, gained its independence in 1994.

The countries of Oceania are working to make life better for their people. In 1971, they formed the South Pacific Forum. It encourages trade and friendship among the countries of the region.

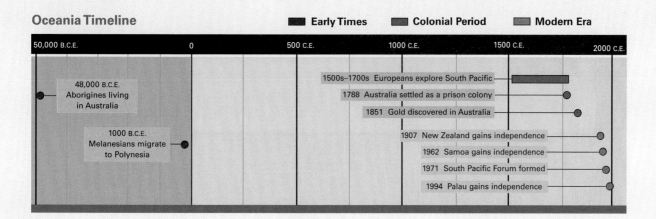

Oceania Timeline   ■ Early Times   ■ Colonial Period   ■ Modern Era

50,000 B.C.E. — 0 — 500 C.E. — 1000 C.E. — 1500 C.E. — 2000 C.E.

48,000 B.C.E. Aborigines living in Australia

1000 B.C.E. Melanesians migrate to Polynesia

1500s–1700s Europeans explore South Pacific

1788 Australia settled as a prison colony

1851 Gold discovered in Australia

1907 New Zealand gains independence

1962 Samoa gains independence

1971 South Pacific Forum formed

1994 Palau gains independence

Population

Oceania and Antarctica is the most thinly settled region in the world. It has less than one percent of the world's population. This small population is growing slowly. No one really lives in Antarctica. But more people visit every year as researchers and tourists.

Seven out of 10 people in Oceania live in **urban** areas. This number varies from place to place. In Australia and New Zealand, close to 9 out of 10 people live in cities. In Polynesia and Melanesia, less than half of the people live in urban areas.

Four out of five people in Oceania are Christians. Two thirds of these Christians belong to Protestant churches. One third are Roman Catholics. The next three largest religious groups are Muslims, Hindus, and Buddhists. A small part of the population still follows traditional religions of the native groups. One out of 10 people in this region practices no religion at all.

Oceania: Major Religions

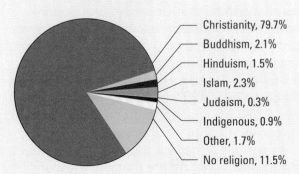

- Christianity, 79.7%
- Buddhism, 2.1%
- Hinduism, 1.5%
- Islam, 2.3%
- Judaism, 0.3%
- Indigenous, 0.9%
- Other, 1.7%
- No religion, 11.5%

Oceania: Urban and Rural Population, 2000

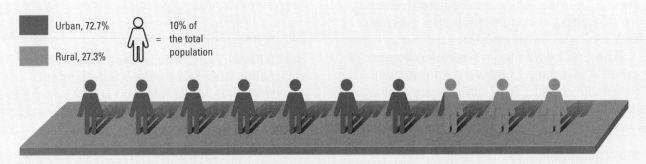

- Urban, 72.7%
- Rural, 27.3%
- = 10% of the total population

Oceania: Population Growth, 1950–2050

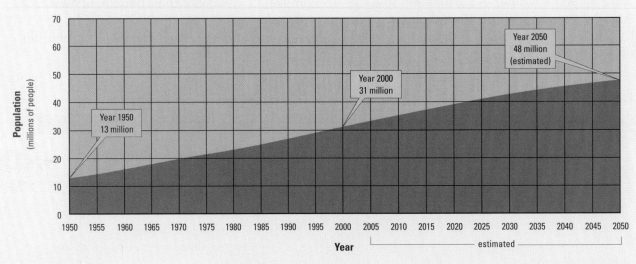

Year 1950 13 million

Year 2000 31 million

Year 2050 48 million (estimated)

Population (millions of people)

Year — estimated

Sources: *Population Division of the Department of Economic and Social Affairs of the United Nations Secretariat,* "World Population Prospects: The 2004 Revision" and "World Urbanization Prospects: The 2003 Revision," esa.un.org/unpp. "Religion," *Encyclopædia Britannica,* 2005, Encyclopædia Britannica Premium Service, www.britannica.com.

Economic Activity

Oceania is rich in minerals and energy resources. Its waters are full of fish. In areas with more land, livestock raising has become an important **economic activity**.

European settlers brought sheep and cattle with them to Oceania. These animals adapted well to conditions in Australia and New Zealand. Today there are 12 sheep for every person living in New Zealand. Wool from New Zealand sheep is used to make carpets, blankets, and fine yarn for knitting. Cattle in Australia provide beef and dairy products, much of which is sold to Asia.

Resources

Precious metals are a key resource for this region. Australia is one of the leading producers of diamonds in the world. Gold, silver, and copper are also mined there. Papua New Guinea also has gold mines.

Fossil fuels are found in many places in this region. Australia has huge resources of oil, coal, and natural gas. But these deposits are far from settlements. It is expensive to get to them. New Zealand and Papua New Guinea have **natural gas** and oil deposits. Both Australia and New Zealand use **hydroelectric power** as a source of energy.

Sheep ranches in Australia and New Zealand produce large amounts of wool. Woolen mills like this one turn that wool into yarn for cloth, sweaters, and carpets.

Land Use

Subsistence farming is common in the Pacific Islands. The biggest **cash crop** is copra, which is dried coconut meat.

Some **commercial farming** takes place on the eastern and southern coasts of Australia. But much of Australia's dry land is used for livestock raising. In New Zealand, half the land is used for farming and livestock raising. **Forestry** thrives in the islands' wooded areas.

Many people depend on **commercial fishing** across this large region. Boats from many countries fish in the waters of the South Pacific.

Trade and manufacturing are centered in the cities of this region. Factories in Australia produce a wide range of goods, including cars, medicines, and electrical appliances.

Processed foods are New Zealand's most valuable manufactured goods. Food processing plants turn milk into butter and cheese. Meat processing plants freeze lamb and beef for export around the world.

Workers shell coconuts at a copra factory in Tonga. The economy of many small South Pacific islands is dependent on copra.

Relative and Absolute Location: What Makes Australia Unique?

33.1 Introduction

Try to picture how Australia must have looked to European explorers when they first arrived on that continent more than 200 years ago. It probably seemed a very odd place. Winter came in July, and summer heat peaked in January. Animals were hopping around, carrying their young in pouches. The land was generally flat and very dry. Even the patterns of the stars in the night sky looked strange.

As you have read, the **absolute location** of a place describes its exact position on Earth. Canberra, the capital of Australia, is located at 35°S latitude and 149°E longitude. The letters S and E refer to **hemispheres**. The latitude reveals to us that the city of Canberra is in the Southern Hemisphere. This location explains why the seasons in Australia are the opposite of those in the United States. The longitude tells us that Canberra is in the Eastern Hemisphere, which means that it is on the opposite side of the world from the United States.

In contrast, the **relative location** of a place describes where it is in relation to other places. Relative location can affect a country's history and way of life in unexpected ways. Australia's nearest neighbors are South Pacific islands, but its language and culture came from quite far away: Great Britain.

In this chapter, you will learn how Australia's location has shaped life there. You will also explore how location has helped make Australia such an interesting place to live and to visit.

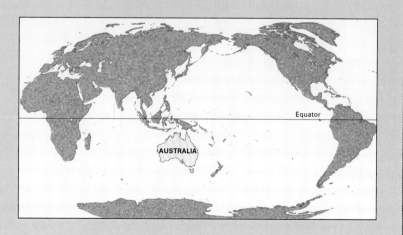

Essential Question

How does a country's location shape life within its borders?

This map puts Australia at the center of the world. It is colored yellow to make it stand out. Notice where Australia is relative to the equator. Also notice how far it is from the other continents. Keep this map in mind as you try to answer the Essential Question.

Graphic Organizer

Equator

AUSTRALIA

◀ The West MacDonald Ranges in the arid center of Australia

Climate Zones of Australia

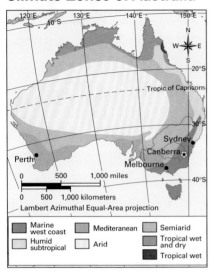

Australia's Seven Climates

Australia has a mix of climate, from tropical to arid. Rain falls mainly near the coast. Most of Australia's interior is a desert.

Rainfall on Six Continents

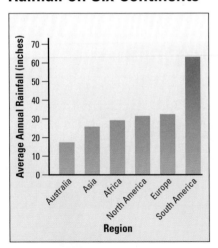

An Arid Continent

Australia is the most arid of the inhabited continents. Droughts are common. So are wildfires during the dry summer months.

33.2 The Geographic Setting

Australia is the only country that is also a continent. It is set off from the rest of the world by the vast Pacific and Indian oceans. Australia gets its name from the Latin word *australis,* which means "southern." Australians also call their country "Down Under" because on maps it lies "under" the equator.

Australia is not quite as large as the United States. Much of it is **desert,** and only the continent of Antarctica is more **arid**. It also has one of the most diverse collections of **flora** and **fauna** in the world. Scientists trace the origins of these unusual plants and animals to Australia's formation as a continent.

How Australia Drifted "Down Under" Scientists hypothesize that Earth did not always have seven continents. About 200 million years ago, all of the land on Earth was joined together in one huge **supercontinent**. Over time, this enormous **landmass** broke apart into a number of **tectonic plates,** which eventually formed the continents we know today. Australia reached its present location after drifting northward for many millions of years.

This **continental drift theory** is based on the theories of a German geographer named Alfred Wegener. He called his supercontinent Pangaea, which is a Greek word that means "all lands." Geographers tell us that the continents are still drifting today, with their average rate of movement being less than an inch a year.

Australia's Biodiversity: From Koalas to Kookaburras One of the first Europeans to study Australia's unusual flora and fauna was a botanist named Joseph Banks. A botanist is a scientist who studies plants. Banks was surprised to find species, or types, of flora and fauna that he had never seen before. One was the small, furry koala, and another was the kookaburra, a bird with a loud laughing call.

The plants and animals that Banks found so surprising are Australia's **native species,** or species that are naturally found in an area. About 80 percent of the continent's plant and animal species are found nowhere else on Earth. This is because Australia broke away from other landmasses about 50 million years ago and slowly, over millions of years, drifted to its present location.

During that extremely long period of time, the plants and animals in Australia developed in isolation. And, until modern times, few species have arrived or have been brought from other continents to contribute to Australia's **biodiversity**.

In the 1800s, Australia became a colony of Great Britain. The colonists brought animals and plants from their homelands to Australia. These introduced plants and animals are called **exotic species**. Many of the imported species had few or no natural enemies in Australia, so their populations quickly multiplied.

In time, exotic species of animals began to compete with native species for food and territory. The result has been a growing number of endangered and threatened species. **Endangered species** are in immediate danger of dying out. **Threatened species** may become endangered if not protected.

▶ Geoterms

continental drift theory the idea that continents are slowly drifting as the tectonic plates that they sit on move. This idea comes from Alfred Wegener, who proposed that Earth once had one giant supercontinent. This supercontinent broke apart into plates that have slowly drifted to their current locations.

endangered species animals or plants that are in danger of dying out in the immediate future

exotic species animals or plants that are brought into an area from somewhere else

native species animals or plants that occur naturally in an area

threatened species animals or plants that are likely to become endangered if not protected

Continental Drift

These maps show how Earth's continents may have moved over time. Notice the east coast of South America. It fits like a giant puzzle piece into the west coast of Africa. According to continental drift theory, both were once part of the same giant landmass. Australia was once joined to Antarctica. It drifted off on its own about 50 million years ago.

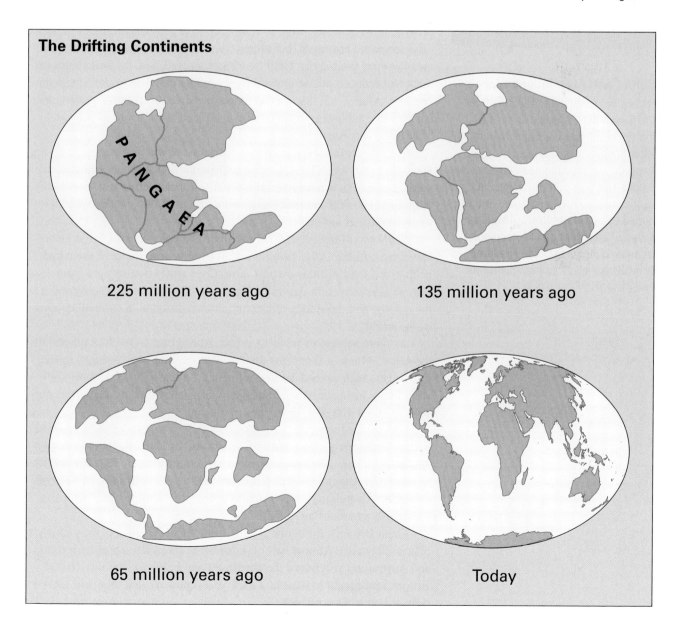

The Drifting Continents

PANGAEA

225 million years ago

135 million years ago

65 million years ago

Today

Before and After Independence

Before independence, Australia flew the British flag, or Union Jack. It is the top of the two flags shown here. After becoming independent in 1901, Australia adopted the new flag shown below. This flag kept the Union Jack as a symbol of Australia's past. But it added the Southern Cross. This is a group of stars that can be seen only from south of the equator. The large star represents Australia's six states and its territories.

33.3 A Land Far from Great Britain

Australia's first people, who are known as Aborigines, arrived in Australia more than 40,000 years ago. Their way of life may be the oldest culture in the world.

The Aborigines believe in a time long ago that they call the Dreamtime, a time before humans when spirits roamed Earth. These spirits formed the land and created people. They told humans how to keep the land alive. The Aborigines consider land to be sacred. When Europeans arrived much later, they saw the land differently, as something to be owned and used.

An Isolated Place to Send Prisoners In 1770, a British sea captain named James Cook discovered Australia while exploring the South Pacific. Cook claimed the land for Great Britain. At that time, however, Great Britain was having trouble with its American colonies. Therefore, the British did nothing with Australia until after the Americans won their independence in 1783.

The loss of the American colonies created a problem for British prisons, most of which were overflowing with convicts. Some of these prisoners were criminals, but others were simply poor people who were unable to pay their debts. Until the Americans rebelled, the British government had reduced prison crowding by sending convicts to the American colonies. After 1783, this was no longer possible. Instead, the government decided to establish a prison colony in a place as far away as possible. That place was Australia.

In 1788, eleven ships from Great Britain arrived in Australia, carrying about 700 convicts. The ships also transported tools, sheep, cattle, and seeds. The convicts built Australia's first European settlement. Eventually, more than 160,000 convicts were sent there, until the practice was formally abolished in 1868.

The new colony grew slowly at first. The convicts supported themselves by farming. After being released from prison, many of them had been given land of their own to farm. Over time, free settlers from Europe also arrived in Australia. Then, in 1851, gold was discovered in the colony, and thousands of treasure hunters flooded in from all corners of the world.

As more settlers came to Australia, Aborigines were often pushed off their land. Many of them also died of diseases that were brought by the Europeans, such as measles and influenza. At least 750,000 Aborigines were living in Australia when the Europeans arrived, but today there may be only about 400,000 Aborigines in the country.

British Influence in Australia Continues In 1901, the people of Australia gained their independence. The country's new flag, however, showed that Australians still felt connected to Great Britain. In one corner of the Australian flag is a small copy of the "Union Jack," which is the British national flag.

Great Britain's influence is still strong today. English is the country's official language. Almost half of Australians claim British or Irish roots, and Australians still honor the British monarch. Finally, almost 10,000 Britons **immigrate** to Australia each year, knowing that they will feel right at home "Down Under."

33.4 New Relationships with Near Neighbors

After achieving their independence, Australians adopted a "white Australia" immigration policy. The purpose of that policy was to keep people of color from entering the country. Any person who wanted to immigrate had to pass a "dictation test." An official read aloud a 50-word statement in a European language, and the prospective immigrant had to write it down word for word. Those who could not pass this test were turned away. This policy was effective in limiting immigration primarily to white Europeans.

Australia Opens Its Doors to the World The "white Australia" policy ended in the 1970s. The country then opened its doors to immigrants from anywhere in the world. By 2005, more than 20 million people lived in Australia. About one of every four was born in another country.

Today Australia welcomes approximately 90,000 immigrants each year, with almost one half of these newcomers arriving from Asia and Africa. People come to Australia for many reasons. Some immigrants are **refugees** who are fleeing wars. Others come seeking an education or a good job.

The opening of Australia to immigrants from the world over has transformed the country. People of color are no longer uncommon. Old ways of life have blended with new cultures. Sometimes this has led to tension between **ethnic groups,** but the main result has been the creation of a lively **plural society**.

New Trading Partners in the Asia-Pacific Region A century ago, more than half of Australia's exports went to Great Britain. Today few exports head toward Europe.

The country now looks closer to home for trade because the cost of shipping goods to nearby countries is much less than shipping to Europe. By 1950, Japan was Australia's most important trade partner. In recent years, South Korea, China, and Taiwan have also increased their trade with Australia.

Australia's Export Markets, 1999

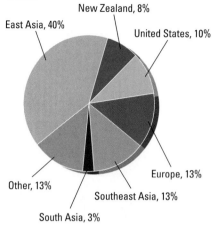

New Zealand, 8%
East Asia, 40%
United States, 10%
Other, 13%
Europe, 13%
Southeast Asia, 13%
South Asia, 3%

Source: *Australian Government, Department of Foreign Affairs and Trade,* www.dfat.gov.au.

Shifting Trade Patterns

Australia's trade with Europe has dropped in recent years. Meanwhile, trade with nearby Asia has increased. More than half of all of Australia's exports are now sold in Asia. Japan has replaced Britain as Australia's most important trade partner.

A Plural Society in the Making

Australia once limited immigration mainly to whites. Today people from all over the world are welcome. This map shows where Australians who were born in other countries came from.

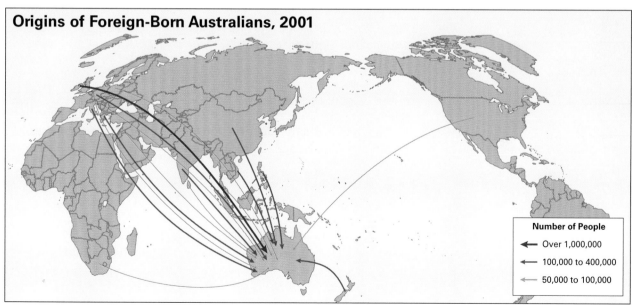

Origins of Foreign-Born Australians, 2001

Number of People

← Over 1,000,000
← 100,000 to 400,000
← 50,000 to 100,000

Source: *Australian Bureau of Statistics,* www.abs.gov.au.

New Year's Eve in Sydney

Australians celebrate New Year's Eve in Sydney with fireworks over the harbor. The unusual structure on the left is the Sydney Opera House. This performing arts center is one of the world's most famous buildings.

33.5 Australia's Reversed Seasons

Australians are celebrating the New Year. Bondi Beach, near the harbor city of Sydney, is packed with families lounging under beach umbrellas. The sky is a clear blue, and temperatures hover around 98°F. Surfers wait patiently for the next big wave while children make sandcastles on the beach. In the evening, families will picnic around Sydney Harbor while awaiting one of the world's great fireworks shows.

Sunny December in the Southern Hemisphere As you recall, Australia is in the Southern Hemisphere. Its seasons are the opposite of those in the northern half of the world. Summer there starts in December and runs through March.

In Chapter 1, you learned that the seasons are caused by the tilt of Earth on its **axis**. Because of this tilt, the Southern Hemisphere receives more sunlight between the months of December and March. These are Australia's warm summer months. Those same months are the winter season north of the equator.

Seasonal Advantages of Living "Down Under" December means bundling up for winter in much of the United States, but in Australia families are preparing to enjoy their summer vacation. Warm days and beautiful beaches attract tourists from north of the equator. More than 6 million people vacation in Australia every year, with many of them coming to escape winter where they live.

The reversed seasons give Australians another advantage. Countries such as the United States and Japan import out-of-season fruits from Australia. Cherries, for example, are a summer fruit in the United States, but they ripen "Down Under" during December and January. Many other fruits are also harvested during these two months. These fruits are shipped to supermarkets north of the equator, enabling them to offer fresh produce all year.

33.6 Australia's Amazing Wildlife

Many unusual animals live in Australia. Miniature penguins waddle ashore each night after dark. The swans gliding across lakes are black, not white. Giant crocodiles are as much at home in the ocean as in **freshwater** ponds. You might even see a very odd animal that looks like a cross between a duck and a beaver. The fairy penguin, black swan, saltwater crocodile, and duck-billed platypus are just a few of the country's curious creatures.

Flora and Fauna Found Only in Australia There are more than 13 million living species of plants and animals throughout the world. About one million species are found in Australia. Many of them exist nowhere else on Earth.

As you read, Australia was separated from the rest of the continents a very long time ago. Its plants and animals were isolated, developing without contact with other species elsewhere.

Within Australia, however, plants and animals have adapted to a wide variety of **climates**. In the hot and humid northeast, you might find the cassowary, a large flightless bird. The arid center of the country is a perfect place for red kangaroos. Kangaroos are marsupials, mammals that carry their young in pouches.

Exotic Species Endanger Many Native Species Early settlers from Europe brought many plants and animals with them. One of the animals was the rabbit. Rabbits adapted easily to the new environment but have had a harmful effect on native species. As the rabbits multiplied, they consumed grasses that native animals needed to survive.

Exotic species have disturbed the natural environment in much of the country. As a result, some of the native species have disappeared. Other native species are in danger of becoming **extinct**. A small marsupial called the *bilby* is an example. Because of competition from rabbits, it may die out.

Australia's Unique Animals

Many unique animal species are found in Australia. Three are shown here: the kangaroo, the bilby, and the platypus. The kangaroo and bilby are marsupials. They raise their babies in pouches on their bellies. The platypus is one of only two mammals that reproduces by laying eggs. The other egg-laying mammal is the echidna, a native of Australia and New Guinea.

Less Ozone, More Skin Cancer
Australia has the highest rate of skin cancer in the world. This is partly because the ozone over nearby Antarctica has been thinning. Ozone protects living things from the sun's harmful rays. Less ozone means that more of these rays reach Earth.

33.7 Living Under an Ozone Hole

Surf's up, mate! In December, Australia's beaches are usually crowded with sunbathers and surfers. It's a common sight to see young people grabbing surfboards and heading for the water. Today's surfers reach for something else as well: sunscreen. They know that because of a hole in Earth's **atmosphere,** they are at risk of getting more than sunburn at the beach.

Air Pollution Creates an Ozone Hole Scientists divide Earth's atmosphere into layers. The lowest layer in the atmosphere contains the air we breathe. The next layer begins about six miles above the planet and contains a gas called *ozone*. You cannot see ozone, but without this gas there would be no life on Earth. Ozone prevents the ultraviolet (UV) rays from the sun from reaching Earth. Ultraviolet rays are harmful to living things. In humans, UV rays cause sunburn, eye disease, and skin cancer.

In 1985, scientists discovered that the ozone over the continent of Antarctica was thinning. They called this thin patch an **ozone hole**. At times, part of this ozone hole has moved north far enough to extend over nearby Australia.

The loss of ozone in the atmosphere is caused mainly by chemicals known as *chlorofluorocarbons* (CFCs). When the ozone hole was discovered, CFCs were widely used in aerosol spray cans, refrigerators, and air conditioners. When released into the air, CFCs destroy ozone. Since 1985, atmospheric CFC levels have been reduced. As a result of this reduction, the ozone hole should slowly shrink. By 2050, it may be gone completely.

"Slip, Slop, Slap" to Prevent Skin Cancer The thinning of the ozone layer has created health problems for Australians. They are used to sunbathing and enjoying outdoor activities, so they are often exposed to harmful rays from the sun. In recent years, skin cancer rates have risen sharply, and two out of three Australians are now likely to develop skin cancer in their lifetime.

The Australian government is working to prevent new cases of cancer. Posters and advertisements advise Australians to "slip, slop, slap" before they venture out into the sun. This slogan is telling them to "slip" on a shirt, "slop" on some sunscreen, and "slap" on a hat to protect their skin. There are also "no-hat, play-in-the-shade" rules at schools. Students are not allowed outside to play if they are not wearing a hat.

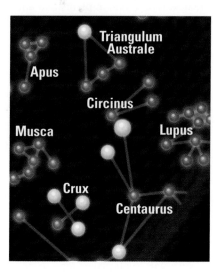

33.8 Australia's Night Sky

Robert Evans, a retired minister, is an expert on Australia's night sky. With the help of a tiny 16-inch telescope, he has spotted 39 supernovas. A supernova is the explosion of a large star like our sun. Despite having much more powerful telescopes, many professional astronomers have not caught a glimpse of even a single exploding star. How has Evans been able to observe what so many astronomers have missed? His location gives him a significant advantage, because the Australian night sky is clear most of the year.

Antarctica's Ozone Hole
The dark blue area on this illustration shows how large the ozone hole over Antarctica has grown.

A Starry Symbol: The Southern Cross The night sky as seen from the South Pole looks quite different from the view at the North Pole. There are several constellations, or groups of stars, that are visible only in the Southern Hemisphere. One of these constellations is called the Southern Cross, or Crux. Since ancient times, its bright stars have been invaluable to sailors, who have used the Crux to find their way in the South Pacific.

33.9 Beginning to Think Globally

In this chapter, you learned what effects location has had on shaping life in Australia. You read that this island continent drifted to its current location millions of years ago and that it has been isolated there ever since. You also learned about some of the unusual animals that are unique to Australia. You discovered that some of these native species are being threatened by exotic species that were introduced by colonists and, as a result, that some natives have become threatened species. Those most at risk are endangered species. If they are not protected, they are likely to disappear altogether.

Australia is not the only country that has threatened flora and fauna species. The World Conservation Union maintains a list of threatened species around the world. These are plants and animals that are likely to disappear if they are not protected. By 2004, the number of species on that list had increased to more than 15,000. Think about this as you examine the world map in the next section that shows where threatened animals are located.

Southern Constellations
The Southern Cross, or Crux, is the smallest constellation in the sky. Four of its five stars, seen above, are so bright that sailors can use them to steer by.

33.10 Global Connections

The map shows the locations of threatened animal species around the world. If nothing is done to protect these species, they could soon become endangered. This means they are in danger of rapid extinction. When a species becomes extinct, it is lost to the world forever.

What do the areas with most of the threatened species have in common? Tropical **regions** are "hot spots" for threatened species. Because of their absolute location near the equator, these areas can support great biodiversity—which means that tropical regions also have the most species to lose. Islands are also at great risk of losing species. Between the years 1500 and 2000, most extinctions took place on islands. Since 2000, however, about half of all extinctions occurred on continents.

What factors pose the greatest dangers to threatened species?
In the past, exotic species posed the greatest risk to native plants and animals. This was especially true on islands and in isolated locations such as Australia. Today, however, **habitat** loss is the greatest danger facing most animals. More than 6 billion people live on Earth today, and the human population is growing by 80 million each year. As humans take over more and more land, animals are crowded out.

How does relative location affect a species' chances of survival?
Animals that live far from human settlements generally have the best chances of survival. Such places tend to be too hot, dry, cold, or high for people to live in large numbers. In northern Russia, for example, there is only about one person per square mile. This leaves a lot of habitat for wolves, reindeer, and other animals.

Threatened Species Around the World

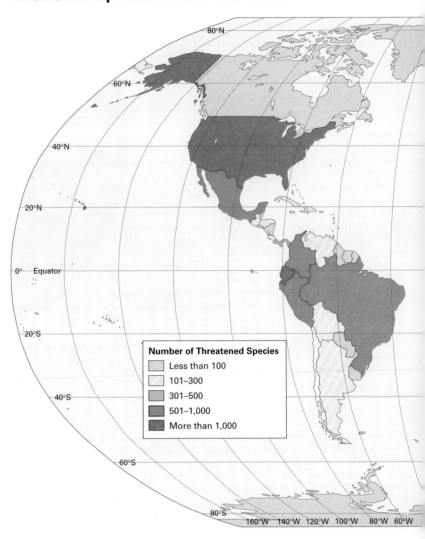

Number of Threatened Species
- Less than 100
- 101–300
- 301–500
- 501–1,000
- More than 1,000

Bald Eagle

Where threatened:
Continental
United States

Estimated population:
3,000 breeding pairs

Ibex

Where threatened:
European Alps

Estimated population:
30,000

Black Rhinoceros

Where threatened:
Africa

Estimated population:
3,600

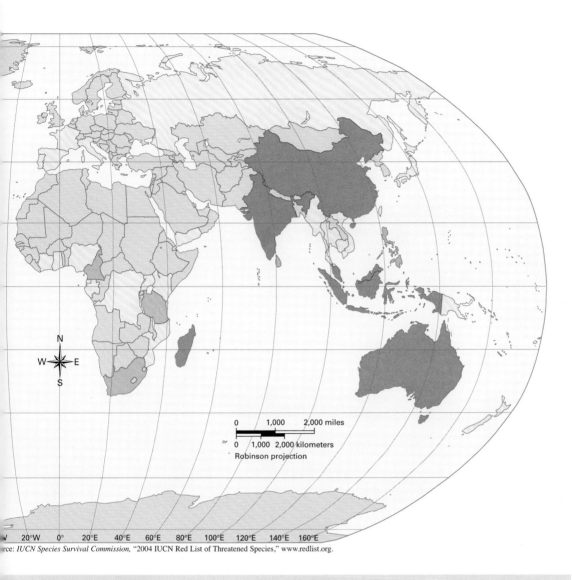

Source: IUCN Species Survival Commission, "2004 IUCN Red List of Threatened Species," www.redlist.org.

Humpback Whale

Where threatened:
The world's oceans

Estimated population:
15,000

Snow Leopard

Where threatened:
Mountains of
Central Asia

Estimated population:
6,000

Long-beaked Echidna

Where threatened: :
New Guinea

Estimated population:
less than 300,000

Giant Panda

Where threatened:
China

Estimated population:
1,000

Relative and Absolute Location: What Makes Australia Unique?   **487**

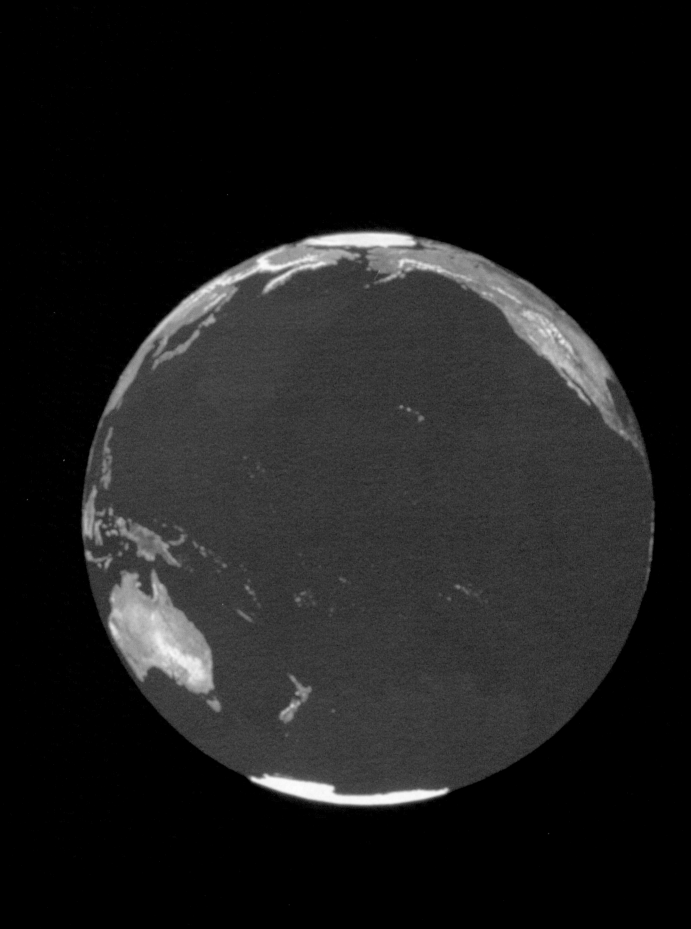

The Pacific Islands: Adapting to Life Surrounded by Ocean

34

34.1 Introduction

It is almost impossible to imagine how vast the Pacific Ocean is. Its enormous size has fascinated travelers for centuries. In 1835, a British scientist named Charles Darwin was shocked at the ocean's expanse as he sailed across the Pacific from Tahiti to New Zealand as part of an almost five-year scientific expedition. The maps he had been using, Darwin wrote, failed to give an accurate sense of the size of the Pacific Ocean. The water seemed to go on forever, and there was far less land than he had imagined.

The Pacific Ocean covers roughly one third of Earth's surface. That is approximately 64 million square miles, an area more than twice the size of the Atlantic Ocean. Tens of thousands of islands are scattered across the vast blue waters of the Pacific Ocean.

These islands were formed in different ways. Volcanoes rising up from the ocean floor created **volcanic islands**. Rings of small islands called **atolls** were formed by coral reefs. **Continental islands** are chunks of land that were once part of a continent.

In this chapter, you will read about the **physical features** of all three types of islands and about the **climate** and economy on a particular island of each type. You will see how winds, water, and ocean resources have combined to shape life in the vast Pacific region. In addition, you will read how the people who make their home on continental islands, volcanic islands, and atolls have adapted to a life surrounded by ocean.

Essential Question

How do people adapt to life in an island region?

This illustration shows the relative size and shape of three types of islands. All three are found in the Pacific Ocean. The largest are continental islands. The second largest are volcanic islands. Atolls are usually quite small. People adapt differently to life on each type of island. Keep this illustration in mind as you try to answer the Essential Question.

Graphic Organizer

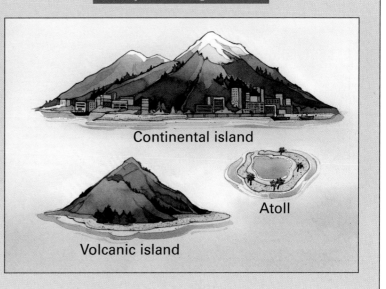

Continental island

Atoll

Volcanic island

◀ Satellite image of the Pacific Ocean and its islands

Travel Across the Pacific

Vast distances separate the Pacific islands. And yet, in time, most islands large enough to support people were settled. The first settlers may have used rafts or oceangoing canoes like this one to go from island to island.

34.2 The Geographic Setting

Thousands of islands dot the central and southern waters of the Pacific Ocean. There may be 20,000 or even 30,000 islands; no one knows for certain. However, if you were to put all of these islands together, they would add up to very little land.

As you read in the introduction to this unit, geographers categorize Pacific islands into three groups: Melanesia (black islands), Micronesia (tiny islands), and Polynesia (many islands). You can see a map of the three groups at the bottom of this page. Within these island groups lie 14 countries and many territories.

A Mix of Island Types The largest islands in this expanse of ocean are the continental islands. These islands were once connected to a continent by a bridge of land, but some of the islands were eventually separated from the larger **landmass** following the last ice age. As **glaciers** melted, sea levels rose until the land bridge was submerged in water. Other continental islands were cut off when ocean waves washed away the land that was connecting them to a continent.

The movement of **tectonic plates** formed still other continental islands. One example is New Zealand, which was once part of a huge landmass. The movement of tectonic plates broke this landmass apart, resulting in the formation of Antarctica, Australia, and several continental islands.

Volcanic islands begin when a volcano erupts on the ocean floor, causing **lava** and ash to slowly build up on the seabed. When enough of this material accumulates, the island rises above sea level. Most volcanic islands are cone shaped with steep slopes rising to a high peak. Fiji, Samoa, and the Hawaiian Islands are all examples of this type of island.

An atoll is a ring of coral islands and reefs surrounding a shallow body of water called a **lagoon**. Atolls begin as coral reefs grow around a volcanic island. Over time, the island sinks beneath the sea. Some islands sink as a result of the movement of tectonic plates. Other islands are covered by water when sea levels rise. Still others gradually erode away over time. The area above the sunken volcano is eventually transformed into a lagoon ringed by coral reefs. Over time, ocean waves break away parts of the reefs, and the bits of broken coral pile up to form flat, sandy islands around the lagoon. The Marshall Islands and most of the Tuvalu Islands are atolls.

The Pacific Islands

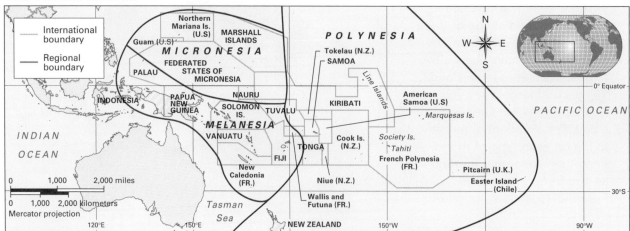

▶ Geoterms

atoll a ring of coral islands and reefs surrounding a shallow body of ocean water

continental island an island that was once part of a continent

lagoon a body of shallow water partly cut off from the ocean by low-lying rock, sand, or coral reefs

volcanic island an island formed when an underwater volcano builds up enough lava and ash to rise above sea level

Atolls

An atoll forms when a volcanic island surrounded by a coral reef sinks beneath the sea. The coral reef remains. But it surrounds a lagoon, not land. Atolls are common in the Indian and Pacific oceans.

Continental Islands

Continental islands were once part of a continent. Some islands are separated when sea levels rise. Some are cut off from a continent by erosion. Others break away when tectonic plates move.

Volcanic Islands

Volcanic islands form when a volcano erupts far beneath the sea. When these volcanoes rise above the ocean's surface, they form islands. Volcanic islands are steep with high peaks.

34.3 The Ocean Shapes Life in the Pacific

Visitors often describe islands in the Pacific Ocean as "paradise." Tourists travel there to relax on the sunny beaches and swim in the warm ocean water. However, the ocean is not always peaceful; in fact, sometimes it can become dangerous.

In 2004, an extremely powerful earthquake shook the floor of the Indian Ocean. The quake triggered a huge wave called a **tsunami** that flooded coastal areas from Asia to Africa. More than 200,000 people perished, and many more were left homeless. For better or worse, the ocean affects every aspect of life in the Pacific region.

Winds and Currents Warm the Islands Winds and ocean currents shape the climate of most Pacific islands. As you read in Chapter 11, winds move around Earth in circular patterns. One group of winds, known as **trade winds,** blows toward the equator from both the north and the south. As trade winds move toward the equator, they shift westward. This directional shift is a result of the rotation of Earth.

When winds blow across the ocean, they move water on the ocean's surface. This moving surface water forms ocean currents that travel in circular patterns, just like the winds. Near the equator, ocean currents move westward with the trade winds, and as these currents move along the equator, the sun warms the water.

When these warm ocean currents encounter land, they are forced to change direction. In the Northern Hemisphere, the currents turn to the north; in the Southern Hemisphere, they turn to the south. As these currents move farther away from the equator, they function as heating systems by warming the air in coastal areas and on islands that might otherwise be cooler.

Heating and Cooling Earth

Ocean currents affect the world's climate. Warm currents can heat places far from the equator that would otherwise be cold. The warm Gulf Stream, for example, brings mild winter weather to the British Isles. Cold currents can cool places near the equator that would otherwise be hot.

Ocean Surface Currents

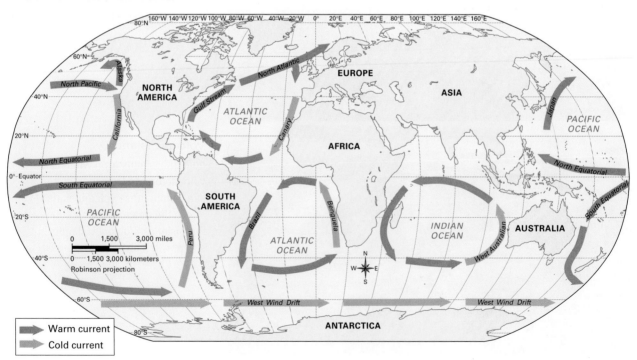

Warm Air and Water Bring Wet Weather
As you learned in Chapter 11, warm air and
warm water combine to create wet weather.
Warm air can hold a large amount of moisture, and at the same time warm ocean
water evaporates easily to provide that
moisture. As the wet, warm air rises in
the atmosphere, it forms rain clouds. Not
surprisingly, Pacific islands that are located
in warm equatorial waters have **tropical
wet** climates, with some receiving rain
every day. In contrast, islands farther from
the equator are both cooler and drier.

Warm ocean temperatures also cause
typhoons, which are **tropical cyclones**
that begin over the Pacific Ocean. Similar
storms that begin over the Atlantic Ocean
are termed **hurricanes**. Typhoons are huge
storms that generate winds of at least
74 miles per hour and drop enormous
amounts of rain, often causing **storm
surges** that can flood coastal areas. For
people who live on Pacific islands, it is
typhoons, not tsunamis, that are the most
frequent **natural disaster**.

The Ocean Is Rich in Resources Pacific islanders have always looked
to the sea for much of their food—and for good reason: there is great
biodiversity in the oceans. Many more kinds of plants and animals can
be found in the sea than on the land. About 13,000 species of fish inhabit
the oceans.

For centuries, Pacific islanders have harvested these fish for their
own use. Today the islanders have been joined in the Pacific by commercial fishing fleets from many countries. About 60 percent of all fish
consumed by humans today comes from the Pacific Ocean.

Scientists are now looking to the sea for new medicines. One drug
that has been developed from a sea sponge is already being used to treat
cancer. A drug that may be used to treat severe pain has been developed
from a marine, or sea, snail. William Speck, a doctor and director of the
Marine Biological Laboratory in Woods Hole, Massachusetts, sees great
promise in medicines from the sea. "I believe marine organisms can be
used to eliminate disease and human suffering," said Speck in a 2001
newspaper interview.

Other resources are also found in the Pacific. Pearls, which are produced in oysters, a type of shellfish, are prized for jewelry. Vast expanses
of the ocean floor in the central Pacific are rich in metal **ores,** such as
manganese, copper, and nickel, that can be mined and processed. And
some areas of the sea have deposits of oil and natural gas.

The occupations of Pacific islanders are often related to the ocean
and its resources. Many local people are employed in the tourist industry,
and **tourism** is now the biggest moneymaker on many islands. Others
work in the fishing industry.

A Great Variety of Fish
Hundreds of species of fish live in the
lagoons and coral reefs of the Pacific.
Tourists come to Pacific islands to see
this marine life. They use snorkels and
scuba diving gear to get a good look at
life beneath the waves.

34.4 Life on a Continental Island: New Zealand

New Zealand, an island country in the South Pacific, is one of the world's most isolated countries. It is separated from its nearest neighbor, Australia, by more than 1,000 miles of ocean.

The first people to settle in New Zealand knew from experience just how distant it was from other places. According to legend, they were at sea for a very long time. Finally, one of them spotted in the distance a long white cloud, a sign that they were approaching land. The settlers named their new home Aotearoa, which in their language meant "Land of the Long White Cloud."

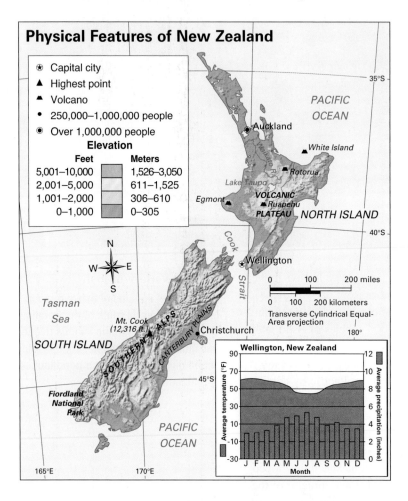

Physical Features New Zealand is made up of two large continental islands and many islands that are much smaller. The two large islands are called the North Island and the South Island. Together they measure approximately 1,000 miles from north to south and 280 miles from east to west, which is roughly the size of the state of California.

Many of the mountains that dominate both large islands are volcanoes. Some of these volcanoes, such as Mount Ruapehu, still erupt on occasion. The mountains of the North Island feature many rivers, lakes, hot springs, steam-spouting **geysers,** and bubbling pools of hot mud. On the South Island, the Southern Alps are high enough to be covered by snow throughout the year. The Southern Alps are also steep enough to provide a challenge to mountain climbers.

The rocky west coast of the South Island is indented with a number of fjords. A fjord is a narrow inlet between two steep cliffs. Long ago, these inlets were carved out of the coastline by glaciers.

A Varied Landscape

New Zealand boasts a great variety of physical features. The North Island is a land of volcanoes, some of which are still active. The South Island's Southern Alps are still growing at the rate of about two fifths of an inch a year.

Climate and Economy New Zealand has a **marine west coast** climate. Temperatures are moderate throughout the year, with few extremes of hot and cold. Most days are sunny, but the islands receive regular rainfall from the warm, moist winds that blow from west to east across the Pacific Ocean.

The rain falls unevenly around New Zealand. As heavy rains drench the west side of the South Island, the western slopes of its mountains receive more than an inch of precipitation per day. By the time the clouds cross the eastern side of the mountains, they have lost most of their moisture. The result is a **rain shadow** east of the mountains. As you know, people living in a rain shadow must adapt to life with very little rain. This area receives only 25 inches of rain per year.

Unlike many island countries, New Zealand is blessed with large expanses of fertile land. Farming and raising livestock form the foundation of the country's economy. New Zealand farmers raise enough meat and dairy products to feed their own country and millions more people worldwide. The most important farm animals are sheep, which are raised both for their meat and their wool. Sheep outnumber people in New Zealand by more than 12 to 1. No other country has so many farm animals compared with its population.

Because New Zealand is surrounded by water, it is not surprising that fishing is also a major contributor to the country's economy. Tuna, marlin, and snapper thrive in the ocean waters. The variety of sea life also attracts tourists, as people from around the world come to watch dolphins, seals, and whales in their natural **habitat**.

Human Adaptations By 2005, around 4 million people lived in New Zealand. The great majority make their home on the North Island. Most New Zealanders live in a few large cities.

Although New Zealand doesn't have extreme temperatures, it does have four distinct seasons. In the summer, New Zealanders might never need to wear more than a light jacket. In the winter, they put on warm clothing when they go outdoors.

New Zealand's extremely varied **landscape** offers numerous opportunities for outdoor recreation. People ski and hike on the snowcapped mountains, and they surf, sail, swim, and fish along the coasts. Rivers provide abundant opportunities for kayaking and white-water rafting, whereas hot springs attract people who want to relax.

New Zealand is fairly large compared with many other Pacific islands. To get around their country, New Zealanders travel by car, train, or bus. Air travel links them to the world beyond their island home.

Living in Auckland

Auckland is New Zealand's largest city. More than 1.3 million people make their home in the city and its suburbs. This is about a third of the country's population. Homes in Auckland are similar to houses you would find in an American city.

34.5 Life on a Volcanic Island: Tahiti

Steep Volcanoes

This map shows why Tahiti is sometimes called a two-part island. Tahiti Iti and Tahiti Nui are inactive volcanoes. Waterfalls tumble down steep mountain slopes. Sunlight often creates rainbows in the spray. Natives call their island "Tahiti of the many-colored waters."

Tahiti is a land of beautiful beaches and sweet-smelling flowers. Tourists from around the world travel to this island to relax, and many of them share the opinions of the first Europeans who arrived in Tahiti hundreds of years ago. They think Tahiti is just about perfect.

Getting to Tahiti takes a long time, even when traveling by airplane. Like many Pacific islands, Tahiti is very far from its neighbors. It is more than 3,000 miles from Australia and almost 6,000 miles from Japan. It is part of the island group called French Polynesia. Once a French colony, Tahiti is now a French territory with its own government.

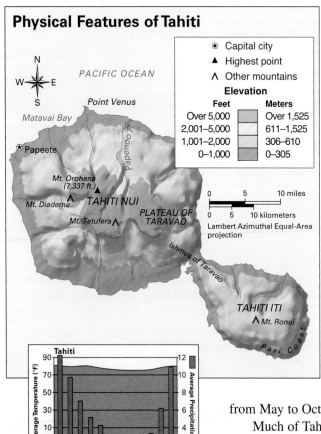

Physical Features Tahiti is the largest island within French Polynesia, but it is only 402 square miles in area, making it one third the size of the tiny state of Rhode Island. From above, the island looks somewhat like a hand mirror with a fat handle. The part of the island that is shaped like a round mirror is known as Tahiti Nui (Big Tahiti), and the fat handle is called Tahiti Iti (Small Tahiti). These two parts are joined together by a narrow **isthmus**.

Both Tahiti Nui and Tahiti Iti were once active volcanoes. The land in both parts of the island rises steeply from the coast. The slopes surround **craters** that once were the volcanoes' centers. The dramatic landscape also features waterfalls and cliffs. The Te Pari cliffs of Tahiti Iti are so steep that they are nearly vertical.

Climate and Economy There are two seasons in Tahiti. During the wet season, which lasts from November to April, Tahiti gets three fourths of its annual rainfall, and temperatures range from 80 to 86 degrees Fahrenheit. The dry season, which lasts from May to October, is slightly cooler.

Much of Tahiti is too steep for farming, with only the coastal plain being flat enough for crop cultivation. Tahiti is known for its breadfruit, a large fruit that takes on the texture of bread when it is baked or roasted. Coconut palms, citrus fruits, and orchids also grow in Tahiti. Coconuts are a versatile plant. The palms are woven into roofs, mats, and baskets. The trunk is used as a building material, and the coconut husk can be made into strong cord. In the past, Tahiti's farms produced enough food to support its people, but as the population has increased, much of the island's food now must be imported.

Tahiti's economy depends on ocean resources in many ways. Its sunny beaches, coral reefs, colorful fish, and sea turtles attract large numbers of tourists, who are a major source of income for the island.

The next most important income source is black pearls, which come from oysters. When a foreign object, such as a bit of sand, gets inside an oyster's shell, the oyster coats it with a substance called *mother of pearl*. Sometimes the result is a lustrous pearl. Pearls can be white, gold, pink, or dark gray—the true color of black pearls.

To encourage oysters to make pearls, Tahitians plant a small bead inside their shells. Ideally a large, dark gray pearl will take shape around the bead over the next two years, but that doesn't happen often. In reality, only 3 oysters out of 100 produce a perfect pearl.

The waters off Tahiti are full of sea life. Many Tahitian natives still fish for tuna, marlin, and shark the old-fashioned way, using poles and lines to catch no more than they will be able to eat.

Commercial fishing is an important part of Tahiti's economy. Fishing fleets from Japan, Korea, and the United States pay Tahiti for permission to fish in its waters. These fleets use electronic equipment to locate fish and huge nets to haul their catch out of the sea.

Human Adaptations More than half of the population of French Polynesia lives on the island of Tahiti. Most live on the island's north coast, which is also the location of Papeete, French Polynesia's capital. Papeete is a crowded modern city, but other parts of Tahiti are less built up, with people living in more traditional villages.

Beginning in the 1700s, outsiders introduced new ways to Tahiti. For example, men and women traditionally wore a wrapped garment called a *pareu,* but today most Tahitians choose to wear casual clothes such as jeans and T-shirts.

Housing has also changed. Traditional one-room houses were made out of coconut trunks and pandanus leaves, but today's houses are larger and constructed of more durable materials. Wealthy Tahitians reside in large concrete houses. In contrast, people who are less well-off live in one- or two-story wooden homes, and houses in the country may have thatched roofs.

Tahiti offers many recreation opportunities. Residents and visitors scuba dive, snorkel, and surf in the water. They hike or ride horses on the volcanic slopes, and some go hang gliding off the steep cliffs. Local people may also participate in traditional dancing and sports.

A modern airport in Papeete brings visitors to Tahiti. Cars and buses provide local transportation. The bus service, called *le truck,* uses trucks that have been converted into open-air buses to transport people around the island.

Bright Colors Everywhere
Traditional Tahitian clothing is made of brightly colored cloth. Both men and woman wore a wraparound garment called a *pareu*.

Tahiti Attracts Artists
Artists from around the world have been coming to Tahiti ever since Europeans came to the island. Paul Gauguin was one of the most famous. He was a French painter during the 1800s. His home, shown here, is a traditional Tahitian house.

34.6 Life on an Atoll: Kwajalein Island

A String of Small Islands

Kwajalein Atoll is part of the Marshall Islands. Kwajalein is also the name of one of the islands in the atoll. Kwajalein Island is ½ mile wide and 2½ miles long.

Imagine living on an island that is about the size of a small town. That's what it's like for the people who make their home on Kwajalein Island. Kwajalein is one of the islands that make up the Kwajalein Atoll, which is located just north of the equator in Micronesia. Kwajalein is part of the Republic of the Marshall Islands, and it is also home to a United States Army base.

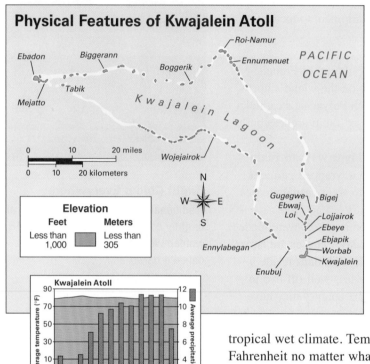

Physical Features of Kwajalein Atoll

Physical Features Kwajalein Atoll is the largest coral atoll in the world, but even so, its 97 islands have a total land area of only 6.5 square miles. The atoll surrounds a lagoon that covers more than 600 square miles. There's a lot more ocean than land in Kwajalein Atoll.

The highest points on Kwajalein Atoll are only 12 to 15 feet above sea level. Because atolls are so low, they can flood easily during storms. Also, there are no rivers or springs to provide fresh water. In the past, islanders had to rely on catching rainwater for drinking. Today **desalinization plants** help some islanders meet their water needs by removing salt from seawater to make it suitable for human use.

Climate and Economy Kwajalein has a tropical wet climate. Temperatures range from about 80 to 88 degrees Fahrenheit no matter what the season, and rain falls every day during both the wet and the "dry" seasons. The difference between the seasons is that the showers do not last as long during the drier months. Tropical storms sometimes blow across Kwajalein, but typhoons are not common. Coral reefs protect the islands from storm surges and also serve as home to sea turtles, sea sponges, and shellfish.

Few crops grow in the atoll's sandy soil, but the islanders are able to raise coconut palms, breadfruit, and a starchy root called *arrowroot*. Copra, or dried coconut meat, is one of Kwajalein's main exports. Processors transform copra into oil that is then used in skin and hair care products and in the soap-making and food-processing industries. Because farming is so limited, the islanders depend on fish for much of their food.

Today, however, the economy of Kwajalein is based mainly on its importance as a U.S. military base in the Pacific. Tourism is also growing, primarily among scuba divers who like to explore old shipwrecks.

Human Adaptations People live on only 14 of Kwajalein Atoll's 97 islands. About 13,500 are citizens of the Marshall Islands, and approximately 3,000 are Americans. Only people who work for the U.S. Army, and their families, are allowed on Kwajalein Island.

Living on Kwajalein Island can be challenging. The constant rain and dampness, combined with the salty air, rusts everything that is constructed from iron. Outdoor barbecues and metal furniture do not last long in this climate.

Damaged Coral Reefs
The coral reefs of Kwajalein Atoll were once used as building material by people living on the islands. In this photograph, you can still see large areas where coral has been removed.

Travel around Kwajalein Island can be tricky. The only cars belong to the U.S. Army. Residents rely on bicycles for transportation, but the dampness can rust a bike in days if it isn't properly cared for. A person who has a bike for three years has been either very careful or very lucky. Ferries and planes link Kwajalein Island with the rest of the atoll and the outside world.

The U.S. Army owns all of the housing on Kwajalein Island, with people living in a mix of trailers, older concrete houses, and newer wooden houses. The most unusual houses are dome homes, which look like white plastic bowls turned upside down. The dome homes are made of materials that resist weather damage and conserve energy.

People on Kwajalein dress like most other Americans, only more casually. Many wear shorts and light shirts to beat the heat.

For those who like sports, there is a lot to do on Kwajalein Island. Scuba divers enjoy exploring the coral reefs with their schools of colorful fish, and water sports such as sailing and windsurfing are popular on the lagoon. Sports fishing is common as well, with tuna, marlin, and skipjack being popular game fish. People also enjoy team sports such as volleyball and softball. Indoor activities range from bowling to movies.

34.7 Beginning to Think Globally

In this chapter, you learned that the ocean affects every aspect of life in the Pacific islands. You also learned about life on three kinds of islands. Continental islands are the largest, with the most usable land. On volcanic islands, people live primarily along the coasts, where the land is flat and fertile. Atolls, in contrast, are difficult places to live because they have very little land and lack fresh water. The ocean is important to all Pacific islanders because it is a major source of food and an attraction for tourists.

Oceans are important to the rest of the world as well. One out of every five people worldwide relies on fish for protein. As the world's population increases, the demand for fish will rise as well. Think about this as you examine the map of regulated fishing zones around the world in the next section.

Oceans Provide Resources
Oceans are important to people around the world. Worldwide, 35 million people earn a living by catching or raising fish for food.

34.8 Global Connections

This map shows regulated fishing areas throughout the world. Each country that borders an ocean has the authority to regulate, or control, the fishing off its coast in an area that extends 200 nautical miles (230 miles) out to sea. These regulated areas are colored dark blue on the map. The light blue areas represent unregulated waters, where under international law anyone is allowed to fish. The map also shows where some species of sea life are in danger of dying out as a consequence of **overfishing**.

What is happening to the world's fish supply and why? The supply of many species of fish has been declining. Pollution and changes in climate may have contributed to this decline, but the most important cause has been overfishing. So many fish are being caught that they cannot replace themselves. Overfishing has been driven by a rising worldwide demand for fish. It is also the result of advances in **technology,** which have enabled fishing crews to catch more fish in less time.

What problems might overfishing cause? Overfishing damages the **ecosystems** of the ocean. The **food web** in oceans changes when a species disappears. In addition, overfishing threatens a food source on which many people rely.

What can be done to prevent overfishing? Countries can attempt to reduce overfishing in the waters that they control. One way is to outlaw fishing methods that catch too many fish. Another is to ban the catch of endangered species. However, individual countries can only regulate limited areas, leaving the rest of the seas unprotected. To stop overfishing, countries must work together to protect the oceans and their resources.

Regulated Fishing Areas Around the World

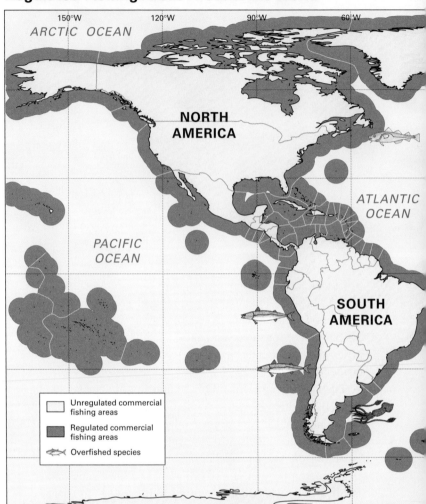

Salmon fishing in Ketchikan, Alaska

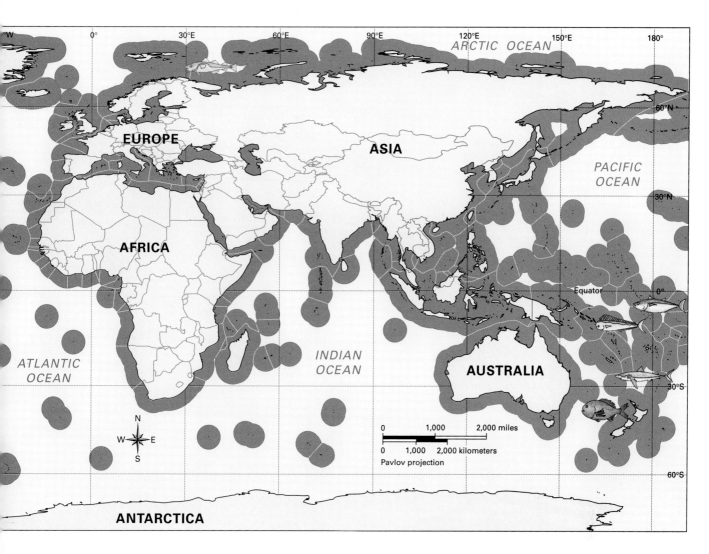

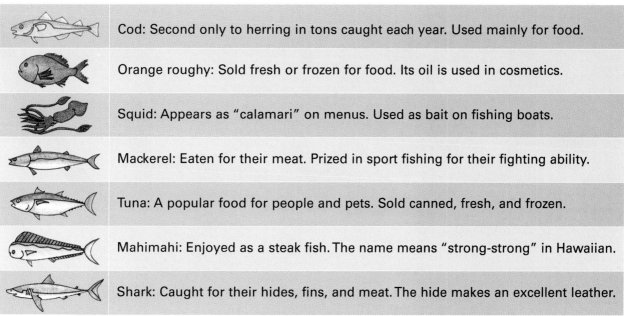

Cod: Second only to herring in tons caught each year. Used mainly for food.

Orange roughy: Sold fresh or frozen for food. Its oil is used in cosmetics.

Squid: Appears as "calamari" on menus. Used as bait on fishing boats.

Mackerel: Eaten for their meat. Prized in sport fishing for their fighting ability.

Tuna: A popular food for people and pets. Sold canned, fresh, and frozen.

Mahimahi: Enjoyed as a steak fish. The name means "strong-strong" in Hawaiian.

Shark: Caught for their hides, fins, and meat. The hide makes an excellent leather.

Antarctica: Researching Global Warming at the Coldest Place on Earth

35.1 Introduction

Antarctica is the coldest continent on Earth. The average temperature at the South Pole is –74°F, a temperature at which spilled coffee can turn to ice before it hits the ground. No one lives year-round on this cold continent. Each summer, though, Antarctica warms up a bit, and during these few warmer months researchers from throughout the world travel to Antarctica to work.

Researchers come to Antarctica to study many things. One of the most important areas of research, however, is **global warming,** a term referring to a slow increase in the temperature of Earth's surface. **Climate** records for the past 25 years have shown a worldwide surface temperature increase of about 0.4°F. However, this warming has not occurred uniformly throughout the world. Some places are warmer, while others are cooler.

Many scientists believe that this warming relates to the **greenhouse effect,** a process that occurs when gases in the **atmosphere** prevent heat from Earth's surface from escaping into space. The trapped heat, the scientists believe, makes Earth warmer. Studies of ice bubbles trapped in polar ice show that amounts of **greenhouse gases** in the atmosphere are increasing, but not all scientists think that this increase explains Earth's warming. In fact, some aren't sure whether the planet is warming at all.

In this chapter, you will consider ideas about global warming and how it may be affecting Antarctica. You will also look at possible effects of global warming on the rest of the world.

Essential Question

How might global warming affect the environment in the world's coldest places?

These two researchers are debating the theory of global warming. One believes that her research in Antarctica supports the theory. The other has doubts based on his research. Think about this debate as you try to answer the Essential Question.

Graphic Organizer

Based on my research in Antarctica, I support the theory of global warming.

My research in Antarctica leads me to doubt the theory of global warming.

◄ Conducting research in Antarctica during the short summer season

A Polar Desert

People think that an ice-capped land must get a lot of rainfall. But Antarctica is a desert. It gets less than three inches of precipitation per year. This polar desert has fewer plants and animals than most desert biomes because it is so cold as well as dry.

35.2 The Geographic Setting

Antarctica surrounds the South Pole, which is the southernmost point on Earth. This icy continent is larger than Australia or Europe. Almost all of its land is buried beneath **glaciers,** and a majority of Earth's fresh water is frozen here as ice.

The Coldest Place on Earth Antarctica can be unimaginably cold. On July 21, 1983, instruments in Antarctica registered a temperature of −128°F, which is the coldest temperature ever recorded on Earth.

Why does Antarctica get so bitterly cold? As the most distant continent from the equator, it receives less sunshine than other parts of the world. On some winter days, the sun never even rises above the horizon. The small amount of **solar energy** that Antarctica does receive is mostly reflected by the vast expanses of ice back into space.

Antarctica also has the distinction of being the world's driest continent, receiving less than two inches of **precipitation** per year. Few living things can survive in such a cold, dry **biome,** or large **ecosystem**. Only two species of flowering plants grow on Antarctica, and no trees or shrubs. However, a variety of animals thrive in the waters surrounding the continent, including seals and whales, as well as penguins and many other kinds of birds.

Glaciers cover approximately 98 percent of Antarctica, with much of this ice measuring well over a mile thick. Moving flows of ice called **ice streams** slide across the surface of this **ice cap,** carrying ice from the center of the continent to the sea. Upon reaching the coast, an ice stream flows outward into the ocean. There it forms an **ice shelf,** or floating sheet of ice, that remains attached to the continent. The largest of these ice shelves, the Ross Ice Shelf, is roughly the size of France. In some places, the Ross Ice Shelf is up to 3,000 feet thick.

A Continent Reserved for International Research In 1978, a woman boarded a plane in Argentina and flew to a research station in Antarctica. While there, she gave birth to a baby boy. He was the first human being to be born on the continent, yet he could not be considered a citizen of Antarctica. That is because Antarctica has no country and no government.

In the past, seven countries have claimed various parts of Antarctica. In 1959, those countries joined with others to sign the Antarctic Treaty, in which the seven countries agreed to set aside any claims to the continent. The treaty stated that Antarctica, in order to promote international cooperation, should be reserved for peaceful activities such as scientific investigation.

More than 4,000 people travel to Antarctica every year to participate in scientific studies. Scientists find Antarctica a good place to do research for many reasons, one of which is that it is the least populated continent on Earth. This helps researchers see how Earth has changed over time without the influence of human activity.

Also, Antarctica's glaciers serve as historic records of climate change. Researchers drill deep into the thick ice and pull up samples called **ice cores,** which can be studied to learn what the climate was like as far back as 420,000 years ago. Researchers use this information to help understand the warming and cooling of Earth over time.

▶ Geoterms

biome a very large ecosystem such as a desert, forest, wetland, or grassland. Each biome is home to its own community of plants and animals.

global warming the gradual increase in the temperature of Earth's surface over time. This warming may be the result of natural causes. It may also be caused by human activity.

greenhouse effect the process by which gases in the atmosphere trap heat from the sun and keep it close to Earth's surface. This trapped heat may contribute to global warming.

ice shelf a large, floating sheet of ice that is attached to the coast. Ice shelves can extend out to sea for hundreds of miles.

A Cool Place for Research

No one owns Antarctica. The Antarctic Treaty makes it a natural reserve. It can be used only for such peaceful purposes as scientific research. Many countries have research stations in Antarctica.

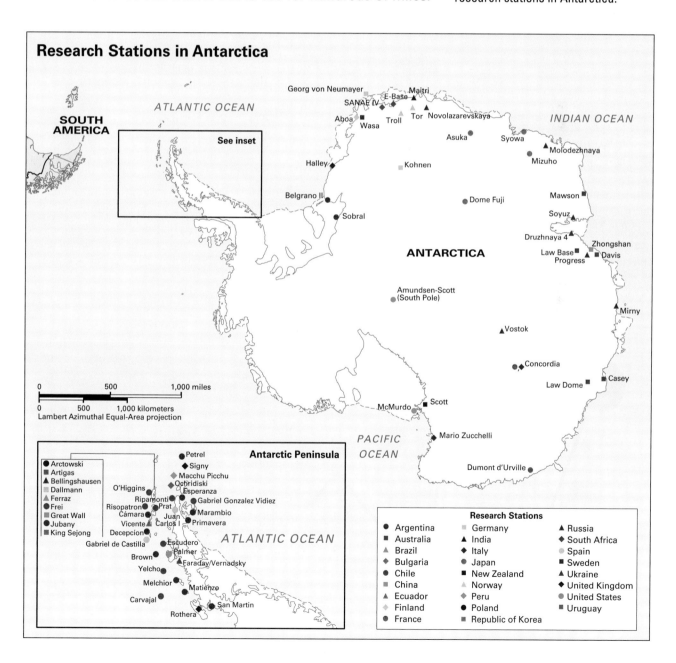

Research Stations in Antarctica

35.3 The Theory of Global Warming

In the past, Earth's climate has had both warm and cool periods. Changes from one period to another were caused by natural events. The last cool period ended about 12,500 years ago. Since then, Earth has been in a warm period. During the past 200 years, however, temperatures seem to have risen faster than usual. The theory of global warming tries to explain why the climate is heating up.

Three Key Ideas About Global Warming The theory of global warming is based on three key ideas. The first is that Earth's climate is getting warmer. The second is that this trend, or change over time, is mainly caused by human activity, not natural causes. The third key idea is that global warming is harmful to people and many biomes. Because of this, many people believe it should be slowed or even stopped.

The Greenhouse Effect Keeps Earth Warm Earth is kept warm by a natural process called the *greenhouse effect*. This process traps energy from the sun in our atmosphere. The atmosphere then acts like a giant greenhouse surrounding Earth. This "greenhouse" keeps Earth's average surface temperature at a warm 59°F. Without it, the temperature could drop to 0°F, or well below freezing.

The greenhouse effect works because of gases in the atmosphere. The most common greenhouse gases are carbon dioxide, methane, and water vapor. They trap heat from the sun in the atmosphere. Otherwise, this heat would escape into space.

Since around 1800, levels of greenhouse gases in the atmosphere have been rising. This increase is due mainly to people burning **fossil fuels** such as coal, oil, and natural gas. When these fuels are burned, they give off carbon dioxide. Many scientists believe that the increase in carbon dioxide and other greenhouse gases is causing Earth to warm. Others are not so sure.

Energy from the Sun

This diagram shows what happens to energy from the sun once it enters Earth's atmosphere. Some energy is absorbed by Earth's surface. Some is reflected back into space. Some is trapped in a layer of gases that surround Earth. This trapped heat may be causing global warming.

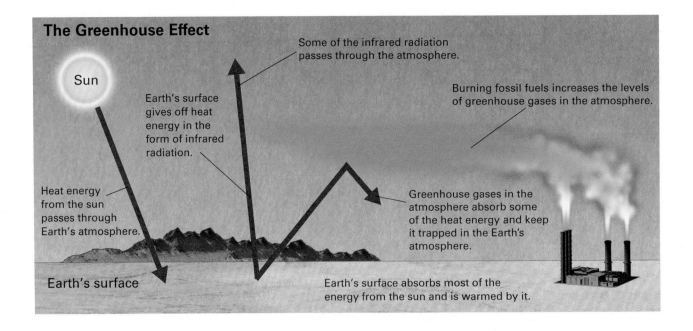

The Greenhouse Effect

Sun

Heat energy from the sun passes through Earth's atmosphere.

Earth's surface gives off heat energy in the form of infrared radiation.

Some of the infrared radiation passes through the atmosphere.

Burning fossil fuels increases the levels of greenhouse gases in the atmosphere.

Greenhouse gases in the atmosphere absorb some of the heat energy and keep it trapped in the Earth's atmosphere.

Earth's surface

Earth's surface absorbs most of the energy from the sun and is warmed by it.

35.4 Support for the Global Warming Theory

Scientists who support the theory of global warming point to three kinds of evidence. The first is climate records. These records show rising surface temperatures in many places. The second is glacier records. They show that glaciers around the world are melting as temperatures rise. The third type of evidence is rising levels of greenhouse gases in the atmosphere. Studies of air bubbles trapped in polar ice show that greenhouse gas levels are the highest they've been in 420,000 years.

Supporters of the global warming theory trace these changes back to the start of the **Industrial Revolution**. During this time, many new machines were invented. Many were powered by the burning of fossil fuels.

Today we use coal, oil, and natural gas to heat our homes, run our cars, and power our factories. As a result of this activity, we add more than 4 billion tons of carbon dioxide to the air every year. This gas will stay in our atmosphere for at least the next 100 years.

The results of global warming, these scientists warn, could have terrible consequences. Some biomes may lose plants and animals that are unable to adapt to warmer conditions. Crop failures may become common, leading to widespread hunger. Ocean levels may rise as polar ice melts. Higher seas may flood low-lying islands and coastal cities.

The best way to prevent these disasters, these scientists say, is to reduce activities that create greenhouse gases. This could mean difficult changes in the way many people today live.

35.5 Doubts About the Global Warming Theory

Not all scientists agree with the global warming theory. Some doubt that Earth's temperature is, in fact, rising at all.

Like supporters, the doubters support their views with evidence. They point out that temperature records of the upper atmosphere show little sign of warming. Most surface temperature records, they argue, come from urban areas. City buildings and pavement absorb more heat from the sun than green spaces. As a result, urban areas get warmer as they grow. What looks like global warming may just be city warming.

The doubters also note that not all glaciers are shrinking. Some are growing.

Some doubters accept evidence that Earth is warming. But they believe this is due to natural causes. Changes in the sun's energy or in ocean currents are far more likely to cause climate change, they believe, than human activity.

Finally, some doubters question whether rising temperatures will be so disastrous. People living in cold climates, they point out, might welcome warmer winters. Areas that are now too cold for crops might become productive farmland. Also, more carbon dioxide in the air may boost plant growth. The result could be faster growing crops and forests. This might be good, not bad, for many biomes.

The Global Warming Debate

Some people believe that global warming will have disastrous effects. They argue for reduced use of fossil fuels to slow climate change. Others don't believe that global warming is a major problem. Some even suggest that warmer weather could benefit people living in cold climate zones.

35.6 Studying Temperatures in Antarctica

The impact of global warming on Antarctica could be dramatic because warmer temperatures could cause glaciers and ice shelves to melt. If the area of the continent that is covered by ice shrinks, less energy from the sun would be reflected back into space. As a consequence, temperatures would rise even more.

To find out whether such temperature changes are probable, scientists have been gathering data on air temperatures in many parts of Antarctica. They compare those data with records from recent years to identify any trends.

Researchers are also collecting information about Antarctica's climate from thousands of years ago. The snow that falls in Antarctica each year doesn't melt. Instead, it piles up in layers, which are thicker in wet years and thinner in dry years.

Researchers drill deep into glaciers to take out cores of ice, each of which looks like a very long pole with thin cross stripes. Each stripe, or layer, represents a year's snowfall. By examining these ice cores, researchers can learn what the climate was like when each layer of snow fell. They can determine how much precipitation fell and what temperatures were like for that particular year. The deeper they drill, the farther back in time they can explore.

Recording Temperatures

The coldest place on Earth is the best place to look for signs of climate change. The slightest rise in Antarctica's air temperature could begin to melt the ice. Annual temperatures are recorded to see whether they are rising.

35.7 Studying Ice Shelves in Antarctica

As you have read, ice shelves are floating sheets of ice that have remained attached to the continent. Ice shelves form approximately half of the coastline of Antarctica and more than a tenth of its surface area. Every summer, the edges of some Antarctic ice shelves break off to form **icebergs,** which are large masses of ice that float around in the ocean.

Researchers in Antarctica study ice shelves to determine whether they are growing or melting. They also watch for large chunks of ice that break off and float away. One way in which they monitor ice shelves is by placing cameras on satellites that orbit, or circle, Earth. These satellite cameras produce images of ice shelves as they form and break apart.

Researchers also spend time at observation posts on or near the ice shelves. From there they can examine how seasonal temperature changes affect the ice shelves.

The Larsen Ice Shelf

The edges of ice shelves often break off to form icebergs. If temperatures rise too much, whole ice shelves might break apart or melt. The Larsen Ice Shelf pictured here is about the size of Rhode Island. In 2002, about 1,500 square miles of this shelf broke off and floated out to sea.

35.8 Studying Penguins in Antarctica

The Adelie is the most common penguin in this polar biome, with nearly 5 million Adelie penguins calling Antarctica home. Each summer these penguins raise their young on the few areas of coastline that are not covered with ice.

Global warming could be harmful for Adelies. Warmer air can hold more moisture, which could lead to increased snowfall in Antarctica. If snow covers the few bare spots that Adelie penguins require for nesting, they might stop breeding.

Researchers are studying how many Adelie penguins return to their nesting grounds each year. They do this by taking a simple **census,** which means counting the number of penguins that return to each nesting site. Researchers also try to track the birds' movements over the year by gluing transmitters on the penguins' feathers and using satellites to track the signals given off.

The Denver Post, 2002.

35.9 Beginning to Think Globally

In this chapter, you learned that Antarctica is a very cold, remote place. Researchers visit Antarctica to study global warming by gathering information on air temperatures, ice shelves, and penguins.

Researchers don't always agree on the significance of their findings. For example, air temperatures are rising in some areas of Antarctica. This may be due to the greenhouse effect, but temperatures are falling in other areas. The significance of these temperature variations is unclear.

In recent years, researchers have observed enormous chunks of ice shelves break off to form icebergs. However, scientists aren't sure what is triggering the breakups or what impact the breakups will have on the polar biome.

Researchers have also observed changes in the penguin populations. There are far fewer Adelies in some areas than in the past, but other penguin species are increasing their numbers. Neither of these changes may be the result of global warming.

Most scientists connect global warming to increasing levels of greenhouse gases within the atmosphere. They argue that this rise is a consequence of human activity, especially the burning of fossil fuels. However, the use of fossil fuels varies significantly from country to country. Think about this as you examine the maps in the next section.

What If Antarctica Melts?

This cartoon looks at what could happen if global warming were to melt the ice over Antarctica. The water trapped there would flow into the ocean, and sea levels would rise. If both polar ice caps were to melt, sea levels could rise by 20 feet or more.

35.10 Global Connections

The cartogram on the opposite page shows greenhouse gases produced by countries throughout the world. Notice the size of the United States. The maps across the bottom show how global warming could impact three parts of the world. The maps show coastlines in each of these places as they appear today and also how those coastlines would change if the polar ice caps were to melt.

How might rising sea levels be connected to greenhouse gases? Greenhouse gases may cause surface temperatures to rise. As Earth warms, glaciers and ice shelves will melt, resulting in a dramatic rise in sea levels around the world.

Are the countries that produce the most greenhouse gases the ones that will be most affected by rising sea levels? The major producers of greenhouse gases are the **developed countries,** such as the United States and Canada. Such countries operate their factories and cars on fossil fuels. Poor **developing countries** such as Bangladesh and Tuvalu have little industry, but because they are at low elevations and relatively flat, they could be severely affected by rising sea levels.

What can people do to reduce the greenhouse gases they add to the environment? People can reduce their production of greenhouse gases by using less energy from fossil fuels. One way to do this is to drive cars that get more miles per gallon of gas. Another step is to use energy-saving fluorescent lights. Still another is to turn lights and televisions off when they are not being used. Each of these steps may seem small, but together they can add up to considerable greenhouse gas savings.

Flooding in Tuvalu

Tuvalu is a small island country in the South Pacific. Scientists warn that in the next 50 years, rising sea levels could swamp Tuvalu's low-lying atolls. Were that to happen, its people would have to leave their flooded homes forever.

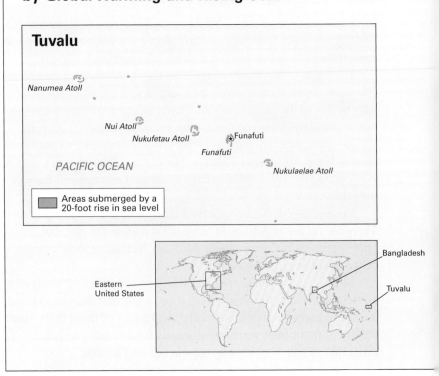

How Three World Areas May Be Affected by Global Warming and Rising Seas

Tuvalu

Nanumea Atoll

Nui Atoll
Nukufetau Atoll
Funafuti
Funafuti
Nukulaelae Atoll

PACIFIC OCEAN

Areas submerged by a 20-foot rise in sea level

Bangladesh

Eastern United States

Tuvalu

Greenhouse Gas Emissions Around the World

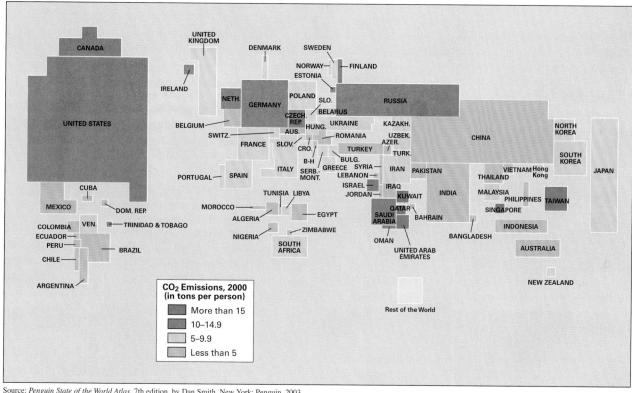

CO₂ Emissions, 2000 (in tons per person)
- More than 15
- 10–14.9
- 5–9.9
- Less than 5

Source: *Penguin State of the World Atlas,* 7th edition, by Dan Smith, New York: Penguin, 2003.

Eastern United States

Areas submerged by a 20-foot rise in sea level

Bangladesh

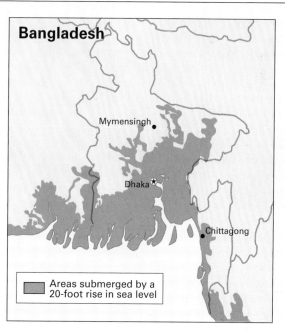

Areas submerged by a 20-foot rise in sea level

The Impact of Rising Seas

These maps show how the melting of the polar ice caps would affect three coastal areas. Many large U.S. cities would be under water. So would much of Bangladesh and all of Tuvalu.

Resources

The photographs introducing each of the eight units in this book were taken around the world. They are all the work of photographer Yann Arthus-Bertrand. For more information about aerial photography, see "Aerial Photographs and Satellite Imagery" in the beginning of this book.

Unit 4: Europe and Russia

Schoolyard in Paris, France The painted symbol of this schoolyard is best seen from above. The French school system begins with three years of pre-elementary for ages 3 to 5. Students then enter elementary school, secondary school, and high school.

Unit 2: Canada and the United States

Agricultural fields near Bozeman, Montana These fields in the north central United States are an example of contour farming. Fields are plowed in strips across the natural slope. Each row acts as a mini-dam, slowing runoff when it rains and reducing soil erosion.

Unit 3: Latin America

Confluence of rivers in Bolivar, Venezuela These two rivers come together in the state of Bolivar, in southern Venezuela. The muddy brown color of the river on the right comes from soil that has been washed out by heavy rains.

Unit 5: Africa

Date palm plantation near Cairo, Egypt On a date palm plantation in northern Egypt, fresh yellow and red dates slowly turn brown as they dry in the sun. Farmers protect the drying dates from wind and water by surrounding them with soil and branches.

Unit 6: Southwest and Central Asia

Tree plantation near Irbid, Jordan
In northern Jordan, olive trees survive in rocky, sandy soil. They need little water and are rarely irrigated. This makes olives a good crop for this area. Jordan is one of the most water-poor countries on the planet.

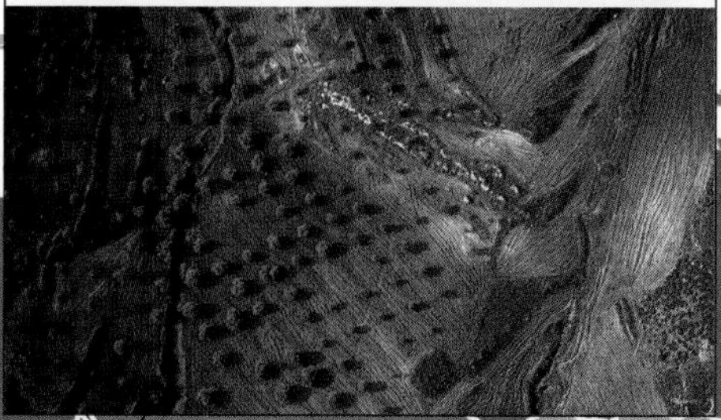

Unit 7: Monsoon Asia

Rice fields in Bali, Indonesia On the island of Bali, farmers have built thousands of terraced fields into the hilly landscape. An elaborate system of canals brings rainwater to irrigate their rice fields.

Unit 1: The Geographer's World

Brick factory near Agra, India At this brick factory in northern India, thousands of terra cotta bricks are stacked in neat rows. These bricks are the main building material used in nearby urban centers.

Unit 8: Oceania and Antarctica

Coral sand beach on Whitsunday Island, Australia In between the northeast coast of Australia and the Great Barrier Reef lie hundreds of tiny islands. The sand on the beaches of these islands is made of coral sediment. This sediment gives the sand its brilliant white color.

Flag	Country	Capital	Total Area (square miles)	Official and Other Major Languages	Major Religions
Canada and the United States					
	Canada	Ottawa	3,849,670	**English, French**	Christian, other
	United States	Washington, D.C.	3,717,796	**English,** Spanish	Christian, other, Muslim, Jewish
Latin America					
	Antigua and Barbuda	Saint John's	170	**English,** local dialects	Christian
	Argentina	Buenos Aires	1,073,514	**Spanish,** English, Italian, German, French	Christian, Jewish, other
	The Bahamas	Nassau	5,359	**English,** Creole	Christian, other
	Barbados	Bridgetown	166	English	Christian, other
	Belize	Belmopan	8,865	**English,** Spanish, Mayan, Garifuna, Creole	Christian, other
	Bolivia	La Paz	424,162	**Spanish, Quechua, Aymara**	Christian

The Global Data Bank contains basic information on every country on the globe. The countries are organized by regions. Within each region, they are listed alphabetically.

On the left-hand page for each region, you will find information that is unlikely to change much over time. These data include the country's name, flag, capital, and area. Each country's major languages and religions are also listed here.

On the right-hand page for each region, you will find information that is more likely to change with time. This includes population data such as population density, life expectancy, and population growth rate. You will also find economic data here. Examples include a country's gross domestic product, televisions per 1,000 people, and Internet users.

The figures on these right-hand pages are the latest available at the time this book went to press. More recent data can be found on the Internet at the Web sites of these organizations:

- CIA World Factbook
- NationMaster
- Population Reference Bureau
- UN Population Information Network

Population	Arithmetic Population Density*	Life Expectancy	Urban Population	Annual Population Growth from Births and Deaths	Gross Domestic Product (per capita, US$)	Literacy Rate	Doctors (per 100,000 people)	Televisions (per 1,000 people)	Internet Users (per 1,000 people)
31,900,000	8	79	79%	0.3%	$29,800	97%	210	691	513
293,600,000	79	77	79%	0.6%	$37,800	97%	549	938	551
100,000	447	71	37%	1.7%	$11,000	89%	17	452	128
37,900,000	35	74	89%	1.1%	$11,200	97%	301	326	112
300,000	59	72	89%	1.3%	$16,700	96%	106	248	268
300,000	1,542	72	50%	0.6%	$15,700	97%	121	346	370
300,000	31	70	49%	2.3%	$4,900	94%	105	175	109
8,800,000	21	63	63%	1.9%	$2,400	87%	73	121	32

*People per square mile

Flag	Country	Capital	Total Area (square miles)	Official and Other Major Languages	Major Religions
	Latin America (continued)				
	Brazil	Brasilia	3,300,154	**Portuguese,** Spanish, English, French	Christian, other
	Chile	Santiago	292,135	Spanish	Christian
	Colombia	Bogotá	439,734	Spanish	Christian, other
	Costa Rica	San José	19,730	**Spanish,** English	Christian, other
	Cuba	Havana	42,803	Spanish	Christian, other
	Dominica	Roseau	290	**English,** French patois	Christian, other
	Dominican Republic	Santo Domingo	18,815	Spanish	Christian, other
	Ecuador	Quito	109,483	**Spanish,** Quechua, other indigenous languages	Christian, other
	El Salvador	San Salvador	8,124	Spanish, Nahua	Christian
	Grenada	Saint George's	131	**English,** French patois	Christian
	Guatemala	Guatemala City	42,042	Spanish, Quiche, Cakchiquel, Kekchi, Mam, Garifuna, Xinca, other indigenous languages	Christian, indigenous
	Guyana	Georgetown	83,000	English, indigenous languages, Creole, Hindi, Urdu	Christian, Hindu, Muslim, other
	Haiti	Port-au-Prince	10,714	**French, Creole**	Christian, other, indigenous
	Honduras	Tegucigalpa	43,278	Spanish, indigenous languages	Christian

Population	Arithmetic Population Density*	Life Expectancy	Urban Population	Annual Population Growth from Births and Deaths	Gross Domestic Product (per capita, US$)	Literacy Rate	Doctors (per 100,000 people)	Televisions (per 1,000 people)	Internet Users (per 1,000 people)
179,100,000	54	71	81%	1.3%	$7,600	86%	206	349	82
16,000,000	55	76	87%	1.2%	$9,900	96%	109	523	272
45,300,000	103	72	71%	1.7%	$6,300	93%	135	303	62
4,200,000	214	79	59%	1.4%	$9,100	96%	173	231	193
11,300,000	263	76	75%	0.5%	$2,900	97%	591	251	11
100,000	238	74	71%	1.0%	$5,400	94%	49	225	160
8,800,000	469	69	64%	1.9%	$6,000	85%	188	97	64
13,400,000	122	71	61%	2.1%	$3,300	93%	148	252	44
6,700,000	826	70	58%	2.0%	$4,800	80%	124	233	84
100,000	807	71	39%	1.2%	$5,000	98%	50	370	169
2,700,000	301	66	39%	2.8%	$4,100	71%	90	145	33
800,000	9	63	36%	1.4%	$4,000	99%	48	98	142
8,100,000	757	51	36%	1.9%	$1,600	53%	25	60	10
7,000,000	162	71	47%	2.8%	$2,600	76%	83	119	25

*People per square mile

Flag	Country	Capital	Total Area (square miles)	Official and Other Major Languages	Major Religions

Flag	Country	Capital	Total Area (square miles)	Official and Other Major Languages	Major Religions
	**Jamaica**	Kingston	4,243	English, English patois	Christian, other
	**Mexico**	Mexico City (Distrito Federal)	756,062	Spanish, Mayan, Nahuatl, other indigenous languages	Christian, other
	**Nicaragua**	Managua	50,193	**Spanish,** indigenous languages	Christian
	**Panama**	Panama City	29,158	**Spanish,** English	Christian
	**Paraguay**	Asunción	157,046	**Spanish, Guarani**	Christian
	**Peru**	Lima	496,224	**Spanish, Quechua,** Aymara, many indigenous Amazonian languages	Christian
	**Saint Kitts and Nevis**	Basseterre	139	English	Christian
	**Saint Lucia**	Castries	239	**English,** French patois	Christian
	**Saint Vincent and the Grenadines**	Kingstown	151	English, French patois	Christian, other
	**Suriname**	Paramaribo	63,039	**Dutch,** English, Sranang Tongo, Hindustani, Javanese	Christian, Hindu, Muslim, indigenous
	**Trinidad and Tobago**	Port of Spain	1,981	**English,** Hindi, French, Spanish, Chinese	Christian, other, Hindu, Muslim
	**Uruguay**	Montevideo	68,498	Spanish, Portuñol, Brazilero	Christian, other, Jewish
	**Venezuela**	Caracas	352,143	**Spanish,** indigenous languages	Christian, other

Population	Arithmetic Population Density*	Life Expectancy	Urban Population	Annual Population Growth from Births and Deaths	Gross Domestic Product (per capita, US$)	Literacy Rate	Doctors (per 100,000 people)	Televisions (per 1,000 people)	Internet Users (per 1,000 people)
2,600,000	623	75	52%	1.4%	$3,900	88%	85	369	228
106,200,000	140	75	75%	2.1%	$9,000	92%	172	282	118
5,600,000	112	69	58%	2.7%	$2,300	68%	164	123	17
3,200,000	109	75	62%	1.8%	$6,300	93%	168	191	41
6,000,000	38	71	54%	2.5%	$4,700	94%	117	218	20
27,500,000	56	69	72%	1.7%	$5,100	91%	117	172	104
50,000	338	70	33%	1.0%	$8,800	97%	118	239	213
200,000	685	72	30%	1.1%	$5,400	67%	518	296	82
100,000	731	72	44%	1.1%	$2,900	96%	88	234	60
400,000	7	70	69%	1.5%	$4,000	93%	45	242	42
1,300,000	664	71	74%	0.6%	$9,500	99%	79	350	106
3,400,000	50	75	93%	0.6%	$12,800	98%	365	530	120
26,200,000	74	73	87%	1.9%	$4,800	93%	194	186	51

*People per square mile

Flag	Country	Capital	Total Area (square miles)	Official and Other Major Languages	Major Religions

Europe and Russia

Flag	Country	Capital	Total Area (square miles)	Official and Other Major Languages	Major Religions
	Albania	Tiranë	11,100	**Albanian,** Greek, Vlach, Romani, Slavic dialects	Muslim, Christian
	Andorra	Andorra la Vella	174	**Catalan,** French, Castilian, Portuguese	Christian
	Austria	Vienna	32,378	**German, Slovene, Croatian, Hungarian**	Christian, Muslim
	Belarus	Minsk	80,154	Belarusian, Russian	Christian, other
	Belgium	Brussels	11,787	**Dutch, French, German**	Christian, other
	Bosnia and Herzegovina	Sarajevo	19,741	Bosnian, Croatian, Serbian	Christian, Muslim, other
	Bulgaria	Sofia	42,822	Bulgarian, other ethnic languages	Christian, Muslim, other
	Croatia	Zagreb	21,830	Croatian	Christian, Muslim, other, Jewish
	Czech Republic	Prague	30,448	Czech	Christian, other
	Denmark	Copenhagen	16,637	Danish, Faroese, Greenlandic, German	Christian, Muslim
	Estonia	Tallinn	17,413	**Estonian,** Russian, Ukranian, Finnish, other	Christian, Jewish
	Finland	Helsinki	130,560	**Finnish, Swedish,** Sami, Russian	Christian, other
	France	Paris	212,934	**French**	Christian, Muslim, Jewish
	Germany	Berlin	137,830	**German**	Christian, other, Muslim

Population	Arithmetic Population Density*	Life Expectancy	Urban Population	Annual Population Growth from Births and Deaths	Gross Domestic Product (per capita, US$)	Literacy Rate	Doctors (per 100,000 people)	Televisions (per 1,000 people)	Internet Users (per 1,000 people)
3,200,000	291	74	42%	1.2%	$4,500	87%	139	318	10
100,000	397	84	92%	0.8%	$19,000	100%	259	462	90
8,100,000	250	79	54%	0%	$30,000	98%	324	646	462
9,800,000	122	69	72%	−0.6%	$6,100	100%	450	362	141
0,400,000	883	79	97%	0.1%	$29,100	98%	418	541	328
3,900,000	197	74	43%	0.1%	$6,100	95%	134	116	26
7,800,000	182	72	70%	−0.6%	$7,600	99%	338	453	206
4,400,000	203	75	56%	−0.2%	$10,600	99%	237	293	232
0,200,000	335	75	77%	−0.2%	$15,700	100%	343	538	268
5,400,000	325	77	72%	0.1%	$31,100	100%	366	859	513
1,300,000	77	71	69%	−0.4%	$12,300	100%	316	507	328
5,200,000	40	79	62%	0.2%	$27,400	100%	311	679	509
0,000,000	282	79	74%	0.4%	$27,600	99%	329	632	366
2,600,000	599	78	88%	−0.2%	$27,600	99%	362	675	473

*People per square mile

Flag	Country	Capital	Total Area (square miles)	Official and Other Major Languages	Major Religions
Europe and Russia (continued)					
	**Greece**	Athens	50,950	**Greek,** English, French	Christian, Muslim
	Hungary	Budapest	35,919	**Hungarian**	Christian, other
	**Iceland**	Reykjavik	39,768	Icelandic, English, Nordic languages	Christian, other
	**Ireland (Republic of)**	Dublin	27,135	English, Gaelic	Christian, other
	**Italy**	Rome	116,320	**Italian,** German, French, Slovene	Christian, Jewish, other
	Latvia	Riga	24,942	**Latvian,** Lithuanian, Russian	Christian
	Liechtenstein	Vaduz	62	**German,** Alemannic dialect	Christian, other
	Lithuania	Vilnius	25,174	**Lithuanian,** Polish, Russian	Christian, Muslim, Jewish
	Luxembourg	Luxembourg	999	**Luxembourgish, German, French**	Christian, Jewish, Muslim
	**Macedonia (Former Yugoslav Republic of)**	Skopje	9,927	Macedonian, Albanian, Turkish, Serbo-Croatian	Christian, Muslim, other
	**Malta**	Valletta	124	**Maltese, English**	Christian
	**Moldova**	Chisinau	13,012	**Moldovan,** Russian, Gagauz	Christian, Jewish
	**Monaco**	Monaco	1	**French,** English, Italian, Monégasque	Christian, other
	Netherlands	Amsterdam	15,768	**Dutch, Frisian**	Christian, Muslim, other

Population	Arithmetic Population Density*	Life Expectancy	Urban Population	Annual Population Growth from Births and Deaths	Gross Domestic Product (per capita, US$)	Literacy Rate	Doctors (per 100,000 people)	Televisions (per 1,000 people)	Internet Users (per 1,000 people)
11,000,000	216	78	60%	0%	$20,000	98%	440	519	150
10,100,000	281	73	65%	−0.4%	$13,900	99%	316	475	232
300,000	7	81	94%	0.8%	$30,900	100%	348	509	675
4,100,000	150	77	60%	0.8%	$29,600	98%	237	694	313
57,800,000	497	80	90%	−0.1%	$26,700	99%	607	494	337
2,300,000	93	72	68%	−0.5%	$10,200	100%	291	859	406
30,000	550	80	21%	0.5%	$25,000	100%	data not available	517	585
3,400,000	136	72	67%	−0.3%	$11,400	100%	403	487	214
500,000	453	78	91%	0.3%	$55,100	100%	255	598	376
2,000,000	205	73	59%	0.5%	$6,700	96%	219	282	48
400,000	3,229	78	91%	0.2%	$17,700	93%	293	566	303
4,200,000	323	68	45%	−0.4%	$1,800	99%	269	358	65
30,000	44,000	79	100%	0.6%	$27,000	99%	586	data not available	494
6,300,000	1,033	79	62%	0.4%	$28,600	99%	329	648	522

*People per square mile

Flag	Country	Capital	Total Area (square miles)	Official and Other Major Languages	Major Religions
Europe and Russia (continued)					
	**Norway**	Oslo	125,050	**Bokmal Norwegian, Nynorsk Norwegian**, Sami, Finnish	Christian, other
	Poland	Warsaw	124,807	**Polish**	Christian, other
	**Portugal**	Lisbon	35,514	**Portuguese, Mirandese**	Christian
	Romania	Bucharest	92,042	**Romanian**, Hungarian, German	Christian, other
	Russia	Moscow	6,592,819	**Russian**	Christian, Muslim, other
	**San Marino**	San Marino	23	Italian	Christian
	**Serbia and Montenegro**	Belgrade	39,448	Serbian, Albanian	Christian, Muslim, other
	**Slovakia**	Bratislava	18,923	**Slovak**, Hungarian	Christian, other
	**Slovenia**	Ljubljana	7,819	Slovenian, Serbo-Croatian	Christian, Muslim, other
	**Spain**	Madrid	195,363	**Castilian Spanish, Catalan, Galician, Basque**	Christian, other
	**Sweden**	Stockholm	173,730	Swedish, Sami, Finnish	Christian, other
	**Switzerland**	Bern	15,942	**German, French, Italian, Romansch**	Christian, other
	Ukraine	Kiev	233,089	Ukrainian, Russian, Romanian, Polish, Hungarian	Christian, Jewish
	**United Kingdom**	London	94,548	English, Welsh, Scottish Gaelic	Christian, Muslim, other

Population	Arithmetic Population Density*	Life Expectancy	Urban Population	Annual Population Growth from Births and Deaths	Gross Domestic Product (per capita, US$)	Literacy Rate	Doctors (per 100,000 people)	Televisions (per 1,000 people)	Internet Users (per 1,000 people)
4,600,000	37	80	78%	0.3%	$37,800	100%	356	884	346
88,200,000	306	75	62%	0%	$11,100	100%	220	229	232
0,500,000	295	77	53%	0%	$18,000	93%	325	413	194
21,700,000	235	71	53%	−0.3%	$7,000	98%	189	694	190
44,100,000	22	65	73%	−0.6%	$8,900	100%	417	538	41
30,000	1,252	80	84%	0.3%	$34,600	96%	4,707	863	531
0,700,000	271	73	52%	0.2%	$2,200	93%	data not available	282	79
5,400,000	284	74	56%	0%	$13,300	100%	326	409	256
2,000,000	255	76	51%	−0.1%	$19,000	100%	219	366	376
2,500,000	218	79	76%	0.1%	$22,000	98%	320	564	239
9,000,000	52	80	84%	0.1%	$26,800	99%	305	965	573
7,400,000	464	80	68%	0.1%	$32,700	99%	352	563	351
7,400,000	203	68	68%	−0.8%	$5,400	100%	297	456	18
9,700,000	630	78	89%	0.1%	$27,700	99%	167	950	423

*People per square mile

Flag	Country	Capital	Total Area (square miles)	Official and Other Major Languages	Major Religions
Africa					
	Algeria	Algiers	919,591	**Arabic,** French, Berber dialects	Muslim
	Angola	Luanda	481,351	**Portuguese,** Bantu, other African languages	Christian, indigenous
	Benin	Porto-Novo	43,483	**French,** Fon and Yoruba, tribal languages	Indigenous, Christian, Muslim
	Botswana	Gaborone	224,606	**English,** Setswana	Indigenous, Christian
	Burkina Faso	Ouagadougou	105,792	**French,** native Sudanic African languages	Muslim, indigenous, Christian
	Burundi	Bujumbura	10,745	**Kirundi, French,** Swahili	Christian, indigenous, Muslim
	Cameroon	Yaoundé	183,568	**English, French,** 24 major African languages	Indigenous, Christian, Muslim
	Cape Verde	Praia	1,556	Portuguese, Crioulo	Christian, indigenous
	Central African Republic	Bangui	240,533	**French,** Sangho, tribal languges	Christian, indigenous, Muslim
	Chad	N'Djamena	495,753	**French, Arabic,** Sara, more than 120 other languages	Muslim, Christian, Animist
	Comoros	Moroni	861	**Arabic, French,** Shikomoro	Muslim
	Congo	Brazzaville	132,046	**French,** Lingala, Monokutuba, Kikongo, other languages and dialects	Christian, indigenous, Muslim
	Côte d'Ivoire	Yamoussoukro	124,502	**French,** Dioula, 60 native dialects	Muslim, indigenous, Christian
	Democratic Republic of the Congo	Kinshasa	905,351	**French,** Lingala, Kingwana, Kikongo, Tshiluba	Christian, indigenous, Muslim

Population	Arithmetic Population Density*	Life Expectancy	Urban Population	Annual Population Growth from Births and Deaths	Gross Domestic Product (per capita, US$)	Literacy Rate	Doctors (per 100,000 people)	Televisions (per 1,000 people)	Internet Users (per 1,000 people)
32,300,000	35	73	49%	1.5%	$6,000	70%	85	171	16
13,300,000	28	40	33%	2.6%	$1,900	42%	8	20	3
7,300,000	167	51	40%	2.7%	$1,100	41%	6	34	10
1,700,000	7	36	54%	0.1%	$9,000	80%	29	44	35
13,600,000	128	45	15%	2.6%	$1,100	27%	4	12	4
6,200,000	580	43	8%	2.2%	$600	52%	5	35	2
16,100,000	88	48	48%	2.2%	$1,800	79%	7	35	4
500,000	300	69	53%	2.3%	$1,400	77%	17	102	44
3,700,000	16	42	39%	1.7%	$1,100	51%	4	5	1
9,500,000	19	49	24%	3.2%	$1,200	48%	3	5	2
700,000	757	56	33%	3.5%	$700	57%	7	24	6
3,800,000	29	48	52%	2.9%	$700	84%	25	13	4
16,900,000	136	42	46%	2.0%	$1,400	51%	9	91	14
58,300,000	64	49	30%	3.1%	$700	66%	7	2	1

*People per square mile

Flag	Country	Capital	Total Area (square miles)	Official and Other Major Languages	Major Religions
	Africa (continued)				
	Djibouti	Djibouti	8,958	**French, Arabic,** Somali, Afar	Muslim, Christian
	Egypt	Cairo	386,660	**Arabic,** French, English	Muslim, Christian
	Equatorial Guinea	Malabo	10,830	**Spanish, French,** English, Fang, Bubi, Ibo	Christian, indigenous
	Eritrea	Asmara	45,405	Afar, Arabic, Tigre, Kunama, Tigrinya, other Cushitic languages	Muslim, Christian
	Ethiopia	Addis Ababa	426,371	Amharic, Tigrinya, Oromigna, Gauragigna, Somali, Arabic, other local languages, English	Muslim, Ethiopian Orthodox Animist, other
	Gabon	Libreville	103,347	**French,** Fang, Myene, Nzebi, Bapounou/Eschira, Bandjabi	Christian, indigenous
	Gambia	Banjul	4,363	**English,** Mandinka, Wolof, Fula, other indigenous	Muslim, Christian
	Ghana	Accra	92,100	**English,** Akan, Mosi-Dagomba, Ewe, Ga, other African languages	Christian, indigenous, Muslim
	Guinea	Conakry	94,927	**French,** ethnic languages	Muslim, Christian, indigenous
	Guinea-Bissau	Bissau	13,946	**Portuguese,** Crioulo, African languages	Indigenous, Muslim, Christian
	Kenya	Nairobi	224,081	**English, Kiswahili,** indigenous languages	Christian, indigenous, Muslim
	Lesotho	Maseru	11,718	**English,** Sesotho, Zulu, Xhosa	Christian, indigenous
	Liberia	Monrovia	43,000	**English,** about 20 ethnic languages	Indigenous, Christian, Muslim
	Libyan Arab Jamahiriya	Tripoli	679,359	Arabic, Italian, English	Muslim

Population	Arithmetic Population Density*	Life Expectancy	Urban Population	Annual Population Growth from Births and Deaths	Gross Domestic Product (per capita, US$)	Literacy Rate	Doctors (per 100,000 people)	Televisions (per 1,000 people)	Internet Users (per 1,000 people)
700,000	79	46	82%	2.3%	$1,300	68%	13	78	10
73,400,000	190	68	43%	2.0%	$4,000	58%	212	229	39
500,000	47	49	45%	2.6%	$2,700	86%	25	116	3
4,400,000	98	53	19%	2.6%	$700	59%	3	53	2
72,400,000	170	46	15%	2.4%	$700	43%	3	7	1
1,400,000	13	57	73%	2.1%	$5,500	63%	29	138	26
1,500,000	355	54	26%	2.9%	$1,700	40%	4	15	19
21,400,000	232	58	44%	2.2%	$2,200	75%	9	51	8
9,200,000	97	49	33%	2.7%	$2,100	36%	9	17	5
1,500,000	110	45	32%	3.0%	$800	42%	17	40	15
32,400,000	145	51	36%	2.3%	$1,000	85%	13	45	13
1,800,000	154	38	17%	1.1%	$3,000	85%	5	35	10
3,500,000	81	42	45%	2.9%	$1,000	58%	2	25	0
5,600,000	8	76	86%	2.4%	$6,400	83%	129	137	29

*People per square mile

Flag	Country	Capital	Total Area (square miles)	Official and Other Major Languages	Major Religions
	Africa (continued)				
	Madagascar	Antananarivo	226,656	**French, Malagasy**	Indigenous, Christian, Muslim
	Malawi	Lilongwe	45,745	**English, Chichewa,** other regional languages	Christian, Muslim, indigenous
	Mali	Bamako	478,838	**French,** Bambara, numerous African languages	Muslim, indigenous
	Mauritania	Nouakchott	395,954	**Arabic,** Pulaar, Soninke, French, Hassaniya, Wolof	Muslim
	Mauritius	Port Louis	788	**English, French,** Creole, Hindi, Urdu, Hakka, Bhojpuri	Hindu, Christian, Muslim
	Morocco	Rabat	172,413	**Arabic,** Berber dialects, French	Muslim, Christian, Jewish
	Mozambique	Maputo	309,494	**Portuguese,** Makhuwa, Tsonga, Lomwe, Sena, numerous indigenous languages	Indigenous, Christian, Muslim
	Namibia	Windhoek	318,259	**English,** Afrikaans, German, Oshivambo, Herero, Nama	Christian, indigenous
	Niger	Niamey	489,189	**French,** Hausa, Djerma	Muslim, indigenous, Christian
	Nigeria	Abuja	356,668	**English,** Hausa, Yoruba, Igbo, Fulani	Muslim, Christian, indigenous
	Rwanda	Kigali	10,170	**Kinyarwanda, French, English,** Bantu, Kiswahili (Swahili)	Christian, Muslim
	São Tomé and Príncipe	São Tomé	371	**Portuguese**	Christian
	Senegal	Dakar	75,954	**French,** Wolof, Pulaar, Jola, Mandinka	Muslim, Christian
	Seychelles	Victoria	174	**English, French,** Creole	Christian, other

Population	Arithmetic Population Density*	Life Expectancy	Urban Population	Annual Population Growth from Births and Deaths	Gross Domestic Product (per capita, US$)	Literacy Rate	Doctors (per 100,000 people)	Televisions (per 1,000 people)	Internet Users (per 1,000 people)
17,500,000	77	55	26%	3.0%	$800	69%	9	18	4
11,900,000	261	44	14%	3.1%	$600	63%	5	6	3
13,400,000	28	48	30%	3.3%	$900	46%	4	27	2
3,000,000	8	54	40%	2.7%	$1,800	42%	14	44	4
1,200,000	1,568	72	42%	1.0%	$11,400	86%	85	333	123
30,600,000	177	70	57%	1.5%	$4,000	52%	48	165	27
19,200,000	62	40	29%	1.7%	$1,200	48%	2	17	3
1,900,000	6	47	33%	1.6%	$7,200	84%	30	79	34
12,400,000	25	45	21%	3.5%	$800	18%	3	10	1
37,300,000	385	52	36%	2.9%	$900	68%	27	68	6
8,400,000	829	40	17%	1.9%	$1,300	70%	2	8	3
200,000	445	69	38%	2.8%	$1,200	79%	47	93	99
0,900,000	143	56	43%	2.6%	$1,600	40%	8	40	22
100,000	460	71	50%	1.0%	$7,800	58%	132	244	145

*People per square mile

Flag	Country	Capital	Total Area (square miles)	Official and Other Major Languages	Major Religions
Africa (continued)					
	Sierra Leone	Freetown	27,699	**English,** Mende, Temne, Krio	Muslim, indigenous, Christian
	Somalia	Mogadishu	246,201	**Somali,** Arabic, Italian, English	Muslim
	South Africa	Tshwane (Pretoria)	471,444	**Afrikaans, English, Ndebele, Pedi, Sotho, Swazi, Tsonga, Tswana, Venda, Xhosa, Zulu**	Christian, indigenous, Muslim, Hindu
	Sudan	Khartoum	967,494	**Arabic,** English, Sranang Tongo, Hindustani, Javanese	Muslim, indigenous, Christian
	Swaziland	Mbabane	6,703	**English, siSwati**	Indigenous, Roman Catholic, Muslim, other
	Tanzania (United Republic of)	Dar es Salaam	364,900	**Swahili, English,** Kiunguju, Arabic, many local languages	Muslim, indigenous, Christian
	Togo	Lomé	21,927	**French,** Ewe, Mina, Kabye, Dagomba	Indigenous, Christian, Muslim
	Tunisia	Tunis	63,170	**Arabic,** French	Muslim, Christian, Jewish
	Uganda	Kampala	93,066	**English,** Ganda, Swahili, Arabic, other Niger-Congo languages, other Nilo-Saharan languages	Christian, indigenous
	Western Sahara*	El Aaiún	97,344	Arabic	Muslim
	Zambia	Lusaka	290,583	**English,** Bemba, Kaonda, Lozi, Lunda, Luvale, Nyanja, Tonga, about 70 other indigenous languages	Christian, Muslim, Hindu
	Zimbabwe	Harare	150,873	**English,** Shona, Sindebele, many tribal dialects	Christian, indigenous

*The country of Morocco considers Western Sahara under its rule.
As of 2005, this rule remains under dispute, awaiting a decision from
the United Nations.

Population	Arithmetic Population Density*	Life Expectancy	Urban Population	Annual Population Growth from Births and Deaths	Gross Domestic Product (per capita, US$)	Literacy Rate	Doctors (per 100,000 people)	Televisions (per 1,000 people)	Internet Users (per 1,000 people)
5,200,000	187	35	37%	2.1%	$500	31%	7	13	2
8,300,000	34	47	33%	2.9%	$500	38%	4	15	9
46,900,000	99	53	53%	1.0%	$10,700	86%	69	177	68
39,100,000	40	57	31%	2.8%	$1,900	61%	16	383	9
1,200,000	162	43	25%	2.0%	$4,900	82%	18	34	26
36,100,000	99	45	22%	2.3%	$600	78%	2	44	7
5,600,000	253	54	33%	2.7%	$1,500	61%	6	123	42
10,000,000	158	73	63%	1.1%	$6,900	74%	70	210	64
26,100,000	280	45	12%	3.0%	$1,400	70%	5	16	5
300,000	3	62	94%	2.1%	data not available	data not available	data not available	data not available	data not available
10,900,000	38	35	35%	1.8%	$800	81%	7	61	6
12,700,000	84	41	32%	1.2%	$1,900	91%	6	66	43

*People per square mile

Flag	Country	Capital	Total Area (square miles)	Official and Other Major Languages	Major Religions
Southwest and Central Asia					
	Afghanistan	Kabul	251,772	**Pashtu,** Afghan Persian, Uzbek, Turkmen, Balochi, Pashai, other ethnic languages	Muslim
	Armenia	Yerevan	11,506	**Armenian,** Russian	Christian, indigenous
	Azerbaijan	Baku	33,436	**Azerbaijani,** Russian, Armenian	Muslim, Christian, other
	Bahrain	Manama	266	Arabic, English, Farsi, Urdu	Muslim
	Cyprus	Nicosia	3,571	Greek, Turkish, English	Christian, Muslim, other
	Georgia	Tbilisi	26,911	**Georgian,** Russian, Armenian, Azeri, other, Abkhaz	Christian, Muslim, other
	Iran (Islamic Republic of)	Tehran	630,575	Persian, Turkic, Kurdish, Luri, Balochi, Arabic, Turkish, other dialects	Muslim, other
	Iraq	Baghdad	169,236	Arabic, Kurdish, Assyrian, Armenian	Muslim, other
	Israel	Jerusalem	8,131	**Hebrew,** Arabic, English	Jewish, Muslim, other, Christian
	Jordan	Amman	34,444	**Arabic,** English	Muslim, Christian, other
	Kazakhstan	Astana	1,049,151	**Kazakh, Russian**	Muslim, Christian, other
	Kuwait	Kuwait	6,880	**Arabic,** English	Muslim, other
	Kyrgyzstan	Bishkek	76,641	**Kyrgyz, Russian**	Muslim, Christian, other
	Lebanon	Beirut	4,015	**Arabic,** French, English, Armenian	Muslim, Christian, other

Population	Arithmetic Population Density*	Life Expectancy	Urban Population	Annual Population Growth from Births and Deaths	Gross Domestic Product (per capita, US$)	Literacy Rate	Doctors (per 100,000 people)	Televisions (per 1,000 people)	Internet Users (per 1,000 people)
28,500,000	113	43	22%	2.7%	$700	36%	19	14	0
3,200,000	279	73	64%	0.2%	$3,500	99%	353	232	53
8,300,000	248	72	51%	0.8%	$3,400	97%	354	334	37
700,000	2,714	74	87%	1.7%	$16,900	89%	160	425	282
900,000	265	78	65%	0.5%	$19,200	98%	298	379	337
4,500,000	168	72	52%	0%	$2,500	99%	391	357	31
67,400,000	107	69	67%	1.2%	$7,000	79%	105	173	72
25,900,000	153	60	68%	2.7%	$1,500	40%	54	83	1
6,800,000	837	79	92%	1.6%	$19,800	95%	391	342	301
5,600,000	163	72	79%	2.4%	$4,300	91%	205	177	83
15,000,000	14	64	57%	0.6%	$6,300	98%	330	338	16
2,500,000	362	78	100%	1.7%	$19,000	84%	153	418	231
5,100,000	66	68	35%	1.4%	$1,600	97%	268	49	30
4,500,000	1,121	73	87%	1.7%	$4,800	87%	325	354	117

*People per square mile

Flag	Country	Capital	Total Area (square miles)	Official and Other Major Languages	Major Religions
Southwest and Central Asia (continued)					
	Oman	Muscat	82,031	**Arabic**, English, Baluchi, Urdu, Indian dialects	Muslim, Hindu
	Pakistan	Islamabad	307,375	**Urdu, English**, Punjabi, Sindhi, Siraiki, Pashtu, Balochi, Hindko, Brahui	Muslim, other
	Qatar	Doha	4,247	**Arabic**, English	Muslim, other
	Saudi Arabia	Riyadh	829,996	**Arabic**	Muslim
	Syrian Arab Republic	Damascus	71,498	**Arabic**, Kurdish, Armenian, Aramaic, Circassian, French	Muslim, Christian, Jewish
	Tajikistan	Dushanbe	55,251	**Tajik**, Russian	Muslim, other
	Turkey	Ankara	299,158	**Turkish**, Kurdish, Arabic, Armenian, Greek	Muslim
	Turkmenistan	Ashgabat	188,456	Turkmen, Russian, Uzbek, other	Muslim, Christian
	United Arab Emirates	Abu Dhabi	32,278	**Arabic**, Persian, English, Hindi, Urdu	Muslim, other
	Uzbekistan	Tashkent	172,741	**Uzbek**, Russian, Tajik, other	Muslim, Christian, other
	Yemen	Sanaa	203,849	Arabic	Muslim, other

Population	Arithmetic Population Density*	Life Expectancy	Urban Population	Annual Population Growth from Births and Deaths	Gross Domestic Product (per capita, US$)	Literacy Rate	Doctors (per 100,000 people)	Televisions (per 1,000 people)	Internet Users (per 1,000 people)
2,700,000	32	74	76%	2.2%	$13,100	76%	126	591	71
159,200,000	518	61	34%	2.4%	$2,100	46%	66	79	10
700,000	175	72	92%	1.6%	$21,500	83%	221	469	197
25,100,000	30	72	86%	3.0%	$11,800	79%	140	279	67
18,000,000	251	70	50%	2.4%	$3,300	77%	140	182	13
6,600,000	120	68	27%	1.9%	$1,000	99%	218	357	1
71,300,000	238	69	59%	1.4%	$6,700	87%	124	409	81
5,700,000	30	67	47%	1.6%	$5,800	98%	317	182	2
4,200,000	130	74	78%	1.4%	$23,200	78%	202	213	275
26,400,000	153	70	37%	1.6%	$1,700	99%	289	280	19
20,000,000	98	60	26%	3.3%	$800	50%	22	308	5

*People per square mile

Flag	Country	Capital	Total Area (square miles)	Official and Other Major Languages	Major Religions
Monsoon Asia					
	Bangladesh	Dhaka	55,598	**Bangala**, English	Muslim, Hindu
	Bhutan	Thimphu	18,147	**Dzongkha**, Tibetan and Nepalese dialects	Buddhist, Hindu
	Brunei Darussalam	Bandar Seri Begawan	2,228	**Malay**, Chinese, English	Muslim, Buddhist, Christian, indigenous, other
	Cambodia	Phnom Penh	69,900	**Khmer**, French, English	Buddhist, other
	East Timor	Dili	5,741	**Tetum, Portuguese**, Indonesian, English, Tetum, Galole, Mambae, Kemak, other indigenous languages	Christian, Muslim, Hindu, Buddhist, indigenous
	India	New Delhi	1,269,340	**Hindi, Bengali, Telugu, Marathi, Tamil, Urdu, Gujarati, Malayalam, Kannada, Oriya, Punjabi, Assamese, Kashmiri, Sindhi, Sanskrit**, English, Hindustani	Hindu, Muslim, Christian, other
	Indonesia	Jakarta	735,355	**Bahasa Indonesia**, English, Dutch, Javanese, other local dialects	Muslim, Protestant, Roman Catholic, Hindu, Buddhist, other
	Japan	Tokyo	145,869	**Japanese**	Buddhist, indigenous, other
	Korea, North	Pyongyang	46,541	**Korean**	Government-sponsored groups and others
	Korea, South	Seoul	38,324	**Korean**, English	Christian, Buddhist, indigenous, other
	Laos	Vientiane	91,429	**Lao**, French, English, many ethnic languages	Buddhist, indigenous, other
	Malaysia	Kuala Lumpur	127,317	**Bahasa Melayu**, Chinese dialects, Tamil, Telugu, Malayalam, Panjabi, Thai, Iban and Kadazan, other indigenous languages	Muslim, Buddhist, indigenous, Hindu, Christian, other
	Maldives	Male	116	**Maldivian Dhivehi**, English	Muslim

Population	Arithmetic Population Density*	Life Expectancy	Urban Population	Annual Population Growth from Births and Deaths	Gross Domestic Product (per capita, US$)	Literacy Rate	Doctors (per 100,000 people)	Televisions (per 1,000 people)	Internet Users (per 1,000 people)
141,300,000	2,542	60	23%	2.1%	$1,900	43%	23	62	2
1,000,000	53	66	21%	2.5%	$1,300	42%	5	29	20
400,000	166	76	74%	1.9%	$18,600	94%	101	629	102
13,100,000	188	57	16%	2.2%	$1,900	69%	16	8	2
800,000	143	49	8%	1.3%	$500	59%	data not available	data not available	63
,086,600,000	856	62	28%	1.7%	$2,900	60%	51	84	17
218,700,000	297	68	42%	1.6%	$3,200	88%	16	153	38
127,600,000	875	82	78%	0.1%	$28,200	99%	201	785	483
22,800,000	489	63	60%	0.7%	$1,300	99%	297	160	data not available
48,200,000	1,258	77	80%	0.5%	$17,800	98%	181	458	610
5,800,000	63	54	19%	2.3%	$1,700	66%	59	54	3
25,600,000	201	73	62%	2.1%	$9,000	89%	70	210	344
300,000	2,573	73	27%	1.4%	$3,900	97%	78	131	53

*People per square mile

Flag	Country	Capital	Total Area (square miles)	Official and Other Major Languages	Major Religions

Flag	Country	Capital	Total Area (square miles)	Official and Other Major Languages	Major Religions
	Mongolia	Ulaanbaatar	604,826	**Khalkha Mongol,** Turkic, Russian	Buddhist, Muslim, indigenous, Christian
	Myanmar (Burma)*	Yangon (Rangoon)	261,228	**Burmese,** other ethnic languages	Buddhist, Christian, Muslim, indigenous
	Nepal	Kathmandu	56,826	**Nepali,** other indigenous languages	Hindu, Buddhist, Muslim
	People's Republic of China	Beijing	3,696,519	Mandarin Chinese, Yue, Wu, Minbei, Minnan, Xiang, Gan, Hakka, other minority languages	Officially atheist
	Philippines	Manila	115,830	**Filipino, English,** Tagalog, Cebuano, Ilocan, Hiligaynon, Bicol, Waray, Pampango, Pangasinense	Christian, Muslim, Buddhist, other
	Singapore	Singapore	239	**Chinese, Malay, Tamil, English**	Buddhist, Muslim, Christian, Hindu, indigenous, other
	Sri Lanka	Colombo	25,332	**Sinhala, Tamil,** other	Buddhist, Hindu, Christian, Muslim
	Taiwan (Republic of China)†	Taipei	13,969	**Mandarin Chinese,** Taiwanese, Hakka dialects	Buddhist-Confucian-Taoist, Christian, other
	Thailand	Bangkok	198,116	**Thai,** English, ethnic dialects	Buddhist, Muslim, other
	Vietnam	Hanoi	128,066	**Vietnamese,** English, French, Chinese, Khmer, indigenous languages	Buddhist, indigenous, Christian, Muslim

*Military authorities in Burma adopted the name Myanmar in 1989. As of 2005, many continue to refer to the nation as Burma.

†Taiwan considers itself an independent nation. The country of China considers Taiwan a province of their country. As of 2005, the United Nations does not officially recognize Taiwan as an independent country.

Population	Arithmetic Population Density*	Life Expectancy	Urban Population	Annual Population Growth from Births and Deaths	Gross Domestic Product (per capita, US$)	Literacy Rate	Doctors (per 100,000 people)	Televisions (per 1,000 people)	Internet Users (per 1,000 people)
2,500,000	4	65	57%	1.2%	$1,800	98%	267	81	58
50,100,000	192	57	28%	1.4%	$1,800	85%	30	7	1
24,700,000	435	59	14%	2.3%	$1,400	45%	5	8	3
,307,300,000	352	71	41%	0.6%	$5,000	91%	164	350	63
83,700,000	722	70	48%	2.0%	$4,600	93%	116	182	44
4,200,000	17,541	79	100%	0.6%	$23,700	93%	140	303	509
19,600,000	772	72	30%	1.3%	$3,700	92%	43	121	12
22,600,000	1,621	76	78%	0.4%	$23,400	96%	data not available	441	391
63,800,000	322	71	31%	0.8%	$7,400	93%	30	283	111
81,500,000	636	72	25%	1.2%	$2,500	90%	53	197	43

*People per square mile

Flag	Country	Capital	Total Area (square miles)	Official and Other Major Languages	Major Religions
Oceania and Antarctica					
	Australia	Canberra	2,988,888	English, indigenous languages	Christian, other
	Fiji	Suva	7,054	**English,** Fijian, Hindustani	Christian, Hindu, Muslim, other
	Kiribati	Tarawa	282	**English,** I-Kiribati	Christian, other
	Marshall Islands	Majuro	69	**Marshallese, English,** Japanese	Christian
	Micronesia (Federated States of)	Palikir	270	**English,** Trukese, Pohnpeian, Yapese, Kosrean, Ulithian, Woleaian, Nukuoro, Kapingamarangi	Christian, other
	Nauru	Yaren District	9	**Nauruan,** English	Christian
	New Zealand	Wellington	104,452	**English, Maori**	Christian, other
	Palau	Koror	178	**English, Palauan, Sonsoralese, Tobi, Angaur, Japanese**	Christian, indigenous
	Papua New Guinea	Port Moresby	178,703	Melanesian Pidgin, Motu, 715 indigenous languages	Indigenous, Christian, other
	Samoa	Apia	1,097	Samoan, English	Christian
	Solomon Islands	Honiara	11,158	Melanesian Pidgin, English, 120 indigenous languages	Christian, indigenous
	Tonga	Nuku'alofa	290	Tongan, English	Christian
	Tuvalu	Funafuti	10	Tuvaluan, English, Samoan, Kiribati	Christian, other
	Vanuatu	Port-Vila	4,707	**English, French, Bislama,** more than 100 indigenous languages	Christian, indigenous

Population	Arithmetic Population Density*	Life Expectancy	Urban Population	Annual Population Growth from Births and Deaths	Gross Domestic Product (per capita, US$)	Literacy Rate	Doctors (per 100,000 people)	Televisions (per 1,000 people)	Internet Users (per 1,000 people)
20,100,000	7	80	91%	0.6%	$29,000	100%	249	722	567
800,000	120	67	39%	1.9%	$5,800	94%	34	117	67
100,000	319	63	43%	1.8%	$800	100%	30	44	23
100,000	820	69	68%	3.7%	$1,600	94%	47	data not available	26
100,000	400	67	22%	2.1%	$2,000	89%	60	25	51
10,000	1,412	61	100%	1.8%	$5,000	95%	149	44	26
4,100,000	39	78	78%	0.7%	$21,600	99%	223	574	526
20,000	118	70	70%	0.8%	$9,000	92%	109	data not available	35
5,700,000	32	57	15%	2.2%	$2,200	65%	5	23	14
200,000	167	73	22%	2.4%	$5,600	100%	70	148	22
500,000	41	61	16%	2.7%	$1,700	77%	13	10	5
100,000	352	71	32%	1.8%	$2,200	99%	35	70	29
10,000	900	68	47%	1.7%	$1,100	98%	data not available	data not available	125
200,000	46	67	21%	2.2%	$2,900	34%	11	13	36

*People per square mile

80°N 160°W 140°W 120°W 100°W 80°W 60°W 40°W

Mt. McKinley
(20,320 ft.
6,194 m)

60°N

ROCKY MOUNTAINS

GREAT PLAINS

NORTH

AMERICA

ATLANTIC
OCEAN

40°N

Mississippi

Tropic of Cancer

20°N

PACIFIC
OCEAN

Amazon R.

AMAZON
BASIN

0° Equator

ANDES MOUNTAINS

SOUTH

BRAZILIAN
HIGHLANDS

20°S

Tropic of Capricorn

AMERICA

Mt. Aconcagua
(22,834 ft.
6,960 m)

PAMPAS

40°S

| 0 | 1,500 | 3,000 miles |
| 0 | 1,500 | 3,000 kilometers |

Robinson projection

60°S

Vinson Massif
(16,067 ft.
4,897 m)

80°S 160°W 140°W 120°W 100°W 80°W 60°W 40°W

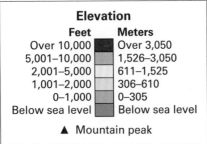

Elevation

Feet	Meters
Over 10,000	Over 3,050
5,001–10,000	1,526–3,050
2,001–5,000	611–1,525
1,001–2,000	306–610
0–1,000	0–305
Below sea level	Below sea level

▲ Mountain peak

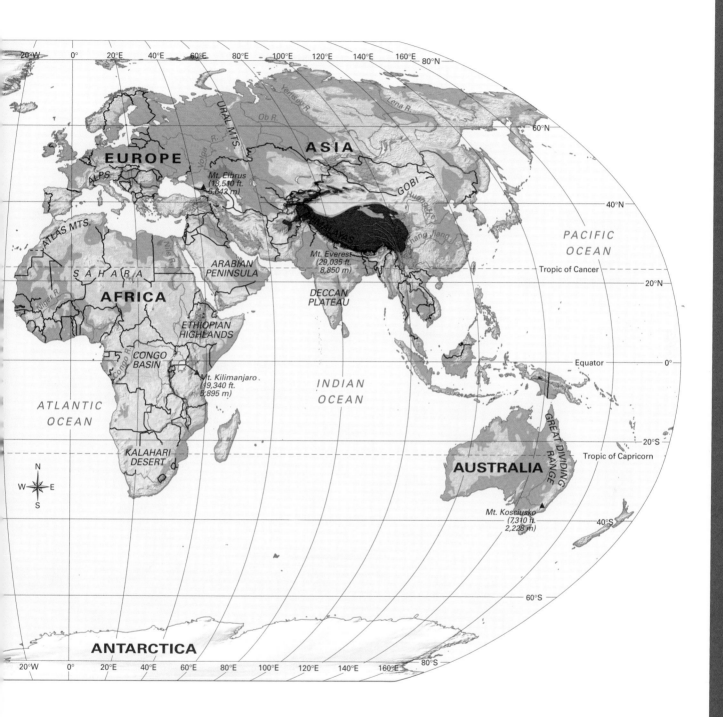

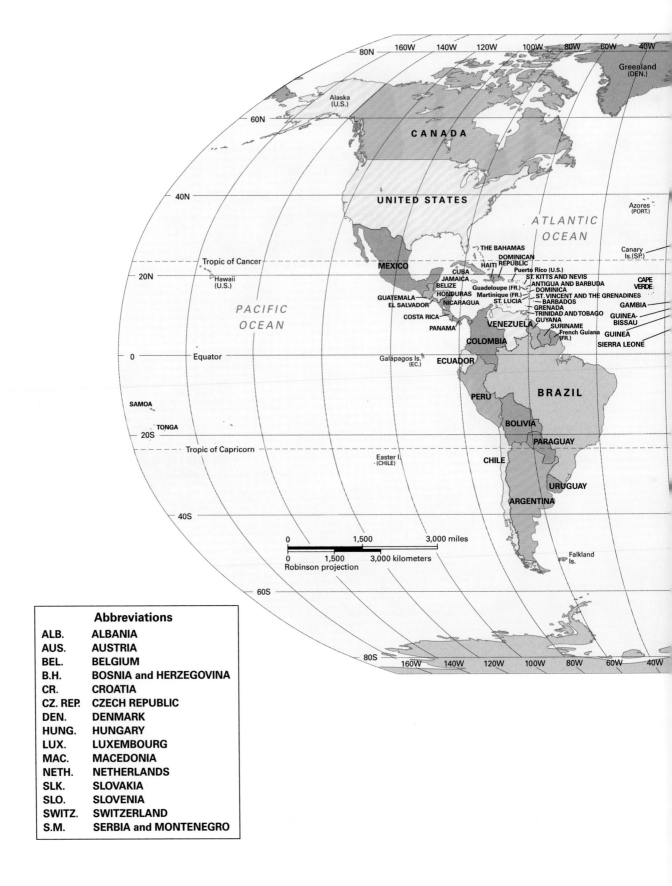

Abbreviations

ALB.	ALBANIA
AUS.	AUSTRIA
BEL.	BELGIUM
B.H.	BOSNIA and HERZEGOVINA
CR.	CROATIA
CZ. REP.	CZECH REPUBLIC
DEN.	DENMARK
HUNG.	HUNGARY
LUX.	LUXEMBOURG
MAC.	MACEDONIA
NETH.	NETHERLANDS
SLK.	SLOVAKIA
SLO.	SLOVENIA
SWITZ.	SWITZERLAND
S.M.	SERBIA and MONTENEGRO

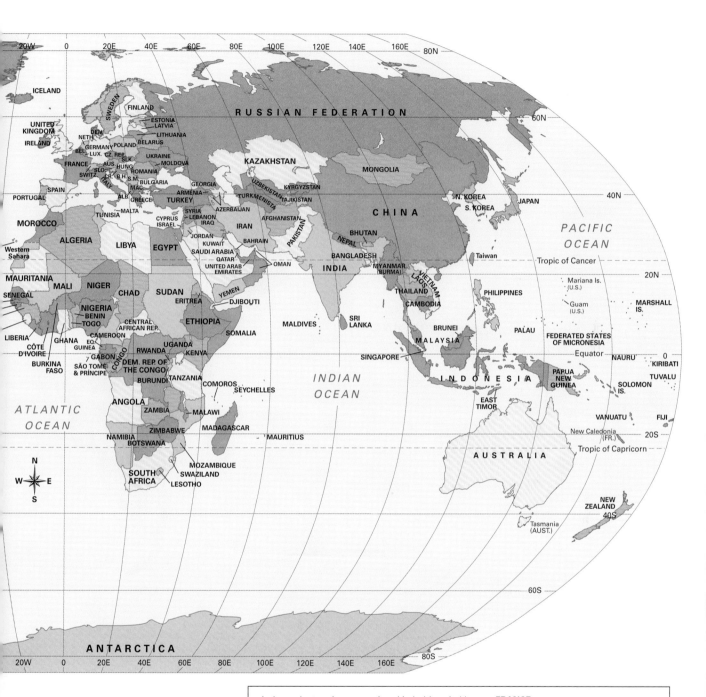

- Independent nations are printed in bold capital letters: **FRANCE**.
- Nations whose independence or governing rule is in dispute are printed in bold type: **Taiwan**.
- Territories, provinces, and the like governed by an independent nation are printed in bold type, with an abbreviation for the ruling nation: **French Guiana (FR.)**.
- Areas whose governing rule is in dispute are printed in nonbold type: Falkland Islands.
- Areas that are part of an independent nation but geographically separated from it are printed in nonbold type, with an abbreviation for the ruling nation: Hawaii (U.S.).

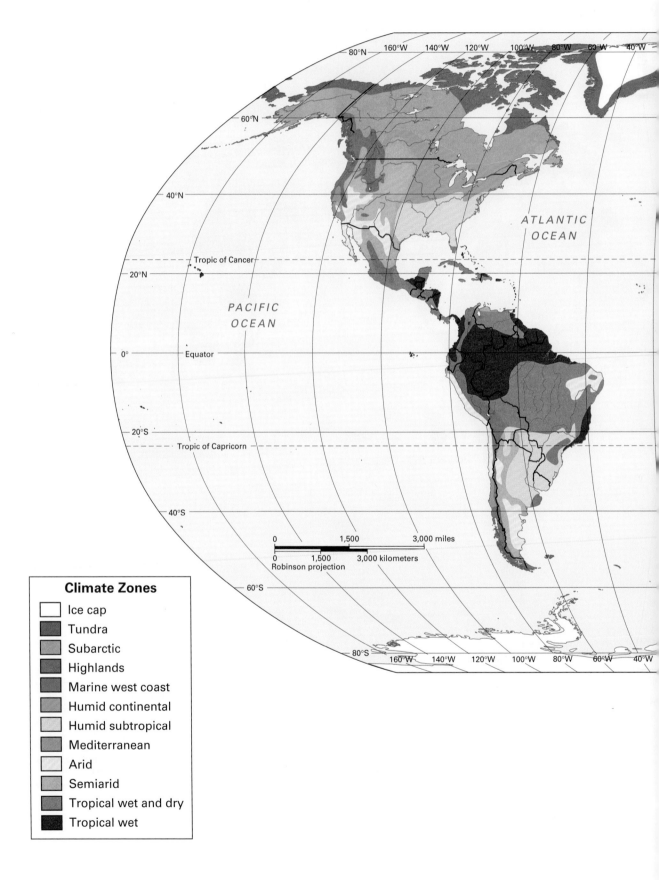

Climate Zones

- Ice cap
- Tundra
- Subarctic
- Highlands
- Marine west coast
- Humid continental
- Humid subtropical
- Mediterranean
- Arid
- Semiarid
- Tropical wet and dry
- Tropical wet

80°N 160°W 140°W 120°W 100°W 80°W 60°W 40°W

60°N

40°N

ATLANTIC OCEAN

Tropic of Cancer

20°N

PACIFIC OCEAN

0° Equator

20°S

Tropic of Capricorn

40°S

0 1,500 3,000 miles
0 1,500 3,000 kilometers
Robinson projection

60°S

80°S 160°W 140°W 120°W 100°W 80°W 60°W 40°W

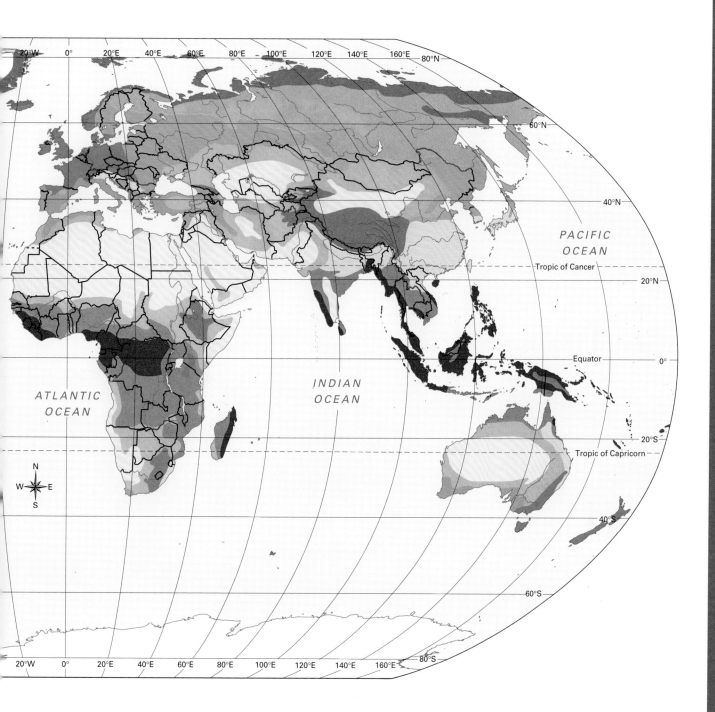

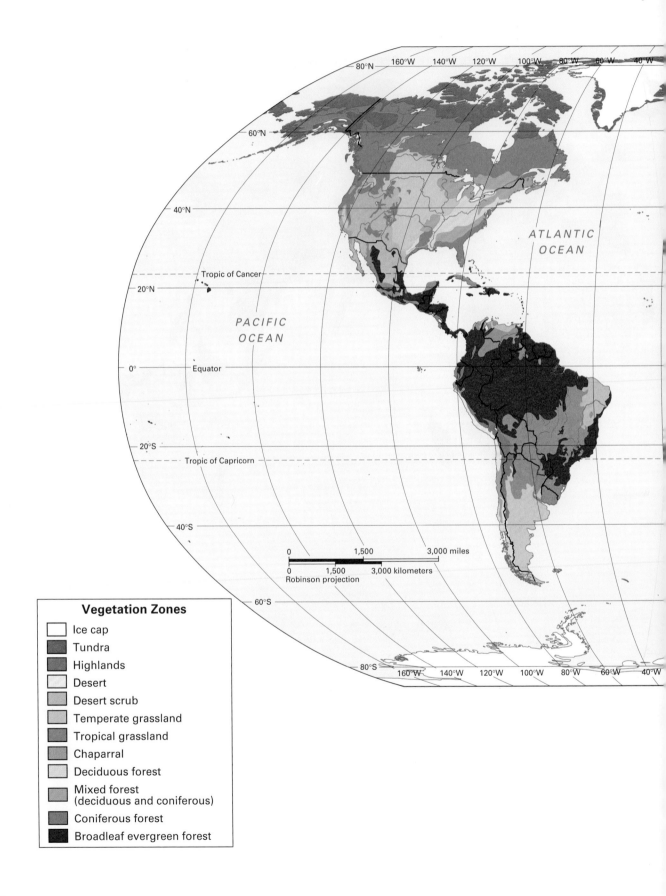

Vegetation Zones

- Ice cap
- Tundra
- Highlands
- Desert
- Desert scrub
- Temperate grassland
- Tropical grassland
- Chaparral
- Deciduous forest
- Mixed forest (deciduous and coniferous)
- Coniferous forest
- Broadleaf evergreen forest

0   1,500   3,000 miles
0   1,500   3,000 kilometers
Robinson projection

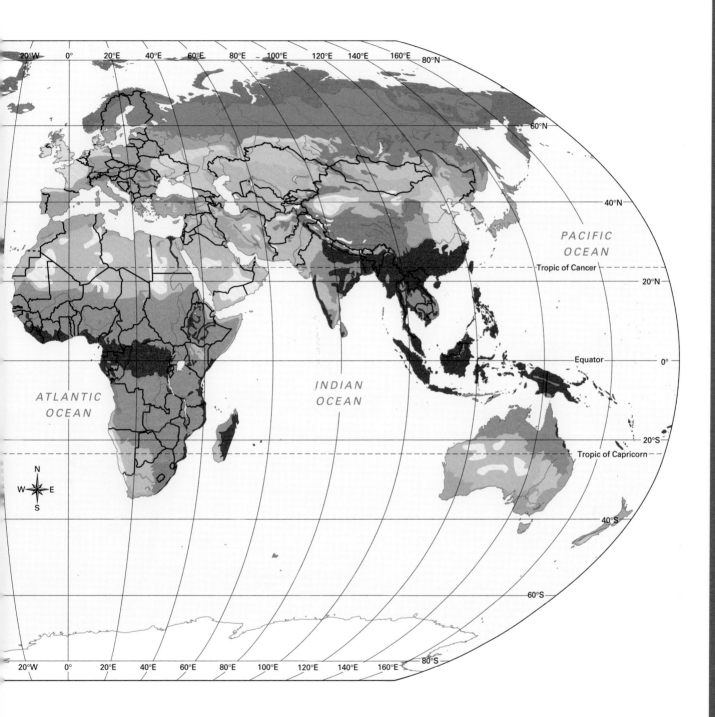

PACIFIC
OCEAN

80°N

60°N

40°N

Tropic of Cancer

20°N

Equator 0°

INDIAN
OCEAN

ATLANTIC
OCEAN

20°S

Tropic of Capricorn

40°S

N
W—E
S

60°S

80°S

20°W 0° 20°E 40°E 60°E 80°E 100°E 120°E 140°E 160°E 80°N

20°W 0° 20°E 40°E 60°E 80°E 100°E 120°E 140°E 160°E 80°S

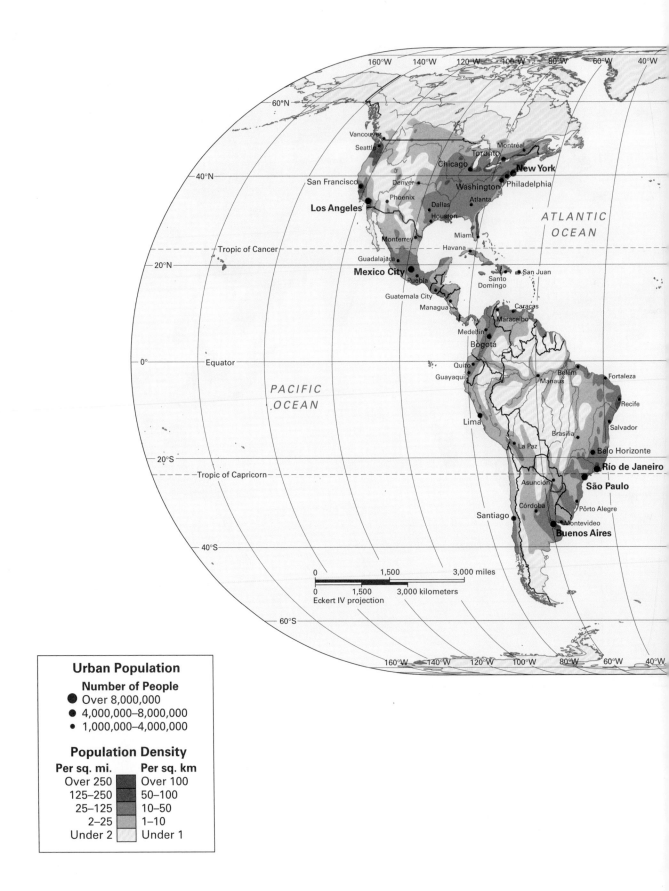

Urban Population

Number of People
- ● Over 8,000,000
- ● 4,000,000–8,000,000
- • 1,000,000–4,000,000

Population Density

Per sq. mi.	Per sq. km
Over 250	Over 100
125–250	50–100
25–125	10–50
2–25	1–10
Under 2	Under 1

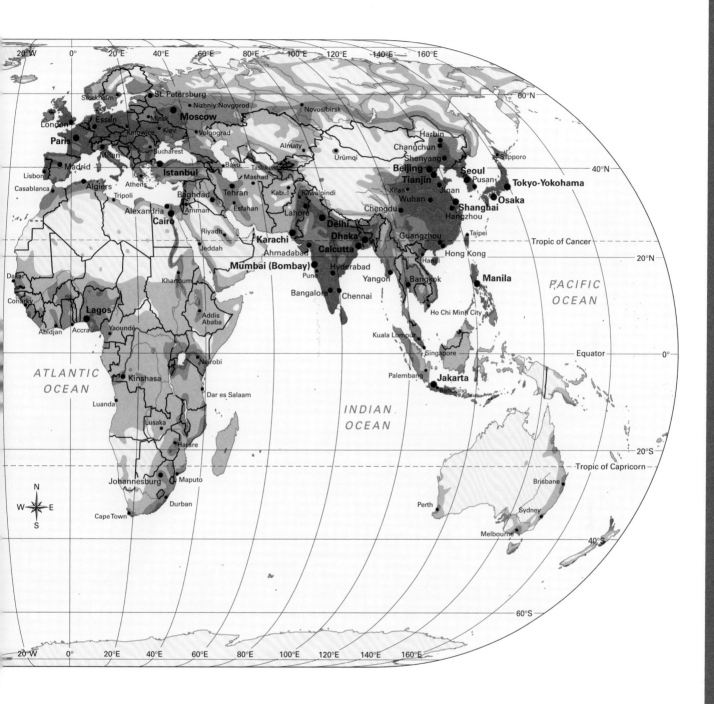

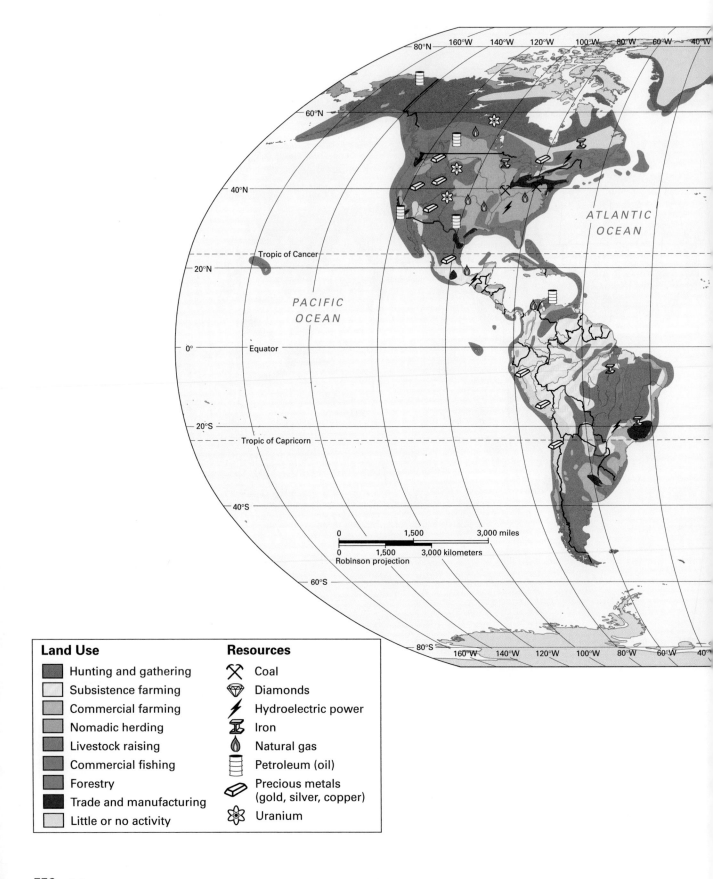

Land Use

- Hunting and gathering
- Subsistence farming
- Commercial farming
- Nomadic herding
- Livestock raising
- Commercial fishing
- Forestry
- Trade and manufacturing
- Little or no activity

Resources

- ⚒ Coal
- ◈ Diamonds
- ⚡ Hydroelectric power
- ⚒ Iron
- ◐ Natural gas
- ▯ Petroleum (oil)
- ▱ Precious metals (gold, silver, copper)
- ✳ Uranium

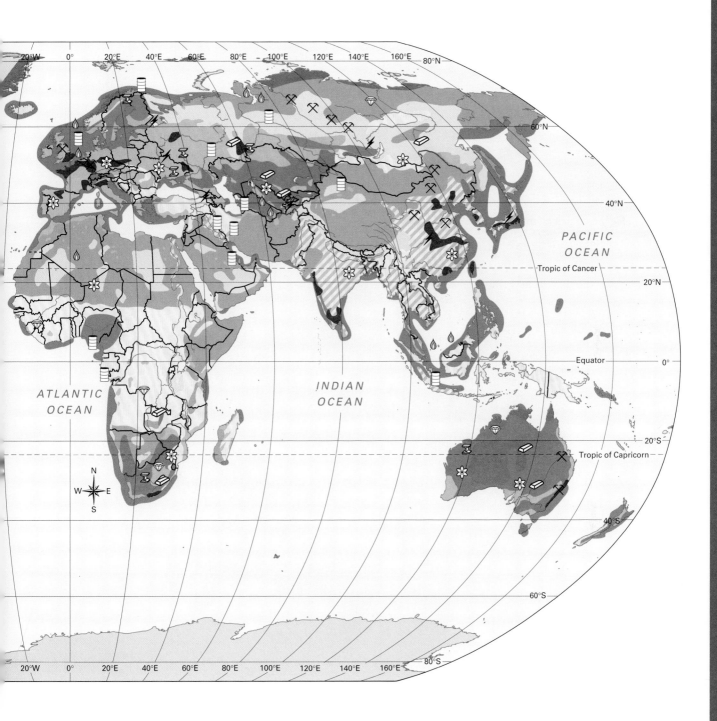

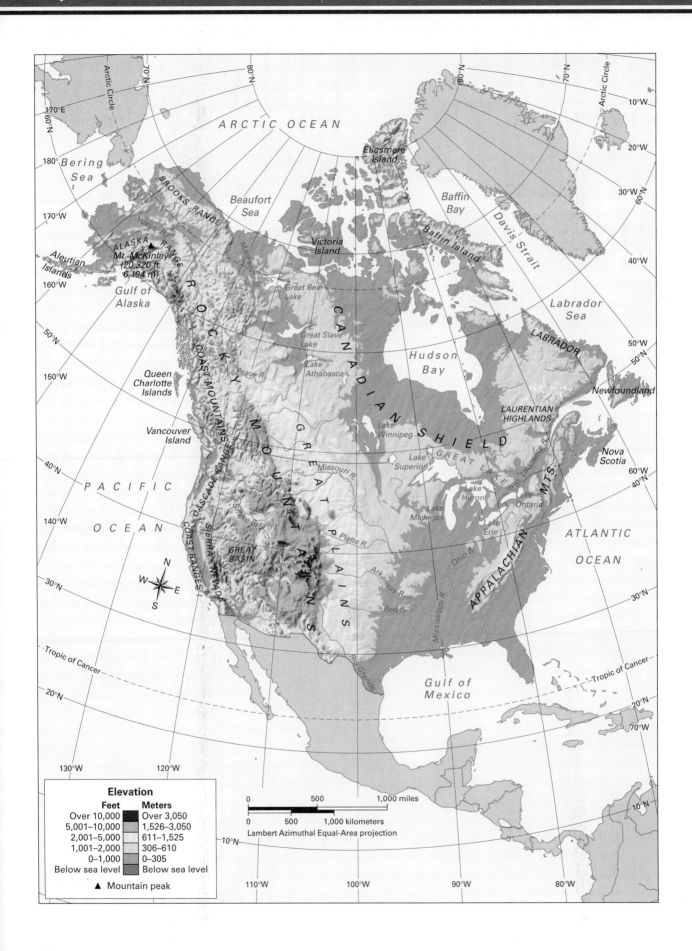

Elevation

Feet	Meters
Over 10,000	Over 3,050
5,001–10,000	1,526–3,050
2,001–5,000	611–1,525
1,001–2,000	306–610
0–1,000	0–305
Below sea level	Below sea level

▲ Mountain peak

0   500   1,000 miles
0   500   1,000 kilometers
Lambert Azimuthal Equal-Area projection

Political Boundaries of Canada and the United States

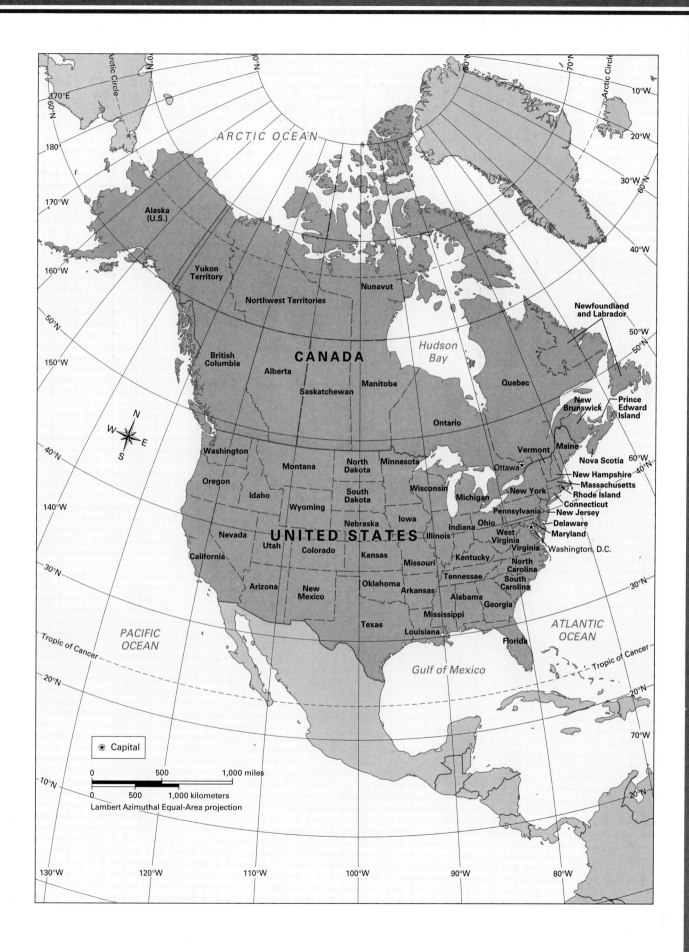

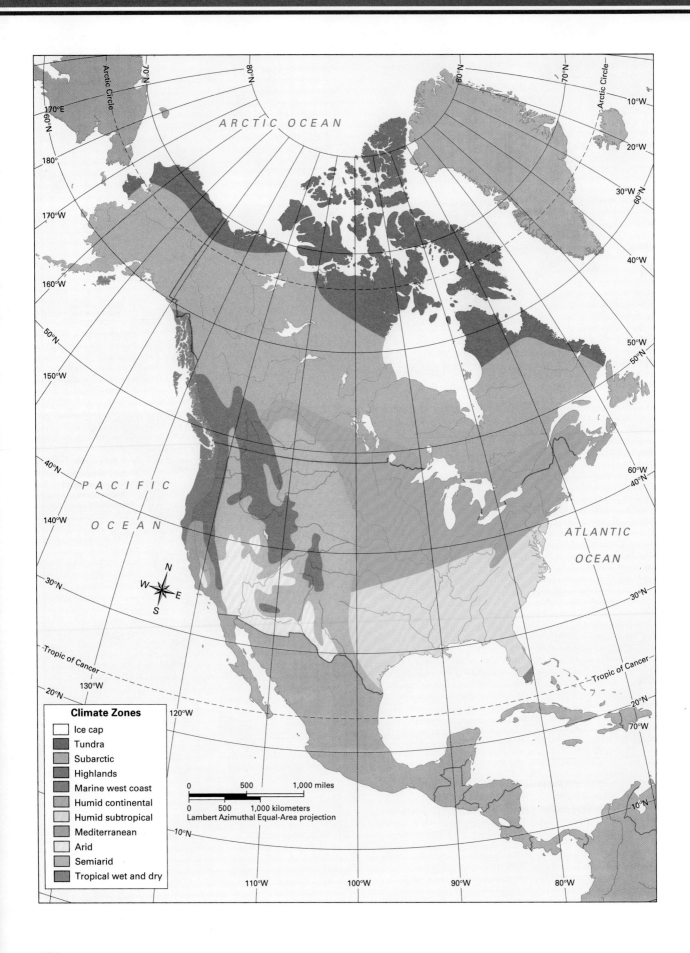

Climate Zones of Canada and the United States

ARCTIC OCEAN

PACIFIC OCEAN

ATLANTIC OCEAN

Arctic Circle

Tropic of Cancer

Climate Zones

- Ice cap
- Tundra
- Subarctic
- Highlands
- Marine west coast
- Humid continental
- Humid subtropical
- Mediterranean
- Arid
- Semiarid
- Tropical wet and dry

0   500   1,000 miles

0   500   1,000 kilometers
Lambert Azimuthal Equal-Area projection

Vegetation Zones of Canada and the United States

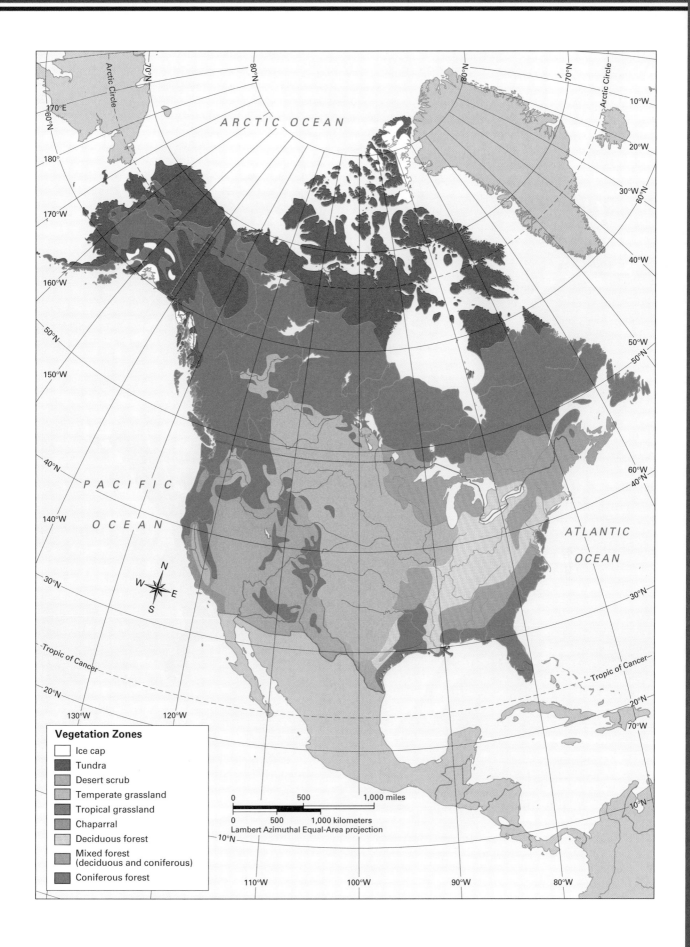

ARCTIC OCEAN

PACIFIC
OCEAN

ATLANTIC
OCEAN

Tropic of Cancer

Tropic of Cancer

Vegetation Zones

- Ice cap
- Tundra
- Desert scrub
- Temperate grassland
- Tropical grassland
- Chaparral
- Deciduous forest
- Mixed forest (deciduous and coniferous)
- Coniferous forest

0   500   1,000 miles

0   500   1,000 kilometers
Lambert Azimuthal Equal-Area projection

Population Density of Canada and the United States

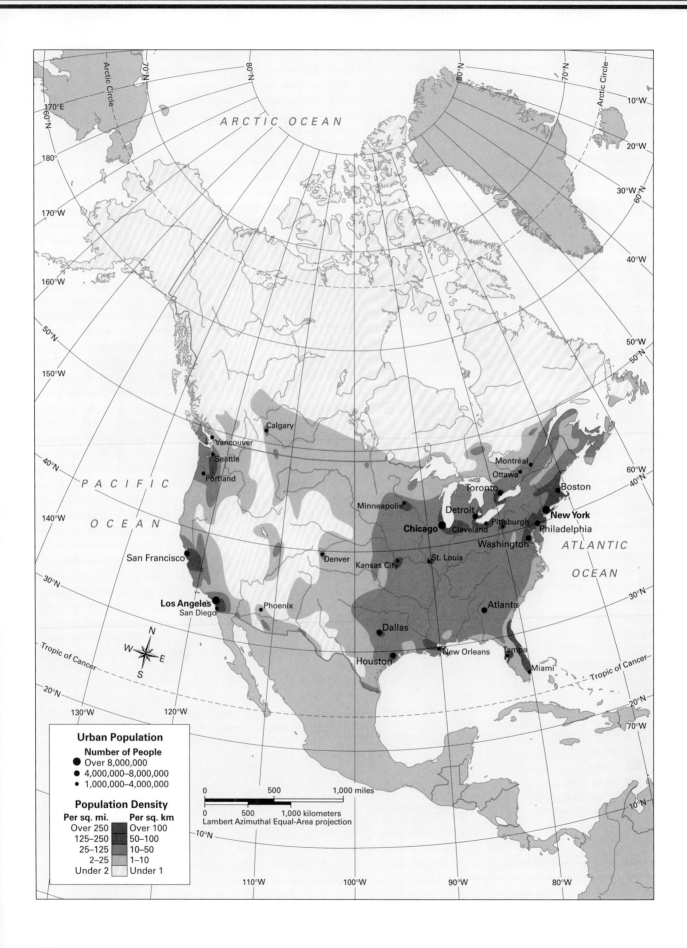

Urban Population

Number of People
- Over 8,000,000
- 4,000,000–8,000,000
- 1,000,000–4,000,000

Population Density

Per sq. mi.	Per sq. km
Over 250	Over 100
125–250	50–100
25–125	10–50
2–25	1–10
Under 2	Under 1

0   500   1,000 miles
0   500   1,000 kilometers
Lambert Azimuthal Equal-Area projection

ARCTIC OCEAN

PACIFIC OCEAN

ATLANTIC OCEAN

Arctic Circle

Tropic of Cancer

Calgary
Vancouver
Seattle
Portland
San Francisco
Los Angeles
San Diego
Phoenix
Denver
Kansas City
Dallas
Houston
Minneapolis
Chicago
St. Louis
New Orleans
Detroit
Cleveland
Pittsburgh
Atlanta
Tampa
Miami
Toronto
Montréal
Ottawa
Boston
New York
Philadelphia
Washington

Economic Activity of Canada and the United States

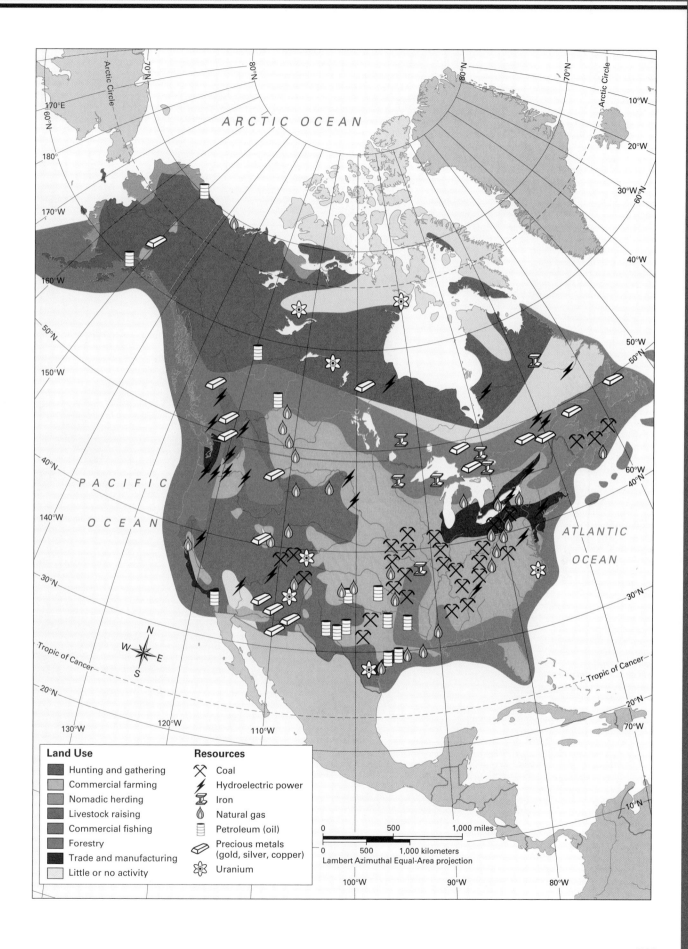

Land Use
- Hunting and gathering
- Commercial farming
- Nomadic herding
- Livestock raising
- Commercial fishing
- Forestry
- Trade and manufacturing
- Little or no activity

Resources
- ⚒ Coal
- ⚡ Hydroelectric power
- ⫯ Iron
- ⬭ Natural gas
- ⬛ Petroleum (oil)
- ▱ Precious metals (gold, silver, copper)
- ✳ Uranium

0   500   1,000 miles

0   500   1,000 kilometers
Lambert Azimuthal Equal-Area projection

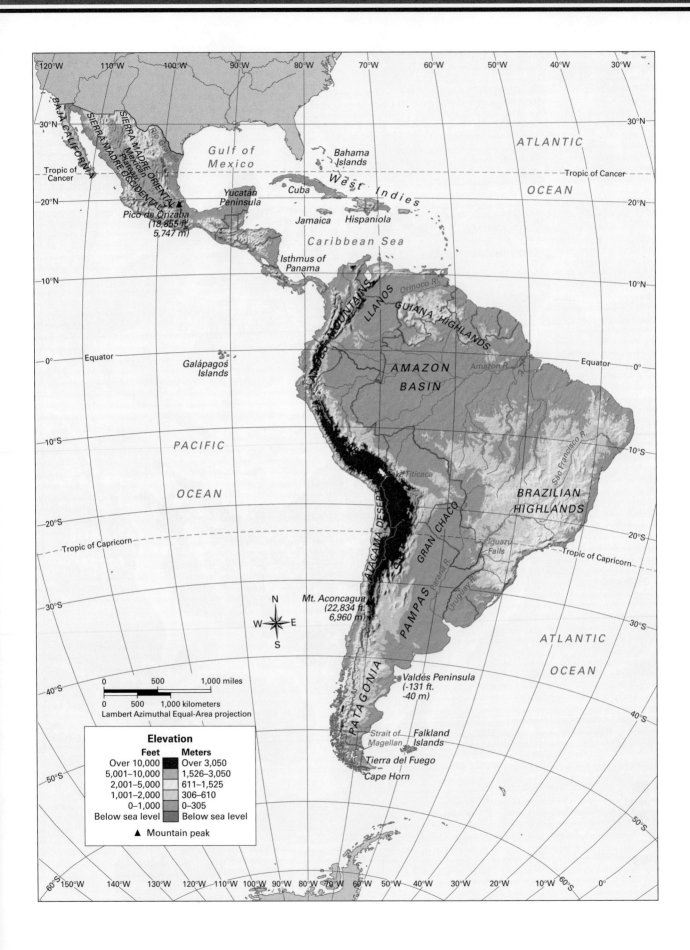

Elevation

Feet	Meters
Over 10,000	Over 3,050
5,001–10,000	1,526–3,050
2,001–5,000	611–1,525
1,001–2,000	306–610
0–1,000	0–305
Below sea level	Below sea level

▲ Mountain peak

0   500   1,000 miles
0   500   1,000 kilometers
Lambert Azimuthal Equal-Area projection

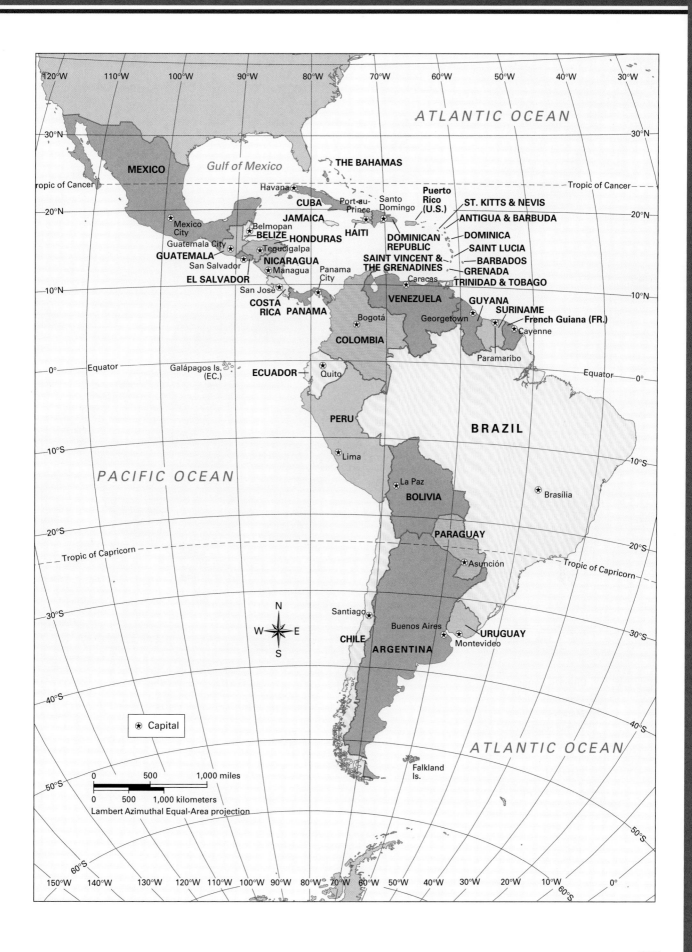

Political Boundaries of Latin America

ATLANTIC OCEAN

Gulf of Mexico

MEXICO

THE BAHAMAS

Tropic of Cancer

Havana ★

Mexico City ★

CUBA

Port-au-Prince

Santo Domingo ★

Puerto Rico (U.S.)

ST. KITTS & NEVIS

ANTIGUA & BARBUDA

JAMAICA

Belmopan ★

HAITI

DOMINICAN REPUBLIC

DOMINICA

BELIZE

HONDURAS

SAINT LUCIA

Guatemala City ★

Tegucigalpa ★

BARBADOS

GUATEMALA

NICARAGUA

SAINT VINCENT & THE GRENADINES

GRENADA

San Salvador ★

Managua ★

Caracas ★

TRINIDAD & TOBAGO

EL SALVADOR

San José ★

VENEZUELA

GUYANA

COSTA RICA

PANAMA

SURINAME

PANAMA City

Bogotá ★

Georgetown ★

French Guiana (FR.)

Cayenne ★

COLOMBIA

Paramaribo ★

Galápagos Is. (EC.)

ECUADOR

Quito ★

Equator

PERU

BRAZIL

Lima ★

PACIFIC OCEAN

La Paz ★

Brasília ★

BOLIVIA

PARAGUAY

Tropic of Capricorn

Asunción ★

N
W ★ E
S

Santiago ★

Buenos Aires ★

URUGUAY

CHILE

Montevideo ★

ARGENTINA

★ Capital

ATLANTIC OCEAN

Falkland Is.

0   500   1,000 miles
0   500   1,000 kilometers
Lambert Azimuthal Equal-Area projection

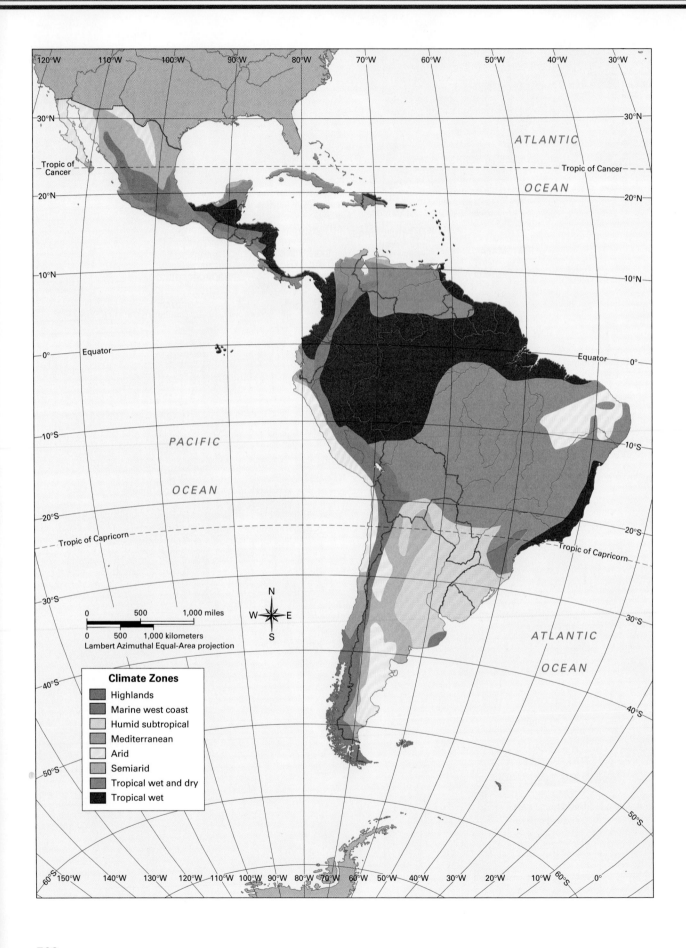

Climate Zones

- Highlands
- Marine west coast
- Humid subtropical
- Mediterranean
- Arid
- Semiarid
- Tropical wet and dry
- Tropical wet

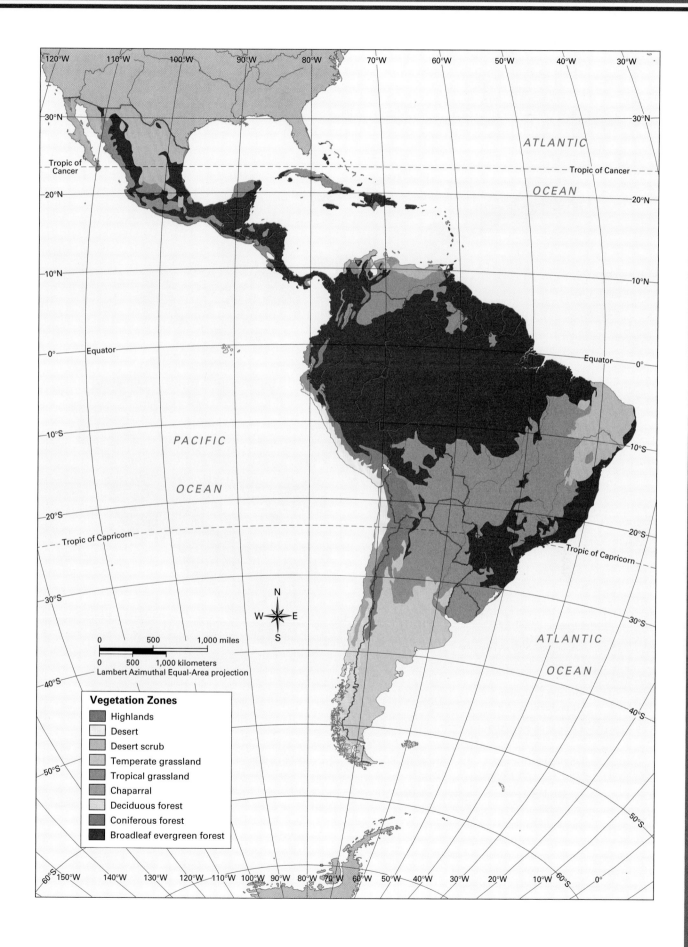

Vegetation Zones

- Highlands
- Desert
- Desert scrub
- Temperate grassland
- Tropical grassland
- Chaparral
- Deciduous forest
- Coniferous forest
- Broadleaf evergreen forest

Lambert Azimuthal Equal-Area projection

0   500   1,000 miles

0   500   1,000 kilometers

Urban Population
Number of People
● Over 8,000,000
● 4,000,000–8,000,000
• 1,000,000–4,000,000

Population Density
Per sq. mi.	Per sq. km
Over 250	Over 100
125–250	50–100
25–125	10–50
2–25	1–10
Under 2	Under 1

0   500   1,000 miles
0   500   1,000 kilometers
Lambert Azimuthal Equal-Area projection

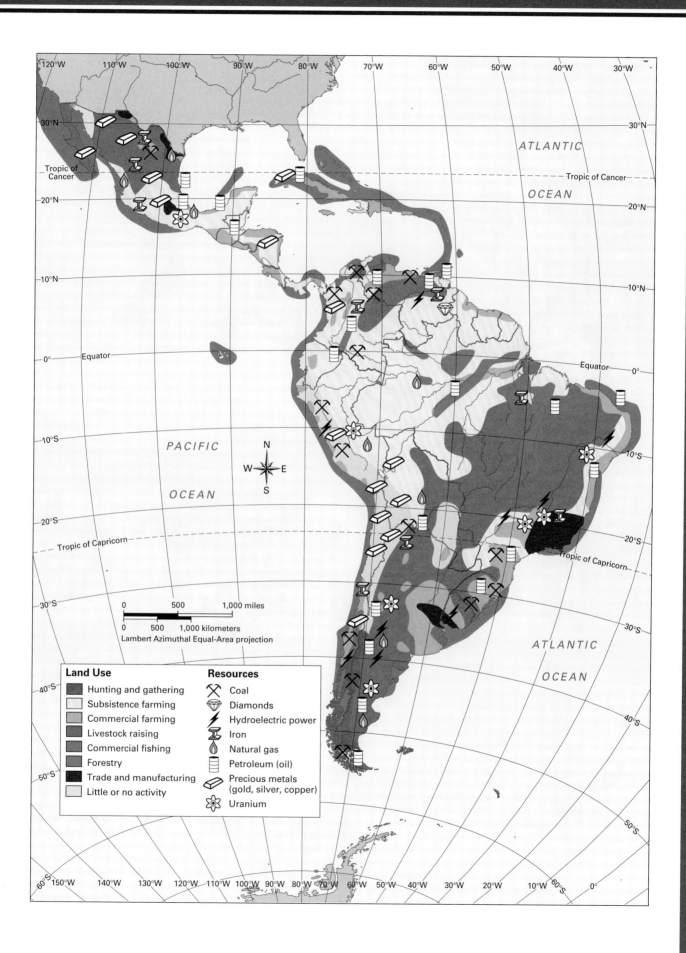

Land Use
- Hunting and gathering
- Subsistence farming
- Commercial farming
- Livestock raising
- Commercial fishing
- Forestry
- Trade and manufacturing
- Little or no activity

Resources
- Coal
- Diamonds
- Hydroelectric power
- Iron
- Natural gas
- Petroleum (oil)
- Precious metals (gold, silver, copper)
- Uranium

0   500   1,000 miles
0   500   1,000 kilometers
Lambert Azimuthal Equal-Area projection

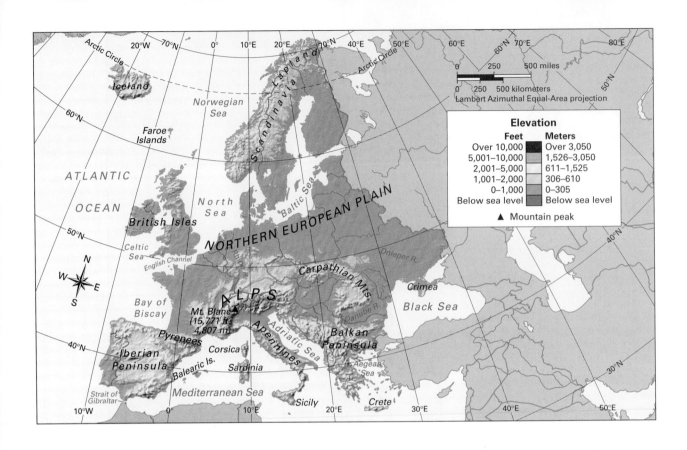

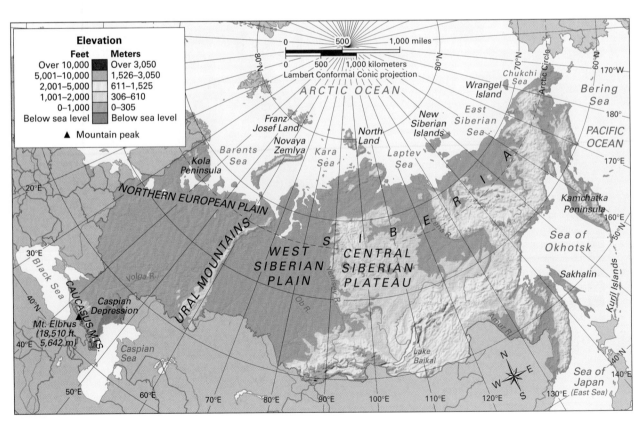

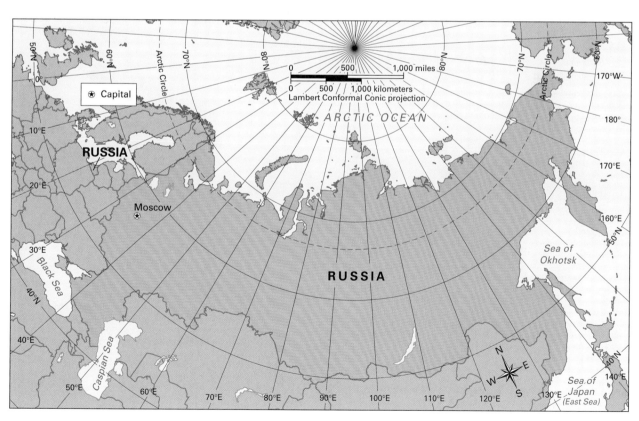

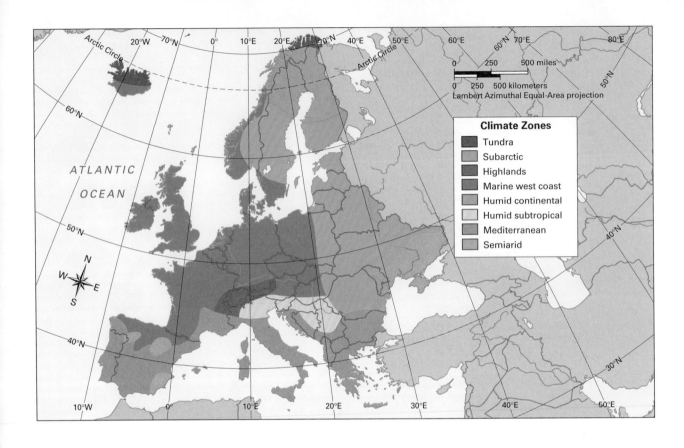

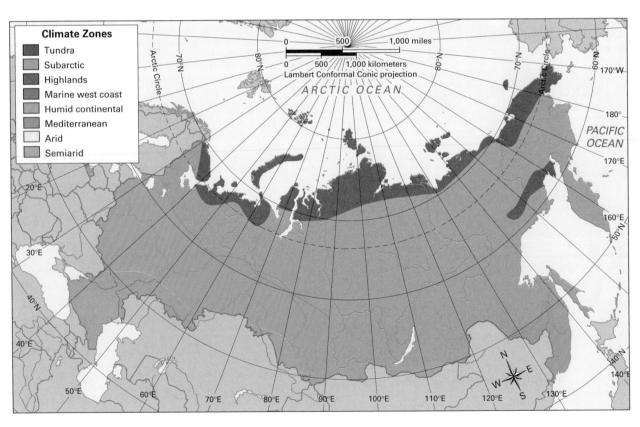

Vegetation Zones of Europe and Russia

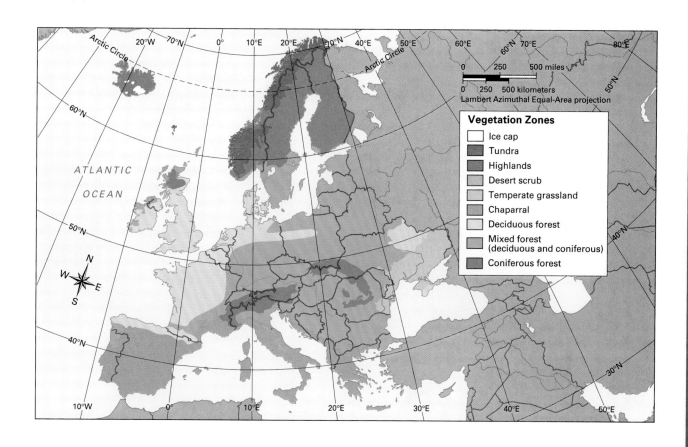

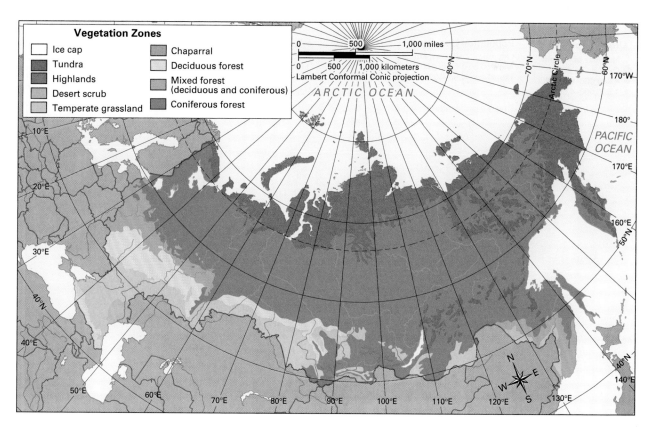

Vegetation Zones
- Ice cap
- Tundra
- Highlands
- Desert scrub
- Temperate grassland
- Chaparral
- Deciduous forest
- Mixed forest (deciduous and coniferous)
- Coniferous forest

Population Density of Europe and Russia

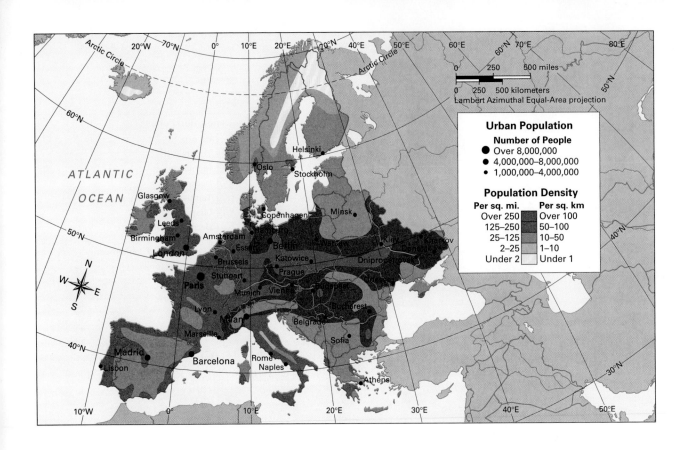

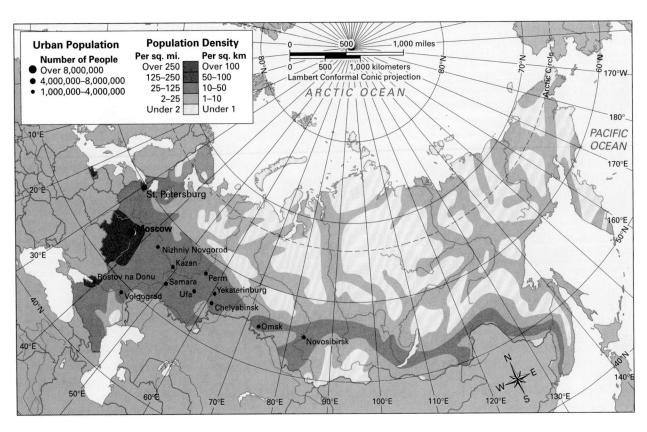

Economic Activity of Europe and Russia

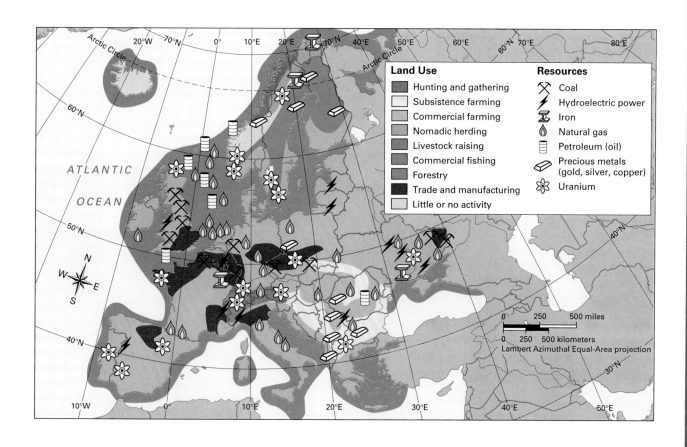

Land Use
- Hunting and gathering
- Subsistence farming
- Commercial farming
- Nomadic herding
- Livestock raising
- Commercial fishing
- Forestry
- Trade and manufacturing
- Little or no activity

Resources
- Coal
- Hydroelectric power
- Iron
- Natural gas
- Petroleum (oil)
- Precious metals (gold, silver, copper)
- Uranium

ATLANTIC OCEAN

0   250   500 miles
0   250   500 kilometers
Lambert Azimuthal Equal-Area projection

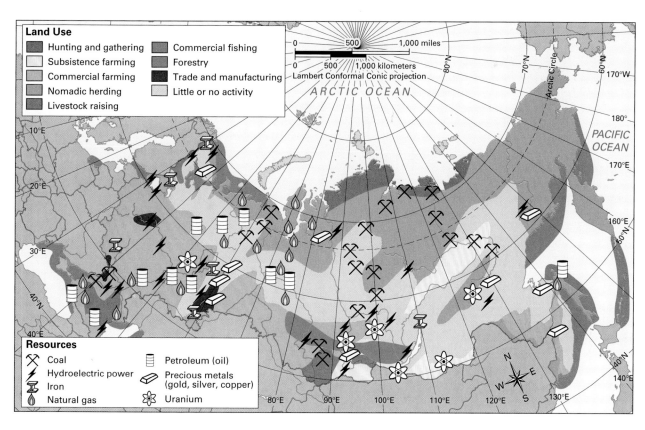

Land Use
- Hunting and gathering
- Subsistence farming
- Commercial farming
- Nomadic herding
- Livestock raising
- Commercial fishing
- Forestry
- Trade and manufacturing
- Little or no activity

Resources
- Coal
- Hydroelectric power
- Iron
- Natural gas
- Petroleum (oil)
- Precious metals (gold, silver, copper)
- Uranium

0   500   1,000 miles
0   500   1,000 kilometers
Lambert Conformal Conic projection

ARCTIC OCEAN

PACIFIC OCEAN

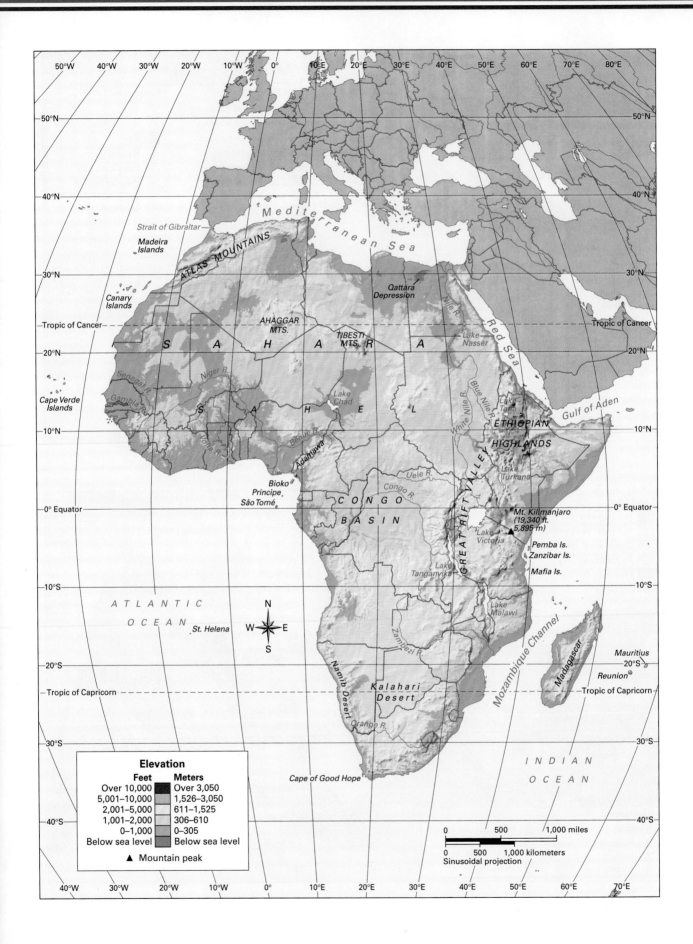

Strait of Gibraltar

Madeira
Islands

Mediterranean Sea

Qattara
Depression

Nile R.

ATLAS MOUNTAINS

Canary
Islands

Tropic of Cancer

AHAGGAR
MTS.

TIBESTI
MTS.

Lake
Nasser

Red Sea

Tropic of Cancer

S A H A R A

Cape Verde
Islands

Senegal R.

Gambia R.

Niger R.

Lake
Chad

Gulf of Aden

S A H E L

Volta R.

Benue R.

White Nile R.

Blue Nile R.

Lake
Tana

ETHIOPIAN

HIGHLANDS

Bioko
Principe
São Tomé

Adamawa

Uele R.

Congo R.

C O N G O

B A S I N

GREAT RIFT VALLEY

Lake
Turkana

Mt. Kilimanjaro
(19,340 ft.
5,895 m)

Lake
Victoria

Pemba Is.
Zanzibar Is.

Mafia Is.

Lake
Tanganyika

Lake
Malawi

A T L A N T I C

O C E A N

St. Helena

N
W E
S

Mozambique Channel

Madagascar

Mauritius

Reunion

Namib Desert

Zambezi R.

Tropic of Capricorn

K a l a h a r i
D e s e r t

I N D I A N

O C E A N

Orange R.

Cape of Good Hope

Elevation

Feet		Meters
Over 10,000		Over 3,050
5,001–10,000		1,526–3,050
2,001–5,000		611–1,525
1,001–2,000		306–610
0–1,000		0–305
Below sea level		Below sea level

▲ Mountain peak

0   500   1,000 miles

0   500   1,000 kilometers
Sinusoidal projection

Political Boundaries of Africa

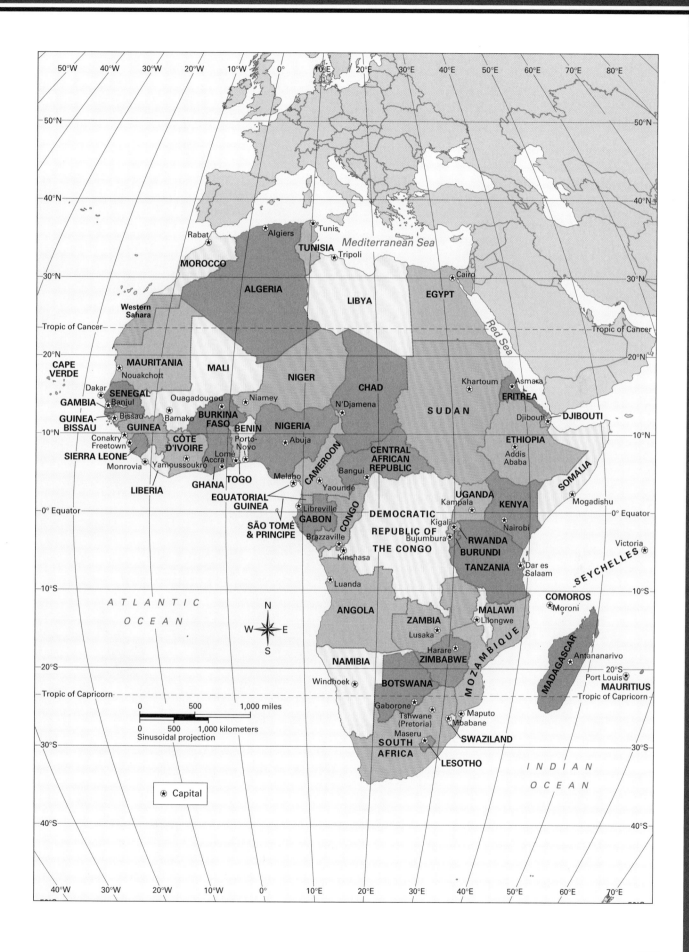

MOROCCO
Rabat ⊛
Algiers ⊛
TUNISIA
Tunis ⊛
Tripoli ⊛
Mediterranean Sea

ALGERIA

Western
Sahara

LIBYA
EGYPT
Cairo ⊛

Red Sea

Tropic of Cancer

CAPE
VERDE
MAURITANIA
Nouakchott ⊛
MALI
NIGER
CHAD
Khartoum ⊛
SUDAN
Asmara ⊛
ERITREA
DJIBOUTI
Djibouti ⊛

Dakar ⊛
SENEGAL
GAMBIA
Banjul ⊛
GUINEA-
BISSAU
Bissau ⊛
Ouagadougou ⊛
Niamey ⊛
N'Djamena ⊛

Bamako ⊛
BURKINA
FASO
GUINEA
Conakry ⊛
Freetown ⊛
SIERRA LEONE
Monrovia ⊛
LIBERIA
CÔTE
D'IVOIRE
Yamoussoukro ⊛
BENIN
NIGERIA
Abuja ⊛
CENTRAL
AFRICAN
REPUBLIC
ETHIOPIA
Addis
Ababa ⊛
SOMALIA

Accra ⊛
Lomé ⊛
Porto-
Novo ⊛
GHANA
TOGO
Malabo ⊛
CAMEROON
Bangui ⊛
Yaoundé ⊛
UGANDA
Kampala ⊛
KENYA
Mogadishu ⊛

EQUATORIAL
GUINEA
Libreville ⊛
GABON
CONGO
DEMOCRATIC
REPUBLIC OF
THE CONGO
Kigali ⊛
Bujumbura ⊛
RWANDA
BURUNDI
Nairobi ⊛
Victoria ⊛
SEYCHELLES

SÃO TOMÉ
& PRINCIPE
Brazzaville ⊛
Kinshasa ⊛
Luanda ⊛
TANZANIA
Dar es
Salaam ⊛

0° Equator

ATLANTIC
OCEAN

N
W E
S

ANGOLA
ZAMBIA
Lusaka ⊛
MALAWI
Lilongwe ⊛
COMOROS
Moroni ⊛

Harare ⊛
ZIMBABWE
MOZAMBIQUE
Antananarivo ⊛
MADAGASCAR
Port Louis ⊛
MAURITIUS

NAMIBIA
Windhoek ⊛
BOTSWANA
Gaborone ⊛
Tshwane
(Pretoria) ⊛
Maputo ⊛
Mbabane ⊛
SWAZILAND
Maseru ⊛
SOUTH
AFRICA
LESOTHO

Tropic of Capricorn

⊛ Capital

INDIAN
OCEAN

0   500   1,000 miles
0   500 1,000 kilometers
Sinusoidal projection

Atlas **577**

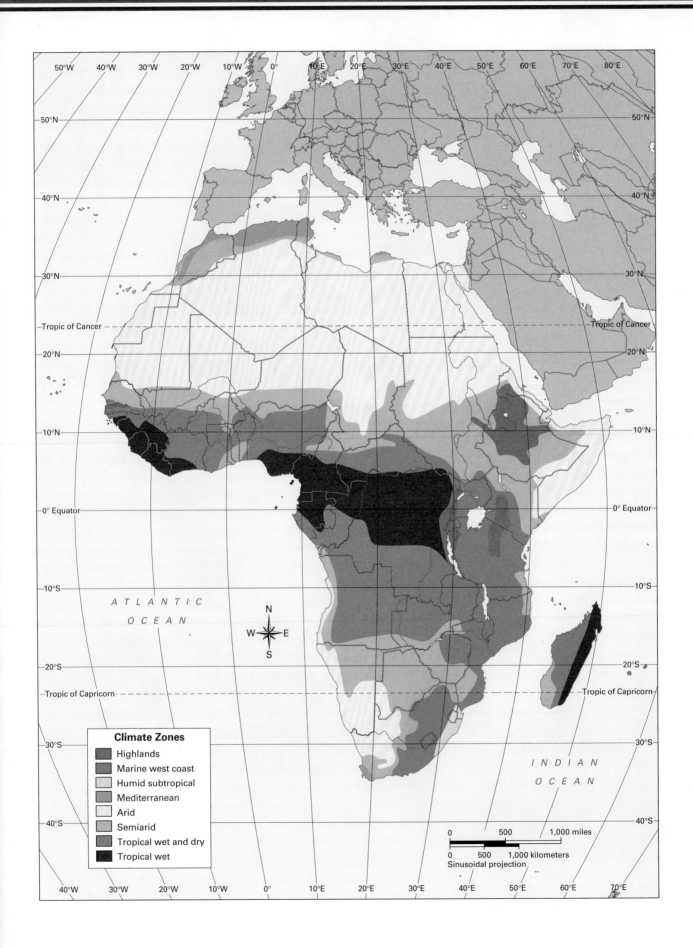

Climate Zones

- Highlands
- Marine west coast
- Humid subtropical
- Mediterranean
- Arid
- Semiarid
- Tropical wet and dry
- Tropical wet

ATLANTIC OCEAN

INDIAN OCEAN

Tropic of Cancer

Tropic of Cancer

0° Equator

0° Equator

Tropic of Capricorn

Tropic of Capricorn

0   500   1,000 miles

0   500   1,000 kilometers

Sinusoidal projection

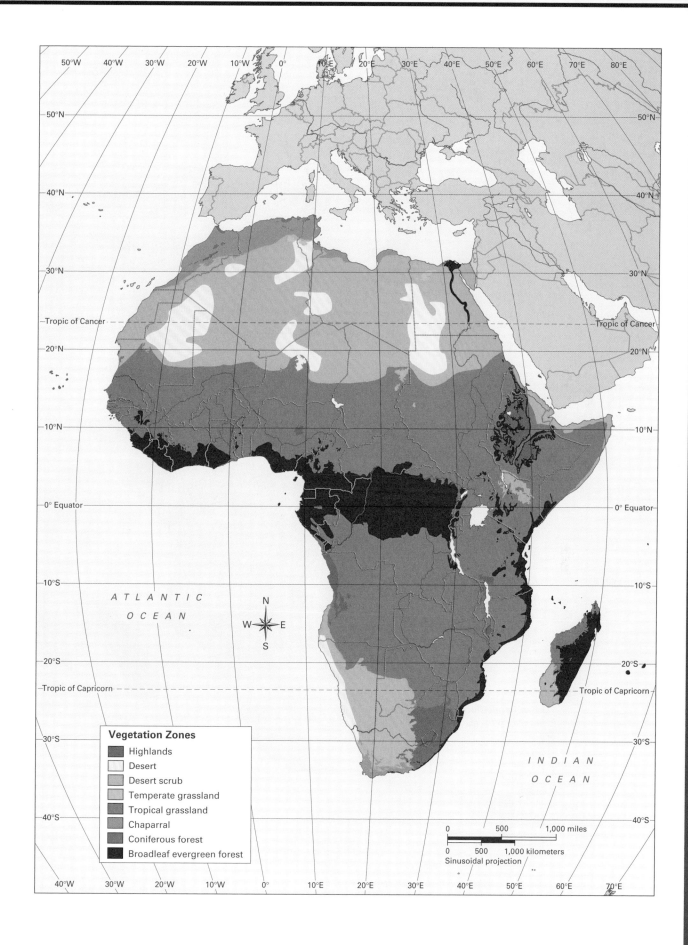

Vegetation Zones
- Highlands
- Desert
- Desert scrub
- Temperate grassland
- Tropical grassland
- Chaparral
- Coniferous forest
- Broadleaf evergreen forest

ATLANTIC OCEAN

INDIAN OCEAN

Tropic of Cancer

0° Equator

Tropic of Capricorn

0   500   1,000 miles
0   500   1,000 kilometers
Sinusoidal projection

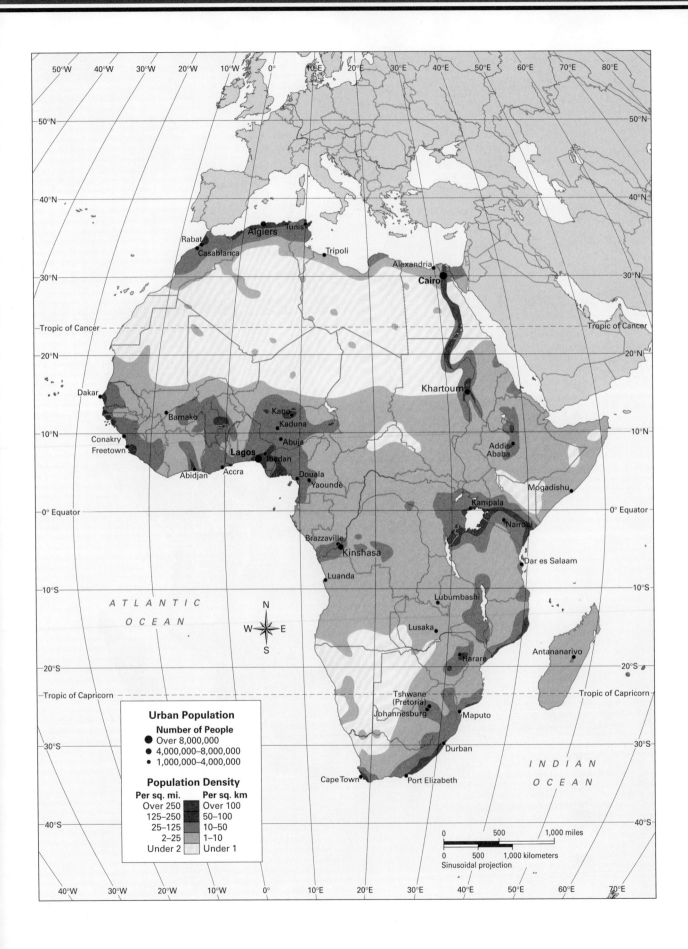

Urban Population

Number of People
- ⬤ Over 8,000,000
- ● 4,000,000–8,000,000
- • 1,000,000–4,000,000

Population Density

Per sq. mi.	Per sq. km
Over 250	Over 100
125–250	50–100
25–125	10–50
2–25	1–10
Under 2	Under 1

Sinusoidal projection

0   500   1,000 miles

0   500   1,000 kilometers

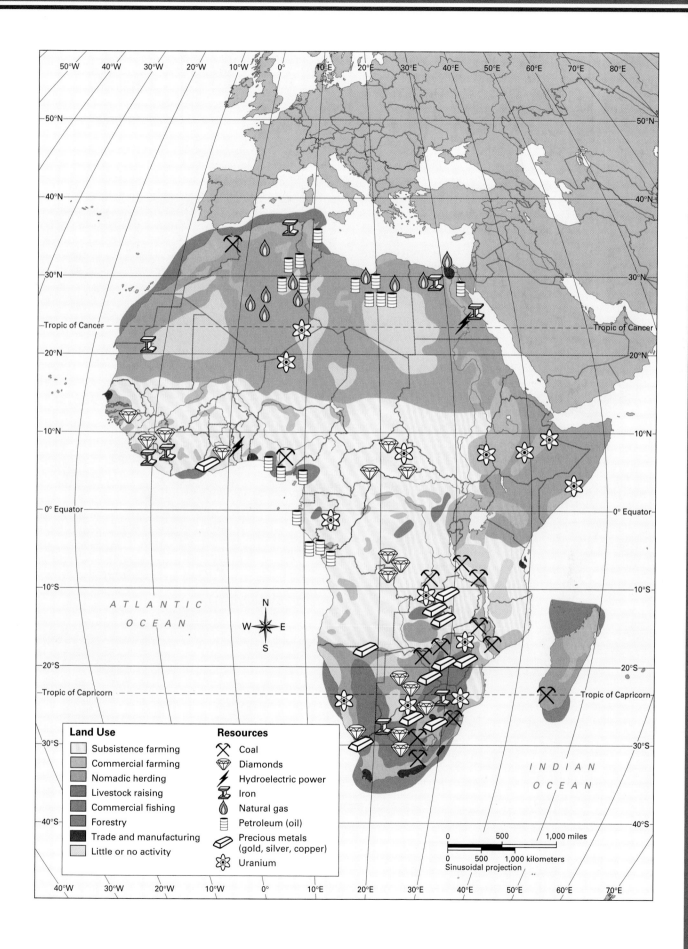

Land Use
- Subsistence farming
- Commercial farming
- Nomadic herding
- Livestock raising
- Commercial fishing
- Forestry
- Trade and manufacturing
- Little or no activity

Resources
- Coal
- Diamonds
- Hydroelectric power
- Iron
- Natural gas
- Petroleum (oil)
- Precious metals (gold, silver, copper)
- Uranium

ATLANTIC OCEAN

INDIAN OCEAN

Tropic of Cancer

Equator

Tropic of Capricorn

0   500   1,000 miles
0   500   1,000 kilometers
Sinusoidal projection

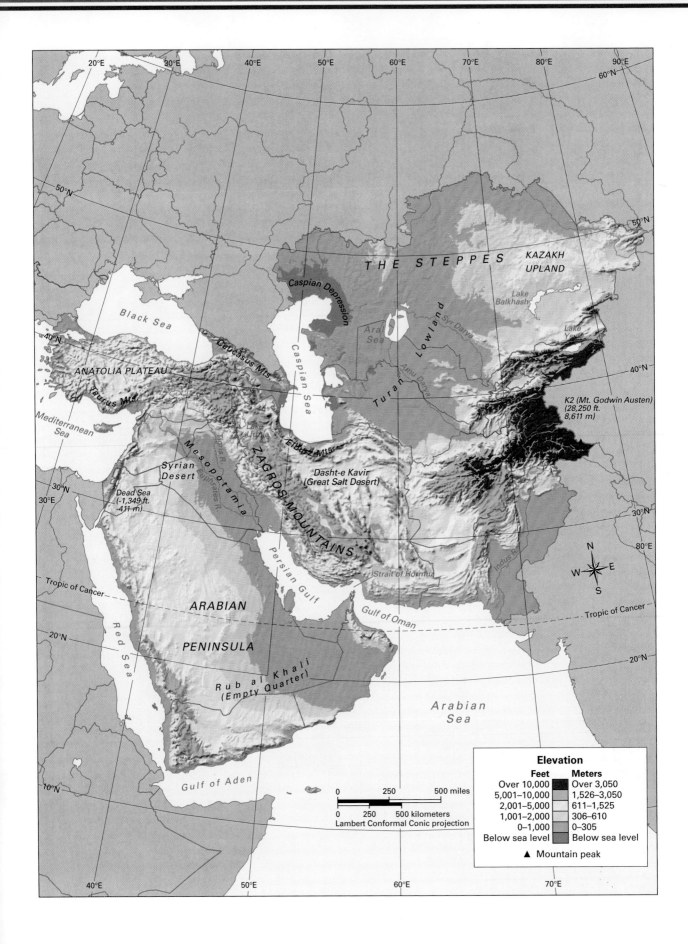

Elevation

Feet	Meters
Over 10,000	Over 3,050
5,001–10,000	1,526–3,050
2,001–5,000	611–1,525
1,001–2,000	306–610
0–1,000	0–305
Below sea level	Below sea level

▲ Mountain peak

0   250   500 miles

0   250   500 kilometers

Lambert Conformal Conic projection

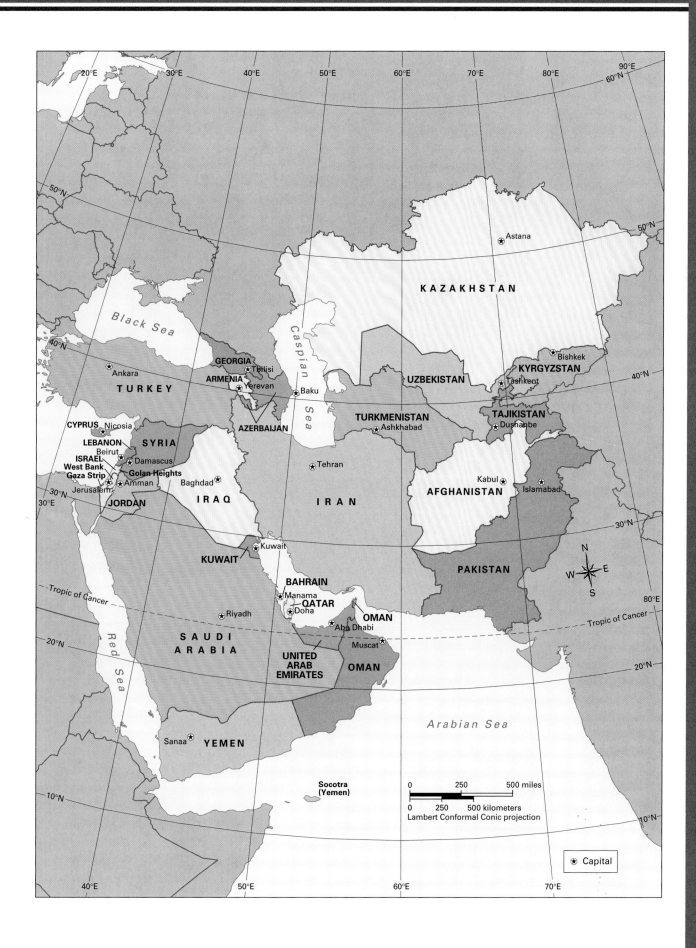

Political Boundaries of Southwest and Central Asia

20°E · 30°E · 40°E · 50°E · 60°E · 70°E · 80°E · 90°E · 60°N

50°N · 50°N

Black Sea

Caspian Sea

★ Astana

KAZAKHSTAN

40°N · 40°N

GEORGIA
★ Tbilisi

Ankara ★

ARMENIA

TURKEY

★ Yerevan

★ Baku

UZBEKISTAN

★ Bishkek

KYRGYZSTAN

★ Tashkent

CYPRUS ★ Nicosia

AZERBAIJAN

TURKMENISTAN

TAJIKISTAN

LEBANON
Beirut ★
SYRIA

★ Ashkhabad

★ Dushanbe

ISRAEL ★ Damascus
West Bank
Gaza Strip ★ Golan Heights
★ Amman
Jerusalem ★

★ Tehran

Kabul ★

★ Islamabad

30°E
30°E

IRAQ

IRAN

AFGHANISTAN

★ Baghdad

JORDAN

30°N

KUWAIT
★ Kuwait

PAKISTAN

N
W · E
S

80°E

BAHRAIN

Tropic of Cancer

★ Manama QATAR
★ Doha

OMAN

★ Riyadh

20°N

Red Sea

SAUDI
ARABIA

★ Abu Dhabi

★ Muscat

Tropic of Cancer

20°N

UNITED
ARAB
EMIRATES

OMAN

Arabian Sea

Sanaa ★ YEMEN

Socotra
(Yemen)

0 · 250 · 500 miles

0 · 250 · 500 kilometers
Lambert Conformal Conic projection

10°N

10°N

40°E · 50°E · 60°E · 70°E

★ Capital

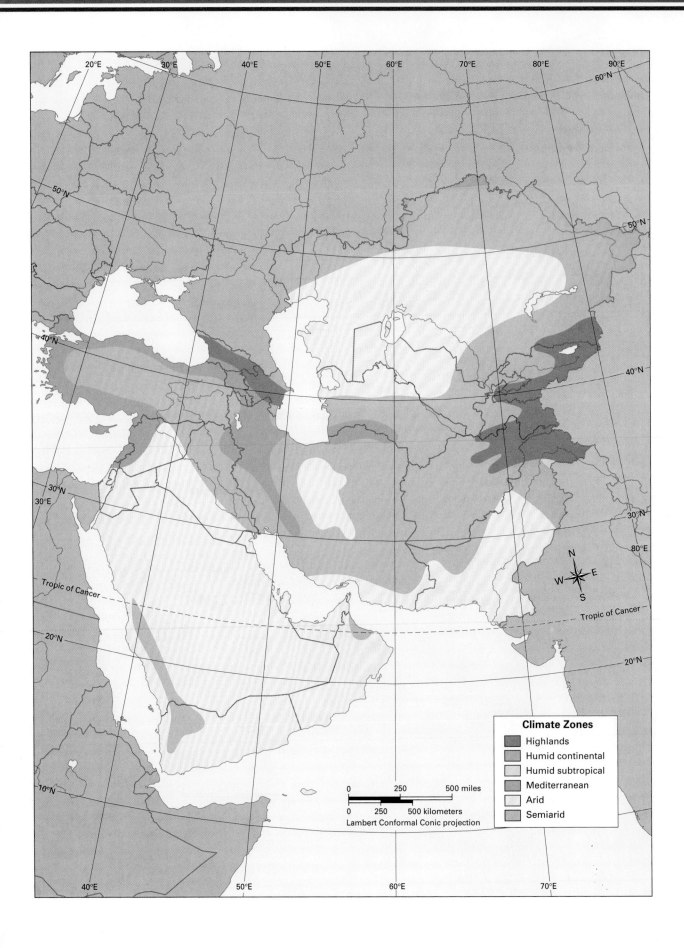

Climate Zones

- Highlands
- Humid continental
- Humid subtropical
- Mediterranean
- Arid
- Semiarid

0   250   500 miles

0   250   500 kilometers

Lambert Conformal Conic projection

Tropic of Cancer

Tropic of Cancer

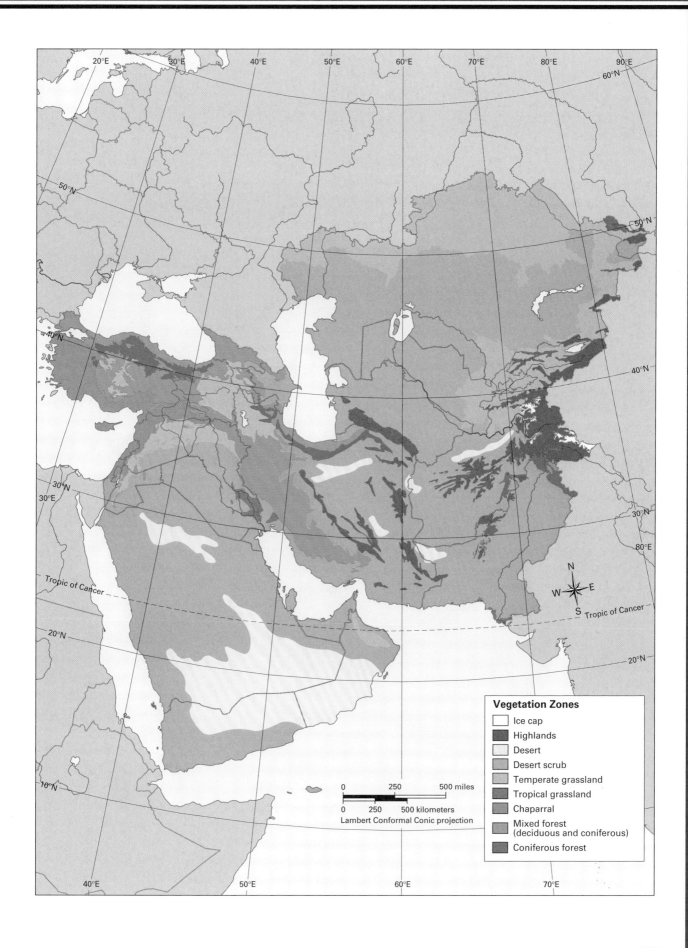

Vegetation Zones

- Ice cap
- Highlands
- Desert
- Desert scrub
- Temperate grassland
- Tropical grassland
- Chaparral
- Mixed forest (deciduous and coniferous)
- Coniferous forest

0   250   500 miles

0   250   500 kilometers
Lambert Conformal Conic projection

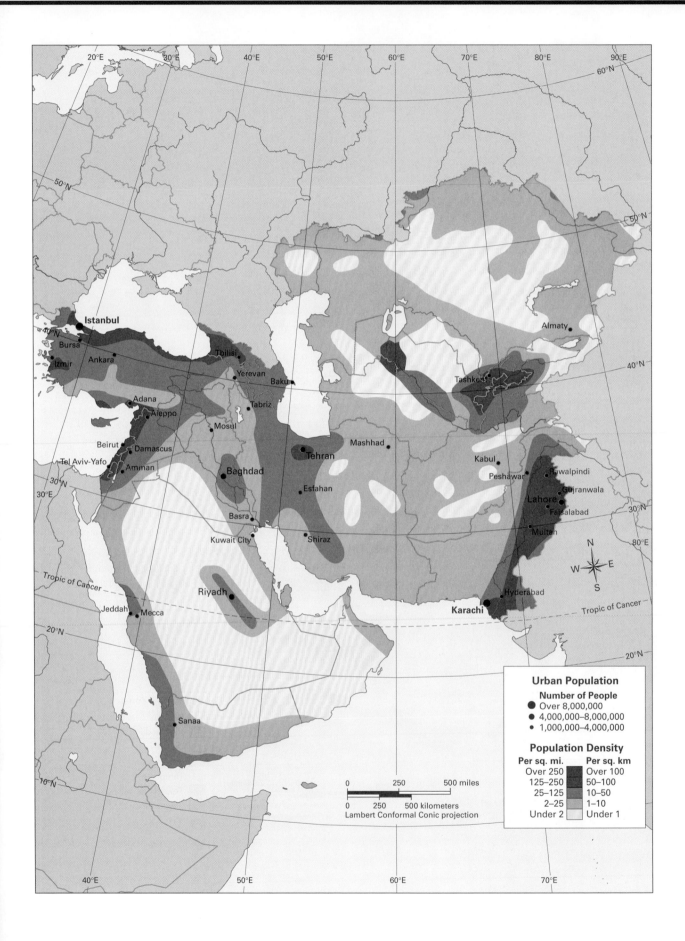

Urban Population

Number of People

- ● Over 8,000,000
- ● 4,000,000–8,000,000
- • 1,000,000–4,000,000

Population Density

Per sq. mi.	Per sq. km
Over 250	Over 100
125–250	50–100
25–125	10–50
2–25	1–10
Under 2	Under 1

0   250   500 miles

0   250   500 kilometers

Lambert Conformal Conic projection

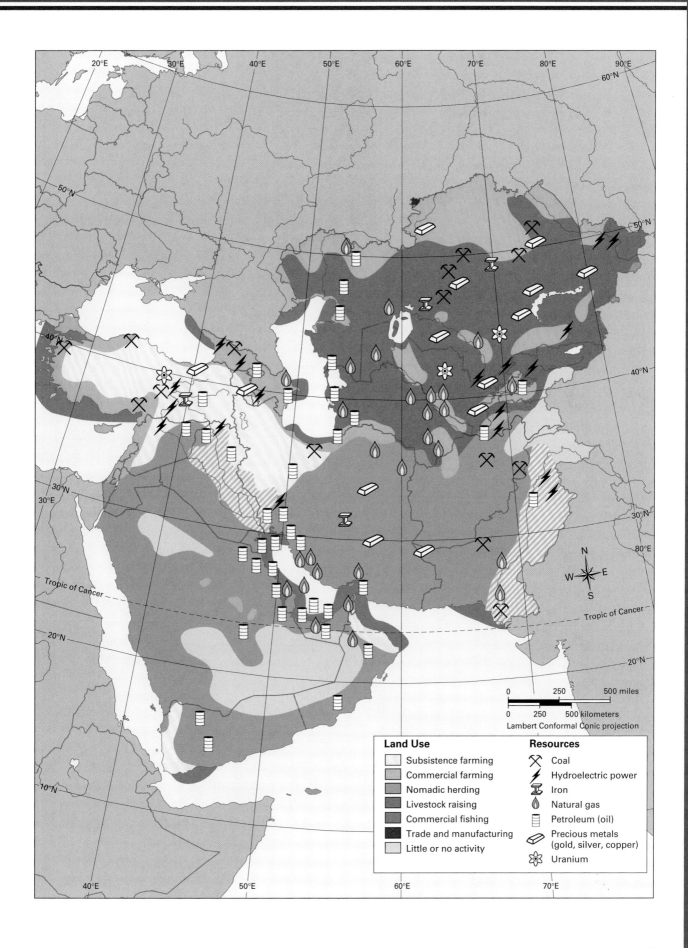

Land Use

- Subsistence farming
- Commercial farming
- Nomadic herding
- Livestock raising
- Commercial fishing
- Trade and manufacturing
- Little or no activity

Resources

- Coal
- Hydroelectric power
- Iron
- Natural gas
- Petroleum (oil)
- Precious metals (gold, silver, copper)
- Uranium

Lambert Conformal Conic projection

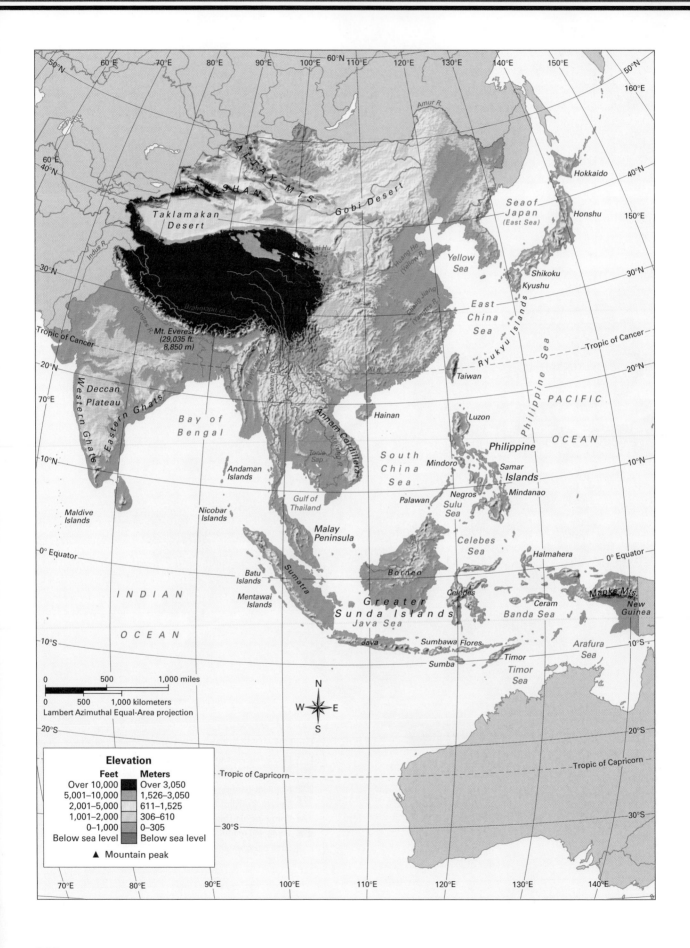

Taklamakan Desert

Tian Shan

Altay Mts.

Gobi Desert

Amur R.

Indus R.

Ganges R.

Brahmaputra R.

Qinghai Hu

Huang He (Yellow R.)

Chang Jiang (Yangtze R.)

Hokkaido

Honshu

Shikoku
Kyushu

Sea of Japan (East Sea)

Yellow Sea

East China Sea

Ryukyu Islands

Tropic of Cancer

Mt. Everest (29,035 ft. 8,850 m)

Deccan Plateau

Western Ghats

Eastern Ghats

Bay of Bengal

Salween R.

Annam Cordillera

Mekong R.

Taiwan

Hainan

Philippine Sea

PACIFIC OCEAN

Luzon

Mindoro

Philippine Islands

Samar

Negros

Mindanao

Andaman Islands

Tonle Sap

South China Sea

Maldive Islands

Nicobar Islands

Palawan

Sulu Sea

Malay Peninsula

Gulf of Thailand

Celebes Sea

Halmahera

Batu Islands

Sumatra

Borneo

Celebes

Ceram

Banda Sea

Maoke Mts.

New Guinea

INDIAN OCEAN

Mentawai Islands

Greater Sunda Islands

Java Sea

Java

Sumbawa Flores

Sumba

Timor

Arafura Sea

Timor Sea

Tropic of Capricorn

Elevation

Feet	Meters
Over 10,000	Over 3,050
5,001–10,000	1,526–3,050
2,001–5,000	611–1,525
1,001–2,000	306–610
0–1,000	0–305
Below sea level	Below sea level

▲ Mountain peak

0   500   1,000 miles
0   500   1,000 kilometers
Lambert Azimuthal Equal-Area projection

N
W   E
S

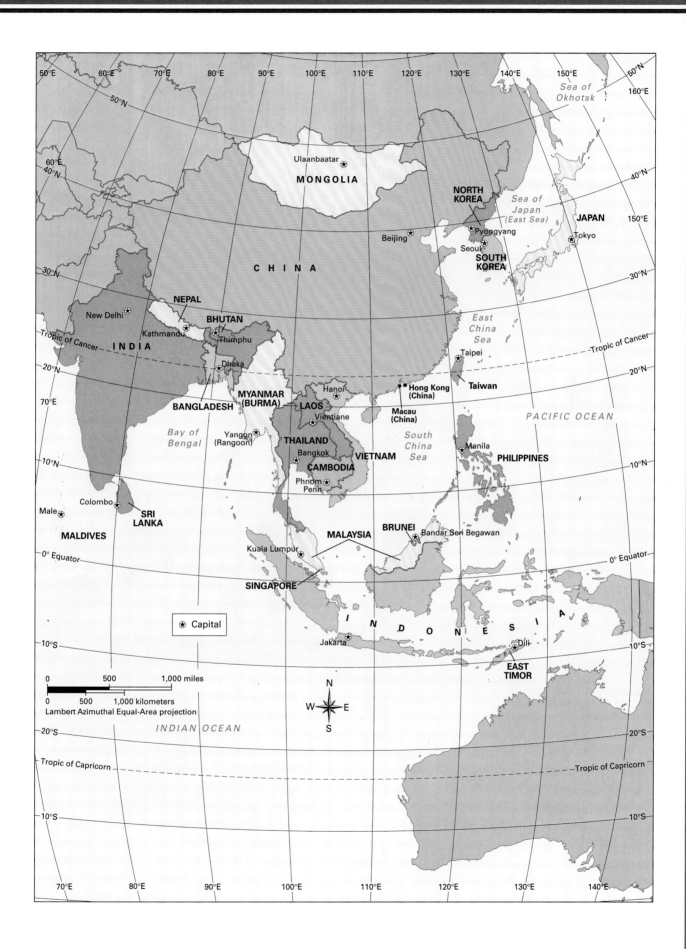

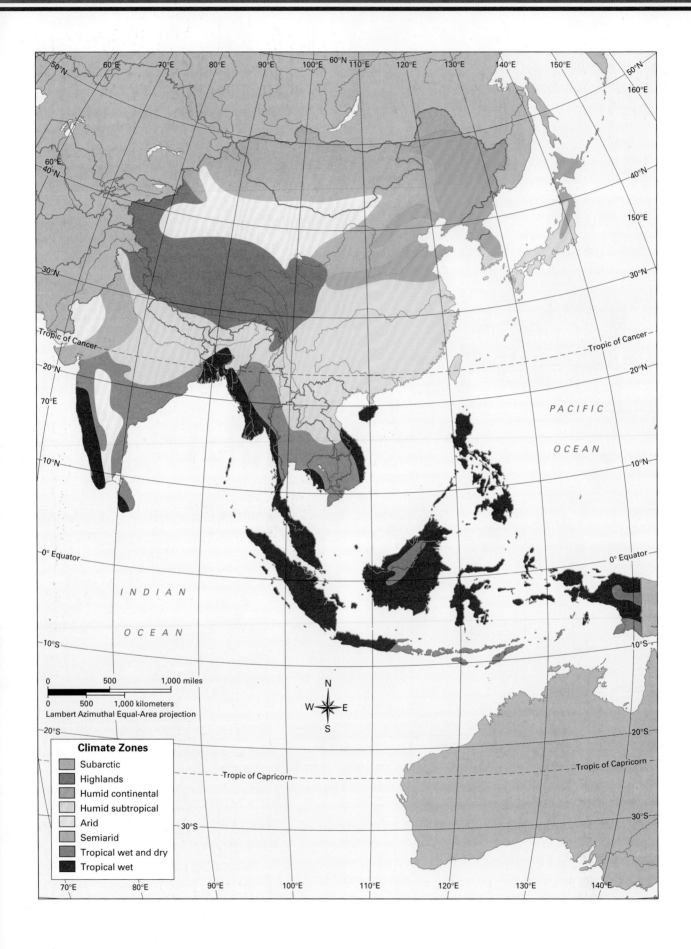

Climate Zones
- Subarctic
- Highlands
- Humid continental
- Humid subtropical
- Arid
- Semiarid
- Tropical wet and dry
- Tropical wet

0   500   1,000 miles

0   500   1,000 kilometers

Lambert Azimuthal Equal-Area projection

PACIFIC OCEAN

INDIAN OCEAN

Tropic of Cancer

Tropic of Capricorn

Equator

Vegetation Zones of Monsoon Asia

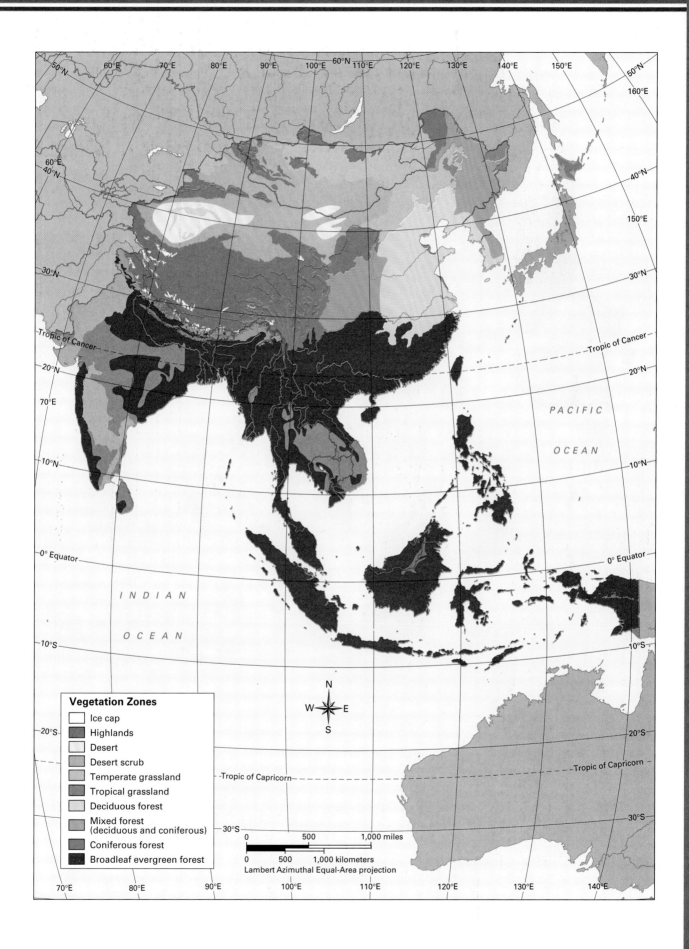

Vegetation Zones

- Ice cap
- Highlands
- Desert
- Desert scrub
- Temperate grassland
- Tropical grassland
- Deciduous forest
- Mixed forest (deciduous and coniferous)
- Coniferous forest
- Broadleaf evergreen forest

N
W E
S

0   500   1,000 miles

0   500   1,000 kilometers
Lambert Azimuthal Equal-Area projection

PACIFIC OCEAN

INDIAN OCEAN

Tropic of Cancer
Equator
Tropic of Capricorn

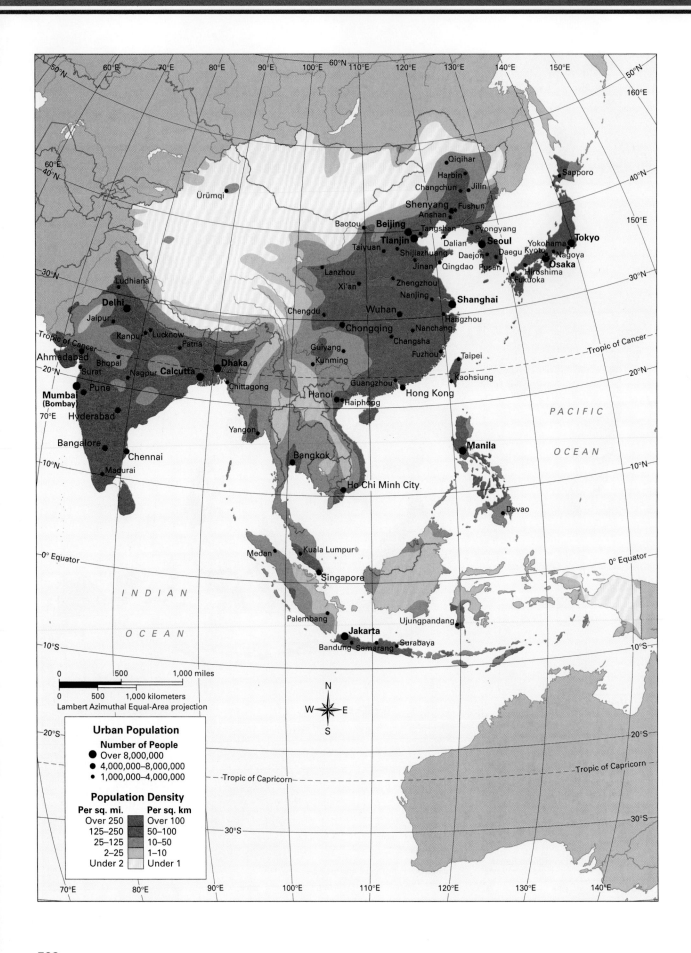

Urban Population

Number of People
- ● Over 8,000,000
- ● 4,000,000–8,000,000
- • 1,000,000–4,000,000

Population Density

Per sq. mi.	Per sq. km
Over 250	Over 100
125–250	50–100
25–125	10–50
2–25	1–10
Under 2	Under 1

0   500   1,000 miles

0   500   1,000 kilometers

Lambert Azimuthal Equal-Area projection

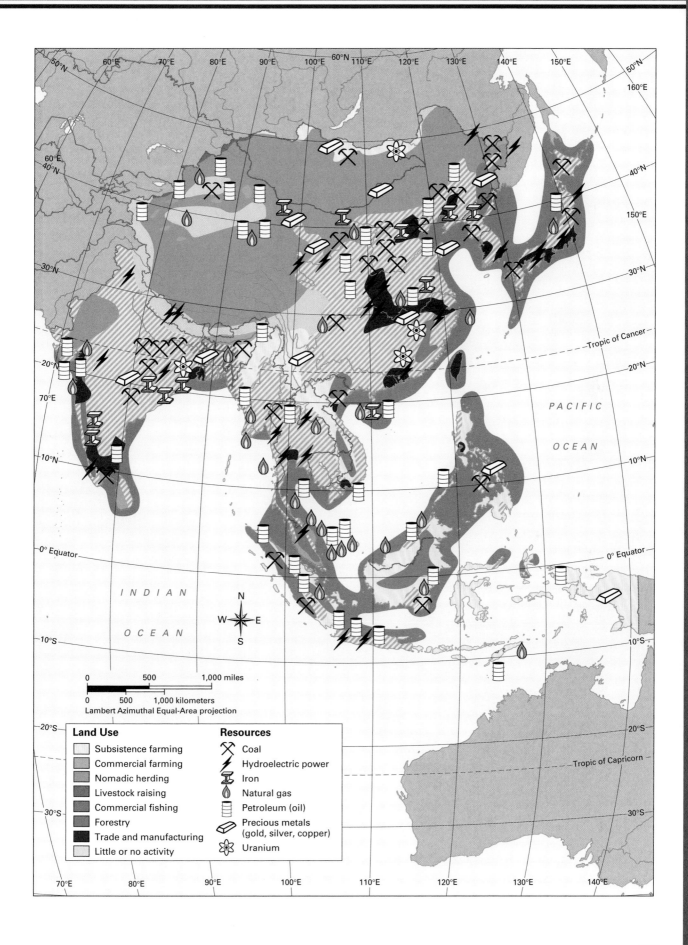

Land Use
- ☐ Subsistence farming
- ☐ Commercial farming
- ☐ Nomadic herding
- ☐ Livestock raising
- ☐ Commercial fishing
- ☐ Forestry
- ■ Trade and manufacturing
- ☐ Little or no activity

Resources
- ⚒ Coal
- ⚡ Hydroelectric power
- ⌶ Iron
- ◊ Natural gas
- ☐ Petroleum (oil)
- ▱ Precious metals (gold, silver, copper)
- ✳ Uranium

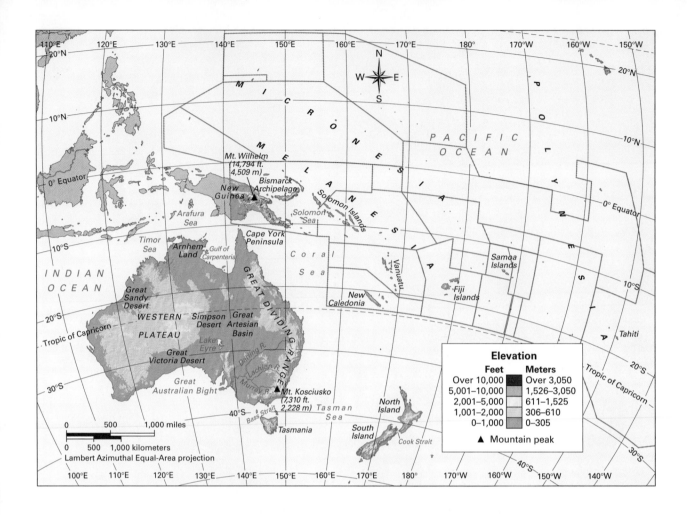

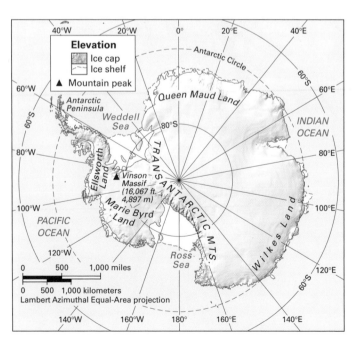

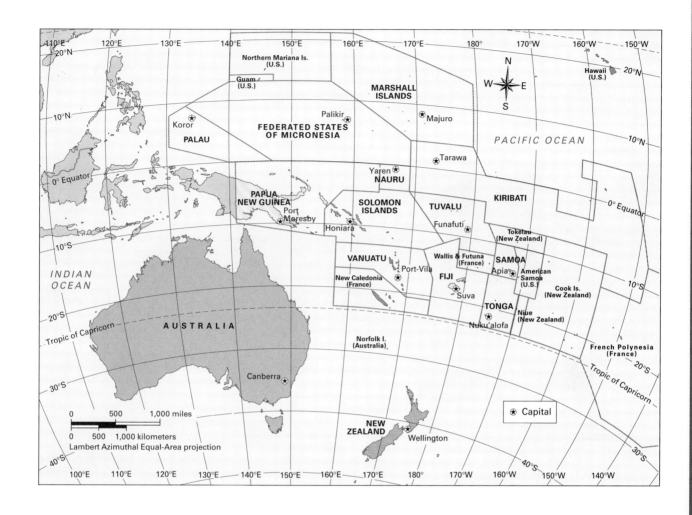

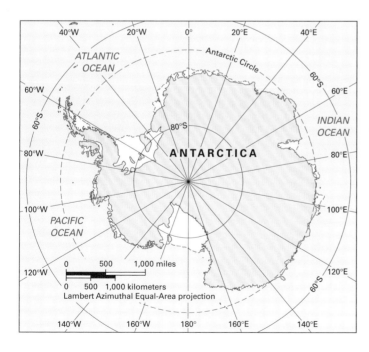

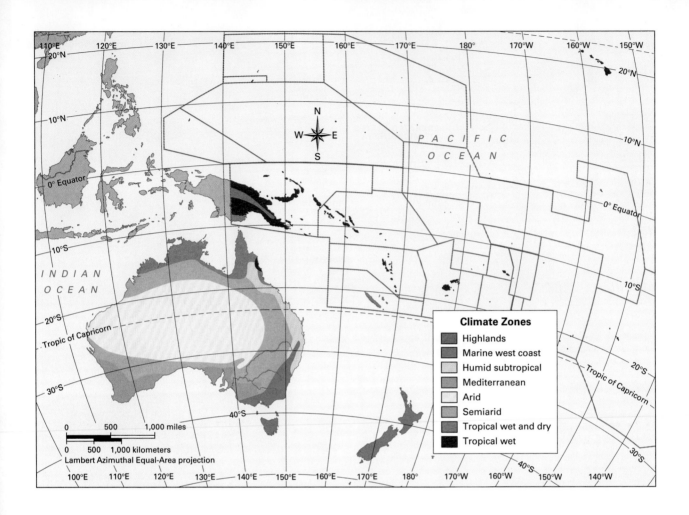

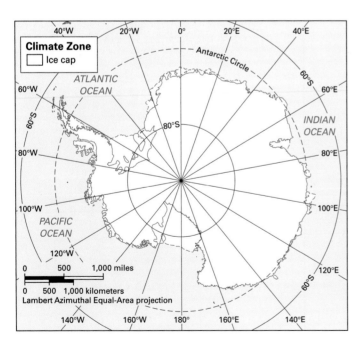

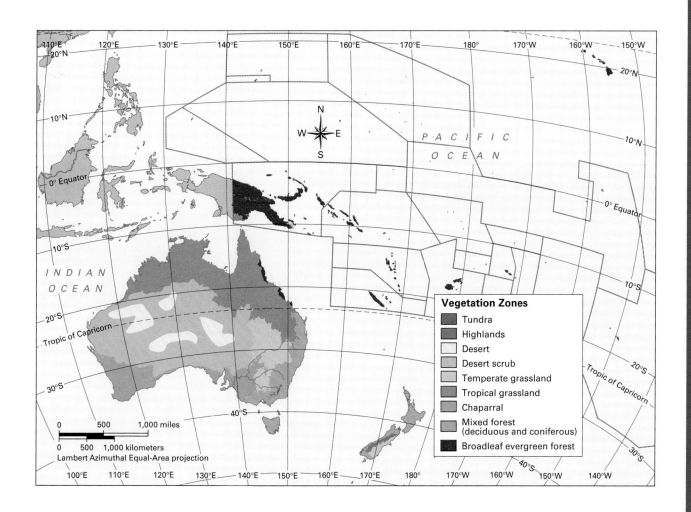

Vegetation Zones
- Tundra
- Highlands
- Desert
- Desert scrub
- Temperate grassland
- Tropical grassland
- Chaparral
- Mixed forest (deciduous and coniferous)
- Broadleaf evergreen forest

Lambert Azimuthal Equal-Area projection

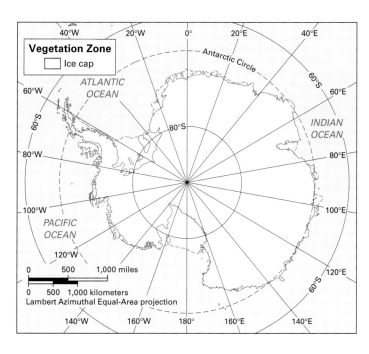

Vegetation Zone
- Ice cap

Lambert Azimuthal Equal-Area projection

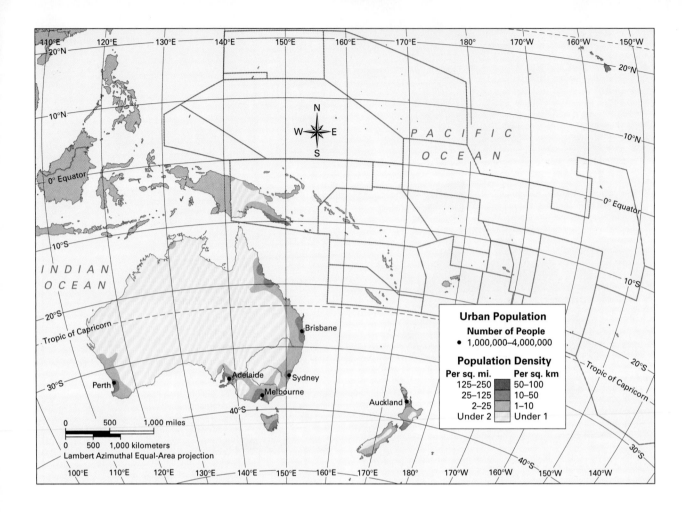

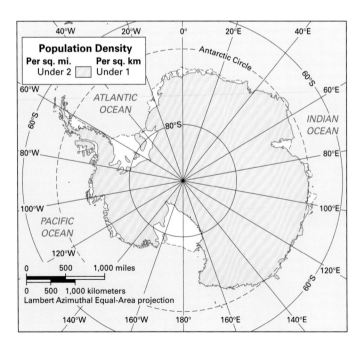

Economic Activity of Oceania and Antarctica

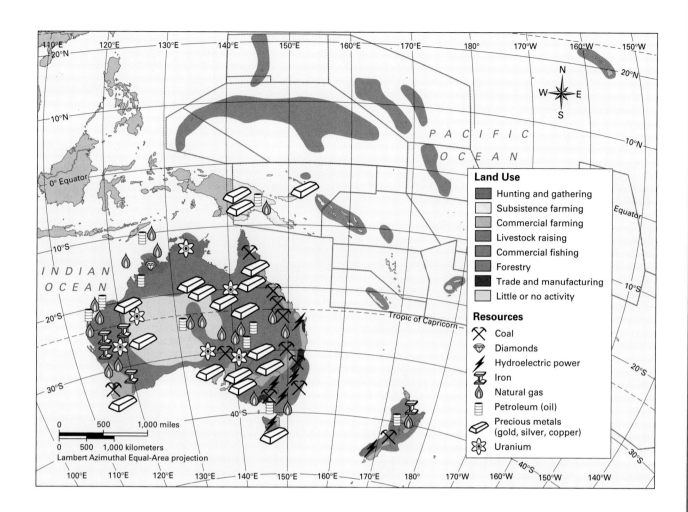

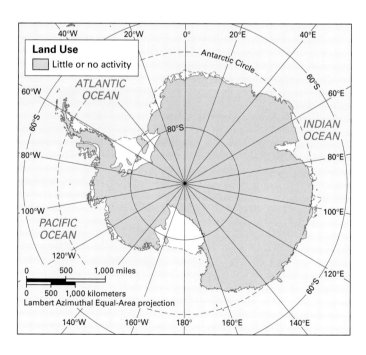

Glossary

Geoterms are in **blue**. Vocabulary words are in **black**.

A

absolute location the precise point where a place is located on Earth

accidental pollution the release of harmful substances into the environment as the result of an accident, such as an oil tanker spilling oil into the sea

acclimatize the process of adjusting to lower oxygen levels at high elevation

acid rain rain that can damage the environment because it contains acid created from chemicals in factory smoke and car exhaust. Acid rain can damage plants, fish, animals, and even buildings.

adaptation a change in a way of life to suit new conditions

adobe a type of brick that is made of clay mixed with straw and dried in the sun

air quality the condition of the air based on the amount of pollution in it

alpine found in high mountains; also describes the mountain **vegetation zone** between the **tree line** and the **snow line**

alpine glacier a **glacier** formed by snowfall in a high, cold mountain valley

altitudinal zonation the division of land into zones based on elevation, which in turn helps determine **climate** and **vegetation**

Antarctic Circle the line of latitude at 60°30′S that marks the boundary of the southern **polar zone**

apartheid the former official South African policy of separating people according to race; it gave most of the political and economic power to whites

aqueduct a pipe or channel built to transport water from one place to another

arable land land suitable for growing crops

archipelago a group or chain of islands

Arctic Circle the line of latitude at 60°30′N that marks the boundary of the northern **polar zone**

arête a sharp, narrow mountain ridge

arid dry or lacking rainfall; also a **climate** or **climate zone** that is hot and dry all year with very little rain

arithmetic population density the population of a country divided by its total land area

atmosphere the layer of air that surrounds Earth

atmospheric pressure the weight of the **atmosphere** pressing down on any point of the surface of Earth

atoll a ring of coral islands and reefs surrounding a shallow body of ocean water

avalanche the sudden movement of a large mass of ice, snow, or rocks and soil down the side of a mountain

axis an imaginary line that runs from the North Pole to the South Pole through the center of Earth

B

baby boom a sudden increase in the **birth rate** of a population

barter conducting trade by exchanging goods or services instead of money

basin a bowl-shaped depression, or hollow, in Earth's surface

biodiversity the variety of plants and animals living in one area, or on Earth

biome a very large **ecosystem** such as a **desert**, forest, **wetlands**, or grassland; home to a community of plants and animals

birth rate the number of births in a year for every 1,000 people in a population

brain drain the loss of well-educated people such as doctors or engineers to another country

broadleaf evergreen forest a **vegetation zone** of mainly tall trees that remain green all year; also refers to the type of vegetation in this zone

C

calorie a measure of the amount of energy in food

canopy the thick layer of overlapping tree branches that make up the top layer of a forest

capital city a city that is the governmental center of a country or **region**

carbon-oxygen cycle the process by which carbon and oxygen cycle among plants, people and animals, and the environment

cardinal directions the four main directions on a **compass rose:** north, south, east, and west

carrying capacity the number of people or animals the environment of an area can support

cash crop a crop that is grown to be sold rather than to be consumed by the farmers and their families

cataract a series of rapids and low waterfalls on a river

census a count of a population

centrifugal forces the forces that divide people and countries

centripetal forces the forces that unite people and countries

chaparral a **vegetation zone** of mainly small trees and bushes adapted to a **Mediterranean climate;** also refers to the type of vegetation in this zone

cirque a deep, bowl-shaped basin on a mountain in which melting ice often forms a lake

civil war a war between groups living in the same country

clear-cut to cut down all of the trees in an area

climagraph a graph that shows the average temperature and **precipitation** in a place over a year

climate the pattern of weather over a long period of time

climate zone a large area of Earth with a particular pattern of weather

cloud forest a type of high-altitude, tropical forest that is usually covered by clouds or mist

cloud seeding the scattering of chemicals into clouds to bring about rain

colonialism a system in which one country rules another area as a colony. The ruling country controls trade with its colony for its own benefit.

commercial farming raising crops for sale, often on large farms

commercial fishing catching fish for sale, often with the use of large ships

common market a group of countries that acts as a single market, without trade barriers between member countries

communal land land that is held in common by a group of people

commute time the amount of time spent traveling to and from work

comparative advantage the ability of one country to produce a good or provide a service at a lower cost or more effectively than another country

compass rose a diagram on a map that shows directions such as north, south, east, and west

condense to lose heat and change from a vapor or gas into a liquid. Moisture, or water vapor, in the air condenses to form rain.

confluence the flowing together of two or more streams

conifer a tree with needles and cones, such as a pine tree

coniferous forest a **vegetation zone** of mainly **evergreen** trees with needles and cones; also refers to the type of vegetation in this zone

conservationist someone who works to protect the beauty and **natural resources** of the environment from destruction or **pollution**

consumption the using up of goods and services; also the purchase and use of goods and services by consumers

continental climate a type of **climate** that occurs in inland areas and other places not affected by the sea; marked by hot summers, cold winters, and relatively little **precipitation**

Continental Divide a series of mountain ridges in North America that separate the streams and rivers that flow west into the Pacific Ocean from those that flow east into the Arctic and Atlantic oceans

continental drift the slow movement of Earth's continents

continental drift theory the idea that continents are slowly drifting as the **tectonic plates** that they sit on move. This idea comes from Alfred Wegener, who proposed that Earth once had one giant **supercontinent**. This supercontinent broke apart into plates that have slowly drifted to their current locations.

continental glacier a large, thick ice sheet that covers a vast area and moves outward in many directions

continental island an island that was once part of a continent

convection the movement, or transfer, of heat through a gas or liquid

coordinates a set of numbers that together describe the exact location of something, such as a place on a map

core the innermost part of Earth, made of solid iron and surrounded by a layer of liquid iron

Coriolis effect the curving pattern of wind and ocean **currents** caused by Earth's rotation

cost of living the average cost of basic necessities, such as food, clothing, and shelter, in a particular place or country

crater a bowl-shaped hole in Earth's surface

crude oil petroleum as it comes out of the ground and before it has been refined or processed into useful products

crust the hard outer layer of Earth

cultural identity a feeling of belonging to a group that shares the same culture, or way of life

cultural region an area that is set apart from other places by the way of life of the people who live there

currency the bills and coins used as money in a particular country or group of countries

current the steady movement of air or water due to **convection**

D

death rate the number of deaths in a year for every 1,000 people in a population

deciduous forest a **vegetation zone** of mainly trees that shed their leaves before winter; also refers to the type of vegetation in this zone

deforestation removing or clearing away the trees from a forest. Deforestation is often done to clear land for farming or ranching.

delta the triangle-shaped deposit of sand and **sediment** that occurs where a river flows into an ocean

demographic transition model a model of how the size of a population changes as a country develops its economy

demography the study of human populations, including how they change due to births, deaths, aging, and migration

dependency ratio the number of old and young people who don't work compared with the working-age population. The higher the ratio, the more young and old people the workers have to support.

desalinization plant a facility that removes salt from seawater to make it suitable for human use

desert a geographic **region** with too little rainfall to support much plant life; also a **vegetation zone**

desertification the process by which land becomes more and more dry until it turns into **desert;** may be caused by **climate** change, human activities, or both.

desert scrub a **vegetation zone** of mainly small trees, bushes, and other plants adapted to a dry **climate;** also refers to the type of vegetation in this zone

developed country a wealthy country with an advanced economy. Developed countries have many industries and provide a comfortable way of life for most of their people.

developing country a poorer country with a less advanced economy. In general, developing countries are trying to increase their industries and improve life for their people.

dialect a version of a language that is spoken in a specific area

dictator a leader who governs by force, without the consent of the people

digital divide the difference in opportunities available to people who have access to computers and the Internet and those who do not

discrimination unfair treatment of a person or group based on class rather than individual worth

distortion a change in shape, size, or position of a place when it is shown on a map

distribution the way people or things are spread out over an area or a space; also the way resources, power, or goods are divided among people or groups

diversity a variety or wide range of differences

doubling time the length of time it takes for a population to double

downwind in the direction that the wind is blowing

drought an unusually long period in which little or no rain falls

E

earthquake-resistant construction techniques building methods used to make structures safer during earthquakes

earthquake zone an area where earthquakes are likely, often where **tectonic plates** meet

economic activity any action that relates to the making, buying, and selling of goods and services

economic interdependence a condition in which countries have strong economic ties and depend on each other for resources, **technology,** trade, and investment

ecosystem a community of all the living things in an area and the environment in which they live

ecotourism a form of **tourism** that brings people to unique **ecosystems** while trying to avoid damage to these special places

ecumene a geographic **region** that is well suited for permanent settlement by people. Areas not included in the ecumene are generally too dry, too cold, or too rugged for permanent human settlement.

El Niño a warm ocean **current** that flows off the west coast of South America every few years. An El Niño event changes weather patterns around the world. It may also cause **extreme weather** in some regions.

emigrate to move from a country. People who leave a country are called **emigrants.**

empire a group of territories, peoples, or **nations** ruled by a single authority

endangered species animals or plants that are in danger of dying out in the immediate future

environmental degradation damage to or destruction of the natural environment. When such damage occurs, **habitats** are destroyed, **biodiversity** is lost, or **natural resources** are used up.

environmentalist a person who works to protect the natural world

erg a great sea of sand with tall sand dunes in the Sahara

erosion the gradual wearing away of Earth's surface by the action of wind, water, ice, and gravity

estate a sizable area of privately owned property with a large house

ethnic diversity a variety of people from different **ethnic groups**

ethnic group a group of people in a country who share a unique culture and identity

euro the unit of currency used in many countries of the **European Union**

European Union (EU) a **supranational organization** through which a number of European countries work together on shared issues

evaporation the process by which a liquid, such as water, turns into a vapor, or gas

exotic species animals or plants that are brought into an area from somewhere else

exposure the harmful effects of cold, wind, or other extreme weather conditions

extended family a family made up of parents, children, grandparents, and sometimes more distant relatives

extinct having completely died out. An extinct species has no living members.

extreme weather severe or unusual weather conditions, such as hurricanes, **tornadoes,** or blizzards

eye the calm area at the center of a hurricane or other **tropical cyclone**

eye wall the ring of thunderstorms that surrounds the **eye,** or center, of a hurricane or other **tropical cyclone**

F

failed state a state that no longer exists or one in which the government is so weak that it has little control over its territory

famine a severe shortage of food that results in widespread hunger

fauna all the animal life in a particular region

fault a line on Earth's surface that results from a deep crack in the **crust**

fault-block mountain a mountain created when a block of Earth's crust tilts upward as a result of **tectonic movement**

fault line a line on Earth's surface that occurs where there is a break in the **crust**

fishery a place where fish are caught, processed, and sold

floodplain the flat area around a river that is covered with **sediment** as a result of frequent flooding

flora all the plant life in a particular **region**

fold mountain a mountain that is created by a folding of Earth's **crust**

food chain a series of plants and animals, each of which depends on the one below it for food. A food chain usually forms part of a much larger **food web.**

food web all of the feeding relationships within an **ecosystem**. Each living thing in a food web provides food energy to other living things within that ecosystem.

foreign investment investment by a person or company based in another country

forest floor the bottom layer, or ground, of a forest

forestry the planting, growing, and harvesting of trees

fossil fuel any fuel, such as petroleum, coal, and natural gas, that is made from the remains of prehistoric plants and animals

free trade the flow of goods and services across national borders, with little or no government control

freshwater made up of water that is fresh, not salty; also describes creatures that live in fresh water, such as freshwater fish

G

GDP See **gross domestic product**.

gender-based division of labor the division of work into two categories based on sex, or gender. The result is that men and women do different kinds of work.

general pollution the release of harmful substances into the environment as a result of everyday activities, such as burning coal to make electricity

geography the study of features on Earth's surface including landforms, water bodies, climate, plants, animals, and peoples

geothermal energy energy produced by steam or hot water from deep inside Earth

geyser a spring that throws a jet of hot water or steam into the air

glaciation the creation and movement of **glaciers**

glacier a large mass of ice found near Earth's poles (**continental glacier**) or in a high, cold mountain valley (**alpine glacier**)

global grid the system of imaginary lines (called **parallels of latitude** and **meridians of longitude**) used to divide the surface of Earth on maps and globes

global warming the gradual increase in the temperature of Earth's surface over time. This warming may be the result of natural causes. It may also be caused by human activities.

globalization the development of a global society in which people, money, information, and goods flow fairly freely across national borders

greenhouse effect the process by which gases in the **atmosphere** trap heat from the sun and keep it close to Earth's surface. This trapped heat may contribute to **global warming**.

greenhouse gas any gas, such as carbon dioxide, that helps to trap heat in Earth's **atmosphere,** contributing to the **greenhouse effect**

gross domestic product (GDP) the total value of goods and services produced in a country in a year

groundwater water lying deep under the ground that supplies wells and springs. Over half the people in the world depend on groundwater for their drinking water.

growth boundary a legal border that separates an area where development is permitted from an area where development is forbidden

gulf a large inlet of the sea that cuts deeply into the land

H

habitable suitable for humans to live in

habitat the natural environment in which a plant or animal lives

hamada a high, rock-covered flatland in the Sahara

hanging valley a small valley carved into a mountainside from which water often cascades in a waterfall

headwaters the stream or streams that make up the beginnings of a river

hemisphere one half of a sphere. Earth can be divided into eastern and western hemispheres or into northern and southern hemispheres.

highlands a mountainous part of a country; a **climate zone** where temperature and **precipitation** vary with latitude and elevation; a **vegetation zone** where the mix of plants varies with latitude and elevation; also refers to the type of vegetation in this zone

horn a sharp mountain peak shaped like a pyramid

human geography the study of how people have spread across Earth

humid continental a **climate** or **climate zone** with warm, rainy summers and cool, snowy winters

humid subtropical a **climate** or **climate zone** with hot, rainy summers and mild winters with some rain

hurricane the name for a tropical cyclone that begins in the Atlantic Ocean

hydroelectric potential the electrical power that can be generated from flowing water

hydroelectric power electricity that is generated from the power of moving water

I

iceberg a large mass of ice floating in the ocean

ice cap a **climate** or **climate zone** that is very cold all year with permanent ice and snow; also a permanent, dome-shaped covering of ice over a large area; also a **vegetation zone** that is too cold to support plant life

ice shelf a large, floating sheet of ice that is attached to the coast. Ice shelves can extend out to sea for hundreds of miles.

ice stream a fast-moving section of a continental glacier

illiterate unable to read or write

immigrate to move to a country. People who move to another country are called **immigrants**.

impermeable rock rock that does not allow liquid or gas to flow through it

indigenous peoples natives of an area who have been conquered or dominated by others who came later

Industrial Revolution the huge social and economic change in Europe and the United States that was produced by the shift from hand tools to machines in the 18th and 19th centuries

infant mortality rate the number of infants, out of every 1,000 babies born in a particular year, who die before reaching age 1

infill the process of filling in empty or run-down parts of a city with new development

infiltration the movement of water from Earth's surface into the soil

informal economy the part of the economy in which goods and services are exchanged outside of government control. People who work in the informal economy often sell goods on the street or in a street market.

information technology (IT) the use of **technology** to move and process information. IT includes computers, communication satellites, cell phones, and the Internet

inland sea a large body of salt water with little or no connection to the ocean

intermediate directions the directions on a compass rose, such as southeast, that are located between the **cardinal directions**

International Date Line the **meridian of longitude** located at 180°. By international agreement, the date is one day earlier to the east of this line.

invasive species nonnative plants and animals that invade an **ecosystem**

isthmus a narrow strip of land that links two larger **landmasses**

L

lagoon a body of shallow water partly cut off from the ocean by low-lying rock, sand, or coral reefs

landform any natural feature of Earth's surface that has a distinct shape. Landforms include major features such as continents, plains, **plateaus,** and mountain ranges. They also include minor features such as hills, valleys, canyons, and dunes.

landlocked surrounded entirely by land

landmass a very large, unbroken area of land

landscape a large area with a particular kind of scenery, such as a desert landscape

land use the ways in which people use a particular area of Earth's surface; for example, for farming, development, or preservation

land use conflict disagreement over how to use a particular area of land

lava molten, or liquid, rock that flows out of a **volcano**

life expectancy the average age that a person in a given population can expect to live to

linguistic group a group of people who share a common language

lithosphere the outermost part of Earth, including a layer of solid rock and Earth's **crust**

livestock raising raising animals for food, milk, wool, or other products

longevity length of a person's life

lower story the middle layer of a forest, consisting of shrubs and trees

lowland an area of land that is flatter or lower than nearby areas

M

magma molten, or liquid, rock that lies beneath Earth's **crust**

mantle the middle layer of Earth that lies between the **core** and the **lithosphere**

map grid a system of imaginary lines that divides up the space on a map

map key another name for **map legend**

map legend a box or other display on a map that explains the meaning of the symbols used on the map

map projection a way of representing the spherical Earth on a flat surface

map scale an element of a map that shows how a unit of distance on the map (such as an inch) relates to actual distance on the surface of Earth

marginal land land that is not well suited for growing crops

marine climate a type of **climate** that is influenced by the sea. This type of climate is marked by relatively mild winters, cool summers, and fairly regular **precipitation**.

marine west coast a **climate** or **climate zone** with warm summers, cool winters, and rainfall all year

Mediterranean a **climate** or **climate zone** with warm to hot, dry summers and mild, rainy winters

megalopolis a very large city

meridian of longitude an imaginary line between the North and South poles that crosses the equator at right angles

meteorology the scientific study of **climate** and weather patterns

metropolitan area a major population center made up of a large city and the smaller **suburbs** and towns that surround it

micro-entrepreneur a person who starts and runs a very small business

micro-enterprise a very small business with few or no employees

migrant worker a person who moves regularly in order to find work, especially in harvesting crops

migrate to move from one **region** or country to another

migration stream the constant flow of migrants from one country into another country. The largest migration stream into the United States today is from Mexico.

mixed forest a type of vegetation or **vegetation zone** that includes both coniferous and deciduous trees

mixed-use development development that combines housing and businesses in one area

monsoon a seasonal wind. Summer monsoon winds in South Asia usually bring rain to that **region**.

moraine a mass of dirt and rock that has been left by a **glacier** as it retreats

multinational corporation a large company that has operations in more than one country

multiracial made up of people from several **ethnic groups**

N

nation a large group of people who share a common history and culture. Not all nations have their own government or control a territory, but the word *nation* often means a country or **nation-state**.

nationalism feelings of loyalty and pride toward one's **nation** or **ethnic group**. Nationalism sometimes includes the belief that one's nation or group is better than all others.

national park a large area of land that a government has set aside in order to preserve it in its natural state

nation-state an independent **state,** or country, whose people mostly share a common identity

native species animals or plants that occur naturally in an area

natural disaster great destruction or loss of life caused by natural forces rather than by human actions

natural gas a gas found beneath Earth's surface that can be burned as fuel for cooking, heating homes, and other purposes

natural resource a useful material that is found in nature, such as water, wood, coal, or oil

navigable lake a lake that is large and deep enough for big ships

nomad a person who wanders from place to place

nomadic herding the raising of livestock for food by moving herds from place to place to find pasture and water

non-point-source pollution **pollution** that does not come from a single location, but rather from many sources such as runoff from farms

nonrenewable resource a resource that takes so long to form that it can't be replaced. Oil, which takes millions of years to form, is such a resource.

nuclear family a family made up of parents and their children

nuclear radiation a form of energy that comes from nuclear reactions. Radiation has no smell or taste, but it can be very harmful to living things. Materials polluted with nuclear radiation are said to be *radioactive*.

nutrient a substance that provides nourishment, such as one of the elements in soil that make it fertile

O

oasis an isolated spot in a **desert** where water is found

oil reserves oil that has been discovered but remains unused in the ground

ore a mineral from which a valuable metal can be mined

orographic effect the **precipitation** that occurs when moist air rises up the side of a mountain. As the air rises, it cools down and releases most of its moisture as rain or snow.

outsource to hire someone outside a company to do work that was once done inside the company. **Information technology** has made it possible to outsource jobs to businesses in other countries.

overfishing taking too many fish from a body of water, so that the supply of fish is used up

ozone hole an area of the upper atmosphere in which the ozone layer has become unusually thin

P

parallel of latitude an imaginary line around Earth that runs parallel to the equator

pastoral nomads groups of herders who move with their animals from place to place in search of pasture and water

peninsula a long, narrow stretch of land that is surrounded by water on three sides

pension a fixed amount of money paid to a retired person by a government or former employer

per capita by or for each person. A per capita figure is calculated by dividing the total amount of something by the number of people in a place.

perennial irrigation a system that allows for the year-round watering of crops

permafrost a layer of soil beneath Earth's surface that is always frozen

persecution unfair treatment of others because of who they are or what they believe

pesticide a chemical substance used to control anything seen as a pest, such as insects, weeds, or rodents

physical feature any natural characteristic of Earth's surface, such as **landforms** and bodies of water

physical geography the study of natural features on the surface of Earth

physical processes natural forces that change Earth's **physical features,** including forces that build up and wear down Earth's surface

physiologic population density the population of a country divided by its **arable land** area

plantation a large farm, especially in a hot area

plateau a raised area of land, such as a hill or mountain, with a flat top

plaza an open square or marketplace

plural society a society in which different cultural groups keep their own identity, beliefs, and traditions

point-source pollution water **pollution** from a single place, such as a discharge pipe at a plant that treats **sewage**

polar zone the area between the **Arctic Circle** and the North Pole or between the **Antarctic Circle** and the South Pole, where the **climate** is generally cold

pollutant something that pollutes, or damages, air, soil, or water

pollution damage to the natural environment caused by harmful substances; also refers to harmful substances

population density the average number of people who live in a unit of area, such as a square mile. Population density measures how crowded an area is.

population distribution where people live in a country, whether crowded together in cities or spread out across the countryside

population pyramid a graph that shows the ages and sexes in a population, with the youngest ages at the bottom. The graph is often shaped like a pyramid.

potable safe for drinking

precipitation moisture that falls from the sky as rain, snow, sleet, or hail

prevailing winds winds that usually blow in a certain direction

primate city the largest and most important city in a country. A primate city has at least twice the population of the next largest city. It is a center of economic power and national culture.

prime meridian the **meridian of longitude** labeled 0 degrees, from which all other degrees of longitude are measured. The prime meridian passes through Greenwich, England.

public transit system a network of buses, trains, and other vehicles used for moving passengers

pull factor something that encourages people to move to a new place

push factor something that encourages people to leave a place behind

R

rainband a band of dense clouds that swirls around the **eye wall** of a hurricane

rainforest a type of thick evergreen forest found in areas of heavy rainfall

rain shadow a dry area on the **downwind** side of a mountain

rate of natural increase the annual rate of population growth. This percentage is calculated by subtracting the **death rate** from the **birth rate**. It does not include people moving into or out of a country.

recycling the process of collecting used materials that would otherwise be thrown away and turning them into raw materials for new uses

reforestation the replanting of trees in a formerly forested area by people or by nature

refugee someone who seeks safety by going to another country

reg a gravel-covered **desert** plain

region an area defined by one or more natural or cultural characteristics that set it apart from other areas

relative location where a place is located in relation to another place

remittance a payment of money sent by an immigrant to a relative in his or her home country

renewable resource a resource that can't be used up or that can be replaced as quickly as it is used up. Sunlight is a renewable resource that cannot be used up. Wood is a renewable resource that can be replaced by planting more trees.

replacement rate the **total fertility rate** needed for a population to replace itself

reserve an area that has been set aside for a specific purpose

reservoir an artificial lake where water is stored

revolution one complete trip by Earth around the sun

ritual a set of actions performed as part of a ceremony

river basin the area drained by a river and its **tributaries**

river system a river and all the **tributaries** that flow into it

rotation the spinning motion of Earth around its **axis**

runoff water from rainfall that is not absorbed into the soil and instead flows into streams or lakes

rural found in or living in areas that are not close to cities

rural decline worsening economic conditions in the countryside, including rising **unemployment** and growing poverty

rural fringe the small towns, farms, and open spaces that lie just beyond a city's **suburbs**

S

saline containing salt

salinization the buildup of salt in soil or water

sanitation the systems that keep an area free of filth and germs that can cause disease

savanna a type of **tropical grassland**

satellite image a view, such as of Earth, created from information gathered by instruments on board a satellite

sediment bits of soil left in a place by moving water

segregation the separation of one group of people from another, such as by race. Segregation can involve laws or customs that require different groups to use different facilities and live in separate areas.

semiarid dry, with little rainfall; also a **climate** or **climate zone** with hot, dry summers and cool, dry winters

sewage solid and liquid waste from homes and other buildings that is carried away by sewers or drains

shantytown a settlement made up of crudely built shacks

shari'a traditional Islamic law

shield the large core of very old rock that lies at the base of each continent

shifting agriculture the practice of clearing one area for farming for a few years and then moving on to another area when the first has lost its fertility

silt sand, mud, or clay made up of fine bits of soil and found at the bottom of a river or lake

site the specific place where something is located, including its physical setting

situation the way a place is positioned in relation to its wider surroundings

slash-and-burn method a way of clearing land for farming that involves cutting down and burning trees and other plants

slum an overcrowded, dirty area of a city where the housing is usually in very poor condition

smog a haze in the air caused by **pollution,** especially the exhaust from cars and other vehicles

snow line the lowest elevation on mountains where snow remains year-round

solar energy energy from the sun that can be converted into heat or electricity

spatial inequality the unequal **distribution** of wealth or resources in a geographic area, so that some places are richer than others

standard of living the overall level of comfort and well-being of a group or a country

state a political unit that controls a particular territory

steppe a vast, grassy plain

storm surge a wall of water that is pushed ashore by a storm

subarctic a **climate** or **climate zone** with cold, snowy winters and cool, rainy summers

subsistence farming farming carried out mainly to provide food for farm families, with little surplus for sale to others

subterranean found or existing under the ground

suburb a developed area at the edge of a city that is mainly homes. Many suburbs also have stores and businesses.

supercontinent a huge **landmass** from which the present continents were formed

superpower an extremely powerful country with more political, economic, or military might than most other countries

supranational cooperation a form of international cooperation in which countries give up some control of their affairs as they work together to achieve shared goals

sustainable development using resources in ways that meet the needs of people today without hurting the ability of future generations to meet their own needs. This means finding ways to use resources without using them up.

T

taiga a large, coniferous forest located in a far northern latitude, just south of the **tundra**

tariff a tax on goods that cross country borders

technology the creation and use of tools to meet practical needs; also refers to the tools themselves

tectonic movement the movement of plates below Earth's surface

tectonic plate a large piece of Earth's **crust** that floats on the liquid **mantle**

temperate moderate or mild, without extremes of hot or cold

temperate grassland vegetation or a **vegetation zone** of mainly grasses and scattered trees adapted to a **tropical wet and dry** climate

temperate zone the area between Earth's **tropical zones** and **polar zones,** where the **climate** is relatively mild

tenement a rundown apartment building

terracing the creation of flat areas on mountain slopes for the purpose of farming

thematic map a map that shows a particular theme, or topic

threatened species animals or plants that are likely to become endangered if not protected

time zone an area that uses the same clock time. Earth is divided into 24 standard time zones. In each zone, clocks are set to the area's own hour and minute.

topographic map a map that uses elevation lines and symbols to show a **region's** physical and human features. These features may include hills, valleys, rivers, lakes, roads, trails, and buildings.

tornado a violent, spinning windstorm that appears as a funnel-shaped cloud

total fertility rate (TFR) the average number of children a woman in a given population will have in her lifetime. This number is different in different countries.

tourism travel for pleasure rather than business or necessity; also, the business of organizing such travel

township in South Africa, a poor urban settlement where blacks were forced to live during **apartheid**

toxic chemical a chemical that is poisonous to humans or other living things

toxic waste waste materials from industry that are poisonous to humans or other living things

trade bloc a group of countries that work together to promote trade with one another

trade winds steady winds in tropical latitudes that blow toward the equator from the north and south

traditional culture customs and ways of life handed down from ancestors

transboundary pollution **pollution** that starts in one country and crosses boundaries into other countries. Generally, transboundary pollution is carried by wind or water.

tree line the highest elevation where trees grow on a mountain

tributary a stream or river that flows into a larger stream or river

tropical cyclone a severe storm with high winds that spiral around a calm center. Depending on where they form, tropical cyclones are called *hurricanes, typhoons,* or *cyclones.*

tropical depression a storm near the equator with winds moving in a circle at speeds of up to 38 miles per hour

tropical disturbance a cluster of thunderstorms near the equator that moves with the **prevailing winds**

tropical grassland vegetation or a **vegetation zone** of mainly grasses and scattered trees adapted to a **tropical wet and dry** climate

tropical rainforest a **broadleaf evergreen forest** found in wet and hot **regions** near the equator

tropical storm a storm near the equator with winds moving in a circle at speeds of 39 to 73 miles per hour

tropical wet a **climate** or **climate zone** that is hot and rainy all year

tropical wet and dry a **climate** or **climate zone** that is hot all year with rainy and dry seasons

tropical zone the area between the equator and the **Tropic of Cancer** and between the equator and the **Tropic of Capricorn,** where the **climate** is generally hot

Tropic of Cancer the northernmost line of latitude where the sun's rays ever beat straight down. This line marks the northern limit of the **tropical zone.**

Tropic of Capricorn the southernmost line of latitude where the sun's rays ever beat straight down. This line marks the southern limit of the **tropical zone.**

tsunami a huge, destructive wave caused by an earthquake or a volcanic eruption

tundra a climate zone with very cold winters, cold summers, and little rain or snow; a vast, treeless plain in the arctic **regions** between the **ice cap** and the **tree line;** also a **vegetation zone** that is a treeless plain with grasses, mosses, and scrubs adapted to a cold climate

typhoon the name for a tropical cyclone, or hurricane, that begins in the western Pacific Ocean

unemployment joblessness

UNESCO a branch of the United Nations. UNESCO stands for United Nations Educational, Scientific, and Cultural Organization.

upwind against the direction that the wind is blowing

urban found or living in a city

urban core the older part of a big city. Often the urban core serves as the downtown or central business district of a city.

urban fringe the ring of small towns and **suburbs** that surround a big city

urban hierarchy a ranking of cities based on their size and the services they offer

urbanization the movement of people from **rural** to **urban** areas, resulting in the growth of urban areas

urban sprawl the rapid, often poorly planned spread of development from an **urban** area outward into **rural** areas

U-shaped valley a valley with a relatively flat bottom, formed by a **glacier**

V

vegetation all the plants and trees in an area

vegetation zone a large area of Earth with a certain mix of plants and trees that are adapted to similar conditions

vertical trade the trading of crops between lowland and highland areas

volcanic activity the formation and eruption of **volcanoes**

volcanic island an island formed when an underwater **volcano** builds up enough **lava** and ash to rise above sea level

volcano a break in Earth's **crust** where **magma** and other material erupts from Earth's interior

V-shaped valley a valley with a relatively narrow bottom, formed by a river

W

wadi the usually dry bed of a river or stream in a **desert** or **semiarid** area

wastewater water that has been used; for example, for washing or producing goods

water cycle the movement of water from the surface of Earth to the **atmosphere** and back again. During this cycle, water evaporates from rivers, lakes, and oceans, rises and **condenses** into clouds, and then falls back to Earth as rain, hail, sleet, or snow. This process is also known as the *hydrologic cycle*.

watershed a geographic area that includes all of the land and waterways that drain into a body of water; also called a *drainage basin*.

water stress the condition that occurs when people don't have enough clean fresh water to meet their everyday needs

water vapor water in the form of a gas, as in steam or moisture in the **atmosphere**

wetland an area where the soil is usually wet or covered with water

wildlife wild animals and birds living in their natural environment

windbreak a wall or hedge that breaks the force of the wind

windward facing the wind

workforce all the people who are available for work, for example, in a country

World Heritage Site a place of great natural or cultural value that has been placed on the **UNESCO** World Heritage List. UNESCO helps countries preserve these sites for future generations.

Z

zero population growth a condition in which the population of a country does not grow but remains stable. This condition comes about when the **birth rate** plus immigration equals the **death rate** plus emigration.

Index

Page numbers in **bold** indicate definitions.

G

gender-based division of labor, 311, **313**
  finding water, 74, 403
  Mayan Indians, 155
  women micro-entrepreneurs in Africa, 311–319
gender equality, in Africa, 313
geographic inquiry process, 5
geography
  field of, 4
  national standards, 7–9
Germany
  car making, 234
  population and labor supply, 233
glaciation, 252, **253,** 260–261
glaciers
  Andes Mountains, 199
  worldwide, 200–201
Global Connections
  acid rain, 248–249
  birth rates and population trends, 236–237
  climate and human adaptation, 406–407
  deserts and desertification, 308–309
  ecumene, 62–63
  El Niño and extreme weather, 174–175
  ethnic conflicts, 332–333
  foreign companies in U.S., 416–417
  foreign investment worldwide, 464–465
  forest gains and losses, 188–189
  freshwater availability, 76–77
  glaciers, retreating, 200–201
  greenhouse gases, 510–511
  HIV/AIDS, 344–345
  indigenous populations, adaptations, 160–161
  international organizations, 222–223
  irrigation and water stress, 386–387
  micro-credit organizations, 320–321
  migration streams, 128–129
  municipal waste production, 116–117
  new nations, 274–275
  overfishing, 500–501
  population density, 452–453
  primate cities, 376–386
  protected lands, 104–105
  rate of natural increase, 440–441
  renewable energy sources, 366–367
  river systems and hydroelectric power, 296–297
  standard of living (HDI), 148–149
  tectonic plates, volcanoes, and earthquakes, 262–263
  threatened species, 486–487
  urban populations, 90–91
  World Heritage sites, 428–429
global ecumene, 62–63
global migration pattern, 120
global trade
  Australia and Asia-Pacific region, 481
global warming, 503, **505**
  Antarctica, effects on, 503–509
  debate about, 507
  and greenhouse effect, 506
  and ice shelves, 508
  introduction, 503
  potential effects, worldwide, 511
  and temperatures, 508
  theory of, 506–507
globalization, 455, **457**
  distribution channels, 461
  future of, 463
  geographic setting, 456
  growth of, in Asia, 456
  introduction, 455
  manufacturing sites, 460
  movement away from U.S., 456
  and offshore production, 460
  product design, 458
  pros and cons of, 462–463
  raw materials, sources of, 459
Goode's Homolosine projections (maps), 23
goods and services
  and funding for micro-enterprises, 316–317
  prices and globalization of production, 462
  and sustainable development in Amazon rainforest, 187
governmental centers, Mayan Indians, 154
Grand Canyon, 95
Great Barrier Reef, 429
Great Britain
  relations with Australia, 480
Great Lakes
  in 1969, 68–69
  geographic setting, 66
  habitat loss, 72–73
  introduction, 65
  invasive species, 69, 72
  pollution challenges, 68–71
  population density, 73
Great Smoky Mountains National Park, 103
greenhouse effect, 503, **505,** 506
greenhouse gas emissions, worldwide, 510

Chapter 1

p. 14: "The Hunting of the Snark," by Lewis Carroll, excerpted from *Project Gutenberg Online Book Catalog,* www.gutenberg.org. **p. 19:** "Watching the World Go By," by Ed Lu, Oct. 22, 2003, at *NASA,* "Earth Observatory," eol.jsc.nasa.gov/EarthObservatory/Watchingtheworldgoby.htm.

Chapter 4

p. 68: *Case Western Reserve University,* www.cwru.edu. **p. 70:** *The Lorax,* by Dr. Seuss, New York: Random House, 1971.

Chapter 5

p. 83: *Oregon Department of Land Conservation and Development,* www.oregon.gov. **p. 86:** *Toronto,* www.toronto.ca. **p. 87:** "Sprawling, Sprawling," by Daniel Pederson et al., *Newsweek,* July 19, 1999. **p. 88:** Pederson et al., 1999.

Chapter 6

p. 94: *National Park Service,* www.nps.gov. *The Yosemite,* by John Muir, New York: Century, 1912. **p. 98:** *Anne of Green Gables,* by Lucy Maud Montgomery, Boston: L.C. Page Co., 1908.

Chapter 8

p. 123: "Lost Boys of Sudan," by Stephanie Kriner, Aug. 14, 2001, *American Red Cross,* www.redcross.org. **p. 124:** Kriner, 2001. **p. 126:** Kriner, 2001. "Valdas Adamkus Biography," *Former President of Republic of Lithuania,* www.adamkus.Lt/en/biography.phtml.

Chapter 11

p. 163: "Hurricane Ivan," *Wikipedia,* www.wikipedia.org. "Eyewitness: Hurricane Ivan," Sep. 10, 2004, *BBC News World Edition,* news.bbc.co.uk. **p. 170:** "Hurricane Hunters," by Beth Geiger, *National Geographic Explorer,* Sep. 2004. **p. 171:** "Reporters' Log: Hurricane Ivan," Sep. 16, 2004, *BBC News World Edition,* news.bbc.co.uk.

Chapter 12

p. 180: *Survival International,* survival-international.org. **p. 185:** "Brazilian Activists Log Major Victory for Amazon Forests," *International Wildlife,* Nov.-Dec. 2000, at *LookSmart Find Articles,* www.findarticles.com.

Chapter 13

p. 198: "Sacred Peaks of the Andes," by Johan Reinhard, *National Geographic,* Mar. 1992. **p. 199:** "Sizing Up the Earth's Glaciers," by Evelyne Yohe, June 22, 2004, at *NASA,* "Earth Observatory," eol.jsc.nasa.gov/EarthObservatory/Watchingtheworldgoby.htm.

Chapter 14

p. 221: "EU Membership and the 'New Europe,'" by Rick Steves and Cameron Hewitt, at *Rick Steves,* www.ricksteves.com.

Chapter 15

p. 232: "United Nations Says Elderly Will Soon Outnumber Young for First Time," by Emma Daly, *New York Times,* Apr. 9, 2002, at *Global Action on Aging,* www.globalaging.org.

Chapter 16

p. 243: *Chernobyl,* by Don Nardo and Brian McGovern (illus.), Farmington Hills, Mich.: Thomson Gale, 1990.

Chapter 17

p. 254: *The Virtual Museum of the City of San Francisco,* www.sfmuseum.net.

Chapter 20

p. 302: *Sahara Unveiled,* by William Langewiesch, New York: Pantheon Books, 1996. **p. 307:** "Niger: Coal, the New Weapon to Stop Desert Advance," UN Office for the Coordination of Humanitarian Affairs, July 1, 2004, at *UN-OCHA Integrated Regional Information Networks,* www.plusnews.org.

Chapter 21

pp. 314–315: "Makeshift 'Cuisinart' Makes a Lot Possible in Impoverished Mali," by Roger Thurow, *Wall Street Journal,* July 26, 2002. **pp. 316–317:** *Women in African Economies: From Burning Sun to Boardroom: Business Ventures and Investment Patterns of 74 Ugandan Women,* by Margaret Snyder, Kampala, Uganda: Fountain Publishers, 2000. **pp. 318–319:** "Women Street Caterers," by Earl P. Scott, *Focus Magazine,* Jan. 1, 1999.

Chapter 23

p. 339: "United in Action: A Short History of the African National Congress (South Africa) 1912–1982," *African National Congress,* www.anc.org.za. "Historical Papers: Archival Collections: Archbishop Desmond Mpilo Tutu," *University of the Witwatersrand,* www.wits.ac.za.

Chapter 26

p. 384: *Chasing the Sea: Lost Among the Ghosts of Empire in Central Asia,* by Tom Bissell, New York: Pantheon Books, 2003.

Chapter 29

p. 419: *Into Thin Air: A Personal Account of the Mt. Everest Disaster,* by Jon Krakauer, New York: Anchor Books, 1998. **p. 420:** *The Mammoth Book of Eyewitness Everest,* by Jon E. Lewis (ed.), New York: Carroll and Graf, 2003. **p. 422:** Krakauer, 1998. **p. 423:** "Quest Everest: Through the Icefall," *NOVA Online Adventure,* www.pbs.org/wgbh/nova/. **p. 424:** Krakauer, 1998. "Everest: The Way to the Summit," *NOVA Online Adventure,* www.pbs.org/wgbh/nova/. **p. 425:** Krakauer, 1998. *MSNCB,* www.msnbc.msn.com. **p. 426:** "Alive on Everest: Into the Death Zone," *NOVA Online Adventure,* www.pbs.org/wgbh/nova/. Lewis, 2003.

Chapter 30

p. 431: "Internal Crises I: Demographic Disasters," *Asia for Educators: Columbia University,* afe.easia.columbia.edu.

Chapter 34

p. 492: "Scientists Seek New Medicines from the Ocean," by Sharon Kay, *The Boston Globe,* Aug. 7, 2001, at National Geographic News, news.nationalgeographic.com.

Global Data Bank

"2004 World Population Data Sheet," *Population Reference Bureau,* www.prb.org.

Global Atlas of the Health Workforce (2004), World Health Organization, www.who.int/GlobalAtlas/home.asp.

Human Development Report 2004, United Nations Development Program, hdr.undp.org/statistics/data/.

"Internet Indicators: Hosts, Users, and Number of PCs" (2004), International Telecommunications Union, *ICT Free Statistics Homepage,* www.itu.int/ITU D/ict/statistics/.

"Population, Health and Human Well-Being Searchable Database" (2004), World Resources Institute, *EarthTrends: The Environmental Information Portal,* earthtrends.wri.org/searchable_db/index.cfm?theme=4.

The World Factbook 2005, United States Central Intelligence Agency, www.cia.gov/cia/publications/factbook/.

Front Cover

b: Yann Arthus-Bertrand/Corbis.
tl: Olivier Coret/Corbis. **tr:** RF/Corbis.
c: Ludovic Maisant/Corbis. **spine:** © Dex Images, Inc./Corbis.

Back Cover

b: Yann Arthus-Bertrand/Corbis.
tl: Jonathan Blair/Corbis. **tr:** ML Sinibaldi/Corbis. **c:** Jonathan Andrew/ Corbis.

Contents (all)

Yann Arthus-Bertrand/Corbis.

Unit 1 Opener

p. 2: Yann Arthus-Bertrand/Corbis.
p. 4 c: Frans Lemmens/Getty Images.
p. 4 l: NASA - Earth Observatory. **p. 4 c:** Robert van de Hilst/Corbis. **p. 5 r:** Getty Images. **p. 6 r:** NOAA. **p. 6 c:** TCI. **p. 7:** James Marshall/Corbis. **p. 8:** GoodShoot/ SuperStock. **p. 9 r:** Peter Essick/Aurora.
p. 9 l: David Turnley/Corbis.

Chapter 1

p. 10: Masterfile. **p. 13 l:** TCI. **p. 16:** Getty Images.

Chapter 2

p. 24: Qin Zhong Yu. **p. 26:** Corbis.
p. 34 r: Ben Mangor/SuperStock. **p. 34 l:** Corbis. **p. 35 c:** Yann Arthus-Bertrand/Corbis. **p. 35 r:** Getty Images. **p. 35 l:** Getty Images. **p. 36 cr:** Jeremy Horner/Corbis. **p. 36 cl:** Bojan Brecelj/ Corbis. **p. 36 l:** Staffan Widstrand/Corbis. **p. 36 r:** Galen Rowell/Corbis. **p. 37 l:** Paul A. Souders/Corbis. **p. 37 cl:** Nik Wheeler/ Corbis. **p. 37 cr:** Gary Braasch/Corbis. **p. 37 r:** Gideon Mendel/Corbis.

Unit 2 Opener

p. 40: Yann Arthus-Bertrand/Corbis.
p. 43: Muench Photography. **p. 44 t:** Earl Adams. **p. 44 t, inset:** Qin Zhong Yu. **p. 45:** QT Luong/Terragalleria.
p. 47: Don Taka. **p. 48 tr:** Qin Zhong Yu.
p. 48 c: Qin Zhong Yu. **p. 48 b:** Qin Zhong Yu. **p. 49 t:** Troy & Mary Parlee/Index Stock Photography. **p. 49 b:** Alan Pitcairn/ Grant Heilman Photography.

Chapter 3

p. 50: NASA. **p.57:** Robert Estall/ Corbis. **p. 58 b:** Richard Nowitz/Corbis.
p. 58 t: Christopher J. Morris/Corbis.
p. 59 c: Robert Holmes/Corbis. **p. 59 t:** Andre Jenny/PictureQuest. **p. 59 ct:** Lee Snider/Corbis. **p. 59 cb:** Dave G. Houser/Corbis. **p. 59 b:** Bryan & Cherry Alexander/Photo Researchers Inc. **p. 61:** Eastcott-Momatiuk/The Image Works.

Chapter 4

p. 64: SeaWiFS Project, NASA/ Goddard Space Flight Center and Orbimage.
p. 65: Len Ebert. **p. 66:** Susan Jaekel.
p. 68: Cleveland State University Library, The Cleveland Press Collection.
p. 69: Ted Spiegel/ Corbis. **p. 70:** RF/TCI #26. **p. 71 tr:** Masterfile. **p. 71 b:** Len Ebert. **p. 72 b:** USGS. **p. 72 t:** GLERL/ NOAA. **p. 73:** The Great Lakes: An Environmental Atlas and Resource Book. **p. 74:** Reuters Pictures Archive.
p. 75: Qin Zhong Yu.

Chapter 5

p. 78: Lester Kefkowitz/Corbis. **p. 79:** Len Ebert. **p. 83:** Rick Schafer/ Index Stock Imagery, Inc. **p. 84:** Steve Terrill/ Corbis. **p. 85:** Scott Tysick/ Masterfile.
p. 86: Toronto Urban Development Services. **p. 86:** Corbis. **p. 89:** Sebastian D'Souza/AFP/Getty Images.

Chapter 6

p. 94 t: QT Luong/Terragalleria. **p. 94 b:** QT Luong/Terragalleria. **p. 95:** Marc Muench/Muench Photography. **p. 96 t:** Lisa McKeon/ USGS. **p. 96 b:** © S. Cyd Read/Natural Born Hikers. All Rights Reserved. **p. 96 c:** Getty Images. **p. 98 c:** Parks Canada. **p. 98 b:** Parks Canada.
p. 99 t: Parks Canada. **p. 101 t:** Muench Photography. **p. 101 c:** Marc Muench/ Muench Photography. **p. 101 b:** Marc Muench/Muench Photography. **p. 102 t:** Kennan Ward/Corbis. **p. 102 c:** NGS/ Getty Images. **p. 102 b:** QT Luong/ Terragalleria. **p. 103 r:** NPS/Visibility Monitoring Program/Air Resource Specialists. **p. 103 l:** NPS/Visibility Monitoring Program/Air Resource Specialists.

Chapter 7

p. 106: Randi Anglin-Syracuse Newspapers/The Image Works.
p. 108: Qin Zhong Yu. **p. 110:** Getty Images. **p. 111 tr:** Qin Zhong Yu.
p. 111 b: Sarah Leen/National Geographic. **p. 112:** Getty Images.
p.113 tr: Qin Zhong Yu. **p. 113 b:** Getty Images. **p. 114:** Qin Zhong Yu. **p. 115:** Getty Images.

Chapter 8

p. 118: Lee Snider/Corbis. **p.121:** Qin Zhong Yu. **p. 122:** AP/Wide World Photos. **p. 123:** Janet Jarman/Corbis. **p. 124 tl:** From the film *Lost Boys of Sudan* (www.lostboysfilm.com.) **p. 124 bl:** Qin Zhong Yu. **p. 125:** Peter Yates/ Corbis.
p. 126: AP/Wide World Photos. **p. 127:** Reuters Pictures Archive.

Unit 3 Opener

p. 130: Y. A. Bertrand/Corbis. **p. 134 b:** Getty Images. **p. 134 t:** Pablo Corral V/Corbis. **p. 134 t, inset:** Qin Zhong Yu. **p. 135 t:** Robert Holmes/Corbis. **p. 137:** Don Taka. **p. 138 tr:** Qin Zhong Yu. **p. 138 c:** Qin Zhong Yu. **p. 138 b:** Qin Zhong Yu.
p. 139 b: Collart Herve/Corbis Sygma. **p. 139 t:** Josef Polleroess/The Image Works.

Chapter 9

p. 140: M. Winkel-Zefa/Corbis. **p. 141 b:** HIRB/Index Stock Imagery. **p. 141 cr:** Stephanie Maze/Corbis. **p. 141 cl:** HIRB/Index Stock Imagery. **p. 142:** Steve Vider/SuperStock. **p. 145:** Stephanie Maze/Corbis. **p. 146:** Getty Images. **p. 147:** Kal Muller/Woodfin Camp & Associates.

Chapter 10

p. 150 background: The Lowe Art Museum, The University of Miami.
p. 150: Jeffrey J. Foxx. **p. 151:** Jeremy Horner/Corbis. **p. 153 c:** Jeffrey J. Foxx.
p. 154: Len Ebert. **p. 155:** SuperStock.
p. 157: AP/Wide World Photos. **p. 158:** Jeffrey J. Foxx. **p. 159:** Jeffrey J. Foxx.

Chapter 11

p. 162: Getty Images. **p. 164:** RF/Corbis.
p. 168 tl: Qin Zhong Yu. **p. 168 tr:** Qin Zhong Yu. **p. 169 tl:** Qin Zhong Yu.
p. 169 tr: Qin Zhong Yu. **p. 170 tl:** AP/ Wide World Photos. **p. 171 tr:** Henry Romero/Corbis. **p. 172:** Anna Martinez-Reuters/Corbis.

Chapter 12

p. 176 b: AP/Wide World Photos. **p. 176 t:** Dave Bartruff/Corbis. **p. 177:** Len Ebert.
p. 180: Joe Cavanaugh/DDB Stock. **p. 181:** Katherine McGlynn/The Image Works.
p. 183: Getty Images. **p. 184:** David Katzenstein/Corbis. **p. 185:** Siri Weber Feeney. **p. 186:** Carl & Ann Purcell/ Corbis. **p. 187 t:** NASA. **p. 187 b:** NASA.

Chapter 13

p. 190: Pablo Corral/Corbis. **p. 192:** Herbert Stadler/Corbis. **p. 194 br:** SuperStock. **p. 195 br:** Pablo Corral Vega/Corbis. **p. 196 bl:** Craig Lovell/ Corbis. **p. 197 tl:** RF/TCI #19. **p. 197 b:** Len Ebert. **p. 198 br:** Jeffrey J. Foxx.
p. 199: NASA. **p. 201:** NASA.

Unit 4 Opener

p. 202: Yann Arthus Bertrand/Corbis.
p. 205: Robert Burrington/Index Stock Imagery. **p. 206 b:** Bryan & Cherry Alexander/Arctic Photo. **p. 206 t:** National Geographic Image Collection.

Mukherjee-AFP/Getty Images. **p. 414 br:** Qin Zhong Yu. **p. 415:** Reuters Pictures Archive. **p. 417 cr:** Qin Zhong Yu.

Chapter 29
p. 418: Jock Montgomery/Bruce Coleman Inc. **p. 419:** Qin Zhong Yu. **p. 420:** Topham/The Image Works. **p. 422:** John Van Hasselt/Corbis. **p. 423 t:** Bobby Model/National Geographic Image Collection. **p. 423 b:** Jake Horton/Mountain World Photography. **p. 424:** Robert Holmes/Corbis. **p. 425:** AP/Wide World Photos. **p. 426:** Jake Norton/Mountain World Photography. **p. 427:** Jake Norton/Mountain World Photography. **p. 428 bl:** QT Luong/Terragalleria. **p. 428 br:** RF/TCI #19. **p. 429 bl:** Martin Land/Photo Researchers, Inc. **p. 429 bc:** Nik Wheeler/Corbis. **p. 429 bcl:** RF/TCI #24. **p. 429 bcr:** RF/TCI #17. **p. 429 br:** RF/TCI #10.

Chapter 30
p. 430: Prisma-V&W/The Image Works. **p. 431:** Qin Zhong Yu. **p. 432 b:** Qin Zhong Yu. **p. 434:** Alain Le Garsmeur/Corbis. **p. 436:** AP/Wide World Photos. **p. 438:** Panorama Images/The Image Works.

Chapter 31
p. 442: Bettmann/Corbis. **p. 443:** Qin Zhong Yu. **p. 444:** Miwako Ikeda/International Stock. **p. 446:** Figaro Magahn/Photo Researchers Inc. **p. 447 t:** Roger Ressmeyer/Corbis. **p. 447 cr:** Qin Zhong Yu. **p. 448:** Robert Essel NYC/Corbis. **p. 449:** Christopher Knowles. **p. 450:** Kenneth Hamm/Photo Japan. **p. 451:** Ron Dahlquist/SuperStock.

Chapter 32
p. 454: Michael S. Yamashita/Corbis. **p. 455:** Qin Zhong Yu. **p. 456:** Rebello Collection. **p. 458:** Brian Sytnyk/Masterfile. **p. 459 tr:** Qin Zhong Yu. **p. 460:** Anna Clopet/Corbis. **p. 461 t:** AP/Wide World Photos. **p. 461 cr:** Qin Zhong Yu. **p. 462:** Bob Krist/Corbis. **p. 463:** Reuters/Corbis. **p. 464 b:** Qin Zhong Yu. **p. 465 b:** Qin Zhong Yu.

Unit 8 Opener
p. 466: Yann Arthus-Bertrand/Corbis. **p. 469:** Michael Patrick O'Neill/Photo Researchers Inc. **p. 470:** Getty Images. **p. 470 inset:** Qin Zhong Yu. **p. 471 b:** Getty Images. **p. 471 t:** Jeremy Woodhouse/Masterfile. **p. 473:** Don Taka. **p. 474 tr:** Qin Zhong Yu. **p. 474 c:** Qin Zhong Yu. **p. 474 b:** Qin Zhong Yu. **p. 475 t:** R. Ian Lloyd/Masterfile. **p. 475 b:** Ted Streshinsky/Corbis.

Chapter 33
p. 476: Ted Mead/PictureQuest. **p. 478 bl:** Qin Zhong Yu. **p. 480 t:** RF/Index Stock. **p. 480 b:** RF-Comstock/Jupiter Images. **p. 482:** Annie Griffiths Belt/National Geographic Image Collection. **p. 483 l:** Medford Taylor/National Geographic Image Collection. **p. 483 r:** Tom McHugh/Photo Researchers Inc. **p. 483 c:** Martin Harvey/Corbis. **p. 484:** Wildlight. **p. 485 t:** NASA. **p. 485 b:** Qin Zhong Yu. **p. 486 r:** Getty Images. **p. 486 c:** Norbert Rosing/National Geographic Image Collection. **p. 487 cl:** T. Kitchin-V. Hurst/Photo Researchers Inc. **p. 487 cr:** Paul A. Souders/Corbis. **p. 487 br:** Getty Images. **p. 487 l:** Paul Nicklen/National Geographic Image Collection. **p. 487 bl:** Tim Laman/National Geographic Image Collection.

Chapter 34
p. 488: Tom Van Sant/Photo Researchers Inc. **p. 489:** Len Ebert. **p. 490:** Anders Ryman/Corbis. **p. 491 t:** Getty Images. **p. 491 c:** Jean-Pierre Pieuchot/Getty Images. **p. 491 b:** Richard Hamilton Smith/Corbis. **p. 493:** Getty Images. **p. 495:** Jeremy Woodhouse/Masterfile. **p. 497 b:** Morton Beebe/Corbis. **p. 497 t:** Douglas Peebles/Corbis. **p. 499 t:** Kevin M. McGrath/McGrath Images. **p. 499 b:** Tom Stewart. **p. 500:** Kevin Fleming/Corbis. **p. 501:** Doug Roy.

Chapter 35
p. 502: Galen Rowell/Corbis. **p. 503:** Len Ebert. **p. 504:** Gordon Wiltsie/National Geographic Image Collection. **p. 506:** Qin Zhong Yu. **p. 507:** ASAY-reprinted by permission of the Gazette in Colorado Springs. **p. 508 t:** Galen Rowell/Corbis. **p. 508 b:** Graham Neden/Corbis. **p. 509 c:** Mike Keefe, The Denver Post, 2002. **p. 509 t:** Peter Essick/Aurora. **p. 510:** Torsten Blackwood-AFP/Getty Images.

Global Data Bank
p. 514: NASA.

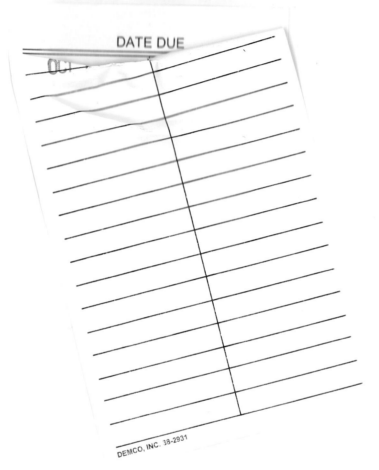

DATE DUE

OCT

DEMCO, INC. 38-2931